C000142861

THE FORD IN BRITAIN Centenary FILE

AN ERIC DYMOCK MOTOR BOOK

DOVE PUBLISHING LTD

THE FORD IN BRITAIN Centenary FILE

AN ERIC DYMOCK MOTOR BOOK

First published in Great Britain in 2011 by
Dove Publishing Limited
Torksey, Lincolnshire LN1 2LS

Book design by Andrew Barron @ thextension

ISBN 978-0-9554909-3-4

British Library Cataloguing-in-Publication Data.
A catalogue record for this book is available from the
British Library

Printed in China by 1010 Printing International Limited

Contents

A centenary. A celebration.

Ford of Britain has been in the fabric of the nation for a hundred years. We celebrate it in this book with cars whose names and numbers have earned affection and admiration in the streets and on the racetrack. Models T, B and Y; Prefect, Anglia, Zephyr and Zodiac became members of the family at weddings, wakes and festivals, on the school run and at work. Transit became a generic name for a carry-all van. Mondeo man entered popular culture. In this book are the Cortinas, Capris, Escorts and Fiestas that provided generations with great motoring and great value.

Eric Dymock is the right person to compile it. He has been writing about cars for half the lifetime of Ford in Britain which, as he says in the history section, "...became integrated so completely into the domestic industrial and manufacturing scene that it was often regarded (sometimes even by Detroit) as quintessentially British."

Well, Ford is now accelerating its standing as a truly global company with leadership that is supremely concentrated on the future of the Ford oval. Ford of Britain is a major pillar of this global strategy and the new world wide Ford Focus, centerpiece of this centenary, features advanced powertrains developed and produced in the UK. Ford of Britain is exporting engines to propel the world as well as playing a leading role in developing the next generation of low carbon technologies to meet global consumer needs in the coming decades. Here's to the next one hundred years.

Joe Greenwell, Chairman,
Ford Motor Company Limited

100 Years of Ford in Britain

Ford Motor Company of America was only months old when the first Fords came to Britain. It had scarcely begun making cars when Henry Ford enquired of a shareholder, president of the Daisy Air Rifle Company Charles H Bennett, how to go about selling them abroad. Bennett referred him to a New York export agent, Robert M Lockwood, who did business with British importer Shippey Brothers. The Shippeys' American Manufacturers Direct Supply Agency had a showroom on Long Acre, London and Arthur Shippey thought he would be able to sell a franchise for Ford cars. Accordingly in March 1904 he arranged for three to be displayed at the Agricultural Hall, Islington.

They appeared on the stand of a subsidiary, the American Motor Car Agency, whose proprietor Aubrey Blakiston quickly ordered a dozen more. Already in the early years of the Twentieth Century cars looked promising and Blakiston offered to exchange shares in his syndicate against a 16-year lease of the showroom at Shippey's Central Emporium. The prospect appealed to Blakiston's employee, Percival Lea Dewhurst Perry.

Blakiston set up the Central Motor Car Company in November 1904, taking over the American Motor Car Agency, and Perry became a minority shareholder the following year. Born at Bristol and raised in Birmingham, Perry gained a scholarship to King Edward's School and in 1896 had gone to work for rascally Harry Lawson in London. Lawson planned a motor industry monopoly, buying patents for car designs in the hope of rich royalties, but by the turn of the century his schemes had collapsed. Disillusioned, Perry returned to a family business in Hull, before going back to London, into partnership with

Blakiston and had been on hand when the first Fords were delivered in wooden crates.

Business was steady rather than brisk. Sales were barely a car a month before the more powerful Ford Model B of 1905 led to an improvement. Blakiston was unconvinced and resigned, leaving Perry in charge of reorganization. He sailed for Detroit in search of support from Henry Ford and although it did not amount to much, the pair formed a strong friendship and the visit led to a key development. Ford of Canada, formed 17 August 1904, owned the concession for the Dominion, British Colonies and the Empire until probably under a little pressure from president Henry Ford, its proprietor Gordon McGregor waived the rights to the United Kingdom. He concluded: "The rest of the Empire is enough," and Perry came back, reassured.

Central sold other cars besides Fords until the early months of 1907, when Perry wound it up to form Perry, Thornton and Schreiber, selling the recently introduced improved Model N. A bargain at £120, 50 were sold after Perry augmented the standard 2-seater with 4-seater or landaulette bodywork. The seven employees relinquished the Shippey connection altogether by moving to Westminster Bridge Road, just in time for the launch of the Model T in October 1908. Eight of the first production batch were sent to London for the Olympia Motor Show.

Results were encouraging. American-made cars were selling well in Britain. Central retailed 400 but it was not enough and Perry imported Reo cars as well in 1909. He went back to Detroit for another meeting with Henry Ford and accepted Ford company secretary James Couzens' advice to liquidate his partnership and create a formal Ford organisation in Britain. In March

1911 Perry set up Ford Motor Company (England) Ltd, from a showroom at 55-59 Shaftesbury Avenue with Models C and F.

There never was a D or E. Cars were delivered in crates, without wheels to reduce shipping space, to Vauxhall Wharf on the Thames. In 1910 Lloyd George's so-called Peoples' Budget raised tax on large cars. A 60HP went up from £5 to £42 (£2000 in modern money) in a move Henry Ford complained was discriminatory and aimed at his principal product.

Fords were practical and solidly made. Since the Model T was projected to sell throughout the world, plans were put in hand for assembly in Britain, and following a visit in 1912, Henry Ford decided this should initially be at Cork in the south of Ireland. He stipulated that his European factories should be accessible by sea; Ireland was then still part of the United Kingdom and Cork seemed a convenient port for America. It was intended to build tractors there although production did not get under way until 1919. Henry had an emotional connection with Ireland; his father had emigrated from County Cork following failure of the potato crop in 1847.

It was still planned to have production on the British mainland. Perry spent £2000 leasing a 5.5acre (2.2hectare) site on a new industrial estate at Trafford Park. American components were brought in by the 40-mile Manchester Ship Canal, which was making Manchester, deep inland, the fourth largest port in Britain after London, Liverpool, and Hull. Steep 19th century port and rail charges had threatened Manchester's cotton-spinning prosperity. It was costing almost as much to send goods and raw materials overland from Liverpool as it had to ship them across the Atlantic and the city's reply was an engineering

wonder of the age, the Canal opened by Queen Victoria in 1894. It followed the River Irwell along the north side of what had been the country estate of Sir Humphrey de Trafford. Two sections of the 1761 Bridgewater Canal had rendered his deer park a picturesque island, Sir Humphrey had grown tired of large ships passing his window and in 1896 disposed of the entire 1200 acres hoping for a development of expensive villas or a racecourse.

Instead the canal management built factories. They could be reached by ocean-going ships and railways, Ford occupying one that had belonged to the British Electric Car Company (BECC), building tramcars for towns from Ayr to Weston-super-Mare and exported them to Egypt and Argentina. BECC was bought and closed down by the rival United Electric Car Company of Preston, leaving empty its buildings on the corner of

OPPOSITE **The 1906 Model N was the first Ford sold in Ireland, France, Germany, Spain and Austria. Shown at Olympia in November at £120 it was the cheapest 4-cylinder on the market. On an 84in (213.4cm) wheelbase its 4-cylinder 2199cc 15bhp (11.2kW) engine was good for 45mph (72.4kph).**
ABOVE **Model T opened new opportunities for travel.**

Westinghouse Road and First Avenue. On
the canal side their neighbour was crane
manufacturer Frederick Henry Royce. Born, like
Henry Ford, in 1863, he also went into cars and
aero engines.

Each factory had its own railway siding.
Trafford Park was at the hub of Britain's rail
network and by 1914 Ford was distributing
vehicles in covered wagons to 1000 dealers. Perry
thought Manchester, "The very best geographical
and economic centre for our business." The
workforce welcomed Ford; it paid the best rates,
10d to 1s 3d (4p to 6.25p) an hour although under
their terms of employment everyone had to
be able to shift from trade to trade. Prosperous
pre-First World War Britain became Ford's second
biggest market after the US, and Ford turned out,
in the long run, more stable and consistent in the
United Kingdom than the indigenous motor

industry. It became integrated so completely into
domestic industrial and manufacturing life that it
was often regarded (sometimes even by Detroit)
as quintessentially British.

Although he had a high regard for Perry's
business acumen, Henry Ford still imposed strict
rules, such as demanding payment for cars as
they were loaded on board ships in New York.
No loose credit arrangements there. Cash flow
could be problematical and Perry had sometimes
to call on loans from his father-in-law. Car
bodywork was light but bulky and freight charges
for importing bodies were high, so one of Perry's
economies was to buy Trafford Park Woodworkers
Ltd and have them made locally.

After 1914 Model Ts were built on moving
assembly lines, as in Detroit, a chain conveyor
114ft (34.75metres) long could move at 15in
(38.1cm) per minute, so producing cars at a rate of

seven cars an hour, it took 90 minutes to make one start to finish. Moving at 21in (53.3cm) per minute 14 cars could be made, or faster still at 27in (68.6cm) per minute or 21 cars an hour. Bodies were spray-painted in three minutes; wheels dipped in a paint vat then spun at speed to throw off the excess.

Local content increased until the cars were wholly British, which was just as well on the eve of the Great War. Morris Motors suffered badly when American-made Continental engines for the 11.9HP Cowley were sunk in the Atlantic. The wartime McKenna Duties made imports that did get through uneconomic. Ford production reached 3,000 in 1912, prices were cut, production doubled, and only the outbreak of war frustrated an increase to 10,000.

The stricture about black paintwork did not, at first, affect British Fords. Applying paint kept in a tank in the roof was an unskilled job at Trafford Park; each of the three coats was dried in a large gas oven and up to 1913 the paintwork was blue. It was then green with black wings, and for 1914 Fords were to be a rich brown but following an edict from Detroit, and the introduction of Manchester's assembly line, they obediently turned black. Japan enamel was the only paint that would dry quickly and thickly, resulting in Henry Ford's famous aphorism that customers could have any colour they liked, so long as they liked black. Nobody was ever sure that he actually said it. Ford accumulated a long lexicon of legend and folklore.

Ford did not invent the moving production line. Instead it combined two well-established American technologies, the interchangeable components developed in the gun-making industry and the conveyor belts used in Chicago's

PART OF 100 CARS = 1 DAY'S OUTPUT

meat trade warehouses. Cars had been assembled on the shop floor; pieces brought to the bare chassis frame and bolted on. Putting the chassis on a conveyor and taking it to the components, rather than the other way round, reduced the time it took to build a car from 12 and a half hours to one and a half. Everything was made to close tolerances, as nearly identical as possible, so that they fitted together perfectly. This was a huge step forward from machining parts roughly to size, then filing and fettling them so that they worked in some sort of harmony. It meant that spare parts could be supplied when originals broke or wore out and they would always fit, something far from routine hitherto.

Percival Perry worked for the British government, as Deputy Controller of Mechanical Warfare at the Ministry of Munitions, throughout the war, earning a CBE in 1917 and a knighthood KBE the following year. Following the Armistice he resigned from Ford over dealer policy, joining a consortium refurbishing 10,000 war-surplus

OPPOSITE **Following a country-wide tour the 250,000th Ford built in Britain went on show at the British Empire Exhibition, where it was inspected by His Majesty King George V (behind car) and Queen Mary (on right). The Ford stand at Wembley stressed Britishness with a miniature production line "making" Model Ts.**
ABOVE **A day's output of Model Ts from Trafford Park, saloons, vans and lorries contribute to the total of 100.**

LEFT **Teutonic air of Model Y convertible with hood irons.**
OPPOSITE **Historic hand-coloured print of Model T van.**

This was to be no piecemeal assembly operation. Ford wanted to build cars from scratch, from raw materials to the finished product, so every operation had to take place on site, as much as possible under one roof. Accordingly, in 1924 the company committed itself to a self contained plant with services, including suppliers feeding components straight on to the assembly line, setting an example car manufacturers the world over followed well into the twenty-first century.

But who was to run it? In 1928, with plans well advanced, Henry Ford was advised to take Sir Herbert Austin into partnership and visited the UK in March. His celebrity tour included lunch with Lloyd George, he was guest of Lady Astor at Cliveden, took tea with the King and Queen and met the Prince of Wales. Ford visited Morris Motors and met Sir Philip Sassoon, the Under-Secretary for Air, but his main task was to persuade Sir Percival Perry to rejoin him. They met on board the White Star liner RSS Majestic at Southampton as Ford made his way home. Perry accepted, and recruited as advisors Patrick Hennessy, general manager and eventual successor, and a former Humber apprentice A Rowland Smith.

After the best part of three decades of motor industry experience, Perry thus installed a dynasty of management that would carry Ford of Britain through most of the next four.

Hennessy was a young Irish purchasing manager from the Cork tractor plant. In 1928 he had saved a major tractor order from Russia from cancellation. Smith had worked with Ford's distributor in Calcutta but been frustrated in a bid to become assistant manager at Trafford Park. He became works manager at Standard Motor Company in 1928-1929, then went back to Ford as

lorries at the 600 acre Slough Motor Transport Depot. This led to setting up Slough Trading Estates so in 1922, greatly enriched, he retired, buying the Channel Island of Herm's lease from novelist Compton Mackenzie. Trafford Park meanwhile prospered. By 1925 it was working to capacity and made its 250,000th vehicle.

Perry's departure had been a setback. Competition was intense, and from being market leader Ford, now making left hand drive Model Ts following a bizarre edict from Henry Ford, dropped to fourth behind Austin, Morris, and Singer. In 1922, the Austin Seven and the reduction of import levies made the challenge even stiffer. A succession of American chief executives came and went. Following establishment of the Irish Free State, castings from Cork suffered a 22 per cent duty. More production was essential to make up lost ground but there was no room to expand at Trafford Park. Britain had to be explored for somewhere by the sea for a new car plant. Cork plant manager Edward Grace was detailed to look for a suitable site; Perry had wanted to build on one by Southampton Water, bought in 1919, but the company settled for 295acres (119.4hectares) of Essex marshland, alongside the Thames near Dagenham.

Perry moved towards production at Dagenham, scheduled for the summer of 1932.

Commercial vehicles had been part of the plans since the Model T and its lorry derivatives. In 1929 production of tractors was moved from Cork to Dagenham. British Ford trucks were much the same as American ones until 1932 when a 1-ton lorry, with a 3-speed gearbox and a 3.3-litre 4-cylinder side-valve engine was introduced, alongside a 10cwt van on a derivative of a car chassis.

Dagenham was Ford's most ambitious expansion outside America. It took four years' planning before Edsel Ford cut the first sod (with a silver spade that bent and had to be hammered straight again) for construction to begin on 17 May 1929. This took another two and a half years. Ford was in no hurry. The timing could scarcely have been worse. The decision to expand in Britain was taken with America on the crest of a wave. In 1927 it had nine million cars, one for every six Americans. In England the ratio was still one to 57, in Germany one to 289. In May, as Charles Lindbergh flew the Atlantic, the 15 millionth Model T rolled off the line in Detroit. In November General Motors declared the biggest profit in American corporate history, and Ford's new Model A went on display at the Waldorf Hotel in New York, with instant orders for 50,000. Secretary of Commerce, Herbert Hoover, asserted in his annual report that American workers' wages were "higher than anywhere else in the world or than at any other time in history".

But in April 1928, within months of Hoover's up-beat assessment, share prices on Wall Street faltered. The market value of General Motors that had soared in the wake of its record profits fell just as swiftly. So did Chrysler's. In May the aircraft

industry was hit by a wave of selling forcing Dodge and Chrysler into a merger. Yet while accepting the Republican Party's nomination for President, the ever-optimistic Hoover looked forward to, "A chicken in every pot, a car in every garage." In December 1928 Ford of Britain was refloated, its £7million capital furnished by still surprisingly confident investors.

Wall Street finally crashed in October 1929. The domestic market collapsed and Ford's overseas investments took on a new significance, even though money to pay for them became scarce. Maurice Sampson in *The Autocar* greeted Dagenham enthusiastically, however: "In a period of difficulty and world wide depression (it) is an example of heroic pluck. It lifts the beckoning hand of faith in a time when many men are losing courage. It is not being built in a period of boom when goods almost sell themselves; it is being erected in a time of depression, its purpose and mission to create international trade."

Too true. Dagenham was a daring act of faith.

OPPOSITE **Royal Albert Hall display in 1934 included special-bodied convertible V8s, vans, new Model C in foreground and an ambulance.**
ABOVE **There were still open fields behind the Dagenham factory when it opened with Thames-side jetty access.**

FORD EIGHT 1937

Its capacity of 1000 to 1500 vehicles a day meant it replaced Detroit as supplier of Fords to Europe, in effect costing American jobs. Dagenham was an Essex job creation scheme on a grand scale. Ford's inward investment was £5million, a lot of money in 1930, for a new complex that included developments on the London Tilbury and Southend Southern Railway (SR) lines, with a London Midland and Scottish (LMS) branch connection. The completed factory covered 600acres (242.8hectares).

A 2000ft (610m) jetty capable of berthing 12,000ton (12,192 metric tonne) ships provided facilities for incoming raw materials and outgoing vehicles. In 1934 Ford inaugurated the only blast furnace with its own coke ovens in the south of England, so made its own iron and steel. Iron ore unloaded at the jetty duly left again as cars.

Reclaiming the marshes involved one of the biggest pile-driving operations ever. Some 22,000 concrete columns between 40ft (12.2metres) and 75ft (22.9metres) were driven into the soggy ground before it was possible to erect buildings, their floors laid with eight million wood blocks. Production stopped at Trafford Park on a Friday with the 301,980th, a Model A van, and

recommenced albeit haltingly, at Dagenham the following Tuesday. Special trains took 2000 employees and their families from Manchester to Essex over the weekend. Trains took production machinery from Trafford Park straight into Dagenham's new railway sidings, where it was unloaded into the factory and bolted into prepared places, ready to restart after the weekend. A ready-made supply of labour came from an imaginative London County Council rehousing programme, directed at still rural Dagenham. Perry had not forgotten trading estate principles learned at Slough; independent suppliers Briggs Motor Bodies and the Kelsey-Hayes Wheel Company set up facilities within the Dagenham complex.

In October 1930 Henry Ford visited the partly completed factory to see where the £5million had gone. Perry moved into offices opposite a new London showroom at 88 Regent Street, and at about the same time Ford Belgium moved to a modest purpose-built factory of its own.

Dagenham's first product was a 30cwt (1524kg) AA truck. Car sales were still so depressed that only five came off the line in the first three months. Sir Percival Perry had to report bad news to Dearborn; Ford of Britain would be insolvent unless there was a new small car. American engines suffered from British Treasury Rating horsepower tax owing to their large cylinder bore and a new model had to be unburdened with it. British manufacturers built engines with small cylinder bores and long strokes, not satisfactory technically but agreeable commercially. A Standard 9, Morris Minor and Austin 7 were hastily bought and shipped to America for appraisal while Laurence Sheldrick, Eugene Turenne and Bob Gregorie began work almost at

RIGHT **Anglia production draws to an end in 1939–1940. War production waits at the side with a WOA2 being made ready on the left.**

once on the Model 19, which would come to market as British Ford Model Y. By the end of the year Rowland Smith crossed the Atlantic to approve the prototype. Henry Ford, now 68, joined in to lend urgency, and by the beginning of February, 14 pre-production cars were on test. It was one of the shortest gestation periods ever for any major Ford, barely ten months elapsing from drawing board to manufacture.

It was just in time. Ford UK lost £681,000 in 1932. The Model Y was also built in Germany in a new plant at Cologne, as well as Barcelona, Spain and Asnières, France. Dagenham did not get it free. Dearborn sent a design bill for $535,360 (£160,287). Following protests it was reduced to $210,000 (£62,874) but still the British end of the business was not out of danger. Ford Holland had to help with £1million of ready cash until production built up from 8260 in 1932, to 33,958 in 1933. Model Y also appeared as a 5cwt van, turning round Ford Britain to a profit of £388,170 in 1933, then to over half a million pounds the following year. The Y was also the basis for the Fordson Tug, a curious 3-wheeler only 10ft (3m) long with a coil-sprung single front wheel.

In 1933 Fordson, a name previously applied to tractors, appeared on trucks with payloads from 5cwt to 2tons. It extended to 6x2 Surrey and 6x4 Sussex variations on the 2-tonner, while the new V8 engine was still only made available for a Ford 20-seat coach, and was offered on a truck in 1936. The V8 became the regular commercial engine from then until the outbreak of war, as the medium and heavy Fordsons were renamed Thames, a title kept until 1965.

Dagenham was making 75,000 cars a year by 1936 and the style of small British Fords looked set to continue even though some features of the

Model Y, like the transverse leaf springs, had been handed down from the Model T. The Y and its progenitors, the Anglia and Popular, stuck with them for another 25 years, making Ford technology look laggardly for some models, yet in the 1930s it scarcely mattered. Price was more important and with its careful attention to cost control Ford was already undercutting most of the industry. Design at Ford tended to evolve according to what could be made on existing machinery. A change of engine was only countenanced if it could be machined with the same bore centres as before.

Quality could be maintained while keeping change to a minimum. Ford was able to introduce the first full-sized £100 car in 1935 and still show a profit. It also demonstrated flair for marketing, as the disconsolate family at the bus stop established in the famous advertisement.

OPPOSITE **Women volunteers staffed emergency Ford Thames vans for wartime schoolboys.** ABOVE **WAAF tractor driver pulls trolley-loads of bombs to waiting aircraft.**

Its message was inescapable. The only way the breadwinner could restore self-respect was with a £100 cheque, or by taking up one of the new "deferred payment" credit schemes. Ford's moves into hire purchase finance made it as much a bank as a car manufacturer.

Still, no manufacturer could get by on a lacklustre range, no matter how worthy. The Model Y and its successor the Model C brought style to a sector of the market from which it had been largely absent. Themes were borrowed from the trend-setting car of the 1930s, the Ford V8, its heart-shaped radiator and curving front bumper evoking a racy, sleek appearance cultured in Hollywood.

The V8 itself was what a later era would call aspirational; not many could afford it but lots admired it. It was too big and used too much petrol for British drivers, yet it lent glamour to smaller Fords in a way that would become an automotive marketing strategy. The first V8s sold in Britain were made by Ford Canada, the Empire-made label a tangible reassurance of United Kingdom credentials.

There was no gainsaying Ford's core market. Henry Ford's disdain for what he termed interest

groups, like Britain's Society of Motor Manufacturers and Traders (SMMT), compelled the company's annual motor shows to be held in the Albert Hall, separate from the industry's main event at Olympia or Earls Court. Here were introduced sturdy 8HP and 10HP saloons that became the Anglia and Prefect, together with upright vans and small trucks. They were always amongst the cheapest on the market, and although price was no reflection on their quality, they were nevertheless widely regarded as utilitarian.

Dagenham persevered with civilian production as long as it could until, when war broke out in 1939 it felt itself, not without cause, in the firing line. The factory was exposed, a landmark on the flat Essex coast to enemy bombers from occupied Europe, suffering attacks and casualties. It retaliated by making 347,371 trucks, tractors, Bren Gun Carriers and numerous associated products including V8 engines used in coastal patrol boats and landing craft. Ford also made 30,000 Rolls-Royce Merlin aero engines at a new factory at Urmston in Manchester, not far from Trafford Park, which had been intended for peacetime truck production.

As a multi-national company during the war Ford faced some discomfiture. The German factory was effectively taken over by the Third Reich, so Ford internationally could have been liable to pay corporation tax twice in different countries. To avoid it Perry set up a temporary holding company, first in Lichtenstein, then in Luxembourg, and finally in German-occupied Channel Islands. Up to the time of Pearl Harbor, executives in Ford Germany and Ford UK could even remain in touch with each other, usually through Dearborn. There were joint "advertising

conferences" in neutral Sweden, to one of which in 1944 J Clayton Young, Dagenham advertising manager, flew in the improvised cabin of a de Havilland Mosquito. A handful of the fighting aircraft were pressed into civilian service with British Overseas Airways Corporation (BOAC). Young suffered from the extreme cold in the unpressurised interior and died soon after the three hour flight.

Jig-boring machinery for the manufacture of the crucial Merlin aero engines had to be obtained from Switzerland. Scrupulously neutral, the Swiss maintained trade with both sides. Each acknowledged the consequences of refusal or impediment, so the huge borers had to be shipped through Vichy France, then by ostensibly neutral but avowedly Fascist Spain, en route to Britain.

Almost as soon as the guns stopped firing in Europe in May 1945, car production recommenced, mostly with the same models as before. Ford had become such an integral part of the British industry that it joined the Society of Motor Manufacturers and Traders, taking part in the first post-war motor show of 1948. The V8 was reintroduced into a market desperate for cars, but the recovery was fraught with difficulties over steel supplies and government restrictions. They were austere times; Britain was obliged to pay off war debts by exporting all it could, and the demand to sell cars abroad (mostly to the Dominions and the near Continent) led to the abolition of the restrictive cylinder bore horsepower tax, which had led to a generation of unsuitable long-stroke engines. The removal encouraged radical designs, pre-eminent among which were the Consul and Zephyr, introduced at the London Motor Show in 1950.

Technical triumphs for the time, they were the first Fords with a unitary, monocoque bodyshell; the first to feature Macpherson strut independent front suspension, and the first Fords with an ohv petrol engine. Fatigued by ten years of wartime and post-war hardship, Britain took the flush-sided American-styled cars to its heart as symbols of a return to peace and prosperity. They became as much part of the national revival as the Festival of Britain, although their design credentials lasted rather better than the tacky exhibitionism on London's South Bank. They were well proportioned and, when the Zephyr Zodiac appeared two years later resplendent in a "two-tone" colour scheme, Ford climbed another rung on the social ladder. "Planned obsolescence", the culture of annual model facelifts, was being

OPPOSITE **Celebrations for the new model's sporting achievements included a gathering of champions at Cortina d'Ampezzo, the ski resort in the Italian Dolomites north of Venice, from which it took its name. Jim Clark, 1963 world champion driver, strained his back in a snowball fight, unexpectedly providing Jackie Stewart with his first Formula 1 drive, in the 1964 Rand Grand Prix at Kyalami where he won his heat.**
LEFT **Ford took up motor sport with enthusiasm, starting with the Anglia on East African Safari.**

LEFT **Transit production began at Langley and moved to Southampton, replacing the 400E Thames Trader made in many guises, including this smart crew bus** RIGHT**, since 1957.**

gradually discredited, but Ford knew it was profitable to raise the profile of a car, lift it up a market segment by adding value, even simply making it bigger. Following the cars' success, employment at Dagenham peaked in 1953 at 40,000.

Ford applied the technique successfully, introducing cars at what were becoming known as entry level prices and then enhancing them, making them better equipped or faster, so that they could be sold at premium prices. The introduction of the 100E Anglia in 1953 was at an entry level price before tax of £360. By the time of the final version, long after the initial investment had been paid off by close on three quarters of a million cars, the 107E Prefect of 1961 (much the same with four doors and an overhead valve engine) cost £438.

Ford's mastery of advertising was matched by a creativity in public relations, which had begun in the 1930s on Percival Perry's visits to Ford's European factories. He took with him a talented linguist fresh from Eton, Maurice Buckmaster. Perry wanted to create a Ford of Europe, with Dagenham as its hub, but found that the other operations wanted autonomy. The time for international co-operation through easy travel and modern communications had not arrived, and the war would see its postponement. During the conflict Buckmaster's fluency in languages brought him to the attention of the Special Operations Executive (SOE) and he returned to Ford afterwards as head of what was henceforth called Public Affairs. His successors included Walter Hayes, a former Fleet Street editor, whose influence on Ford in Europe and the United States went well beyond the customary boundaries of motor industry PR. The gifted Hayes elevated the science of Public Affairs to new heights and he went on to senior management taking charge of Aston Martin in 1991 following its purchase by Ford.

In 1955 commercial vehicle production passed 50,000, and although vans and light trucks still had side-valve engines, they came to enjoy the comfort of independent front suspension and hydraulic brakes, as well as the thrift of Ford's first diesel. Tractors and commercial vehicles had been offered with a Perkins P6 until the advent of a 3.6-litre ohv compression ignition engine of 52.2kW (70bhp). The 1957 Thames Trader range had synchromesh gearboxes, hypoid back axles, and all its engines were Ford-made, the 4-cylinder joined by a petrol 4.9-litre 85.75kW (115bhp) and a 5.4-litre diesel of 80.5kW (108bhp).

In 1960 commercial vehicle operations were transferred to Langley, west of London, where by 1965 it was making over 85,000 units including buses. From 1971 the Transit was made in Southampton, and D-series forward control trucks

with tilt cabs and inclined engines covered the 2 to 9-ton market. In 1966 Ford was Britain's leading producer of commercial vehicles, with 113,623 units.

The landmark Cortina of 1962 was created under executive product planner Terry Beckett. The name Caprino was wisely rejected, although Cortina still turned out inappropriate for Italy, where it meant curtains. Its success led Becket to chairmanship of Ford UK, a knighthood and chairmanship of the Confederation of British Industry (CBI). Sir Terence Beckett summed up the achievement: "The Cortina came in under cost and most significantly, we did it in record time. I believe we took just 21 months from full-size clay style to Job 1, which was then an all time record for the industry. We needed a bigger body shell and also more wheel movement. We decided that we would provide a proper boot – in a way we overdid that, but it was perfect for a rep who wanted to take samples, and it was perfect for the family motorist." A straight-panelled middle market family saloon, Cortina grew in size and speed from fleet "repmobile" to the sophisticated executive car of the 1970s. In September 1982 Sam Toy drove the last, 4,279,079th Cortina, off the Dagenham line.

The Capri became a social icon, proof that a sporty car was no longer exclusive to a privileged class. And in the face of opposition from Ferrari, Ford won the Le Mans 24 Hours race, perhaps the most prestigious event on the world motor sporting calendar. The secure prestige of the other classic makes, Porsche, Jaguar, Alfa Romeo and Bentley would never be as secure again.

Formula 1 came to be dominated by Ford. The Cosworth-Ford DFV, evolved by the genius of Keith Duckworth and Cosworth Engineering, may have

only been paid for by Ford, but it said FORD on the cam covers. Walter Hayes's astute management of Public Affairs ensured the connection was strongly made. Lotus Cortinas and Sierra Cosworths won races and rallies. Ford was in the performance league; the youth market belonged to Ford, the Capri was not a flash in the pan with a long bonnet and a tiny engine. It was part of a well-constructed policy that refuted the picture of Ford as mass-market or, worse, down-market.

No self-respecting car manufacturer was without its own research and development centre. Ford in Britain had been self sufficient in most ways since the 1930s but from time to time had had to turn to Detroit for inspiration, as with the 1950s Consul and Zephyr. The Mark II Zephyr and Zodiac were designed in Dagenham on the platform of the Mark I under Sir Patrick Hennessey, who succeeded Sir Rowland Smith in 1956. The Three Graces, as they were known, established a British style and character, which proved more enduring than some less distinctive although arguably better-built strains developed in Cologne.

OPPOSITE **In 1969 Ford took to the high seas with a team of power boats using 6.0 litre turbocharged Ford marine diesels. The 28-foot Fairey Huntsman Seaspray won 16 major awards.**
ABOVE **1968 Le Mans, postponed until September owing to French strikes, won by the John Wyer Automotive GT40 running in Gulf colours, driven by Pedro Rodriguez and Lucien Bianchi. Two Wyer cars were out by midnight but the third held a lead it never lost.**

Ford in Britain outgrew existing research and development facilities so new ones were laid down close to Dagenham, at Dunton in Essex. The Government directed Ford to expand in the provinces if it wanted development grants for manufacturing, and Anglia production went to the new plant on Merseyside at Halewood. In 1960 Ford USA bought all privately-held Ford of Britain shares, paying £7.25 for each £1 ordinary share, an estimated £128.5million. Meanwhile Ford-Britain engineers engaged in styling, designing and building prototypes moved into a purpose-built facility at Aveley, Essex.

Sam Toy became chairman as Ford launched a new Escort, which had cost £1250million to develop. It was hoped to guarantee continuing success in Europe and increase Ford's share of the depressed United States market, but at Halewood, where the Escort was built, output was only 65 per cent of its target; the new chairman complained that efficiency and productivity were twice as good at Ford's German plant. Industrial disputes slowed production and Toy threatened that unless matters improved the Escort could be the last car launched there. In 1981 he warned that Nissan's plan to build in Britain could be catastrophic for Britain's motor industry: "If we can't meet [the Japanese] and beat them we're dead".

Milestones under Toy's management included resisting EEC proposals to harmonise car prices. Toy supported the government's Youth Training Scheme offering jobs to teenagers at Ford plants and dealerships, and was in charge when Ford Britain lent Ford US £961million. High American interest rates made it cheaper to borrow from the British company, which was able to fund it from retained profits and reserves.

Ford cars became bigger and faster. In 1967 the convergence of Ford Britain and Ford Germany had been formalized, creating Ford of Europe. Common resourcing took years, however. Cortina and Taunus programmes gradually found common ground, so did the Escort and Granada, reaching success throughout the 1970s and 1980s. By then the big Fords could get no bigger leading to the creation of the 1990s' Premier Automotive Group embracing Jaguar, Land Rover, Volvo, Aston Martin and Lincoln. This was not like Ford's takeover of Ghia in 1973. The Italian coachbuilding house had been devalued as no more than a label for luxury interiors and shiny embellishments, a job that could easily have been done in-house. Ford paid £1.6billion for Jaguar in 1989, and $6.5billion for Volvo ten years later. This time there would be no devaluing.

Walter Hayes confirmed his motor industry credentials at Aston Martin in the new factory established by Tom Walkinshaw, away from the impossibly cramped and antiquated premises at Newport Pagnell, creating the exquisite DB7 on the basis of the underrated Jaguar XJS platform.

LEFT **Ford's romance with Jaguar from 1989 to 2008 left both with a long lasting commercial and engineering legacy, highlighted by the 1595kg (3516.3lb) aluminium XK8 of 2006.**
OPPOSITE **Thames Traders were made between 1957 and 1965 with 4 or 6-cylinder petrol or diesel engines. The distinctive cab was based on an American design.**

Tough, dependable, economical...

HAMES TRADERS

30 cwt. 2, 3, 4, 5 & 7 tonners   built by FORD

By the 21st century Ford UK factories and offices extended well beyond Essex to Bristol, Croydon, Daventry, Edinburgh, Halewood, Leamington, Leeds, Southampton, and Trafford House in Manchester. The Dunton Technical Centre became the largest automotive design and engineering facility in Britain and one of the most advanced in the whole of Europe. It was home to over 5000 engineers, designers, and support staff who, together with colleagues in Cologne, were responsible for design and development of small and medium cars and vans, and commercial vehicles, throughout the world. After 21 years, in 2001 the Bridgend engine plant made its ten millionth engine, and investment of £225million created new jobs doubling engine production to more than a million annually in 2004. There was investment of £345million for a new Transit at Southampton. In 2001 Ford had been Britain's best-selling brand for 25 years, 36 as medium commercial vehicle market leader, and 23 as light commercial vehicle market leader.

At Dagenham, Ford's British home for over 70 years, production ended after 10,980,368 vehicles. Following a £375 million programme a new assembly hall increased diesel engine capacity from 650,000 to 900,000. Together with Bridgend production, this meant that one in four of all Fords world wide were equipped with British made engines.

Ford continued its pursuit of success in rallying. Colin Steele McRae joined in 1999 after a successful career with Subaru, with whom he won the World Rally Championship (WRC) drivers' title in 1995, and helped bring three consecutive manufacturers' titles. Ford made him the highest-earning rally driver ever, but although his 2002 win of the Safari Rally posted a record in WRC

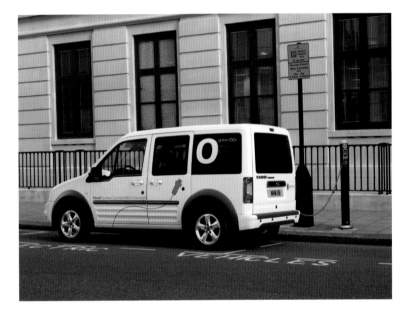

events the top world title eluded him. When he left after four years European director of motorsport Martin Whitaker had to thank him and his co-driver Nicky Grist for strenuous efforts. McRae died piloting his helicopter in 2007.

In July 2004 Martin Smith, formerly with Porsche, Audi and Vauxhall/Opel was made executive director of design in a major reorganization of European Ford design staff. Smith was instrumental in the introduction of Kinetic Design, meaning clean angles and complex surfacing that gave Fords a more dynamic appearance. In February 2005 Sir Nick Scheele retired from the presidency, Chairman Bill Ford paying tribute: "When I became chief executive officer three years ago I turned to trusted Ford veterans such as Nick to help steer this company back to the basics of our business. Not only did Nick help us overcome many of our

OPPOSITE **Tipping Transit and projected Tourneo BEV battery electric** ABOVE **charging from the kerbside. The silent zero-emission BEV was shown at Frankfurt Motor Show in 2010 in partnership with Smith Electric Vehicles (Tanfield group).**

challenges, he helped set the stage for a new generation of leaders that is making Ford the most competitive global automaker."

Progress quickened towards concentrating on the Ford brand world wide in March 2008, following agreement that the Jaguar Land Rover business was to be sold to Tata Motors. On closing the deal the total cash paid by Tata of US$2.3billion coincided with a contribution by Ford of around US$600million to Jaguar Land Rover pension plans. Alan Mulally, president and CEO of Ford Motor Company acknowledged the great quality of the brands into which Ford had put such strenuous efforts: "We are confident that they are leaving our fold with products, plan, and team to continue to thrive under Tata. It is time for Ford to integrate the Ford brand globally." He said much the same in 2010 when Ford concluded the sale of Volvo to Zhejiang Geely Holding Group for $1.8 billion.

Part of both transactions was an undertaking to continue the supply of power trains, stampings and components, as well as a variety of technology, engineering support, information, accounting and other services. The integration of engine manufacture would take years to work through. In one of his last pronouncements before his untimely death, Jaguar Land Rover CEO Geoff Polites expressed confidence in the team that had delivered significant improvements in the company's business performance.

Plans for a £1.5billion investment in four UK engineering and manufacturing facilities over five years followed a £450million loan to Ford from the European Investment Bank (EIB). The loan was signed off at Ford's Dunton Technical Centre in Essex following an announcement in March that the UK government was to provide a £360million loan guarantee. Business Minister, Mark Prisk, European Investment Bank vice president, Simon Brooks and Ford of Britain chairman, Joe Greenwell, signed contracts for the guarantee and the loan, repayable on commercial terms, to pay for projects that improve fuel efficiency and reduce emissions. Engines assembled at Ford Dagenham emitting as little as 98g CO_2/km were installed in Fiesta and Focus ECOnetic models. Fuel-saving ECOnetic technology was also extended to commercial vehicles. Ford Bridgend produced the 1.6-litre Ford EcoBoost petrol engine, which offered CO_2 and fuel savings of up to 20 per cent compared with conventional petrol engines and equipped the C-MAX range in the autumn. Ford of Britain chairman, Joe Greenwell, said: "This European Investment Bank loan, and the loan guarantee from the government, will help to unlock up to £1.5billion in low-carbon and environmentally friendly engine and vehicle technology investment over the next five years."

In 45 years 2.1million Transits were sold in the UK, six million world wide and in 2010 the first of a limited edition Transit Sapphire was presented to Paul Hendy of Hendy Group, Britain's first Ford dealer, celebrating its centenary.

LEFT **Ford aimed for five plug-in hybrid electric and battery vehicles in America by 2012 and Europe the following year. The Focus Electric could charge its lithium-ion battery pack from either a standard 240V or 120V charging station.**
OPPOSITE **Dagenham made engines for the world of Ford.**

1908
Model T

Convinced of the Model T's worldwide appeal, Henry Ford shipped the first eight for display at Olympia in London, on 13 November 1908, and then on to Paris. Fords had been imported to Britain since 1903, yet the Model Ts coming in through The Central Motor Car Company Ltd, of 117 Long Acre, London WC, represented a fresh approach. Among their radical features were cylinders cast in one block, and an integral engine, clutch and gearbox. The epicyclic gears drew inspiration from the works of Frederick Lanchester, along principles that would form the basis of the modern automatic transmission. There were three pedals; the middle one engaged reverse, the left engaged low when pressed, high when released, and the right operated the transmission brake. A steering column throttle controlled engine speed and mounting the road springs transversely meant only two were needed instead of four, a useful economy. Crosswise springing also offered less resistance to side-roll and twisting on corners. Following European practice American carmakers had put the steering wheel on the right. Henry Ford decided it was more logical, where the rule of the road was keep right, to have it on the left. He was a passionate advocate of vanadium steel, which he believed would make cars stronger and lighter. He used it for the Model T's frail looking but sturdy drop forged front axle, spindly crankshaft, and parts of the transmission. His confidence was thoroughly justified.

INTRODUCTION 27 September 1908, produced until 26 May 1927.
BODY Various body styles; 2 or 4-seats; weight 1200lb (544kg).
ENGINE 4-cylinders, in-line, front; 3.75in (95.25mm) x 4in (101.6mm), 2896cc (176.7 cu in); compr 4.5:1; 20bhp (14.91kW) @ 1800rpm; 6.9bhp (5.1kW)/l.
ENGINE STRUCTURE L-head side valve; gear-driven camshaft; non-adjustable tappets; detachable cast iron cylinder head and block; Holley or Kingston updraught single jet carburettor, mixture adjustable by driver; low-tension flywheel magneto, low tension distributor and separate trembler coil for each cylinder, standby battery for starting; splash lubrication; gravity fuel feed; 3-bearing crankshaft; cooling by multi-tube radiator (brass shell in UK until 1916, thereafter black), thermosyphon, and fan.

TRANSMISSION rear wheel drive; epicyclic 2-speed and reverse gearbox, steel disc clutches for low speed and reverse by contracting bands on epicycle drums; multi-disc clutch for direct drive top; propeller shaft enclosed in torque tube; final drive passenger cars and light vans straight-tooth bevel gears; ratio 3.64:1 high 10:1 low
CHASSIS straight steel channel-section chassis; transverse leaf springs front and rear with radius rods; mechanical brakes foot – contracting band on direct-drive clutch, hand – expanding shoes in rear wheel drums; steering by epicyclic reduction gear in steering wheel boss, drop arm on end of steering column, transverse drag link, 1.25 turns lock to lock; 10gal (45.46l) fuel tank; 30 x 3in front, 30 x 3.5in rear, variations on balloon and straight-sided tyres; hickory-spoked

artillery wheels, non-detachable, fixed rims; detachable rims after 1919.
DIMENSIONS wheelbase 100in (254cm); track 56in (142.2cm) later 60in (152.4cm); length 134in (340.4cm); width 66in (167.6cm); ground clearance 10.5in (76.2cm).
EQUIPMENT 1909–1915 no electrical system; 1915–1919 8v headlamps and horn from flywheel magneto; 1919–1927 dynamo and battery for 6v starting and lighting.
PERFORMANCE maximum speed 45mph (72.2kph) approx, claim by Ford, 15mph (24kph) in low; 27.2kg/bhp (36.5kg/kW); fuel consumption 28mpg (10.1l/100km).
PRICE in the US $850, reduced to $600 in 1913, by 1918 $360. UK price 1910 £220.
PRODUCTION 15,007,033 in US and Canada, total from all sources about 16,500,000.

1911
Trafford Park Model T

Five hundred cars a year was good business, so Ford Motor Company (England) Ltd was established at Trafford Park. The first British Ford assembled from imported parts was produced on 23 October 1911. Ford's Irish factory supplied chassis items until Joseph Sankey, of Hadley Shropshire, could take over so by the 1920s Model Ts were made from home grown components. A moving production line came in September 1914. Assembly had been a stationary affair with axles and chassis laid out on the floor and building a Model T took 12 hours. Moving assembly tracks had been used elsewhere, but Ford waited until components could be made accurately enough to be interchangeable. Build time was cut to an hour and a half. The following year the flywheel magneto operated an electric lighting set, not altogether satisfactorily, since being dependent on engine speed, the lights grew dim when driving slowly. The Model T's success was overwhelming. All other Fords were discontinued to try meeting the demand. A quarter of a million Model Ts came off the line at the new Detroit Highland Park plant; 3000 a year made Ford Britain's biggest car maker. Historian Anthony Bird wrote: "To say of the Model T Ford that it was a remarkably bad car would be tantamount to doubting the judgement of the 15,007,033 satisfied customers who bought the Lizzie during her production life of 19 years. To placate their shades and turn aside the howls of angry derision which must greet the statement let it be rephrased, to say that Henry Ford, like Carl Benz before him, was an obstinate man whose undeniable ingenuity was tinged with perversity, with the result that his masterpiece was marred by some curiously maladroit features."

INTRODUCTION 27 September 1908, produced until 26 May 1927.
BODY Various styles; 2 or 4-seats; weight 1200lb (544kg).
ENGINE 4-cylinders, in-line; front; 3.75in (95.25mm) x 4in (101.6mm), 2896cc (176.7 cu in); compr 4.5:1; 20bhp (14.91kW) @ 1800rpm; 6.9bhp (5.1kW)/l.
ENGINE STRUCTURE L-head side valve; gear-driven camshaft; non-adjustable tappets; detachable cast iron cylinder head and block; Holley or Kingston single jet updraught carburettor, mixture adjustable by driver; low-tension flywheel magneto, distributor and separate trembler coil for each cylinder, standby battery for starting; splash lubrication; gravity fuel feed; 3-bearing crankshaft; cooling by multi-tube radiator (brass shell in UK until 1916 thereafter black), thermosyphon, and fan.

TRANSMISSION rear wheel drive; epicyclic 2-speed and reverse gearbox, steel disc clutches for low speed and reverse by contracting bands on epicycle drums; multi-disc clutch for direct drive top; propeller shaft enclosed in torque tube; final drive passenger cars and light vans straight-tooth bevel gears; ratio 3.64:1 high 10:1 low.
CHASSIS straight steel channel-section chassis; transverse leaf springs front and rear with radius rods; mechanical brakes foot – contracting band on direct-drive clutch, hand – expanding shoes in rear wheel drums; steering by epicyclic reduction gear in steering wheel boss, drop arm on end of steering column, transverse drag link, 1.25 turns lock to lock; 10gal (45.46l) fuel tank; 30 x 3in front, 30 x 3.5in rear, variations on balloon and straight-sided tyres; hickory-spoked

artillery wheels, non-detachable, fixed rims; detachable rims after 1919; wire-spoked wheels 1925.
DIMENSIONS wheelbase 100in (254cm); track 56in (142.2cm) later 60in (152.4cm); length 134in (340.4cm); width 66in (167.6cm); ground clearance 10.5in (76.2cm).
EQUIPMENT from 1909-1915 no electrical system; 1915-1919 8v headlamps and horn from flywheel magneto; 1919-1927 dynamo and battery for 6v starting and lighting.
PERFORMANCE maximum speed 45mph (72.2kph) approx, claim by Ford, 15mph (24kph) in low; 27.2kg/bhp (36.5kg/kW); fuel consumption 28mpg (10.1l/100km).
PRICE Various models, roadster, tourer, 2-door, 4-door saloons, and town car, chassis 1919 £170, 1921 £250, 1924 2-seater £110.
PRODUCTION 300,000.

1916
Military Model T

Almost as soon as the assembly line was installed, Trafford Park went over to war production, supplying 30,000 vehicles during hostilities. The Model T served on the Western Front and was endorsed by Lawrence of Arabia during his campaign in Mesopotamia, along with his armoured Rolls-Royce Silver Ghost. Blakes of Liverpool was appointed a Ford dealer in 1910, making bodies for Model T ambulances, 2645 of which were produced between 1915 and 1920. The army devised a more aggressive role, mounting a Vickers machine-gun on the scuttle and using the Model T as a reconnaissance patrol car. Others were fitted with flanged wheels, to act as railway trolleys on narrow-gauge lines, and after the war M Kègresse evolved one into a half-track all-terrain vehicle, but it failed to find favour with the forces. The Royal Flying Corps developed a Model T chemical fire engine with extinguisher canisters in the rear. Also for the RFC, Captain Bentfield C (Benny) Hucks of Scarborough, a test pilot for the Airco company of Hendon, designed a mechanism to start aircraft engines off the Model T's epicyclic transmission. A chain drive from the rear of the gearbox to an overhead shaft spun the propeller, which was a good deal safer than having it swung by a hapless aircraftsman. A Model T with a Hucks starter was displayed in the Imperial War Museum Hanger 4 at Duxford.

INTRODUCTION 1916–1918.
BODY 2-seat panel van with C-cab or open truck; weight approx 1540lb (698.5kg).
ENGINE 4-cylinders, in-line; front; 3.75in (95.25mm) x 4in (101.6mm), 2896cc (176.7 cu in); compr 4.5:1; 20bhp (14.91kW) @ 1800rpm; 6.9bhp(5.1kW)/l.
ENGINE STRUCTURE L-head side valve; gear-driven camshaft; non-adjustable tappets; detachable cast iron cylinder head and block; Holley or Kingston single jet updraught carburettor, mixture adjustable by driver; low-tension flywheel magneto, low tension distributor and separate trembler coil for each cylinder, standby battery for starting; splash lubrication; gravity fuel feed; 3-bearing crankshaft; cooling by multi-tube radiator, thermosyphon, and fan.
TRANSMISSION rear wheel drive; epicyclic 2-speed and reverse gearbox, steel disc clutches for low speed and reverse by contracting bands on epicycle drums; multi-disc clutch for direct drive top; propeller shaft enclosed in torque tube; final drive light van straight-tooth bevel gears; 1-ton truck overhead worm and wheel; ratio 3.64:1 high 10:1 low.

CHASSIS straight steel channel-section chassis; transverse leaf springs front and rear with radius rods; mechanical brakes foot – contracting band on direct-drive clutch, hand – expanding shoes in rear wheel drums; steering by epicyclic reduction gear in steering wheel boss, drop arm on end of steering column, transverse drag link, 1.25 turns lock to lock; 10gal (45.46l) fuel tank; 30 x 3in front, 30 x 3.5in rear, variations on balloon and straight-sided tyres; hickory-spoked artillery wheels, non-detachable, fixed rims.
DIMENSIONS wheelbase 100in (254cm); track 56in (142.2cm) later 60in (152.4cm); length 134in (340.4cm); width 66in (167.6cm); ground clearance 10.5in (76.2cm).
EQUIPMENT 1915-1918 8v headlamps and horn from flywheel magneto.
PERFORMANCE maximum speed 45mph (72.2kph) approx, 15mph (24kph) in low 34.9kg/bhp (46.9kg/kW); fuel consumption 28mpg (10.1l/100km).
PRODUCTION approximately 30,000.

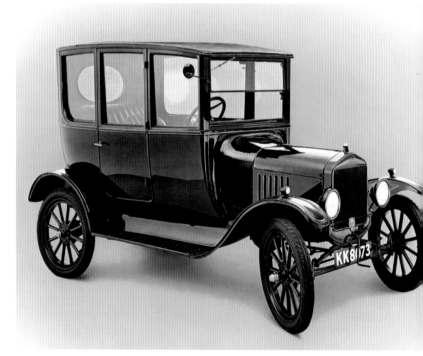

1918
Model T 1-Ton

Ford's first British-built commercial vehicle was a delivery van introduced in 1912. It could carry loads up to 7cwt (355.6kg) and became the basis of Model T commercials. By 1924 these had outstripped production of cars. The delivery van often replaced horse-drawn carts and was adequate for light loads such as bakeries doing door-to-door business, but it was too short for a proper truck. Proprietary conversions were offered from 1914, which took a chain drive to a second axle mounted on half-elliptic springs. Payload increased to 1ton (1016kg) and the conversion cost £92. In 1919 Ford introduced its own Model TT truck with the frame extended by 24in (60.96cm), a stronger back axle on the familiar transverse spring and the choice of solid rear tyres or smaller-diameter pneumatics. Trafford Park sold complete Ton Vans, as they were known, as well as the TT chassis for proprietary bodywork. Over 1000 were bought as Post Office vans and the chassis also made a platform for charabancs, furniture vans, and even petrol tankers. The British American Import Company (BAICO), which carried out extended-chassis conversions, produced the Extendatonna with a 1.5ton (1512kg) capacity, and the Supertonna capable of taking 2.5tons (2540kg). The feeble power unit needed all the help it could get to move such a load, so an extra three-speed gearbox provided even lower gearing.

INTRODUCTION 1918, produced until 1927.
BODY 2-seat panel van with C-cab, or all-steel cab after 1924; weight approx 1540lb (698.5kg).
ENGINE 4-cylinders, in-line; front; 3.75in (95.25mm) x 4in (101.6mm), 2896cc (176.7 cu in); compr 4.5:1; 20bhp (14.91kW) @ 1800rpm; 6.9bhp(5.1kW)/l.
ENGINE STRUCTURE L-head side valve; gear-driven camshaft; non-adjustable tappets; detachable cast iron cylinder head and block; Holley or Kingston single jet updraught carburettor, mixture adjustable by driver; low-tension flywheel magneto, low tension distributor and separate trembler coil for each cylinder, standby battery for starting; splash lubrication; gravity fuel feed; 3-bearing crankshaft; cooling by multi-tube radiator, thermosyphon, and fan.

TRANSMISSION rear wheel drive; epicyclic 2-speed and reverse gearbox, steel disc clutches for low speed and reverse by contracting bands on epicycle drums; multi-disc clutch for direct drive top; propeller shaft enclosed in torque tube; final drive light van straight-tooth bevel gears; 1-ton truck overhead worm and wheel lower ratio 3.64:1 high 10:1 low.
CHASSIS straight steel channel-section frame; transverse leaf springs front and rear with radius rods; mechanical brakes foot – contracting band on direct-drive clutch, hand – expanding shoes in rear wheel drums; steering by epicycle reduction gear in steering wheel boss, drop arm on end of steering column, transverse drag link, 1.25 turns lock to lock; 10gal (45.46l) fuel tank; 30 x 3in front, 30 x 3.5in rear, variations on balloon and

straight-sided tyres; hickory-spoked artillery wheels, non-detachable, fixed rims; detachable rims after 1919.
DIMENSIONS wheelbase 100in (254cm), TT 124in (314.9cm); track 56in (142.2cm) later 60in (152.4cm); length 134in (340.4cm); width 66in (167.6cm); height 71in (180.34cm); ground clearance 10.5in (76.2cm).
EQUIPMENT 1915–1919 8v headlamps and horn from flywheel magneto; 1919-1927 dynamo and battery for 6v starting and lighting.
PERFORMANCE maximum speed 45mph (72.2kph) approx, claim by Ford, 15mph (24kph) in low; 34.9kg/bhp (46.9kg/kW); fuel consumption 28mpg (10.1l/100km).
PRICE Various, chassis only 1919 £170, 1921 £250.
PRODUCTION 37,556 Trucks; 11,307 Ton Vans, 56,301 chassis.

1918
Fordson Model F tractor and Model T racer

Fordson was the telegraphic address of Henry Ford & Son Company, which Henry Ford and his son Edsel established to make tractors, after the main board opposed the idea. The world's first light weight mass produced tractor, the Model F had a bigger engine than the Model T and a 3-speed gearbox in the back axle. The structure combined engine block, transmission, and rear axle, the inspiration of Ford's Hungarian engineer Eugene Farkas. The British Government Board of Agriculture was under pressure to increase wartime food production. As soon as the prototype Fordson was demonstrated to the members, it was put into production at the Cork factory, using components shipped directly from the United States. Henry Ford made a gift of the drawings and patent rights to Britain for the duration of the conflict. The fierce clutch and short wheelbase made starting off alarming and it had a tendency to rear over backwards, if its plough encountered an obstruction. Cork proved unable to meet the demand so the Ministry of Munitions ordered a further 6000 from Detroit, for British farms.

A Model T racer like Frank Kulick's could average 107.8mph (173kph) on the frozen surface of Lake St Clair in the winter of 1912. His Super T was not much more than a chassis, with the engine in a box on top, and a pointed radiator. This was a popular feature of T Torpedo Runabouts and the 1912 Speedster looked every inch a sportsman's car.

INTRODUCTION production 1917–1927 and 1933-1946.
BODY Open; no doors, 1-seat; weight 2710lb (1229.26kg) 1920; 3175lb (1440.18kg) 1926 with ballast. Specification material based on Nebraska tractor test laws 1920 and 1926.
ENGINE 4-cylinders, in-line; front; 4in (101.6mm) x 5in (127mm), 251cu in (4118cc); 18.2bhp (13.57kW) gross at power take-off @ 1100rpm in 1920. 22.3bhp (16.63kW); 4.41bhp(3.3kW)/l in 1926.

ENGINE STRUCTURE L-head side valve; gear-driven camshaft; non-adjustable tappets; detachable cast iron cylinder head and block; Ford brass single jet carburettor, kerosene mixture adjustable by driver, with gasoline for starting; low-tension flywheel magneto, low tension distributor and separate trembler coil for each cylinder, standby battery for starting; splash lubrication; gravity fuel feed; 3-bearing crankshaft; cooling by multi-tube 11gal (50litre) radiator, thermosyphon, and fan.

TRANSMISSION Rear wheel drive; multiple disc in oil clutch; 3-speed manual gearbox; worm and wheel reduction gear final drive.
CHASSIS Unitary bolted and cast structure of engine, transmission and axle; no suspension; drop arm on end of steering column to drag link, 1.25 turns lock to lock; saddle fuel tank; steel wheels by Whitehead & Kales and Kelsey; solid rubber optional.
PERFORMANCE maximum speed 6.5mph (10.5kph); 64.6kg/bhp (86.6kg/kW) 1926; fuel consumption 7.32 hp/hour per gallon 1920, 9.63 hp/hour per gallon 1926 (Nebraska test)
PRICE $750
PRODUCTION Cork from July 4 1919 63001 – 63200 and 65001 – 65103. 1920 65104 – 65500 and 105001 – 108229. 1921 108230 – 109672. 1922 109673 – 110000 and 170958 – 172000 and 25001 – 250300 and 253001 – 253552

1923
Model T

Model Ts were mostly blue, green, or grey. Black was not an option until the production line created Henry Ford's aphorism about customers having cars any colour they wanted, provided they liked black. Speed of production was essential to meet demand and the quickest-drying paint was black japan enamel. Body-painting was done 24 hours ahead of assembly with coats of colour varnish and finishers. Trafford Park was obliged to become self-sufficient, particularly in wartime, and radiators and wings were made on the premises although chassis and engines were shipped from the United States until 1921, when they became available from Cork. The following year, after the foundation of the Irish Free State, new import duties were imposed and once again Manchester was encouraged to become autonomous. On 17 April 1925 it made its 250,000th Model T, advertised as, "a British car made of British parts by British labour." By the time production ended in August 1927 the Model T was more sophisticated, with a rounded nickel-plated radiator and lower, more comfortable bodywork. Problems with the electrical system persisted, and in winter the clutch tended to seize and hand-cranking the engine produced unwanted creep which could run an unwary crankist over. Accessory firms sold Model T-specific items such as cradles and supports to strengthen the notoriously weak engine bearers. Colour options came back in 1926.

INTRODUCTION 27 September 1908, produced until 26 May 1927.
BODY Various styles; 2-door; 2 or 4-seats; weight 1540lb (698.5kg).
ENGINE 4-cylinders, in-line; front; 3.75in (95.25mm) x 4in (101.6mm), 2896cc (176.7 cu in); compr 4.5:1; 20bhp (14.91kW) @ 1800rpm; 6.9bhp(5.1kW)/l.
ENGINE STRUCTURE L-head side valve; gear-driven camshaft; non-adjustable tappets; detachable cast iron cylinder head and block; Holley or Kingston single jet updraught carburettor, mixture adjustable by driver; low-tension flywheel magneto, low tension distributor and separate trembler coil for each cylinder, standby battery for starting; splash lubrication; gravity fuel feed; 3-bearing crankshaft; cooling by black-painted multi-tube radiator, thermosyphon, and fan.

TRANSMISSION rear wheel drive; epicyclic 2-speed and reverse gearbox, steel disc clutches for low speed and reverse by contracting bands on epicyclic drums; multi-disc clutch for direct drive top; propeller shaft enclosed in torque tube; final drive passenger cars and light vans straight-tooth bevel gears; 1-ton truck overhead worm and wheel; ratio 3.64:1 high 10:1 low.
CHASSIS straight steel channel-section frame; transverse leaf springs front and rear with radius rods; mechanical brakes foot – contracting band on direct-drive clutch, hand – expanding shoes in rear wheel drums, 8in later 11in with asbestos linings; steering by epicycle reduction gear in steering wheel boss, drop arm on end of steering column, transverse drag link, 1.25 turns lock to lock; 10gal (45.46l) fuel tank; 30 x 3in front, 30 x 3.5in rear, 4.40 x 21 balloon in 1927 tyres; wire-spoked wheels 1926.
DIMENSIONS wheelbase 100in (254cm); track 56in (142.2cm) later 6in (152.4cm); length 134in (340.4cm); width 66in (167.6cm); ground clearance 10.5in (76.2cm).
EQUIPMENT Fordor body added 1923; 8v headlamps and horn from flywheel magneto; 1919–1927 dynamo and battery for 6v starting and lighting.
PERFORMANCE maximum speed 45mph (72.2kph) approx, claim by Ford, 15mph (24kph) in low; 34.9kg/bhp (46.9kg/kW); fuel consumption 28mpg (10.1l/100km).
PRICE Various models, roadster, tourer, 2-door, 4-door saloons, and town car, chassis 1919 £170, 1921 £250, 1924 2-seater £110.
PRODUCTION 300,000.

1927
Model A 3285cc 22HP

If the Model T was a motor industry Holy Grail, a single design that could be sold the world over, the Model A that came next showed such universalism was no longer tenable. In Europe cars were taxed by engine size, petrol was becoming expensive, roads were small, narrow and congested, and no sooner had Ford introduced the Model A than market differences became obvious. In the United States a big 3-litre engine was fine for open roads and fuel was cheap, even in the wake of the Depression. However once production got under way at Cork, Southern Ireland and at Trafford Park Manchester, a smaller-engine option the AF (for Model A-Foreign) (qv) had to be introduced in response to

a cautious market. Model A innovations included abandonment of the epicyclic gearbox, but the transverse leaf springs, torque tube transmission, and stout channel-section chassis of the Model T remained. The body shape was not unlike the Model T, although a bigger radiator and engine cowling made it seem bigger. Enclosure of all rotating parts from the starting handle to the back axle was a strong sales point, in an era when whirring chains and shafts, along with exposed oscillating valves, were not uncommon. Top gear pulling power was robust but when changes did need to be made, it had, as The *Autocar*'s testers marvelled, "a gear control simply made for caressing."

INTRODUCTION 1927 produced until 1932.
BODY 2-seat 2-door, 4-seat tourer, 2-door 4-seat Tudor saloon or coupe; 2-door 4-seat sports coupe and 4-door 4-seat saloon Fordor; weight 22.75cwt (1155.7kg) (2547.8lb).
ENGINE 4-cylinders, in-line; front; 98mm (3.875in) x 108mm (4.25in), 3285cc; compr 5.2:1; 40bhp (29.8kW) @ 2200rpm; 12.2bhp(9.1kW)/l.
ENGINE STRUCTURE side valves; gear-driven camshaft; cast iron detachable cylinder head and block; coil ignition; gravity fuel supply; automatic multi-jet needle valve carburettor; 3-bearing crankshaft; cooling by thermosyphon, later with centrifugal water impeller.
TRANSMISSION rear wheel drive; multi-disc clutch, later single dry plate; 3-speed manual gearbox, synchromesh later; freewheel later; torque tube; spiral bevel final drive 4.66:1.
CHASSIS pressed steel channel frame; front and rear suspension transverse leaf spring; Houdaille hydraulic dampers; radius rods front and rear; mechanical 4-wheel drum brakes; worm and sector steering 11.25:1; 8gal (36.4l) fuel tank; 30 x 4.5in tyres, 21in later 19in wire wheels.
DIMENSIONS wheelbase 103.5in (262.9cm); length 151.5in (384.8cm); width 66in (167.6cm); ground clearance 9in (22.9cm); turning circle 17ft (5.18m).
EQUIPMENT stop-lamp, hand throttle, hand ignition control, Triplex glass standard, theft-proof ignition cable, 6 volt electrical system.
PERFORMANCE maximum speed 65mph (105kph); 28.9kg/bhp (38.8kg/kW); fuel consumption 19.4mpg (14.5l/100km).
PRICE chassis £120, 2-seater £145, tourer £150, Tudor saloon or coupe £185, sports coupe and Fordor £215.
PRODUCTION in Britain 14,516; total 4,320,466.

1928
Model AF 2038cc 14.9HP

The AF engine had a smaller 3.05in (77.47mm) bore but the same stroke as the regular A, yet in a world of small long-stroke treasury-rated horsepower (HP) Eights and Tens, a 2038cc of 14.9HP was too much of a good thing. Despite an anomalous £5 premium on the price, it outsold the full-size 3295cc 23.8 HP Model A on account of a cheaper Road Fund Licence. Production continued for a while at Trafford Park following inauguration of the new Dagenham plant, where it took three months to build the first five cars. The number of leaves in the chrome alloy steel transverse leaf springs depended on what body it was going to have. There was no independent braking system at first; a Model A's footbrake and handbrake actuated the same mechanism, slots on the ends of the connecting rods enabling one to be applied without the other. Authorities in Britain, France and Germany objected on safety grounds and the system was redesigned with an independent handbrake. Another early modification was the adoption of three instead of four engine mounts to reduce vibration, but the steel body remained obstinately noisy. The interior was plain with an unwinding ribbon speedometer and a central throttle pedal. Transverse leaf springing was all very well on the lightweight Model T but Ford's continued dedication to it in the heavier A (it represented a big saving on springs) invited body roll on corners.

INTRODUCTION 1927 produced until 1932.
BODY Saloon; 4-doors, 5-seats; weight 22cwt (1117.6kg) (2463.9lb).
ENGINE 4-cylinders, in-line; front; 77.5mm x 108mm, 2038cc; compr 5.2:1; 28bhp (20.88kW) @ 2600rpm; 13.7bhp(10.2kW)/l.
ENGINE STRUCTURE side valves; gear-driven camshaft; cast iron detachable cylinder head and block; coil ignition; gravity fuel feed; automatic multi-jet needle valve carburettor; 3-bearing carbon manganese steel crankshaft, cooling by thermosyphon, later with centrifugal water impeller.
TRANSMISSION rear wheel drive; multi-disc clutch at first, later single dry plate; 3-speed manual gearbox, synchromesh later; freewheel later; torque tube; spiral bevel final drive 4.66:1.
CHASSIS pressed steel channel frame; front and rear suspension transverse leaf spring; Houdaille double acting hydraulic dampers; radius rods front and rear; mechanical 4-wheel drum brakes; worm and sector steering 11.25:1; 8gal (36.4l) fuel tank; 30 x 4.5in tyres, 21in later 19in wire wheels.
DIMENSIONS wheelbase 103.5in (262.9cm); track 56in (142.2cm); length 151.5in (384.8cm); width 66in (167.6cm); ground clearance 9in (22.9cm); turning circle 17ft (5.18m).
EQUIPMENT stop-lamp, hand throttle, hand ignition control, Triplex glass standard, theft-proof ignition cable, 6-volt electrical system.
PERFORMANCE maximum speed AF 54mph (87kph) *The Autocar*; 39.9kg/kW (53.3kg/bhp); fuel consumption 27.4mpg (10.3l/100km).
PRICE £185, 2-door saloon; £135 chassis.
PRODUCTION of Models A and B in Britain 14,516; world total 4,320,466.

1931
Fordson 30-40cwt AA truck

First off the Dagenham line, driven by general manager RA (later Sir Rowland) Smith was AA4791110, a 1½ ton truck. British and American Ford trucks were the same until 1932. The AA was based on the Model A car, differences included longitudinal rear springs (stronger for different applications), and a 4-speed gearbox. There were complications with the torque tube transmission. Owing to the fixed length connection to the axle, the spring seating had to move on bump and rebound, so a crown wheel and pinion replaced the A's worm drive. Pressed steel wheels gave a sturdy appearance with a roomy cab, drop sides and a tailboard that lowered, "in a trice". Payloads went up to 40cwt (2032kg), and among the body

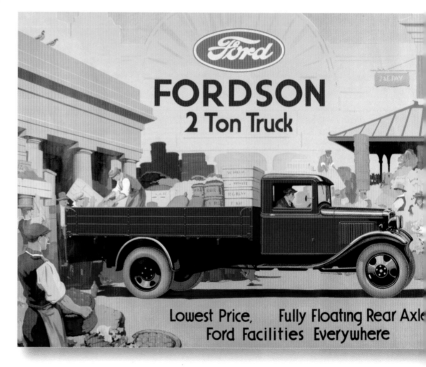

options was the "Luton" van, "...of a type originally laid down for the service of the hat-makers after whose metropolis it is named." Twin rear wheels were an option on short or long chassis to "facilitate the operation of the truck on soft yielding surfaces (such, for example, as those of a newly-opened building estate) and also reduce very considerably any possibility of skidding, or side-slip, on greasy, wet, or frost-rimed roads." All six wheels were interchangeable so only one spare was needed. The Boarded Tilt van was for laundrymen, departmental stores and, "users whose loads can be damaged by even a sharp shower because its loading space is protected by a rear curtain, extensible over hampers or crates on the tailboard."

INTRODUCTION 1931 production to 1935.
BODY Flatbed truck and cab; 2-doors, 2-seats; chassis weight 27cwt (1371.6kg), vehicle 3370lb (1528.6kg) to 33.5cwt (1701.8kg). hydraulic tipper 42.5cwt (2159kg).
ENGINE 4-cylinders, in-line; front; 98mm (3.875in) x 108mm (4.25in), 3285cc; compr 5.2:1; 52bhp (38.78kW) @ 2600rpm; 11.8bhp(15.8kW)/l.
ENGINE STRUCTURE side valves; Bakelised fabric gear-driven camshaft; cast iron detachable cylinder head and upper block; automatic ignition; fuel supply cam-driven pump for tank beneath driver's seat; automatic multi-jet needle valve carburettor; 3-bearing crankshaft; cooling by thermosyphon with centrifugal water impeller.

TRANSMISSION rear wheel drive; single plate clutch; 4-speed manual gearbox; torque tube; spiral bevel final drive 8.7:1; low ratio 11.13:1.
CHASSIS pressed steel 6in (15.2cm) side-member; 7in (17.8cm) with 3in (7.6cm) flanges on 2-tonner; channel frame; front suspension transverse leaf spring; rear cantilever half-elliptic graduated-thickness springs; radius rods front and rear; mechanical 4-wheel 14in (35.6cm) drum brakes; worm and sector steering 11.25:1; 12gal (54.55litres) fuel tank; wired-on cord 20 x 6in front tyres, 32 x 6in rear (6 x 20 all round with twin rear wheels); perforated steel wheels.
DIMENSIONS wheelbase 131.5in (334cm) or 157in (398.8cm); track front 55.1in (139.9cm), rear 68.8in (174.75cm); length 206.5in (524.5cm),

Luton van 228in (579.12cm); width 73.5in (186.7cm); height 71in (180.3cm); ground clearance 8in (20.32cm); turning circle 47ft (14.3metres).
EQUIPMENT 6-volt electric system; safety glass windscreen; windscreen wiper; petrol gauge, speedometer, toolkit, electrical lighting and starting.
PERFORMANCE Legal maximum speed 20mph (32.11kph); 26.4kg/bhp (35.4kg/kW)
PRICE chassis only £174 swb, £181.10s (£181.50p) with twin rear wheels, to £190 lwb; truck £210 ex-works Manchester; Boarded Tilt van £230, Luton van £260, hand-tipping truck £227, hydraulic tipper £277.10s (277.50p), farm utility truck £238
PRODUCTION world-wide 1928–1931 124,966

1932
Model B 2043cc and 3285cc

INTRODUCTION 1932 production to 1935.

BODY Roadster, cabriolet, tourer, Tudor, Fordor; 2/4-doors, 2/4-seats; weight approx 1464lb (1117.6kg).

ENGINE Model AB 4-cylinders, in-line; front; 98mm (3.875in) x 108mm (4.25in), 3285cc; compr 5.2:1; 48bhp (35.79kW) @ 2400rpm; 14.6bhp(10.9kW)/l. Model BF: 77.5mm x 108mm, 2038cc; compr 5.2:1; 41bhp (30.6kW) @ 3000rpm; 20.1bhp(15kW)/l.

ENGINE STRUCTURE side valves; gear-driven camshaft; cast iron detachable cylinder head and block; automatic ignition; mechanical fuel pump; automatic multi-jet needle valve carburettor; 3-bearing crankshaft; cooling by thermosyphon and centrifugal water impeller.

TRANSMISSION rear wheel drive; multi-disc clutch at first, later single dry plate; 3-speed manual gearbox, synchromesh; torque tube; spiral bevel final drive 4.66:1.

CHASSIS pressed steel channel frame; front and rear suspension transverse leaf spring; Houdaille hydraulic dampers; radius rods front and rear; mechanical 4-wheel drum brakes; worm and sector steering 11.25:1; 8gal (36.4l) fuel tank; 5.25 x 18 tyres, big-hub wire wheels.

DIMENSIONS wheelbase 106in (269.2cm); track 56in (142.2cm); length 142in (360.7cm); width 67.5in (171.4cm).

EQUIPMENT 6 volt electrical system.

PERFORMANCE maximum speed ABF 57mph (91.5kph) AB 65mph (104.3kph); 23.3kg/bhp (31.2kg/kW), BF 27.3kg/bhp (36.5kg/kW); fuel consumption ABF 32mpg (8.8l/100km), AB 19.4mpg (14.6l/100km).

PRICE ABF Tudor £180; Fordor £210; deluxe £225; AB Tudor £190, Fordor £220, deluxe £235.

PRODUCTION 8784

Still quite a big car by British standards, the Model B shared its 106in (269.2cm) wheelbase chassis with the new V8 and had more powerful versions of the two Model A engine options. Chassis improvements were scant, retaining the transverse springing familiar since the Model T, but the body sheet metal, pressed and assembled alongside the Dagenham production line by Briggs Motor Bodies, was carefully designed to have a more appealing style, with a more rounded grille. Although not as sleek as its American counterpart, it acknowledged the increasing importance for sales of keeping up appearances. The petrol tank was at the back instead of in the scuttle, by 1934 the wings were curvier and skirted, with streamlined sidelights, and the instruments were moved to the driver's line of sight. The headlamp tie-bar was straight instead of bent, fatter tyres gave a smoother, quieter ride and all the improvements incorporated in later Model As, such as synchromesh gears, were passed on. Ford's official chassis-plate designations were Model AB for the larger engined car, and Model ABF for the smaller, titles generally discarded in favour of plain Model B. Success did not attend it in Britain where taxation and the economic depression conspired to favour smaller cars. It was just as well that the truck side was flourishing and new small Fords were on their way.

Stylish Coupe. Most Model Bs were upright staid saloons.

1932
V8 18 30HP Victoria, Tudor, Fordor, Coupe, Convertible

Ford did not invent the V8 engine. Although it might have felt like it at the time, that distinction belonged to Clément Ader, whose *Societé Industrielle des Téléphones-Voitures Automobiles systèm Ader* evolved the first (really two V4s coupled together), for the 1903 Paris-Madrid race. M.Ader's three 32HP V8s made the finish at Bordeaux. De Dion Bouton, Cadillac, Lincoln, and NAG followed, then in the 1930s Cord, Riley, Horch and Standard made the V8 trustworthy. Ford's V8 was so overwhelmingly successful that the two became synonymous, and references to "the V8" usually meant, "the Ford". It was generic as Hoover or Mini. Show business stars welcomed the V8, along with racing drivers (Richard Seaman among them) who wanted a turn of speed together with the security of Ford's service network. Pan-European travellers found that when the classic makes to which they were accustomed broke down, spares could be problematic and expert dealers few and far between. A Ford V8 could be fixed as easily in Nice as Nottingham, its reliability was exemplary and it could negotiate Alpine passes, even though the flexible chassis of the V8 18 had to be reinforced before it could be taken on the Monte Carlo Rally. More likely to be described as racy than thoroughbred, the engine was used in some reputable sports cars, remaining in production for the best part of a quarter century.

TOP **Early Ford publicity picture of open cabriolet by Admiralty Arch.**

INTRODUCTION October 1932 produced to October 1933, Treasury rating 30HP.

BODY Victoria, Tudor, Fordor, Coupe, Convertible; 2/4-doors, 2/4-seats; weight 23cwt (1168.4kg) (2575.8lb).

ENGINE 8-cylinders in 90deg V; 77.8mm x 95mm, 3622cc; compr 5.5:1; 65bhp (48.5kW) @ 3400rpm; 17.9bhp (13.4kW)/l; 130lbft (176 Nm) @ 1250rpm.

ENGINE STRUCTURE side valves; centre gear-driven 3-bearing camshaft; cast iron detachable cylinder heads, blocks and upper crankcase unitary cast iron; engine weight 581lb (263.5kg); 1.25in (3.2cm) downdraught carburettor, coil ignition, camshaft-driven distributor; AC fuel pump; 3-bearing cast steel crankshaft; thermosyphon cooling, two belt-driven pumps, pressure lubrication by camshaft pump.

TRANSMISSION rear wheel drive; 9in (22.9cm) sdp clutch; 3-speed manual gearbox, synchromesh on 2 gears; helical bevel final drive 4.11:1, 3.78 optional.

CHASSIS steel frame with 4 cross-members; suspension by transverse leaf springs; 4 hydraulic lever arm dampers; mechanical drum brakes; worm and sector steering; 11.5gal (52.3l) rear-mounted fuel tank; 5.25 - 18 tyres.

DIMENSIONS wheelbase 106in (269.2cm); track 56in (142.2cm); length 165in (419.1cm); width 67.5in (171.45cm).

PERFORMANCE maximum speed 76mph (122kph), 0-60mph (96kph) 17.0sec; 18kg/bhp (24.1kg/kW); fuel consumption 16mpg (17.6l/100km).

PRICE Tudor sal £230; Coupe £295; Victoria Coupe £285; Fordor sal £260; Cabriolet £295; Fordor with sunroof £275; leather upholstery £7 10s (£7.50) extra.

PRODUCTION 911 including V8-40.

1932
Model Y

Inheriting features from the Model T, the Model Y dynasty passed them on to several generations of small Fords well into the 1950s. Except during the Second World War, Ford made a car with transverse leaf springs, a side valve 4-cylinder engine, torque tube transmission and mechanical brakes until 1959. The Y was conceived in the aftermath of the Great Depression and its basic recipe survived until the end of production for the Popular 103E. It arrived at a critical time for Dagenham. Model A sales were collapsing, and although the factory was in theory up and running, between its first AA truck on 1 October 1931 and the end of the year it produced only a handful of cars. Drawn up by Dearborn, hurriedly built prototypes of Model Y were introduced at the Royal Albert Hall, London, on 18 February 1932 and the car was rushed into production inside six months. Its heart-shaped radiator grille, ten degree sloping windscreen and curvy lines looked rakish against contemporary upright and angular small cars. Before long it accounted for two out of every five 8HP cars sold in Britain. The production Y was given 2in (5.1cm) more elbow room than the prototype, the fuel tank was located aft, fuel filler and radiator filler caps concealed and a fine moulded coach line introduced to make it look longer. To Dagenham's relief the engine was rated at 7.9HP making the annual road tax £8. Fourteen of the American prototypes were shipped to Europe, with body dies, jigs and fittings to equip Dagenham and the adjacent Briggs Motor Bodies factory. Three British cars, an Austin 7, Standard 9, and Morris Minor had been sent to Dearborn, for comparison with what was known in America as Model 19. It was changed to Model Y as part of Sir Percival Perry's plans to sell cars in Europe. Prototype engines had 2-bearing cranks, quickly changed to 3-bearing after tests.

INTRODUCTION August 1932 produced to August 1937.
BODY Saloon; 4-seats; 2-door Tudor weight 1630lb (739.4kg); 4-door Fordor, 1660lb (752.9kg).
ENGINE 4-cylinders, in-line; 56.6mm x 92.5mm, 933cc; compr 6.2:1; 23.4bhp (17.45kW) @ 4000rpm; 25.1bhp (18.7kW)/l; 36.5lbft (49.5Nm) @ 2300rpm.
ENGINE STRUCTURE side valve; gear-driven camshaft; cast iron detachable cylinder head and block; cast aluminium sump; aluminium pistons; Zenith downdraught carburettor; coil ignition, and mechanical fuel pump; 3-bearing crankshaft; thermosyphon cooling; splash and pressure lubrication.
TRANSMISSION rear wheel drive; 7.4in (18.7cm) sdp clutch; 3-speed manual gearbox, later synchromesh on 2 and 3; torque tube; spiral bevel final drive 5.43:1 to Sep 1933 later 5.5:1.
CHASSIS pressed steel channel-section frame with three crossmembers; suspension, transverse leaf springs front and rear with triangulated radius arms;

dampers round Luvax hydraulic to 1933, pear-shaped Luvax to 1937; rod actuated 10in (25.4cm) drum brakes; planetary steering gearbox to November 1932, then Burman worm and nut; 6.5gal (29.5l) rear fuel tank; 4.50 – 17 Firestone tyres; steel spoke welded wheels.
DIMENSIONS wheelbase 90in (228.6cm); track 45in (114.3cm); length 143in (363.2cm); width 57in (144.8cm); height 63in (160cm); ground clearance 8.25in (20.9cm); turning circle 31ft (9.45m).
EQUIPMENT 6 volt electrical system; 7 optional colours; Rexine or leather upholstery.
PERFORMANCE maximum speed 59mph (94.7kph); 0-50mph (80.26kph) 34sec; 31.6kg/bhp (42.4kg/kW); fuel consumption 35mpg (8l/100km) to 45mpg (6.3l/100km) at normal speeds.
PRICE Tudor £120, Fordor £135 5cwt van £115.
PRODUCTION 135,244 all Model Ys.

Continuity in publicity. Hand-coloured Model Y picture with Chelmsford EV registration 4 digits away from V8 18 opposite.

1933
Fordson tractor

There was little change in the Fordson tractor between 1917 and 1928, and not much after production moved to Dagenham in 1933. Built in the United States to meet British government wartime needs, it was the world's first mass produced tractor, using assembly techniques learned with the Model T. Identifiable by the perforated ladder-type radiator sides, early Model Fs were sold cheaply in the 1920s, to the discomfiture of the indigenous tractor industry. Production continued at Cork as the model N from 1919 until 1923, restarted in 1929 but was then moved out of what had become the Irish Free State, after which production dropped to 50-60 tractors a week. UK improvements included discarding the troublesome trembler coil ignition, increasing the cylinder bore and the size of the bearings, and providing a water pump. Dagenham tractors had a ribbed pattern on the radiator header tank and Fordson was cast into the side panels. Production continued into the Second World War for the Royal Air Force, which used them for towing aircraft. Several hundred Roadless half-tracks were made with rubber jointed tracklaying at the back, some even with full-length tracks round the front wheels as well. Roadless Fordsons, sold off as RAF war surplus, came with instructions for dismantling the 1-ton hand operated crane mounted over the front wheels, used for loading bombs.

INTRODUCTION Dagenham production, February 19 1933 to 1945.
BODY open; 0-doors, 1-seat; weight 3000lb (1360.8kg). 1300lb (589.7kg) on front wheels. 1850lb (839.2kg) on rear.
ENGINE 4-cylinders, in-line; 4.125in (104.78mm) x 5in (127mm), 4380cc; Model F 20.19bhp (15.1kW); Model N 23.24bhp (17.3kW) @ 1000rpm on kerosene; 29.1bhp (21.7kW) on petrol; 6.6bhp(5kW)/l.
ENGINE STRUCTURE side valves; side camshaft gear-driven from crankshaft; iron cylinder head, block; Holley model 234 vaporiser for kerosene, Zenith carburettor for petrol, ignition by low-tension flywheel magneto and trembler coils, later Bosch FU4 magneto; gravity fuel feed; 3-bearing crankshaft; cooling by thermosyphon, fan, and (later) impeller; flat-type airwasher; oilbath air cleaner from 1938.

TRANSMISSION rear wheel drive; multi-plate clutch; constant-mesh; 3-speed manual gearbox; low, intermediate, and high; transmission brake; underslung worm final drive; four pinion differential.
CHASSIS integral engine clutch, gearbox, final drive; front axle buffer; mechanical brakes, front, rear drums; worm and sector steering; 16gal (72.7l) fuel tank; wheels standard agricultural; rear spoked with cleats or spade lugs, Land Utility with cast centres for Dunlop, Firestone, Goodyear or French & Hecht tyres; cast front wheels; Rowcrop Vee formation optional, with independent pedal-operated brakes.
DIMENSIONS wheelbase 63in; length 102in (259.1cm); width 62.75in (159.38cm); height 54.5in (138.43cm); ground clearance 11.625in (29.53cm); turning circle 21ft (6.4m).
EQUIPMENT Dearborn grey, red oxide wheels, Cork grey or blue, Dagenham darker blue with red

wheels; orange from December 1938 then green in October 1940.
PRICE £130 lowest in 1920s, 1933 £155, Rowcrop £187, Land Utility £175
PRODUCTION 750,000 1917–1928

Around half of 1930s Land Utility Fordson tractors were on fourteen spoke steel wheels with spade lugs. The Cork colour scheme of light blue gave way to dark blue for Dagenham-built machines. This Model N was built in Cork. It was used as a prime mover on a farm raising cattle and horses, hauling hay and for belt power on silo and thresher. Photo Don Clough, West Gardiner, Maine.

V8 40 30HP Victoria, Tudor, Fordor, Roadster, Coupe

As a result of an obscure bargain struck by Henry Ford in 1904, Ford of Canada had supplied the V8-18s that introduced British drivers to eight-cylinder motoring. The V8-40, which replaced it in 1933, was assembled in Cork and Cologne and although better handling thanks to a stronger X-braced chassis, it sold only in small numbers. Despite being probably the best looking of the series, the stiff British horsepower tax and heavy fuel consumption produced the anomaly of a car cheap to buy but costly to run. Specialist coachbuilders such as Jensen could make it costly to buy as well. A team of three was run in the 1934 Ards TT without much success. Jensen's links with Ford, which began with the Mistral Model Y for Bristol Street Motors flourished, with around 30 Jensen V8s made over three years. One was ordered, although not actually bought, by screen star Clark Gable. From there it was but a step to fully fledged Jensen cars on modified V8 chassis, of which 50 were sold at between £645 and £765 in the years up to 1941. The V8-40's heart-shaped radiator and flared wings were reproduced in the Model Y. Available as a roadster, saloon, or 3-window coupe, it might have looked as though Ford was getting above itself. Hollywood star Joan Crawford had a white 1934 Model 40 specially made with white steering wheel and white leather upholstery.

RIGHT ABOVE **Fur-clad Miss Finland 1934 is about to drive off in a left hand drive roadster, styled by ET Gregorie at the behest of Edsel Ford. Ford folklore remained divided on whether it was a scaled-up Model Y or vice versa.**
RIGHT BELOW **Monte Carlo Rally V8 of Javanese-Dutch Bud Bakker Schut finished seventh in 1935. He won in 1938 driving a V8 78.**

INTRODUCTION October 1933 production to June 1934, Treasury rating 30HP.
BODY Coupe, Victoria, Tudor, Fordor, Roadster; 2/4-doors, 2/4-seats; weight 23cwt (1168.4kg) (2575.8lb).
ENGINE 8-cylinders in 90deg V; 77.8mm x 95mm, 3622cc; compr 6.3:1; 75bhp (55.9kW) @ 3800 rpm; 20.7bhp (15.44kW)/l; later 85bhp (63.4kW); 23.47bhp (17.5kW)/l; 145lbft (197Nm) @ 1500rpm.

ENGINE STRUCTURE side valves; centre gear-driven 3-bearing camshaft; aluminium detachable cylinder heads, blocks and upper crankcase unitary cast iron; engine weight 581lb (263.5kg) Stromberg 48 twin choke downdraught carburettor, coil ignition, camshaft-driven distributor; AC fuel pump; 3-bearing cast steel crankshaft; thermosyphon cooling, two belt-driven pumps, pressure lubrication by camshaft pump.

TRANSMISSION rear wheel drive; 9in (22.9cm) sdp clutch; 3-speed manual gearbox, synchromesh on 2 gears; final drive 4.11:1, 3.78 optional.
CHASSIS steel X-braced with 4 cross-members; suspension by transverse leaf springs; 4 hydraulic lever arm dampers; mechanical drum brakes; worm and sector steering; 11.5gal (52.28l) rear-mounted fuel tank; 5.25-18 tyres.
DIMENSIONS wheelbase 112in (284.5cm); track 56in (142.24cm); length 176in (447cm); width 67.5in (171.45cm).
PERFORMANCE maximum speed 81mph (130kph); 15.6kg/bhp (20.9kg/kW); later 13.8kg/bhp (18.4kg/kW); fuel consumption 16mpg (17.6l/100km).
PRICE Tudor sal £230; Coupe £295; Victoria Coupe £285; Fordor sal £260; Cabriolet £295; Fordor with sunroof £275; leather upholstery £7 10s (£7.50) extra
PRODUCTION 911 including V8-18.

1934
Model C and CX 10HP

In the era of Art Deco, the Bauhaus, Chrysler Airflow, streamlined trains and a new design consciousness, the Model C was made to resemble the successful and emblematic V8. There was even talk of a small V8 engine, which never came to pass. The Model C was designed, like the Model Y, in Dearborn where it was known as Model 20. Dagenham called it the 10HP De Luxe to distinguish it from the £100 Popular. Although the chassis had cross members and was plated to form a sort of platform, it kept cheap and practical transverse springing. Similarity to the Model Y enabled it to be built on the same Dagenham track. The 1172cc cylinder block had the same 92.5mm stroke as the 933cc so it could be machined on the same tools, yet Henry Ford's opposition to adjustable tappets remained, despite the production difficulties imposed throughout the engine's life. The De Luxe made more of a fashion statement, especially with racy two-colour paint. After a season the CX came in with a small important styling change; horizontal bars on the radiator grille made it look more like a mini-V8 than ever. Suction operated screen wipers, which almost ceased working when needed most accelerating or climbing hills, were a persistent problem. Not exactly a failure and certainly a fashion pointer, the Model C never reached Ford's ambitious expectations in sales, so was never regarded as a complete success.

INTRODUCTION Model C October 1934 to 31 October 1935, CX to March 1937.
BODY Fordor, Tudor, and 4-seat Tourer; weight Tudor 1828lb (829.2kg).
ENGINE 4-cylinders, in-line; 63.5mm x 92.56mm, 1172cc; compr 6.16:1; 30bhp (22.4kW) @ 4000rpm; 25.6bhp (19kW)/l; 60lbft (81Nm) @ 2000rpm.
ENGINE STRUCTURE side valves; gear-driven side camshaft; cast iron cylinder head and block; aluminium pistons; Ford downdraught carburettor; coil ignition; mechanical fuel pump; 3-bearing crankshaft; thermosyphon cooling; splash and pressure lubrication.

TRANSMISSION rear wheel drive; sdp clutch; 3-speed manual gearbox, synchromesh on 2 and 3; torque tube; spiral bevel final drive 5.5:1.
CHASSIS pressed steel channel-section frame with three crossmembers; suspension, transverse leaf springs front and rear with triangulated radius arms; Luvax hydraulic dampers; rod actuated 10in (25.4cm) drum brakes; worm and nut steering; 6.5gal (29.5l) fuel tank; 4.50 – 17 Firestone tyres; steel spoke bolt-on welded wheels.
DIMENSIONS wheelbase 90in (228.6cm); track 45in (114.3cm); length 147in (373.4cm); width 57in (144.8cm); height 63in (160.02cm); ground clearance 8.25in

(20.9cm); turning circle 33ft (10.06m).
EQUIPMENT 6 volt electrics; rear window blind, clock, driver's sun visor, roof net, interior roof light; optional leather upholstery, sliding roof, both £5.
PERFORMANCE maximum speed 65.45mph (105.07kph) The Autocar; 0-60mph (96kph) 39sec; 27.6kg/bhp (37kg/kW); fuel consumption 32-35mpg (8.8-8.1l/100km).
PRICE 1936 Tudor £135, Fordor £155.
PRODUCTION 21,340 including 3699 CKD.

1935
Model Y The £100 Ford

INTRODUCTION October 1935 to August 1937.

BODY Saloon; 4-doors, 2-doors, 4-seats; weight 1630lb (739.4kg) Tudor, 1660lb (753kg) Fordor.

ENGINE 4-cylinders, in-line; 56.6mm x 92.5mm, 933cc; compr 6.2:1; 23.4bhp (17.45kW) @ 4000rpm; 25.1bhp (18.7kW)/l; 36.5lbft (49.5Nm) @ 2300rpm.

ENGINE STRUCTURE side valve; gear-driven camshaft; cast iron detachable cylinder head and block; aluminium pistons; Zenith downdraught carburettor; coil ignition, and mechanical fuel pump; 3-bearing crankshaft later counterbalanced; thermosyphon cooling; splash and pressure lubrication.

TRANSMISSION rear wheel drive; 7.375in (18.73cm) sdp clutch; 3-speed manual gearbox, synchromesh on 2; torque tube; spiral bevel final drive 5.5:1.

CHASSIS pressed steel channel-section frame with three crossmembers; suspension, transverse leaf springs front and rear with triangulated radius arms; pear-shaped Luvax; rod actuated 10in (25.4cm) drum brakes; Burman worm and nut steering; 6.5gal (29.5l) rear fuel tank; 4.50 - 17 Firestone tyres; steel spoke welded wheels.

DIMENSIONS wheelbase 90in (228.6cm); track 45in (114.3cm); length 143in (363.2cm); width 57in (144.78cm); height 63in (160.02cm); ground clearance 8.25in (20.95cm); turning circle 31ft (9.45m).

EQUIPMENT 6 volt electrical system; 2 optional colours; Rexine or leather upholstery, Lissen radio £10, sliding roof, luggage rack.

PERFORMANCE maximum speed 59mph (94.7kph); 0-50mph (80.26kph) 34sec; 31.6kg/bhp (42.4kg/kW); fuel consumption 35-45mpg (8l/100km-6.3l/100km) at normal speeds.

PRICE Tudor £100, Fordor £112.10s (£112.50) 5cwt van £115. In July 1937 the Tudor price went up to £105.

PRODUCTION 135,244 all Model Ys.

It can be yours –

THE £100 FORD SALOON

The first Y had a straight bumper and short radiator. From 1933 it took on some of the V8's character, with a longer radiator and curved bumper. Planetary gearbox steering was abandoned, the speedometer read up to 80mph instead of 70mph and there was an electric fuel gauge. It had better brakes and following the introduction of the 10HP Model C, in October 1935, the price was reduced to £100. The specification was not downgraded, it became known as the Popular and there was nothing to match it. Morris had a £100 car in 1932 but that was a 2-seat tourer. The 1934 Austin Opal was also a 2-seater and the closest 4-seater was the Austin Ruby at £118. Among the options offered were a sliding roof,

luggage rack, and with customary Ford whimsy that named 4-door cars Fordor and 2-doors Tudor, there was a radio set called the Lissen. Sir Percival Perry proposed that Briggs, which made the body, should reduce its price by £2 with a view to doubling sales. The target was not reached, but the Popular increased Ford's share of the 8HP market from 22 per cent to 41 per cent with the engine's official rating of 7.9HP setting annual tax at £8. Road test reports of the £100 Ford were almost all eulogistic, *The Light Car* struck a critical note: "It would be too much to expect an electric screen wiper on a car of such low price, but more than once during heavy rain we had occasion to wish that this were a £101 Ford…".

1935
Model Y Fordson 5cwt van and Tug 3-wheeler

The Model Y made a good van with 50cuft (1416l) of space within a floor 51.2in (130cm) long and 43.5in (110.5cm) wide. Objects 42.5in (107.9cm) across x 36.5in (92.7cm) tall could be loaded through the back doors. There was no passenger seat, making access to the load space easier during door to door deliveries, but these early models were criticised for no rearward-facing windows or (a production economy measure) driver's door. The front half cab and engine from the Model Y was used for the Ford Tug, based on a design by County Commercial Cars with a heavy-duty chassis. Horse haulage was by no means a thing of the past in the 1930s, so mechanical horses harnessed to different vans and carts for short-haul deliveries from railway goods-yards or docksides, were logical. A mechanical horse could make a journey with one trailer, while its next cargo was being loaded-up (or unloaded) on another. Made first as a Ford then a Fordson, with a single fat sprung front wheel, it had a reduction gearbox behind the 8HP engine, and the steering drop-arm was mounted in the stout chassis side member behind a bulge on the side of the bodywork. It was effectively a Model Y shorn of its wings. The Tug made its debut at the Royal Albert Hall on October 17 1935 billed without a trace of irony as, "an entirely new transport unit."

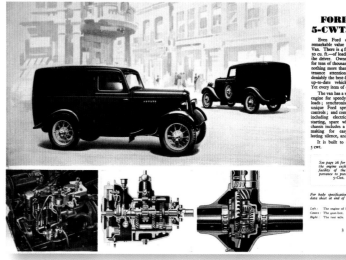

FORDSON 5-CWT. VAN

INTRODUCTION August 1932 production to August 1937, Tug September 1935 to September 1937.
BODY van; 1 (later 2)-doors, 1-seat (passenger seat optional); weight 1316lb (596.9kg) Tug 14cwt (711kg).
ENGINE 4-cylinders, in-line; 56.6mm x 92.5mm, 933cc; compr 6.2:1; 23.4bhp (17.45kW) @ 4000rpm; 25.1bhp (18.8kW)/l; 36.5lbft (49.1Nm) @ 2300rpm.
ENGINE STRUCTURE side valve; gear-driven camshaft; cast iron detachable cylinder head and block; cast aluminium sump; aluminium pistons; Zenith downdraught

carburettor; coil ignition, and mechanical fuel pump; 3-bearing crankshaft; thermosyphon cooling; splash and pressure lubrication.
TRANSMISSION rear wheel drive; 7.375in (18.73cm) sdp clutch; 3-speed manual gearbox, later synchromesh on 2 and 3; torque tube, roller bearings; spiral bevel final drive; 5.5:1. Tug reduction gearbox behind engine and final drive 4.11:1.
CHASSIS pressed steel channel-section frame with three crossmembers; Tug heavy duty A-frame; suspension, transverse 8-leaf springs front, 12-leaf rear with triangulated radius arms; dampers Ford-made; rod actuated 10in (25.4cm) drum brakes (Tug, rear wheels only, 12in (30.5cm) drums); Burman worm and nut steering; 6.5gal (29.5l) rear fuel tank; tyres 4.50 – 17, Tug front 18in x 7in oval section; steel spoke welded wheels.
DIMENSIONS wheelbase 90in (228.6cm); track 45in (114.3cm); length 135.75in (344.8cm); width 54in (137.2cm); height 65in (165.1cm); ground clearance 8.35in (21cm); turning circle 31ft (9.45m)

Tug 21ft (6.4m) with trailer, 16ft (4.88m) without.
EQUIPMENT 6-volt electrical system; 7 optional colours, Rexine upholstery; Tug vineyard green; front bumper semi-circular spring steel. Optional standard 2-wheel trailer, 131in (332.7cm) Fordson truck dropside body.
PERFORMANCE maximum speed 59mph (94.7kph) Tug maximum legal, 20mph (32.1kph), design top speed; 24mph (38.53kph); 0-30mph (48.16kph) 10.5sec; 24.4kg/bhp (34.1kg/kW); fuel consumption 40mpg (7.06l/100km) *Commercial Motor* 18mpg (15.69l/100km) *Modern Transport*
PRICE 5cwt van £115 Tug £185.
PRODUCTION 135,244 Model Ys. 111Tugs.

1935–1937
van, truck, and bus

In the middle of the 1930s Ford's commercial range went from 5cwt to 3tons and before long up to 5tons. There were 4-cylinder (or 4-cylindered as the brochures said), and V8s of two sizes, 3.6litre for power, 2.2litre for economy. The 4-cylinder Model A engine came straight from the car with 40bhp (29.83kw) @ 2200rpm, and it was installed in vans and trucks without modification, the only concession to its new role a four-speed gearbox. From 1933 six rear wheels were an option on the 131.5in (334cm) and 157in (398.8cm) wheelbases. These were developed jointly with County Commercial Cars Ltd of Fleet, with the drive to one axle or both, through double spiral bevel drives. They continued as Surrey or Sussex models right up to the war. The commercials' straight-sided chassis frame, inherited from the American designs with which Ford started the 1930s, was used for any number of applications, tall vans, dropside trucks, tippers, or from 1932 as a 20-seat coach, the first commercial application of the V8 engine. The 6in (15.24cm) side-members

were increased to 7in (17.8cm) with 3in (7.6cm) flanges on the 2-tonner and went up to 17in (43.2cm) in places on the heaviest six-wheelers. Forward-control trucks had been available as proprietary conversions for operators wanting more space for payload until, in 1934, the first production forward control Ford entered service as the BBE 2-tonner.

DAGENHAM COMMERCIAL VEHICLES 1928–1939
1928–1932 A van 3.2litre 4-cylinder 10cwt
1928–1932 AF van 2.0litre 4-cylinder 10cwt
1928–1935 AA and AAF 3.2litre 4-cylinder 1ton and 30cwt trucks, vans, chassis
1932–1935 B van 3.2litre 4 cylinder 10-12cwt
1932–1935 BF van 2.0litre 4 cylinder 10-12cwt
1932–1936 BB and BBF 3.2litre 4-cylinder; 3.6litre V8 2-tonner
1933–1935 BB Sussex 3.2litre 4-cylinder and 3.6litre V8 6-wheeler double drive
1933–1935 BB Surrey 3.2litre 4-cylinder and 3.6litre V8 6-wheeler single drive
1934–1938 BBE 3.6litre V8 2-ton forward control
1933–1937 Model Y van 933cc 4-cylinder 5cwt
1935 Model 50 3.6litre V8 15cwt van
1935 Model 60E 2.2litre V8 15cwt van
1936 Model 51 3.6litre V8 2- and 3-tonners
1936 Model 51 Sussex 3.6litre V8 6-wheeler double drive
1936 Model 51 Surrey 3.6litre V8 6-wheeler single drive
1936–1939 Model 61 2.2litre V8 25cwt forward control
1936 Model 67 V8 15cwt van
1936–1937 Tug 933cc 4-cylinder 3-wheeler mechanical horse
1937–1939 933cc 4-cylinder 5cwt van
1937 Model 73 2.2litre V8 15cwt van
1937 Model 77 3.6litre V8 15cwt van
1937 Model 79 3.2litre 4-cylinder, 3.6litre V8 2- and 4-tonner
1937 Model 79 Sussex 3.2litre 4-cylinder and 3.6litre V8 6-wheeler double drive
1937 Model 79 Surrey 3.2litre 4-cylinder and 3.6litre V8 6-wheeler single drive
1937–1946 Model 7V 3.2litre 4-cylinder and 3.6litre V8 2- 3- 5-ton forward control
1937–1939 Model 7V Sussex 3.2litre 4-cylinder and 3.6litre V8 6-wheeler double drive
1937–1939 Model 7V Sussex 6-wheeler forward control

1936–1937 MY
4-cyl 5cwt light van 90in wheelbase £112 road tax £10
V8 15cwt light van 112in wb £220 road tax £20 (also with 2.2litre V8)
V8 25cwt truck 106in wheelbase £200 road tax £20
V8 25cwt van 106in wb dual rear wheels £240 road tax £20
4-cyl or V8 2-ton truck 131.5in wb dual rear wheels £236 road tax £25
4-cyl or V8 hand tipper 131.5in wb dual rear wheels £246 road tax £30
4-cyl or V8 hydraulic 3-way 2ton tipper 131.5in wb dual rear wheels £294 road tax £30
forward control V8 2ton truck 118in wb £250 road tax £25
forward control V8 2ton van 118in wb £286 road tax £25
4-cyl or V8 3ton truck 131.5in wb dual rear wheels £271 road tax £30
4-cyl or V8 3ton hydraulic 3-way tipper 131.5in wb dual rear wheels £345 road tax £30
4-cyl or V8 3ton hydraulic end tipper 131.5in dual rear wheels £325 road tax £30
4-cyl or V8 3ton truck 143.5in wb dual rear wheels £295 road tax £30
Fordson-Surrey-Sussex V8 118in wb forward control 131.5in normal control

1935
V8 48 30HP Tudor, Fordor, Cabriolet, Utility

A short-lived model, introduced seven months behind Detroit, the first V8 made at Dagenham was also the first to have an all purpose van-like body, known as a Shooting Brake or Utility, depending on what part of the market it was aiming at. The good looking varnished wood body demonstrated Ford's ambition to go for quality clientele as a counterbalance to its well established reputation for low-cost economical family saloons. With a resemblance to the Model C and CX, through the broad radiator grille with horizontal bars, the V8-48 had the engine up close to the front wheel centre line, increasing room inside and bringing the occupants within the wheelbase. This was an innovation Ford described as "centrepoise riding". The sweeping wings and rounded lines "...strike a very modern note without being blatant," according to *The Motor*, and the seat cushions were softer, "... to damp out road shocks". An all-synchromesh gearbox was a welcome improvement, and touring saloons de luxe had additional built-in luggage containers against the ordinary saloons' sweeping tail with externally mounted spare wheel. Rated at 30HP, the 3622cc V8 attracted an annual tax of £22.10s (£22.50). At almost 10 per cent of the car's purchase price this was an important consideration. Special-bodied V8s for 1935 included Dagenham Motors' special saloon at £395 and a 2-door sports saloon with fat tyres, extravagant bonnet louvres, spotlights and ornate bonnet mascot at £425.

INTRODUCTION March to November 1935.
BODY Saloons Tudor and Fordor 5-6-seat, cabriolet 2-seat, coupe 2-seat, utility 4-door 5-6-seat; coupe weight 23cwt (1168.4kg) (2576lb).
ENGINE 8-cylinders in 90deg V; 77.8mm x 95mm, 3622cc; compr 6.3:1; 80bhp (59.6kW) @ 3500 rpm; 22.1bhp (16.5kW)/l; 140lbft (190Nm) @ 1500rpm.
ENGINE STRUCTURE side valves; centre gear-driven 3-bearing camshaft; aluminium detachable cylinder heads, blocks and upper crankcase unitary cast iron; engine weight 581lb (263.5kg); Stromberg 48 twin choke downdraught carburettor, coil ignition, camshaft-driven distributor; mechanical fuel pump; 3-bearing cast steel crankshaft; thermosyphon cooling, two belt-driven pumps, pressure lubrication by camshaft pump.
TRANSMISSION rear wheel drive; 9in (22.9cm) sdp clutch; 3-speed manual all-synchromesh gearbox; final drive 4.11:1.
CHASSIS steel X-braced frame with 4 cross-members; suspension by transverse leaf springs; 4 hydraulic lever arm dampers; mechanical drum (non-scoring alloy) brakes; worm and sector steering; 11.5gal (52.28l) rear-mounted fuel tank; 6.00-16 tyres.
DIMENSIONS wheelbase 112in (284.5cm); track 56in (142.2cm); length 183in (464.8cm); width 67.5in (171.4cm).
EQUIPMENT 6-volt electrics, cigar lighter, smokers' companion, self-cancelling trafficators, leather upholstery £7 10s (£7.50) extra, twin horns.
PERFORMANCE maximum speed 86mph (138kph); 0-60mph (96kph) 17sec; 14.6kg/bhp (19.6kg/kW); fuel consumption 16mpg (17.6l/100km).
PRICE Touring Tudor £235, Touring Fordor £250, Cabriolet £240, Coupe £230, Utility £245
PRODUCTION 616

1935
V8 60 22HP

Ford's antipathy to trade associations persisted into the 1930s, preventing it from joining the Society of Motor Manufacturers and Traders (SMMT), which organised the London Motor Show at Olympia. As a result, from 1928 to 1938 Ford held its own motor exhibition every autumn, coinciding with the SMMT show, usually in the Royal Albert Hall on Kensington Gore, barely a mile and a half away. At the 1935 event, acknowledging the difficult economic circumstances of the country, Ford introduced the £100 Model Y, together with a 22HP V8 with reduced bore and stroke, which brought the annual Road Fund tax down from the 3622cc V8's £22.10s (£22.50) to £16 10s (£16.50). The V8 60 was outwardly identical to the V8 48 but the crucial cylinder bore, on which the Treasury

RAC horsepower was calculated, came down from 77.8mm to 66mm. The stroke was shorter as well, bringing the capacity to 2227cc. The engine had been designed for the French Matford as the Alsace before being pressed into service, with some success, in Britain where its gearing was lower. The resulting car was by no means slow. The transverse springs were now rubber-mounted, the rear one behind the back axle. Coupes and Cabriolets were 2-seaters with dickey seats in the sweeping tail. For 1936 Jensen had a stylish 4-seat open sports, with deeply cutaway doors, on a shortened 22HP chassis sold through Bristol Street Motors. The Harris V8 special saloon with hide upholstery was listed at £575. The engine went on to the US market in 1937.

INTRODUCTION September 1935 – June 1936.
BODY Saloons Tudor and Fordor 5-6-seat, cabriolet 2-seat, roadster 2-seat, coupe 2-seat, utility 4-door 5-6-seat; coupe weight 23cwt (1168.4kg) (2575.85lb).
ENGINE 8-cylinders in 90deg V; 66mm x 81.28mm, 2227cc; compr 6.3:1; 60bhp (44.7kW) @ 3500 rpm; 26.9bhp(20.1kW)/l.
ENGINE STRUCTURE side valves; centre gear-driven 3-bearing camshaft; aluminium detachable cylinder heads, 17-stud blocks and upper crankcase unitary cast iron; engine weight 581lb (263.5kg); Stromberg 48 twin choke downdraught carburettor, coil ignition, camshaft-driven distributor; electric fuel pump; 3-bearing cast steel crankshaft; thermosyphon cooling, two belt-driven pumps, pressure lubrication by camshaft pump.
TRANSMISSION rear wheel drive; 9in (22.9cm) sdp clutch; 3-speed manual all-synchromesh gearbox; final drive 4.77:1.
CHASSIS steel X-braced frame with 4 cross-members; suspension by transverse leaf springs; 4 hydraulic lever arm dampers; mechanical drum (non-scoring alloy) brakes; worm and sector steering; 11.5gal (52.28l) rear-mounted fuel tank; 6.00-16 tyres.
DIMENSIONS wheelbase 112in (284.5cm); track 56in (142.2cm); length 183in (464.8cm); width 67.5in (171.4cm).
EQUIPMENT 6-volt electrics, cigar lighter, smokers' companion, self-cancelling trafficators, leather upholstery £7 10s (£7.50) extra, twin horns.
PERFORMANCE maximum speed 76mph (122kph); 19.5kg/bhp (26.1kg/kW); fuel consumption 20-25mpg (14.1-11.3l/100km).
PRICE Saloon 2-door £215, 4-door £230, Touring saloon £235, Coupe, Roadster £215, Tourer £225, Utility £230
PRODUCTION 2807

LEFT **Mariette Hélène Delange, racing driver, exotic danceuse as Mlle Hellé Nice, the Bugatti Queen, (right) won the Coupe des Dames in the 1937 Monte Carlo Rally with co-driver Mlle Marinivich.**

1936
V8 68 30HP

The ritual of annual facelifts was started in the 1930s by America with elaborate marketing plans. Sales campaigns ruled. The V8 68 was not much more than a well-groomed V8 60, yet it was the most successful of all the pre-war V8s. One feature determined by the US was the continuous fall, between 1932 and 1939, of all V8 steering ratios. The Model 18 of 1932 had been relatively quick and responsive, but as the demand for lighter steering grew, five turns lock to lock, as with this car, became commonplace. The virtue of engine flexibility remained, however, and *The Autocar* of 3 July 1936 enthused that it was: "...almost fantastically fast and lively for its price ... (yet) figures alone do not convey the whole meaning. A V8 is virtually a unique motoring experience. It suits the laziest driving mood with its top gear running abilities." Drivers in the 1930s did not enjoy changing gear, shifts were ponderous and clutches heavy so it was welcome when the lusty torque of the V8 enabled first and second to be engaged for a few yards, "...and then the engine will at once pick up and pull away smoothly on the quite high top gear ratio. It runs thereafter, even in slow-moving traffic and on right-angle corners, without the slightest need for a change down to be made." Praise indeed.

INTRODUCTION November 1935 – December 1936.
BODY Saloons Tudor and Fordor 5-6-seat, cabriolet 2-seat, coupe 2-seat, utility 4-door 5-6-seat; coupe weight 23cwt (1168.4kg) (2575.854lb), 4-door touring saloon 28cwt (1422.4kg) (3135.823lb).
ENGINE 8-cylinders in 90deg V; 77.8mm x 95mm, 3622cc; compr 6.3:1; 80bhp (59.6kW) @ 3500 rpm; 22.1bhp (16.5kW)/l; 140lbft (190 Nm) @ 1500rpm.
ENGINE STRUCTURE side valves; centre gear-driven 3-bearing camshaft; aluminium detachable cylinder heads; blocks and upper crankcase unitary cast iron; engine weight 581lb (263.5kg); Stromberg 48 twin choke downdraught

carburettor, coil ignition, camshaft-driven distributor; mechanical fuel pump; 3-bearing cast steel crankshaft; thermosyphon cooling, two belt-driven pumps, pressure lubrication by camshaft pump.
TRANSMISSION rear wheel drive; 9in (22.86cm) sdp clutch; 3-speed manual gearbox with synchromesh 2 and 3; final drive 4.11:1.
CHASSIS steel X-braced frame with 4 cross-members; suspension by transverse leaf springs; 4 hydraulic lever arm dampers; mechanical drum (non-scoring alloy) brakes; worm and sector steering; 11.5gal (52.28l) rear-mounted fuel tank; 6.00-16 tyres.
DIMENSIONS wheelbase 112in (284.5cm); track 55in (139.7cm);

length 185in (470cm); width 67.5in (171.45cm); height 68in (172.7cm) touring saloon; ground clearance 8.5in (21.6cm); turning circle 40ft (12.2m).
EQUIPMENT 6-volt electrics, cigar lighter, smokers' companion, self-cancelling trafficators, leather upholstery £6 extra, twin horns.
PERFORMANCE maximum speed 83.9mph (134.68kph) *The Autocar*; 0-60mph (96kph) 17.5sec; 14.6kg/bhp (19.6kg/kW); fuel consumption 18mpg (15.69l/100km).
PRICE Chassis £195, Touring Tudor £235, Touring Fordor £250, Cabriolet £240, Coupe £230, Utility £245
PRODUCTION 4527

1937
7Y Eight

The first British-designed body defined the entry level Ford for 20 years. The 7Y was rated at 8HP, the closely related 7W announced two months later was 10HP. On the short wheelbase of the original Model Y, the 7Y Eight had a one-piece waterfall grille instead of three vertical slats. Marketing called it "Completely new", and while steel slotted wheels and bodywork with a crease in the front door to make it look longer were new, the mechanical specification was thoroughly familiar. The chassis was stronger owing to steel panelling under the rear seat and floor, and the springs were longer to provide a more resilient ride. However the car had put on weight and at 105lb (47.6kg) felt less lively. *The Motor* thought it notable for, "its unusually spacious interior considering the fact that it is only an Eight, its new and attractive lines and its enclosed luggage accommodation." A 5cwt (254kg) van, produced on the same assembly line, had the front of the saloon and a sheet steel rear with a wooden frame and floor. It weighed under 12cwt (609.6kg) and had 52cu.ft (1473litres) of load space. The GPO was a big customer, and among the special bodies built on the 7W chassis, was one by Bonallack & Son of East London. First displayed at the Smithfield Show its Utilecon was an ancestor of many years' small Ford estate cars and camper vans.

INTRODUCTION August 1937 production to September 1939.
BODY Saloon; 2-doors, 4-seats; weight 1735lb (787kg).
ENGINE 4-cylinders, in-line; 56.6mm x 92.5mm, 933cc; compr 6.2:1; 23.4bhp (17.45kW) @ 4000rpm; 36.5lbft (49.5Nm) @ 2300rpm; 25.1bhp (18.7kW)/l.
ENGINE STRUCTURE side valve; gear-driven camshaft; cast iron detachable cylinder head and block; aluminium pistons; Zenith downdraught carburettor; coil ignition, and mechanical fuel pump; 3-bearing counterbalanced crankshaft; thermo-syphon cooling; splash and pressure lubrication.
TRANSMISSION rear wheel drive; 7.375in (18.7cm) sdp clutch; 3-speed manual gearbox, synchromesh on 2; torque tube; spiral bevel final drive 5.5:1.
CHASSIS pressed steel channel-section frame with three crossmembers and central box-section; suspension, transverse leaf springs front and rear with triangulated radius arms; pear-shaped Luvax dampers; rod actuated 8in (20.3cm) front 7in (17.8cm) rear drum brakes; Burman worm and nut steering; 6.5gal (29.5l) rear fuel tank; 4.50 – 17 Firestone tyres; steel spoke welded wheels.
DIMENSIONS wheelbase 90in (228.6cm); track 45in (114.3cm); length 148in (375.9cm); width 57in (144.8cm); height 63in (160.02cm); ground clearance 6.25in (15.87cm); turning circle 36ft (10.97m).
EQUIPMENT 6volt electrical system; fixed-rate charging; 10amps at 30mph; leathercloth upholstery, leather trim and sliding roof optional.
PERFORMANCE maximum speed 59mph (94.7kph); 0-50mph (80.26kph) 35sec; 33.6kg/bhp(45kg/kW); fuel consumption 35-45mpg (8-6.3l/100km) at normal speeds
PRICE Standard 2-door £117.10s (£117.50), de luxe £127.10s (£127.50).
PRODUCTION 59,598 plus 5,500CKD.

1937
7W Ten

The new Ten announced in April 1937, replacing the Model C, had the same stiffened frame as the Eight. To avoid the charge of over half a million dollars Dearborn had asked of its British subsidiary for the design of the Model Y, Dagenham director Percival Perry elected to have the new range designed in Britain. The Americans nearly forbade it until purchasing manager, 37 year old Patrick Hennessy, persuaded Edsel Ford. The new model's middle was braced by a strong welded and riveted box that included the propeller shaft tunnel, and there was an extra 4in (10.16cm) of wheelbase to provide a 4-door body. The robust frame allowed an open 4-seat Tourer with cutaway doors. A roadster had been planned back in 1932, and some were built by outside coachbuilders but this Tourer, *The Motor* thought, would "appeal to open car enthusiasts (to be) used with a measure of success in trials and competitions." Innovations included front-hinged doors, hitherto been difficult to hang on raked windscreen pillars, but safer and giving better access to the back. In August the 7W Ten was joined by a de luxe version of the Eight. Running boards, a sort of step under the door dating from an era of taller cars, ran from the trailing edge of the front wing to the leading edge of the rear wing, and were done away with in 1938 for non-de luxe cars.

INTRODUCTION Production October 1937 to September 1939.

BODY Saloon; 2-doors, 4-doors, 4-seats, Tourer 2-door 4-seats; weight (2-door) 1735lb (787kg).

ENGINE 4-cylinders, in-line; 63.5mm x 92.5mm, 1172cc; compr 6.6 x:1; 30bhp (22.4kW) @ 4000 rpm; 60lbft (81Nm) @ 2000rpm; 25.6bhp(19.1kW)/l.

ENGINE STRUCTURE side valve; gear-driven camshaft; cast iron detachable cylinder head and block; aluminium pistons; Zenith downdraught carburettor; coil ignition, and mechanical fuel pump; 3-bearing counterbalanced crankshaft; thermo-syphon cooling; splash and pressure lubrication.

TRANSMISSION rear wheel drive; 7.37in (18.73cm) sdp clutch; 3-speed manual gearbox, synchromesh on 2; torque tube; spiral bevel final drive 5.5:1.

CHASSIS pressed steel channel-section frame with three crossmembers and central box-section; suspension, transverse leaf springs front and rear with triangulated radius arms; pear-shaped Luvax dampers; rod actuated 10in (25.4cm) drum brakes; Burman worm and nut steering; 6.5gal (29.5l) rear fuel tank; 4.50 – 17 Firestone tyres; steel spoke Easiclean welded wheels.

DIMENSIONS wheelbase 94in (238.8cm); track 45in (114.3cm); length 156in (396.2cm); width 57in (144.8cm); height 63in (160cm); ground clearance 6.25in (15.87cm); turning circle 36ft (10.97m).

EQUIPMENT 6volt electrical system; two wipers, facia clock, metal spare wheel cover, interior light, map pocket, chrome hubcaps and windscreen frame, trafficators, glovebox lid, and opening windscreen; leathercloth upholstery, leather trim and sliding roof optional.

PERFORMANCE maximum speed 59mph (94.7kph); 0-50mph (80.26kph) 35sec; fuel consumption 35mpg (8l/100km) to 45mpg (6.3l/100km) at normal speeds.

PRICE 2-door £150, 4-door and Tourer £162 10s (£162.50).

PRODUCTION 59,598 plus 5,500CKD all 7Y and 7W.

1937
V8 78 30HP

It looked as though the Ford V8 was going to emulate the Lincoln Zephyr V12. Perhaps the classiest-looking of all the pre-war V8s, the Model 78's front strongly resembled the Zephyr's sloping headlamps sunk in the wings beside a stylish "fencer's mask" grille. It conformed to a trend that was making American cars admired in Europe, and the home grown Ford competed with the imported Hudson Terraplane (from £299), Dodge (£345), Oldsmobile, Chrysler, Packard, Pontiac, Buick and the Lincoln itself from within Ford. The Zephyr with a V12 engine, essentially a Ford V8 with four extra cylinders, started at £475 under the handicap of a Treasury rating of 37HP and annual tax of £22 10s (£22.50). A 6-cylinder Nash cost £445 and a 4-cylinder Willys Coupe £252. The V8 78 was regarded as vaguely mid-Atlantic, British made perhaps, but by an American company in an American idiom. It was profitable, for while import duty was responsible for a large part of the price difference between home and imported cars, a V8 could cost as little as $500 (£100) in America and $1300 (£260) in Britain. Henry Ford still would not sanction a change to hydraulic brakes, but with the 78 rod operation gave way to cable without much effect on comfort or efficiency.

INTRODUCTION January 1937 produced until June 1938
BODY Saloons Tudor and Fordor 5-6-seat, cabriolet 2-seat, coupe 2-seat, utility 4-door 5-6-seat; coupe weight 23cwt (1168.4kg) (2575.8lb), 4 door touring saloon 28cwt (1422.4kg) (3135.8lb).
ENGINE 8-cylinders in 90deg V; 77.8mm x 95mm, 3622cc; compr 6.3:1; 80bhp (59.6kW) @ 3500 rpm; 140lbft (190Nm) @ 1500rpm; 22.1bhp (16.5kW)/l.
ENGINE STRUCTURE side valves; centre gear-driven 3-bearing camshaft; aluminium detachable cylinder heads, blocks and upper crankcase unitary cast iron; engine weight 581lb (263.5kg); Stromberg 48 twin choke downdraught

carburettor, coil ignition, camshaft-driven distributor; mechanical fuel pump; 3-bearing cast steel crankshaft; thermosyphon cooling, two belt-driven pumps, pressure lubrication by camshaft pump.
TRANSMISSION rear wheel drive; 9in (22.86cm) sdp clutch; 3-speed manual gearbox with synchromesh 2 and 3; final drive 4.11:1.
CHASSIS steel X-braced frame with 4 cross-members; suspension by transverse leaf springs; 4 hydraulic lever arm dampers; mechanical drum (non-scoring alloy) brakes; worm and sector steering; 11.5gal (52.3l) rear fuel tank; 6.00-16 tyres.
DIMENSIONS wheelbase 112in (284.48cm); track 55in (139.7cm); length 185in (470cm); width 67.5in (171.45cm); height 68in (172.7cm)

touring saloon; ground clearance 8.5in (21.6cm); turning circle 40ft (12.2m).
EQUIPMENT 6-volt electrics, cigar lighter, smokers' companion, self-cancelling trafficators, leather upholstery £6 extra, twin horns.
PERFORMANCE maximum speed 87mph (139.66kph); 0-60mph (96kph) 17sec; fuel consumption 16mpg (17.6l/100km) see text.
PRICE October 1937 Chassis £195, Touring Tudor £245, Touring Fordor £260, Club Cabriolet £255, Coupe £235, Club Coupe £250, Utility £280
PRODUCTION 4331

1937
V8 62 22HP 2227cc

Most prolific of the pre-war V8s, the 62 reinforced the French connection that had been created by putting the Alsace engine of the Matford in the V8 60. It adopted the Matford body as well, except for its rear-hinged doors. The Model 62 had a revised chassis frame, it was 10in (25.4cm) shorter than before and the roofline 2.5in (6.35cm) lower. A few were even made in 1941, and impressed into service as WOA staff cars for the military. Early cars had the spare wheel on the sloping tail, with luggage space access from the back seat. After 1938 there was a projecting luggage boot, with the spare wheel recessed on the external downwards-folding lid under a metal cover. The engine was carried even further forward, over the front wheels, to provide more room inside. Free-standing headlamps, horn grilles, and V8 insignia everywhere, made this essentially mid-sized Ford easily identifiable, and its lively acceleration established it as a firm favourite with keen drivers wanting as much punch per pound as they could. Among the attractions at Ford's 1937 exhibition at the Royal Albert Hall was the spectacle of two mechanics dismantling a V-8 engine in six minutes and reassembling it in nine minutes. The middle section of the 22HP survived the war as the basis of the Ford Pilot and the woody estate car set a fashion that endured for generations.

INTRODUCTION June 1936 – February 1941.
BODY Saloons Tudor and Fordor 5-6-seat, cabriolet 2-seat, roadster 2-seat, coupe 2-seat and utility 4-door 5-6-seat; coupe weight 23cwt (1168.4kg) (2575.8lb).
ENGINE 8-cylinders in 90deg V; 66mm x 81.28mm, 2227cc; compr 6.3:1; 60bhp (44.7kW) @ 3500 rpm; 100lbft (134.1Nm) @ 1500rpm; 26.9bhp (20.1kW)l; Treasury rating 21.63HP annual tax £16 10s (£16.50).
ENGINE STRUCTURE side valves; centre Celeron helical-cut gear-driven 3-bearing camshaft; aluminium detachable cylinder heads, blocks and upper crankcase cast iron; Stromberg 48 twin choke downdraught carburettor, coil ignition, camshaft-driven distributor; electric fuel pump; 3-bearing cast steel crankshaft; thermosyphon cooling, two belt-driven pumps, pressure lubrication by camshaft pump.
TRANSMISSION rear wheel drive; 9in (22.86cm) sdp cushioned clutch; 3-speed manual all-synchromesh gearbox; spiral bevel final drive 4.55:1.
CHASSIS steel X-braced frame with 4 cross-members; suspension by transverse leaf springs; 4 hydraulic lever arm dampers; mechanical drum (non-scoring alloy) brakes; worm and sector steering; 12.5gal (56.82l) rear fuel tank; 5.75-16 tyres; electrically welded steel disc wheels.

DIMENSIONS wheelbase 108.25in (274.9cm); track 55.25in (140.34cm) front 58in (147.32cm) rear; length 173.25in (440.05cm); width 69.5in (176.53cm); height 68in (172.7cm); ground clearance 8.25in (20.9cm); turning circle 40ft (12.2m)
EQUIPMENT 6-volt electrics; combined ignition and steering column lock; body colours Black, Cordoba Tan, Gunmetal Grey, Vineyard Green.
PERFORMANCE maximum speed 76mph (122kph); 14.4mph (23.2kph) @ 1000rpm; 0-60mph (96kph) 19sec; fuel consumption 20mpg (14.1l/100km) - 25mpg (11.3l/100km).
PRICE 1936 introduction Saloon 4-door £210 (1937 £240), Chassis £180,
PRODUCTION 9239

1938
V8 81A 30HP

It was perhaps just as well that the V8 81A was relatively short-lived. It tried to catch up with Dearborn on style, sinking the headlamps downwards and inwards, extending the bulge of the front wings rearwards, giving the grille the appearance of a liner's bow-wave, but the result was compromised. Among the UK-specific items found necessary were semaphore direction indicators on the windscreen pillars and wing-mounted sidelamps. A basic no-frills model was sold in America but only the de luxe was available in the UK. The saloons were straight-backed, a retrograde step following the Model 78's external-booted body bulge, but Dagenham acknowledged the growing popularity of wood-framed estate car-style bodies by making the 30HP V8s available on a chassis-only basis. A number of these utilitarian multi-purpose vehicles were supplied to the British Army, with wide-section tyres for cross-country use. A talented carpenter could construct one cheaply, and with a third row of seats and fibre-board lining inside, the Woody (a title not adopted until much later) became fashionable on the grouse moor as well as practical as an urban people carrier. Coachbuilders Corsica, better known for lightweight low-slung sports bodies on Daimler Double-Six, Triumph Dolomite, Squire and Bugatti chassis did build a seven-seat limousine on one V8 81A. Heavily American, unwieldy for Europe, the 81A failed to make its mark and was quickly superseded.

ABOVE **Remarkable Cars sold this 72 year old "woody" V8 for $105,000.**

INTRODUCTION April–November 1938.

BODY Saloons Tudor and Fordor 5-6-seat, cabriolet 2-seat, coupe 2-seat, utility 4-door 5-6-seat; coupe weight 23cwt (1168.4kg) (2575.8lb), 4 door touring saloon 28cwt (1422.4kg) (3135.8lb).

ENGINE 8-cylinders in 90deg V; 77.8mm x 95mm, 3622cc; compr 6.3:1; 80bhp (59.6kW) @ 3500 rpm; 140lbft (190Nm) @ 1500rpm; 21.8bhp (16.5kW)/l.

ENGINE STRUCTURE side valves; centre gear-driven 3-bearing camshaft; aluminium detachable cylinder heads, blocks and upper crankcase unitary cast iron; engine weight 581lb (263.5kg); Stromberg 48 twin choke downdraught carburettor, coil ignition, camshaft-driven distributor; mechanical fuel pump; 3-bearing cast steel crankshaft; thermosyphon cooling, two belt-driven pumps, pressure lubrication by camshaft pump.

TRANSMISSION rear wheel drive; 9in (22.86cm) sdp clutch; 3-speed manual gearbox with synchromesh 2 and 3; final drive 4.11:1.

CHASSIS steel X-braced frame with 4 cross-members; suspension by transverse leaf springs; 4 hydraulic lever arm dampers; mechanical drum (non-scoring alloy) brakes; worm and sector steering; 11.5gal (52.28l) rear fuel tank; 6.00-16 tyres, 9.00-13 on Station Wagons.

DIMENSIONS wheelbase 112in (284.48cm); track 55in (139.7cm); length 185in (470cm); width 67.5in (171.4cm); height 68in (172.7cm) touring saloon; ground clearance 8.5in (21.6cm); turning circle 40ft (12.2m).

EQUIPMENT 6-volt electrics,

PERFORMANCE maximum speed 87mph (139.66kph); 0-60mph (96kph) 17sec; fuel consumption 16mpg (17.6l/100km).

PRICE Chassis £195, Touring Tudor £245, Touring Fordor £260, Club Cabriolet £255, Coupe £235, Club Coupe £250, Utility £280

PRODUCTION 1200

Fordson E83W10cwt. Renamed Thames, 1953

The E38W had the saloon car's 1172cc engine offset to the left, providing a forward-control driving position but leaving little foot room for a passenger. The accelerator pedal was between and beneath clutch and brake. A roomy panel van, it was obtainable as a chassis-cab for specialist bodywork, and put to any number of uses including hand-operated tipper refuse collector and dropside truck. During the war it served as ambulance, Auxiliary Fire Service (AFS) tender and in utility service roles. It became well known as the Ford Emergency Food Van, with 450 paid for personally by Henry and Edsel Ford, equipped with tall bodywork so that occupants could stand upright in the back where they cooked food and served through a hatch in the side. The vans were operated by the YMCA, Salvation Army, Church Army, and Society of Friends and were on hand at air raids. They went to outlying sites such as anti-aircraft or barrage balloon posts, docks, workshops, farms, schools, and aerodromes. It was calculated that they served nearly 82 million meals. Ford dealers maintained them free of charge. The E83W was only replaced by the Consul-engined 400E, a forerunner of the 1960s Transit. The E of the title referred to English build, 8 the year of introduction (1938), 3 the engine designation (1 and 2 were V8s) and W indicated forward control.

INTRODUCTION March 1938 production to September 1957.
BODY semi forward control van; 2-doors, 2-seats; weight approx 16cwt (813kg).
ENGINE 4-cylinders, in-line; 63.5mm x 92.5mm, 1172cc; compr 6.6 x:1; 30bhp (22.4kW) @ 4000 rpm; 46.4lbft (62.2Nm) @ 2400rpm; 25.6bhp(19.1kW)/l.
ENGINE STRUCTURE side valve; gear-driven camshaft; cast iron detachable cylinder head and block; aluminium pistons; Zenith downdraught carburettor; coil ignition, and mechanical fuel pump; 3-bearing counterbalanced crankshaft; thermo-syphon cooling; splash and pressure lubrication.

TRANSMISSION rear wheel drive; 7.5in (19cm) sdp clutch; 3-speed synchromesh gearbox; torque tube; final drive spiral bevel,6.83:1; three-quarter floating axle.
CHASSIS pressed steel channel-section frame with three crossmembers and central box-section; separate composite wood and metal cab and panel van by Briggs Motor Bodies; suspension, transverse leaf springs front and rear with triangulated radius arms; Armstrong lever arm dampers; I-beam front axle, live rear axle; differential offset to left; Girling mechanical brakes, 11in (27.9cm) drums; 7gal (31.8l) fuel tank on left side; 5-18 tyres.

DIMENSIONS wheelbase 90in (228.6cm); track front 50.5in (128.27cm) rear; load length 80in (203.2cm); capacity 110cuft; width 64in (162.6cm).
EQUIPMENT 6 volt electrical system 63amp battery.
PERFORMANCE maximum speed approx 60mph (96kph); 0-30mph (48kph) 15sec fuel consumption 25-30mpg (11.3-9.4l/100km).
PRICE £168
PRODUCTION 188,577

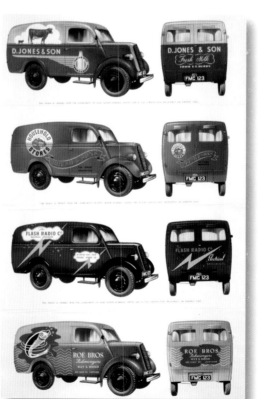

LEFT **Creative artistry of Ford marketing invented livery for small traders, customers for an adaptable van that survived two decades.**

1939
V8 91A 30HP

The last V8 before the Second World War was more Dearborn than ever. It was based on the 1939 Mercury with the grille abbreviated and headlamps moved to the wingtips. Its major technical novelty represented a break with tradition when it was provided at last with hydraulic brakes. Henry Ford's distrust of hydraulics was well known and he clung to rod or cable-operated systems for as long as his slogan, "the safety of steel from toe to wheel," would last, but in the end the market demanded change. There were changes too in the flathead V8. After nearly a decade it still tended to consume too much oil and relocating the water pumps had not altogether cured its tendency to overheat. The petrol pump was moved away from the warmth, the distributor away from the wet, and the 21

studs holding down the cylinder heads increased to 24. Less than two thousand 91As were made. The September 5 1939 issue of *The Motor* advertised used V8s at bargain levels. A one owner 30HP Club Cabriolet with brown leather, and 6,000 miles on the clock, was "almost as new" for £165. A 1939 22HP saloon only a month old was £195, a new unregistered one £240. A 1936 V8 Cabriolet could be picked up for £30, a 1937 22HP for £5 deposit or 45Gns (£47.25p) cash.

ABOVE **The Finishing Straight in front of the Brooklands clubhouse became a parade ground for the Ford range, including V8s featured on the pedestrian bridge, at a 1939 Ford dealer festival.**

INTRODUCTION December 1938 production to January 1940.
BODY Saloons Fordor 5-6-seat, convertible 2-seat, utility 4-door 5-6-seat; 4 door touring saloon 28cwt (1422.4kg) (3135.8lb).
ENGINE 8-cylinders in 90deg V; 77.8mm x 95mm, 3622cc; compr 6.3:1; 80bhp (59.6kW) @ 3500 rpm; 140lbft (190Nm) @ 1500rpm; 21.8bhp (16.5kW)/l.
ENGINE STRUCTURE side valves; centre gear-driven 3-bearing camshaft; aluminium detachable cylinder heads, 24-stud blocks and upper crankcase unitary cast iron; engine weight 581lb (263.5kg); Stromberg 48 twin choke downdraught carburettor, coil ignition, camshaft-driven spiral bevel gear to distributor; mechanical fuel pump; 3-bearing nodular iron crankshaft; thermosyphon cooling, two belt-driven pumps, pressure lubrication by camshaft pump.
TRANSMISSION rear wheel drive; 9in (22.86cm) sdp clutch; 3-speed manual gearbox with synchromesh 2 and 3; final drive 4.11:1.
CHASSIS steel X-braced frame with 4 cross-members; suspension by transverse leaf springs; 4 hydraulic lever arm dampers; hydraulic drum (non-scoring alloy) brakes; worm and sector steering; 11.5gal (52.3l) rear fuel tank; 6.00-16 tyres, 9.00-13 on Station Wagons.
DIMENSIONS wheelbase 112in (284.48cm); track 55in (139.7cm); length 185in (470cm); width 67.5in (171.45cm); height 68in (172.7cm) touring saloon; ground clearance 8.5in (21.6cm); turning circle 40ft (12.2m).
EQUIPMENT 6-volt electrics,
PERFORMANCE maximum speed 87mph (139.66kph); 0-60mph (96kph) 17sec; fuel consumption 16mpg (17.6l/100km).
PRICE September 1939, Touring Fordor £280, Convertible Coupe £300, Estate Car £325, Commercial Utility Car £325.
PRODUCTION 1878

1938
Prefect E 93 A

The first Ford with a name, not a letter or number, could still claim Model T pedigree with transverse leaf springs, side valve engine and torque tube transmission. Despite prodigious advances in production techniques, enabling Fords to be made at prices the rest of industry envied, the model that (owing to the war) was to span the family car market for ten years was still made to roughly the specification of the Model Y. Stretched to accommodate four doors, its chassis was less Model Y than Model C, with a dip in the middle, the floor and rear seat wells reinforced by steel panelling. The engine casting was wider than the Y to accommodate larger bore cylinders, and it could still be machined on the same ingenious transfer equipment as smaller counterparts. Non-adjustable tappets were another legacy of Henry Ford's technical stubbornness and it still had six-volt electrics. There were however, some innovations. The cheap vacuum-operated screen wipers acquired the luxury of a vacuum tank, so that they did not stop quite so profoundly at inconvenient times, such as when overtaking. Unlike the Model C, the additional length was turned to advantage, with an extra window in the rear quarters. Running boards, a narrow step enabling people to get in and out more easily, were reinstated, and the boot had a let-down door on leather straps providing a platform for luggage.

INTRODUCTION October 1938, civilian production to July 1940, wartime production until February 1942. Manufacture recommenced June 1945 to January 1949.
BODY Saloon: 2-doors, 4-doors, 4-seats, Tourer 2-door 4-seats; weight (4-door) 15cwt (762kg) (1679.9lb) The Autocar.
ENGINE 4-cylinders, in-line; 63.5mm x 92.5mm, 1172cc; compr 6.6:1; 30bhp (22.4kW) @ 4000 rpm; 60lbft (81Nm) @ 2000rpm; 25.6bhp (19.1kW)/l.
ENGINE STRUCTURE side valve; gear-driven camshaft; cast iron detachable cylinder head and block; aluminium pistons; Zenith downdraught carburettor; coil ignition, and mechanical fuel pump; 3-bearing counterbalanced crankshaft; thermo-syphon cooling; splash and pressure lubrication.
TRANSMISSION rear wheel drive; 7.375in (18.73cm) sdp clutch; 3-speed manual gearbox, synchromesh on 2; torque tube; spiral bevel final drive 5.5:1.
CHASSIS pressed steel channel-section frame with three crossmembers and central box-section; suspension, transverse leaf springs front and rear with triangulated radius arms; pear-shaped Luvax dampers; rod actuated 10in (25.4cm) drum brakes; Burman worm and nut steering; 6.5gal (29.5l) rear fuel tank; 4.50 – 17 Firestone tyres; steel spoke welded wheels.
DIMENSIONS wheelbase 94in (238.76cm); track 45in (114.3cm); length 155.5in (395cm); width 57in (144.78cm); height 63in (160.02cm); ground clearance 6.25in (15.87cm); turning circle 36ft (10.97m).
EQUIPMENT 6volt electrical system; fixed-rate charging; 10amps at 30mph; leathercloth upholstery, leather trim and sliding roof optional.
PERFORMANCE maximum speed 65mph (104.34kph); 0-50mph (80.26kph) 35sec fuel consumption 35mpg (8l/100km) to 45mpg (6.3l/100km) at normal speeds.
PRICE 2-door £150, 4-door and Tourer £162 10s (£162.50).
PRODUCTION 1938–1949 120,505, including 1028 tourers, 667 coupes, 10,163 Tudor, 37,502CKD.

1938
Bren Gun Carrier V8 3622cc, later Universal Carrier

Vickers' 1934 tracked gun-towing vehicle, the Light Dragon (from drag-gun) Tractor, with an Armstrong Siddeley air-cooled V8, and later a Meadows 6-cylinder, was redeveloped in 1936 as an infantry carrier. It mounted a Vickers machine gun and, following the introduction of the Bren light machine-gun, the superstructure was modified and in 1938 10 were issued per infantry battalion as "Carrier, Bren, No 2 Mark 1". In 1938 it was "Carrier, Scout" for mechanised cavalry regiments then "Carrier, Cavalry" with lighter armour and accommodation for six under a canvas tilt. The "Carrier, Armoured, OP" for Royal Artillery forward observation officers had a radio and a telephone cable wound off a drum at the back to report fall of shot to the gunners. In 1940 it was developed as the Universal Carrier, with various option kits, and better armour. Steering was by a novel track warping arrangement, activated by steering wheel, enabling it to be driven on the road like a wheeled vehicle. It also had a brake on the differential that allowed it to slew around in its own length. Experimental models carried 2-pdr, 6-pdr and 25-pdr guns and various multiple machine guns without seeing service. Universal Carriers with Canadian, British or American Ford V8s were made by Thornycroft Basingstoke, Morris Cowley, Sentinel Steam Wagon Company Shrewsbury, Aveling Barford, and Ford at Dagenham. They were also made at Windsor Ontario and by GM New Zealand, the New Zealand State Railways Workshop, and Australia. The Americans made 2,500 of a more powerful, but ultimately unsatisfactory T16.

INTRODUCTION 1936 production in small numbers as machine gun carrier, 1936 as Bren carrier, 1940 as Universal Carrier
BODY Open-topped; 0-doors, up to 6-seats; weight 3810kg (8400lb) payload 55kg (1212lb); weight of Universal 4318kg (9520lb); front armour 10mm (.393in); side 7mm (.275in)
ENGINE 8-cylinders, in 90deg V; mid; 77.79mm x 95.25mm, 3622cc; compr 5.5:1; 63.38kW (85bhp) @ 3500rpm; approx 130lbft (176Nm) @ 1250rpm; 21.7bhp (16.2kW)/l. US engine 95bhp (70.84kW); UK 65bhp (48.5kW).
ENGINE STRUCTURE side valves; centre gear-driven 3-bearing camshaft; aluminium detachable cylinder heads, 24-stud blocks and upper crankcase unitary cast iron; twin choke downdraught carburettor, coil ignition, camshaft-driven spiral bevel gear to

distributor; mechanical fuel pump; 3-bearing nodular iron crankshaft; thermosyphon cooling, two belt-driven pumps, pressure lubrication by camshaft pump.
TRANSMISSION rear drive sprockets; front idlers; single dry plate clutch; 4-speed and reverse manual gearbox; final drive 5.883:1.
CHASSIS steel monocoque; suspension 3 bogie wheels to tracks, leading and trailing arms, coil springs and hydraulic dampers; mechanical hydraulic servo drum brakes; steering by track braking; optional 120gal (545.5l) fuel tank for flamethrower; steel linked track-laying.
DIMENSIONS track width to centres 62.5in (158.75cm); length 144in (365.8cm) Universal 148in (375.9cm); width 69in (175.3cm) Universal 71in (180.34cm); height 57in (144.8cm) Universal 63in (160cm); ground

clearance 8.75in (22.2cm); turning circle, tracks-length
EQUIPMENT Optional OP sliding shutter in lieu of gun port, rifle racks, ammunition boxes, fire extinguishers, smoke canisters, starting handle, Verey pistol; Universal, mud deflectors over tracks, armour plating on engine compartment, steps for entry at rear, optional flame-thrower or mortars, mountings for .55in Boys anti tank rifle, Wasp Mark2 model with "Ronson" flamethrower.
PERFORMANCE maximum speed 30mph (48kph); range 110mls (177km) approx
FORD PRODUCTION 13,942. Caption: The ten thousandth Universal Carrier made by Ford between 1940 and 1945 undergoes pre-delivery field trials.

1940
Ford WOA1 saloon

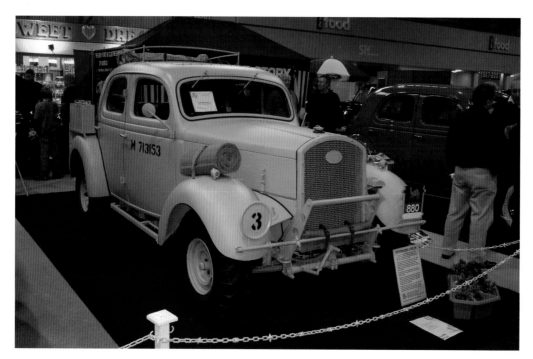

Using the 4-light body of the 22HP Model 62, with an austere military-pattern grille, the WOA1 staff car with a 30HP engine saw service throughout the Second World War. Designated WOA1 and WOA1/A principally for the army, they were used by all three services, together with 81 and 91 saloons and estate cars from a variety of sources including Canada. Allocation of staff cars to senior officers could be contentious, especially to those of field rank, sensitive about their status when turning up at conferences. Field Marshal Viscount Montgomery of Alamein made his open Humber Super Snipe "Old Faithful" famous in the desert campaign and later in Northern Europe, but preferred his Rolls-Royce Phantom III with unusual reverse-raked windscreen body by

HJ Mulliner. Formerly Field Marshall Lord Gort's car, it passed to "Monty" and became his personal property. Fords were for middle-ranking officers although Field Marshal Earl Alexander of Tunis hung on to his Canadian-made Ford C11AD with US 3.9litre 70.8kW (95bhp) V8. The bodywork was a combination of estate car framed doors and open top, with reinforcements to compensate for the absence of the steel roof. Wartime regulations demanded headlight hoods for the black-out and white-painted bumpers, wings, and running boards to help pedestrians see them. Home-based army vehicles were given a matt khaki finish, RAF cars were light blue, those for the Royal Navy dark blue.

INTRODUCTION production 1941-1944.
BODY Saloon Fordor 5-6-seat weight 25cwt (2800lb) (1279kg).
ENGINE 8-cylinders in 90deg V; 77.8mm x 95mm, 3622cc; compr 6.3:1; 59.6kW (80bhp) @ 3500 rpm; 22.1bhp (16.5kW)/l; 140lbft (190Nm) @ 1500rpm.
ENGINE STRUCTURE side valves; centre gear-driven 3-bearing camshaft; aluminium detachable cylinder heads, blocks and upper crankcase unitary cast iron; engine weight 581lb (263.5kg); Stromberg 48 twin choke downdraught carburettor, coil ignition, camshaft-driven distributor; mechanical fuel pump; 3-bearing cast steel crankshaft; thermosyphon cooling, two belt-driven pumps, pressure lubrication by camshaft pump.
TRANSMISSION rear wheel drive; 9in (22.9cm) sdp cushioned clutch; 3-speed manual all-synchromesh gearbox; spiral bevel final drive 4.55:1.
CHASSIS steel X-braced frame with 4 cross-members; suspension by transverse leaf springs; 4 hydraulic lever arm dampers; mechanical drum (non-scoring alloy) brakes; worm and sector steering; 12.5gal (56.8l) rear fuel tank; 5.75-16 or 9.00-13 or 6.50-16 (Model WOA1/A) tyres; electrically welded steel disc wheels.
DIMENSIONS wheelbase 108.25in (275cm); track 55.25in (140.3cm) front 58in (147.3cm) rear; length 173.25 (440cm); width 69.5in (176.5cm); turning circle 40ft (12.19m).
EQUIPMENT 6-volt electrics, body colours according to service
PERFORMANCE maximum speed 76mph (122kph); 0-62mph (100kph) 17sec; fuel consumption 20-25 mph (14.1-11.3l/100km).

ABOVE **Staff car by modeller Alan McNeilly used tall radiator instead of faired-in grille of standard saloon.**

1940
WOA2 heavy utility

An upright rugged shooting brake style of body on a reinforced Model 62 chassis, with an austere military-pattern grille, the WOA2 had a 30HP engine and many survived the war as commercial workhorses. Production continued for several more years, and long before the introduction of leisure 4x4s they became general purpose vehicles for off-road use. Despite not having four wheel drive, wide tyres with deep treads provided useful grip in heavy going. The Post Office Telephones Home Counties Division bought them for essential line maintenance during the war and in 1946 added ex-military reconditioned war-surplus stock to carry on the work. The body had a horizontally split tailgate and there were two rows of seats with two more tip-up chairs in the rear. Equipment varied according to service demands. A folding map table could be installed behind the front seats when used as a staff car, and many were modified as open tourers for service in the desert. The WOA2 was adapted as a 15cwt GS truck known as the WOT2, using the same bonnet and radiator, with forward control that resulted in a narrow toe-board for the driver. As a result the accelerator pedal had to be mounted aft of the front wheel arch. The simplified cab had canvas top and doors, and individual small windscreens; later versions had fully enclosed cabs and evolved into proper trucks. A number of WOT2s were equipped as fire appliances and used by the National Fire Service

INTRODUCTION production May 1941–1947
BODY Saloon 5-door 7-seat weight 4790lb (2173kg).
ENGINE 8-cylinders in 90deg V; 77.8mm x 95mm, 3622cc; compr 6.3:1; 80bhp (59.6kW) @ 3500 rpm; 140lbft (190Nm) @ 1500rpm; 22.1bhp (16.5kW)/l.
ENGINE STRUCTURE side valves; centre gear-driven 3-bearing camshaft; aluminium detachable cylinder heads, blocks and upper crankcase unitary cast iron; engine weight 581lb (263.5kg); Stromberg 48 twin choke downdraught carburettor, coil ignition, camshaft-driven distributor; mechanical fuel pump; 3-bearing cast steel crankshaft; thermosyphon cooling, two belt-driven pumps, pressure lubrication by camshaft pump.
TRANSMISSION rear wheel drive; 9in (23cm) sdp cushioned clutch; 3-speed manual all-synchromesh gearbox; spiral bevel final drive 4.55:1.
CHASSIS steel X-braced frame with 4 cross-members; suspension by transverse leaf springs; 4 hydraulic lever arm dampers; mechanical drum brakes; worm and sector steering; 12.5gal (56.82l) rear fuel tank; 9.00-13 or 6.50-16 tyres; electrically welded steel disc wheels.
DIMENSIONS wheelbase 108.25in (274.9cm); track 55.25in (140.3cm) front 58in (147.3cm) rear; length 173.25in (440.05cm); width 75in (190.5cm); height 70in (177.8cm).
EQUIPMENT 6-volt electrics, body colours according to service
PERFORMANCE fuel consumption 20mpg (14.1l/100km)
PRODUCTION 11,754

ABOVE **RL Davey's 1944 Dagenham-built WOA2 re-enacts a WWII military convoy at Trucks and Troops Show at National Motor Museum, Beaulieu.**

1944
Ford Merlin V12

In 1933 the ailing Sir Henry Royce persevered with a V12 aero engine in the face of Air Ministry indifference and prevarication. The PV (for Private Venture) 12 was a straightforward upright V12 of a sort with which Rolls-Royce was familiar. An inverted layout was considered, which might have given the pilots of the single seater monoplane fighters a better view forward, but lubrication was difficult. Sir Henry Royce did not like novelties, and the idea was dropped. The great engineer died on 22 April 1933 just as the final drawings were being completed. The first engine ran on 15 October and Royce's vision resulted in one of the most significant aircraft power units of the Second World War. Developed from the Kestrel and the R-type that had been successful in the Schneider Trophy Supermarine S6 racing seaplanes, the Merlin was not named after the legendary wizard, but was one of a series designated by birds of prey. It was used not only in

the front-line fighters in the Battle of Britain, the Hawker Hurricane and Supermarine Spitfire, but also in Avro Lancaster and de Havilland Mosquito. Later ones were developed to produce substantial power increases at high altitude and by the end of the war specialist versions were turning out 2640bhp (1969kW). Rolls-Royce did not have capacity at Derby, Crewe, and Hillington Glasgow to meet the demand. Four times as many Merlins were needed to equip the new 4-engined bombers. Packard made them in America and Ford was invited to set up a plant at Urmston, Manchester, not far from Trafford Park. Rowland Smith guessed it would cost £7m, telling Rolls-Royce chairman Lord Hives that Ford could not build engines from the drawings supplied by Rolls-Royce. The tolerances were far too wide. Ford production machinery worked to closer limits than Rolls-Royce managed on hand-finished engines.

ENGINE 12-cylinders, 60deg V; 5.4in (137.1mm) x 6in (152.4mm), 1649 cu in (27,021cc); compr 6.0:1; 1030bhp (768kW) @ 3000rpm @ 16,250ft (4940m) Merlin I, to 1480bhp (1104kW) @ 3000rpm @ 6000ft (1830m), to 12,250ft (3740m) from Merlin XX; weight 1385lb (629kg) Merlin I, 1450lb (647kg) Merlin XX, 1640lb (744kg) for 1565bhp (1167kW) Merlin 61 onwards, 57.9bhp (43.2kW)/l.

ENGINE STRUCTURE 4 inclined 45deg KE965 steel valves per cylinder (4 valves parallel from Merlin G); sodium-cooled exhaust valves; Stellited ends to inlet valves; double valve springs; Silchrome valve seats screwed into heads; one shaft bevel gear-driven 7-bearing overhead camshaft per bank; 2 2-piece cylinder blocks cast in RR50 aluminium alloy; detachable cylinder heads; wet high carbon steel cylinder liners; aluminium crankcase split horizontally; twin choke updraught R-R/SU carburettor with anti-ice heating; gear-driven centrifugal supercharger, 2-speed from Mark X; liquid-cooled intercooler; 2 mechanical fuel pumps on quill shafts; 2 magnetos; one-piece 6-throw chrome molybdenum steel 7-bearing crankshaft; dry sump lubrication; 70% water 30% ethylene glycol cooling; centrifugal pump; electric starter; air compressor take-off for aircraft services.

TRANSMISSION single plain spur 0.477:1 or 0.42:1 reduction gears to propeller from front of crankshaft.

PRODUCTION over 30,000.

1939–1945
Anglia E04 A

Pool petrol, rationing, the end of car production for all but the military, shortages of many things hitherto regarded as essential; the onset of war changed everything except the specification of the smallest Ford. One innovation was a name, Anglia, unmistakably British even though Dagenham was more Essex than Anglian. War broke out on September 3 1939, yet until the real conflict began nobody knew what to do. Ford went ahead and introduced a new car. The upright square grille gave it good proportions, and although a coupe was proposed and prototypes built with independent front suspension, it never reached production. The return to peacetime manufacture was planned well in advance, and barely three weeks after the guns stopped firing in Europe Dagenham began making cars for the biggest seller's market in history. A small luggage boot was added but running boards deleted, windscreens no longer opened, the front bumper was plain straight not cranked and there were no indicators until 1948, but cars were once again in production and Ford was making the cheapest. It was fairly nimble. With one and three quarter turns of the steering lock to lock, changes of direction were quite swift and, despite the high gearing, it was not heavy to drive. For the post-war export drive Anglias shipped to North America had the 1172cc 10HP engine and, astonishingly for such a narrow car with a central gearshift, a bench front seat.

INTRODUCTION October 1939, production until November 1948 (chassis nos Y278543-Y369249, final wartime 1941 Anglia Y287241, first postwar May 25 1945 Y291482).
BODY saloon; 2-doors, 4-seats; weight 1940 1735lb (787kg), 1945 1706lb (774kg).
ENGINE 4-cylinders, in-line; 56.6mm x 92.5mm, 933cc; comp 6.2:1; 23.4bhp (17.5kW) @ 4000rpm; 25.1bhp (18.7kW)/l; 36.5lbft (49.5Nm) @ 2300rpm.
ENGINE STRUCTURE side valve; gear-driven camshaft; cast iron detachable cylinder head and block; aluminium pistons; Zenith downdraught carburettor; coil ignition, and mechanical fuel pump; 3-bearing counterbalanced crankshaft; thermo-syphon cooling; splash and pressure lubrication.
TRANSMISSION rear wheel drive; 7.4in (187mm) sdp clutch; 3-speed manual gearbox, synchromesh on 2; torque tube; spiral bevel final drive 5.5:1.
CHASSIS pressed steel channel-section frame with three crossmembers and central box-section; suspension, transverse leaf springs front and rear with triangulated radius arms; pear-shaped Luvax dampers; rod actuated 10in (254mm) drum brakes; Burman worm and nut steering; 6.5 gal (29.5l) rear fuel tank; 4.50-17 Firestone tyres; steel spoke welded wheels.
DIMENSIONS wheelbase 90in (228.6cm); track 45in (114.3cm); length 152in (386.1cm); width 57in (144.8cm); height 63in (160cm); ground clearance 6.25in (15.9cm); turning circle 36ft (11m).
EQUIPMENT 6 volt electrical system; fixed-rate charging; 10amps at 30mph; leathercloth upholstery, leather trim optional, sliding roof optional for £3 in 1940; vacuum reservoir for wipers.
PERFORMANCE maximum speed 59mph (94.7kph) (*The Autocar* 1940); 0-50mph (80.3kph) 35sec; 33.6kg/kW (45kg/kW) 1940, 33.1kg/bhp (44kg/kW) 1945; fuel consumption 35-45mpg (8-6.3l/100km) at normal speeds.
PRICE 1940 de luxe £140; 1945 £293.
PRODUCTION 46,745 plus 9062 CKD.

RIGHT **Wartime regulations demanded blackout masks on headlights of this 1940s Anglia.**

1945
Prefect E93A

Dagenham's millionth car was an E93A Prefect. The rounded grille and so-called "alligator" front-opening bonnet lent it a vaguely exotic air when it was relaunched only as a 4-door. Tourers were unwanted interruptions to the serious business of resuming car production. With rationing still in force economy was important, even though low-quality Pool petrol was only 2 shillings (10p) a gallon, but Purchase Tax at 33.3 per cent raised car prices against those of 1939. An annual road tax based on cubic capacity had been proposed but it was not invoked until 1946. The distorted market reversed the pre-war position in which Anglia outsold Prefect. Now the 10HP car outsold the 8 by almost two to one, although both were

virtually unchanged from 1939. The Prefect had a bigger dynamo and the seats tubular frames, which were not only cheaper to make but also more comfortable. There were minor differences in trim and colour but by 1948 The Autocar was finding the Prefect noisy and the handling indifferent. There was body roll on corners and a lot of pitching. "The system of suspension," it observed icily, "gives comfortable riding in the sense that it takes the shock out of poor surfaces, and allows the car to be driven over really bad surfaces, without causing one to feel it is being done any harm." Post-war designs were appearing with unitary construction and independent front suspension.

INTRODUCTION October 1938, production to January 1949.
BODY saloon; 4-doors, 4-seats; weight 15.7cwt (797.6kg) (1758lb).
ENGINE 4-cylinders, in-line; 63.5mm x 92.5mm, 1172cc; compr 6.6:1; 30bhp (22.4kW) @ 4000 rpm; 25.6bhp (19.1kW)/l; 97.8lbft (132.6Nm) @ 2400rpm.
ENGINE STRUCTURE side valve; gear-driven camshaft; cast iron detachable cylinder head and block; aluminium pistons; Zenith downdraught carburettor; coil ignition, and mechanical fuel pump; 3-bearing counterbalanced crankshaft; thermo-syphon cooling; splash and pressure lubrication.
TRANSMISSION rear wheel drive; 7.375in (18.73cm) sdp clutch; 3-speed manual gearbox, synchromesh on 2; torque tube; spiral bevel final drive 5.5:1.
CHASSIS pressed steel channel-section frame with three crossmembers and lowered central box-section; suspension, transverse leaf springs front and rear with triangulated radius arms; pear-shaped Luvax dampers; rod actuated 10in (25.4cm) drum brakes; Burman worm and nut steering; 7 gal (31.8l) fuel tank; 5.00-16 tyres; steel spoke welded wheels.
DIMENSIONS wheelbase 94in (238.8cm); track 45in (114.3cm); length 155.5in (395cm); width 57in (144.8cm); height 63in (160cm); ground clearance 8.75in (22.2cm); turning circle 36ft (10.97m).
EQUIPMENT 6 volt electrical system; fixed-rate charging; 10amps at 30mph; rear window blind; cloth upholstery, leather trim £7 13s 4d (£7.67p).
PERFORMANCE maximum speed 59.7mph (95.8kph) The Motor; 0-50mph (80.3kph) 26.9sec; 26.6kg/bhp (35.6kg/kW); fuel consumption 33.8mpg (8.3l/100km).
PRICE 4-door £275 plus PT £77 2s 9d, £352 2s 9d (£352.77p).
PRODUCTION 1938-1949 120,505 including 1028 tourers, 667 coupes, 10,163 Tudors, 37,502CKD.

1945
Fordson Major E27N

When tractor production restarted after the war, the Model N's replacement used the same engine and a new axle, later incorporated in the 1952 New Fordson Major. Modern farm machinery required a driving force and the W27N had an optional central Power Take Off (PTO), a hydraulic power lift and sufficient ground clearance for rowcrop as well as general agriculture. Diesel tractors were still in a minority despite Ford's efforts to promote multi-fuel until 1948 when the Perkins P6 TA became an option. Its 45bhp (33.6kW) was the greatest power of any tractor based on the 1917 design principles of Eugene Farkas, Ford's Hungarian-born chief engineer. Practical styling came in with a radiator cowl with vertical slats and lights and it was available with a wide range of attachments, including a Roadless half-track kit and the County Full Track (CFT). Ford had been working on its own diesel engine since 1944 but farmers proved reluctant to endorse diesels owing to their reputation for difficult starting. Following the success of the Perkins, however, Ford was encouraged to introduce the New Major in 1951 with curved styling and a 4-cylinder 3.6-litre with a compression ratio ranging from 4.35:1 to 16:1. It could thus be used with petrol, petrol-TVO, or diesel fuel. The same diesel engine was also employed in Thames Trader commercials.

INTRODUCTION March 19 1945, production to 1952.
BODY open; 0-doors, 1-seat; weight 4000lb (1814.4kg); 4500lb (2041.2kg) with Perkins P6.
ENGINE 4-cylinders, in-line; 4.125in (104.78mm) x 5in (127mm), 4380cc; 27bhp (20.1kW) @ 1200rpm; 6.2bhp (4.6kW)/l. Perkins P6 6-cylinders; 3.5in (88.9mm) x 5in (127mm); 4730cc; 45bhp (33.6kW) @ 1500rpm; 9.5bhp (7.1kW)/l.
ENGINE STRUCTURE side camshaft gear-driven from crankshaft; iron cylinder head, block; vaporiser for TVO, Zenith carb for petrol, ignition Lucas high tension magneto; gravity fuel feed; 3-bearing crankshaft; cooling by pump and fan; flat-type air-washer. P6 valve in-head with high level camshaft; indirect injection by CAV in-line pump, swirl pre-combustion chambers; starting by Ki-gas pump and heater plug.
TRANSMISSION rwd; wet single-plate clutch; constant-mesh; 3-speed manual gearbox; low, intermediate, and high; slewing brakes on bull pinion shafts; transmission brake; spiral bevel final drive; four pinion differential.
CHASSIS integral engine clutch, gearbox, final drive; front axle buffer; mechanical brakes, front drums; worm and sector steering, later worm and nut with PAS optional; 16 gal (72.7l); standard agricultural wheels; rear, optional steel spoked with cleats or spade lugs, Land Utility with cast centres for Dunlop, Firestone, Goodyear or French & Hecht tyres; cast front wheels; Rowcrop Vee formation optional, with independent pedal-operated brakes.
DIMENSIONS wheelbase 63in (160cm); length 102in (259.1cm); width 62.75in (159.4cm); height 54.5in (138.4cm); ground clearance 11.6in (29.5cm); turning circle 21ft (6.4m).
EQUIPMENT optional electric starter; dark blue with orange wheels, later light blue. Cab optional from 1960.
PRICE Standard agricultural £237 on metal wheels; Land Utility on rubber tyres £281; Row Crop £255-£285.

BELOW **Rudimentary enclosure of the driver, pneumatic tyres, power take-offs, and a fetching colour scheme were on offer to farmers by the 1950s.**

1947
Pilot E71A

First new model after the war was derived from the 1937 22HP V8-62, with a distinctive radiator grille designed by new Australian chief body engineer Don Ward plus lockable boot and outside spare wheel. With cylinder dimensions of 65mm x 95mm (the old 22HP was 66mm x 81mm) giving 2535cc, but with only 66bhp (49.22kW) it was too slow or, as Ford put it at the time, "after further research into overseas markets, it was decided not to proceed with a 2.5-litre". The 95mm stroke version was retained, even though the 3.6-litre's fuel consumption seemed inappropriate in an era of austerity and shortages. Among the innovations were a front anti-roll bar and a Clayton Dewandre heater, with demisting and de-icing vents under the windscreen, as standard. The Smith's Jackall four wheel jacking system had hydraulic rams that could be pumped down to raise the car for wheel-changing. The Pilot chassis-cab that continued into 1952 as the E71C commercial, encouraged production of wood-paneled estate cars and even pick-ups. King George VI had a Pilot shooting brake, on a rare long wheelbase chassis, preserved at Sandringham. A 12-volt electrical system was produced for export police cars, and heavy-duty clutch and high capacity water pumps were optional. Several Pilots appeared in Monte Carlo Rallies, in which V8s had done well before the war, and Ken Wharton used one to win the 1950 Tulip Rally.

INTRODUCTION August 1947, production to May 1951.
BODY saloon, 4-door, 5-6-seat, weight 29cwt (1473kg) (3248lb).
ENGINE 8-cylinders in 90deg Vee; 77.8mm x 95.3mm, 3622cc; compr 6.15:1; 85bhp (63.4kW) @ 3500 rpm; 23.5bhp (17.5kW)/l; 140lbft (190Nm) @ 1500rpm; Treasury rating 30.01HP.
ENGINE STRUCTURE side valves; centre Celeron helical-cut gear-driven 3-bearing camshaft; cast iron detachable cylinder heads, blocks and upper crankcase unitary cast iron; Solex twin choke downdraught carburettor, coil ignition, camshaft-driven distributor; electric fuel pump; 3-bearing cast steel crankshaft, separate bearings for each big-end; thermosyphon cooling, two belt-driven pumps, pressure lubrication by camshaft pump.
TRANSMISSION rear wheel drive; 9in (23cm) sdp cushioned clutch; 3-speed manual gearbox, synchromesh on 2 and 3; steering column change; torque tube; spiral bevel final drive 4.11.
CHASSIS steel X-braced frame with 4 cross-members; suspension by transverse leaf springs; front anti-roll bar; 4 hydraulic lever arm dampers; hydro-mechanical drum brakes; worm and sector steering; 12.5 gal (56.8l) rear fuel tank; 6.00-16 tyres; bolt-on pierced steel wheels.
DIMENSIONS wheelbase 108.25in (275cm); track 55.25in (140.3cm) front, 58in (147.3cm) rear; length 174.75in (444cm); width 69.5in (176.5cm); height 66in (167.6cm); ground clearance 8.25in (21cm); turning circle 40ft (12.19m).

EQUIPMENT 6 volt electrics; automatic voltage control, cloth upholstery, leather £16 extra; interior heater; radio optional; combined ignition and steering column lock; floor carpets; hydraulic jacks; colours available black, dark blue, beige, or light green.
PERFORMANCE maximum speed 82.5mph (132.4kph) The Autocar; 0-60mph (96kph) 20.5 sec; 17.3kg/bhp (23.2kg/bhp); fuel consumption 17-20mpg (16.6-14.1l/100km).
PRICE £585 plus PT £163 5s, £748 5s (£748.25p).
PRODUCTION 21,487, 668CKD.

1948
Anglia E494A

The solitary British car with a basic price under £250, the Anglia still gained only minor changes for 1949. The grille became an erect oval with a divider down the middle. However there was not much cheer for Ford in the first post-war motor show at Earls Court, following the introduction of the Morris Minor at only £358 10s 7d (£358.53). The Minor still had side-valves but it had modern full-width styling, a roomy interior, independent front suspension, rack and pinion steering, a 4-speed gearbox, generous luggage accommodation and exemplary ride and handling. The writing was surely on the wall for Model T technology as Nuffield and Austin announced the "constant interchange of information and pooling of resources," that would lead to the formation of the British Motor Corporation. *The Autocar* found it increasingly difficult to write about the Anglia kindly: "(The Fords) have years of experience behind them and the resources of the great plant at Dagenham, which is synonymous with service. All three models are lively in their respective classes, as their construction is light, and their engines reliable and willing." Faint praise. Ford hoped to keep the price the same as the outgoing Anglia, £242 + PT £67 19s 5d making £309 19s 2d (£309.97p). By the motor show it was £255 + PT £71 11s 8d making it £326 11s 8d, perilously close to the Morris.

INTRODUCTION November 1948, production to October 1953.
BODY saloon; 2-doors, 4-seats; weight 1940 1735lb (787kg), 1945 1706lb (774kg).
ENGINE 4-cylinders, in-line; 56.6mm x 92.5mm, 933cc; compr 6.2:1; 23.4bhp (17.5kW) @ 4000rpm; 25.1bhp (18.7kW)/l; 36.5lbft (49.5Nm) @ 2300rpm.
ENGINE STRUCTURE side valve; gear-driven camshaft; cast iron detachable cylinder head and block; aluminium pistons; Zenith downdraught carburettor; coil ignition, and mechanical fuel pump; 3-bearing counterbalanced crankshaft; thermo-syphon cooling; splash and pressure lubrication.
TRANSMISSION rear wheel drive; 7.375in (18.7cm) sdp clutch; 3-speed manual gearbox, synchromesh on 2; torque tube; spiral bevel final drive 5.5:1.
CHASSIS pressed steel channel-section frame with three crossmembers and central box-section; suspension, transverse leaf springs front and rear with triangulated radius arms; pear-shaped Luvax dampers; rod actuated 10in (25.4cm) drum brakes; Burman worm and nut steering; 6.5 gal (29.5l) fuel tank; 4.50-17 tyres; steel spoke welded wheels.
DIMENSIONS wheelbase 90in (229cm); track 45in (114.3cm); length 152in (386.1cm); width 57in (144.8cm); height 63in (160cm); ground clearance 6.25in (15.9cm); turning circle 36ft (10.97m).
EQUIPMENT 6 volt electrical system; fixed-rate charging; 10amps at 30mph; cloth upholstery, leather trim optional; vacuum reservoir for wipers.
PERFORMANCE maximum speed 59mph (94.7kph) (*The Autocar* 1940); 0-50mph (80.3kph) 35sec; 33.6kg/bhp (45kg/kW); fuel consumption 35-45mpg (8-6.3l/100km).
PRICE £255 plus PT £71 11s 8d, £326 11s 8d (£326.58p).
PRODUCTION 108,000.

ABOVE **Smethwick garage proprietor Ken Wharton was a versatile racing and rally driver, winning the 1949 Tulip Rally with co-driver Joy Cooke.**

TOP **Coats of Robbialac paints came in many colours.**

1949
Prefect E493A

As an indication that Ford was aware of the need for change, the facelifted Prefect at the 1949 London Motor Show had an upright Pilot-style grille, and headlamps faired into the wings. It was not much, in the light of what was to follow, but it was a start. The swage line in the front doors that had served little purpose but imitate a longer front wing was discarded. Style was becoming important as the post-war seller's market began to decay, while cars were still in short supply and subject to a Covenant forbidding resale and profiteering. As the 1950s began, competition increased. The Prefect still did not have a heater, even as an option, but in 1948 it acquired swiveling instead of fixed scuttle vents so that the air inside the car, even if not heated, was at least fresh. Export Prefects were equipped with an optimistic bench-type 3-abreast seat. Yet no sooner was the new improved Prefect on the road than there was a 4-door Morris Minor. It had been restyled with high-mounted headlamps, and as a result of the nascent BMC merger, an overhead valve Austin A30 engine was waiting in the wings. The Minor's price went up to £429 including Purchase Tax but the pressure of competition was starting to tell. Only bargain hunters were now going for Fords.

INTRODUCTION December 1948, production to September 1953.
BODY saloon; 4-doors, 4-seats; weight 1808lb (820.1kg).
ENGINE 4-cylinders, in-line; 63.5mm x 92.5mm, 1172cc; compr 6.6:1; 30bhp (22.4kW) @ 4000 rpm; 25.6bhp (19.1kW)/l; 97.8lbft (133Nm) @ 2400rpm.
ENGINE STRUCTURE side valve; gear-driven camshaft; cast iron detachable cylinder head and block; aluminium pistons; Zenith downdraught carburettor; coil ignition and mechanical fuel pump; 3-bearing counterbalanced crankshaft; thermo-syphon cooling; splash and pressure lubrication.
TRANSMISSION rear wheel drive; 7.375in (18.7cm) sdp clutch; 3-speed manual gearbox, synchromesh on 2; torque tube; spiral bevel final drive 5.5:1.
CHASSIS pressed steel channel-section frame with three crossmembers and lowered central box-section; suspension, transverse leaf springs front and rear with triangulated radius arms; pear-shaped Luvax dampers; rod actuated 10in (25.4cm) drum brakes; Burman worm and nut steering; 7 gal (31.8l) fuel tank; 5.00-16 tyres; steel spoke welded wheels.
DIMENSIONS wheelbase 94in (238.8cm); track 45in (114.3cm); length 155.5in (395cm); width 55.75in (141.6cm); height 63in (160cm); ground clearance 8.75in (22.2cm); turning circle 36ft (10.97m).
EQUIPMENT 6 volt electrical system; fixed-rate charging; 10amps at 30mph; rear window blind; cloth upholstery, leather trim £7 13s 4d (£7.67p).
PERFORMANCE maximum speed 59.7mph (95.8kph) The Motor; 0-50mph (80.3kph) 26.9sec; 27.3kg/bhp (36.7kg/kW); fuel consumption 33.8mpg (8.35l/100km).
PRICE 4-door £310 plus PT £86 17s 3, £396 17s 3d (£396.86p).
PRODUCTION 117,206, 75,023 CKD.

1950
Consul EOTA saloon and estate

Almost overnight in 1950 Ford was transformed from a manufacturer of small, mostly black, cheap, working class cars into a design conscious, *avant garde* fashion house. The new Consul and Zephyr not only had the glamour and elegant proportions of the 1949 American Fords, they had innovative engineering as well. They were the first mass-market cars to make something out of the abolition of the old RAC Treasury rating for road tax; their new overhead valve engines were over-square, with a bore/stroke ratio of 0.96:1, which reduced piston speed from that of their long-stroke forebears. They were the first Fords with unitary structures, 12volt electrics, 13in wheels, a hydraulic clutch and independent front suspension employing a new layout – the brainchild of American engineering vice-president Earle Steele MacPherson. The ingenious and widely copied MacPherson strut distributed the suspension loads throughout the front of the monocoque, and the bottom link incorporated an anti-roll bar that bent as well as twisted. The design work was done in Detroit, bringing in new production techniques that manufactured engines twice as fast, by automatically transferring the cylinder blocks from one machining operation to another. The cheaper 4-cylinder Consul was 10.2cm (4in) shorter than the 6-cylinder Zephyr with its longer bonnet and additional chrome.

INTRODUCTION Motor Show October 1950, production January 1951 until February 1956.
BODY saloon; 4-doors, 5-seats; weight 1080kg (2380lb).
ENGINE 4-cylinders, in-line; 79.37mm x 76.2mm, 1508cc; compr 6.8:1; 35kW (47bhp) @ 4400rpm; 23.2kW (31.2bhp)/l; 98Nm (72lbft) @ 2400rpm.
ENGINE STRUCTURE pushrod ohv chain-driven camshaft; cast iron cylinder head and block; 30mm downdraught carburettor, 12v coil ignition AC mechanical fuel pump; 3-bearing cast iron counterweighted crankshaft.
TRANSMISSION rear wheel drive; 203mm (8in) single plate hydraulic clutch; 3-speed manual synchromesh (on 2nd and top) gearbox; steering column shift; hypoid final drive 4.625:1.
CHASSIS steel monocoque structure; ifs by coil springs and hydraulic telescopic dampers integral with kingpins; single track control arms located by triangulated anti-roll bar; live rear axle with half-elliptic springs and piston dampers; Girling hydraulic 22.9cm (9in) drum brakes, 2 leading shoe at front; Burman worm and peg steering; 40.9l (9 gal) fuel tank; steel disc wheels, 5.90 x 13in tyres.
DIMENSIONS wheelbase 254cm (100in); track front 127cm (50in); 124.5cm (49in) rear; length 412.8cm (162.5in); width 162.6cm (64in); height 164.3cm (60.75in); ground clearance 17.1cm (6.75in); turning circle right 12.5m (41ft), left 12m (39.5ft).
EQUIPMENT bench front seat, radio optional, heater optional £10.
PERFORMANCE maximum speed 120.4kph (75mph); 23.9kph (14.9mph) @ 1000rpm; 0-96kph (60mph) 31.1sec; 30.8kg/kW (23kg/bhp); fuel consumption 11.8-10.1 l/100km (24-28mpg).
PRICE £425 plus £118.16s 2d purchase tax, £543.16s 2d (£543.81).
PRODUCTION 231,481.

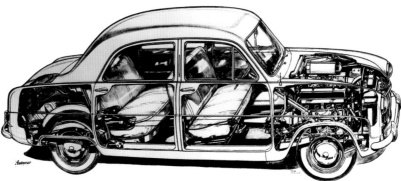

1950
Zephyr Six EOTTA saloon and estate

The first British Ford with 6 cylinders, the Zephyr had a longer bonnet than the Consul to accommodate two more cylinders and a distinctive front grille. Both cars had bench seats front and rear that could accommodate three occupants abreast. From the B-post rearwards the bodies were identical, so with more weight in front Zephyrs had a reputation for readiness to spin their rear wheels on loose surfaces. Unaccustomed to copious power from a smooth-revving engine, some drivers carried ballast in the boot to try and keep a grip on things. Firestone Town and Country tyres were a popular palliative. Proving the Zephyr had satisfactory ride and handling, Dutch driver Maurice Gatsonides won

the 1953 Monte Carlo Rally in VHK194, standard except for an elaborate glare-shield over the battery of fog lights, and an adjustable jet carburettor. At the 1954 motor show ED Abbott, a small Farnham coach-building firm, brought out an estate car version of Consul and Zephyr. Abbott had made high-class coachwork for Daimlers and Lanchesters since the 1920s, and had a strong commercial line in bus bodies. Under the proprietorship of Gordon Sutherland, formerly of Aston Martin and owner of Friary Motors, which did estate car conversions throughout the 1950s, the estate car roof extension was developed using concrete dies to form the roof pressing. The estate car with side-hinged tailgate cost only £145 extra.

INTRODUCTION Motor Show October 1950, production February 1951 to February 1956.
BODY saloon; 4-doors, 5-seats; weight 1187.5kg (2618lb).
ENGINE 6-cylinders, in-line; 79.37mm x 76.2mm, 2262cc; compr 6.8:1; 50.7kW (68bhp) @ 4000rpm; 22.4kW (30.1bhp)/l; 152Nm (112lbft) @ 2000rpm.
ENGINE STRUCTURE pushrod ohv chain-driven camshaft; cast iron cylinder head and block; 30mm downdraught carburettor, 12v coil ignition AC mechanical fuel pump; 4-bearing cast iron counterweighted crankshaft.
TRANSMISSION rwd; 203mm (8in) single plate hydraulic clutch; 3-speed manual synchromesh (on 2nd and top) gearbox; steering column shift; hypoid final drive 4.375:1.
CHASSIS steel monocoque structure; independent front suspension by coil springs and hydraulic telescopic dampers integral with kingpins; single track control arms located by triangulated anti-roll bar. Live rear axle with half-elliptic springs and piston dampers; Girling hydraulic 22.9cm (9in) drum brakes, 2 leading shoe at front; Burman worm and peg steering; 40.9l (9 gal) fuel tank; steel disc wheels, 6.40 x 13in tyres.
DIMENSIONS wheelbase 264.2cm (104in); track front 127cm (50in), 124.5cm (49in) rear; length 431.8cm (170in); width 162.6cm (64in); height 154.3cm (60.75in); ground clearance 17.1cm (6.75in); turning circle right 12.5m (41ft), left 12m (39.5ft).
EQUIPMENT bench front seat, radio optional, heater optional £10.
PERFORMANCE maximum speed 130kph (81mph); 26.3kph (16.4mph) @ 1000rpm; 0-96kph (60mph) 21.1sec; 23.4kg/kW (17.5kg/bhp); fuel consumption 12.3-11.3l/100km (23-25mpg).
PRICE £475 plus £132.13s 11d purchase tax £607.13s 11d (£607.70). 1953 with pvc upholstery £667, £684 with leather.
PRODUCTION 152,677.

Maurice Gatsonides (of the Gatso speed camera) removed the glare-shield from the front of his Zephyr for the final test on the Monte Carlo Rally. Engine cooling on the 21km (13mile) descent of the Col de Castillon was at a premium. So was brake cooling. Teams of helpers on slow corners threw cold water on hot drums.

1951
Consul and Zephyr Convertibles

Prototype Convertibles were shown a year after the saloons' introduction, but they did not make it into production for a further two years, while problems with reinforcing the monocoque structure were dealt with. This work was entrusted to one of the oldest contract coachworks in the industry, Carbodies of Coventry. As specialists in convertibles, Carbodies had been supplier to Alvis, MG and Rover, as well as making Hillman Minx dropheads from 1932. Post-war it made London taxis, worked for Singer and Standard, and bodied the Austin Somerset and Hereford convertibles, so it was a natural choice for the complex task of designing a cross-bracing underneath the Fords, stiffening them in the absence of a steel roof. The shells were modified with 2 instead of 4 doors and trimmed by Carbodies, but final assembly took place at Dagenham. Like Carbodies' contemporary Daimler and Lanchester, the Ford Convertible top could be rolled back in the intermediate "de ville" position and both cars were catalogued with an electro-hydraulic power-operated roof, optional on the Consul. The rear seat back was repositioned about an inch forwards, making way for the hood stowage and the front seat backs hinged, giving access to the rear. In 1954, as work on the Ford contract got under way, its proprietors sold Carbodies to the BSA group.

SPECIFICATION FOR CONSUL
INTRODUCTION Motor Show October 1951, production 1953 until February 1956.
BODY Convertible; 2-doors, 5-seats.
ENGINE 4-cylinders, in-line; 79.37mm x 76.2mm, 1508cc; compr 6.8:1; 35.1kW (47bhp) @ 4400rpm; 23.2kW (31.2bhp)/l; 98Nm (72lbft) @ 2400rpm.
ENGINE STRUCTURE pushrod ohv chain-driven camshaft; cast iron cylinder head and block; 30mm downdraught carburettor, 12v coil ignition AC mechanical fuel pump; 3-bearing cast iron counterweighted crankshaft.

TRANSMISSION rear wheel drive; 20.3cm (8in) single plate hydraulic clutch; 3-speed manual synchromesh (on 2nd and top) gearbox; steering column shift; hypoid final drive 4.625:1.
CHASSIS steel monocoque structure with additional X-bracing; ifs by coil springs and hydraulic telescopic dampers integral with kingpins; single track control arms located by triangulated anti-roll bar. Live rear axle with half-elliptic springs and piston dampers; Girling hydraulic 229mm (9in) drum brakes, 2 leading shoe at front; Burman worm and peg steering; 40.9l (9 gal) fuel tank; steel disc wheels, 5.90 x 13in tyres.
DIMENSIONS wheelbase 254cm (100in); track front 127cm (50in), 124.5cm (49in) rear; length 412.75cm (162.5in); width 162.6cm (64in); height 154.3cm (60.75in); ground clearance 17.1cm (6.75in); turning circle right 12.5m (41ft), left 12.1m (39.5ft).

EQUIPMENT bench front seat, radio optional, heater optional £10.
PERFORMANCE maximum speed 120.4kph (75mph); 23.9kph (14.9mph) @ 1000rpm; 0-96kph (60mph) 31.15sec; fuel consumption 11.8-10.1 l/100km (24-28mpg).
PRICE 1953 Consul £809 with pvc and manual hood, £890 power hood and leather; Zephyr £960 pvc, £981 leather (including purchase tax).
PRODUCTION 3749 Consul 4048 Zephyr

1953
Popular 103E

Last survivor of the 1932 Y-type, indeed the last of a lineage that could be traced to the Model T, the 1949 Anglia was relaunched as back-to-basics family transport with a solitary screen wiper without vacuum reservoir, three instrument dials in a plain body-coloured facia, undersized 24w headlamps, silver-painted wheels, bumpers without over-riders, and a choice of four colours. The only concession to decoration was a thin chrome strip round the radiator grille. The parcel shelf under the facia and the plywood boot floor were deleted and only the passenger seat tipped for access to the rear. Luggage was laid on top of the spare wheel or tied to the bootlid, which was opened by a carriage key, and let down on stout straps. There were no door map pockets, and winding windows allowed the driver hand signals in the absence of mechanical direction indicators. The 1172cc engine, hitherto available on export Anglias, was kept for the tough and reliable Popular, the last British car catalogued at a retail price of under £400. The newly imported Volkswagen was nearly twice the price at £739, the Series II Morris Minor £530, and the new Standard Eight £481. A heater and a second wiper, with vacuum reservoir to keep it working on hills, were amongst the options that could take the Popular's price over £400.

INTRODUCTION October 1953, produced until 1959.
BODY saloon; 2-doors, 4-seats; weight 737kg (1624lb).
ENGINE 4-cylinders, in-line; 63.5mm x 92.5mm, 1172cc; compr 6.16:1; 22.4kW (30.1bhp) @ 4000rpm; 19.1kW (25.7bhp)/l; 63Nm (46.4lbft) @ 3000rpm.
ENGINE STRUCTURE side valve; chain-driven camshaft; cast iron cylinder head and block; downdraught Zenith carburettor, coil ignition, AC mechanical fuel pump; 3-bearing crankshaft.
TRANSMISSION rear wheel drive; single dry plate 187.3mm (7.375in) clutch; 3-speed manual gearbox, synchromesh on 2nd and top; torque tube; spiral bevel final drive 5.5:1.
CHASSIS Pressed steel channel-section chassis; transverse semi-elliptic springs front and rear; double-acting lever arm damper; Girling mechanical 25.4cm (10in) drum brakes; worm and nut steering; 31.8l (7 gal) fuel tank; 4.50-17 tyres; perforated steel disc wheels.
DIMENSIONS wheelbase 228.6cm (90in); track 114.3cm (45in) front and rear; length 384.8cm (151.5in); width 143.5cm (56.5in); height 163.2cm (64.25in); ground clearance 22.2cm (8.75in); turning circle 10.6m (34.75ft).
EQUIPMENT 6 volt electrical system, plastic-faced felt floor covering, no ashtrays, no interior light.
PERFORMANCE maximum speed 96kph (60mph); 22.3kph (13.9mph) @ 1000rpm; 0-80.3kph (50mph) 29.2sec; 32.9kph/kW (24.5kg/bhp); fuel consumption 8.1l/100km (35mpg).
PRICE 1954 £275 plus £115.14s 2d purchase tax, £390 14s 2d (£390.71p).
PRODUCTION 155,350.

1953
Anglia 100E

The next Ford milestone after the 1950 Consul and Zephyr was the redesigned Anglia and Prefect of 1953. The old reinforced chassis frame was discarded for integral construction, "without the interposition of any chassis frame," as *The Motor* put it with customary elegance, giving a low build. "No attempt is made to conceal every joint between body panels, but these joints are part of the lines of the car". Out went transverse leaf springs, in came MacPherson strut independent front suspension, and although the cylinder dimensions of the side-valve engine remained the same it was a new smoother running and more powerful unit with bigger valves and bearings, and at long last adjustable tappets. Dedication to 63.5mm x 92.5mm was only determined by the need for cylinder blocks to be machined on the same production plant. The styling replicated bigger Fords, the handling was transformed, and the accommodation enhanced. Two facelifts took place during the model's 6-year span. In 1955 the indirect gear ratios were lowered and the instrument panel enlarged. A new mesh grille and a bigger rear window came in 1957, together with NewtonDrive semi-automatic transmission, but only about 50 100Es were ever made with it. The Anglia was a nimble club rally car, and even won its class in the 1956 Safari Rally, although the brisk performance was bought at the expense of fuel consumption that was no better than average.

INTRODUCTION October 28 1953, produced until September 4 1959.
BODY saloon; 2-doors, 4-seats; weight 774.75kg (1708lb).
ENGINE 4-cylinders, in-line; 63.5mm x 92.5mm, 1172cc; compr 7.0:1; 26.8kW (36bhp) @ 4400rpm; 22.9kW (30.7bhp)/l; 70.5Nm (52lbft) @ 2500rpm.
ENGINE STRUCTURE side valve; chain-driven camshaft; cast iron cylinder head and block; downdraught Solex 26ZIC carburettor, 12volt coil ignition, AC mechanical fuel pump; 3-bearing crankshaft.
TRANSMISSION rear wheel drive; single dry plate 7.38in hydraulic clutch; 3-speed manual gearbox, synchromesh on 2nd and top; Hardy Spicer open prop shaft; spiral bevel final drive 4.429:1.
CHASSIS steel monocoque structure; independent front suspension by MacPherson struts; live rear axle with half-elliptic springs; telescopic dampers; Girling hydraulic 17.8cm (7in) drum brakes, 2LS at front; anti-roll bar; Burman worm and peg steering; 31.8l (7 gal) fuel tank; 5.20 x 13in tyres steel disc wheels.
DIMENSIONS wheelbase 220.9cm (87in); track front 121.9cm (48in), rear 120.7cm (47.5in); length 384.2cm (151.25in); width 153.7cm (60.5in); height 150.5cm (59.25in); ground clearance 17.8cm (7in); turning circle 9.8m (32.25ft).
EQUIPMENT sun visor, screen wiper, 4 body colours, self-cancelling flashing indicators, pump, fan, and thermostat cooling, baulk-ring synchromesh, moulded rubber floor covering, heater extra.
PERFORMANCE maximum speed 109kph (68.3mph) (*The Autocar*); 23.9kph (14.9mph) @ 1000rpm; 0-96kph (60mph) 33.2sec; 28.9kg/kW (21.5kg/bhp); fuel consumption 29.7mpg (9.5 l/100km).
PRICE £360 plus £151 2s 6d purchase tax, £511 2s 6d (£511.12fhp).
PRODUCTION 279,203 plus 66,638 as assembly kits.

1953
Prefect 100E

Essentially the same as the Anglia, with 4 doors, superior trim and better equipment such as facia instrumentation, the Prefect was some 22.7kg (50lb) heavier, and identifiable by chrome headlight surrounds and slatted grille. Among detail features welcomed by *The Autocar* were its hydraulic clutch and pendant pedals. Most cars still had pedals sprouting through the toe-board with consequent problems of sealing from wind and water. Not so the new Fords with their hydraulic cylinder mounted on the clutch housing. The only sour note was struck by the vacuum operated wipers, which still "stopped in a most irritating fashion when the engine was pulling hard." The drive was taken up smoothly

and firmly, although a rapid take-off from rest could spin the rear wheels if the rear seat was not occupied. Yet for a small car the 100E's refinement was a revelation. Relatively narrow-section tyres did not set up much resonance through the monocoque structure, the engine was relatively small and quiet, there was not much wind noise at 60-odd mph, bulkhead sealing was quite good, and the three-box configuration absorbed vibrations well. There was a useful amount of luggage boot room with the spare wheel on the floor and the fuel tank to one side. The bonnet opened to a vertical position from the windscreen end, providing excellent engine accessibility.

INTRODUCTION December 17 1953, produced until September 15 1959. **BODY** saloon; 4-doors, 4-seats; weight 796kg (1755lb). **ENGINE** 4-cylinders, in-line; 63.5mm x 92.5mm, 1172cc; compr 7.0:1; 26.8kW (36bhp) @ 4400rpm; 22.9kW (30.7bhp)/l; 70.5Nm (52lbft) @ 2500rpm. **ENGINE STRUCTURE** side valve; chain-driven camshaft; cast iron cylinder head and block; downdraught Solex 26ZIC carb, 12volt coil ignition, AC mechanical fuel pump; 3-bearing crank. **TRANSMISSION** rwd; single dry plate 7.38in hydraulic clutch; 3-speed manual gearbox, synchromesh on 2nd and top; Hardy Spicer open prop shaft; spiral bevel final drive 4.429:1. **CHASSIS** steel monocoque; ifs by MacPherson struts; live rear axle with half-elliptic springs; telescopic dampers; Girling hydraulic 17.8cm (7in) drum brakes, 2LS at front; anti-roll bar; Burman worm and peg; 31.8l (7 gal); 5.20 x 13in tyres, steel disc wheels. **DIMENSIONS** wheelbase 220.9cm (87in); track 121.9cm (48in) front, 120.7cm (47.5in) rear; length 384.2cm (151.25in); width 153.7cm (60.5in); height 150.5cm (59.25in); ground clearance 17.8cm (7in); turning circle 9.8m (32.25ft). **EQUIPMENT** horn ring, interior light, 2 sun visors, 2 screen wipers, 5 colours, self-cancelling flashing indicators, pump, fan, thermostat cooling, baulk-ring synchromesh, heavy moulded rubber floor covering, heater extra. **PERFORMANCE** maximum 108.9kph (67.7mph) (*The Autocar*); 23.9kph (14.9mph) @ 1000rpm; 0-96kph (60mph) 38.9sec; 29.7kg/kW (22.1kg/bhp); 8.3l/100km (33.8mpg). **PRICE** £395, purchase tax £165 14s 2d, total £560 14s 2d (£560.71). **PRODUCTION** 178,750 plus 76,905 as assembly kits.

1954
Zodiac EOTTA

Two-tone paintwork, white sidewall tyres, 9-carat gold-plated script, leather upholstery in two colours matching the exterior, chrome wing mirrors, Lucas "flamethrower" driving lamp and foglamp, the Zodiac was the very epitome of 1950s style. As compelling an automotive icon as the E-type Jaguar or the Mini, it was a flash of glamour in a new Elizabethan age, inspiring a host of really quite inappropriate accessories, such as a slatted blind for the big back window and a sun visor over the windscreen. It was all a bit more appropriate to Marbella than Marylebone, yet to a nation only just breaking the habit of buying cars in black or, for a showy fringe perhaps gunmetal grey; the two-colour Zodiac was a revelation. It was symptomatic of the British discovering that they were not dull at all, and the nation relished the high-compression engine with its valve cover painted red, allegedly for identification but in reality to give the underbonnet a touch of class. Ferrari was not the first to think of Testa Rossa. By 1955 the axle ratio of the Zephyr had been raised slightly and the Zodiac's higher compression took advantage of increasingly available premium-quality fuel. The reversing light was not turned on simply by engaging reverse, but by a separate switch with, as required by law, an illuminated tell-tale to prevent it being left alight inadvertently.

INTRODUCTION Motor Show October 1953, production November 1953 until February 1956.
BODY saloon; 4-doors, 5-seats; weight 1206.5kg (2660lb).
ENGINE 6-cylinders, in-line; 79.37mm x 76.2mm, 2262cc; compr 7.5:1; 52.9kW (71bhp) @ 4200rpm; 23.4kW (31.4bhp)/l; 152Nm (112lbft) @ 2000rpm.
ENGINE STRUCTURE pushrod ohv chain-driven camshaft; cast iron cylinder head and block; 30mm downdraught carburettor, 12v coil ignition AC mechanical fuel pump; 4-bearing cast iron counterweighted crankshaft.

TRANSMISSION rear wheel drive; 203mm (8in) single plate hydraulic clutch; 3-speed manual synchromesh (on 2nd and top) gearbox; steering column shift; hypoid final drive 4.44:1.
CHASSIS steel monocoque; ifs by coil springs and hydraulic telescopic dampers integral with kingpins; single track control arms located by triangulated anti-roll bar. Live rear axle with half-elliptic springs and piston dampers; Girling hydraulic 22.9cm (9in) drum brakes, 2 leading shoe at front; Burman worm and peg steering; 40.9l (9 gal) fuel tank; steel disc wheels, 6.40 x 13in tyres.

DIMENSIONS wheelbase 264.2cm (104in); track front 127cm (50in), rear 124.5cm (49in); length 431.8cm (170in); width 162.6cm (64in); height 154.3cm (60.75in); ground clearance 17.1cm (6.75in); turning circle right 12.5m (41ft), left 12m (39.5ft).
EQUIPMENT radio optional £47 17s 1d (£47.85fhp); heater, screenwasher, whitewall tyres standard.
PERFORMANCE maximum speed 130kph (81mph); 25.9kph (16.2mph) @ 1000rpm; 0-96kph (60mph) 20.4sec; 22.8kg/kW (17kg/bhp); 11.91/100km (23.7mpg) (*The Autocar*).
PRICE £600 plus £251 2s 6d purchase tax 1955, £851 2s 6d (851.12fhp).
PRODUCTION 22,634.

Thames, 1950s Thames Trader

Thames was applied to Ford and Fordson medium and heavy trucks early in 1939. After the war and until 1965, it became the brand name for all Ford's commercial activities. First came the established 5 and 10cwt vans and forward-control V8 2.5tonners, replaced in 1949 by Thames 4x2s, 6x4s, articulated units, and a Public Service Vehicle (PSV) chassis. Payloads ranged from 2 to 8tons, hydraulic brakes were introduced, with vacuum servos for heavy versions; there were semi-elliptic springs at the front, and the option of a Perkins P6 diesel. The petrol V8 continued until 1953. The advent of a 3.6-litre ohv 5-bearing 4-cylinder of 52.2kW (70bhp) would also form the basis of Ford's first diesel in 1954. The heaviest range, 4 tons and over, retained the V8 until 1957 when the Thames Trader came in. This had a synchromesh gearbox and hypoid final drive, and was the first wholly British designed and developed British Ford commercial range, carrying the type number 508 suffixed E for England. The Trader's engines were all Ford-built, the 4-cylinder and 6-cylinder petrol 4.9-litre 85.8kW (115bhp), and a 5.4-litre 80.5kW (108bhp) diesel. The first 2ton to 5ton forward control range embraced tippers and an articulated tractor unit, later extending to low frame models, 4x4 conversions by Vickers, and 6x2 and 6x4 reworkings by County Commercial Cars along the lines of the pre-war Surrey and Sussex models. There was also a 41-seater PSV chassis, one of which, equipped with a singular double-deck body, was assigned to take cyclists through the Dartford-Purfleet Tunnel. By the middle 1950s Ford had forward control vehicles from 2 to 7tons. The range was augmented by a series of normal control Traders with a cab from Germany, Cologne having ceased commercial vehicle production. From 1957 a new van, the 10/12cwt 400E, used a

commercial version of the Consul 4-cylinder 1508cc following the withdrawal of the long-lasting 10cwt E83. The 400E had integral construction, forward control, side loading, 3-speed gearbox with steering column shift, independent front suspension, and hypoid final drive. It remained in production into the 1960s with the option of a Perkins diesel and, in 1964, a fourth gear. Commercial vehicle assembly moved to Langley, next to what was still in 1960 the Cromwell Road Extension, the first part of the M4. The move marked an assault on the heavy end of the truck business that lasted well into the 1970s. By the time the M4 stretched to Wales in the west, and a link established to the nearby M25 and the rest of the motorway network, Langley faced closure.

1955
Escort and Squire

Ford's first production estate car was no in-house saloon conversion but a stand-alone new model, with the underpinnings of the 100E Anglia and Prefect. It met a growing demand for carrying capacity for the hobbyist or small business. The rear doors were split horizontally, so there was no confusion with the Thames 5cwt van, and as a means of emphasising its saloon car credentials there were two models. Both were 3-door, the higher-priced Prefect-equivalent Squire denoting its place in the class structure by appliqué timber strips on the body sides. The less grand Escort had fewer frills (and certainly no wood). It was a cheaper model with mesh grille, less chrome and less elaborate side windows. Testers complained that the bluff rear tended to suck along exhaust fumes, which had to be directed out again by the sliding side windows. The only mechanical difference from the saloons was stiffer rear springs, making the back axle hop a bit. The saloons' lower gearing was largely offset by the estates' larger-section tyres and economy was aided by the engines' ability to run on cheaper low-grade fuel, equivalent in cost to an extra 56.5l/100km (5mpg). The increase in weight resulted in some loss of performance.

INTRODUCTION both models September 1955. Escort produced to April 1961, Squire discontinued September 1959.
BODY estate; 3-doors, 4-seats; weight 838.25kg (1848lb).
ENGINE 4-cylinders, in-line; 63.5mm x 92.5mm, 1172cc; compr 7.0:1; 26.8kW (36bhp) @ 4400rpm; 22.9kW (30.7bhp)/l; 70.5Nm (52lbft) @ 2500rpm.
ENGINE STRUCTURE side valve; chain-driven camshaft; cast iron cylinder head and block; downdraught Solex 26ZIC carburettor, 12volt coil ignition, AC mechanical fuel pump; 3-bearing crankshaft.

LEFT **In October 1957 the Squire lost its much derided wooden strips, and was amalgamated with the Escort in 1959.**
ABOVE **BEA Thames was the commercial equivalent.**

TRANSMISSION rear wheel drive; single dry plate 7.4in hydraulic clutch; 3-speed manual gearbox, synchromesh on 2nd and top; Hardy Spicer open prop shaft; spiral bevel final drive 4.429:1.
CHASSIS steel monocoque structure; independent front suspension by MacPherson struts; live rear axle with half-elliptic springs; telescopic dampers; Girling hydraulic 20cm (8in) drum brakes, 2LS at front; anti-roll bar; Burman worm and peg steering; 31.8l (7 gal) fuel tank; 5.60 x 13in tyres steel disc wheels.
DIMENSIONS wheelbase 220.9cm (87in); track 121.9cm (48in) front, 120.7cm (47.5in) rear; length 361.3cm (142.25in); width 153.7cm (60.5in); height 160cm (63in); ground clearance 17.8cm (7in); turning circle 9.14m (30ft).

EQUIPMENT 8 body colours, pump, fan, and thermostat cooling, baulk-ring synchromesh, rubber floor covering, pvc plastic upholstery, leather extra, heater extra, Ecko radio extra.
PERFORMANCE maximum speed 112.2kph (69.9mph) The Motor; 24.2kph (15.1mph) @ 1000rpm; 0-96kph (60mph) 33.8sec; 31.3kg/kW (23.3kg/bhp); fuel consumption 7.9l/100km (35.7mpg).
PRICE 1956 Squire £445 plus purchase tax £223 16s, £668 16s (£668.80p). 1959 Escort £434, £615.96p.
PRODUCTION Escort 30,976, 2155 as assembly kits; Squire 15,952, 1860 as kits.

1956
Consul Mark II 204E

The momentum of the Consul and Zephyr was maintained by an inspired second edition. Planned obsolescence was still in vogue, new shapes and new fashions were brought in so slightly hooded headlights and a hint of tail fins arrived. The Mark IIs exemplified the transformation of British motoring, with Ford repositioning itself in a market that in the 1930s had been dominated by Morris. It was a market where Ford had shared second place with Austin followed by Rootes and Standard. Vauxhall remained a distant sixth and imports negligible, until Ford caught up and then overtook the combined Austin and Morris British Motor Corporation. It progressively moved away from its bargain basement position by keeping cars like the Consul updated and re-skinned with eye-catching styles, colours, and trim. Price competition was maintained by manufacturing efficiency, which meant long production runs for engines and transmissions as well as, so far as possible, a car's basic platform and running gear. The Mark II Consul and Zephyr carried forward the Mark I's principle of a common central bodyshell, differences confined to front, back and trim. Body stiffness was improved and the new cars were roomier with wider track, longer wheelbases and more deeply curved windscreen and rear windows. "Well-styled and spacious," was *The Motor's* verdict, "showing the swing in contemporary design from the curvilinear to the rectilinear."

INTRODUCTION February 1956, production until April 1962.
BODY saloon; 4-doors, 5-seats; weight 1143kg (2520lb).
ENGINE 4-cylinders, in-line; 82.55mm x 79.5mm, 1702cc; compr 7.8:1; 44kW (59bhp) @ 4200rpm; 25.8kW (34.7bhp)/l; 124Nm (91lbft) @ 4400rpm.
ENGINE STRUCTURE pushrod inclined ohv: chain-driven camshaft; cast iron cylinder head and block; Zenith 34WIA downdraught carburettor, centrifugal and vacuum ignition; mechanical fuel pump; 3-bearing hollow-cast counterweighted crankshaft.
TRANSMISSION rear wheel drive; 20.3cm (8in) sdp clutch; 3-speed manual gearbox with steering column shift; synchromesh on 2nd and top; optional Borg Warner

overdrive; Hardy Spicer open prop shaft; final drive 4.11:1.
CHASSIS steel monocoque structure; independent front suspension by MacPherson struts; anti-roll bar; live rear axle with half-elliptic springs and lever arm dampers; Girling hydraulic 22.9cm (9in) drum brakes, 2LS at front; worm and peg steering, recirculating ball after 1958; 50l (11 gal) fuel tank; 5.90-13 tyres.
DIMENSIONS wheelbase 265.4cm (104.5in); track front 134.6cm (53in), rear 132.1cm (52in); length 438.2cm (172.5in); width 170.2cm (67in); height 151.1cm (59.5in); ground clearance 16.5cm (6.5in); turning circle 9.7m (32ft).
EQUIPMENT vacuum operated wipers; Optional fresh-air heater with demister, radio, screenwash, electric clock, cigar lighter, overdrive.

Oct 1957: Consul de luxe 2-tone paintwork, cigar lighter, leather and nylon weave upholstery standard.
PERFORMANCE maximum speed 127.3kph (79.3mph) *The Motor*; 26.7kph (16.6mph) @ 1000rpm; 0-96kph (60mph) 23.2sec; 26kg/kW (19.4kg/bhp); fuel consumption 12.8l/100km (22.1mpg).
PRICE £520, purchase tax £261 7s 0d, total £781 7s 0d (£781.35) 1956. De luxe 1958 £871.35.
PRODUCTION 290,951 saloons assembled 59,293 kits of parts.

1956
Consul Convertible, Estate car

Soft-top versions of popular cars were always a small proportion of production, yet they were important for Ford to enhance the range in keeping with the abandonment of its old smokestack image. Again Carbodies was enlisted for their manufacture; strong flitch-plates reinforced the sills and transmission tunnel, making them stiffer than the Mark I to ensure closer door shut-lines. The engineering used up some rear seat and boot space, and *The Motor* was disappointed with the power-operated hood on a Consul it tested in 1958. The switch-controlled electrical power system only moved the hood from the "de ville" position and the testers complained about the effort involved in

rolling up or restoring the forward part. A fully manual hood, they concluded, would be lighter, better, and cheaper. Complete bodyshells were brought to Carbodies' works at Holyhead Road Coventry where the roof and doors were removed, new rear wings and doors manufactured, underbody reconstruction and reinforcement carried out, and the hood installed. The bodies were painted and trimmed, then taken back to Dagenham for wiring and assembly with the mechanical units. The estate car was once more entrusted to Abbott of Farnham with extended roof, new side panels with windows behind the rear doors, and a single piece tailgate.

INTRODUCTION October Motor Show 1956, production to Feb 1962.
BODY convertible; 2-doors, 5-seats; weight 1206.5kg (2660lb).
ENGINE 4-cylinders, in-line; 82.55mm x 79.5mm, 1702cc; compr 7.8:1; 44kW (59bhp) @ 4200rpm; 25.8kW/l (34.7bhp/l); 123Nm (91lbft) @ 4400rpm.
ENGINE STRUCTURE pushrod inclined ohv; chain-driven camshaft; cast iron cylinder head and block; Zenith 34WIA downdraught carb, centrifugal and vacuum ignition; mechanical fuel pump; 3-bearing hollow-cast counterweighted crankshaft.
TRANSMISSION rwd; 8in sdp clutch; 3-speed gearbox with steering column shift; synchro on 2nd and top; optional Borg Warner overdrive; Hardy Spicer open prop shaft; final drive 4.11:1.
CHASSIS steel monocoque; ifs by MacPherson struts; anti-roll bar; live rear axle with half-elliptic springs and lever arm dampers; Girling hydraulic 9in drum brakes, 2LS at front; worm and peg steering, recirculating ball after 1958; 47.7l (10.5 gal) fuel tank; 5.90-13 tubeless tyres.
DIMENSIONS wheelbase 265.4cm (104.5in); track front 134.6cm (53in), rear 132cm (52in); length 438.2cm (172.5in); width 170.2cm (67in); height 151.1cm (59.5in); ground clearance 16.5cm (6.5in); turning circle 9.7m (32ft).
EQUIPMENT vacuum operated wipers; pile carpet; 8 body colours. Optional fresh-air heater with demister, radio, screenwash, electric clock, cigar lighter, overdrive.
PERFORMANCE maximum speed 125.4kph (78.1mph) *The Motor*; 26.7kph (16.6mph) @ 1000rpm; 0-96kph (60mph) 24.2sec; 27.4kg/kW (20.4kg/bhp); 11.4l/100km (24.7mpg).
PRICE including power-operated roof £713, purchase tax £357 17s 0d, £1070 17s 0d (£1070.85) manual hood total £991.35).
PRODUCTION 9398 convertibles, 5643 estates including Zephyrs

1956
Zephyr Mark II 206E

Consul, Zephyr, and Zodiac underwent a number of changes over six years, besides the lowering of the roofline in 1959. The instrument panel was flattened out, interiors redesigned and stainless steel was used for roof guttering and windscreen surrounds. Safety received more than lip service, with the scuttle topped off in soft padded plastic material and sun visors with collapsing frames. In 1960 the entire range was given the option of disc front brakes after they were tried successfully on works rally cars. By the following year discs were standard, along with sealed-beam headlamps. The bench front seat was retained despite some antipathy; handling and roadholding was now so good that the occupants slid from side to side

uncomfortably on corners. The concomitant steering column shift was one of the best of its kind; as well it ought, having only three forward speeds to select. Suspension tuning that induced understeer and curbed body roll subdued earlier models' tiresome rear wheel skittishness, and the change to recirculating ball restored some feel to the steering. Engine changes from the Mark I included an extra 3.175mm (0.125in) on the bore and stroke, and a new cylinder head with inclined valves in wedge-shaped combustion chambers, giving much the same power output as before but at lower rpm, to the advantage of high-geared economy and refinement.

INTRODUCTION February 1956, production to April 1962.
BODY saloon; 4-doors, 5-seats; weight 1218kg (2695lb).
ENGINE 6-cylinders, in-line; 82.55mm x 79.5mm, 2553cc; compr 7.8:1; 64.1kW (86bhp)gross @ 4200rpm; 25.1kW(33.7bhp)/l; 184Nm (136lbft) @ 2000rpm.
ENGINE STRUCTURE pushrod inclined ohv; chain-driven camshaft; cast iron cylinder head and block; Zenith 36WIA downdraught carburettor, centrifugal and vacuum ignition; mechanical fuel pump; 4-bearing hollow-cast counterweighted crankshaft.
TRANSMISSION rear wheel drive; 8in sdp clutch; 3-speed manual gearbox with steering column shift; synchromesh on 2nd and top; optional Borg Warner overdrive; Hardy Spicer open prop shaft; final drive 3.9:1, 2.83:1 overdrive; automatic optional.
CHASSIS steel monocoque structure; ifs by MacPherson struts; anti-roll bar; live rear axle with half-elliptic springs and lever arm dampers; Girling hydraulic 9in drum brakes, 2LS at front, from 1960 servo-assisted disc brakes; worm and peg steering, recirculating ball after 1958; 50l (11 gal) tank; 6.40-13 tyres; 4fhJ rim steel wheels.
DIMENSIONS wheelbase 271.8cm (107in); track 134.6cm (53in) front, 132.1cm (52in) rear; length 453.4cm (178.5in); width 170.2cm (67in); height 151.8cm (59.75in); ground clearance 17.1cm (6.75in); turning circle 10.9m (36ft).
EQUIPMENT optional radio £30; heater £14; overdrive £64, automatic transmission.
PERFORMANCE maximum 135.7kph (84.5mph) overdrive top *The Autocar*; 29.5kph (18.4mph) @ 1000rpm, 40.6kph (25.3mph) in overdrive; 0-96kph (60mph) 17.9sec; 19kg/kW (14.2kg/bhp); 11.7l/100km (24.1mpg).
PRICE £580, purchase tax £292, total £872.
PRODUCTION 301,417 including Zodiac.

1956
Zephyr Mark II Estate car, Convertible, pick-up

Abbott-built Zephyr Estates had a wide but shallow tailgate aperture, as it was important not to dispense with the stiffening effect of the transverse panel between the tail-lights. Customers could specify a heavy wooden floor over the boot platform of the original saloon, with the spare wheel underneath. Access was gained through a trapdoor. Alternatively, the existing boot floor could remain the basis of a large though uneven rear compartment, with the spare wheel upright at the side. The rear seat was liberated by draw-bolts and could be lifted out and placed vertically behind the front seat back or removed altogether. It was an unsophisticated arrangement but it worked, and the easily

removable seat cushion was available for picnics or impromptu grandstand comfort at sporting events. The increasing popularity of the estate car as a fashion accessory was country-pursuit led. There was a small loss in performance from the saloon Zephyr through the addition of 68kg (150lb) in weight and although there was more rearwards weight bias, the handling was not much affected. An unlikely variation on the Zephyr platform resulted from Dagenham building Knock-Down (KD) kits for assembly in Australia. This was a pick-up truck that proved popular among rural customers and of which 46 were exported as built-up vehicles.

INTRODUCTION February 1956, produced to April 1962.

BODY estate car, 5-doors, 5-seats; weight 1287kg (2838lb); convertible, 2-doors, 5-seats, 1270kg (2800lb).

ENGINE 6-cylinders, in-line; 82.55mm x 79.5mm, 2553cc; compr 7.8:1; 64.1kW (86bhp) gross @ 4200rpm; 25.1kW (33.7bhp)/l; 184Nm (136lbft) @ 2000rpm.

ENGINE STRUCTURE pushrod inclined ohv; chain-driven camshaft; cast iron cyl head and block; Zenith 36WIA downdraught carb, centrifugal and vacuum ign; mechanical fuel pump; 4-bearing hollow-cast counterweighted crankshaft.

TRANSMISSION rear wheel drive; 8in sdp clutch; 3-speed manual gearbox with steering column shift; synchromesh on 2nd and top; optional Borg Warner overdrive; Hardy Spicer open prop shaft; final drive 3.9:1, 2.83:1 overdrive; optional automatic.

CHASSIS steel monocoque structure; ifs by MacPherson struts; anti-roll bar; live rear axle with half-elliptic springs and lever arm dampers; Girling hydraulic 9in drum brakes, 2LS at front, from 1960 servo-assisted disc brakes; worm and peg

steering, recirculating ball after 1958; 50l (11 gal) fuel tank, Convertible 10.5 gal; 6.70-13 tyres; 4fhJ rim steel wheels.

DIMENSIONS wheelbase 271.8cm (107in); track 134.6cm (53in) front, 132.1cm (52in) rear; length 453.4cm (178.5in); width 170.1cm (67in); height 151.8cm (59.75in); ground clearance 17.1cm (6.75in); turning circle 10.9m (36ft).

EQUIPMENT optional radio £30; heater £16; overdrive £64.

PERFORMANCE max 133.6kph (83mph) direct top The Autocar, 128.7kph (80mph) overdrive, Con 141.75kph (88.3mph) The Motor; 30.8kph (19.2mph) @ 1000rpm in top, 43.9kph (27.4mph) overdrive; 0-96kph (60mph) 18.7sec, Con 17sec; 20.1kg/kW (15kg/bhp), Con 19.8kg/kW (14.8kg/bhp); 11.3l/100km (25mpg).

PRICE £817 10s, purchase tax £410 2s, total £1227 12s (£1227.60); Convertible £841 10s plus purchase tax £351 15s, total £1193 5s (£1193.25p).

PRODUCTION 5643, including Consul estates

1956
Zodiac Mark II 206E

Wide front-hinged doors, a generous boot, and all four extremities visible from the driving seat, were among the practical aspects of the cleverly proportioned Mark 2 body. As bench seats and 3-speed gearboxes with steering column control lost their appeal, relief arrived with the development of a 3-speed automatic by Borg Warner, its modest power losses appropriate for a 2½-litre engine. Once manufacture started in the UK, the Borg Warner 35 found its way into an increasing number of British cars, automatic transmission matching the vaguely mid-Atlantic temperament of the 6-cylinder Fords perfectly and setting new standards of refinement. The

gearbox weighed an extra 63.5kg (140lb) and absorbed more power than a conventional gearbox, so although fuel consumption was not much affected, acceleration suffered. An option at around 15% of the purchase price on the Zephyr, automatic was eventually standard on the Zodiac. By the late 1950s heaters were usually fitted as standard, but it was not until the effects of Japanese imports were felt that radios followed suit. Ford's own-brand radio, the optional Enfo, had an amplifier behind the rear seats. If it was loud enough for the driver to hear, it was usually too noisy for rear-seat passengers. The Enfo, even on the Zodiac, only had manual tuning.

INTRODUCTION February 1956, production until April 1962.
BODY saloon; 4-doors, 5-seats; weight 1311kg (2891lb).
ENGINE 6-cylinders, in-line; 82.55mm x 79.5mm, 2553cc; compr 7.8:1; 63.4kW (85bhp) net @ 4400rpm; 24.8kW (33.3bhp)/l; 180Nm (133lbft) @ 2000rpm.
ENGINE STRUCTURE pushrod inclined ohv; chain-driven camshaft; cast iron cylinder head and block; Zenith 36WIA downdraught carburettor, centrifugal and vacuum ignition; mechanical fuel pump; 4-bearing hollow-cast counterweighted crankshaft.
TRANSMISSION rear wheel drive; sdp clutch, 3-speed manual gearbox; optional 3-speed automatic Borg Warner 35 gearbox; Hardy Spicer open prop shaft; final drive 3.9:1; overdrive optional.
CHASSIS steel monocoque; ifs by MacPherson struts; anti-roll bar; live rear axle with half-elliptic springs and lever arm dampers; Girling hydraulic 9in drum brakes, 2LS at front, from 1960 servo-assisted disc brakes; worm and peg steering, recirculating ball after 1958; 47.7l (10.5 gal) tank; 6.70-13 tyres; 4.5J rim steel wheels.
DIMENSIONS wheelbase 271.8cm (107in); track 134.6cm (53in) front, 132.1cm (52in) rear; length 458.5cm (180.5in); width 170.2cm (67in); height 151.8cm (59.75in) (low roofline); ground clearance 17.1cm (6.75in); turning circle 10.9m (36ft).
EQUIPMENT vacuum-operated wipers; screenwash; fresh air heater.
PERFORMANCE maximum speed 141.5kph (87.9mph) *The Motor*; 29.5kph (18.3mph) @ 1000rpm; 0-96kph (60mph) 17.1sec; 20.7kg/kW (15.4kg/bhp); 13.1l/100km (21.5mpg).
PRICE £645 plus purchase tax £323 17s, total £968 17s (£968.85).
PRODUCTION 301,417 including Zephyr.

1959
Popular 100E

Ford continued to make the cheapest car in Britain into the 1960s, with a Popular version of the 100E Anglia. Just as the previous Popular had continued after a replacement Anglia came out, so the well-liked Anglia became the Popular by slightly de-trimming it, discarding the parcels shelf and opening quarter lights. It was no more than a gesture. The new Popular was an Anglia at a discount and owed nothing to the Model T heritage of the old Popular with its transverse leaf springing and rod-operated brakes. Road testers obediently compared it with this car rather than the 100E whose genes it really inherited. It was up to date, notwithstanding its side-valve engine and Hardura floorcloth. Vindication of continuing production after its Anglia years came with the extension of its lifespan to nearly a decade and the manufacture of nearly half as many examples again. While the long list of extras explains some of the cost-cutting to get the price not only under £500 but also below the new Mini (by barely £1), the Popular did have up to date equipment where appropriate. The brakes were enlarged and 4-ply tubeless tyres fitted to meet contemporary standards. Most buyers equipped Populars with the de luxe extras including no less than three ashtrays. Chief demerit was that by the 1960s much of the competition was smoother-riding and had four gears.

INTRODUCTION August 25 1959, produced until June 1962. **BODY** saloon; 2-doors, 4-seats; weight 749kg (1652lb). **ENGINE** 4-cylinders, in-line; 63.5mm x 92.5mm; 1172cc; compr 7.0:1; 26.8kW (36bhp) @ 4500rpm; 22.9kW (30.7bhp)/l; 70.5Nm (52lbft) @ 2500rpm. **ENGINE STRUCTURE** side valve; chain-driven camshaft; cast iron cylinder head and block; downdraught Solex 26ZIC2 carburettor, 12 volt coil ignition, AC mechanical fuel pump; 3-bearing crankshaft. **TRANSMISSION** rear wheel drive; single dry plate 7.4in hydraulic clutch; 3-speed manual gearbox, synchromesh on 2nd and top; Hardy Spicer open prop shaft; spiral bevel final drive 4.429:1. **CHASSIS** steel monocoque structure; independent front suspension by MacPherson struts; live rear axle with half-elliptic springs; telescopic dampers; Girling hydraulic 20.3cm (8in) drum brakes, 2LS at front; anti-roll bar; Burman worm and peg steering; 31.8l (7 gal) fuel tank; 5.20 x 13in 4-ply tubeless tyres, steel disc wheels. **DIMENSIONS** wheelbase 220.9cm (87in); track 121.9cm (48in) front, 120.7cm (47.5in) rear; length 384.2cm (151.25in); width 153.7cm (60.5in); height 150.5cm (59.25in); ground clearance 17.8cm (7in); turning circle 9.8m (32.25ft). **EQUIPMENT** 8 exterior colours, 11 on de luxe, sun visor, 2 screen wipers, pump, fan, and thermostat cooling, baulk-ring synchromesh, moulded rubber floor covering. Heater, screenwashers, radio, roof rack, wheel trims, bumper overriders, interior light, cigar lighter, carburettor air cleaner, underbody spare wheel carrier, tool kit, reversing lamp, boot handle extra. **PERFORMANCE** maximum speed 109kph (68.3mph) The Autocar; 23.9kph (14.9mph) @ 1000rpm; 0-96kph (60mph) 33.2sec; 27.9kg/kW (20.8kg/bhp); fuel consumption 9.5 l/100km (29.7mpg). **PRICE** £348 plus purchase tax £146 2s 6d, total £494 2s 6d (£494.12fhp). **PRODUCTION** 120,815, 5300279,203 plus 66,638 as assembly kits.

1959
Anglia 105E

Features like tailfins became part of the stylist's stock-in-trade, but the reverse-rake rear window was gimmicky from the start. Drawn up by peripatetic American designer Elmwood Engel, and advertised as providing a clear view behind on a bad day, it may have gone down well at design clinics but it got short shrift by customers who could see no rationale for it beyond a perverse desire to be different. The new Anglia was more notable for its overhead valve engine and long-legged high-geared performance than for a back window whose only real merits lay in a bigger luggage boot aperture, and more headroom in the back. An important feature was the 80-bore engine, more over-square in its cylinder dimensions (0.6:1) than anything hitherto, and high gearing anticipating the opening of Britain's new motorways. The new Anglia may not have been as technically *avant garde* as other 1959 Earls Court debutants the Mini and the Triumph Herald, yet it transcended both in build quality. The result was a saloon, with an estate car launched in 1961 that sold more than a million. Production was transferred in March 1963 to a new factory at Halewood on Merseyside. The Anglia's significance lay well beyond its immediate lifespan; like the Model T it became the basis for Ford models several generations ahead.

INTRODUCTION September 3 1959, produced until November 1967.
BODY saloon; 2-doors, 4-seats; weight 737kg (1624.8lb), 5 door estate 786kg (1732.8lb).
ENGINE 4-cylinders, in-line; 80.96mm x 48.41mm, 996.6cc; compr 8.9:1; 29.1kW (39bhp) @ 5000rpm; 29.2kW (39.1bhp)/l; 71Nm (52.5lbft) @ 2700rpm.
ENGINE STRUCTURE pushrod ohv, chain-driven camshaft; cast iron cyl head and block; Solex downdraught 30ZIC2 carb, centrifugal and vacuum ignition; AC mechanical fuel pump; 3-bearing hollow-cast crankshaft.
TRANSMISSION rwd; 18.4cm (7.25in) sdp clutch; 4-speed manual gearbox, synchro on 3; Hardy Spicer open prop shaft; hypoid bevel final drive 4.12:1.
CHASSIS steel monocoque; ifs by MacPherson struts with Armstrong double-acting integral dampers and anti-roll bar; live rear axle with half-elliptic springs and Armstrong lever arm dampers; hydraulic 203mm (8in) drum brakes; recirculating ball steering; 31.8l (7 gal) fuel tank; 5.20-13 tubeless tyres; 5.60-13 estate.
DIMENSIONS wheelbase 229.2cm (90.25in); track 117.5cm (46.25in); length 390.5cm (153.75in), estate 392cm (154.3in); width 143.5cm (56.5in); height 142.2cm (56in); ground clearance 15.2cm (6in); turning circle 9.9m (32.4ft).
EQUIPMENT 8 exterior colours on standard spec, 12 single and 4 dual-tone on de luxe; heater £14.17; moulded rubber floor covering, 2-colour pvc upholstery on de luxe, one colour on standard; radio, screenwasher, leather upholstery optional.
PERFORMANCE maximum speed 123.3kph (76.8mph) *The Autocar*; 25.8kph (16.1mph) @ 1000rpm; 0-96kph (60mph) 29.4sec; 25.3kg/kW (18.9kg/bhp), estate 27kg/kW (20.2kg/bhp); 7.8l/100km (36.1mpg).
PRICE £430, purchase tax £180 5s 10d, total £610 5s 10d (£610.29).
PRODUCTION 1,083,960 including 129,528 estates.

1959
Prefect 107E

Ford was good at ringing the changes in its model range, and while the new Anglia borrowed the 100E's MacPherson strut suspension and other running gear, the old Prefect 4-door bodyshell inherited the 107E overhead valve engine for a new lease of life than lasted two more years. The new Anglia was a 2-door only, the Classic was a relatively large car, and so the 107E was invoked to keep Ford in the small 4-door saloon market. Distinguishable from the old side-valve Prefect by means of chrome side strips and optional 2-colour paintwork, it was available only in de luxe form with more comfortable seats, carpets, and the Anglia's 4-speed gearbox. Its clientele remained faithful, and although the engine was of 15 per cent smaller displacement, its modern design and over-square cylinder dimensions gave it just as much torque and far more power. It was good value and even if the body styling had begun to look a bit staid and upright, it was a practical 3-box shape, easy to get in and out of with a useful boot and its performance and economy were ideal for the family motorist. *The Motor* found the ride a bit lively when there was little weight aboard and although there was "quite fair" insulation against shock, the testers were agreeably surprised to find no "exaggerated softness to make passengers queasy."

INTRODUCTION May 5 1959, produced until June 1961.
BODY saloon; 4-doors, 4-seats; weight 800kg (1764lb).
ENGINE 4-cylinders, in-line; 80.96mm x 48.41mm, 996.6cc; compr 8.9:1; 29.1kW (39bhp) net @ 5000rpm; 29.2kW (39.1bhp)/l; 71Nm (52.5lbft) @ 2700rpm.
ENGINE STRUCTURE pushrod overhead valve, chain-driven camshaft; cast iron cylinder head and block; Solex downdraught 30ZIC2 carburettor, centrifugal and vacuum ignition; AC mechanical fuel pump; 3-bearing hollow-cast crankshaft.
TRANSMISSION rwd; 18.4cm (7.25in) sdp clutch; 4-speed gearbox, synchromesh on 3; Hardy Spicer open prop shaft; hypoid bevel final drive 4.429:1.
CHASSIS steel monocoque structure; ifs by MacPherson struts; live rear axle with half-elliptic springs; telescopic dampers; Girling hydraulic 17.8cm (7in) drum brakes, 2LS at front; anti-roll bar; Burman worm and peg steering; 31.8l (7 gal) tank; 5.20 x 13in tubeless tyres, steel disc wheels.
DIMENSIONS wheelbase 220.9cm (87in); track 121.9cm (48in) front, 120.7cm (47.5in) rear; length 384.2cm (151.25in); width 153.7cm (60.5in); height 150.5cm (59.25in); clearance 17.8cm (7in); turning circle 9.8m (32.25ft).
EQUIPMENT Heater extra £13 9s 2d, leather trim £14 3s 4d, 2-colour paint £7 1s 8d, whitewall tyres £5 13s 4d, also bumper overriders, wheel trims, hub cap medallions, exhaust deflector, seat covers, cigar lighter, vanity mirror, radiator blind, screenwashers standard, carpets, 12 exterior colours, four 2-colour.
PERFORMANCE maximum speed 117kph (72.9mph) *The Motor*; 23.9kph (14.9mph) @ 1000rpm; 0-96kph (60mph) 27.2sec; 27.5kg/kW (20.5kg/bhp); 9.4l/100km (30.1mpg).
PRICE £438, purchase tax £183 12s 6d, total £621 12s 6d (£621.62fh).
PRODUCTION 38,154 including 10,840 in kit form.

1961
Consul Classic 315 109E

The reverse-rake rear window of the Anglia was perpetuated on the Classic, arguably a good car condemned to mediocrity by this flight of fancy. Filling a vacancy between the Anglia and the now grown-up Consul, and essentially a stop-gap in anticipation of the Cortina, the Classic was not expected to have a long life span. In this respect Ford planners were not disappointed, the 1340cc lasting a year and the 1500 only a year on from that. A production run for the combined Classic and Capri of less than 130,000 was hardly up to par, and the best that could be said was that the model had been used as a test-bed for innovation.

It had the appearance, feel, and luggage capacity of a larger car, and it returned Ford gear levers firmly to the floor, although with true marketing caution the steering column change was retained as an option. The engine was essentially Anglia with the same bore and longer stroke. Separate front seats, disc brakes, electric screen wipers, four headlamps, a choice of two or four doors, and a good standard of trim for only just over £800 (the 2-door was under £750) raised the stakes in the market. Even if the customers eventually turned down the radical styling, there was quite a lot to be said for the Classic in the evolution of Ford.

INTRODUCTION 4-door and de luxe 2-door April 1961-July/August 1962; standard 2-door June 1961-August 1962.

BODY saloon; 2 and 4-doors, 5-seats; weight 920kg (2025lb) 2-door, 945kg (2080 lb) 4-door.

ENGINE 4-cylinders, in-line; 80.96mm x 65.07mm, 1340cc; compr 8.5:1; 40.3kW (54bhp) @ 4900rpm; 30.1kW (40.3bhp)/l; 100Nm (74lbft) @ 2500rpm.

ENGINE STRUCTURE pushrod overhead valve, chain-driven camshaft; cast iron cylinder head and block; Zenith 32VN downdraught carburettor, centrifugal and vacuum ignition; AC mechanical fuel pump; 3-bearing hollow-cast crankshaft.

TRANSMISSION rear wheel drive; 18.4cm (7.25in) hydraulic sdp clutch; 4-speed gearbox, synchromesh on 3; hypoid bevel final drive 4.13:1.

CHASSIS steel monocoque structure; ifs by MacPherson struts and anti-roll bar; live rear axle with half-elliptic springs and lever arm dampers; Girling hydraulic non-servo 24.1cm (9.5in) disc front, 22.9cm (9in) drum rear brakes; recirculating ball steering; 41l (9 gal) fuel tank; 5.60-13 tyres.

DIMENSIONS wheelbase 252cm (99in); track 126cm (49.5in); length 434cm (170.8in); width 166cm (62.2in); height 142cm (56in); ground clearance 15cm (5.9in); turning circle 10.36m (34ft).

EQUIPMENT fresh-air heater, leather upholstery, push-button or manual control radio optional extras; screenwasher standard, pvc upholstery, carpet, 12 body colours, seven 2-colour choices.

PERFORMANCE maximum speed 125.8kph (78.4mph) The Motor; 26.4kph (16.45mph) @ 1000rpm; 0-96kph (60mph) 22.5sec; 22.8kg/kW (17.1kg/bhp) 2-door, 23.4kg/kW (17.5kg/bhp) 4-door; fuel consumption 9.9l/100km (28.6mpg).

PRICE 4-door £565, purchase tax £236 10s 10d, total £801 10s 10d (£801.54).

PRODUCTION 84,694.

1961
Capri 109E

The voluptuous lines of the Capri were a surprise to a British market that regarded 2+2s as sports cars and was unfamiliar, even uncomfortable, with the concept of a car in which appearance took precedence over passenger space. It was legitimate if space was sacrificed to speed, but a rear window raked at 40 degrees and an enormously long rear deck just for appearances' sake was somehow too contrived. The name outlasted the model. It had been used on a Lincoln, and Ford now applied it to a version of the Classic intended for export, but to which the home market eventually and unexpectedly warmed. 5cm (2in) lower than the saloon, its small frontal area gave it an advantage in top speed, but it had no real sporting pretensions. Rather thin cushions could be specified for the rear shelf, normally carpeted as an addition to the enormous boot, enabling it to serve as a back seat when absolutely necessary. Luggage room was even bigger than the Classic and the boot floor, which was of pick-up truck proportions, was rubber-covered. The front seats were better shaped than the saloon's and finished in two colours of pvc. Like the Classic, however, the Capri driver was still required to do a certain amount of home maintenance to ensure satisfactory running. Ten points required attention with a grease-gun every 1000 miles.

INTRODUCTION July 1961 – August 1962.

BODY coupe; 2-doors, 2+2-seats; weight 2055lb (932.1kg).

ENGINE 4-cylinders, in-line; 80.96mm x 65.07mm, 1340cc; compr 8.5:1; 40.3kW (54bhp) @ 4900rpm; 30.1kW (40.3bhp)/l; 100Nm (74lbft) @ 2500rpm.

ENGINE STRUCTURE pushrod overhead valve, chain-driven camshaft; cast iron cylinder head and block; Zenith 32VN downdraught carburettor, centrifugal and vacuum ignition; AC mechanical fuel pump; 3-bearing hollow-cast crankshaft.

TRANSMISSION rear wheel drive; 18.4cm (7.25in) hydraulic sdp clutch; 4-speed gearbox, synchromesh on 3; hypoid bevel final drive 4.13:1.

CHASSIS steel monocoque structure; ifs by MacPherson struts and anti-roll bar; live rear axle with half-elliptic springs and lever arm dampers; Girling hydraulic non-servo 24.1cm (9.5in) disc front, 22.9cm (9in) drum rear brakes; recirculating ball steering; 41l (9 gal) fuel tank; 5.60-13 tubeless tyres.

DIMENSIONS wheelbase 252cm (99in); track 126cm (49.5in); length 434cm (170.8in); width 166cm (62.2in); height 137.2cm (54in); ground clearance 15cm (5.9in); turning circle 10.36m (34ft).

EQUIPMENT fresh-air heater, leather upholstery, push-button or manual control radio optional extras; screenwasher standard, pvc upholstery, carpet, 12 body colours, seven 2-colour choices.

PERFORMANCE maximum speed 130.35kph (81.2mph) *The Autocar*; 26.4kph (16.5mph) @ 1000rpm; 0-96kph (60mph) 21.3sec; 30.9kg/kW (17.3kg/bhp); 10.1l/100km (27.9mpg).

PRICE £627, purchase tax £288 12s, total £915 12s (£915.60).

PRODUCTION 11.143 including 1291 kits.

1962
Classic 116E

Despite being the beneficiary of the new strain of Ford engines, the Classic's second year of production began its decline. Five main bearings made for smooth running, there was 10 per cent more pulling power and an increase in top speed, yet the Classic spent a shorter time in production than any Ford since the war. It was all very well to claim it was never meant to survive long and that the body dies were made of short-duration Kirksite, not case-hardened steel. Its reception from the press was lukewarm and customers failed to materialise in their customary numbers. Ford had enjoyed unbroken success since the Consul and Zephyr of 1950, its transformation

from working-class to middle-class complete, but the Classic was a salutary reminder that sustained effort and good judgment were required to remain on top of the market. The engine was the third (105E, 109E and 116E) to use the same cylinder block, with a bore of 1.187in, variations being attained by lengthening the stroke from 1.906in, to 2.562in and finally 2.86in. This last had the cylinder top face raised by .66in (16.76mm) and the change to five main bearings was accompanied by a change to a solid crankshaft rather than a nodular cored-out one. Cylinder heads were not interchangeable, however and the combustion chambers were fully machined.

INTRODUCTION July 1962, production until September 1963.
BODY saloon; 2 and 4-doors, 5-seats; weight 2-door 935kg (2058lb), 4-door 955kg (2106 lb).
ENGINE 4-cylinders, in-line; 80.96mm x 72.7mm, 1499cc; compr 8.3:1; 44.4kW (59.5bhp) @ 4600rpm; 29.6kW (39.7bhp)/l; 110.5Nm (81.5lbft) @ 2300rpm.
ENGINE STRUCTURE pushrod overhead valve, chain-driven camshaft; cast iron cylinder head and block; Zenith 33VN downdraught carburettor, centrifugal and vacuum ignition; AC mechanical fuel pump; 5-bearing crankshaft.
TRANSMISSION rear wheel drive; 18.4cm (7.25in) hydraulic sdp clutch; 4-speed synchromesh gearbox; hypoid bevel final drive 4.13:1.
CHASSIS steel monocoque structure; ifs by MacPherson struts and anti-roll bar; live rear axle with half-elliptic springs and lever arm dampers; Girling hydraulic non-servo 24.1cm (9.5in) disc front, 22.9cm (9in) drum rear brakes; recirculating ball steering; 41l (9 gal) fuel tank; 5.60-13 tubeless or tubed tyres.
DIMENSIONS wheelbase 252cm (99in); track 126cm (49.5in); length 434cm (170.8in); width 166cm (62.2in); height 142cm (56in); ground clearance 15cm (5.9in); turning circle 10.36m (34ft).
EQUIPMENT fresh-air heater, leather upholstery, push-button or manual control radio optional extras; screenwasher standard, pvc upholstery, carpet, 12 body colours, seven 2-colour choices.
PERFORMANCE maximum speed 129.6kph (80.7mph) The Motor; 26.4kph (16.5mph) @ 1000rpm; 0-96kph (60mph) 20.1sec; 21.1kg/kW (15.7kg/bhp) 2-door, 21.5kg/kW (16.1kg/bhp) 4-door; fuel consumption 11l/100km (25.8mpg).
PRICE £565, purchase tax £212 17s 9d, total £777 17s 9d (£777.89p) 4-door.
PRODUCTION 24,531, 2000KD. standard 4-door 1770; de luxe 2-door 6742; de luxe 4-door 17,179.

LEFT **Classic in tranquil Inveraray.**

1962
Capri 116E, Capri GT

The Capri 335 inherited the Classic's 5-bearing engine and all-synchromesh gearbox and managed to outlast the saloons by almost a year. It was all part of Ford's repositioning of itself, the GT invoking what Ford liked to call a spirit of fun, which meant more speed and style, better handling, and just a whiff of sportiness. The 105E engine was already the mainstay of Formula Ford racing; the sturdy 5-bearing engine with its robust bottom end encouraged tuners and special builders. The 116E for the GT was equipped with a twin-choke Weber carburettor, essential to any engine with competition aspirations in the 1960s, a 4-branch exhaust and a high-lift camshaft designed by a new name in high performance engines, Keith Duckworth. The co-founder of Cosworth Engineering, Duckworth had a close relationship with Ford. "I hadn't designed many cams," he said later. "I had read all the books on cam design and believed them, but they only tended to mislead me. I decided it was better to work things out from first principles." His engineering genius was yet to reach full flower, and although the Capri GT was a lively performer with 30 per cent more power and 12 per cent more torque, it never really found a role as a sporty car and only 412 were sold in its final year.

INTRODUCTION July 1962, produced until September 1963; GT February 1963 until July 1964.
BODY coupe; 2-doors, 2+2-seats; weight 946.7kg (2087lb).
ENGINE 4-cylinders, in-line; 80.96mm x 72.7mm, 1499cc; compr 8.3:1; 44.4kW (59.5bhp) @ 4600rpm; 29.6kW (39.7bhp)/l; 110.5Nm (81.5lbft) @ 2300rpm. GT compr 9:1; 58.2kW (78bhp) @ 5200rpm; 38.8kW (52bhp)/l; 123Nm (91lbft) @ 3600rpm.
ENGINE STRUCTURE pushrod ohv, chain-driven camshaft; cast iron cyl head and block; Zenith 33VN downdraught carb, centrifugal and vacuum ignition; AC mechanical fuel pump; 5-bearing crank. GT Weber 28/36 DCD22 2-choke compound downdraught carb.

TRANSMISSION rear wheel drive; 18.4cm (7.25in) hydraulic sdp clutch; 4-speed synchromesh gearbox; hypoid bevel final drive 4.13:1.
CHASSIS steel monocoque structure; ifs by MacPherson struts and anti-roll bar; live rear axle with half-elliptic springs and lever arm dampers; Girling hydraulic non-servo (GT Servo) 24.1cm (9.5in) disc front, 22.9cm (9in) drum rear brakes; recirculating ball steering; 41l (9 gal) fuel tank; 5.60-13 tubeless tyres.
DIMENSIONS wheelbase 252cm (99in); track 126cm (49.5in); length 434cm (170.8in); width 166cm (62.2in); height 142cm (56in); ground clearance 15cm (5.9in); turning circle 10.36m (34ft).

EQUIPMENT fresh-air heater standard, Cirrus or leather/pvc upholstery, push-button (£33 3s 11d, £33.20) or manual control radio optional; screenwasher standard, pvc upholstery, carpet, safety belts £4 15s 0d (£4.75p), occasional seat cushion £9. 9s 0d (£9.45p).
PERFORMANCE max speed GT 149.8kph (93.3mph) *The Motor*; 26.4kph (16.5mph) @ 1000rpm; 0-96kph (60mph) 20sec, GT 14.1sec; 21.3kg/kW (15.9kg/bhp); fuel consumption GT 10.4l/100km (27.1mpg).
PRICE £864 total with purchase tax. GT £745, purchase tax £155 15s 5d, total £900 15s 5d (£955.77p).
PRODUCTION 6868 plus 705 in kits, 2002 total GTs.

1962
Anglia Super 123E

The Anglia Super was presented as a high performance luxury version with a 1200cc engine. Only two weeks later its new place in the scheme of things was revealed when the cheapest Cortina was announced at £639 a bare £40 dearer. Like the Cortina, the Anglia Super had synchromesh on all 4 gears, with the ratio of first raised to make the most of it. Wider brake drums were fitted, and it had a popular distinguishing feature, duo-tone paintwork. Wheel trims were included in the price, which was £60 over the standard Anglia. The result was a good deal livelier than the 105E but used more fuel. Customers, soon to be exposed to Oriental imports with radios, heaters,

and suchlike included in the price, now expected better equipment from domestic producers, although they had to wait until 1964 for a built-in radio and seat belt attachments. The Anglia Super had pleated pvc upholstery (whose silvery finish *The Motor's* road testers found slippery during cornering), woven-cord carpet, padded dashboard, screenwashers and a cigarette lighter. Production was transferred to Halewood in March 1963, in 1965 the estate car gearing was standardised on saloons, and the Anglia went on to have an eight-year run of success. In 1966 Ford introduced an in-house carburettor to replace the original Solex downdraught.

INTRODUCTION September 1962, production until November 1967.
BODY saloon; 2-doors, 4-seats; weight 778kg (1715lb).
ENGINE 4-cylinders, in-line; 80.96mm x 58.17mm, 1198cc; compr 8.7:1; 36.5kW (49bhp) @ 4800rpm; 30.5kW (40.9bhp)/l; 86Nm (63lbft) @ 2700rpm.
ENGINE STRUCTURE pushrod overhead valves, chain-driven camshaft; cast iron cylinder head and block; Solex B30 PSEI-2 downdraught carburettor, centrifugal and vacuum ignition; AC mechanical fuel pump; 3-bearing hollow-cast crankshaft.

TRANSMISSION rear wheel drive; Borg & Beck 18.4cm (7.25in) clutch; 4-speed synchromesh gearbox; Hardy Spicer series 1140 prop shaft; hypoid bevel final drive 4.125:1.
CHASSIS steel monocoque structure; ifs by MacPherson struts and anti roll bar; live rear axle with half-elliptic springs, lever arm damper; Girling hydraulic 20.3cm (8in) drum brakes; Burman recirculating ball steering; 31.8l (7 gal) fuel tank; 5.20-13 tubeless tyres.
DIMENSIONS wheelbase 229.2cm (90.25in); track 117.5cm (46.25in); length 390.5cm (153.75in), estate 392cm (154.3in); width 143.5cm (56.5in); height 142.2cm (56in); ground clearance 15.2cm (6in); turning circle 9.88m (32.4ft).

EQUIPMENT manual pump screenwashers, self-parking wipers, heater, carpets standard, Ford manual or push-button radio optional, eight duo-tone colours.
PERFORMANCE maximum speed 131.3kph (81.8mph) *The Motor*; 25.2kph (15.7mph) @ 1000rpm;

0-96kph (60mph) 21.6sec; 21.3kg/kW (15.9kg/bhp); fuel consumption 33mpg (8.56l/100km).
PRICE de luxe £495, purchase tax £103 13s 9d, total £598 13s 9d (£598.69p).
PRODUCTION 79,223.

1962
Cortina 113E 2-door, 4-door, Estate Car

The Classic appeared first as a Consul Classic and the Cortina a Consul Cortina, meeting an obscure concern in the marketing department for continuity with names. Consul was soon dropped; the Cortina never needed spin-doctoring. It was one of the most successful Fords ever and outshone more technically adventurous competitors. It even outshone a front wheel drive that rival Ford Germany was developing jointly with Detroit, codenamed Cardinal. Ford of Britain mischievously gave its project the codename Archbishop, for a straightforward front-engined, rear-drive, three box car, the highest-tech feature of which was a monocoque shell designed to new heights of aerospace excellence. Stress requirements were calculated so precisely that surplus metal, and thus surplus weight, could be discarded. The

process saved some 68kg (150lb), making the Cortina cheaper, faster and more economical than anything in its class. It was claimed that the weight saved was equivalent to the weight of an adult occupant. Roy Brown was responsible for the shape (as he was for the Mk III Zephyr) and got the proportions right. The Cortina was *Auto Universum's* car of the year, priced at the level of many 1-litre cars, and as roomy as lots of 1.5-litre cars. Analogous with the Classic, the 1.2 Cortina 2-door was a revelation. It could seat 6, with the optional bench seat and the ingenious cable-operated steering column gearshift, even though buyers mostly preferred it on the floor. Introduced with a rather severe interior of painted metal and rubber-covered floor it was not long before the Cortina moved up-market with better furnishings and a higher price.

INTRODUCTION 2-door Nov 1962, then 4-door and estate; produced until Nov 1966.
BODY saloon 2-door, 4-door, estate 5-door, 5-seats; wt 4-door 809kg (1783.5lb), 2-door 794kg (1750.5lb), estate 912kg (2010.6lb).
ENGINE 4-cylinders, in-line; 80.96mm x 58.17mm, 1198cc; compr 8.7:1; 36.5kW (49bhp) @ 4800rpm; 30.5kW (40.9bhp)/l; 85Nm (63lbft) @ 2700rpm.
ENGINE STRUCTURE pushrod overhead valve, chain-driven camshaft; cast iron cylinder head and block; Solex B30 PSEI-2 downdraught carburettor, centrifugal and vacuum ignition; AC mechanical fuel pump; 3-bearing hollow-cast crankshaft.
TRANSMISSION rear wheel drive; Borg & Beck 18.4cm (7.25in) clutch; 4-speed synchromesh gearbox; Hardy Spicer series 1140 prop shaft; hypoid bevel final drive 4.125:1. CHASSIS steel monocoque structure; ifs by MacPherson struts and anti roll bar; live rear axle with half-elliptic springs, telescopic dampers; Girling hydraulic 20.3cm (8in) drum brakes; Burman recirculating ball steering; 31.8l (7 gal) fuel tank; 5.20-13 tubeless tyres.
DIMENSIONS wheelbase 249cm (98in); track 126cm (49.6in), estate front 127cm (50in); length 427.5cm (168.3in), estate 428cm (168.5in); width 159cm (62.6in); height 144cm (56.7in), estate 146cm (57.5in); ground clearance 16cm (6.3in), estate 17cm (6.7in); turning circle 9.6m (31.5ft).
EQUIPMENT 8 exterior colours, 6 duotone at extra cost; bench seat with steering column gearchange, heater, radio, whitewall tyres, leather upholstery optional extras.
PERFORMANCE maximum speed 123.2kph (76.5mph) *The Autocar*; 25.8kph (16.1mph) @ 1000rpm; 0-96kph (60mph) 22.4sec; 22.2kg/kW (16.5kg/bhp); fuel consumption 9.4l/100km (30.2mpg).
PRICE £484, purchase tax £182 10s 3d, £666 10s 3d (£666.51p).
PRODUCTION 1,013,391 all Mark 1.

Zephyr 4 Mark III 211E saloon, Estate Car

The Mark III Zephyr marked a further step into the premium priced large car market, although at the entry level it was promoted as a Consul replacement, until the name was at last abandoned, and it became plain Zephyr 4. Stylist Canadian Roy Brown, whose predilection for ovoid shapes had helped fashion the ill-starred Edsel, took over after in-house and Frua designs were abandoned, designing a homely family of cars with sufficient tailfin and good balance to be almost in vogue. The Zephyr 4 was plainest, with a one-piece grille and less brightwork, even though it offered the same room inside and had the same boot and bonnet. Rear legroom was less than generous however, and had to be increased with a package of modifications within nine months of launch, when the interior was improved cosmetically with simulated wood like the 6. There were a few technical innovations such as a new sort of recirculating ball steering, with variable ratio to make it lighter at parking speeds. There was not much demand for technical novelty. Once again Farnham did the estate car conversions using Zodiac bodyshells, which had more appropriate rear window configuration, and adding a rear tailgate in glass reinforced plastic (grp). A floor gearshift was introduced for the 1964 model year, with better-class simulated wood interior in American walnut grain effect.

INTRODUCTION January 1962, production until January 1966.
BODY saloon; 4-doors, 5-seats; weight 1163kg (2564lb).
ENGINE 4-cylinders, in-line; 82.55mm x 79.5mm, 1703cc; compr 8.3:1, 7.0:1 optional; 50.7kW (68bhp) @ 4800rpm; 29.8kW (39.9bhp)/l; 127Nm (94lbft)) @ 2000rpm.
ENGINE STRUCTURE pushrod overhead valve, chain-driven camshaft; cast iron cylinder head and block; Zenith 36VN downdraught carburettor, centrifugal and vacuum ignition; AC mechanical fuel pump; 5-bearing crankshaft.
TRANSMISSION rear wheel drive; hydraulic sdp clutch; 4-speed synchromesh gearbox; overdrive and Borg Warner automatic optional; hypoid bevel final drive 3.9:1; 4.11:1 with overdrive; 3.545:1 with auto.
CHASSIS steel monocoque structure; ifs by Macpherson telescopic damper and coil spring strut, lower wishbone incorporating anti roll bar; rear half elliptic leaf springs with Armstrong lever arm dampers; Girling hydraulic servo disc front 24.8cm (9.75in) and drum rear 22.9cm (9in) brakes; Ford-Burman recirculating ball steering; 12.5 gal (56.8l) fuel tank; 6.40-13 4-ply tubeless tyres.
DIMENSIONS wheelbase 271.8cm (107in); track 135.25cm (53.25in) front, 135.6cm (53.5in) rear, later 140.3cm (55.25in); length 458.5cm (180.5in); width 175.3cm (69in); height 146cm (57.5in); ground clearance 15.2cm (6in); turning circle 10.67m (35ft).
EQUIPMENT electric windscreen wipers, heater optional, radio optional pvc upholstery leather extra, rubber floor covering, 12 colour options.
PERFORMANCE maximum speed 126.7kph (78.9mph) automatic *The Motor*; 31.9kph (19.9mph) @ 1000rpm (auto); 0-96kph (60mph) 22.8sec (auto); 22.9kg/kW (17.1kg/bhp); fuel consumption 10.4l/100km (27.2mpg).
PRICE £695, PT £261 12s 9d, total £956 12s 9d (£956.64).
PRODUCTION 106,810 saloons, 13,628 estate cars.

RIGHT **Following the styling triumphs of Zephyr and Zodiac I and II, Ford tried hard. Frua was rejected for Mark III. Initiatives by Colin Neale, who designed the Mark II, and Detroit's Elwood Engel were likewise discarded. Roy Brown won the day and although the result was less than dazzling, he did achieve an identity for Zephyr and Zodiac.**

1962
Zephyr 6 Mark III 213E saloon, Estate Car

By the Mark III the Zephyr was losing some of its piquancy. The competition was catching up. Despite the stylists' best efforts, to say nothing of the long-running TV police series Z-Cars, the gaping grille was neither trend setting nor cute. It was even getting a bit late in the day for fins. Large overhangs made the Zephyr III seem bigger than it was, and although generously proportioned, space inside was constrained by the steeply raked windscreen, big boot, and low roof. Curved side windows enhanced elbowroom, but not enough, and rear seat legroom became an issue. Marketing had decreed a boot of 6.2cu m (22cu ft), to catch the eye

of the fleet business driver, still a major influence in the British market. The penalty was shortage of passenger space. The floor pan had to be urgently reworked, the rear bulkhead moved back to provide 5.1cm (2in) more legroom, the wheel arches were modified, and a new axle casing and half shafts resulted in an increase in rear track by 4.5cm (1.75in). It was a major undertaking only months after launch. Throughout its five year life the Mark III Zephyr needed constant promotion and the estate was probably the most successful with a torsion bar counterbalanced glass reinforced plastic tailgate, yet even it failed to sell in large numbers.

INTRODUCTION Jan 1962, production until Jan 1966.
BODY saloon; 4-doors, 5-seats; weight 1223kg (2696lb).
ENGINE 6-cylinders, in-line; 82.55mm x 79.5mm, 2553cc; compr 8.3:1 7:1 optional; 73.1kW (98bhp) @ 4750rpm; 28.6kW (38.4bhp)/l; 182Nm (134lbft) @ 2000rpm.
ENGINE STRUCTURE pushrod ohv, chain-driven camshaft; cast iron cylinder head and block; Zenith 36WIA-2 downdraught carb, centrifugal and vacuum ignition; AC Delco mechanical fuel pump; 7-bearing crankshaft.
TRANSMISSION rwd; hydraulic sdp clutch; 4-speed synchromesh gearbox; overdrive and Borg Warner 3-speed automatic optional; hypoid bevel final drive 3.545:1.
CHASSIS steel monocoque; ifs by Macpherson telescopic damper and coil spring strut, lower wishbone incorporating anti roll bar; rear half elliptic leaf springs with Armstrong lever arm dampers; Girling hydraulic servo disc front 24.8cm (9.75in) and drum rear 22.9cm (9in) drum brakes; Ford-Burman recirculating ball steering; 56.8l (12.5 gal) fuel tank; 6.40-13 4-ply tubeless tyres.
DIMENSIONS wheelbase 271.8cm (107in); track front 135.25cm (53.25in), rear 135.6cm (53.5in), later 140.3cm (55.25in); length 458.5cm (180.5in); width 175.3cm (69in); height 146cm (57.5in); ground clearance 15.2cm (6in); turning circle 10.67m (35ft).
EQUIPMENT electric windscreen wipers, screen washers, heater optional, radio optional pvc upholstery leather extra, carpet, individual front seats optional, 12 colour options.
PERFORMANCE maximum 140.3kph (87.4mph) *The Motor*, automatic 31.9kph (19.9mph) @ 1000rpm; 0-96kph (60mph) 17.5sec; 16.7kg/kW (16.7kg/bhp); 17.6-14.9l/100km (16-19mpg).
PRICE £772 plus PT £161 7s 11d, total £933 7s 11d 9 (£933.58p).
PRODUCTION 107,380, estate 1632.

1962
Zodiac Mark III saloon, Estate Car

Two-colour paintwork may have become passé but the Zodiac still had allure. Four headlamps, a shiny mouth-organ grille, a subtle change from the Zephyr's side elevation with six windows, and gold-plated badges could still command attention. With an extra 8.2kW (11bhp) available from the Zephyr engine, Ford's first catalogued 100mph model still cost less than £1000. The gearshift was firmly back on the floor and although the steering was a bit lifeless the handling was safe, predictable and the ride smooth. The new gearshift did not earn universal praise. Marketing was still nervous about individual front seats, yet a floor change made a third occupant of a bench seat problematical, so the gear lever was angled towards the driver and its movement canted over uncomfortably. In January 1965 the Zodiac's prestige as a businessman's saloon was enhanced when a new name was coined for the top of the range. "Executive" as in keys to the washroom, desks, office suites, jet aircraft and airport lounges carried cachet. The Zodiac Executive had a push-button Motorola radio, extra lights, seat belts, high-output dynamo, black crushed hide upholstery, and among the five colours were two acrylic metallics. Although in some respects it was a perfectly run-of-the-mill Zodiac, the Executive label remained in Ford model nomenclature for a generation and became a shorthand term throughout the industry.

INTRODUCTION December 1961, production until January 1966, estate car from November 1962.
BODY saloon; 4-doors, 5-seats; weight 1288kg (2839.5lb).
ENGINE 6-cylinders, in-line; 82.55mm x 79.5mm, 2553cc; compr 8.3:1 7:1 optional; 81.3kW (109bhp) @ 4800rpm; 31.8kW (42.7bhp)/l; 191Nm (140.5lbft) @ 2400rpm.
ENGINE STRUCTURE pushrod overhead valve, chain-driven camshaft; cast iron cylinder head and block; Zenith 42WIA-2 downdraught carburettor, centrifugal and vacuum ignition; AC Delco mechanical fuel pump; 7-bearing crankshaft.
TRANSMISSION rear wheel drive; Ford Borg & Beck hydraulic 20.9cm (8.25in) sdp clutch; 4-speed synchromesh gearbox; overdrive and Borg Warner 3-speed automatic optional; Hardy Spicer needle roller propeller shaft; hypoid bevel final drive 3.545:1.
CHASSIS steel monocoque structure; independent front suspension by Macpherson telescopic damper and coil spring strut, lower wishbone incorporating anti roll bar; rear half elliptic leaf springs with Armstrong lever arm dampers; Girling hydraulic servo disc front 24.8cm (9.75in), drum rear 22.9cm (9in) brakes; Ford-Burman recirculating ball steering; 16.8l (12.5 gal) fuel tank; 6.40-13 4-ply Nylon Sport tubeless tyres.
DIMENSIONS wheelbase 271.8cm (107in); track 135.25cm (53.25in) front, 135.6cm (53.5in) rear, later 140.3cm (55.25in); length 458.5cm (180.5in); width 175.3cm (69in); height 146cm (57.5in); ground clearance 15.2cm (6in); turning circle 10.7m (35ft).
EQUIPMENT electric windscreen wipers, screen washers, heater, radio optional, pvc upholstery, leather extra, carpet, individual front seats optional, 12 colour options (but see Executive).
PERFORMANCE maximum speed 160.8kph (100.2mph) *The Motor*, automatic 31.9kph (19.9mph) @ 1000rpm; 0-96kph (60mph) 13.4sec; 15.8kg/kW (11.8kg/bhp); fuel consumption 15.6l/100km (18.1mpg).
PRICE £813 plus PT £169 18s 9d, total £982 18s 9d (£982.94p).
PRODUCTION 77,709, estates 1576.

1963
Cortina Super and GT 118E

It was not long before Cortina production ramped up, as motor industry jargon had it, to hopeful levels and the 1.5-litre Super arrived with bigger brakes, better trim and chrome strips along the flanks. Crucially, in view of its impressive performance and influence on the Cortina's public perception, came the Cortina GT with a camshaft designed by Cosworth. Grand Touring was as much a part of the motoring lexicon of the 1960s as Chummy and Sedanca de Ville had been in the 1930s. It needed no explanation. It was lower, faster, racier and lighter. It was also more expensive and had a silvered facia, with lots of round important-looking instruments. The Cortina GT became the basis of Ford's flourishing rally programme with a significant win in the 1964 Safari Rally, which had acquired a reputation as one of the toughest and fastest rallies in the world. Vic Preston had won in a Zephyr in 1955 since when it had been dominated by Volkswagen, Mercedes-Benz, and Peugeot, all cars renowned for their strength and vigour. Ford had won team prizes in the Safari, but now outright victory by Kenyan Ford importer Peter Hughes, with the Cortina barely into its stride, gave it a magnificent start. In 1965 notable progress in comfort for production saloon cars was made with the adoption of Aeroflow fresh air ventilation

INTRODUCTION Super Jan 1963, GT April 1963, production to Oct 1966.
BODY saloon 2-door, 4-door; estate 5-door, 5-seats; weight 4-door 850kg (1874b), 2-door 835kg (1841lb), GT 794kg (1750lb).
ENGINE 4-cylinders, in-line; 80.96mm x 72.75mm, 1498cc; compr 8.3:1 (GT 9.0:1); 44.7kW (59.9bhp) @ 4600rpm; 29.8kW (40bhp)/l; 111Nm (81.5lbft) @ 2300rpm. GT 58.2kW (78bhp) @ 5200rpm; 123Nm (91lbft) @ 3600rpm.
ENGINE STRUCTURE pushrod ohv, chain-driven camshaft; cast iron cyl head and block; Zenith 33VN2 downdraught carb, GT Weber DCD1 dual barrel; centrifugal and vacuum ign; AC mechanical fuel pump; 5-bearing crank.

TRANSMISSION rwd; Borg & Beck 18.4cm (7.25in) clutch; 4-speed synchromesh gearbox; Hardy Spicer open prop shaft; hypoid bevel final drive 3.9:1; Borg Warner Model 35 -auto optional.
CHASSIS steel monocoque; ifs by MacPherson struts and anti roll bar - GT 1.9cm (0.75in); live rear axle with half-elliptic springs, telescopic dampers; Girling hydraulic 22.9cm (9in) front 20.3cm (8in) rear drum brakes; GT 24.1cm (9.5in) front discs; Burman recirculating ball steering; 36.4l (8 gal); 5.6 (saloon) 6 (estate) -13, 6-ply tubeless tyres; GT 5.60-13 4-ply.
DIMENSIONS wheelbase 249cm (98in); track 126cm (49.6in), 127cm (50in) estate front; length 427.5cm (168.3in), estate 428cm (168.5in);

width 159cm (62.6in); height 144cm (56.7in), estate 146cm (57.5in), GT 140.3cm (55.25in); ground clearance 16cm (6.3in), estate 17cm (6.7in); 9.6m (31.5ft) turning circle.
EQUIPMENT heater standard, radio, whitewall tyres optional, pvc upholstery, carpets, 11 colours, five 2-tone optional (not GT).
PERFORMANCE maximum 129.7kph (80.8mph); GT 146.9kph (91.5mph) The Motor; 25.8kph (16.1mph) @ 1000rpm; 0-96kph (60mph) 19.0sec, GT 12.1sec; 19kg/kW (14.2kg/bhp), GT 13.6kg/kW (10.2kg/bhp); 10.4l/100km (27.2mpg), GT 10.8l/100km (26.1mpg).
PRICE totals 4-door Super £670, Estate £785, GT £767.
PRODUCTION Super saloon 77,753, GT 76,947, estate 108,219.

1963
Lotus Cortina

Colin Chapman's designs were long on inspiration but short on quality and reliability. He produced some of the most stimulating cars of the 20th century, but they were betrayed by frailty and inconsistency. It was the same for his Lotuses, as well as his consultancy designs like the A-framed coil-sprung rear suspension and transmission he drew up for the Lotus Cortina. Together with other modifications, such as a partly aluminium-panelled body that Lotus made on the small assembly line in the factory at Cheshunt, they transformed the Cortina into a sporting car with astonishing handling and roadholding. Its merit was demonstrated by Jim Clark when, even with a front wheel about a foot off the ground on corners, the Lotus Cortina was the fastest car on the circuit. It was less satisfactory on real roads, as were later leaf-sprung versions, but on a smooth-surfaced track it was peerless. The twin cam conversion of the strong 5-bearing engine was equally effective and fortunately less frail. Designed by Harry Mundy, whose racing engine design experience encompassed ERA, BRM, and work with Walter Hassan at Coventry-Climax and Jaguar, it gave a stirring performance. Achieving reliability should have been a matter of development, but the axle's endemic shortcomings, including its effect on the carefully designed production body shell, could not be tolerated. Patience with Chapman ran out and production reverted to Ford. "A car of very strong personality..." *The Motor*.

INTRODUCTION Announced January, delivered summer 1963, produced until November 1966.

BODY saloon, 2-door; 4-seats; weight 775kg (1709lb).

ENGINE 4-cylinders, in-line; 82.55mm x 72.75mm, 1558cc; compr 9.5:1; 79kW (106bhp) @ 5500rpm; 50.7kW (68bhp)/l; 146Nm (108lbft) @ 4000rpm.

ENGINE STRUCTURE two valves per cylinder, two chain-driven overhead camshafts; cast iron block aluminium cylinder head; two Weber 40DCOE twin choke compound carburettors; centrifugal and vacuum ignition; AC mechanical fuel pump; 5-bearing crankshaft.

TRANSMISSION rear wheel drive; diaphragm spring 20.3cm (8in) sdp clutch; 4-speed synchromesh gearbox; BRD single piece open prop shaft; hypoid bevel final drive 3.9:1, optional 4.1:1.

CHASSIS steel monocoque structure; ifs by MacPherson struts and anti roll bar; live rear axle with coil springs, A-bracket, radius arms, telescopic dampers; From June 1965 half-elliptic leaf springs, twin radius arms; Girling hydraulic 24.1cm (9.5in) front discs, 20.3cm (8in) rear drum brakes; Burman recirculating ball steering; 36.4l (8 gal) fuel tank; 6.00-13 Dunlop C41 tyres, 5.5in rims.

DIMENSIONS wheelbase 249cm (98in); track 130.8cm (51.5in) front, 128.8cm (50.5in) rear; length 427.5cm (168.3in); width 159cm (62.6in); height 136.5cm (53.75in); ground clearance 15.2cm (6in); turning circle 10.4m (34ft).

EQUIPMENT radio optional, safety belts optional, pvc upholstery, moulded rubber floor covering, one only exterior colour white and green, rev limiter at 6500rpm.

PERFORMANCE max speed 173.4kph (108mph) *The Motor*; 25.8kph (17.2mph) @ 1000rpm; 0-96kph (60mph) 10.1sec; 9.8kg/kW (7.3kg/bhp); fuel consumption 13.3l/100km (21.3mpg).

PRICE £910, PT £190 2s 11d, total £1100 2s 11d (£1100.15).

PRODUCTION 3301.

Bengt Söderström winner 1966 RAC Rally.

1963
Corsair 120E, GT, 120GT

The basis for the Corsair was a Cortina platform with 7.6cm (3in) extra on the wheelbase, a stylish body and a higher price. Commercially it performed a double function; it made more volume for the Cortina parts it used and it provided an upmarket profit. If the Cortina could be said to replace the old Consul, the Corsair was half way towards a Zephyr. Sir Terence Beckett (above) who, as plain Terry Beckett, was Ford's project engineer in charge of the development of the Cortina, recalled to author Graham Robson: "We needed a replacement for the Classic and we thought of an extension of the Cortina as a way of doing this. It was a useful stopgap and it wasn't expensive. There was a lot of commonality with the Cortina." At 50kg (110.2lb) heavier the Corsair felt more substantial, a perception the self-consciously Thunderbird styling did little to dispel. Commonality with the Cortina extended to scuttle, bulkhead, windscreen, and inner engine bay panels. Ford managed to make a virtue out of the extra floor pan length in the rear, claiming the double skinning of the transmission tunnel was invoked to aid refinement. Corsair suspension was based on GT Cortina components, a steering column gearshift was optional on the 120E, but a floor shift was standard on the GTs.

INTRODUCTION Oct 1963, production until Sept /Oct 1965.
BODY saloon 2-door, 4-door, estate 5-door, 5-seats; 2-door weight 890kg (1962lb), 4-door 896kg (1975lb), GT 4-door 928kg (2046lb).
ENGINE 116E and 116 E/GT: 4-cylinders, in-line; 80.96mm x 72.75mm, 1498cc; compr 8.3:1, 7.0:1 optional (GT 9.0:1); 44.7kW (59.9bhp) @ 4600rpm; 29.8kW (40bhp)/l; 110.5Nm (81.5lbft) @ 2300rpm. GT 58.2kW (78bhp) @ 5200rpm; 38.8kW (52.1bhp)/l; 123Nm (91lbft) @ 3600rpm.
ENGINE STRUCTURE pushrod ohv, chain-driven camshaft; cast iron cyl head and block; Zenith 33VN2 downdraught carb; GT Weber 28/36 DCD16/18 dual barrel; centrifugal and vacuum ign; AC mechanical fuel pump; 5-bearing crank.

TRANSMISSION rear wheel drive; Borg & Beck 18.4cm (7.25in) clutch; 4-speed synchromesh gearbox; Hardy Spicer open prop shaft; hypoid bevel final drive 3.9:1; Borg Warner Model 35 automatic optional.
CHASSIS steel monocoque structure; ifs by MacPherson struts and anti roll bar, GT 19mm (0.75in) dia; live rear axle with half-elliptic springs, Armstrong telescopic dampers; Girling hydraulic 24.1cm (9.5in) front discs, 20.3cm (8in) rear drum brakes; GT vacuum servo; Burman recirculating ball steering; 36.4l (8 gal) fuel tank; 5.60-13, 4-ply tubeless tyres.
DIMENSIONS wheelbase 256.5cm (101in); track 127cm (50in) front, 126cm (49.6in) rear; length 449cm (176.8in); width 161cm (63.4in); height 145cm (57.1in); ground clearance 17cm (6.7in); turning circle 10.2m (33.5ft).

EQUIPMENT heater, radio optional, individual front seats, pvc upholstery, loop pile carpets, 11 colours, five 2-tone.
PERFORMANCE maximum speed 134.5kph (83.8mph) *The Motor*, GT 147.9kph (92.1mph); 27.9kph (17.4mph) @ 1000rpm; 0-96kph (60mph) 19sec, GT 12.8sec; 20kg/kW (15kg/bhp), GT 16kg/kW (11.9kg/bhp); 26mpg (9.2l/100km).
PRICE de luxe saloon £580, PT £121 7s 11d, £701 7s 11d (£701.40p). GT £847.40p.
PRODUCTION 120E saloons 137,734, GT 21,857.

RIGHT **Ford publicity photo-shoot with Corsair, world champion Jim Clark and model Jean Shrimpton.**

1964
GT40 Mark I
(prototypes, later Mark II, some converted from Mark I)

In 1962 Henry Ford II rescinded American car manufacturers' agreement not to take part in motor racing. It was abrogated at first only in America, but it was not long before Ford, having failed to buy Ferrari for $10million, mounted a challenge in Europe. The Le Mans 24 Hours race was opened to manufacturers' prototypes and Ford created a car to fit the bill. The 1962 Mustang 1 was a 1.7-litre, mid-engined open 2-seater designed by Roy Lunn, while in Britain Eric Broadley had designed the Lola GT, a closed coupe along similar lines. Ford brought them together in Ford Advanced Vehicles, a subsidiary set up in Slough, and by the beginning of 1964 the first cars were finished. Events moved quickly and two crashed the first time out on a track at the Le Mans test weekend. However in June a GT40, driven by Richie Ginther and Masten Gregory, led the French classic race before retiring, and another driven by Phil Hill set a new circuit record at 211.4kph (131.7mph). Despite the resources expended on the GT40 design, including new computer aided technology, Lunn was forced to admit that: "...some stability phenomenon existed that had not become apparent during the design analytical phase." What this meant was that at speed the car generated some 317.5kg (700lb) of aerodynamic lift, threatening at best instability, and at worst flight.

INTRODUCTION April 1964.
BODY coupe; 2-doors, 2-seats; weight 832.4kg (1835lb) dry, 1111.3kg (2450lb) on startline without driver; distribution 43 front 57 rear.
ENGINE 8-cylinders, 90deg V; mid; 95.5mm (later 101.6mm) x 72.9mm, 4195cc (later 4736cc); compr 12.5:1; 261kW (350bhp) @ 7200rpm, later 291kW (390bhp) @ 7000rpm; 62.2kW (73.9bhp)/l, later 61.4kW (82.3bhp)/l; 373Nm (275lbft) @ 5600rpm, later 441Nm (325lbft) @ 5000rpm.
ENGINE STRUCTURE pushrod ohv from central camshaft; aluminium cylinder head and block; 4 Weber 48mm dual-choke carburettors; 5-bearing crankshaft, wet-sump. (prototypes of April 1964 had dry-sump 4.2-litre 261kW (350bhp) engine).
TRANSMISSION rwd; 216mm (8.5in) Borg & Beck 3-plate clutch; 4-speed manual Colotti gearbox, no synchro, in unit with transaxle; from 1965 5-speed ZF all-synchromesh.
CHASSIS semi-monocoque hull, 23swg sheet steel, 60mm (.024in) with square tube stiffening, grp body panels from 1968 carbon filament reinforced; ifs by double wishbones, coil springs, telescopic dampers, anti roll bar; independent rear suspension by double trailing arms, transverse top link and lower wishbone, coil springs, telescopic dampers, anti-roll bar; hydraulic servo disc brakes, from 1968 ventilated discs, 29.2cm (11.5in); rack and pinion; 139l (30.6 gal) door sill fuel tanks; 6.00-15 front, 9.00-15 rear, later 10.30-15 and 13.50-15 tyres.
DIMENSIONS wheelbase 241.3cm (95in); track front and rear 137.2cm (54in); length 418.1cm (164.6in); width 177.8cm (70in); height 102.9cm (40.5in); ground clearance 12.2cm (4.8in).
EQUIPMENT cockpit and driver's seat ventilation by air-duct front high-pressure point under nose.
PERFORMANCE maximum speed (1966) timed on Mulsanne 301kph (187.5mph), design estimate 337.1kph (210mph), still air maximum of early GT40 likely 316.2kph (197mph); 3.2kg/kW (2.4kg/kW), later 2.9kg/kW (2.4kg/bhp).
PRICE n/a.
PRODUCTION 12 prototypes and 87 production GT40s.

RIGHT **Ford's first foray at Le Mans.**

1965
Corsair V4 and GT

INTRODUCTION October 1965; GT 2000 produced to 1969, 1700 de luxe to 1965.

BODY saloon 2-door, 4-door; estate 5-door, 5-seats; weight 2-door 967kg (2131.8lb), 4-door 981kg (2162.7lb), GT 4-door 995kg (2193.6lb).

ENGINE 2720E, GT 2724E; 4-cylinders, 60deg V; 93.66mm x 60.35mm, 1663cc; compr 9.1:1, 7.1:1 optional; 57.1kW (76.5bhp) @ 4750rpm; 34.3kW (46bhp)/l; 127Nm (94lbft) @ 3000rpm. GT 93.7mm x 72.4mm, 1996cc; 65.6kW (88bhp) @ 4750rpm; 32.9kW (44.1bhp)/l; 158Nm (116.5lbft) @ 3600rpm.

ENGINE STRUCTURE pushrod ohv, gear-driven camshaft; cast iron cylinder head and block; Zenith 36 IV downdraught carburettor; centrifugal and vacuum ignition; AC mechanical fuel pump; 3-bearing crankshaft.

TRANSMISSION rear wheel drive; Borg & Beck 8in (20.3cm) clutch; 4-speed synchromesh gearbox; Hardy Spicer open prop shaft; hypoid bevel final drive 3.78:1; automatic optional.

CHASSIS steel monocoque structure; ifs by MacPherson struts and anti roll bar; live rear axle with half-elliptic springs and radius arms on the GT, Armstrong telescopic dampers; Girling hydraulic 24.4cm (9.6in) front discs 22.9cm (9in) rear drum brakes; GT vacuum servo; Burman recirculating ball steering; 45.46l (10 gal) fuel tank; 5.60-13 tyres, 4in rims.

DIMENSIONS wheelbase 256.5cm (101in); track 127cm (50in) front, 126cm (49.6in) rear; length 449cm (176.8in); width 161cm (63.4in); height 145cm (57.1in); ground clearance 17cm (6.7in); turning circle 10.2m (33.5ft).

EQUIPMENT heater, radio optional, individual front seats, pvc upholstery, loop pile carpets, 11 colours, 5 two-tone.

PERFORMANCE maximum speed 141.3kph (88mph) The Motor, GT 141.3kph (88mph) The Autocar; 28.3kph (17.6mph) @ 1000rpm; 0-96kph (60mph) 15.6sec, GT 14.7sec; 17.2kg/kW (12.8kg/bhp), GT 14.6kg/kW (11.3kg/bhp); fuel consumption 12.6l/100km (22.4mpg).

PRICE £650, PT £135 8s 4d, £785 8s 4d (£785.42); GT total £909.

PRODUCTION 135,000 including GT.

The Corsair's success was based on what marketing called aspirational owners, who liked the practicality of a Cortina but were looking for something whose doors shut with the comforting clunk of a slam-door railway carriage. In its second incarnation the Corsair became the test-bed for a new generation of Ford engines. The V4 was designed to take up less room than a straight four, not that it mattered much in the Corsair, which had an engine bay the same size as before. Even with a Lanchester style counter-rotating balancer shaft (right) it was no smoother than a straight four; it was heavier, slower, used more fuel, and the GT was little livelier than the ordinary 1700. The Motor was exasperated: "the new engine is a little harsh at idling speed ... willing ... (but) some resonant periods." Furthermore fuel consumption had deteriorated by 70.6l/100km (4mpg). Aeroflow ventilation and better décor was all very well, but there was little disguising the Transit van refinement, and the extra weight brought woolly lower-geared steering and nose-heavy understeer. Interior improvements included clear round instruments instead of the old model's architectural ovals and strip-type speedometer. Boot space was generous at 3.3cu m (11.7cu ft). Individual seats and a tall transmission tunnel banished even the option of the bench-style seating treasured by marketing departments since 1946.

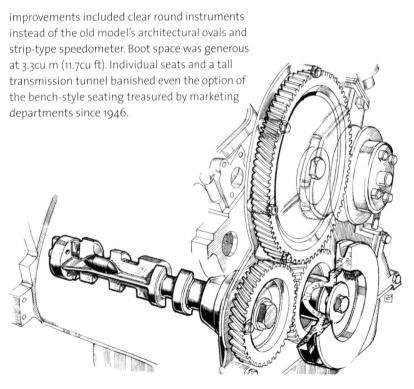

1965
Transit

Transits were used as fire engines, ambulances, motor caravans, breakdown vehicles, tipper trucks and dropside lorries. They were made with platforms for cherry-pickers, auxiliary power units, generator sets, mobile workshops, security vans, riot police vans, radio and television studios, dustcarts and milk floats. Their versatile rear-drive structure was integral when they were a van, with the floor welded to inverted full length top-hat section longerons, or when a chassis-cab with closures turning the top-hats into box-section load-bearers. Short wheelbases had plain ladder frames, long wheelbases cruciform bracing. There was a choice of two V4 engines or a Perkins diesel, and any number of options on the standard bodywork including sliding doors, side-loading doors, high roofs, and for buses different trim varying from hard-wearing and practical to luxury. Six basic models (there were 44 different versions) varied in load capacity from 610kg (12cwt) to 1780kg (35cwt), coaches from 9-seaters to 15-seaters. Short wheelbases came with single rear wheels, long ones with twins. Engineered and built at Langley by a team including Terry (later Sir Terence) Becket and Alex (later Sir Alex) Trotman, production moved to Southampton in 1971. A V6 was added to the engine range, then an automatic, the V4s got more power, and the 2.4-litre Ford diesel replaced the Perkins engine.

INTRODUCTION October 1965.
BODY van or chassis-cab; 2-doors, 1 or 2-seats; weight 1837kg (4050lb) to 3266kg (7200lb).
ENGINE 4-cylinders, 60deg V; 93.6mm x 60.35mm, 1660cc; compr 8.0:1; 48.47kW (65bhp) @ 4750rpm; 29.2kW (39.2bhp)/l; 117Nm (86.5lbft) @ 3000rpm. 2.0: 93.6 x 72.4mm; 1996cc; compr 8.9:1; 65.62kW (88bhp) @ 4750rpm; 34.4kW (44.1bhp)/l; 167Nm (123.5lbft) @ 2750rpm. Perkins 4/99 diesel; 1760cc; compr 22:1; 4-cylinders; 30.4kW (40.7bhp) @ 3700rpm; 17.2kW (23.1bhp)/l; 97Nm (71.5lbft) @ 2250rpm.
ENGINE STRUCTURE V4s pushrod ohv; gear-driven side cam, gear-driven balancer shaft; cast iron cyl head, block; single carb, centrifugal and vacuum ign; AC mech fuel pump; 3-bearing crank.

TRANSMISSION rwd; Borg & Beck 21.6cm (8.5in) diaphragm spring clutch; 4-speed synchromesh gearbox; hypoid bevel final drive 4.111, 4.444, 4.625, 5.143, 5.125:1 according to application; one-piece prop shaft swb, two piece lwb.
CHASSIS steel monocoque (but see text); front and rear semi-elliptic springs; differences in dimensions and spring leaves according to application, lwb with slipper-ended rear springs; telescopic dampers, heavy-duty option; Lockheed hydraulic brakes, vacuum servo optional, front-rear ratio according to wheelbase and application; 2-leading shoes at front; 22.9cm (9in) or 25.4cm (10in) drums; recirculating ball steering; 42.1l (9.25 gal) fuel tank swb; 68.2l (15 gal) lwb; 6.50, 7.00, 7.50-14YY tyres depending on application.

DIMENSIONS wbase 269.2cm (106in) and 299.7cm (118in); track front 163.8cm (64.5in), rear 153.9cm (60.6in) (twin rear wheels); bodywork length swb to 236.2cm (93in), lwb to 312.4cm (123in); typical van overall length 517.4cm (203.7in); width 205.7cm (81in); height 207.3cm (81.6in); circle 10.4m (34ft) swb, 11.3m (37ft) lwb.
PERFORMANCE maximum 125.2kph (78mph) *Commercial Motor* 30cwt van 2.0-litre; 0-50mph (80kph) 26.1sec; 23.9-12.3l/100km (11.8-23mpg) depending on application.
PRICE from £545.

BELOW **boxer Henry Cooper with his 1965 Transit Custom.**

1965
D-series truck and 1967 D1000 heavy truck

Essentially a corollary to the introduction of the Transit, for capacities from 12cwt to 35cwt, the D-series met requirements at the heavy end of the commercial market in three stages. First was a range covering capacities from 2 to 8tons, tippers, forward-control tilt-cab inclined engine 6-wheelers, chassis-cab units for special bodywork, together with an articulated tractor unit for gross vehicle weights (gvw) up to 20tons. There were new engines, a 4161cc 4-cylinder, 5948cc 6-cylinder, and turbo-diesel 5948cc 6-cylinder. Two years later the next stage was 4-wheelers with gvws up to 16 tons, and an articulated tractor of 28tons. Cummins and Ford Model 511 V8 diesels were introduced in stage two together with, for a time, 6-cylinder 96.2kW (129bhp) and 111kW (149bhp) imported American engines. Heavy-duty vehicles had air-hydraulic brakes as standard and custom cabs were a popular option in the D-series that also extended to PSV chassis. The R192 and R226 (the figures indicating wheelbase in inches), the more powerful available with a 5-speed, could carry up to 53 passengers. Midland Red ordered 100 in 1970 alone and within two years 220 were in service with, from 1978, 107.38kW (144bhp) turbo-diesels.

The former Thames Trader market (below D-series but heavier than Transit) was filled in 1973 with the A-series, a range of Transit-related light commercials from 30cwt to 5 tons that included tippers, large vans, and small artics. Their engines came from the passenger car range, 2.0-litre V4s, 3.0-litre V6s and 2.4-litre 4-cylinder diesel. There was also the 3.6-litre ohv 4-cylinder 52.2kW (70bhp) diesel dating back to 1954. Standard dual-circuit servo braking systems, optional 4- or 5-speeds for the gearbox, and an unprecedented standard of comfort for the

occupants were important novelties.

Beside the D-series came a parallel redesigned normal control chassis with the same range of engines and capacities, known as the K-series, made until 1973. Stage 3 in heavy vehicles was the H-series Transcontinental of 1975, chassis-cabs and trucks between 16-19 tons gvw for 4-wheelers, 24 tons for 6-wheelers, and articulated tractor units of both sorts up to 42 tons. Made in Holland, this was a big range with forward control 3-man tilt cabs, twin-plate clutches, 9-13-speed Fuller constant-mesh gearboxes, single reduction hypoid rear axles, power steering and air brakes. In the absence of a suitable engine of its own, Ford turned to Cummins for a 264.7kW (355bhp) 14-litre 6-cylinder diesel with turbocharger and aftercooler. In 1977 Ford was making the nation's best-selling car (the Cortina) its best selling tractor, and best-selling commercial vehicle range.

1966
Corsair V4 2000, 2000E saloon, Estate Car

Second thoughts on the V4 Corsair came not a moment too soon. The estate car introduced at the 1966 Geneva show was not a success; the loading platform was too high. "Not a maid-of-all-work designed to take pigs to market," said *The Autocar*. "The load space is fully carpeted and the sides are trimmed in padded pvc." It was doubtful about the GT badges that still adhered to the Estate Car but a good deal was changed in January 1967 when the Corsair's up-market credentials were reinforced by the 2000E. This was essentially a de luxe with the 'E' package for an extra £76. This gained it Executive status, and at only a little over £1,000, it had walnut veneer facia, black leather-looking upholstery, black vinyl roof (with the Aeroflow ventilation extractor vents in the rear quarters tastefully finished black), and fancy wheel trims. The chrome strips were removed from the sides, enhancing dignity, and the individual front seats had reclining backrests. Engine power was raised 5.2kW (7bhp) by means of a progressive double-choke Weber carburettor and new camshaft with 50deg of overlap instead of 34deg. Brake servo, and wide radial-ply Pirelli Cinturato or Goodyear G800 tyres completed a specification that could happily have kept the GT appellation. The back axle radius arms, deleted when the GT was dropped, could be specially requested.

INTRODUCTION 2000 November 1966, production until June 1970; 2000E January 1967, production to June 1970; estate 1966-1968.
BODY saloon 4-door, estate 5-door, 5-seats; weight 4-door 992kg (2187lb), estate 1050kg (2314.8lb).
ENGINE 3006E; 4-cylinders, 60deg V; 93.7mm x 72.4mm, 1996cc; comp 8.9:1; 65.6kW (88bhp) @ 4750rpm; 32.9kW (44.1bhp)/l; 158Nm (116.5lbft) @ 3600rpm. After 1967 72.3kW (97bhp) @ 5000rpm; 36.2kW (48.6bhp)/l; 153Nm (113lbft) @ 3000rpm.
ENGINE STRUCTURE pushrod overhead valve, gear-driven camshaft; cast iron cylinder head and block; Zenith 36 IV downdraught, 2000E compound Weber 32 DIFA; centrifugal and vacuum ignition; AC mechanical fuel pump; 3-bearing crankshaft.

TRANSMISSION rear wheel drive; Borg & Beck 20.3cm (8in) clutch; 4-speed synchromesh gearbox; Hardy Spicer open prop shaft; hypoid bevel final drive 3.78:1; automatic optional.
CHASSIS steel monocoque structure; ifs by MacPherson struts and anti roll bar; live rear axle with half-elliptic springs, (stiffer on estate) Armstrong telescopic dampers; Girling hydraulic 24.4cm (9.6in) front discs 22.9cm (9in) rear drum brakes; vacuum servo; Burman recirculating ball steering; 45.5l (10 gal) fuel tank; 5.60-13, 2000E 165-13, 4.5J rims, estate 6.00-13.

BELOW **Ford dealers Eric Jackson (left) and Ken Chambers challenged Union Castle from Capetown to Southampton in 1967. They posed with Captain Hart of the RMS Windsor Castle after Ford Public Affairs chief Walter Hayes conceded a draw because the Corsair 2000E had been airlifted over African bureaucracy. West Sussex police complained about the dirty number plate.**

DIMENSIONS wheelbase 256.5cm (101in); track 127cm (50in) front, 126cm (49.6in) rear; length 449cm (176.8in); width 161cm (63.4in); height 145cm (57.1in), estate 146cm (57.5in); ground clearance 17cm (6.7in); turning circle 10.21m (33.5ft).
EQUIPMENT radio standard, cut pile carpet, crushable facia coaming, carpeted boot.
PERFORMANCE maximum speed 146.1kph (91mph) *The Autocar* (estate); 28.3kph (17.6mph) @ 1000rpm; 0-96kph (60mph) 14.0sec; 15.1kg/kW (11.3kg/bhp); fuel consumption 11.4l/100km (24.8mpg).
PRICE £650, PT £135 8s 4d, £785 8s 4d (£785.42); estate total £1112.
PRODUCTION 331,095 all Corsair; 171,144 all V4s; 2000E 31,566; estate car 940.

1966
Zephyr 4 Mark IV 3010E V4 saloon and Estate Car

Bigger than ever, the last Zephyr and Zodiac were bold. They had independent rear suspension, a long bonnet, short tail, and used compact Vee engines, shifting the occupants rearwards instead of giving them more legroom. Shortening the bonnet was bad for a car's proportions, according to the stylists, so the spare wheel was put right at the front, ahead of the radiator, instead of in the boot. The result was radical; distinctive rather than memorable. Disc brakes with a servo optional on fours, standard on sixes, optional floor shift, overdrive, or automatic transmissions and the availability of power steering provided a specification that with fuel injection and catalytic converter could have been written in the 1990s. Alas for the shortcomings. Independent rear suspension had been contentious in Europe for

years and no car with pretensions could afford to be without it, but Ford adopted a system with less than perfect geometry. Hinged obliquely it had a short link, designed to inhibit rear wheel steer, but not sufficiently so. There was still no consensus on independent rear suspension beyond suspicion of swing axles, like those on

VWs or Renaults, and doubt about Mercedes-Benz's low-pivot. Yet even on the press launch of the Mark IV Zephyr in North Africa, it began to look as though Ford had not got its variant quite right.

INTRODUCTION Dec 1965, production until Dec 1971.
BODY saloon 4-door, estate 5-door, 5-seats; weight 4-door 1250kg (2755.75lb).
ENGINE 3006E; 4-cylinders, 60deg V; 93.7mm x 72.4mm, 1996cc; comp 8.9:1; 61.5kW (82.5bhp) @ 4750rpm; 30.8kW (41.3bhp)/l; 158Nm (116.5lbft) @ 3600rpm.
ENGINE STRUCTURE 3010E pushrod overhead valve, gear-driven camshaft; cast iron cylinder head and block; Zenith 36 IVT downdraught; centrifugal and vacuum ignition; AC mechanical fuel pump; automatic choke; 5-bearing crankshaft.
TRANSMISSION rear wheel drive; hydraulic sdp clutch; 4-speed synchromesh gearbox; optional Laycock de Normanville overdrive or 3-speed automatic; final drive 4.4:1.
CHASSIS steel monocoque structure; independent front suspension McPherson struts with co-axial coil springs and dampers and anti roll bar; rear independent semi-trailing arms, coil springs telescopic dampers; hydraulic servo optional, Girling 24.4cm (9.6in) disc brakes, vacuum servo; recirculating ball steering; PAS optional; 68.2l (15 gal) fuel tank; 6.40-13 tyres.
DIMENSIONS wheelbase 292cm (115in); track 145cm (57.1in)front, 147cm (57.9in) rear; length 470cm (185in); width 181cm (71.3in); height 148cm (58.3in); ground clearance 15cm (5.9in); turning circle 11.58m (38ft).
EQUIPMENT safety belts optional; pvc seats, headlining; loop-pile carpet; heater standard.
PERFORMANCE maximum speed 140kph (87.2mph); 31.1kph (19.4mph) @ 1000rpm; 0-96kph (60mph) 17.7sec; 20.3kg/kW (15.1kg/bhp); fuel consumption 12 l/100km (23.5mpg).
PRICE £933 at launch.
PRODUCTION 41,386.

1966
Zephyr 6 Mark IV 3008E V6 saloon and Estate Car

The narrow-angle Vee engines were settling down and the greater smoothness of a 6-cylinder against a 4-cylinder provided quite refined motoring even if never in the same league as a straight six. The articulated fixed length drive shafts and alloy wishbones at the back designed under Harley Copp the new director of engineering, were expected to control camber and toe-in both during cornering and with changes in passenger loads. It was quite successful when the car was heavily laden, the long heavy spare wheel-encumbered front ploughing on, understeering gently but consistently. Unladen the Zephyr oversteered, sometimes alarmingly, as the rear wheels assumed steep angles and the tyre treads broadly lost contact with the road. In 1967 the suspension

camber angles were changed to try and reduce the tendency but not wholly successfully. The Zephyr rode bumps badly, transmitting road noise through the body, and defeating the refinement achieved by the big engine. As tyres became wider, power steering became almost essential. Without it, at parking speeds the steering was unpleasantly heavy so non power-steered cars were given six turns lock to lock to compensate. Following the 1967 facelift, in which the front was enhanced and Hydrosteer PAS included as standard, things improved. While production trends for other manufacturers increased, the Mark IV Zephyr's decline continued. In its first year 50,593 were made but by 1971 production had shrunk by two-thirds.

PRODUCTION 1966-1971.
BODY saloon; 4-doors, 5-seats; weight 1300kg (2866lb), estate 1385kg (3053.3lb).
ENGINE 6-cylinders, 60deg V; 93.66mm x 60.35mm, 2495cc; compr 9.1:1; 83.5kW (112bhp) @ 4750rpm; 33.5kW (44.9bhp)/l; 186Nm (137.5lbft) @ 2750rpm.
ENGINE STRUCTURE 3006E pushrod overhead valve, gear-driven camshaft; cast iron cylinder head and block; Zenith 38 IVT downdraught; centrifugal and vacuum ignition; AC mechanical fuel pump; automatic choke; 4-bearing crankshaft.
TRANSMISSION rwd; hydraulic sdp diaphragm spring clutch; 4-speed synchromesh gearbox; optional Laycock de Normanville overdrive or 3-speed automatic Ford C4 or Borg Warner 35; final drive 3.9:1.
CHASSIS steel monocoque structure; ifs by McPherson struts with co-axial coil springs and dampers and anti roll bar; rear independent semi-trailing arms, coil springs, telescopic dampers; Girling 24.4cm (9.6in) disc brakes, vacuum servo; recirculating ball steering; PAS optional, standard after 1967; 68.2l (15 gal) fuel tank; 6.70-13 tyres; 14in after 1967.
DIMENSIONS wheelbase 292cm (115in); track 145cm (57.1in) front, 147cm (57.9in) rear; length 470cm (185in); width 181cm (71.3in); height 148cm (58.3in); ground clearance 15cm (5.9in); turning circle 11.9m (39ft).
EQUIPMENT heated rear window optional.
PERFORMANCE maximum speed 154.1kph (96mph) *The Autocar*; 31.1kph (19.4mph) @ 1000rpm; 0-96kph (60mph) 14.6sec; 15.6kg/kW (11.6kg/bhp), estate 16.6kg/kW (12.4kg/bhp); fuel consumption 14.6l/100km (19.4mpg).
PRICE £832, PT £173, total £1005
PRODUCTION 61,031.

1966
Zodiac Mark IV 3012E saloon, estate and Executive

Quad headlights, broad dummy grille bars, turbine-style wheel trims, reclining seats, power steering and a level of furnishing usually found only in American cars, kept the Zodiac among the luxury car leaders. Among the standard fittings were a headlamp flasher, reversing lights, cigar lighter, coat hooks and a vanity mirror behind the passenger side sun visor. There were 3-point safety harnesses with locking inertia reels and the rather large steering wheel was adjustable for height, although not by much more than an inch. The instrument array looked like an aircraft flight deck; the seats were so big that there were complaints about sliding about on corners. Aeroflow, once described as a primitive system of air conditioning, was so effective that road testers gleefully reported there was no need to open windows. Cars were becoming easier to maintain. A Zodiac II of the 1950s demanded application of a grease gun every 1000 miles to 11 places, as well as engine oil and gearbox oil changes. The Mark IV needed fresh gearbox oil at 3000 miles then never again, the engine oil intervals stretched to 6000 miles, brakes and clutch were expected to adjust themselves for wear with only annual inspections. Modern oils and sealed for life bushes had removed many chores. ED Abbott conversions, with stylish vinyl roof concealing the joins, were claimed to be the biggest estate cars made in Britain at the time. Executives had walnut trim on the expansive facia and door cappings.

PRODUCTION 1966-1971.
BODY saloon; 4-doors, 5-seats; weight 1333kg (2938.7lb), estate 1442kg (3179lb).
ENGINE 6-cylinders, 60deg V; 93.66mm x 72.41mm, 2994cc; compr 8.9:1; 95.5kW (128bhp) @ 4600rpm; 31.9kW (42.8bhp)/l; 239Nm (176lbft) @ 3000rpm.
ENGINE STRUCTURE 3012E pushrod overhead valve, gear-driven camshaft; cast iron cylinder head and block; Weber 40 DFA twin choke downdraught; centrifugal and vacuum ignition; AC mechanical fuel pump; automatic choke; 4-bearing crankshaft.
TRANSMISSION rear wheel drive; hydraulic sdp diaphragm spring clutch; 4-speed synchromesh gearbox; optional Laycock de Normanville overdrive or 3-speed automatic Ford C4 or Borg Warner 35; final drive 3.7:1.
CHASSIS steel monocoque structure; independent front suspension McPherson struts with co-axial coil springs and dampers and anti roll bar; rear independent semi-trailing arms, coil springs telescopic dampers; Girling disc brakes 24.4cm (9.6in) front 25.2cm (9.9in) rear, vacuum servo; recirculating ball steering; PAS standard; 68.2l (15 gal) fuel tank; 6.70-13 tyres; 14in after 1967.
DIMENSIONS wheelbase 292cm (115in); track 145cm (57.1in) front, 147cm (57.9in) rear; length 472cm (185.8in); width 181cm (71.3in); height 148cm (58.3in); ground clearance 15cm (5.9in); turning circle 11.9m (39ft).
EQUIPMENT heated rear window, cut pile carpet, upholstery cirrus vinyl, leather optional, steering column lock optional, 2 speed wipers.
PERFORMANCE maximum speed 164.5kph (102.5mph) *The Motor*; 19.7mph (31.6kph) @ 1000rpm; 0-60mph (96kph) 11.0sec; 14kg/kW (10.4kg/bhp), estate 15.1kg/kW (11.3kg/bhp); fuel consumption 18.4mpg (15.4l/100km).
PRICE £1010, PT £218 4s 0d, total £1228 4s 0d (£1228.20p).
PRODUCTION 48,846 (including Executive).

1966
GT40 Le Mans winner Mark II works cars

INTRODUCTION February 1966.
BODY coupe; 2-doors, 2-seats; weight 1136.3kg (2505lb), startline 1206.6kg (2660lb).
ENGINE 8-cylinders, 90deg V; mid; 107.5mm x 96.1mm, 6997cc; compr 10.5:1; 361.7kW (485bhp) @ 6200rpm; 69.3bhp (51.7kW)/l; 644Nm (475lbft) @ 5000rpm.
ENGINE STRUCTURE pushrod ohv; aluminium cylinder head, cast iron block; Holley 4-choke carburettor; 5-bearing crankshaft, dry-sump.
TRANSMISSION rear wheel drive; Long 2 dry plate clutch; 4-speed Ford T-44 synchromesh gearbox in unit with transaxle.
CHASSIS semi-monocoque hull, 23swg sheet steel (.024in) with square tube stiffening, grp body panels reinforced with carbon filament; independent front suspension by double wishbones, coil springs, telescopic dampers, anti roll bar; independent rear suspension by double trailing arms, transverse top link and lower wishbone, coil springs, telescopic dampers, anti-roll bar; hydraulic servo disc brakes, ventilated discs, 29.2cm (11.5in); rack and pinion steering; 159l (35 gal) door sill fuel tanks; cast magnesium wheels, 8.00-15 front, 9.50-15 rear.
DIMENSIONS wheelbase 241.3cm (95in); track 144.8cm (57in) front, 142.3cm (56in) rear; length 414cm (163in); width 177.8cm (70in); height 102.8cm (40.5in); ground clearance 10cm (3.94in).
EQUIPMENT cockpit and driver's seat ventilation by air-duct front high-pressure point under nose
PERFORMANCE maximum speed timed on Mulsanne 301kph (187.5mph), design estimated 337kph (210mph), still air maximum of early GT40 likely 316.2kph (197mph); 3.1kg/kW (2.3kg/bhp).
PRODUCTION about 10.

No sooner was 1965 out of the way then work began on GT40 Mark 11. Winning the following year was now the aim. By midnight the Ford effort had been in ruins; all that was achieved was a lap record and the fastest speed on Mulsanne. Development continued with the 7 litre Galaxie V8 used in American saloon car racing. It was not a sophisticated engine, a pushrod with one 4-choke carburettor and only gave around 52.2kW (70bhp) per litre against a top flight competitor's 74.6kW (100bhp) per litre. It was heavy, at 272.2kg (600lb) despite aluminium cylinder heads, but reaching peak power at a leisurely 6200rpm, made it extremely reliable, with massive torque

that only needed four gears. Kar Kraft of Detroit developed a strong transaxle from the production Galaxie and the result was race-ready almost at once. A big, tough, enormously competent car, it competed at the Daytona 24 Hours in February 1966, led almost all the way and took the first three places. It won again at Sebring, came second at Spa, then set new speed records at Le Mans, finishing first, second and third. Critics complained that Ford overwhelmed the opposition, yet Ferrari had around the same number of cars at the start, and all those in with a chance were out by dawn on the second day.

ABOVE **Chris Amon waves from the winning car he shared with Bruce McLaren.**

1966
GT40 Mark III road car

The GT40 could not go on competing as a prototype; it had to graduate to production with 50 cars laid down in order to qualify. However those produced were by no means all the same, Marks proliferated and many cars that started as Mark Is were converted to Mark IIs, some that began as road cars were converted for racing and many were substantially altered. Only a car-by-car study could provide precise numbers and detailed specifications. A total of 31 Mark I road cars were built, but many raced, including the first prototype, chassis GT40/P1013, that competed (and finished) in virtually road-going condition with some 50,000miles (approx 80,000kms) on

the clock in Portugal's Villa Real 6-hours race. The Mark III was the definitive road-going GT40. Twenty were planned, seven were made, of which 4 were kept by Ford. The engine was detuned, more effective silencers installed, the springing was made more agreeable, the cockpit properly trimmed and although there was no real luggage space, a box in the engine compartment could be pressed into service (although not for anything likely to be affected by heat). The result was surprisingly tractable. Ford ran SNO 250D on the press fleet and it was possible to use it on the road without causing too much consternation.

INTRODUCTION 1966.
BODY coupe; 2-doors, 2-seats; weight 998kg (2200lb).
ENGINE 8-cylinders, 90deg V; mid; 101.6mm x 72.9mm, 4736cc; compr 10.5:1; 228.2kW (306bhp) @ 6000rpm; 48.2kW (64.6bhp)/l; 446Nm (329lbft) @ 4200rpm.
ENGINE STRUCTURE pushrod ohv; aluminium cylinder head, cast iron block; Holley 4-choke carburettor; 5-bearing crankshaft, wet-sump.
TRANSMISSION rear wheel drive; Borg & Beck 2 dry plate clutch; 5-speed ZF 5DS-25 synchromesh gearbox in unit with transaxle.
CHASSIS semi-monocoque hull structure, 23swg sheet steel (.024in) with square tube stiffening, grp body panels with carbon filament reinforcement; independent front suspension by double wishbones, coil springs, telescopic dampers, anti roll bar; independent rear suspension by double trailing arms, transverse top link and lower wishbone, coil springs, telescopic dampers, anti-roll bar; hydraulic servo disc brakes, ventilated discs, 29.2cm (11.5in) front, 28.5cm (11.2in) rear; rack and pinion steering; 125.5l (27.6 gal) door sill fuel tanks; Borrani wire or cast magnesium wheels, 6.50-15 front, 8.00-15 rear.
DIMENSIONS wheelbase 242.6cm (95.5in); track front and rear 135.3cm (53.25in); length 429.3cm (169in); width 177.8cm (70in); height 104.1cm (41in); ground clearance 10cm (3.94in).
EQUIPMENT cockpit and driver's seat ventilation by air-duct front high-pressure point under nose.
PERFORMANCE maximum speed by design 247kph (154mph), on test approx 257kph (160mph) *The Motor*; 1st 93.1kph (58mph), 2nd 144.5kph (90mph), 3rd 203.9kph (127mph), 4th 228kph (142mph); 0-96kph (60mph) 5.3sec; 0-160.5kph (100mph) 11.8sec; 4.4kg/kW (3.3kg/bhp).
PRODUCTION 7 plus 7 post-production cars, 5 built by Alan Mann Racing.

1966
Cortina Mark II 1300, 1500

Determination to sustain the Cortina's momentum brought a facelift in 1964. The 1966 launch of the Mark II was within the four year model cycle Ford had imposed on itself following, by a month, production of the millionth Mark I in September. Mark II was essentially the same platform with a new superstructure, and although the 249cm (98in) wheelbase and 426.7cm (168in) overall length were unchanged, the new body was a useful 61mm (2.4in) wider. The engine bay presswork, the suspension pick-up points, the steelwork round the transmission and the suspension and steering were much the same as before. Yet what a change the new body made. The flat-sided origami-style Cortina was now quite voluptuous, with a full-width grille incorporating the headlights, and now that the opposition was enthusiastically embracing better heating and fresh-air ventilation systems, Ford enhanced Aeroflow with 25 per cent more through-put. Softer springing and better handling enhanced the car's appeal, while the old 1198cc 3-bearing engine was retained only for some export markets. It was replaced by a 5-bearing 1300, really a short-stroke adaptation of the Mark 1's 1500, with a short block but the same head. Automatic transmission was an option but it made the 1300 so feeble it was not popular. Servicing was simplified, greasing points eliminated and engine servicing intervals were 5,000 miles. Negative earth electrics were adopted but the battery for UK market cars was small.

INTRODUCTION October 1966, produced to 1970 (Kent engine from 1967).
BODY saloon; 2-doors, 4-doors 4-seats; estate car 5-door from February 1967; weight from 861kg (1898lb).
ENGINE (1300) 4-cylinders, in-line; 80.96mm x 62.99mm, 1298cc; compr 9.0:1; 39.9kW (53.5bhp) @ 5000rpm; 30.7kW (41.2bhp)/l; 96Nm (71lbft) @ 2500rpm. 1500: 80.96 x 72.8; 1498cc; 8.3:1; 45.5kW (61bhp) @ 4700rpm; 30.4kW (40.7bhp)/l; 120Nm (88.5lbft) @ 2500rpm.
ENGINE STRUCTURE pushrod ohv; chain-driven camshaft; cast iron cyl head and block; Ford GPD downdraught carburettor; centrifugal and vacuum ign; mechanical fuel pump; 5-bearing crank.

TRANSMISSION rear wheel drive; diaphragm spring cable operated clutch; 4-speed synchromesh gearbox; 3-speed automatic optional; hypoid bevel final drive 4.125:1 (1300) 3.89:1 (1500).
CHASSIS steel monocoque; ifs by MacPherson struts and anti roll bar; live rear axle with half-elliptic springs, telescopic dampers, (lever arm on estate cars' rear); Girling hydraulic 22.9cm (9in) disc brakes at front, 20.3cm (8in) rear drums; Burman recirculating ball steering; 45.5l (10 gal) tank; 5.20-13 or 6.00-13 cross-ply, 4in or 4.5in rims.
DIMENSIONS wheelbase 249cm (98in); track front 133cm (52.5in) rear 130cm (51in); length 426.7cm (168in); width 165cm (64.9in); height 144cm (56.5in); ground clearance 13.3cm (5.25in); turning circle 8.53m (28ft).

EQUIPMENT fresh air heater, manual plunger screenwasher, knitweave vinyl upholstery, rubber mat floor covering.
PERFORMANCE maximum speed 129.7kph (80.8mph) (1300) *The Motor*; 25.4kph (15.8mph) @ 1000rpm; 0-96kph (60mph) 20.3sec; 21.6kg/kW (16.1kg/bhp); fuel consumption 27.9mpg (10.1l/100km).
PRICE 1300 4-door £544, £123 13s 4d PT, £668 13s 4d (£668.67p); 1500 Super £755.
PRODUCTION all Mark IIs 1,027,869; standard saloon 14,324 2-door, 4,914 4-door; de luxe 251,537 2-door, 347,462 4-door.

1966
Cortina GT Mark II

The GT designation, now well established, was launched with the Mark II Cortina. Four extra instruments over and above the standard facia layout were added, as well as a stiffer, lower suspension and, from the beginning of 1967, revised gear ratios. Early cars carried over the old Cortina gear ratios, which, even with second held to valve bounce, provided a sluggish response in third. Second was too high or third too low, depending how you looked at it, and while it mattered little on other models, it was an irritant on the GT. The ratios had been amended for the 1965 Corsair V4 and the Lotus Cortina within the same gearbox casing, so they were quickly applied to the Mark II GT to go with the revised sporty floor gearshift, soon made standard throughout the range. In the autumn of 1967 the entire Mark II array was re-equipped with the Kent engine, increasing the GT's power by a useful 7.5kW (10bhp) and enhancing performance to close on 160.5kph (100mph) for the saloon and not much less for the estate car, introduced as a somewhat surprising stable-mate. Sporty estate cars like the Lancia High Performance Estate (HPE), Reliant Scimitar GTE, and Volvo 1800ES still lay in the future when Ford applied the GT label to an estate car. "Expensive for a Cortina," said *Autocar*, "but not for what it offers."

INTRODUCTION October 1966, produced until 1970 (Kent engine from 1967).

BODY saloon; 2-doors, 4-doors 4-seats; estate car 5-door from February 1967; weight 2-door 908kg (2002lb).

ENGINE (1300) 4-cylinders, in-line; 80.96mm x 72.8mm, 1498cc; compr 9.0:1; 58.2kW (78bhp) @ 5200rpm; 38.8kW (52.1bhp)/l; 131.5Nm (97lbft) @ 2500rpm. Kent engine stroke 77.62mm; 1599cc, 65.6kW (88bhp) @ 5200rpm; 41kW (55bhp)/l; 130Nm (96lbft) @ 3600rpm.

ENGINE STRUCTURE pushrod ohv; chain-driven camshaft; cast iron cylinder head and block; Weber 28/36. DCD1 (32 DFM Kent) dual choke carburettor; centrifugal and vacuum ignition; mechanical fuel pump; 5-bearing crankshaft.

TRANSMISSION rear wheel drive; diaphragm spring cable-operated clutch; 4-speed synchromesh gearbox; hypoid bevel final drive 3.89:1.

CHASSIS steel monocoque structure; ifs by MacPherson struts and anti roll bar; live rear axle with half-elliptic springs, radius arms until 1968, telescopic dampers, (lever arm on estate cars' rear); Girling hydraulic 24.4cm (9.62in) disc brakes at front, 22.9cm (9in) rear drums; Burman recirculating ball steering; 45.5l (10 gal) fuel tank; 5.60-13 cross-ply or 165-13 radial-ply, 4in or 4.5in rims.

DIMENSIONS wheelbase 249cm (98in); track front 133cm (52.5in), rear 130cm (51in); length 426.7cm (168in), estate car 431.8cm (170in); width 165cm (64.9in); height 144cm (56.5in); ground clearance 13.3cm (5.25in); turning circle 8.53m (28ft).

EQUIPMENT fresh air heater, manual screenwasher, reclining front seats £25.

PERFORMANCE maximum (estate) 154.1kph (96mph) *Autocar*; 28.1kph (17.5mph) @ 1000rpm; 0-96kph (60mph) 13.0sec; 15.6kg/kW (11.6kg/bhp); 10.9l/100km (26mpg).

PRICE September 1967 GT 2-door £704, PT £161 6s 8d, total £865 6s 8d (£865.33). Estate 1968 total £1084 3s 11d (£1084.20).

PRODUCTION GT 2-door 62,592, 4-door 54,538.

1967
Zodiac Mark IV Executive 3022E

Buyers regarding Zodiacs as aspirational may have been in decline, yet the model remained a status symbol despite the lugubrious handling, partly a result of the 57 per cent forward weight bias. Announced at the 1966 Motor Show for the 1967 model year, the Executive was mechanically identical to the Zodiac, with the exception of the transmission and steering. The C4 Ford 3-speed automatic provided a certain amount of manual over-ride in L (holding first or second for swift acceleration), D1 (for normal driving), and D2 (smoother running in traffic, better traction on snow and ice, engaging only two and three speeds). The Borg Warner fitted later was smoother. Power steering reduced the effort at parking speeds, and the opportunity was taken to raise the ratio to 18.4:1, making for less wheel-twirling. The Executive brought back the sunroof, a popular feature of British cars of the 1930s and 1940s until discredited by rust and leaks. Ford promised it had been thoroughly tested at MIRA's dust tunnel in Arctic and tropical weather; it was wound into position by a foldaway handle. Crushed hide or nylon cloth could be specified for the upholstery, the facia was finished in burr walnut, and the radio had an additional speaker under the rear parcels shelf with a novel control for adjusting the front to rear balance.

INTRODUCTION October 1966, produced until 1971.
BODY saloon; 4-doors, 5-seats; weight 1333kg (2938.7lb).
ENGINE 6-cylinders, 60deg V; 93.66mm x 72.41mm, 2994cc; compr 8.9:1; 95.5kW (128bhp) @ 4600rpm; 31.9kW (42.8bhp)/l; 239Nm (176lbft) @ 3000rpm.
ENGINE STRUCTURE 3012E pushrod overhead valve, gear-driven camshaft; cast iron cylinder head and block; Weber 40 DFA twin choke downdraught; centrifugal and vacuum ignition; AC mechanical fuel pump; automatic choke; 4-bearing crankshaft.
TRANSMISSION rear wheel drive; 3-speed automatic Ford C4, later Borg Warner 35; 4-speed manual gearbox to special order; overdrive optional; final drive 3.7:1.
CHASSIS steel monocoque structure; independent front suspension McPherson struts with co-axial coil springs and dampers and anti roll bar; rear independent semi-trailing arms, coil springs telescopic dampers; Girling disc brakes 24.4cm (9.6in) front 25.6cm (9.9in) rear, vacuum servo; Hydrosteer PAS; 68.2l (15 gal) fuel tank; 6.70-14in. radial ply tyres.
DIMENSIONS wheelbase 292cm (115in); track 145cm (57.1in) front, 147cm (57.9in) rear; length 472cm (185.8in); width 181cm (71.3in); height 148cm (58.3in); ground clearance 15cm (5.9in); turning circle 11.9m (39 ft).
EQUIPMENT heated rear window, cut pile carpet, leather optional, steering column lock optional, two speed wipers, sunroof.
PERFORMANCE maximum speed 153.4kph (95.4mph) *The Motor*; 32.1kph (20mph) @ 1000rpm; 0-96kph (60mph) 13.4sec; 14kg/kW (10.4kg/bhp); fuel consumption 15.7l/100km (18mpg).
PRICE 1970 £1414, PT £432 1s 2d, total £1846 1s 2d (£1846.6p).
PRODUCTION 48,846 (all Zodiac).

1967
GT40 Mark IV and J-car

By 1967 developments and redesigns of the GT40 were proliferating along with the outside companies involved making them. The cars were bigger and faster, and while known as J-car and Mark IV in their various guises, the common ingredients were an increase in engine size to 7.0-litre and a hull made of expanded aluminium honeycomb. By the 1967 Le Mans race there were seven 7.0-litre cars, Carroll Shelby and Holman & Moody with 2 Mark IVs and an improved Mark 2 apiece; Ford France a Mark 2. There were two 5.7-litre cars made by John Wyer at Slough and now called Mirages, and three more GT40s running in Group 2 Sports, making 12 cars in all. Dan Gurney and AJ Foyt not only won at record speed, exceeding 5000km (3107miles) for the first time, but also won the Index of Thermal Efficiency, a distinction highly regarded in France, and usually won by small fuel efficient French cars. The Mirages proved unreliable and raced with 4.7-litre engines, but one of them won outright for the following two years, the first time Le Mans had ever been won by the same car twice. This sustained the competitive life of the design until the end of the decade in the face of determined opposition by Porsche. Ferrari's domination of Le Mans, which it had won eight times, including an unbroken run from 1960–1965, was over.

INTRODUCTION 1967.

BODY coupe; 2-doors, 2-seats; 839kg (1850lb) J, 1000kg (2205lb) Mk IV.

ENGINE 8-cylinders, 90deg V; mid; 107.5mm x 96.1mm, 6997cc; compr 10.5:1; 372.9kW (500bhp) @ 5000rpm; 53.3kW/l (71.5bhp/l); 637Nm (470lbft) @ 5000rpm.

ENGINE STRUCTURE pushrod ohv; aluminium cylinder head, cast iron block; two Holley 4-choke carburettors; 5-bearing crankshaft, dry-sump.

TRANSMISSION rwd; Long 2 dry plate clutch; Ford T-44 4-speed manual synchromesh gearbox in unit with transaxle.

CHASSIS semi-monocoque hull structure, with expanded aluminium honeycomb panels 13mm (.5in) and 25mm (1in) thick with square tube stiffening, grp body panels with carbon filament reinforced; ifs by double wishbones, coil springs, telescopic dampers, anti roll bar; irs by double trailing arms, transverse top link and lower wishbone, coil springs, telescopic dampers, anti-roll bar; hydraulic servo disc brakes, ventilated discs, 292mm (11.5in) front and rear; rack and pinion steering; 154.6l (34 gal) door sill fuel tanks; cast magnesium wheels, 8.00-15 front, 12.00-15 rear.

DIMENSIONS wheelbase 241.3cm (95in); track 140cm (55in); length 416.6cm (164in) J, 434.3cm (171cm) Mk IV; width 175.3cm (69in) J, 179cm (70.5in) Mk IV; height 97.8cm (38.5in); ground clearance 10cm (3.94in).

PERFORMANCE maximum 338.7kph (211mph); 2.2kg/kW (2.2kg/bhp) J-car, 2.7kg/kW (2kg/bhp) Mk IV.

PRODUCTION 12 J-cars, 3 Mirages.

LEFT **Gurney and Foyt led for 23 of the 24 hours.**

Cortina Mark II 1300 and 1500 Kent engine

The entire rationale of Ford production engineering was to use as many components as many times as possible. Introduced to improve the Mark II Cortina's performance by widening the spread of torque, the Kent engine of 1967 went on to become one of the best-performing Ford engines. For the next 16 years, besides several marks of Cortina, it saw service in Fiestas, Escorts, and Capris. Its basis was a singularly robust 5-bearing bottom end, and a cylinder block, whose bore centres already matched the Ford production machinery. Its chief novelty lay in a new cylinder head of crossflow pattern; that is with the inlet ports on one side and the exhaust on the other. It was better known as the Crossflow than the Kent. The 1.3 cylinder head was completely flat and the 1.6 had only small recesses. The combustion chambers were entirely contained within the pistons, and the result was a free-revving and almost unburstable engine, which not only became the basis of Ford's mainstream production cars, but was also a resounding success in motor sport. It was used for Formula Ford single seaters and its crankcase and crankshaft were the building blocks for the BDA Ford Cosworths, giving 85.8kW (115bhp) in road tune and anything up to 212.5kW (285bhp) @ 9000rpm for racing.

INTRODUCTION September 1967, produced until 1970.
BODY saloon; 2-doors, 4-doors 4-seats; estate car 5-door; weight 2-door 1600 875kg (1929lb).
ENGINE (1300) 4-cylinders, in-line; 80.98mm x 62.99mm, 1298cc; compr 9.0:1; 43.3kw (58bhp) @ 5000rpm; 33.3kW (44.7bhp)/l; 97Nm (71.5lbft) @ 2500rpm. 1600 engine: stroke 77.62mm; 1599cc; 53kW (71bhp) @ 5200rpm; 33.1kW (44.4bhp)/l; 124Nm (91.5lbft) @ 2500rpm.
ENGINE STRUCTURE pushrod ohv; chain-driven camshaft; cast iron cylinder head and block; Ford GPD downdraught carburettor (1600 GT-Weber); centrifugal and vacuum ignition; mechanical fuel pump; 5-bearing crank.

TRANSMISSION rwd; diaphragm spring cable-operated 7.5in (19cm) clutch; 4-speed synchromesh gearbox; hypoid bevel final drive 4.13:1.
CHASSIS steel monocoque; ifs by MacPherson struts and anti roll bar; live rear axle with half-elliptic springs, radius arms until 1968, telescopic dampers, (lever arm on estate cars' rear); Girling hydraulic 24.1cm (9.5in) disc brakes at front, 20.3cm (8in) rear drums; Burman recirculating ball steering; 45.5l (10 gal) fuel tank; 5.20-13 radial-ply, 4in rims (1600 5.60-13).
DIMENSIONS wheelbase 249cm (98in); track front 133cm (52.5in), rear 130cm (51in); length 426.7cm (168in), estate car 431.8cm (170in); width 165cm (64.9in); height 144cm 56.5in); ground clearance 16cm (6.3in); turning circle 8.53m (28ft).

EQUIPMENT fresh air heater, manual plunger screenwasher, pvc upholstery, carpet, reclining front seats £25 extra.
PERFORMANCE maximum 140kph (87.2mph) 1600 The Motor; 25.4kph (15.8mph) @ 1000rpm, 1600 28kph (17.5mph) @ 1000rpm; 0-96kph (60mph) 15.1sec; 16.5kg/kW (12.3kg/bhp) 1600; 10.6l/100km (26.5mpg).
PRICE September 1967 2-door de luxe £589, plus PT £134 19s 7d, total £723 19s 7d (£723.98p); 4-door Super £659, plus PT £151 0s 5d, total £810 0s 5d (£810.02p).
PRODUCTION Super 2-door saloon 18,950, 4-door 116,143; estate cars 90,290.

1967
Comuta

The history of electric cars was littered with might-have-beens. The Comuta showed Ford was aware of electric cars 40 years before the 21st century's environmental alarms, taking the possibilities seriously and accumulating engineering expertise. It was good for public relations, with the ecology lobby lending what weight it had to alternative forms of transport, but just as importantly it demonstrated what technology was up against in contemplating the abandonment of the internal combustion engine.
The Comuta provided a convincing demonstration of the difficulty of storing sufficient energy in a self-

contained small automobile to provide adequate range, adequate performance in adequate comfort and safety. If Ford Motor Company, with its huge resources in money and manpower, could not solve the electric car's problems it began to look as though they were a long way off. Driving the Comuta was simple enough; it had an "ignition" switch, a forwards and reverse lever, two pedals, a handbrake and a steering wheel, and whirred quietly into action, although not for long. It broke no new ground in the storage of electrical power and the technology was not much advanced from that of the milk-float. There were plans to make the electric motors bigger to improve the performance, but it was not speed that was the problem as much as endurance. Ford's assistant managing director Leonard Crossland dismissed any hopes of putting the Comuta into immediate production, although tried to sound optimistic: "We expect electrical cars to be commercially feasible within the next 10 years, although we believe that they will be primarily city centre delivery vans and suburban shopping cars."

INTRODUCTION 1967.
BODY saloon; 2-doors, 2+2-seats; weight 1200lb (544.3kg).
ENGINE 0-cyls, rear; 5bhp (3.7kW) @ 2000rpm; combined 81Nm (60lbft).
ENGINE STRUCTURE 2 aircraft auxiliary series-wound DC electric motors 147mm (5.5in) dia; transversely mounted; thyristor control.
TRANSMISSION rwd; motors drive inwards through pinion to helical gear driving each rear wheel independently; no differential; final drive 4.05:1.
CHASSIS welded steel backbone chassis forming duct for interior heater; grp bodywork; ifs by forward-facing oblique arms on Neidhart rubber suspension bushes; irs by trailing arms on Neidhart rubber suspension bushes; telescopic dampers; hydraulic drum brakes; 4 mid-mounted 12 volt 85 amp hour lead-acid batteries; 4.40 radial ply Goodyear tyres 10in wheels.
DIMENSIONS wheelbase 135.9cm (53.5in); track 111.8cm (44in); length 203.2cm (80in); width 125.7cm (49.5in); height 142.2cm (56in); turning circle 5.49m (18ft).
EQUIPMENT recirculating and fresh air interior heater.
PERFORMANCE max 64.2kph (40mph); 0-48kph (30mph) 12.5-14.0sec; 20.1kph (12.5mph) @ 1000rpm; range 64.4km (40 miles) at 40kph (25mph); restart gradient 1 in 5.
PRODUCTION 2.

ABOVE **Twiggy was enlisted to promote the pioneering electric.**

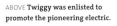

1967
Cortina 1600E

A Cortina aimed at the emerging executive grade, the 1600E (Ford's third E for Executive), was introduced at the 1967 Paris Motor Show. It had the GT engine, Lotus suspension, a luxury interior and wide-rimmed Rostyle wheels, whose chrome brightwork allegedly replicated those on Chairman Len Crossland's wife's car. One-off version of production cars, trimmed by traditional coachbuilders, was a fad of the 1960s, a sort of social commentary enabling pop stars, supermodels and minor royalty to appear democratic without entirely giving up their well-furnished limousines. They had "ordinary" cars, like Minis, painted re-equipped and embellished by their customary coachbuilder. They were not designed to deflect attention, quite the reverse,

and the quality was only skin deep, but the idea caught on. Ford had a classless Cortina suitably trimmed by Hooper as a motor show special. Author Graham Robson described Ford Public Affairs executives Walter Hayes and Harry Calton as the driving forces. The 1600E was the production result, with a tasteful coach line, wood-trimmed facia, wood-capped doors, leather-look pvc and central locker armrest. The carpets were thick, the seats reclined, and it did not much matter that the Kent engine's noise problems had not yet been solved and the driveline was harsh. *Autocar* was critical of the ride and found it, "unexpectedly noisy for its price," but customers then, and collectors later, loved it.

INTRODUCTION 1967, produced until 1970.
BODY saloon; 4-doors (some 2-doors exported); 4-seats; weight 924kg (2037lb).
ENGINE 4-cylinders, in-line; 81.0mm x 77.62mm, 1599cc; compr 9.0:1; 65.6kW (88bhp) @ 5400rpm; 41kW (55bhp)/l; 130Nm (96lbft) @ 3600rpm.
ENGINE STRUCTURE pushrod ohv; chain-driven camshaft; cast iron cylinder head and block; Weber 32DFM compound carburettor; centrifugal and vacuum ignition; AC mechanical fuel pump; 5-bearing crankshaft.
TRANSMISSION rear wheel drive; diaphragm spring cable-operated Borg & Beck 19cm (7.5in) clutch; 4-speed synchromesh gearbox; hypoid bevel final drive 3.91:1.
CHASSIS steel monocoque structure; ifs by MacPherson struts and anti roll bar; live rear axle with half-elliptic springs, upper radius arms, telescopic dampers; Girling hydraulic 24.1cm (9.5in) disc brakes at front, 23cm (9in) rear drums; Burman recirculating ball steering; 45.5l (10 gal) fuel tank; 165-13 radial-ply tyres, 5.5J rims.
DIMENSIONS wheelbase 249cm (98in); track front 133cm (52.5in), rear 130cm (51in); length 426.7cm (168in), estate car 431.8cm (170in); width 165cm (64.9in); height 144cm (56.5in); ground clearance 14cm (5.5in); turning circle 8.53m (28ft).
EQUIPMENT pvc upholstery, carpet, reclining front seats, radio £27.
PERFORMANCE maximum speed 154.4kph (96.2mph) *The Motor*; 27.6kph (17.2mph) @ 1000rpm; 0-96kph (60mph) 11.8sec; 14.1kg/kW (10.5kg/bhp); fuel consumption 12.2l/100km (23.1mpg).
PRICE February 1968 £799, PT £183 2s 1d, total £982 2s 1d (£982.10).
PRODUCTION 57,524, plus 2563 2-door.

1967
Lotus Cortina Mark II, Cortina Twin Cam

Although it lost some of the Mark 1 Lotus-Cortina's glamour, the Mark II's refinement and reliability made it more practical. Production moved to Dagenham, to the barely concealed relief of Ford executives in charge of warranty claims, and the car was made available in a variety of body colours. Traditionalists could still have it in white with a Lotus green stripe, but only to special order. There was even some equivocation over the name, Lotus-Cortina gradually giving way to Cortina-Lotus and finally Cortina Twin Cam, in conformity with its close contemporary the Escort Twin Cam of the following year. The Cortina Lotus's ride height was only about an inch lower than a Cortina GT, there were no aluminium body panels, no lightweight transmission casings (except those homologated for motor sport regulations), no frail A-bracket rear suspension and since the weight had gone up a substantial 144kg (31.5lb) from the Mark I Lotus-Cortina's 775kg (1709lb) it was no longer employed as a front-line competition car by the works team. It did not even have a wood rimmed steering wheel. The fat 5.5in wheels and tyres remained, the grille was painted black, the ride was still firm, the gearshift a delight and the new-found reliability brought it fresh customers. Besides the homologated features it was possible to specify a Special Equipment Lotus engine and an ultra-close ratio gearbox for racing.

INTRODUCTION March 1967, production to 1970.
BODY saloon; 2-doors, 4-seats; weight 919kg (2026lb).
ENGINE 4-cylinders, in-line; 82.57mm x 72.82mm, 1560cc; compr 9.5:1; 81.7kW (109.5bhp) @ 6000rpm; 52.3kW (70.2bhp)/l; 144Nm (106.5lbft) @ 4500rpm.
ENGINE STRUCTURE twin chain-driven overhead camshafts; aluminium cylinder head, cast iron block; Two Weber 40DCOE twin-choke sidedraught carburettors; centrifugal and vacuum ignition; AC mechanical fuel pump; 5-bearing crankshaft.
TRANSMISSION rear wheel drive; Borg & Beck 8in sdp clutch; 4-speed synchromesh gearbox; semi-floating hypoid bevel final drive 3.77:1.
CHASSIS steel monocoque structure; ifs by MacPherson struts and anti roll bar; live rear axle with half-elliptic springs, radius arms, telescopic dampers; Girling hydraulic 24.4cm (9.62in) disc brakes at front, 23cm (9in) rear drums; Burman recirculating ball steering; 45.5l (10 gal) fuel tank; 165 x 13 radial-ply tyres, 5.5J rims.
DIMENSIONS wheelbase 249cm (98in); track front 133cm (52.5in) rear 130cm (51in); length 426.7cm (168in); width 165cm (64.9in); height 141.2cm (55.6in); ground clearance 14cm (5.5in); turning circle 8.53m (28ft).
EQUIPMENT homologated list of 21 high performance racing and rally options, pvc upholstery, carpet.
PERFORMANCE maximum speed 168.7kph (105.1mph) *The Motor*; 28.3kph (17.6mph) @ 1000rpm; 0-96kph (60mph) 9.9sec; 11.2kg/kW (8.4kg/bhp); fuel consumption 12.73l/100km (22.2mpg).
PRICE £869, plus PT £199 2s 11d, total £1068 2s 11d (£1068.15p).
PRODUCTION 4032.

LEFT **Roger Clark and Jim Porter scored a rare victory for the Mark II Lotus Cortina in the Scottish Rally, driving with characteristic vigour that buckled the body shell.**

1967
Lotus-Ford 49

The inspiration behind Ford in Formula 1 lay with Walter Hayes, a former national newspaper editor who became a notable Director of Ford Public Affairs. Hayes was among the first to recognise Colin Chapman's astonishing talent for innovative engineering and was determined that Ford should reap the benefit. Instrumental in achieving the meeting of minds indispensable to a remarkable project was Keith Duckworth, gifted racing engine designer, co-founder of Cosworth

Engineering and already developing racing engines from Ford components. On Ford's behalf Hayes commissioned an engine, the V8 DFV, and Lotus built a car for it. A key feature was that the engine should form a stressed integral part of the Lotus 49 and in a feat unprecedented in modern motor racing it won a world championship race on its first appearance. Two cars were driven in the Dutch Grand Prix at Zandvoort on 4 June 1967, by Graham Hill (left) and Jim Clark. Clark had done little testing, and Hill led for ten laps before retiring with broken timing gear teeth. Even though still unfamiliar with the car, Clark's driving genius brought him through the field from 6th place to take the lead, finishing half a minute ahead of Jack Brabham's Repco Brabham. It was an almost unbelievable achievement and the Lotus-Ford 49 remained a front line competitor until 1970. The Cosworth-Ford DFV, and its derivatives, became the most successful engine in the history of motor racing, providing Ford with a primacy in the sport not seen since Mercedes-Benz and Auto Union in the 1930s.

INTRODUCTION April 1967.
BODY open-wheeled racing, 0-doors, 1-seat; weight 500kg (1102lb) dry, 708.5kg (1562lb) on startline.
ENGINE 8-cylinders, 90deg V; mid; 85.74mm x 64.77mm, 2995cc; compr 11.0:1; 305.7kW (410bhp) @ 9000rpm; 102.1kW (136.9bhp)/l.
ENGINE STRUCTURE 2 gear-driven ohcs per bank, 4 valves per cyl; aluminium cyl head, block, and crankcase; wet cast iron liners; dry sump; Lucas low pressure fuel injection, Lucas transistorised ign, one 10mm Autolite plug per cyl; 5-bearing single plane crank, engine weight 167.8kg (370lb).
TRANSMISSION rwd; Borg & Beck 18.4cm (7.25in) twin plate clutch, Ferodo ceramic lining; ZF 5DS 12 all-synchromesh manual; spiral bevel final drive, various ratios BRD tubular half shafts.
CHASSIS monocoque in 18swg Alclad, front sub-frame, grp body panelling; cantilevered engine; ifs by unequal length wishbones, inboard coil springs and Armstrong telescopic dampers, anti-roll bar; irs by unequal length wishbones, twin radius arms, outboard coil springs, Armstrong telescopic dampers, anti roll bar; Girling hydraulic disc brakes 30.5cm (12in) ventilated later solid; Alford & Adler rack and pinion; 68.2l (15 gal) rubber bag fuel tanks in monocoque side boxes, 45.5l (10 gal) tank under driver's seat; Firestone tyres, Lotus cast magnesium wheels; 305mm (12in) rims front, 406mm (16in) rear.
DIMENSIONS wheelbase 241.3cm (95in); track 152.4cm (60in) front, 154.9cm (61in) rear; length 401.3cm (158in); height 73.7cm (29in).
PERFORMANCE maximum approx 297kph (185mph); 0-96kph (60mph) approx 4sec; 2.3kg/kW (1.7kg/bhp) on startline.
PRODUCTION 9.

1968
Escort 1100 de luxe, 1300 Super

When planning for the Escort began in 1964, the success likely to attend the Cortina could scarcely have been imagined. There had been a lingering suspicion that Ford was technically in arrears; rivals with front wheel drive and fluid suspension had caught the imagination. Yet Dagenham stuck to its guns and in 1968 the Anglia replacement was built in new factories on Merseyside in England and at Saarlouis in Germany. By launch 11,300 Escorts had been made and 500 were being made every day. The Escort was conventional front engine rear-drive, with novelty confined to how it was constructed, body sides aft of the B-post pressed in one piece to ensure precise close-fitting door and window apertures. There was a new administration to build it, Ford of Europe, a joined-up reorganisation of dissimilar factories that up till the middle of 1967 had been providing different cars for different markets. Soon after the launch, following a press appraisal in Morocco that would become the exemplar for similar events over the next 30 years, it was obvious that not only was the Escort, in the well-worn cliché of *Daily Express* motoring correspondent Basil Cardew "... another winner for Britain." It was a winner for Europe. Production began at Halewood on 17 November 1967, and by announcement day, 17 January 1968 11,300 had been made, 2-door saloons only at first, with 500 turned out every day.

INTRODUCTION January 1968, produced until to 1974.
BODY saloon; 2-door, 4-door (from 1969); 4-seats; weight 745kg (1642lb), 754kg (1662lb) 1300 Super.
ENGINE 4-cylinders, in-line; 81mm x 53.3mm, 1098cc; compr 9.0:1; 35.8kW (48bhp) @ 6000rpm; 32.6kW (43.7bhp)/l; 79Nm (58.5lbft) @ 3000rpm. 1300 Super: 80.97 x 62.99; 1298cc; 43.25kW (58bhp) @ 5000rpm; 33.3kW (44.7bhp)/l; 97Nm (71.5lbft) @ 2500rpm.
ENGINE STRUCTURE pushrod ohv; chain-driven camshaft; cast iron cylinder head and block; Ford GDP downdraught carburettor, mechanical fuel pump; 5-bearing crankshaft.
TRANSMISSION rear wheel drive; Borg & beck diaphragm spring clutch, 16.5cm (6.5in) 1100, 19cm (7.5in) 1300; 4-speed synchromesh gearbox; hypoid bevel final drive 4.125:1.

CHASSIS steel monocoque; ifs by MacPherson struts; lower links; telescopic dampers; rear live axle with semi-elliptic leaf springs and telescopic dampers; hydraulic 20.3cm (8in) drum brakes, servo optional; rack and pinion steering; 40.9l (9.0 gal) fuel tank 5.50-12 cross ply tubeless tyres, 4.5in rim and 155-12 radial ply tyres £12.29p extra.
DIMENSIONS wheelbase 240cm (94.5in); track front 124.5cm (49in), rear 127cm (50in); length 397.8cm (156.6in); width 157cm (61.8in); height 134.6cm (53in); ground clearance 16cm (6.3in); turning circle 8.84m (29ft).
EQUIPMENT 1100 floor rubber-covered, 1300 carpet; fresh air-blending heater standard; seat belt anchorages built-in; mandatory seat belts £8; inertia reel belts £13; radio £20; metallic paint £6, brake servo £15.37p.

PERFORMANCE maximum 127kph (79mph) 1100 *The Autocar*; 24.6kph (15.3mph) @ 1000rpm; 0-96kph (60mph) 22sec; 20.8kg/kW (15.5kg/bhp), 17.4kg/kW (13kg/bhp) 1300; 10.2l/100km (27.6mpg).
PRICE totals with tax; de luxe £635 9s 7d (£635.48p); Super £666 4s 2d (£666.21p) 1300 Super £690 15s 10d (£690.79p)
PRODUCTION 2-door 611,305, 4-door 153,660, estate 130,908.

1968
Escort 1300 GT

After eight years and 1,300,000 Anglia 105Es, Ford decided that its small car needed more high-performance variants. They had been recognised as generating showroom traffic and provided high-volume versions with a bit of glamour – a halo effect, marketing called it. Accordingly a 1300GT Escort was planned. The Kent engine was provided with a high-lift camshaft, a special inlet manifold, a compound dual-choke Weber carburettor and the fabricated exhaust manifold already used in the Cortina 1600GT. The GT was the only Escort with two exhaust silencers, one ahead of and one behind the back axle; disc front brakes with vacuum servo were standard. Its close-ratio gearbox was ingeniously accomplished by altering the constant mesh and third gear train by one tooth in each case, raising all the gear ratios by around 10per cent. Changing third from 26/21 to 25/22 almost restored its original value, thus contriving sporting characteristics at minimum cost. Another novel measure was the deletion, carried throughout the Escort range, of the customary front anti-roll bar, which had effectively formed one leg of the lower wishbone in the MacPherson strut. Instead, the Escort had a compression strut angled back to the body shell under the scuttle and a track control arm pivoting on the main front cross-member. Spring rates for the GT were 135lb/in, on the 1100/1300 115lb/in, against the old Anglia's 80lb/in.

INTRODUCTION January 1968, produced until 1974.

BODY saloon; 2-door, 4-seats; weight 778kg (1715lb); 4-door from 1969 weight 835kg (1841lb).

ENGINE 4-cylinders, in-line; 80.97mm x 62.99mm; 1298cc; compr 9.0:1; 53kW (71bhp) @ 6000rpm; 40.8kW (54.7bhp)/l; 95Nm (70lbft) @ 4300rpm.

ENGINE STRUCTURE pushrod ohv; chain-driven camshaft; cast iron cylinder head and block; Weber compound twin choke downdraught carburettor, mechanical fuel pump; 5-bearing crankshaft.

TRANSMISSION rear wheel drive; Borg & Beck diaphragm spring clutch, 19cm (7.5in); 4-speed synchromesh gearbox; hypoid bevel final drive 4.125:1.

CHASSIS steel monocoque structure; independent front suspension by MacPherson struts; lower links; telescopic dampers; rear live axle with semi-elliptic leaf springs and telescopic dampers; Girling hydraulic 21.8cm (8.6in) front disc brakes, rear 20.3mm (8in) drum, vacuum servo standard; rack and pinion steering; 40.9l (9.0 gal) fuel tank; 5.5in rim and 155-12 radial ply tyres.

DIMENSIONS wheelbase 240cm (94.5in); track front 124.5cm (49in), rear 127cm (50in); length 397.8cm (156.6in); width 157cm (61.8in); height 134.6cm (53in); ground clearance 15.2cm (6in); turning circle 8.84m (29ft).

EQUIPMENT fresh air-blending heater and heated rear window standard, inertia reel seat belts £15, centre console, £5, radio £35, fabric seat trim £7.

PERFORMANCE maximum speed 154kph (96kph) *The Autocar*; 24.1kph (15mph) @ 1000rpm; 0-96kph (60mph) 12.4sec; 14.7kg/kW (14.2kg/bhp); fuel consumption 10l/100km (28mpg).

PRICE total with tax 1971 £966.11p.

PRODUCTION 1,082,472 Halewood Escorts.

1968
Escort Twin Cam

Journalists jostled on the Escort press testing in Morocco for the privilege of driving the Twin Cam, of which there was only one or two. It was not only the most exciting Escort; it was one of the most exciting small cars of its time and the ancestor of a dynasty of fast Fords. An important asset of a competitions department was its capacity for intrepid experiment and it was the Ford competitions department that spotted a prototype pushrod Escort on test at Boreham, speculating on what it would be like with a Lotus Cortina unit in the small engine bay. An Escort was 136kg (300lb) lighter than a Cortina so an engine was duly fitted in a strengthened wide wheel-arch type 48 Escort bodyshell. Halewood-made production cars were type 49s, homologated for Group 3 competiton and with taut handling, stiff structure and good balance, they provided the ingredients for a remarkable run of sporting successes. The Twin Cam Escort was faster than an MGB or a Lotus Cortina, a Mini Cooper S or a Sunbeam Rapier. At the new legal British speed limit of 70mph it was tolerably quiet, although above it, the resonant noises of a classic competition engine tended to obtrude. It scarcely mattered. The Twin Cam ushered in a new era of small sports saloons and a six year dynasty of competition Escorts.

INTRODUCTION January 1968, produced until 1971.
BODY saloon; 2-door, 4-seats; weight 785kg (1731lb).
ENGINE 4-cylinders, in-line; 82.55mm x 72.8mm; 1558cc; compr 9.5:1; 81.7kW (109.5bhp) @ 6000rpm; 52.4kW (70.3bhp)/l; 144Nm (106.5lbft) @ 4500rpm.
ENGINE STRUCTURE chain-driven twin overhead camshaft; aluminium cylinder head and cast iron block; two Weber twin choke horizontal 40DCOE carburettors, mechanical fuel pump; 5-bearing crankshaft.
TRANSMISSION rear wheel drive; Borg & Beck diaphragm spring clutch, 20.3cm (8in); 4-speed synchromesh gearbox; hypoid bevel final drive 3.77:1.
CHASSIS steel monocoque; ifs by MacPherson struts; lower links; telescopic dampers, anti-roll bar; rear live axle and half-elliptic leaf springs with telescopic dampers and radius arms; Girling hydraulic 24.4cm (9.6in) front disc brakes, rear 22.9cm (9in) drum, vacuum servo standard; rack and pinion steering; 40.9l (9.0 gal) fuel tank; 5.5in rim and 165-13 radial ply tyres.
DIMENSIONS wheelbase 240cm (94.5in); track 129.5cm (51in) front, 132.1cm (52in) rear; length 397.8cm (156.6in); width 157.5cm (62in); height 138.4cm (54.5in); ground clearance 15.2cm (6in); turning circle 8.84m (29ft).
EQUIPMENT fresh air-blending heater standard, carpeted floor inertia reel seat belts £15, radio £35, wide range of homologated competition extras, rev limiter at 6500rpm.
PERFORMANCE maximum speed 178.7kph (111.3mph) *Motor*; 28.3kph (17.6mph) @ 1000rpm; 0-96kph (60mph) 8.75sec; 9.6kg/kW (7.2kg/bhp); fuel consumption 12l/100km (23.4mpg).
PRICE total with tax and delivery £1123.17p.
PRODUCTION 1,082,472 Halewood Escorts.

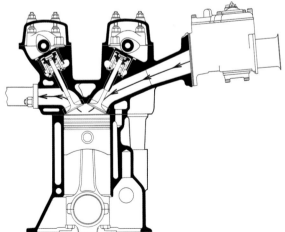

1968
3-litre Group 6 F3L Sports Prototype

Short-lived, shapely, but in the end disastrous, the F3L designed by Len Bailey and built by Alan Mann at Weybridge seemed promising. Essentially a 2-seater Formula 1 car with a Cosworth DFV engine, the prototypes resplendent in red and gold were entered in the BOAC 500, a Brands Hatch 6-hour sports car race, against Porsches, older GT40s, Lola-Chevrolets and Ferraris, and a gas turbine Howmet. Walter Hayes: "Jimmy Clark was going to drive it. Then he rang me up and said 'I can't do it. I know I promised, but Colin (Chapman) says I've got to go to Hockenheim.'"

It led for the first two hours, giving Bruce McLaren a rough ride on the uneven track surface. When Mike Spence took over it broke a half-shaft. By then news of Clark's death had arrived from Hockenheim. Walter Hayes: "It was one of the very bad moments of my life, standing in the pits at Brands and hearing that Jimmy had died." Hayes had persuaded Ford Motor Company to create the Ford-Cosworth DFV whose purpose, besides giving Ford a new image, had been to win the world championship for Jim Clark. The F3L reappeared at the Nürburgring but crashed heavily, badly injuring Chris Irwin. "It was the only car I ever hated in my life," said Hayes. "Alan Mann said he could do it and it would be cheap, and we thought that we needed to replace the GT40 although on reflection we didn't. Sports cars were in decline. I killed that car out of sheer hatred."

INTRODUCTION March 1968.
BODY coupe; 2-doors, 2-seats; weight 671kg (1480lb).
ENGINE 8-cyl, 90deg V; mid; 85.74mm x 64.77mm, 2995cc; compr 11.0:1; 306kW (410bhp) @ 9000rpm; 102kW (137bhp)/l.
ENGINE STRUCTURE two gear-driven ohcs per bank, 4 valves per cylinder; aluminium head, block, and crankcase; wet cast iron liners; dry sump; Lucas low pressure fuel injection, Lucas transistorised ignition, one 10mm Autolite plug per cylinder; 5-bearing single plane crank, engine weight 167.8kg (370lb).
TRANSMISSION rear wheel drive; Borg & Beck 18.4cm (7.25in) twin plate clutch, Ferodo ceramic lining; 5-speed Hewland manual gearbox; spiral bevel final drive, various ratios; BRD tubular half shafts.
CHASSIS monocoque 0.03in (.76mm) malleable aircraft aluminium alloy main longitudinal members, side sponsons containing fuel tanks; deep central backbone; scuttle and toeboard as main front cross member, forming roll cage with the narrow roof; double wishbone welded tube ifs with Rose-type inboard joints, co-axial spring and damper units, provision for 4WD; rear suspension Broadley 4-link with trailing radius arms and adjustable transverse links with co-axial spring and damper units; hydraulic 29.2cm (11.5in) disc brakes; body panelled in light alloy with a frontal area 14sqft (1.3sqm).
DIMENSIONS wheelbase 221cm (87in); length 421.6cm (166in); height 90.2cm (35.5in).
EQUIPMENT aerodynamic downforce 272kg (600lb); internal ducting behind water radiator; NACA air inlets engine and oil rads.
PERFORMANCE maximum speed 321kph (200mph); 2.2kg/kW (1.6kg/bhp).
PRODUCTION 2.

1969
Capri 1300, 1300GT, 1600, 1600GT

The Car You Always Promised Yourself had a profound effect. It was like the original Capri of 1961, neither a sports car in the accepted sense, nor an everyday saloon. It created its own niche as a sort of European Mustang, a clever marketing ploy that enjoyed success. The long bonnet, 2+2 seating and unique style gave it a cachet hardly any car had enjoyed before, and not many would again. The basis was mostly Cortina; only the top half was really new. The first engines were wide-ranging and an important innovation was an array of X, L, XL and R custom pack options, giving customers a wide choice of upholstery and equipment so that they could, in theory at any rate, tailor their Capri to suit themselves. There were dummy air scoops, chrome wheel trims, reclining seats, map-reading light, extra driving lamps and special paint schemes with anti-glare matt black on the bonnet just like real rally cars. The appliqué components could be derided as tasteless but the customers loved them. Launch prototypes were shown with BDA 16-valve twin cam engines (the Escort was first to get it) that never went into regular cars. The Capri's reputation was founded on Ford's mastery of production engineering, relying mostly on components already in production. It would be made in Britain and Germany with getting on for two million sold in 17 years.

INTRODUCTION November 1968, produced until December 1973. **BODY** coupe; 2-doors, 2+2-seats; weight 1300 880kg (1940lb), 1300 900kg (1984lb), 1600 GT 920kg (2028lb). **ENGINE** 1300 4-cylinders, in-line; 80.98mm x 62.99mm, 1298cc; compr 9.0:1; 42.5kW (57bhp) @ 5500rpm; 91Nm (70lbft) @ 2500rpm; 32.8kW (43.9bhp)/l. 1300GT 53.7kW (72bhp) @ 5500rpm. 1600 87.65 x 66mm; 1593cc; 53.7kW (72bhp). GT 65.6kW (88bhp) @ 5700rpm **ENGINE STRUCTURE** pushrod overhead valve, chain-driven camshaft; cast iron cylinder head and block; Ford GPD carburettor; centrifugal and vacuum ignition; mechanical fuel pump; 5-bearing crankshaft. 1300GT and 1600 Weber 320 carburettor; 1600GT Weber compound.

TRANSMISSION rear wheel drive; 19cm (7.5in) diaphragm spring cable-operated clutch; 4-speed synchromesh gearbox; hypoid bevel final drive 4.125:1 (1300) 3.89:1 (1600). Borg Warner 35 automatic available 1300 GT, 1600, final drive 1600GT 3.777:1. **CHASSIS** steel monocoque structure; independent front suspension by MacPherson struts and anti roll bar; live rear axle with half-elliptic springs and radius rods, telescopic dampers; Girling hydraulic 24.1cm (9.5in) disc brakes at front (optional 1300s), 24.4cm (9.6in) GT and 1600; 20.3cm (8in) rear drums; dual circuit; vacuum servo; rack and pinion steering; 48l (10.6 gal) fuel tank; 6.00-13 cross-ply 1300, 165-13 GT and 1600 radial-ply, 4.5rims. **EQUIPMENT** SLR pack £79 12s 10d (£79.64p); fixed seat belts £8.49p, inertia reel belts £14.01p.

DIMENSIONS wheelbase 256cm (100.8in); track front 134.5cm (53in), rear 132cm (52in); length 426cm (167.7in); width 164.5cm (64.8in); height 129cm (50.8in) GT and 1600 128cm (50.4in); ground clearance 11.5cm (4.5in); turning circle 9.75m (32ft). **PERFORMANCE** maximum speed 1300 138kph (86mph), 1300GT and 1600 150kph (93.4mph), 1600GT 160kph (99.7mph); 1300 26.2kph (16.3mph) @ 1000rpm, 1600GT 28.8kph (17.94mph); 0-100kph (62mph) 19sec; 1600 GT 13sec; 16.8kg/kW (12.5kg/bhp); fuel consumption 9.1l/100km (31mpg), 9.8l/100km (28.8mpg) 1600GT **PRICE** 1300, £682, £890 7s 10d (£890.39p) including PT; 1300GT £985 70p; 1600 £936.9p; 1600GT £1041.83p. **PRODUCTION** 374,700 UK Capris.

1969
Capri 2000 GT, 3000 GT

The one-shape-fits-all recipe of the Capri was well judged. Buyers rang the changes with engines and accessory packs to their hearts' content. Rear axle radius arms had been deleted from Cortina GTs on the grounds of road noise; they were reinstated on the Capri to provide GT handling, and developed with care so that there was negligible sacrifice in noise vibration and harshness, the celebrated NVH that Ford took seriously to compete with classic makes in the sporting, semi-sporting or even quasi-sporting field. By the dawn of the 1970s it did not much matter if a car was sporting or not but it had to be refined, smooth-running, and if not completely quiet, at least make the right noises. The 2000GT V4 was not quite ready at launch but went into production in March, the V6 3.0-litre following in September. The first addition to the range was the 3000E, technically the same as the 3000GT, but cosmetically upmarket and better equipped. In 1971 the 3.0-litre Essex V6 was revised with better breathing to provide more torque and 138bhp (102.9kW) instead of 128bhp (95.5kW), a change never applied to the same engine fitted in soon-to-be-replaced Zodiacs. The German Capri RS2600 was not sold in Britain and only 248 of the dramatic RS3100 with big-bore V6 of 1973 were ever made.

INTRODUCTION November 1968, produced until December 1973.
BODY coupe; 2-doors, 2+2-seats; weight 2000GT 960kg (2116lb), V6 1057kg (2330lb).
ENGINE 2000 4-cylinders, 60deg V; 93.66mm x 72.44mm, 1996cc; compr 8.9:1; 68.6kW (92bhp) @ 5250rpm; 34.4kW (46.1bhp)/l; 141Nm (104lbft) @ 3600rpm. V6 93.66 x 72.4mm; 2994cc, 8.9:1; 95.45 kW (128bhp) @ 4750rpm; 31.9kg (42.8bhp)/l; 235Nm (173lbft) @ 3000rpm.
ENGINE STRUCTURE pushrod ohv, gear-driven camshaft; cast iron cylinder head and block; Weber 40 compound carburettor; centrifugal and vacuum ignition; mechanical fuel pump; 4-bearing crankshaft. V6 Weber 40DFA carburettor.
TRANSMISSION rear wheel drive; 22.9cm (9.0in) diaphragm spring cable-operated clutch; 4-speed synchromesh gearbox; hypoid bevel final drive 3.545:1; Borg Warner 35 auto available. V6 3.22:1 final drive.
CHASSIS steel monocoque structure; ifs by MacPherson struts and anti roll bar; live rear axle with half-elliptic springs and radius rods, telescopic dampers; Girling hydraulic disc brakes front, 24.4cm (9.6in); 20.3cm (8in) rear drums; dual circuit; vacuum servo; rack and pinion steering; 48l (10.6 gal) fuel tank; 165-13 radial-ply tyres, 4.5 rims.
DIMENSIONS wheelbase 256cm (100.8in); track 134.5cm (53in) front, 132cm (52in) rear; length 426cm (167.7in); width 164.5cm (64.8in); height 128cm (50.4in); ground clearance 11.5cm (4.5in); turning circle 9.75m (32ft).
EQUIPMENT SLR pack £79 12s 10d (£79.64p); fixed seat belts £8.49p, inertia reel belts £14.01p.
PERFORMANCE maximum speed 171kph (106.5mph), V6 183kph (114mph); 30.6kph (19.1mph) @ 1000rpm, V6 33.4kph (20.8mph); 0-100kph (62mph) 11.3sec, V6 9.2sec; 14kg/kW (10.4kg/bhp); fuel consumption 12.3l/100km (23mpg), V6 12l/100km (23.5mpg).
PRICE £833, £1087 10s 7d (£1087.53p) including PT.
PRODUCTION 374,700 UK Capris.

Ford Capri: the car you always promised yourself.

From £914.

CAPRI Ford

1970
Escort RS1600

Engine development, inspired by the connections with Cosworth, developer of the brilliantly successful DFV Formula 1 engine, went on apace. Four valves per cylinder, twin overhead camshaft engines, once the prerogative of the no-expense-spared grand prix car, now became available on a competitively priced popular small saloon. The engine's ancestry was the Cosworth FVA (Four Valve type A) that developed into the Formula 2 unit, half of which in turn was the prototype of the DFV (Double Four Valve). The new Escort engine was analogous to the Cosworth Formula 2 unit, derated and with toothed belts, instead of gears, driving the overhead camshafts. It was thus known as the BDA (Belt Drive type A). The RS was

derived from Rallye or Renn Sport, evidence of the growing European and in particular German influence on Ford operations. Furthermore, while the Twin Cam block was based on the old 1500cc Ford, the BDA was built round the 1600cc Kent block. The small facility at Aveley Essex known as Ford Advanced Vehicles Operation (AVO) could make up to 30 cars a day using body shells and components from Halewood and outside suppliers. The RS1600 was the first AVO car, virtually hand-assembled on a small production track. As the Twin Cam was run down, the RS1600 took its place, as the front-running Ford sports and competition car. Graham Hill (above) joins in the celebrations at Aveley.

INTRODUCTION 1970, production until 1974.

BODY saloon; 2-door, 4-seats; weight 785kg (1731lb).

ENGINE 4-cylinders, in-line; 80.97mm x 77.6mm; 1601cc; compr 10:1; 89.5kW (120bhp) @ 6500rpm; 55.9kW (75bhp)/l; 152Nm (112lbft) @ 4000rpm.

ENGINE STRUCTURE belt-driven twin overhead camshafts; 4 valves per cylinder; aluminium cylinder head and cast iron block (aluminium block from 1972); two Weber twin choke horizontal 40DCOE 48 carburettors, mechanical fuel pump; 5-bearing crankshaft.

TRANSMISSION rear wheel drive; Borg & Beck diaphragm spring clutch, 20.3cm (8in); 4-speed synchromesh gearbox; hypoid bevel final drive 3.77:1.

CHASSIS steel monocoque structure; independent front suspension by MacPherson struts; lower links; telescopic dampers, anti-roll bar; rear live axle and half-elliptic leaf springs with telescopic dampers and radius arms; Girling hydraulic 24.4cm (9.6in) front disc brakes, rear 22.9cm (9in) drum, vacuum servo standard; rack and pinion steering; 40.9l (9.0 gal) fuel tank; 5.5in rim and 165-13 radial ply tyres.

DIMENSIONS wheelbase 240cm (94.5in); track front 129.5cm (51in), rear 132.1cm (52in); length 397.8cm (156.6in); width 157.5cm (62in); height 138.4cm (54.5in); ground clearance 15.2cm (6in); turning circle 8.84m (29ft).

EQUIPMENT fresh air-blending heater standard, wide range of homologated competition extras, rev limiter at 6500rpm.

PERFORMANCE maximum speed 182kph (113.4mph) *Motor*; 28.25kph (17.6mph) @ 1000rpm; 0-96kph (0-60mph) 8.3sec; 8.8kg/kW (6.5kg/bhp); fuel consumption 11.2l/100km (25.2mpg).

PRICE total with tax and delivery £1447.

PRODUCTION 947.

1970
Escort Mexico

The 1968 London-Sydney 10,000mile (approx 16,000km) Marathon had been surprisingly successful. Encouraged, the Daily Mirror sponsored a rally from London, where the 1966 World Cup football series had been staged, to Mexico, where the 1970 competition was being held. Timed special stages would be decisive, but this time with 16,000miles (approx 26,000kms) in prospect, the competitions department needed an Escort to be not only fast but also last the distance. The overhead camshaft engines were now less brittle than their Lotus forbears but, to be on the safe side, a team of cars was built with enlarged 1558cc Kent pushrod engines. Of the 99 competitors who started from Wembley Stadium, 71 reached Lisbon a week later for shipping to South America. The survivors re-started from Rio de Janeiro, Hannu Mikkola taking the lead in his Escort as the field was further depleted. The event was a triumph for Ford, with the manufacturers' team prize, and Escorts first, third, fifth and sixth. AVO at once went into production with replicas, the Mexico filling the gap in the sporting range between the GT and the Twin Cam, and with its heavy-duty body becoming a firm favourite with amateur racing and rally drivers. Retailed through a new network of Rallye Sport dealers in 1972, the Mexico's trim was improved to that of the RS1600.

ABOVE **Eric Dymock racing an Escort Mexico at Brands Hatch. After leading throughout he was overtaken on the last lap, finishing second.**

INTRODUCTION 1970, produced until 1974.

BODY saloon; 2-door, 4-seats; weight 891kg (1964lb).

ENGINE 4-cylinders, in-line; 80.98mm x 77.62mm; 1599cc ("1601"cc for competition); compr 9.0:1; 64.8kW (86.9bhp) @ 5500rpm; 40.5kW (54.3bhp)/l; 125Nm (92lbft) @ 4000rpm.

ENGINE STRUCTURE pushrod ohv; chain-drive camshaft; 2 valves per cyl; cast iron cyl head and block; Weber 32DFM twin choke compound carb, mechanical fuel pump; 5-bearing crank.

TRANSMISSION rwd; Borg & Beck diaphragm spring clutch, 19cm (7.5in); 4-speed manual all synchro gearbox; hypoid bevel final drive 3.77:1.

CHASSIS steel monocoque; ifs by MacPherson struts; lower links; telescopic dampers, anti-roll bar; rear live axle and half-elliptic leaf springs with telescopic dampers and radius arms; Girling hydraulic 24.4cm (9.6in) front disc brakes, rear 22.7cm (9in) drum, vacuum servo; rack and pinion; 40.9l (9.0 gal) fuel tank; 5.5in rim and 165-13 radial ply tyres.

DIMENSIONS wheelbase 240cm (94.5in); track 129.5cm (51in) front, 132.1cm (52in) rear; length 397.8cm (156.6in); width 157.5cm (62in); height 138.4cm (54.5in); ground clearance 15.2cm (6in); turning circle 8.8m (29ft).

EQUIPMENT heater standard, homologated competition extras, Minilites £109, vinyl seats, pvc headlining; carpets and "Mexico" graphics delete options, Contour driver's seat £18.50, passenger's reclining seat £32.37p, Cibie Oscar lights £7.75p each.

PERFORMANCE maximum 159kph (99mph) *Autocar*; 28.3kph (17.6mph) @ 1000rpm; 0-96kph (60mph) 10.7sec; 13.8kg/kW (10.3kg/bhp); 10.3l/100km (27.5mpg).

PRICE inc tax and delivery £1150.

PRODUCTION 9382, RS2000 4324.

1970
Cortina Mark III 1297cc, 1599cc

The 4-year model cycle seemed to be working and Ford confidently moved the third generation Cortina upmarket to enhance profitability, then instead of four years made it last nearly six. The final facelift in 1975 was no more than black grilles, cloth trim, heated rear windows and cosmetics. As a result the Cortina remained the best-selling car in Britain four years running and the millionth Mark III came that October. The pinched-waist, so called Coke-bottle style and wide range of options proved successful and although the car looked bigger, it was the same length as before even though 5cm (2in) wider and 10.2cm (4in) lower. Improved Kent engines with larger inlet valves, new camshaft, changed piston bowl profile and six to ten per cent more power were used for the 1300 and 1600. British and German Escorts were virtually identical but Cologne Cortinas had Teutonic style. Germany used its own 1300 and 1600 ohc engines and the Taunus 20M a V6. As part of Ford's multi-national culture the Mark III was dimensioned metrically. The MacPherson strut front suspension that had served well for 20 years was replaced by conventional double wishbone ifs, curiously translated into Fordspeak as SLA (short and long arm). Arguably the most important innovation was new rear suspension with variable rate coil springs and twin trailing and semi-trailing arms. The springs were made from wire drawn out, so that its cross-section tapered and it worked at near constant frequency regardless of load. The firm axle location improved ride and handling, and reduced body roll.

INTRODUCTION October 1970, produced until 1976.
BODY saloon; 4-doors, 2-doors, 5-seats; estate car 5-doors; weight 2-door 945kg (2083.4lb), 4-door 965kg (2127.4lb), estate 1040kg (2292.8lb).
ENGINE 1300 4-cyls, in-line; 80.97mm x 62.99mm, 1298cc; cr 9.0:1; 42.5kW (57bhp) @ 5500rpm; 32.7kW (43.9bhp)/l; 91Nm (67lbft) @ 3000rpm; 1600 stroke 77.62mm; 1599cc; 50.7kW (68bhp) @ 5200rpm; 115Nm (85lbft) @ 2600rpm.
ENGINE STRUCTURE pushrod ohv; chain-driven camshaft; cast iron cylinder head and block; Ford GPD downdraught carburettor; centrifugal and vacuum ignition; mechanical fuel pump; 5-bearing crankshaft.

TRANSMISSION rwd; diaphragm spring cable operated 7.5in sdp clutch; 4-speed single selector rail synchromesh gearbox; 3-speed Borg Warner Model 35 automatic optional on 1600; one-piece prop shaft; final drive 1300, 4.11:1; 1600, 3.89:1.
CHASSIS steel monocoque; ifs by coil springs, wishbones, anti-roll bar; rear live axle with coil springs, trailing and semi-trailing radius arms; telescopic dampers; hydraulic servo 24.4cm (9.6in) disc front brakes, 20.3cm (8in) rear drums; rack and pinion steering; 54.6l (12 gal) fuel tank; 5.60-13 4-ply on 4.5J rim, radial-ply, various size options.
DIMENSIONS wheelbase 257.7cm (101.5in); track 142.2cm (56in) front and rear; length 426.7cm (168in); width 170.2cm (67in); height 132.1cm (52in); ground clearance 17.8cm (7in); turning circle 10.36m (34ft).

EQUIPMENT 14 exterior colours, fabric seat trim optional, L Pack, XL Pack options.
PERFORMANCE maximum speed 135.7kph (84.3mph) 1300XL *The Motor*; 24.7kph (15.4mph) @ 1000rpm; 0-96kph (60mph) 18.1sec; 22.2kg/kW (16.6kg/bhp); fuel consumption 12l/100km (23.5mpg).
PRICE at launch: 2-door 1300 £700, total inc PT £913 17s 10d (£913.89p); 1300 XL Estate £1159.33; 1600XL 4-door £1094.6p. Feb 1972: 1300XL £962.50p, with XL Pack £1080, with styled wheels, radial-ply tyres and cloth trim £1150.73p.
PRODUCTION 1,126,559 all Mark III.

1970
Cortina Mark III 1593cc, 1993cc

The 248.9cm (98in) wheelbase platform of the first Cortina lasted through two incarnations, eight years, and the 257.8cm (101.5in) wheelbase (within half an inch of the Corsair) remained the length of Cortinas to come for the next 12. The Mark III was also intended to replace the Corsair, which accounts for its move upmarket and the stretched platform required to provide more room inside. Developed under chief engineer Harley Copp it was also completely new, not only the platform and suspension, but the drivelines too, with the latest thing – overhead cam engines with cogged belt-drive camshafts. Even the Kent 1300 and 1600 engines were brought up to date, but since the ohc engines were 1600 and 2000, it meant that the range had two 1600s. The ohc units were accordingly known as 1600GT and 2000GT; they scarcely equated to previous GT Cortinas, but it proved a useful notation to distinguish Cortinas with the US-designed Pinto engine. Planned for an American compact car, the Pinto became part of Ford's new international programme and was used in Taunus, Escort, Capri, Granada, and was even adapted for the Transit van. Tall and 8.16kg (18lb) heavier than the Kent, it required some in-service development before it was as reliable. Unlike the Kent, the combustion chambers were in the head, not in the pistons. Within a year Cortinas were outselling any other model on the British market.

INTRODUCTION October 1970, produced until 1976.
BODY saloon; 4-doors, 2-doors, 5-seats; estate car 5-doors; weight 2-door 960kg (2116.4lb), 4-door 980kg (2160.5lb), 1600 estate 1085kg (2392lb).
ENGINE 1600 4-cylinders, in-line; 87.75mm x 66mm, 1593cc; compr 9.2:1; 65.6kW (88bhp) @ 5700rpm; 41.2kW (55.2bhp)/l; 125Nm (92lbft) @ 4000rpm. 2000 90.8mm x 76.95mm; 1993cc; 73.1kW (98bhp) @ 5500rpm; 36.7kW (49.2bhp)/l; 151Nm (111lbft) @ 4000rpm.
ENGINE STRUCTURE single ohc; toothed belt; opposed ohv; cast iron cyl head and block; Weber 32/36 DGAV (DFAVH 2000) downdraught twin choke carb; centrifugal and vacuum ign; mechanical fuel pump; 5-bearing crank.

TRANSMISSION rwd; diaphragm spring cable operated 21.6cm (8.5in) sdp clutch; 4-speed single selector rail synchromesh gearbox; 3-speed Borg Warner Model 35 automatic optional; two-piece prop shaft; hypoid bevel final drive, 3.89 (1600) and 3.444:1 (2000).
CHASSIS steel monocoque; ifs by coil springs, wishbones, anti-roll bar; rear live axle with coil springs, trailing and semitrailing radius arms; telescopic dampers; hydraulic servo 24.4cm (9.6in) disc front brakes, 20.3cm (8in) rear drums; rack and pinion steering; 54.6l (12 gal) fuel tank; 5.60-13 4-ply on 4.5J rim; radial-ply, various size options.
DIMENSIONS wheelbase 257.8cm (101.5in); track 142.2cm (56in) front and rear; length 426.7cm (168in); width 170.2cm (67in); height 132.1cm

(52in); ground clearance 17.8cm (7in); turning circle 10.36m (34ft).
EQUIPMENT 14 exterior colours, fabric seat trim optional, L Pack, XL Pack options.
PERFORMANCE maximum 162.5kph (101mph) 2000XL Estate *The Motor*; 26.2kph (16.3mph) @ 1000rpm; 0-96kph (60mph) 14.1sec; 14.6kg/kW (10.9kg/bhp); 7.6l/100km (37.2mpg).
PRICE at launch: 2000 2-door £787, total with PT £1027 9s 5d (£1027.47p); 2000GXL 4-door £133819p; 2000XL; Estate £1272.92p. February 1972: £1388.08p with XL Pack, sports wheels, cloth trim.
PRODUCTION 1,126,559 all Mark III.

1970
GT70

After the works Escorts were badly beaten in the Monte Carlo Rally, competitions manager Stuart Turner and works driver Roger Clark saw a need for a car to restore Ford's reputation for exciting engineering. Something more than a motor show concept car was required to take on the Renault Alpine and Porsche 911 in high-speed rallies, or where snow and ice put the Escort at a disadvantage, so the Competitions Department produced a rakish mid-engined coupe. Placing the engine amidships gave the driver more options in varying conditions, and a prototype was built with a steel platform, glass reinforced plastic body, independent suspension, and a choice of 1.6BDA or V6 RS2600 engines, with a 5-speed ZF transaxle. A potential rally championship winner, six were planned to study its practicality for production. Regular components were used where possible both for expediency and so that AVO could make 500 if it was a success. The design was by Len Bailey, who had been chief designer of the GT40, and World Cup Rally winners Hannu Mikkola and Gunnar Palm were engaged as consultants. Bailey drew up the graceful body, whose efficiency was confirmed by wind-tunnel evaluation, although the cockpit would have been cramped and hot for a rally car. Walter Hayes wrote persuasively to Stan Gillen that a run of 500 would make a profit but the project was scrapped during production workers' strikes.

INTRODUCTION Brussels Motor Show 1971.
BODY coupe; 2-doors; 2-seats; weight 762kg (1680lb).
ENGINE 6-cylinders, 60deg V; mid; 90mm x 66.8mm, 2520cc; compr 9.0:1; 125bhp (93.2kW) @ 5300rpm; 37kW (49.6bhp)/l; 201Nm (148lbft) @ 3000rpm (prototype). BDA engine 4-cylinders, in line; 80.98mm x 77.62mm, "1601cc" for competitions; compr 10:1; 89.5kW (120bhp) @ 6,500rpm; 152Nm (112lbft) @ 4000rpm.
ENGINE STRUCTURE pushrod ohv, gear-driven camshaft; cast iron cyl head and block; Solex twin choke 35/35 EEIT carb; mechanical fuel pump; 4-bearing crank. BDA 16 valve, toothed belt dohc; 2 Weber 40DCOE; cast iron block, aluminium head; 5-bearing crank.

TRANSMISSION rear wheel drive; sdp 21.6cm (8.5in) hydraulic clutch; 5-speed ZF5 DS25 synchromesh gearbox; final drive 4.22:1 (optional Taunus 17M).
CHASSIS perimeter rail 16g steel chassis, floor pan 22g, roll hoop 18g steel tube; (Cortina) ifs by coil springs and double wishbones (with Escort joints); provision for anti roll bar; telescopic dampers; (Zodiac IV) rear independent by upper link and trailing arm, coil springs and anti-roll bar; brakes, hydraulic no servo (Cortina) disc front 24.4cm (9.6in) rear (Zodiac IV) 25.1cm (9.9in); (Cortina) rack and pinion steering; 54.6l (12 gal) fuel tank; 195/70VR tyres 7J rims.
DIMENSIONS wheelbase 111.8cm (44in); track 142.2cm (56in) front, 139.7cm (55in) rear; length 388.6cm (153in); width 172.7cm (68in); height 111.8cm (44in); ground clearance 15.2cm (6in); turning circle 9.45m (31ft).

EQUIPMENT laminated windscreen, optional 1600GT engine, optional Essex V6; luggage capacity 283cu m (10cu ft), retractable headlights, contoured ventilated seats, retractable seat belts; (Capri) handbrake switchgear and electricals; (Anglia) heater.
PERFORMANCE maximum speed est for competition version 289kph (180mph); 32.1kph (20mph) @ 1000rpm.
PRICE estimated for a production version, $5000.
PRODUCTION 6 prototypes planned, 5 completed.

ABOVE **The V6 engine proved too heavy for handling. Final version tuned for French tarmac special stages had the BDA with a Hewland gearbox.**

1972
Consul Granada V4 1996cc

Zephyrs and Zodiacs had kept their place in the luxury car world through a certain flamboyance but by 1971 it was not enough. Pedigree rivals like BMW were becoming more affordable, making executive-class buyers ask why they were paying premium prices for Fords. Premium customers could no longer be fobbed off with indifferent handling or a quirky appearance. A new range was introduced, using the old Consul name, at first, in conjunction with the novel title Granada. Manufactured in West Germany and Britain with a completely new and rather better proportioned body shell than the Mark IVs, the range had a wide choice of engines and a more sophisticated independent rear suspension that did away with the old car's rear wheel steer. It also reverted to drum brakes at the back. The first ones were all 4-door saloons, followed by estates some 18 months later. More compact than the Mark IV, at 12.7cm (5in) shorter and 11.2cm (4.4in) lower, UK cars had V4 and V6 engines, with German-market cars also having the option of an ohc in-line 4-cylinder. Similar dimensions to the Triumph 2000 and Mercedes-Benz 220 indicated Granada's aspirations; the 147.3cm (58in) shoulder room was generous even though headroom was not, on account of the low build, with a low roll-centre only 14cm (5.5in) above the ground.

INTRODUCTION March 1972, production December 1971 to 1974.
BODY saloon; 4-doors, 5-seats; weight 1185kg (2612lb).
ENGINE 4-cylinders, 60deg V; 93.7mm x 72.4mm, 1996cc; compr 8.9:1; 60.8kW (81.5bhp) @ 5000rpm; 30.5kW (40.8bhp)/l; 144Nm (106lbft) @ 3000rpm.
ENGINE STRUCTURE pushrod ohv; gear-driven camshaft; cast iron cylinder heads and block; Ford GPD carburettor, centrifugal and vacuum ignition; mechanical fuel pump; 3-bearing crankshaft.
TRANSMISSION rear wheel drive; 21.6cm (8.5in) sdp clutch; 4-speed synchromesh gearbox; optional automatic; hypoid bevel final drive 3.89:1.
CHASSIS steel monocoque structure; independent front suspension, coil springs and double wishbones, anti roll bar; independent rear by semitrailing arms, coil springs, telescopic dampers; hydraulic vacuum servo dual circuit brakes front disc 26.2cm (10.3in), rear drum 22.9cm (9in); rack and pinion steering; 65l (14.3 gal) fuel tank; 4-ply cross-ply 6.45-14 tyres, 6J wheels optional.
DIMENSIONS wheelbase 277cm (57in); track 151cm (59.5in) front, 154cm (60.6in) rear; length 457cm (179.9in), width 179cm (70.5in); height 137cm (53.9in); ground clearance 13cm (5.1in); turning circle 11m (36ft).
EQUIPMENT cut pile carpet, toughened glass windscreen, safety belts, automatic transmission, sunroof extra, radial ply tyres and 6in rims £57.12, metallic paint £8.84.
PERFORMANCE maximum speed 154kph (95.9mph) *Autocar*; 28.6kph (17.8mph) @ 1000rpm; 0-100kph (62mph) 14.0sec; 19.5kg/kW (14.5kg/bhp); fuel consumption 11.8l/100km (24mpg).
PRICE £1126; £1376.01 incl PT.
PRODUCTION in Britain 58,969, 6002 estates.

1972
Consul Granada V6 2495cc, 2995cc

The Granada not only replaced the Mark IV Zephyr and Zodiac, it also replaced the Taunus 17M, 20M, and 26M in Germany, so it had to cover a wide choice and there was only one bodyshell with which to do it. Germany, however, had an estate car from the beginning and also the racy 2-door fastback. Comfort was emphasised with long suspension travel, 19.6cm (7.7in) at the front and 22.9cm (9in) at the back, while soft springing and anti-dive geometry gave a supple well controlled smooth ride. Cam Gears made the steering rack with integral power ram, and the rotary valve supplied by Adwest Engineering was similar to the component it supplied to Jaguar. The 2.5-litre car could be a Consul (standard or L trim) or Granada (standard or GXL); the 3.0-litre could be a Consul GT (heavy-duty suspension, 6J wheels, radial-ply tyres, Granada instruments and extra lamps), or Granada with a smarter grille with horizontal chrome bars, smarter side mouldings and GXL spec. Power steering and automatic transmission was standard with the GXL together with tinted windows, bumper overriders and a vinyl roof. A heated rear window and radio were also standard, which was welcomed for real gains in comfort, refinement, and roomy boot within a wheelbase the same as a Jaguar XJ6 and a slightly wider track.

INTRODUCTION March 1972, produced from December 1971-1974. **BODY** saloon; 4-doors, 5-seats; 2500 1270kg (2800lb), 3000 1300kg (2866lb). **ENGINE** 2500 6-cyls, 60deg V; 93.7mm x 60.3mm, 2495cc; compr 9.0:1; 89.5kW (120bhp) @ 5000rpm; 35.9kW (48.1bhp)/l; 179Nm (132lbft) @ 3000rpm. 3000: 93.7x72.4mm; 2995cc; 102.9kW (138bhp) @ 5000rpm; 34.4kW (46.1bhp)/l; 235Nm (173lbft) @ 3000rpm. **ENGINE STRUCTURE** pushrod ohv; gear-driven camshaft; cast iron cyl heads and block; Weber twin choke carb, centrifugal and vacuum ignition; mechanical fuel pump; 4-bearing crank. **TRANSMISSION** rwd; 24.1cm (9.5in) sdp clutch; 2-piece propeller shaft; 4-speed synchromesh gearbox; optional automatic; hypoid bevel final drive 3.45:1.

CHASSIS steel monocoque; ifs, coil springs and double wishbones, anti roll bar; independent rear by semi-trailing arms, coil springs, telescopic dampers; hydraulic vacuum servo dual circuit brakes front disc 26.2cm (10.3in) ventilated on 3000, rear drum 22.9cm (9in); rack and pinion PAS optional; 65l (14.3 gal); 4-ply cross-ply 6.95S-14 tyres 2500, radial ply 175HR-14 185HR optional 3000; 6J wheels. **DIMENSIONS** wheelbase 277cm (57in); track 151cm (59.5in) front, 154cm (60.6in) rear; length 457cm (179.9in); width 179cm (70.5in); height 137cm (53.9in); ground clearance 13cm (5.1in); turning circle 11m (36ft). **EQUIPMENT** sunroof, cut pile carpet, toughened glass windscreen, safety belts, automatic transmission. optional 6in rims £57.12, metallic paint £8.84.

PERFORMANCE 2500: maximum speed 2500 175kph (109mph) *Autocar*; 31.6kph (19.7mph) @ 1000rpm; 0-100kph (62mph) 10.4sec; 14.2kg/kW (10.6kg/bhp); 3.5l/100km (21mpg). 3000: maximum 182kph (113.4mph) GXL auto *Autocar*; 33.6kph (20.9mph) @ 1000rpm; 0-100kph (62mph) 9.1sec; 12.6kW/l (9.4bhp/l); GXL 4.8l/100km (19.1mpg). **PRICE** 2500L £1416 GXL, automatic £1934. **PRODUCTION** in Britain 50,747, 7650 estates. **PRODUCTION** 374,700 UK.

1973
Escort RS2000

The last Mark I Escort to be built at Aveley, before AVO became a casualty of the continuing oil crisis in 1975, used the American designed Pinto engine first seen in the Mark III Cortina 2000 of 1970. Ringing the changes with engines was now well established, and a 2.0-litre Escort was a logical development, aimed at sustaining sales right down to the advent of the Mark II Escort in 1975. The new model's underpinnings were already incorporated in Mark I production during 1973, as part of Ford's Europeanisation programme, and the result was the most refined of all the sporting Mark I Escorts. A small increase in power was achieved over the engine's Cortina installation by introducing an electric fan, and a new aluminium sump and oil pick-up were required to clear the Escort's cross-member. An aluminium bell housing was provided to raise the engine's resonance threshold to over 6000rpm, where in theory it would rarely be heard. Ford works racing driver Gerry Birrell helped in developing the suspension, stiffening the front spring rates by 30 per cent and the rear by 10 per cent. Damper rates were changed to suit, and the ride height lowered, "...working wonders for the comfort and making the RS2000 much more progressive when driven to the limits of adhesion," according to *Autocar*.

INTRODUCTION July 1973, production to 1975.
BODY saloon 2-door, 4-seats; weight 915kg (2017.2lb).
ENGINE 4-cylinders, in-line; 90.82mm x 76.95mm; 1993cc; compr 9.2:1; 74.6kW (100bhp) @ 5750rpm; 37.4kW (50.2bhp)/l; l 108lbft (146Nm) @ 3500rpm.
ENGINE STRUCTURE single overhead camshaft, toothed belt drive, opposed ohv; cast iron cylinder head and cast iron block; Weber 32/36 downdraught twin choke carburettor; centrifugal and vacuum ignition; mechanical fuel pump; 5-bearing crankshaft.
TRANSMISSION rear wheel drive; cable operated diaphragm spring clutch, 21.6cm (8.5in); 4-speed synchromesh gearbox; hypoid bevel final drive 3.54:1.

CHASSIS steel monocoque structure; independent front suspension by MacPherson struts; lower links; telescopic dampers, anti-roll bar; rear live axle and half-elliptic leaf springs with telescopic dampers and radius arms; Girling hydraulic 24.4cm (9.62in) front disc brakes, rear 20.3cm (8in) drum, vacuum servo standard; rack and pinion steering; 40.9l (9 gal) fuel tank; 5.5in rim RS alloy optional wheels; 165-13 radial ply tyres.
DIMENSIONS wheelbase 240cm (94.5in); track front 124.5cm (49in), rear 127cm (50in); length 397.8cm (156.6in); width 157.5cm (62in); height 138.4cm (54.5in); ground clearance 15.2cm (6in); turning circle 8.8m (29ft).

EQUIPMENT fresh air-blending heater, heated rear window, cloth seats pvc headlining; carpeted floor inertia reel seat belts, wide range homologated competition extras, rev limiter at 6500rpm.
PERFORMANCE maximum speed 173.4kph (108mph) *Autocar*; 30kph (18.7mph) @ 1000rpm; 0-96kph (60mph) 9.0sec; 12.3kg/kW (9.2kg/bhp); fuel consumption 10.6l/100km (26.6mpg).
PRICE total with tax and delivery in London £1586.
PRODUCTION 4324 including production at Saarlouis.

1973
Capri RS3100

There were two Capri "homologation specials". International competition rules required 1000 to be built to qualify for motor sport, and Ford Germany produced its RS2600 with the 2637cc V6. This was raced successfully and eventually taken to 2.9litres, 111.9kW (150bhp) with Kugelfischer fuel injection. The first 50 were light in weight for racing, but even fully equipped road versions could reach 120mph (192.6kph). The RS2600 was not sold in Britain but was essentially the prototype of the final Capri, the 3.8i, many years later. Its Halewood equivalent was the RS3100, which in racing form had the Ford-Cosworth 3.4-litre quad cam V6 conversion. Production never reached 1000, the regulations were loosely applied, and cars passed provided it looked as though manufacturers had tried. Sales were overtaken by the Mark II Capri in 1974. Only some 200 road-going cars were ever completed using an overbored gas-flowed 3.0-litre (3091cc) V6 with a Weber carburettor, a rear spoiler soon identified as "ducktail", cast alloy wheels, and racy-

looking front quarter bumpers. The basis of the car was largely 3000GT but included ventilated disc brakes as on the RS2600 and incorporated the September 1972 improvements such as a Granada-style facia and matt black panels under the doors. It had firmer, rather than the softer springing used for most of the range.

INTRODUCTION Glasgow Motor Show Nov 1973.
BODY coupe; 2-doors, 2+2-seats; weight 1078kg (2376.6lb).
ENGINE 6-cylinders, 60deg V; 95.19mm x 72.4mm, 3091cc; compr 9.0:1; 110.4kW (148bhp) @ 5000rpm; 35.7kW (47.9bhp)/l; 254Nm (187lbft) @ 3000rpm.
ENGINE STRUCTURE pushrod ohv; gear-drive camshaft; cast iron cylinder head, block; downdraught Weber twin choke carburettor, centrifugal and vacuum ignition; mechanical fuel pump; 4-bearing crankshaft.
TRANSMISSION rear wheel drive; sdp clutch; 4-speed synchromesh gearbox; final drive 3.09:1.
CHASSIS steel monocoque structure; ifs by MacPherson struts and anti roll bar; live rear axle with half-elliptic springs anti roll bar, telescopic dampers; Girling hydraulic disc brakes at front, 24.4cm (9.6in); 22.9cm (9in) rear drums; dual circuit; vacuum servo; rack and pinion steering; 48l (10.6 gal) fuel tank; 185-70HR 13 radial-ply tyres, 4.5 rims.
DIMENSIONS wheelbase 256cm (100.8in); track 134.5cm (53in) front, 132cm (52in) rear; length 430.3cm (169.4in); width 164.5cm (64.8in); height 128cm (50.4in); ground clearance 11.5cm (4.5in); turning circle 9.75m (32ft).
PERFORMANCE maximum speed 200kph (125mph) approx; 36.3kph (22.6mph) @ 1000rpm; 0-100kph (62mph) 8.0sec approx; 9.8kg/kW (7.3kg/bhp); fuel consumption approx 10.5l/100km (26.9mpg).
PRICE £2412.64
PRODUCTION 200.

1973
Cortina 2000E

The Cortina's mid-term facelift came just as the first world oil crisis broke. Inflation, loss of confidence and international tension hardly made it the best time to move upmarket. However, improvements to the range went ahead and yet another Executive model, the 2000E, was introduced. The two-bay instrument panel was replaced by a comprehensively equipped one, extending the width of the car and furnished, in the case of the 2000E, tastefully in teak. The surviving Kent engine was the 1300, the 1600 Kent replaced by a Pinto, now of 53.7kW (72bhp). Gear ratios, a persistent difficulty with Cortinas, were revised and every model now had anti-roll bars. Spring rates were revised, stiffening the GT and reducing understeer. The 2000E, in addition to deep pile carpets and tree wood (as opposed to lookalike plastic wood) luxury interior was provided with a 1970s fashion statement, a vinyl roof. Shiny wheels, shiny rubbing strips, and door casings to match the Savannah nylon upholstery completed a package instrumental in moving the family car up the aspirational ladder. The 2000E's ride, handling, and performance were well up to the mark. All that lay between it and a real (more expensive) luxury car were refinement and longevity. Ford engineers knew where the NVH (Noise Vibration Harshness) was coming from, but often found it impossible to eliminate at the price.

INTRODUCTION 1973, production to 1976.
BODY saloon; 4-doors, 2-doors, 5-seats; estate car 5-doors; weight 4-door 1130kg (2491.2lb).
ENGINE 4-cylinders, in-line; 90.8mm x 76.95mm; 1993cc; 73.1kW (98bhp) @ 5500rpm; 36.7kW (49.2bhp)/l; 150Nm (111lbft) @ 4000rpm.
ENGINE STRUCTURE single overhead camshaft; toothed belt; opposed overhead valve; cast iron cylinder head and block; Weber 32/36 DFAVH downdraught twin choke carburettor; centrifugal and vacuum ignition; mechanical fuel pump; 5-bearing crankshaft.
TRANSMISSION rear wheel drive; diaphragm spring cable operated 21.6cm (8.5in) sdp clutch; 4-speed single selector rail synchromesh gearbox; 3-speed Borg Warner Model 35 automatic optional; two-piece propshaft; hypoid bevel final drive, 3.54:1.

CHASSIS steel monocoque structure; independent front suspension by coil springs, wishbones, anti-roll bar; rear live axle with coil springs, trailing and semi-trailing radius arms, anti-roll bar; telescopic dampers; hydraulic vacuum servo 24.4cm (9.6in) disc front brakes, 20.3cm (8in) rear drums; rack and pinion steering; 54.6l (12 gal) fuel tank; optional 185/70-13,radial-ply 165-13 standard, 5.5in rims.
DIMENSIONS wheelbase 257.8cm (101.5in); track 142.2cm (56in) front and rear; length 426.7cm (168in); width 170.2cm (67in); height 132.1cm (52in); ground clearance 17.8cm (7in); turning circle 10.36m (34ft).
EQUIPMENT rectangular quartz halogen headlamps, centre console, push-button radio standard, seat belts £17.05p, laminated windscreen £28.78p, metallic paint £8.17p; delivery charge included in price.

PERFORMANCE maximum speed 163.7kph (102mph) *Autocar*; 29.3kph (18.2mph) @ 1000rpm; 0-96kph (60mph) 10.3sec; 15.5kg/kW (11.5kg/bhp) 4-door; fuel consumption 10.5l/100km (27mpg).
PRICES 1974 Cortina 1300 £1114; 1300L £1165; 1600XL £1350; 2000E £1637.76p.
PRODUCTION 1,126,559 all Mark III.

ABOVE **Anti-roll bars were incorporated at both ends of the Cortina from 1973, enabling lower rate springs to improve the ride. There had been only one at the front of GTs and GXLs. The 2000E Estate Car was available in 14 colours, six metallic, with the vinyl roof in either black or tobacco. Tinted glass standard from 1974.**

1973
Escort 1300E

Soon after the Escort's launch in 1968, the range was widened by the addition of 1100 and 1300 estates, although a 4-door saloon did not reach production until the following October. Smooth running of the production lines at Halewood brooked no interruption, so Ford Advanced Vehicles was set up at Aveley in Essex to make special versions. Almost a factory within the Ford factory, it was responsible for the racy editions, and also for the first 5000 Executive Escorts following up the successes with premium-priced Cortinas, Corsairs and Zephyrs. The 1300E was a costlier 2-door Escort fitted up with pile carpet, woody facia, extra instruments, coach lines, fancy wheel trims, and halogen auxiliary lamps. To emphasise its exclusiveness it was offered with special paintwork that included venetian gold, amber gold metallic, or a fetching metallic purple that set off chrome flashing round the windows and black vinyl roof. It was based on the Sport, with 13in wheels rather than the full GT, but its "E" for Executive tag (as opposed to "GT") seemed to make insurance companies less suspicious. Revisions in 1971 brought modest power increases to the range through changes in cam profiles and improvements in combustion chamber design. The de luxe and Super names were abandoned in favour of L and XL, and all were carpeted and better trimmed.

INTRODUCTION 1973 to 1974.

BODY saloon; 2-door, 4-seats; weight 815kg (1796.8lb).

ENGINE 4-cylinders, in-line; 80.97mm x 62.99mm; 1298cc; compr 9.2:1; 53.7kW (72bhp) @ 6000rpm; 41.3kW (55.5bhp)/l; 92Nm (68lbft) @ 4000rpm.

ENGINE STRUCTURE pushrod ohv; chain-driven camshaft; cast iron cylinder head and block; Weber twin choke downdraught carburettor, mechanical fuel pump; 5-bearing crankshaft.

TRANSMISSION rear wheel drive; Borg & beck diaphragm spring clutch, 19.1cm (7.5in); 4-speed synchromesh gearbox; hypoid bevel final drive 4.125:1.

CHASSIS steel monocoque structure; independent front suspension by MacPherson struts; lower links; telescopic dampers; rear live axle with semi-elliptic leaf springs and telescopic dampers; Girling hydraulic 21.8cm (8.6in) front disc brakes, rear 20.3cm (8in) drum, vacuum servo standard; rack and pinion steering; 40.9l (9.0 gal) fuel tank; 5.5in rim and 165-13 radial ply tyres.

DIMENSIONS wheelbase 240cm (94.5in); track 124.5cm (49in) front, rear 127cm (50in); length 397.8cm (156.6in); width 156cm (61.8in); height 134.6cm (53in); ground clearance 15.2cm (6in); turning circle 8.84m (29ft).

EQUIPMENT fresh air-blending heater standard, carpeted boot; seat belt anchorages built-in; mandatory seat belts £8; inertia reel belts £13; radio £20; metallic paint £6.

PERFORMANCE maximum speed 149.3kph (93mph) *Motor*; 26.2kph (16.3mph) @ 1000rpm; 0-96kph (60mph) 13.1sec; 15.2kg/kW (11.3kg/bhp); fuel consumption 9.7l/100km (27.3mpg).

PRICE total with tax: £1180.

PRODUCTION 5,000 approx.

1974
Granada Coupe 2994cc, Granada Ghia

Granada up to the waist, The Coupe was a brave entry by Ford Germany to the autobahn-cruiser market. Its racy looking 2-door body had a long sloping roof and it was sold in Britain only with Ghia trim. A 2.olitre was discontinued in the spring of 1976. Most Coupes were V6s with automatic transmission and the body style did not survive after 1977. In April 1973 the 2.5litre saloon was discontinued and the Ghia made both as a saloon and Coupe. The Ghia's distinguishing feature, besides the luxurious interior, was a die-cast grille and headlamp casing, which true to Ford's habit, took the model up the aspirational ladder, encouraging customers to pay a premium in 1974 for a car that cost very little more to make than it had in 1973. The vinyl roof could be black or a tasteful leather grained tobacco brown. Upholstery that looked like traditional West of England broadcloth was really specially treated brushed nylon Beaumont cloth from which, said Ford, oil, coffee, melted chocolate and all the usual motoring stains could be easily removed. Footwells were provided with foam underlays to enhance the feeling of cosseted luxury. Granadas' heating and ventilation was revised and the automatic became the C3 unit from Ford Bordeaux, similar to the American C4 but retuned for European driving.

INTRODUCTION January 1974, produced to 1977.
BODY saloon; 2-doors, 5-seats; weight coupe 2.3 1295kg (2855lb), Ghia 3.0 1385kg (3053.4lb).
ENGINE 6-cylinders, 60deg V; 93.7mm x 72.4mm, 2995cc; compr 9.0:1; 102.9kW (138bhp) @ 5000rpm; 34.4kW/l (46.1bhp/l); 235Nm (173lbft) @ 3000rpm.
ENGINE STRUCTURE pushrod ohv; gear-driven camshaft; cast iron cylinder heads and block; Weber twin choke carburettor, centrifugal and vacuum ignition; mechanical fuel pump; 4-bearing crankshaft.
TRANSMISSION rear wheel drive; 24.1cm (9.5in) sdp clutch; 2-piece propeller shaft; 4-speed synchromesh gearbox; optional C3 automatic; hypoid bevel final drive 3.45:1.

CHASSIS steel monocoque structure; independent front suspension, coil springs and double wishbones, anti roll bar; independent rear by semi-trailing arms, coil springs, telescopic dampers; hydraulic vacuum servo dual circuit brakes front disc 26.2cm (10.3in) ventilated, rear drum 22.9cm (9in); rack and pinion PAS; 65l (14.3 gal) (17.2 US gal) fuel tank; radial ply 175HR-14 185HR optional185-14 Michelin ZX.
DIMENSIONS wheelbase 277cm (57in); track 151cm (59.5in) front, 154cm (60.6in) rear; length 457cm (179.9in); width 179cm (70.5in); height 137cm (53.9in); ground clearance 13cm (5.1in); turning circle 11m (36ft).

EQUIPMENT sunroof, cut pile carpet, toughened glass windscreen, safety belts, automatic transmission. optional sports wheels £51.54, metallic paint £10.60, laminated windscreen £31.20, manual transmission delete option £114.31.
PERFORMANCE maximum speed Ghia saloon 171kph (106.5mph) *Autocar*; 33.4kph (20.8mph) @ 1000rpm; 0-100kph (62mph) 10.7sec; 13.5kg/kW (10kg/bhp) Ghia 3.0; fuel consumption 13.5l/100km (20.9mpg).
PRICE Ghia saloon £2478.71, £2892 incl car tax and VAT.
PRODUCTION in Britain 50,747 all Granada.

1974
Capri II 1300, 1600

With the world in the grip of the first oil crisis, manufacturers seized the opportunity to put new model announcements on hold. Not Ford. It took the plunge with the already successful Capri introducing styling changes, providing more room inside and, while keeping it a strictly 2+2, introducing a hatchback to make the car more practical. Folding the rear seat flat gave huge luggage capacity and as a bonus the backrest was split 50:50, which meant it could accommodate one occupant and large items such as skis. It was surprising really that it had not been done in the first place following the example of the MGB GT. The crease along the body side was discarded, and the dummy air intakes ahead of the rear wheel arch dispensed with, giving a smoother, more sophisticated, appearance. Slimmer windscreen pillars and bigger windows gave better visibility all round, and although the innovations with their attendant reinforcement round the double-skinned gas-strutted tailgate increased body weight by 27.2kg (60lb), they were well worthwhile. Using much the same Cortina underpinnings, the 1300 had a pushrod crossflow Kent engine and the 1600 the latest Pinto overhead camshaft engine, providing a lively turn of speed. The array of trim packs available with the first Capri was reduced; buyers had been confused and in many cases dealers ordering cars for stock failed to identify the most popular options.

INTRODUCTION December 1973, production to October 1976 in Britain and January 1978 in Germany. **BODY** coupe; 2-doors, 2+2-seats; weight 1010kg (2226.7lb), 1600 1040kg (2292.8lb). **ENGINE** 4-cylinders, in-line; 80.98mm x 62.99mm, 1297cc; compr 9.2:1; 42.5kW (57bhp) @ 5500rpm; 32.8kW (44bhp)/l; 91Nm (67lbft) @ 3000rpm. 1600 87.7 x 66mm; 1593cc; 53.7kW (72bhp) @ 5200rpm; 33.7kW (45.2bhp)/l; 118Nm (87lbft) @ 3000rpm. 1600GT 65.6kW (88bhp). **ENGINE STRUCTURE** 3034E pushrod ohv; chain-driven camshaft; cast iron cylinder head, block; Ford GPD carb, centrifugal and vacuum ignition; mechanical fuel pump; 5-bearing crank. 1600 ohc, 1600GT Weber carb.

TRANSMISSION rear wheel drive; 19.1cm (7.5in), 1600 GT 21.6cm (8.5in) diaphragm spring cable-operated clutch; 4-speed synchromesh gearbox; hypoid bevel final drive 4.125:1, 1600 3.77:1, 1600GT 3.75:1. **CHASSIS** steel monocoque; ifs by MacPherson struts and anti roll bar; live rear axle with half-elliptic springs and anti-roll bar, telescopic dampers; Girling hydraulic disc brakes at front, 24.4cm (9.6in); 20.3cm (8in) rear drums, 1600 22.9cm (9in); dual circuit; optional vacuum servo (1600 std); rack and pinion steering; 57.7l (12.7 gal) fuel tank; 165-13; 185/70-13 optional radial-ply tyres, 5Jrims. **DIMENSIONS** wbase 256cm (100.8in); track front 135.4cm (53.3in), rear 138.4cm (54.5in); length 434.1cm (171in); width 169.9cm (66.9in); height 129.8cm (51.1in); ground clearance 10.4cm (4.1in); turning 10.67m (35ft).

EQUIPMENT toughened glass windscreen, laminated extra, brushed nylon seats extra. **PERFORMANCE** maximum speed 167kph (104mph) 1600, *Autocar*, 1300 26.2kph (16.3mph), 1600 28.6kph (17.8mph); 1600GT 28.7kph (17.9mph) @ 1000rpm; 0-100kph (62mph) 11.4sec; 1300 23.8kg/kW (17.7kg/bhp), 1600 19.4kg/kW (14.5kg/bhp); 10.2l/100km (27.7mpg). **PRICE** 1300L £1336.25, 1600L £1415.83, 1600GT £1632.92. **PRODUCTION** 84,400 all Capri II in Britain.

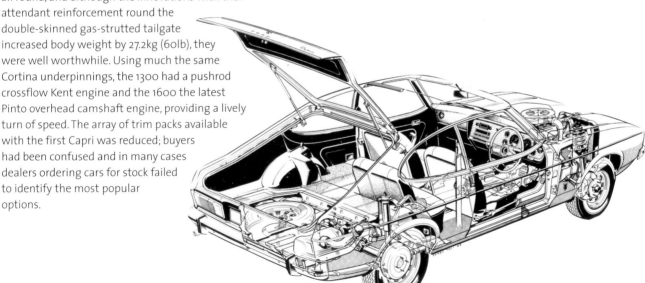

1974
Capri II 2000, 3000

The 2.0-litre overhead camshaft Pinto 4-cylinder engine from the Cortina replaced the V4, and the 3.0-litre V6 Capri was enhanced by an extra 10bhp. Power steering and automatic transmission were popular options, and buyers began taking Capris seriously as competent long distance touring cars once their racing pedigree and resulting development improved the performance and handling. The facia and controls had been revised in 1972 and softer spring rates were among radical changes made in the rear suspension to improve the ride. The rear radius arms were replaced by an anti-roll bar, and the rear track was widened by 5.8cm (2.3in). The millionth Capri was made in 1973, in Cologne, and the Mark II's revised body shape was subtly reshaped to make it less susceptible to side winds. The 3.0-litre had a new power steering option and bigger brakes. A Ghia Capri went on sale from May 1974 with moulded side rubbing strip, alloy wheels with 5.5J rims and a vinyl roof, tinted glass, and an extra coat of clear lacquer. The seats were high-backed and the facia panel had a vinyl covering, colour-keyed was the marketing term, to the Rialto material (a velvet-finished brushed nylon) used for the upholstery. Shown at the 1975 Geneva Motor Show as a limited edition, the Capri S had firmer springing, proving so popular it became generally available for 1976.

ABOVE **Uwe Bahnsen FRSA, Design Vice President,** was responsible for the Taunus 17M, Capri, Escort 3, Sierra and Scorpio.

INTRODUCTION December 1973, production to October 1976 in Britain and January 1978 in Germany.
BODY coupe; 2-doors, 2+2-seats; weight 2.0 1065kg (2348lb), 3.0 1170kg (2579.3lb).
ENGINE 4-cyls, in-line; 90.8mm x 76.95mm, 1998cc; compr 9.2:1; 73.1kW (98bhp) @ 5200rpm; 36.6kW (49bhp)/l; 151Nm (111lbft) @ 3500rpm. 3000: 6-cyls, 60deg V; 93.7 x 72.4mm 9.0:1 compr; 2994cc; 102.9kW (138bhp) @ 5000rpm; 34.4kW (46.1bhp)/l; 236Nm (174lbft) @ 3000rpm.
ENGINE STRUCTURE chain driven ohc; cast iron cyl head, block; Weber carb, centrifugal and vacuum ignition; mechanical fuel pump; 5-bearing crankshaft. V6 4-bearing; pushrod ohv.

TRANSMISSION rear wheel drive; 21.6cm (8.5in), V6 24.4cm (9.6in) diaphragm spring cable-operated clutch; 4-speed synchromesh gearbox; hypoid bevel final drive 3.44:1, V6 3.09:1.
CHASSIS steel monocoque; ifs by MacPherson struts and anti roll bar; live rear axle with half-elliptic springs and anti-roll bar, telescopic dampers; Girling hydraulic disc brakes at front, 24.5cm (9.6in), V6 24.8cm (9.75in); rear drums 22.9cm (9in); dual circuit; vacuum servo; rack and pinion (PAS optional V6); 57.7l (12.7 gal) fuel tank; 165-13; 185/70-13 optional radial-ply tyres, 5Jrims. V6 185/70-13 standard.

DIMENSIONS wheelbase 256cm (100.8in); track front 135.4cm (53.3in), rear 138.4cm (54.5in); length 434cm (170.9in); width 169.9cm (66.9in); height 129.8cm (51.1in); ground clearance 10.4cm (4.1in); turning circle 10.67m (35ft).
EQUIPMENT toughened glass windscreen, laminated extra, brushed nylon seats extra.
PERFORMANCE maximum speed V6 194.2kph (121mph); 31.3kph (19.5mph) @ 1000rpm, V6 35.2kph (21.9mph) @ 1000rpm; 0-100kph (62mph) V6 8.2sec; fuel consumption Touring DIN V6 10.7l/100km (26.4mpg).
PRICE 2000GT £1687.50, 3000GT £1931.66.
PRODUCTION 84,400 all Capri II in Britain.

1975
Escort Mk II 1098cc

Ford's pan-European policy meant that the underpinnings of the Mark II Escort were introduced for some versions in 1973, two years before the demise of the Mark I. The Mark II was essentially a re-skin of the later Mark Is and provided nearly 25 per cent more window area, and more legroom in the back. Instead of the curvy Mark I, it was fashionably upright and square-cut. The basic layout remained largely Anglia 105E; nothing was changed at Ford unless it was absolutely essential, a principle since Model T days, so handling and general roadworthiness remained good. The platform was adaptable enough to encompass 19 different models at launch. The 1100 was the basic fleet model and soon after it was announced, in July 1975 with the market in deep shock as a result of the unrelenting oil crisis, Ford took the precaution of introducing a cut-price version. This was the Escort Popular 2-door at £1299, with cross-ply tyres and reduced engine power (Autocar complained of an engine flat-spot and of having to rev it a lot to make much progress), but it was short-lived. Estate Escorts were Mark II as far as the A pillars; the slightly curved waistline of the Mark I seemed to blend quite well with the front and it was cheaper to keep it. Side mouldings and Sport wheels maintained differentials between L and GL trim options.

INTRODUCTION January 1975, production 1974 to 1980.
BODY saloon, 2-door, 4-door; estate, 4-seats; weight 2-door 875kg (1929lb), estate 1300 920kg (2028.2lb).
ENGINE 4-cylinders, in-line; 81mm x 53.3mm, 1098cc; compr 9.0:1; 35.8kW (48bhp) @ 6000rpm; 32.6kW (43.7bhp)/l; 79Nm (58.5lbft) @ 3000rpm. Popular 30.6kW (41bhp) @ 5300rpm; 70.5Nm (52lbft) @ 3000rpm.
ENGINE STRUCTURE pushrod ohv; chain-driven camshaft; cast iron cyl head and block; Ford GDP downdraught carburettor 34mm barrel (Popular 30mm barrel), mechanical fuel pump; 5-bearing crankshaft.
TRANSMISSION rwd; diaphragm spring clutch, 19cm (7.5in) 4-speed synchromesh gearbox; hypoid bevel final drive 4.125:1, Popular 3.89:1.

CHASSIS steel monocoque; ifs by MacPherson struts; lower links; telescopic dampers; rear live axle with semi-elliptic leaf springs and telescopic dampers; hydraulic 20.3cm (8in) front drum brakes (discs on L-spec cars), 22.9cm (9in) rear drums; rack and pinion steering; 40.9l (9.0 gal) fuel tank; 155-12 on 4.5rim; or 155-13 steel-braced radial ply tyres, 5in (12.7cm) rim Popular cross-ply 6.00-12.
DIMENSIONS wheelbase 240cm (94.5in); track front 127cm (50in), rear 129.5cm (51in); length 397.8cm (156.6in); width 153.7cm (60.5in); height 141cm (55.5in); ground clearance 14cm (5.5in); turning circle 9.45m (31ft).
EQUIPMENT radio £63.47; remote control door mirror £15.60; rear fog warning lamp £15.80; Popular, rubber floor mats, black-painted trim.
PERFORMANCE maximum speed 1300 149.3kph (93mph) Autocar, Popular 123kph (76.6mph) Motor; 1300 25.5kph (15.9mph) @ 1000rpm,

Popular 26kph (16.2mph); 0-96kph (60mph) 1300 13.5sec, Popular 21.8sec; 25.7kg/kW (19.2kg/bhp) 1300, 28.8kg/kW (21.3kg/bhp) Popular); fuel consumption 1300 9.6l/100km (29.3mpg), Popular 12.2l/100km (34.5mpg).
PRICE totals with tax; 1100 2-door £1440.45; Popular £1299, Popular Plus (radial ply tyres, carpet, etc) £1399.
PRODUCTION Halewood total 960,007, Saarlouis 848,388.

1975
Escort Mk II 1297cc, 1599cc

The mainstream replacements for the 7-year-old Mark I Escort were the 1300 and 1600 with the same pushrod Kent engine as before. The 1600 was an innovation for the Mark II with identical cylinder centres (so the blocks could be bored on the same machines), a longer stroke and a Weber twin choke carburettor. Price inflation was beginning to distort the market, and a midrange Ford (even a Ghia model) at over £2000 was surprising. It was the start of a spiral that would make quarterly price increases commonplace. Although the Mark II had only put on around 100lb (45.4kg) over the previous model, a lot of it accounted for by the burden of bigger windows, the 1100's performance was leisurely for the 1970s. Even fleet buyers tended to go for 1300s. But Ford was now firmly established as meeting the demands of performance-oriented customers, so first and second gearbox ratios were raised and the 1600 and 1600 Sport were welcome. Sport models had reduced ride height and stiffer springs. To keep vibrations from the long-stroke engine in check, a two-piece propeller shaft was introduced for the 1600. Following the introduction of the Mark II Escort, Ford abandoned its policy of including delivery charges in new car prices. Nobody had followed its example, it said, and that had made its prices look uncompetitive.

INTRODUCTION January 1975, produced 1974 to 1980.
BODY saloon; 2-door, 4-door, estate, 4-seats; 1300 2-dr 885kg (1951lb), estate 920kg (2028lb), 1600 Ghia 4-dr 955kg (2105.4lb), Sport 930kg (2050.3lb).
ENGINE 4-cyls, in-line; 80.98mm x 62.99mm, 1297cc; cr 9.2:1; 42.5kW (57bhp) @ 5500rpm; 32.8kW (43.9bhp)/l; 91Nm (67lbft) @ 3000rpm. 1300GT: 52.2kW (70bhp) @ 5500rpm; 92Nm (68lbft) @ 4000rpm. 1600: 80.98 x 77.62; 1598cc; 9.0:1; 62.6kW (84bhp) @ 5500rpm; 39.2kW (52.6bhp)/l; 125Nm (92lbft) @ 3500rpm.
ENGINE STRUCTURE pushrod ohv; chain-driven camshaft; cast iron cyl head and block; Ford GDP downdraught carb 1300GT & 1600 Weber twin-choke; mechanical fuel pump; 5-bearing crankshaft.

TRANSMISSION rwd; diaphragm spring clutch, 19cm (7.5in) 4-speed synchromesh gearbox; hypoid bevel final drive 3.89:1; GT, 1600 Sport 4.125:1; 1600 GT 3.54:1.
CHASSIS steel monocoque; ifs by MacPherson struts; lower links; telescopic dampers; rear live axle with semi-elliptic leaf springs and telescopic dampers; hydraulic 24.4cm (9.6in) front disc brakes, 20.3cm (8in) or 22.9cm (9in)rear drums, vacuum servo, divided hydraulic circuits; rack and pinion; 40.9l (9.0 gal) (10.8 US gal); 155SR-13in tyres, 5in rims. Sport 175/70SR-13in.
DIMENSIONS wbase 240cm (94.5in); track front 127cm (50in), rear 129.5cm (51in); length 397.8cm (156.6in); width 153.7cm (60.5in); height 141cm (55.5in); clearance 14cm (5.5in); turning circle 9.45m (31ft).
EQUIPMENT Ford Bordeaux automatic £145.67; radio £63.47; remote control door mirror £15.60; rear fog warning lamp £15.80.

PERFORMANCE maximum 149.3kph (93mph) 1300 *Autocar*; 27.5kph (17.1mph) 1300, 26.2kph (16.3mph) @ 1000rpm GT; 30.5kph (19mph) 1600; 0-96kph (60mph) 13.5 sec; 20.8kg/kW (15.5kg/bhp) 1300; 9.6l/100km (29.3mpg).
PRICE totals with tax; 1300 4-door £1558.62; 1300 Ghia 4-door £2067.57; 1600 Sport 2-door £1860.48.
PRODUCTION Halewood total 960,007, Saarlouis 848,388.

BELOW During a 1970s fuel crisis, an Escort 1297cc with skinny high pressure tyres set fuel consumption records at the Boreham test track. It managed 2.38l/100km (118.7mpg) under specialist driving, involving long slow spells accelerating and prolonged coasting.

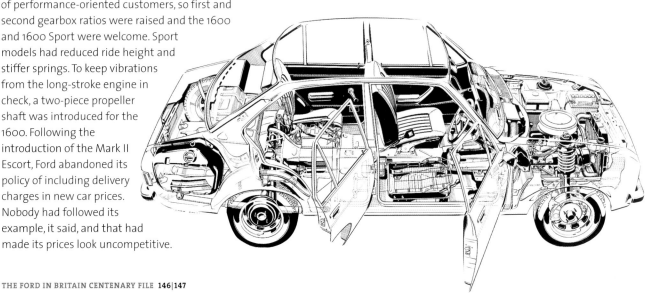

1975
Escort RS1800; 1976 RS 2000

All sporting Escorts had lapsed, so when the Mark II appeared there were no Mexicos or RS models. In March 1975 the Pinto engined RS2000, due for production by the end of the year, was shown together with the prototype BDA-engined RS1800 that went on sale in June in the small numbers befitting a hand-built competition car. With AVO closed down, high performance Escorts with all three engine options (the RS Mexico would follow in 1976), were built at Saarlouis. The successful RS2000, which had a restyled sloping polyurethane front unlike the RS1800, was shown at the 1975 Geneva Motor Show. Both had 2-door reinforced body shells with stronger suspension pick-ups and a heavy-duty front cross-member. The new front claimed improved aerodynamics, reducing front-end lift by 25 per cent, (it was also declared to be more pedestrian-friendly) while the small back spoiler was said to diminish lift at the rear by 60 per cent. Overall aerodynamic drag was down 16 per cent. The gearbox was the standard close-ratio GT and two radius arms replaced the front anti-roll bar, so Ford said, to improve the ride of the firmly sprung car. The interior continued the competition theme with black headlining, black cloth trim and carpet, and lightweight seats. In September 1978 an enhanced RS 2000 Custom was brought out with Recaro seats and alloy wheels.

INTRODUCTION March 1975 and 1976. Production to 1978.
BODY saloon; 2-door; RS1800 900kg (1984.1lb), RS2000 925kg (2039.3lb).
ENGINE 4-cylinders, in-line; 86.75mm x 77.62mm, 1837cc; compr 10.0.1; 85.8kW (115bhp) @ 6000rpm; 46.7kW (62.6bhp)/l; 163Nm (120lbft) @ 4000rpm. RS2000: 90.8 x 76.95; 1993cc; 9.2:1; 82kW (110bhp) @ 5500rpm; 41.2kW (55.2bhp)/l; 161Nm (119lbft) @ 3500rpm.
ENGINE STRUCTURE RS1800 BDA twin belt-driven ohc; 16-valve; 2000 single belt driven ohc 8-valve; 1800 aluminium block and head, 2000 cast iron block, aluminium head; downdraught Weber twin-choke carb; mechanical fuel pump; 5-bearing crank.

TRANSMISSION rwd; diaphragm spring clutch, 19cm (7.5in) 4-speed synchromesh gearbox (RS2000 Type E) (RS1800 close-ratio); hypoid bevel final drive 3.54:1.
CHASSIS steel monocoque; ifs by MacPherson struts; lower links, anti-roll bar; telescopic dampers; rear live axle with semi-elliptic leaf springs, radius arms, and telescopic dampers; hydraulic 24.4cm (9.6in) front disc brakes, 20.3cm (8in) or 22.9cm (9in) rear drums, vacuum servo, divided hydraulic circuits; rack and pinion steering; 40.9l (9.0 gal) fuel tank; cast aluminium alloy wheels 155SR-13in tyres 5.5in (1800) and 6in (2000) rims. Sport 175/70HR-13in.
DIMENSIONS wheelbase 240cm (94.5in); track front 127cm (50in), rear 129.5cm (51in); length 397.8cm (156.6in); width 157cm (61.8in); height 141cm (55.5in); ground clearance 14cm (5.5in); turning circle 9.45m (31ft).

EQUIPMENT Ford Bordeaux automatic £145.67; radio £63.47; remote control door mirror £15.60; rear fog warning lamp £15.80.
PERFORMANCE maximum speed RS2000 173.7kph (108.2mph) Motor; 29.7kph (18.5mph) @ 1000rpm; 0-96kph (60mph) 8.5sec; 10.5kg/kW (7.8kg/bhp) 1800, 11.3kg/kW (8.4kg/bhp) RS2000; 37.7kph (23.5mph).
PRICE totals with tax; 1975 RS2000 £2857, 1977 £3519. 1977 RS1800 £3786.
PRODUCTION RS1800 109 sold UK; RS2000 10,039 sold UK.

1976
Escort RS Mexico

The Mark II Escort Mexico, with a 1.6-litre Pinto engine and looking much like any other Escort, never quite caught on. The RS 2000 was almost as fast as the small-scale production RS 1800, but the Mexico never seemed to find its niche and was discontinued in 1978, with a hybrid RS2000 produced instead with Mexico interior and steel wheels. The rationale behind the original Mexico had been a competition car with stamina, so the engine had been a regular cast iron Kent crossflow. The Mark II inherited a Pinto ohc engine with two valves per cylinder, much like the RS2000's but smaller, with its own cylinder block casting. The gearbox in the first series of Mark II

Mexicos was the Ford Type 3 three rail shift; later cars had the German Type E single rail shift as used for the RS2000. Some Mexicos were badged 1600GT and some were redesignated RS Mexico. The interior had the facia layout of the Sport pack on 1300 and 1600, against the RS models' centre consoles and clocks. Towards the end of the Mark II's production, special editions came thick and fast, such as the Escort Harrier, which was a series of 1500 cars based on the 1600 Sport with Recaro seats, rear spoiler, and alloy RS wheels to commemorate the Escort's eighth successive win in the RAC Rally.

INTRODUCTION 1976, production to 1978.

BODY saloon; 2-door; weight 920kg (2028.2lb).

ENGINE 4-cylinders, in-line; 87.65mm x 66mm, 1593cc; compr 9.2:1; 70.8kW (95bhp) @ 5750rpm; 44.5kW (59.6bhp)/l; 125Nm (92lbft) @ 4000rpm.

ENGINE STRUCTURE single belt driven ohc 8-valve; cast iron block, aluminium head; downdraught Weber twin-choke carburettor; mechanical fuel pump; 5-bearing crankshaft.

TRANSMISSION rear wheel drive; diaphragm spring clutch, 19cm (7.5in) 4-speed synchromesh gearbox; hypoid bevel final drive 3.54:1.

CHASSIS steel monocoque structure; independent front suspension by MacPherson struts; lower links, anti-roll bar; telescopic dampers; rear live axle with semi-elliptic leaf springs, radius arms, and telescopic dampers; hydraulic 24.4cm (9.6in) front disc brakes, 22.cm (9in) rear drums, vacuum servo, divided hydraulic circuits; rack and pinion steering; 40.9l (9.0 gal) fuel tank; cast aluminium alloy wheels 175/70HR-13in tyres, 6in rims (steel wheels optional).

DIMENSIONS wheelbase 240cm (94.5in); track front 127cm (50in), rear 129.5cm (51in); length 397.8cm (156.6in); width 157cm (61.8in); height 141cm (55.5in); ground clearance 14cm (5.5in); turning circle 9.45m (31ft).

EQUIPMENT radio £63.47; remote control door mirror £15.60; rear fog warning lamp £15.80.

PERFORMANCE maximum speed 172kph (107.1mph) Ford; 29.7kph (18.5mph) @ 1000rpm; 13kg/kW (9.7kg/bhp); 0-96kph (60mph) 10.55sec; fuel consumption 9.2l/100km (30.71mpg).

PRICE totals with tax; 1977 Mexico £2978.

PRODUCTION approx 2290 UK registered

1976
Cortina Mark IV 1297cc, 1593cc, 1993cc

By the middle of the 1970s the Coke-bottle fashion was passing. Ford's new designer Uwe Bahnsen was given the job of coordinating Cortina design for Ford Europe using the existing platform. The German and British editions were now almost fully integrated, sporty versions were dropped in favour of business and executive versions, and, as before, a wide range of options meant Cortina customers could, in theory at any rate, tailor their cars to their precise specifications. As ever theory and practice did not always coincide, and choosy customers often found that ringing too many changes on what was on offer at a dealer delayed delivery. The Mark IV had a more European stance than the Detroit-inspired Mark III, it was crisper and more upright, with 15 per cent more glass. And because Cologne and Dagenham were not yet completely in step, the German Taunus range appeared 6 months ahead of Britain's. Also the bigger engined versions in Germany still used the 1999cc and 2293cc Cologne V6, and no Taunus had the UK-only Kent 4-cylinder. In the aftermath of the oil crisis some economy models were introduced. There was an entry-level 36.9kW (49.5bhp) 1300 Kent engine and a 44kW (59bhp) 1600 Pinto, but they sold slowly.

INTRODUCTION October 1976, produced to 1979.

BODY 1300 saloon, 2-dr, 4-dr; 1600 and 2000 4-door, estate; 5-seats; 1300 1000kg (2205lb), 1600 1035kg (2282lb).

ENGINE 1300 4-cyls, in-line; 81mm x 63mm, 1297cc; compr 9.2:1; 36.9kW (49.5bhp) @ 5000rpm; 28.5kW (38.2bhp)/l; 87Nm (64lbft) @ 3000rpm. 1600 87.7m x 66mm; 1593cc; 44kW (59bhp) @ 4500rpm or 53.7kW (72bhp) @ 5000rpm; 111 or 118Nm (82 or 87lbft) torque.

ENGINE STRUCTURE Kent pushrod ohv; Pinto single ohc; toothed belt; opposed ohv; cast iron cyl head, block; Ford GPD carb (2000 Weber 32/36 DGAV downdraught twin choke); mechanical fuel pump; 5-bearing crank.

TRANSMISSION rwd; diaphragm spring cable-operated 21.6cm (8.5in) sdp clutch; 4-spd single selector rail synchromesh gearbox; 3-speed Borg Warner Model 35 auto optional (not 1300 or economy 1600); 2-piece prop shaft (not 1300, 1600); hypoid bevel final drive, 4.11 (1300); 3.78 and 3.89 (1600s); 3.75:1 (2000).

CHASSIS steel monocoque; ifs by coil springs, wishbones, anti-roll bar; rear live axle with coil springs, trailing and semi trailing radius arms; telescopic dampers; hydraulic vacuum servo 24.8cm (9.75in) disc front brakes, 20.3cm (8in) rear drums, 22.7cm (9in on 2000); rack & pinion, PAS opt 2000; 54.6l (12 gal); opt 185/70-13, radial-ply 165-13 standard, 4.5 or 5.5in rims.

DIMENSIONS wb 257.8cm (101.5in); track front 144.5cm (56.9in), rear 142.2cm (56in); l 432.6cm (170.3in); w 170.2cm (67in); h 132cm (52in); clearance 17.8cm (7in); turning 10.4m (34ft).

EQUIPMENT heated rear window, radial-ply tyres, brake servo, front discs, 2-speed wipers, electric screenwash, reversing lights, cigar lighter, dipping mirror, carpets standard through range.

PERFORMANCE maximum 160.5kph (100mph) 2000 Ghia *Autocar*; 28.7kph (17.9mph) @ 1000rpm; 0-96kph (60mph) 11sec; 1600 23.5kW/kg (17.5kg/bhp); 11.7l/10km (24.1mpg).

PRICE at launch 1300 2-door £1950.39, 4-door £2029.95; 1600GL 4-door £2548.26, estate £2822.04; 2000 Ghia 4-door £3120.97.

PRODUCTION 1,131,850 all Mark IV.

1976
Fiesta 957cc, 1117cc

INTRODUCTION 1976, produced until 1983.
BODY saloon; 2-doors, 4-seats; weight 730kg (1609.4lb).
ENGINE 4-cylinders, transverse; 74mm x 55.7mm, 957cc; compr 9.0:1; comp 8.3:1; 29.8kW (40bhp) @ 6000rpm; 33.6kW (45bhp) @ 6000rpm; 35kW (47bhp)/l; 65Nm (47.7lbft) @ 3000rpm. 1.1: 74 x 65mm; 1117cc; 39.52kW (53bhp) @ 6000rpm; 35.4kW (47.4bhp)/l; 80Nm (59lbft).
ENGINE STRUCTURE pushrod ohv; chain-driven camshaft; cast iron cylinder head, block; Ford sonic idle carburettor, mechanical fuel pump; 3-bearing crankshaft.
TRANSMISSION front wheel drive; 16.5cm (6.5in) sdp clutch; 4-spd synchromesh gearbox; final drive helical spur, 957cc 4.29:1; 1117cc 4.056:1.
CHASSIS steel monocoque structure; independent front suspension by MacPherson struts, coil springs; rear suspension dead axle, trailing links, Panhard rod; telescopic dampers; hydraulic, vacuum servo 22cm (8.7in) front disc brakes; rear drums 17.8cm (7.0in); rack and pinion steering; 34l (7.5 gal) fuel tank; Michelin ZX radial-ply 135-12 or 145-12 tyres.
DIMENSIONS wheelbase 228.6cm (90in); track 133.5cm (52.6in) front, 132cm (52in) rear; length 356.5cm (140.4in); width 156.5cm (61.6in); height 136cm (53.5in); ground clearance 14cm (5.5in); turning circle 9.45m (31ft).
EQUIPMENT pvc upholstery, cloth on Ghia, carpets, laminated windscreen.
PERFORMANCE maximum speed 957cc 126.8kph (79mph), 1117cc 138kph (86mph) *Autocar*; 24kph (15mph) or 24.9kph (15.5mph) @ 1000rpm; 0-100kph (62mph) 19.6sec or 15.7sec; 21.7kg/kW (16.2kg/bhp); fuel consumption 8l/100km (35.3mpg) or 8.4l/100km (33.6mpg).
PRICE basic Fiesta £1856, L £2079, Ghia £2657; 1.1L £2179, 1.1 Ghia £2757.
PRODUCTION Fiesta in Britain 307,600.

Ford's return to the market for small cars was previewed as the Bobcat, a supermini prototype, for which studios in Turin, Dunton, Merkenich and Dearborn submitted designs throughout the early 1970s. The first front wheel drive Ford, first transverse-engined Ford and the smallest capacity Ford since the 1950s, it was notable for the diversity of the places that produced it. Bodies and engines were made in two new plants at Valencia, Spain, transmissions at Bordeaux, France, cylinder blocks and radiators at Dagenham and carburettors in Belfast. Assembly was at Valencia, Cologne, Saarlouis Belgium and later Dagenham, and it quickly became Europe's fastest-selling car, with half a million made in the first year and three million by the time of its first

face-lift in 1984. Technically not very daring, it remained a 3-door hatchback until 1989, with no automatic option until Continuously Variable Transmission (CVT) became available. The design brief specified a 228.6cm (90in) wheelbase, which was 7.6cm (3in) longer than a Fiat 127 (to which the Fiesta bore a striking resemblance), and 11.4cm (4.5in) shorter than an Escort. To achieve the necessary economy and performance, the weight target was 700kg (1543.2lb). Fiestas went on sale in most of Europe during 1976, right hand drive models reaching Britain in February 1977 in base, S, and Ghia configurations. A 1978 special edition coincided with the 75th anniversary of Ford Motor Company.

1977
Fiesta 1297cc

The engine for the first Fiesta was essentially a crossflow Kent, dating back to the 105E Anglia, and turned sideways. Kents invariably had a bore of 81mm, whatever their capacity, and the same cylinder spacing, a legacy of the machinery on which they were produced. The Fiesta had a shrunken Kent with 74mm bores and a shorter block; hence it had a shorter crankshaft, which Ford decided could manage perfectly well on three main bearings instead of the usual five. The strokes chosen were 55.7mm, giving a capacity of 957cc, and 65mm, giving 1117cc. By 1977 the engineering work necessary to get a five main bearing, markedly over-square, 81mm bore power unit to fit into the Fiesta's engine space had been carried out, notwithstanding the difficulty that faced dealers carrying out overhauls of changing the clutch without first removing the engine. This had been thought essential for the fleet buyer market in small capacity classes. Among the modifications necessary for the change were new engine and gearbox mountings, a bigger radiator and a higher final drive ratio. The 1300 was available as an S with thicker anti-roll bar, stiffer springs, adjustable dampers, and trendy (for a time at any rate) striped upholstery rather like a deckchair. The alternative was a Ghia with all-round comfort and luxury trim. Both models had 155SR-12 tyres and the same rather wide-ratio gearbox.

INTRODUCTION 1976, produced until 1983.
BODY saloon; 2-doors, 4-seats; weight 885kg (1951lb).
ENGINE 4-cylinders, transverse; 81mm x 63mm, 1298cc; compr 9.2:1; 49.2kW (66bhp) @ 5600rpm; 37.9kW (50.8bhp)/l; 92Nm (68lbft) @ 3250rpm.
ENGINE STRUCTURE pushrod ohv; chain-driven camshaft; cast iron cylinder head, block; Weber dual choke carburettor, mechanical fuel pump; 5-bearing crankshaft.

TRANSMISSION front wheel drive; sdp clutch; 4-speed synchromesh gearbox; final drive helical spur, 3.842:1.
CHASSIS steel monocoque structure; ifs by MacPherson struts, coil springs; rear suspension dead axle, trailing links, Panhard rod; telescopic dampers; hydraulic vacuum servo 22.1cm (8.7in) front disc brakes; rear drums 17.8cm (7.0in); rack and pinion steering; 34l (7.5 gal) fuel tank; Michelin ZX radial-ply 155SR-12 tyres; aluminium alloy wheels.
DIMENSIONS wheelbase 228.6cm (90in); track 133.5cm (52.6in) front, 132cm (52in) rear; length 356.5cm (140.4in); width 156.5cm (61.6in); height 136cm (53.5in); ground

clearance 14cm (5.5in); turning circle 9.45m (31ft).
EQUIPMENT pvc upholstery, cloth on Ghia, carpets, laminated windscreen.
PERFORMANCE maximum speed 151kph (94.1mph) *Autocar*; 26.97kph (16.8mph) @ 1000rpm; 0-100kph (62mph) 13.7sec; 18kg/kW (13.4kg/bhp); fuel consumption 8.9l/100km (31.7mpg).
PRICE 1300S £2844.
PRODUCTION Fiesta in Britain 307,600.

1977
Cortina Mark IV V6 2293cc

Ford Cologne and Ford Dagenham both developed 60-degree V6 engines pre-rationalisation. A common policy seemed unnecessary in the 1960s. The markets were different, the cars were different; it was assumed they would remain different. The Cologne engine was compact and light, and in the tradition of the Ford V8 since the 1930s the drive to the central camshaft was by gears. The Essex engine was strong but it was heavy, and in view of the Cologne engine's scope for development (it had already been used successfully in racing) it was chosen for the most up-market Cortina yet. Under inflationary pressure it was the first Cortina to cost more than

£4000. As a measure of how money had been devalued, when the first Cortina came out in 1962, £4,000 would have bought an Aston Martin DB4 or gone two-thirds of the way towards a Rolls-Royce Silver Cloud. Changed days. Yet the Cortina IV 2300 was more than 15 years ahead of Cortina I in terms of equipment, furnishings, technical sophistication, and performance. S for Sport was largely a trim and suspension term, not a measure of speed, and the extra weight of the V6 meant uprated front springs anyway. Gas-filled dampers came in and the S had seats striped in the style of seaside deck chairs.

PRODUCTION September 1977, production to 1979.
BODY saloon, 4-door; 5-seats; estate, 5-door; weight saloon 1090kg (2403lb).
ENGINE 6-cylinders, 60deg V; 90mm x 60.14mm, 2294cc; compr 8.75:1; 80.5kW (108bhp) @ 5000rpm; 35.1kW (47.1bhp)/l; 176Nm (130lbft) @ 3000rpm.
ENGINE STRUCTURE pushrod ohv, gear-driven camshaft; cast iron cylinder head and block; Solex twin choke 35/35 EEIT carburettor; mechanical fuel pump; 4-bearing crankshaft.
TRANSMISSION rear wheel drive; diaphragm spring cable operated 21.6cm (8.5in) sdp clutch; 4-speed single selector rail synchromesh gearbox; 3-speed Borg Warner Model 35 automatic optional; 2-piece prop shaft; hypoid bevel final drive, 3.44:1.
CHASSIS steel monocoque structure; ifs by coil springs, wishbones, anti-roll bar; rear live axle with coil springs, trailing and semi-trailing radius arms; telescopic dampers; hydraulic vacuum servo 24.8cm (9.75in) disc front brakes, 23cm (9in) rear drums; rack and pinion steering; (PAS standard); 54.6l (12 gal) fuel tank; 185/70-13, radial-ply tyres; 5.5in rims.
DIMENSIONS wheelbase 257.8cm (101.5in); track front 144.5cm (56.9in), rear 142.2cm (56in); length 432.6cm (170.3in); width 170.2cm (67in); height 132.1cm (52in); ground clearance 17.8cm (7in); turning circle 10.36m (34ft).
EQUIPMENT heated rear window, radial-ply tyres, brake servo, front discs, 2-speed wipers, electric screenwash, reversing lights, cigar lighter, dipping mirror, carpets standard alloy wheels optional.
PERFORMANCE maximum speed 158.9kph (99mph) 2.3 Ghia auto *Autocar*; 31.6kph (19.7mph) @ 1000rpm; 0-96kph (60mph) 12.2sec; 13.5kg/kW (10.1kg/bhp); fuel consumption 12.4l/100km (22.8mpg).
PRICE £4126 S, £4445 Ghia.
PRODUCTION 1,131,850 all Mark IV.

1977
Granada Mark II 1993cc, 2293cc

Retaining much of the original platform and suspension, the Mark II Granada took on a crisper appearance as designer Uwe Bahnsen forged a closer relationship in the appearance of the Ford family of cars. Since it was assembled in Germany, the UK V6 engines were discarded in favour of smaller and lighter German ones, and fuel injection and electronic ignition introduced to cope with increasingly demanding American emission legislation. In anticipation of its adoption in Europe, new techniques enabled better control of the combustion process. Ford was among the advocates of lean-burn, to reduce noxious emissions by more complete combustion, but was over-ruled by those who bargained for catalytic converters at the expense of heavy fuel consumption. The 2.0-litre in-line four was no longer offered in its 55.9kW (75bhp) economy form, and it was joined by a 2.3-litre V6 with only 6.7kW (9bhp) extra but a good deal more torque. The German V6 was nearly 22kg (48.5lb) lighter than the older Essex, and although incapable of stretching beyond 2.8-litres, it was much smoother and free-revving. Practical benefits of the new big Fords included Ghias with electric windows and central locking, and an extension of the intervals between major services to 12,000 miles. The new 2.0-litre weighed a useful 50kg (110lb) less than its predecessor through the increasing enlightenment conferred by computer aided design.

INTRODUCTION production December 1976–1978 in Cologne. **BODY** saloon; 4-doors, 5-seats; weight 2.0 1300kg (2866lb), 2.3 1310kg (2888lb), 5-door estate 1395kg (3075.4lb). **ENGINE** 2.0: 4-cylinders, in-line; 90.8mm x 76.95mm, 1998cc; compr 9.2: 73.8kW (99bhp) @ 5200rpm; 37kW (49.5bhp)/l; 151Nm (111lbft) @ 4000rpm. 2.3: 60deg V6; 90 x 60.14mm; 2294cc; compr 8.75; 80.5kW (108bhp) @ 5000rpm; 35.1kW (47.1bhp)/l; 176Nm (130lbft) @ 3000rpm. **ENGINE STRUCTURE** belt-driven overhead camshaft; cast iron cylinder head, block; Weber twin choke variable carburettor, mechanical fuel pump; 5-bearing crankshaft. V6 chain-driven camshaft, pushrod ohv; Solex twin choke; 4-bearing crank.

TRANSMISSION rear wheel drive; diaphragm spring sdp clutch; 4-speed synchromesh gearbox; C3 automatic optional £320.70; final drive hypoid bevel 3.89:1. V6 3.64:1. **CHASSIS** steel monocoque structure; ifs by coil springs and double wishbones; irs by coil springs and semi-trailing arms; front anti roll bar; telescopic dampers; hydraulic vacuum servo brakes, front 26.2cm (10.3in) discs rear 23cm (9in) drums; dual circuit; rack and pinion steering, PAS optional; 65l (14.3gal) (17.2 US gal) fuel tank; radial-ply 175SR-14 tyres 5.5in rims. V6 185-14. **DIMENSIONS** wheelbase 277cm (109in); track 151.5cm (59.7in) front, 153cm (60.2in) rear; length 463.3cm (182.4in); width 179cm (70.5in); height 142cm (55.9in); ground clearance 15cm (5.9in); turning circle 11.2m (36.75ft).

EQUIPMENT seat belts standard, optional central locking (£111.57), remote control mirror (£93.59), electric aerial (£39.88), sun roof (£174.26), front electric windows £141.02), PAS (£210.50). **PERFORMANCE** maximum 164kph (102.2mph), V6 automatic 158kph (98.4mph) *Autocar*, 29.7kph (18.5mph) @ 1000rpm, V6 31.5kph (19.6mph) @ 1000rpm; 0-100kph (62mph) 11.9sec, V6 auto 14.5sec;17.6kg/kW (13.1kg/bhp); fuel consumption 13.4l/100km (21.1mpg), V6 13.7l/100km (20.6mpg). **PRICE** £4516.54, 2.3V6 £5260.94. **PRODUCTION** total Granada 639,440.

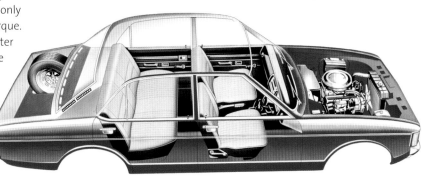

1977
Granada Mk II 2.8, 2.8Fi

Bosch K-Jetronic fuel injection was already available in Germany when it was included in the specification of the Granada. The additional 18.6kW (25bhp) made a marked difference in speed and acceleration with scarcely any penalty in fuel consumption; such was the efficiency that attended it with the same overall gearing. One of the new body's novelties, a consequence of an era in which drag coefficients were being bandied about indiscriminately, was its Cd. Ford claimed the new car had 3.2 per cent less drag than its predecessor, which may not have been saying much, but a good deal of the improvement was said to come from the rearwards slant of the radiator grille. Its slats were cunningly arranged to admit cooling air at slow speeds when it was needed most, but built up a boundary-layer that rendered the grille aerodynamically solid at high speeds, diverting air over the nose of the car. The grille was supplemented by a small beard-type spoiler that swept the slipstream aside, reducing rear-end lift by a remarkable 38 per cent. In August 1979 the 2.3-litre came in for a number of modifications, the engine power was increased to 85 kW (114bhp) and there were improvements to trim and equipment. In 1981 the entire range was revised with major alterations to the suspension settings and cosmetic details inside.

INTRODUCTION production Dec 1976–1978 in Cologne.
BODY saloon; 4-doors, 5-seats; 1360kg (2998.3lb), estate 1455kg (3207.7lb).
ENGINE 6-cylinders, 60deg V; 93.0mm x 68.5mm, 2792cc; compr 9.2:1; 100.7kW (135bhp) @ 5200rpm; 36.1kW (48.4bhp)/l; 216Nm (159lbft) @ 3000rpm. 2.8i: 119.3kW (160bhp) @ 5700rpm; 221Nm (163lbft) @ 4300rpm.
ENGINE STRUCTURE pushrod ohv, chain-driven camshaft; Solex twin choke carb; cast iron cyl head, block; mechanical fuel pump; 4-bearing crank, 2.8i Bosch K-Jetronic mechanical fuel injection.
TRANSMISSION rwd; diaphragm spring sdp clutch; 4-speed synchromesh gearbox; automatic option; final drive hypoid bevel 3.45:1.
CHASSIS steel monocoque; ifs by coil springs and double wishbones; irs by coil springs and semi-trailing arms; front anti roll bar; telescopic dampers; hydraulic vacuum servo brakes, front 26.2cm (10.3in) ventilated discs rear 23cm (9in) drums; dual circuit; rack and pinion PAS; 65l (14.3 gal) fuel tank; radial-ply 175SR-14 tyres 5.5in rims. V6 185-14.
DIMENSIONS wheelbase 277cm (109.1in); track 151.5cm (59.7in) front, 153cm (60.2in) rear; length 463.3cm (182.4in); width 179cm (70.5in); height 142cm (55.9in); ground clearance 15cm (5.9in); turning circle 11.2m (36.75ft).
EQUIPMENT seat belts standard, optional central locking (£107.38), remote control mirror (£22.50), sunroof (£167.80), tinted glass £52.33.
PERFORMANCE max speed 2.8i 187.8kph (117mph) *Autocar*; 33.2kph (20.7mph) @ 1000rpm; 0-100kph (62mph) 8.9sec; 13.5kg/kW (10.1kg/bhp); 13.6l/100km (20.8mpg).
PRICE 2800GL automatic std £5913; 2800i GL£6150 2800i Ghia £7315; 2800iGL Estate £6849.
PRODUCTION total Granada 639,440.

1977
Granada Mk II 2.1D

Ford's plans to make its own diesel developed somewhat behind market demand, especially in Continental Europe, and Ford turned to Peugeot in search of a suitable engine for the Granada. Ford's own light commercial diesels could not be made sufficiently refined for a car, so the 4.90 used in the Peugeot 504 was adapted instead. It was used both as a 1.9-litre and 2.1-litre, with only the larger sold in Britain, after some detail work to make it fit the Granada. The sump was redesigned, engine accessories repositioned, and the power of the glow-plugs was increased to speed cold starts. Ford also installed bigger air, oil, and fuel filters with the objective of extending the interval between oil changes to match that of petrol-engined cars. It was not quite achieved. Oil changes were still required every 3000miles (4828km) filters at 6000miles (9656km) and fuel filters frequently. Peugeot's altruism in the sale of an important engine to a rival did not extend to offering Ford the new 2.3-litre diesel it had developed. *Autocar* reported that its existence was revealed only after Ford had signed up to the existing engines, leaving it a generation behind in a growing European market. Diesel cars were still regarded with some reserve in Britain, suitable at best as taxis, but the increasing cost of fuel was leading to much change.

INTRODUCTION production December 1976-1978 in Cologne. **BODY** saloon; 4-doors, 5-seats; weight 1310kg (2888lb). **ENGINE** 4-cylinders, in-line; 88mm x 80mm, 1948cc; compr 21.8:1; 47kW (63bhp) @ 5200rpm; 24.1kW (32.3bhp)/l; 122Nm (90lbft) @ 2000rpm. **ENGINE STRUCTURE** pushrod ohv, chain-driven camshaft; Bosch fuel injection; cast iron cylinder head, block; mechanical fuel pump; 5-bearing crankshaft. **TRANSMISSION** rear wheel drive; diaphragm spring sdp clutch; 4-speed synchromesh gearbox; final drive hypoid bevel 3.89:1. **CHASSIS** steel monocoque structure; ifs by coil springs and double wishbones; independent rear suspension by coil springs and semi-trailing arms; front anti roll bar; telescopic dampers; hydraulic vacuum servo brakes, front 26.2cm (10.3in) discs rear 23cm (9in) drums; dual circuit; rack and pinion steering, PAS optional; 65l (14.3gal) fuel tank; radial-ply 175SR-14 tyres 5.5in rims. **DIMENSIONS** wheelbase 277cm (109.1in); track front 151.5cm (59.7in), rear 153cm (60.2in); length 463.3cm (182.4in); width 179cm (70.5in); height 142cm (55.9in); ground clearance 15cm (5.9in); turning circle 11.2m (36.75ft). **EQUIPMENT** seat belts standard, PAS (£219.50), optional central locking (£111.57). **PERFORMANCE** maximum speed 2.8i 187.8kph (117mph) Autocar; 29.7kph (18.5mph) @ 1000rpm; 0-100kph (62mph) 27.2sec; 27.9kg/kW (20.8kg/bhp); fuel consumption 9.4l/100km (30.1mpg). **PRICE** £5087. **PRODUCTION** total Granada 639,440.

1978
Capri III 1600, 2000

Not much sheet metal changed for the 1978 Capri facelift. The front was tidied up with four round headlamps instead of two rectangular ones, and a spoiler and a slatted grille were added. Aerodynamics improved the drag factor by six per cent (12.6 per cent with the rear spoiler) from Cd 0.4 to 0.374 and, together with recalibration of the carburettor, gave a small saving in fuel but little in the way of increased speed. Although Ford's official figures (given here) made the car's weight much the same as the Mark II, road test weighbridge figures showed the increase that invariably followed the introduction of the new model. The 1600GT of 65.6kW (88bhp) was dropped in 1980, and the 1300, restored to normal Kent specifications giving 42.5kW (57bhp) @ 5500rpm and 91Nm (67lbft) of torque, was discontinued in 1982. All models except the 1300 gained Bilstein gas-filled dampers, and the 1600 and 2000 were available in GL or S trim. S-specification cars had a bootlid spoiler, a shaded "sidewinder" stripe and Recaro competition style seats with head restraints incorporating a mesh-filled ring to help rearwards visibility. Wider tyres made the steering heavier but the firmer suspension proved popular with keen drivers. The Capri generated a lot of special editions, among them the 1600cc Capri GT4 of which 1500 were made in February 1980.

INTRODUCTION 1978, production to 1986.
BODY coupe; 2-doors, 4-seats; weight 1600 1050kg (2314.8lb), 2000 1060kg (2336.9lb).
ENGINE 4-cylinders, in-line; 87.6mm x 66mm, 1593cc; compr 9.2:1; 53.7kW (72bhp) @ 5200rpm; 33.7kW (45.2bhp)/l; 118Nm (87lbft) @ 2700rpm. 1600GT/S: 65.62kW (88bhp) @ 5700rpm. 2000: 90.82 x 76.95; 1993cc; 68.6kW (92bhp) @ 5200rpm; 34.4kW (46bhp)/l.
ENGINE STRUCTURE ohc, toothed belt; cast iron cylinder head, block; Ford single venturi carburettor, GT/S 2000 Weber twin-choke; 5-bearing crankshaft.

TRANSMISSION rear wheel drive; sdp clutch; 4-speed synchromesh gearbox; optional C3 automatic; final drive 3.77, GT/S 3.75, 2000 3.44:1, auto 3.75, 3.44, 3.09.
CHASSIS steel monocoque structure; independent front suspension by MacPherson struts; rear suspension semi-elliptic springs; anti roll bars; gas-filled telescopic dampers; hydraulic vacuum servo brakes, front disc 24.4cm (9.6in) dia, rear 23cm (9in) drums, dual circuit; rack and pinion steering; 57.7l (12.7 gal) fuel tank; 165SR-13 radial-ply tyres, 5Jrims.
DIMENSIONS wheelbase 256cm (100.8in); track front 135.5cm (53.4in), rear 138.5cm (54.5in); length 437.5cm (172.2in); width 170cm (66.9in); height 136cm (53.5in); ground clearance 11.5cm (4.5in); turning circle 10.8m (35.43ft).

EQUIPMENT 2-speed wipers; hazard warning lights; electric screenwash; cloth upholstery; laminated windscreen.
PERFORMANCE maximum speed 1600S 159kph (99mph), 2000 167kph (104mph) *Autocar*; 1600 28.6kph (17.8mph) @ 1000rpm, 1600S 28.9kph (18mph) @ 1000rpm, 2000 31.3kph (19.5mph) @ 1000rpm; 0-100kph (62mph) 1600 12.7sec, 2000 11.2sec; 1600 19.6kg/kW (14.6kg/bhp), 2000 15.5kg/kW (11.5kg/bhp); fuel consumption 10.2-9.8l/100km (27.7-28.8mpg).
PRICE Sept 1978 1300£2959, 1600S £3069, 2000S £4192.
PRODUCTION Cologne (all Capris 1,886,647).

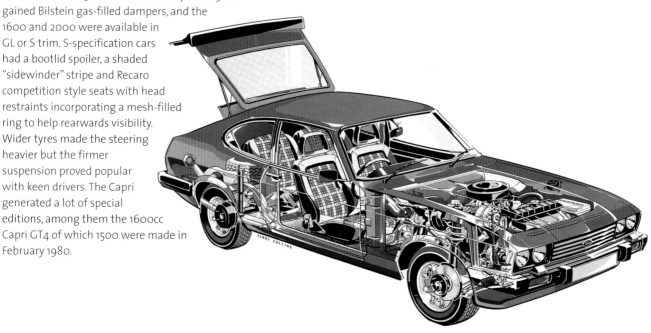

TERRY COLLINS

1978
Capri III 3000; 1981 2.8i

Identifiable by the louvred aerofoil grille and four headlamps, the integral chin spoiler and reprofiled bonnet improved the Capri's aerodynamics. The New Look Capri had wide rubbing strips except for the base model 1.3 and the S, which had a wide strobe cosmetic with an "S". The L was available with either 1.3 or 1.6 ohc engines, GL with 1.6 or 2.0, S with 1.6, 2.0 or 3.0V6, and Ghia with 2.0 or 3.0. In March 1981 the more efficient and clean-burning fuel injected 2.8i was announced, first fruit of the newly established Special Vehicle Engineering department at Dunton, although it was another three months before it went on sale. The 2.8i was a comprehensive improvement over the 3.0; the engine was a high revving 160bhp (119.3kW) Cologne V6, the suspension was stiffened, and the ventilated alloy wheels had wider tyres. Handling was much improved, fresh paintwork and graphics made the car look better, and while these changes failed to sustain Capri sales in the long run, they helped the model's reputation throughout its final phase. In January 1983 the 2.8i was given a 5-speed gearbox and later the same year the entire range was re-trimmed. L, GL, and Ghia were discontinued leaving only 1.6LS, 2.0S, and the last, best Capri of all, the 2.8i to become a real collectors' item.

INTRODUCTION 1978, production to 1986.
BODY coupe; 2-doors, 4-seats; weight 1170kg (2579.4lb).
ENGINE Essex 6-cylinders, 60deg V; 93.7mm x 72.4mm, 2994cc; compr 9.0:1; 102.9kW (138bhp) @ 5000rpm; 34.4kW (46.1bhp)/l; 236Nm (174lbft) @ 3000rpm.
ENGINE STRUCTURE pushrod ohv, gear-drive camshaft; cast iron cylinder head and block; Weber twin-choke downdraught carburettor; 4-bearing crankshaft.
TRANSMISSION rear wheel drive; sdp clutch; 4-speed synchromesh gearbox; optional C3 automatic; final drive 3.09:1.
CHASSIS steel monocoque structure; independent front suspension by MacPherson struts; rear suspension semi-elliptic springs; anti roll bars; gas-filled telescopic dampers; hydraulic vacuum servo brakes, front

disc 24.8cm (9.75in) dia, rear 23cm (9in) drums, dual circuit; rack and pinion PAS; 57.7l (12.7 gal) fuel tank; 185/70 HR-13 radial-ply tyres, 5.5J rims.
DIMENSIONS wheelbase 256cm (100.8in); track front 135.5cm (53.4in), rear 138.5cm (54.5in); length 437.5cm (172.2in); width 170cm (66.9in); height 136cm (53.5in); grd clearance 11.5cm (4.5in); turning circle 10.8m (35.4ft).
EQUIPMENT 2-speed and intermittent wipers; hazard warning lights; electric screenwash; cloth upholstery; laminated windscreen.
PERFORMANCE maximum speed 188kph (117mph) Autocar; 35kph (21.8mph) @ 1000rpm; 0-100kph (62mph) 8.6sec; 11.4kg/kW (8.5kg/bhp); fuel consumption 14.5l/100km (19.5mpg).
PRICE Mar 1978 £4422. 2.8i June 1981 £7993.
PRODUCTION Cologne (all Capris 1,886,647) (Capri III 324,045).
LAST CAPRI 1981 2.8i:

WEIGHT 1230kg (2711.6lb)
ENGINE Cologne V6; 93.0 x 68.5mm; 2792cc; compr 9.2; breakerless ignition; Bosch K-Jetronic fuel injection; 119.3kW (160bhp) @ 5700rpm; 42.7kW (57.3bhp)/l; 220Nm (162lbft) @ 4200rpm.
TRANSMISSION diaphragm spring clutch.
CHASSIS 24mm (0.9in) front, 14mm (0.55in) rear anti-roll bars; 26.2cm (10.3in) ventilated front discs; 59.1l (13 gal) fuel tank; 205/60VR-13 tyres 7in rims, alloy wheels.
PERFORMANCE max speed 203.9kph (127mph); 0-62 7.9sec; 34kph (21.2mph) @ 1000rpm; 10.3kg/kW (7.7kg/bhp); 13.3l/100km (21.3mpg).
PRODUCTION 1987 Capri 280,500.

1979
Cortina Mark V 1297cc

Cortinas were built in four European factories, Dagenham (from 1962), Genk in Belgium (from 1977), Amsterdam (1967-1975) and Cork (from 1978). Dagenham also sent CKD kits to Australia and South Africa, but the sales peak of 290,972 in 1967 was not repeated and 1975, in the wake of the first oil crisis, represented a low point of 141,060, even though one new car in three sold in Britain was a Ford. Nevertheless it looked as though its best days were behind it, and a shot in the arm was required to see it through to the 1980s. The Mark V, known as the Cortina 80, broadly kept the platform that began with the Mark III, with detail changes to freshen the

appearance. Following the second great world oil crisis, better fuel economy was pursued by reducing weight and the styling grew closer to the Granada (and Taunus). Ford cheerfully admitted copying details, such as tail light clusters, from Mercedes-Benz as signals of quality. There was indeed a big effort to improve quality. Customers were growing disillusioned over European cars' readiness to rust, and many Japanese imports were more reliable for longer than their UK counterparts. Ford was by no means the worst culprit for body decay but it was time to improve matters, and Cortinas were now wax-injected and had chip-resistant pvc underneath.

INTRODUCTION September 1979, produced until 1982.
BODY saloon, 2-door, 4-door; 5-seats; weight 965kg (2127.4lb).
ENGINE 4-cylinders, in-line; 81mm x 63mm, 1297cc; compr 9.2:1; 45.6kW (61.2bhp) @ 6000rpm; 35.2kW (47.2bhp)/l; 92Nm (68lbft) @ 3000rpm.
ENGINE STRUCTURE pushrod ohv; chain-driven camshaft; cast iron cylinder head and block; Ford Motorcraft constant vacuum VV carburettor; mechanical fuel pump; 5-bearing crankshaft.
TRANSMISSION rear wheel drive; diaphragm spring cable operated 21.6cm (8.5in) sdp clutch; 4-speed single selector rail synchromesh gearbox; one-piece prop shaft; hypoid bevel final drive, 4.44:1.
CHASSIS steel monocoque structure; independent front suspension by coil springs, wishbones, anti-roll bar; rear live axle with coil springs, trailing and semitrailing radius arms; gas-filled telescopic dampers; hydraulic vacuum servo 24.8cm (9.75in) disc front brakes, 20.3cm (8in) rear drums; rack and pinion steering; 54.6l (12 gal) fuel tank; optional 165-13, radial ply tyres, 4.5 or 5.5in rims.
DIMENSIONS wheelbase 257.8cm (101.5in); track front 144.5cm (56.9in), rear 142.2cm (56in); length 432.6cm (170.3in); width 170.2cm (67in); height 132.1cm (52in); ground clearance 17.8cm (7in); turning circle 10.36m (34ft).
EQUIPMENT heated rear window, radial-ply tyres, brake servo, 2-speed wipers, electric screenwash, reversing lights, cigar lighter, dipping mirror, carpets standard throughout range, viscous fan drive, laminated windscreen.
PERFORMANCE maximum speed 139.7kph (87mph) Ford; 24.2kph (15.1mph) @ 1000rpm; 0-96kph (60mph) 16.1sec; 21.2kg/kW (15.8kg/bhp); fuel consumption approx 11.3l/100km (25mpg).
PRICE at launch 4-door £3475; L £3677; L 4-door £3806.
PRODUCTION 1,131,850 all Mark IV and V.

KEY TO IMPROVEMENTS
1 Viscous-coupled thermostatic fan for better economy and less noise.
2 Variable-venturi carburettor in 1300 and 1600 (except 91PS).
3 Improved heating and ventilation with centre fresh-air vents and side-window demisting.
4 Open-frame head restraints.
5 Increased glass area.
6 Wrap-round tail lamp clusters, with integral fog lamps on saloons.
7 Tough plastic bumper end-caps front and back.
8 New corrosion protection system integrated with multi-stage painting.
9 More comfortable seats of sprung platform construction, infinitely variable backrests and seat-mounted belt stalks.
10 Revised spring and damper settings; S pack option in lieu of S derivatives.
11 New wrap-round front indicators.
12 Deeper front spoiler

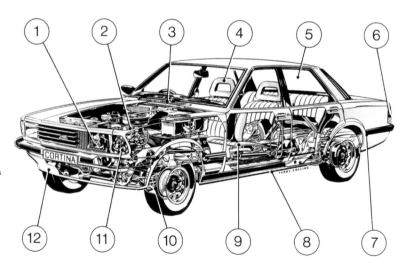

1979
Cortina Mark V 1593cc, 1993cc

The Kent engine fitted to the 1300 Mark V Cortina was something of an aberration. An essential element of the change from Mark IV to V was the harmony achieved with Cologne, whose 1300 had a small Pinto engine. Throughout the rest of the range, however, engines proliferated. The 1600 was available in two states of tune and the 2000 increased in power through reduced valve spring loading and running the fan through a viscous coupling. When the engine was cold the fan ran slowly, using scarcely any engine power, when hot it was speeded up but never to more than 3000rpm, saving more than 2bhp (1.5kW) and quite a lot of fuel. The economy 1600 used the ingenious new downdraught Ford/Motorcraft VV constant vacuum carburettor, a complex instrument designed on similar principles to the well-established sidedraught SU, or Zenith-Stromberg. In the 1970s it still looked as though emission control regulations might be met without resorting to fuel injection by means of this variable venturi (hence VV). Ford claimed it reduced carbon monoxide emissions by 30 per cent. The 1600 for Ghia saloons and estate cars had a different cam profile and a Weber compound dual-choke carburettor, giving it more power than the former Cortina GT. The usual equipment packs of L, GL, and Ghia remained on offer.

INTRODUCTION September 1979, production to 1982.
BODY saloon, 2-door, 4-door; 5-seats estate car 5-door; weight saloon 1060kg (2336.9lb) or 1085kg (2392lb).
ENGINE 1600 4-cylinders, in-line; 87.7mm x 66mm; 1593cc; 9.2:1; 56.3kW (75.5bhp) @ 5500rpm or 92.5bhp (69kW) @ 5900rpm; 35.3kW (58.1bhp)/l or 43.3kW (58.1bhp)/l; 119Nm (87.5lbft) @ 2800rpm or 126Nm (93lbft) @ 4000rpm. 2000 90.8 x 76.95; 1993cc; 76.1kW (102bhp) @ 5400rpm; 38.2kW (51.2bhp)/l; 155Nm (114lbft) @ 4000rpm.
ENGINE STRUCTURE Pinto single ohc; toothed belt; opposed ohv; cast iron cylinder head and block; Ford/Motorcraft VV carburettor (or Weber 32/36 downdraught twin choke); mechanical fuel pump; 5-bearing crankshaft.

TRANSMISSION rear wheel drive; diaphragm spring cable operated 21.6cm (8.5in) sdp clutch; 4-speed single selector rail synchromesh gearbox; 3-speed Borg Warner Model 35 automatic optional; 2-piece prop shaft; hypoid bevel final drive, 3.78, 3.89, and 3.45:1, automatic 3.89, and 3.75.
CHASSIS steel monocoque structure; ifs by coil springs, wishbones, anti-roll bar; rear live axle with coil springs, trailing and semi-trailing radius arms; telescopic dampers; hydraulic vacuum servo 24.8cm (9.75in) disc front brakes, 20.3cm (8in) rear drums, 22.9cm (9in) on 2000; rack and pinion steering; (PAS optional); 54.6l (12 gal) fuel tank; optional 185/70-13, radial ply tyres 165-13 standard, 4.5 or 5.5in rims.

DIMENSIONS wheelbase 257.8cm (101.5in); track front 144.5cm (56.9in), rear 142.2cm (56in); length 432.6cm (170.3in); width 170.2cm (67in); height 132.1cm (52in); ground clearance 17.8cm (7in); turning circle 10.36m (34ft).
EQUIPMENT heated rear window, radial-ply tyres, brake servo, 2-speed wipers, electric screenwash, reversing lights, cigar lighter, dipping mirror, carpets standard throughout range.
PERFORMANCE 1600L maximum speed 146.1kph (91mph) *Autocar*; 28.4kph (17.7mph) @ 1000rpm 0-96kph (60mph) 13.6sec; 18.8kg/kW (14kg/bhp); fuel consumption 9.6l/100km (29.3mpg).
PRICE 1600 4-door £3675; 1600L 4-door £4006; 1600GL £4394; 2000GL £4634; 2000 Ghia £5380; 1600 Estate £4083; 2000GL Estate £5080.
PRODUCTION 1,131,850 all Mark IV and V.

1979
Cortina Mark V V6 2293cc

One of the marketing ploys for the final fling of the Cortina was a redistribution of specification packs. There was no base-level or L-spec 2300, no 2-door version, and only GLs or Ghias. There was a profound rationale for this; flagship cars had to keep their dignity, and once the customer went for an expensive model it helped profitability to load it up with options. More options made it more expensive but since it was possible to price many of the items at a premium, it was good business. L-spec replaced the base model's rubber floor mats with carpet, and brightwork was added. GL brought seat head restraints, map pockets in the door casings, a clock, central console, wooden instrument panel, and a proper side moulding on the body, not just a painted line. A Ghia had cut-pile carpet, cloth-faced door casings, wooden door cappings, a light in the boot, a light in the glovebox, alloy wheels, fatter tyres and the extra cachet of Ghia heraldry and script to let everybody see it was the most expensive Cortina you could get. The run-out phase produced some special editions of the 1300, 1600 and 2000. Chairman Sam Toy drove the final Cortina off the line at Dagenham on Thursday 22 July 1982; 20 years after the first one and after 4,279,079 of all five Marks had been built.

INTRODUCTION September 1979, production to 1982.
BODY saloon, 4-door; 5-seats; estate car 5-door; weight saloon 1080kg (2381lb).
ENGINE 6-cylinders, 60deg V; 90mm x 60.14mm, 2294cc; compr 9.2:1; 86.5kW (116bhp) @ 5500rpm; 37.7kW (50.6bhp)/l; 178Nm (131.5lbft) @ 3000rpm.
ENGINE STRUCTURE pushrod ohv, gear-driven camshaft; cast iron cylinder head and block; Solex twin choke 35/35 EEIT carburettor; mechanical fuel pump; 4-bearing crankshaft.
TRANSMISSION rear wheel drive; diaphragm spring cable operated 21.6cm (8.5in) sdp clutch; 4-speed single selector rail synchromesh gearbox; 3-speed Borg Warner Model 35 automatic optional; 2-piece prop shaft; hypoid bevel final drive, 3.44:1.

CHASSIS steel monocoque structure; ifs by coil springs, wishbones, anti-roll bar; rear live axle with coil springs, trailing and semi-trailing radius arms; telescopic dampers; hydraulic vacuum servo 24.8cm (9.75in) disc front brakes,23cm (9in) rear drums; rack and pinion steering; (PAS standard); 54.6l (12 gal) fuel tank; 185/70-13, radial-ply tyres; 5.5in rims.
DIMENSIONS wheelbase 257.8cm (101.5in); track front 144.5cm (56.9in), rear 142.2cm (56in); length 432.6cm (170.3in); width 170.2cm (67in); height 132.1cm (52in); ground clearance 17.8cm (7in); turning circle 10.36m (34ft).
EQUIPMENT heated rear window, radial-ply tyres, brake servo, front discs, 2-speed wipers, electric screenwash, reversing lights, cigar lighter, dipping mirror, carpets standard alloy wheels optional.

PERFORMANCE maximum speed 176kph (109.6mph), automatic 168kph (104.7mph) Ford; 31.4kph (19.6mph) @ 1000rpm; 0-96kph (60mph) 10.3sec, automatic 12.2sec; 12.5kg/kW (9.3kg/bhp); fuel consumption 10.9km/l (30.7mpg).
PRICE at launch 2300 Ghia 4-door £5989 GL Estate £5,689.
PRODUCTION 1,131,850 all Mark IV and V.

1980
Escort III 1117cc, 1296cc ohc

The third Escort was launched just as Britain was poised for the Metro. Press and government created a lot of interest in a car that was expected to decide the fate of British Leyland, so a fortnight before it was to be launched, Ford replaced its best-selling Escort with another best-selling Escort. The Metro was not eclipsed, but technically the Escort was more than a match for it, having at last gone over to front wheel drive and appearing with a new range of Compound Valve Angle Hemispherical chamber (CVH) ohc engines. Only the 1100 Escort came with a Valencia Fiesta pushrod engine and 3-door, 5-door, and 3-door estate versions were available from the start, closely followed by a van. New from end to end, the well-rounded model programme was a triumph of production engineering but no sooner had the car appeared than the press raised heavy criticism of its ride. Developed at Dunton and tested exhaustively on Ford's extensive proving ground at Lommel in Belgium, it was too firmly sprung, so spring rates and damper settings had to be quickly modified to take account of the complaints. Promoted not very effectively as a "world car" the Escort bore little resemblance to its North American counterpart of the same name but did use the same gearbox as the (now 25 per cent Ford-owned) Mazda 323.

IINTRODUCTION September 1980, production to 1986.
BODY saloon; 3 or 5-doors, 5-seats; weight 3-door 765kg (1686.5lb); 5-door 835kg (1840.8lb); estate 820kg (1807.8lb).
ENGINE 4-cylinders; transverse; 73.96mm x 64.98mm, 1117cc; compr 9.0:1; 40.6kW (54.4bhp) @ 5700rpm; 36.3kW (48.7bhp)/l; 80Nm (59lbft) @ 4000rpm. 1300 CVH 79.96 x 64.62mm; 1295cc; 9.5:1; 43.5kW (58.3bhp) @ 6000rpm; 33.6kW (45bhp)/l; 84Nm (62lbft) @ 4000rpm.
ENGINE STRUCTURE 1100 Valencia pushrod, chain-drive camshaft; iron head and block. 1300 CVH, belt-driven overhead camshaft; hydraulic tappets; aluminium cylinder head; Motorcraft VV carburettor; 1100 3-bearing 1300 5-bearing crankshaft.
TRANSMISSION front wheel drive; sdp diaphragm spring clutch; gearbox 4-speed synchromesh; final drive 4.06:1, 1300 3.84:1.
CHASSIS steel monocoque; MacPherson strut independent front suspension; independent rear by coil springs, pressed lateral arms and trailing tie-bars; 1300 front anti-roll bar; telescopic dampers; hydraulic (1300 servo) brakes, front 24cm (9.45in) dia discs, rear 18cm (7.09in) drums, dual circuit, rack and pinion steering; 40l (8.8 gal) fuel tank; 145SR13, 155SR13, or 175/70 SR/ HR13 tyres 4.5 or 5J rims.
DIMENSIONS wheelbase 239.5cm (94.3in); track 138.5cm (54.5in) front, 143cm (56.3in) rear; length 397cm (156.3in), estate 411.5cm (162in); width 164cm (64.6in); height 140cm (55.1in), estate 137.5cm (54.1in); ground clearance 14cm (5.5in); turning circle 10.5m (34.45ft).
PERFORMANCE maximum speed 146kph (90.9mph), 1300 160kph (99.7mph); 26.8kph (16.69mph), 1300 29kph (18.1mph) @ 1000rpm; 0-100kph (62mph) 13.6sec, 1300 11.3sec; 18.8kg/kW (14.1kg/bhp); fuel consumption 8l/100km (35.3mpg), 1300 7.7l/100km (36.7mpg).
PRICE 1.1 3-door £3374; 1.3 3-door £3543; 1.3 Ghia 5-door£4876.
PRODUCTION 1,857,000 all Mk III

1980
Escort III 1596cc, 1608cc diesel

The notchback was either an inspired innovation, or else designers were unable to decide between a 2-box or 3-box car. Ford preferred to call Escort's two and a half box rear a "bustle". The term did not catch on. Escort III was much the same size as its rear-drive predecessor, although the roof was 5.08cm (2in) lower and track 10.16cm (4in) wider. By the 1980s mathematical analysis of design by computers was becoming commonplace and, with the demand for fuel economy, saving weight was a priority. The Mark III Escort with no long propeller shaft or rear axle casing achieved a useful reduction of around 15 per cent, 108.9kg (240lb), getting down to a competitive weight for its class. Codenamed Erika, it required an investment of £500 million and occupied 500 engineers for five years, their work made easier by the establishment in 1978 of a data link between Merkenich in Germany, Dunton in Essex, and Dearborn. The body stress model was calculated so carefully that, as famously described by Egon Gögel, chief of vehicle programmes engineering, "The roof is an inactive area – it only serves to keep the rain out." Stout roof edge framing carried the body stresses and the roof itself had no cross-bracing. The same went for the boot floor. "If we didn't need it to keep the luggage in, we'd take it out."

INTRODUCTION September 1980, production to 1986; diesel introduced 1983.
BODY saloon; 3 or 5-doors, 5-seats; weight 3-door 795kg (1752.7lb); 5-door diesel 915kg (2017.2lb).
ENGINE 4-cylinders; transverse; 79.96mm x 79.52mm, 1597cc; compr 9.5:1; 70.5kW (94.5bhp) @ 5700rpm; 44.1kW (59.2bhp)/l; 132Nm (97lbft) @ 4000rpm - option 58kW (77.8bhp) @ 5800rpm). Diesel 80 x80mm; 1608cc; compr 21.5:1; 39.5kW (53bhp) @ 4800rpm; 24.6kW (32.9bhp)/l; 95Nm (70lbft) @ 3000rpm.
ENGINE STRUCTURE 1600 CVH, belt-driven ohc; hydraulic tappets; aluminium cyl head; Weber twin choke DFT or Motorcraft VV carburettor; electronic ignition; 5-bearing crankshaft. Diesel Ford KHD ohc.

TRANSMISSION front wheel drive; sdp diaphragm spring clutch; gearbox 4-speed synchromesh; final drive Weber CVH 3.84:1, VV 3.58:1. diesel 3.58:1.
CHASSIS steel monocoque; ifs by MacPherson strut; irs by coil springs, pressed lateral arms and trailing tie-bars; front anti-roll bar; telescopic dampers, Weber car Bilstein gas-filled; hydraulic servo brakes, front 24cm (9.5in) dia ventilated (not diesel) discs, rear 18cm (7.1in) drums, dual circuit, rack and pinion steering; 40l (8.8 gal) fuel tank; tyres 185/60HR14 5.5J rims or 175/70HR13 5J rims; diesel 155SR13, or 175/70 SR/HR13 tyres.

DIMENSIONS wheelbase 239.5cm (94.3in); track 138.5cm (54.5in) front, 143cm (56.3in) rear; length 397cm (156.3in), estate 411.5cm (162in); width 164cm (64.6in); height 140cm (55.1in), estate 137.5cm (54.1in); ground clearance 14cm (5.5in); turning circle 10.5m (34.5ft).
EQUIPMENT Weber car alloy wheels.
PERFORMANCE maximum 182kph (113.4mph), diesel 146kph (90.9mph); 29kph (18.1mph) diesel 39kph (24.3mph) @ 1000rpm; 0-100kph (62mph) 9.7sec, diesel 18.1sec; 11.3kg/kW (8.4kg/bhp), diesel 23.2kg/kW (17.3kg/bhp); 8.9l/100km (31.7mpg) diesel 5.8l/100km (48.7mpg).
PRICE 1.6GL 3-door £4021, Ghia 5-door £5033; 1985 1.6 GL diesel 5-door £7075.
PRODUCTION 1,857,000 all Mk III.

1981
Fiesta XR2

The first 100mph Fiesta, second product of Dunton's Special Vehicle Engineering, was based on the 1300S, with a 1.6-litre Kent engine and stiffened suspension. It was introduced in September following a series of Fiesta challenge races, and the cars were built with competitions department at Boreham-designed X-pack parts. The engine already had considerable success in North America, and was a combination of the Federal US specification bottom end and a 1600GT cylinder head and camshaft, as used on Mark II Cortinas and some Escorts. The 32/34 DFTA Weber carburettor was mounted on a 1300-pattern (but bigger bore) manifold, and the exhaust was a unique four-into-two cast iron arrangement. Novel breakerless ignition was introduced, exemplifying the trend towards an increasing use of electronics. The gearbox was an Escort pattern, and the perforated aluminium alloy wheels were Wolfrace Sonics like those of the 2.8i Capri, except an inch narrower. The 1300S spring rates were retained with the same anti-roll bar at the back, and the ride height lowered by an inch at the front by altering the spring pan on the MacPherson strut. The tie bar to the front frame was also lowered to reduce rearwards pitch on acceleration, not so much for occupant comfort as to lessen changes in driveshaft angles that created torque steer, often a nuisance with lightly laden powerful front wheel drive cars.

INTRODUCTION 1981, production to 1983.
BODY saloon; 3-doors, 5-seats; weight 800kg (1763.7lb).
ENGINE 4-cylinders; transverse; 80.98mm x 77.62mm, 1599cc; compr 9.0:1; 62kW (83.1bhp) @ 5500rpm; 38.8kW (52bhp)/l; 125Nm (92lbft) @ 5500rpm.
ENGINE STRUCTURE Kent; pushrod, chain-driven camshaft; 2 valves; cast iron cylinder head and block; Weber 34DFTA carburettor, transistorised ignition; 5-bearing crankshaft.
TRANSMISSION front wheel drive; sdp clutch; gearbox 4-speed synchromesh; final drive 3.58:1.
CHASSIS steel monocoque structure; ifs by MacPherson struts, coil springs; anti-roll bar; rear suspension dead axle, trailing links, Panhard rod; telescopic dampers; hydraulic, vacuum servo 24.7cm (9.7in) front disc brakes; rear drums 17.8cm (7in); rack and pinion steering; 34l (7.5 gal) fuel tank; 185/60HR 13 tyres; aluminium alloy wheels, 6J rims.
DIMENSIONS wheelbase 228.6cm (90in); track 133.5cm (52.6in) front, 132cm (52in) rear; length 356.5cm (140.4in); width 156.5cm (61.6in); height 136cm (53.5in); ground clearance 14cm (5.5in); turning circle 9.45m (31ft).
PERFORMANCE maximum speed 170kph (105.9mph); 29.7kph (18.5mph) @ 1000rpm; 0-100kph (62mph) 10.1sec; 12.8kg/kW (9.6kg/bhp); fuel consumption 8.6l/100km (32.9mpg).
PRICE 1982 £5150.
PRODUCTION April 1981: Fiesta production passed 2m.

1981
Probe III

As a result of two world oil crises, the spiraling cost of fuel, and apprehension over the future of fossil fuels, car buyers sought economy. They did not want to give up the customary comfort, convenience and speed of the cars they had, so designers began exploring new ways to meet their requirements. Good aerodynamics was a logical solution. A slippery shape not only improved fuel consumption, it could be turned to advantage by providing cars with a fresh new look and it could be done at once and publicly. Coefficients of wind resistance (Cd) had hitherto been largely academic; it scarcely mattered that a Cortina was something like 0.44. When Probe III was shown as a concept car, there was little attempt to disguise its relationship with the approaching Cortina replacement. A good deal of education was required to prepare public taste. Executives in charge of the project realised it was fairly radical and were uncertain if the customers were ready for it. Probe III's body was a complex of features, few of which would have made much difference aerodynamically on their own. Flush windows, the shape of the corner pillars, elimination of roof gutters and drip channels, flush wheel discs, rear spats, and plastic skirts, wings and spoilers combined to give a drag coefficient of 0.22. The curved side windows only wound down after the glass had first been moved inwards, rather like an aircraft door. Underneath, the airflow was managed just as carefully as it was on top. The exhaust was entirely enclosed within the under-tray, and elaborate arrangements were made for insulating its heat and noise. The under-car air management system involved a scoop that would need to be retracted on rough roads or to clear town-road obstructions such as manhole covers as it would only work if it

were close to road level. That was not all, however. Probe III was equipped with car-of-the future features, including digital instruments and the Auto Leading and Information (ALI) system built into the facia, giving the driver route instructions to a programmed destination by means of arrows on an animated diagram. Ford had satellite navigation in mind 20 years before its time. It was said that the aerodynamics were so good that a 1600cc engine, suitably geared, would drive Probe III at 190kph (about 120mph) and provide spectacular economy at lower speeds. Probe III was not a runner. It only had one opening door. Probes IV and V were even more radical, built in America in 1983 and 1985 with more extreme aerodynamics including enclosure of the front wheels by plastic membranes, they had Cd figures of 0.15 and 0.137. Pure research vehicles, they explored design initiatives but were well removed from any production capability.

1981
Escort III XR3, XR3i

Ahead of the launch of the Mark III Escort, the old RS (Renn Sport) models were formally discontinued except for a Group B homologation special, RS1700T, with 16 valves and a turbocharger. The road-going version had 150kW (200bhp), the competition car shown at Frankfurt in 1981, 246kW (330bhp). The RS was replaced by the XR3, which appeared first using the 1600 CVH hydraulic tappet engine. In October 1982 the XR3 became the XR3i with fuel injection, having already gained the 5-speed gearbox that had become available throughout the Escort range. The XR3 accounted for one Escort in 10 and was entirely separate from the RS1600i, a competition tuned specialist road car sold in small numbers in 1982-1983. Besides fuel injection, the XR3i gained a new high efficiency exhaust system and an oil-water intercooler to withstand prolonged operation at high speeds. The electronic ignition was provided with an over-run cutoff to avoid fuel wastage, and reprogrammed with a revised advance curve. Girth of the front anti-roll bar was increased from 22mm (.87in) to 24mm (.94in) and at the back linear rate springs replaced dual rate. Ride heights were reduced by 30mm (1.2in) in front and 20mm (.8in) at the rear and the struts were now Girling Monotubes. Following environmental concerns about asbestos, the XR3i was one of the first Fords to use brake linings free of the material. In 1982 the Escort was voted European Car of the Year.

INTRODUCTION 1981, production to 1986.
BODY saloon; 3-doors, 5-seats; weight 895kg (1973lb).
ENGINE 4-cylinders; transverse; 80mm x 79.5mm, 1598cc; compr 9.5:1; 70.5kW (94.5bhp) @ 6000rpm; 44.1kW (59.1bhp)/l; 132Nm (97lbft) @ 4000rpm. XR3i 77kW (103.3bhp) @ 6000rpm; 48.1kW (64.6bhp)/l; 138Nm (102lbft) @ 4800rpm.
ENGINE STRUCTURE CVH; belt-driven ohc; 2 valves, hydraulic tappets; aluminium cyl head, iron block; twin choke Weber DFT carburettor, transistorised ignition; 5-bearing crank. XR3i Bosch K-Jetronic fuel injection.
TRANSMISSION front wheel drive; sdp clutch; gearbox 5-speed synchromesh gearbox; final drive 3.84:1. XR3i 4.29:1.

CHASSIS steel monocoque; MacPherson strut independent front suspension; independent rear by coil springs, pressed lateral arms and trailing tie-bars; front anti-roll bar; telescopic dampers, Bilstein gas-filled; hydraulic servo brakes, front 24cm (9.5in) dia ventilated discs, rear 18cm (7.1in) drums, dual circuit, rack and pinion steering; 40l (8.8 gal) fuel tank; tyres 185/60HR14 5.5J rims or 175/70HR13 5J rims.
DIMENSIONS wheelbase 239.5cm (94.3in); track front 138.5cm (54.5in), rear 143cm (56.3in); length 397cm (156.3in), estate 411.5cm (162in); width 164cm (64.6in); height 140cm (55.1in), XRi 137cm (53.9in); ground clearance 14cm (5.5in); turning circle 10.5m (34.45ft).

EQUIPMENT cloth seats, carpet standard. rear seats belts, central locking, electric windows, manual sunroof £247, radio cassette player £136, optional extras.
PERFORMANCE maximum speed 182kph (113.4mph), XR3i 186kph (115.9mph); 29kph (18.1mph), XR3i 32.5kph (20.2mph) @ 1000rpm; 0-100kph (62mph) 9.7sec, XR3i 9.6sec; 12.7kg/kW (9.5kg/bhp); fuel consumption 7.7l/100km (36.7mpg), XR3i 8.1l/100km (34.9mpg).
PRICE 1981 XR3 £5750; 1983 XR3i £6278.
PRODUCTION 1,857,000 all Mk III.

1982
Sierra 1294cc, 1593cc

The Sierra was in many respects an unwelcome contrast to the dapper and fashionable Cortina, which had been crisp, dignified and a byword for the stylish family car. The Sierra's principal demerit lay in not being front wheel drive. Ford still had a disparate family of engines, not many of which could be satisfactorily turned sideways and mounted on suitable transmissions, so claimed rear wheel drive was a matter of preference. It did not ring true. The market wanted front wheel drive; Vauxhall had brought in a front drive Cavalier, making Ford look behindhand technically. Probe III's flush-fitting windows were abandoned. Sierra's radical styling had gone badly wrong due, it was said, to

managerial faint-heartedness just as the design was frozen for production. The 1981 Probe had not been well received, yet it was not long before rivals, like Audi with the 0.3Cd 100 were following Ford's aerodynamic example. An economy version of the 1.6 offered at launch had identical power and torque, employing a sophisticated ignition system similar in principle to that used with the Bosch Motronic fuel injection. A 1984 version known as E-Max was a development of this with an 81.3 x 77mm, 1599cc engine. Once again power remained at 55.9kW (75bhp) but developed at 5300rpm instead of 4300rpm. Torque increased to 122 Nm (90lbft) and fuel savings were between seven and 13 per cent.

INTRODUCTION September 1982, production to 1987.
BODY saloon; 5-doors, 5-seats; weight 990kg (2182.6lb), estate 1040kg (2292.8lb).
ENGINE 4-cylinders, in-line; 79mm x 66mm, 1294cc; compr 9.1:1; 44kW (59bhp) @ 5700rpm; 34kW (45.6bhp)/l; 98Nm (72lbft) @ 3100rpm. 1.6: 87.65 x 66mm; 1593cc; 9.2:1; 55kW (73.8bhp) @ 5300rpm; 34.5kW (46.3bhp)/l; 120Nm (88.5lbft) @ 2900rpm.
ENGINE STRUCTURE belt driven overhead camshaft; 2 valves; iron cylinder head, block; Ford variable venturi carburettor, breakerless electronic ignition; 5-bearing crankshaft.
TRANSMISSION rear wheel drive; sdp diaphragm spring clutch; 4-speed synchromesh, 5-speed optional; final drive 3.77:1. 1.6: C3 3-speed automatic optional, 3.61:1 or 3.92:1, estate 1.6 4-speed manual, 3.62:1; economy model 3.14:1, estate 3.92. 5-speed 3.62, 3.38, 3.92.
CHASSIS steel monocoque; ifs by MacPherson struts; independent rear suspension by semi-trailing arms and coil springs; front anti roll bar; telescopic dampers; hydraulic servo brakes, front 24cm (9.5in) dia disc, rear 20.3cm (8in) dia drums, dual circuit; rack and pinion steering; 60l (13.2 gal) fuel tank; 165SR13 or 185/70SR13 tyres 4.5 or 5.5J rims. 1.6: 195/70HR13.
DIMENSIONS wheelbase 261cm (102.8in); track 145cm (57.1in) front, 147cm (57.9in) rear; length 439.5cm (173in), estate 449cm (176.8in); width 170cm (66.9in); height 136cm (53.5in), estate 139cm (54.7in); ground clearance 12cm (4.7in); turning circle 10.6m (34.78ft).
EQUIPMENT cloth trim, laminated windscreen standard. 5-speed £150.
PERFORMANCE maximum speed 152kph (94.7mph), 1.6: 165kph (102.8mph); 29kph (18mph) @ 1000rpm, 1.6 various; 0-100kph (62mph) 18.1sec. 1.6 14sec, automatic 17.2sec; 22.5kg/kW (16.8kg/bhp); fuel consumption 7.9l/100km (35.8mpg).
PRICE 1.3 £4783; 1.6 £5071; estate £5548; 1.6 Ghia £7365.

1982
Sierra 1993, 1998cc

Better-class Sierras got 5-speed gearboxes, all four of the straight-4s were Pinto-engined and all were hatchbacks, unlike the Vauxhall Cavalier, which gave customers the choice of a 4-door. The Sierra's behaviour in cross winds brought an early modification with small "ears" in the rear quarters, aerodynamic spoilers said to keep the car straight and stable. Cost-effective independent rear suspensions had proved elusive on mid-size and large Fords, so the Sierra had an ingenious 7cm (2.75in) dia bent tube sub-frame combined with modestly angled semi trailing arms. Compromise had to be reached on the angle, as 26deg for the Granada had brought too much camber change, so the Sierra was pitched at 18deg. The aluminium final drive casing was bolted to the frame front and rear and the rear dampers were repositioned within the springs on estate cars, which also had the option of Nivomat ride height levelling. At the front, crash test requirements brought the 24mm (0.94in) anti-roll bar behind the wheel line instead of ahead, as was customary with MacPherson struts. The Sierra lost Ford primacy in a market it had dominated for 20 years. It would be a decade before it found its feet again with the Mondeo and, in mounting a defence of the styling, had to issue a denial that it was planning an emergency re-skin to prop up sales.

INTRODUCTION September 1982, production to 1987.
BODY saloon; 5-doors, 5-seats; weight 1025kg (2260lb), estate 1065kg (2348lb), V6 saloon 1070kg (2359lb).
ENGINE 4-cylinders, in-line; 90.82mm x 76.95mm, 1993cc; compr 9.2:1; 77kW (103.3bhp) @ 5200rpm; 38.6kW (51.8bhp)/l; 157Nm (116lbft) @ 4000rpm. V6: 84 x 60.1mm; 1998cc; 9.1:1; 66kW (88.5bhp) @ 5000rpm; 33kW (44.25bhp)/l; 150 Nm (111lbft) @ 3000rpm.
ENGINE STRUCTURE belt driven overhead camshaft; 2 valves; iron cyl head, block; Weber 32/36DGAV carburettor, breakerless electronic ignition; 5-bearing crank. V6 gear-driven central camshaft, 4-bearing crank, twin-choke Solex EEIT carburettor.

TRANSMISSION rwd; sdp diaphragm spring clutch; 4-speed synchro, 5-speed optional; final drive 3.38:1. C3 3-speed auto optional, 3.38:1. V6 manual 3.38:1, estate 3.62:1, also auto.
CHASSIS steel monocoque; ifs by MacPherson struts; irs by semi-trailing arms and coil springs; front anti roll bar; telescopic dampers; Nivomat ride height levelling option on estate cars; hydraulic servo brakes, front 24cm (9.45in) dia ventilated disc, rear 22.9cm (9in) dia drums, dual circuit; rack and pinion steering, PAS optional; 60l (13.2 gal) fuel tank; 165HR13 or 175/70HR13 tyres 4.5 or 5.5J rims. Estate 175 or 195/70HR13.

DIMENSIONS wheelbase 261cm (102.8in); track 145cm (57.1in) front, 147cm (57.9in) rear; length 439.5cm (173in), estate 449cm (176.8in); width 170cm (66.9in); height 136cm (53.5in), estate 139cm (54.7in); ground clearance 12cm (4.7in); turning circle 10.6m (34.8ft).
EQUIPMENT cloth trim, laminated windscreen standard. 5-speed £150.
PERFORMANCE maximum speed 185kph (115.2mph), V6 176kph (109.6mph); 32.3kph (20.1mph), V6 32.3kph (20.1mph) @ 1000rpm; 0-100kph (62mph) 10.4sec, auto 12.8sec; fuel consumption 7.9l/100km (35.8mpg), V6 9.7l/100km (29.1mpg).
PRICE 2.0GL £6524.

1982
Sierra diesel 2304cc

Partly owing to the transition to Ford of Europe and a legacy of too many power units, Sierra engines were something of a muddle. The petrol range comprised three 4-cylinder in-line Pintos, four including the economy model, and 2.3 and 2.8 Cologne V6s. One of the Pintos was 1993cc and one V6 1998cc, an anomaly explained by a German market preference for a V6, even though it gave less power and was heavier, at 167.8kg (370lb) against 137kg (302lb) for the 1993cc. In the absence of its own diesel, not due until 1984, Ford turned to Peugeot, one of Europe's main producers of car-sized diesel engines, for something suitable. Peugeot's 2.1-litre was already installed in the Granada and, since it had just

moved on to a 2.5-litre engine for its own cars, it was able to offer Ford the 2.3-litre. Diesels were still relatively unsophisticated, so hydraulically damped mountings that extended throughout the petrol range as well were welcome. All models had underbonnet sound-damping material, the thickness of which was increased to 30mm (1.18in) on the diesel. With little more power than a 1.3-litre, a heavy flywheel, and ponderous handling due to the heavy weight over the front wheels, the diesel was so sluggish that press road tests were avoided where possible. The 3-door Sierra, available with every engine except the V6, was discontinued after three years.

INTRODUCTION Sept 1982, production to 1987.
BODY saloon; 5-doors, 5-seats; weight 1156kg (2548.5lb), estate 1195kg (2634.5lb).
ENGINE 4-cylinders, in-line; 94mm x 83mm, 2304cc; compr 22.2:1; 49kW (65.7bhp) @ 4200rpm; 21.3kW (28.5bhp)/l; 139Nm (102.5lbft) @ 2000rpm.
ENGINE STRUCTURE LXD2; pushrod ohv, chain-driven camshaft; 2 valves; aluminium cylinder head, iron block inclined 20deg right; Bosch EP/VAC injection; 5-bearing crankshaft.
TRANSMISSION rear wheel drive; sdp diaphragm spring clutch; 5-speed synchromesh; final drive 3.14:1.
CHASSIS steel monocoque; ifs by MacPherson struts; independent rear suspension by semi-trailing arms and coil springs; front anti roll bar; telescopic dampers; estate, self-levelling rear; hydraulic servo brakes, front 24cm (9.5in) dia ventilated disc, rear 22.9cm (9in) dia drums, dual circuit; rack and pinion steering, PAS optional; 60l (13.2gal) fuel tank; 165SR13 or 175/70SR13 tyres 4.5 or 5.5J rims, estate 175 or 195/70HR13.
DIMENSIONS wheelbase 261cm (102.8in); track 145cm (57.1in) front, 147cm (57.9in) rear; length 439.5cm (173in), estate 449cm (176.8in); width 170cm (66.9in); height 136cm (53.5in), estate 139cm (54.7in); ground clearance 12cm (4.7in); turning circle 10.6m (34.8ft).
EQUIPMENT cloth trim, laminated windscreen standard, 5-speed £150.
PERFORMANCE maximum speed 155kph (96.6mph); 42.2kph (26.3mph) @ 1000rpm; 0-100kph (62mph) 19.1sec; 23.6kW/kW (17.6kg/bhp), estate 24.4kg/kW (18.2kg/bhp); fuel consumption 6.7mpg (42.2l/100km).
PRICE 3-door £5749, 5-door L £6421, GL Estate £7711.

1982
Sierra 2.3 V6

Unlike the V6 Cortina, which had sold well, the V6 Sierra survived only two years. The Ghia V6 was given the further refinement of self-levelling suspension, but it was not enough and by 1984 it was discontinued. A 1979 novelty on the Taunus/Cortina V6 engine was breakerless transistorised ignition using a magnetic reluctance triggering system. Extended now to the entire range except the 1.6 economy version, the ignition was set on the production line using microwaves, directed through a spark plug, to detect TDC with the engine running on the test bed. A crank angle probe over the flywheel ring gear then set the ignition timing within a tolerance of half a degree. Automatic

transmission did not contribute towards a vigorous performance and economy was not a strong point either, with one road test recording a worst of 15.4l/100km (18.3mpg), so with a meagre 59.1l (13gal) fuel tank the useful range was less than 400km (about 250mls). The best of the Ghia Sierra lay in the 1980s advances in refinement and comfort that included details which would in due course be taken for granted, but which were only now appearing on popular cars. Delayed action interior lights, illuminated vanity mirrors, footwell-mounted lights, lockable compartments, a carpeted boot and cassette holders for the built-in radio/cassette player were still by no means commonplace.

INTRODUCTION September 1982, production to 1987.
BODY saloon; 5-doors, 5-seats; weight 1115kg (2458lb), estate 1155kg (2546.3lb).
ENGINE 6-cylinders, 60deg V; 90mm x 60.1mm, 2294cc; compr 9:1; 84kW (112.6bhp) @ 5300rpm; 36.6kW (49.1bhp)/l; 176Nm (130lbft) @ 3000rpm.
ENGINE STRUCTURE gear-driven central camshaft; pushrod ohv; 2 valves; iron cylinder head, block; Solex 35/35 EEIT carburettor; breakerless ignition; 4-bearing crankshaft.
TRANSMISSION rear wheel drive; sdp diaphragm spring clutch; 4-speed synchromesh; final drive 3.14:1; estate 3.38:1; optional 5-speed, optional C3 automatic.
CHASSIS steel monocoque structure; ifs by MacPherson struts; independent rear suspension by semi-trailing arms and coil springs; front anti roll bar; telescopic dampers; estate, self-levelling rear; hydraulic servo brakes, front 24cm (9.5in) dia ventilated disc, rear 22.9cm (9in) dia drums, dual circuit; rack and pinion steering, PAS optional; 60l (13.2gal) fuel tank; 165HR13 or 175/70HR13 tyres 4.5 or 5.5J rims, estate 175 or 195/70HR13.
DIMENSIONS wheelbase 261cm (102.8in); track 145cm (57.1in) front, 147cm (57.9in) rear; length 439.5cm (173.1in), estate 449cm (176.8in); width 170cm (66.9in); height 136cm (53.5in), estate 139cm (54.7in); ground clearance 12cm (4.7in); turning circle 10.6m (34.78ft).
EQUIPMENT PAS £355.66, rear seat belts £93.87, heated driver's seat £71.59, electric rear windows £126.13, trip computer £195.25.
PERFORMANCE maximum speed 190kph (118.4mph), automatic 182kph (113.4mph); 34.8kph (21.7mph) @ 1000rpm; 0-100kph (62mph) 10.5sec; 13.3kg/kW (9.9kg/bhp), estate 13.8kg/kW (10.3kg/bhp); fuel consumption 9.2l/100km (30.7mpg), auto 10l/100km (28.25mpg).
PRICE GL £8061, Ghia £9355, GL Estate £8597.

1983
Fiesta II 957cc, 1117cc

Second thoughts on the Fiesta produced detail changes. Ford would have been forgiven for pressing on with none at all, since the car had sold well since 1977. Late special editions such as the Fiesta Finesse ran to 12,000 and over 300,000 were built in Britain alone. The facelift gave it a less erect front, in the interests of slipperier aerodynamics, despite adding to overall length, and also provided extra crushable material to meet the ever more demanding legislation governing impact tests. The two Valencia engines gained little in power, but achieved a small improvement in torque, and new 5-speed gearboxes permitted higher gearing. The suspension was revised to accommodate high-

pressure 13in instead of 12in tyres, and comfort and equipment improved. Useful gains in economy were previewed in 1981 with the Fuel Economy Research Vehicle (FERV), which was the result of much laboratory work evaluating 11 different inlet port types and three sorts of combustion chamber. This resulted in a new cylinder head with smaller-section inlet ports and smaller valves. The objective was improved swirl for better combustion and increased compression. New cam profiles and an exhaust system that kept the flow from adjoining cylinders apart, to reduce back pressure, improved consumption by 18-22 per cent at 75mph and 11-34 per cent on the urban cycle.

INTRODUCTION August 1983, production to 1989.
BODY saloon; 3-doors, 5-seats; weight 750kg (1653.5lb), 1.1 755kg (1664.5lb).
ENGINE 4-cylinders; transverse; 73.96mm x 55.7mm, 957cc; compr 8.5:1; 33kW (44.25bhp) @ 5750rpm; 34.5kW (46.2bhp)/l; 68Nm (50lbft) @ 3700rpm. 1.1: 73.96 x 64.98mm; 1117cc; 9.5:1; 37kW (49.6bhp) @ 5000rpm; 33.1kW (44.4bhp)/l; 83Nm (61lbft) @ 2700rpm.
ENGINE STRUCTURE pushrod ohv; chain-driven camshaft; 2-valves; iron cylinder head, block; inverse Ford-Motorcraft carburettor; 3-bearing crankshaft. 1.1: VV carburettor.
TRANSMISSION front wheel drive; sdp clutch; 4-speed synchro; final drive 4.06:1, or 4.29 or 3.84. 1.1: 3.583:1 or 3.842:1 with optional 5-speed.
CHASSIS steel monocoque structure; ifs by MacPherson struts, coil springs; rear suspension dead axle, trailing links, Panhard rod; telescopic dampers; hydraulic, vacuum servo 22.1cm (8.7in) front disc brakes; rear drums 17.8cm (7in); rack and pinion steering; 34l (7.5gal) fuel tank; radial-ply 135SR-13 tyres or 155/70SR13, 4.5 or 5J rims.
DIMENSIONS wheelbase 228.6cm (90in); track 136.5cm (53.7in) front, 132cm (52in) rear; length 365cm (143.7in); width 158.5cm (62.4in); height 136cm (53.5in); ground clearance 14cm (5.5in); turning circle 10.3m (33.8ft).
PERFORMANCE maximum speed 137kph (85.4mph); 25.9kph (16.1mph) @ 1000rpm (4.06:1); 0-100kph (62mph) 19.8sec; 22.7kg/kW (16.9kg/bhp), 1.1 20.4kg/kW (17kg/bhp); fuel consumption 6.4l/100km (43.9mpg).
PRICE L £4320, 1.1 Ghia £5100.
PRODUCTION 1,980,100 all Fiesta II.

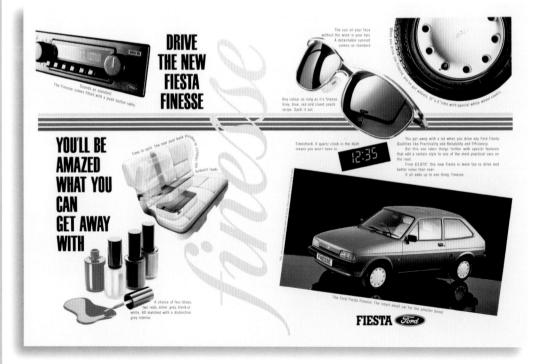

1983
Fiesta II 1298cc, (from 1986) 1392cc

The 1.3 added to the range, and the 1.4 Compound Valve Hemispherical (CVH) ohc hydraulic tappet engines were an effort to regain Ford's reputation for technical innovation, somewhat lost when the Sierra remained in the shrinking world of rear wheel drive. Alterations to the front presswork were not merely cosmetic; they were necessary to provide space for the extra length of the transverse CVH engine and five-speed transaxle. Aft of the A-pillars Fiesta was largely unaltered, but the new front gave a marginal Cd improvement through smoother lines at the critical front corners. Fuel economy was of growing importance in Britain, where the price of petrol was about to pass £0.22 a litre (£1 a gallon)

and looked like doubling. It did so within the year, so the Fiesta's overdrive fifth gear, standard on the CVH and diesel and an optional extra on the 1100, was timely. The 13in tyres were run at 2.67kg-cm (38psi) front and 2.88kg-cm (41psi) rear to lower rolling resistance, the resulting harsher ride being countered by a more compliant bush for the front suspension tie rod. The tyre treatment was claimed to give a 2.5 per cent improvement in economy, and among the suspension and steering changes were non-stiction top mounts for the front struts, a 3.3cm (1.3in) wider track, and revised rack and pinion steering.

INTRODUCTION August 1983, production to 1989.
BODY saloon; 3-doors, 5-seats; weight 775kg (1708.5lb).
ENGINE 4-cylinders; transverse; 79.96mm x 64.5mm, 1297cc; compr 9.5:1; 50.5kW (67.7bhp) @ 6000rpm; 39.2kW (52.2bhp)/l; 100Nm (78lbft) @ 4000rpm. Replaced 1986 by "lean-burn" 77.24 x 74.3mm; 1392cc; 9.5:1; 55kW (73.76bhp) @ 5600rpm; 39.5kW (53bhp)/l; 109Nm (80lbft) @ 4000rpm. With catalytic converter compr 8.5:1; 51.5kW (69.1bhp); 37kW (49.6bhp)/l; 103Nm (76lbft).
ENGINE STRUCTURE CVH belt-driven overhead camshaft, hydraulic tappets; 2-valves; aluminium cylinder head, iron block; inverse Ford-Motorcraft VV carburettor; 5-bearing crankshaft. Lean-burn, Weber DFM. Catalytic converter, fuel injection.
TRANSMISSION front wheel drive; sdp clutch; 5-speed synchromesh; final drive 3.842:1.
CHASSIS steel monocoque structure; ifs by MacPherson struts, coil springs; lean-burn car anti-roll bar; rear suspension dead axle, trailing links, Panhard rod; telescopic dampers; hydraulic, vacuum servo 22.1cm (8.7in) front disc brakes; rear drums 17.8cm (7in); rack and pinion steering; 34l (7.5 gal) fuel tank; radial-ply 155/70SR-13 tyres, 4.5 or 5J rims.
DIMENSIONS wheelbase 228.6cm (90in); track 136.5cm (53.7in) front, 132cm (52in) rear; length 365cm (143.7in); width 158.5cm (62.4in); height 136cm (53.5in); ground clearance 14cm (5.5in); turning circle 10.3m (33.8ft).
PERFORMANCE maximum speed 163kph (101.5mph), lean-burn 165kph (102.8mph), catalyser 161kph (100.3mph); 34.7kph (21.6mph) @ 1000rpm; 0-100kph (62mph) 12.2sec. (12.1sec) (13sec); 15.3kg/kW (11.4kg/bhp); fuel consumption 7.5l/100km (37.9mpg), cat 7.6l/100km (37.2mpg).
PRICE L £5336, Ghia £5657. 1986 1.4 Ghia £6507.
PRODUCTION 1,980,100 all Fiesta II.

1983
Fiesta II diesel 1608cc

INTRODUCTION August 1983, production to 1989.
BODY saloon; 3-doors, 5-seats; weight 835kg (1840.8lb).
ENGINE 4-cylinders; transverse; 80mm x 80mm, 1608cc; compr 21.5:1; 39.5kW (53bhp) @ 4800rpm; 24.6kW (32.9bhp)/l; 95Nm (70lbft) @ 3000rpm.
ENGINE STRUCTURE Ford/KHD; 2 in-line valves, belt-driven overhead camshaft; iron cylinder head and block; mechanical fuel injection; 5-bearing crankshaft.
TRANSMISSION front wheel drive; sdp clutch; 5-speed synchromesh; final drive 3.333:1.
CHASSIS steel monocoque structure; ifs by MacPherson struts, coil springs; rear suspension dead axle, trailing links, Panhard rod; telescopic dampers; hydraulic, vacuum servo 22.1cm (8.7in) front disc brakes; rear drums 17.8cm (7in); rack and pinion steering; 34l (7.5 gal) fuel tank; radial-ply 155/70SR-13 tyres.
DIMENSIONS wheelbase 228.6cm (90in), track 136.5cm (53.7in) front, 132cm (52in) rear; length 365cm (143.7in), width 158.5cm (62.4in); height 136cm (53.5in); ground clearance 14cm (5.5in); turning circle 10.3m (33.8ft).
PERFORMANCE maximum speed 148kph (92.2ph); 39.8kph (24.8mph) @ 1000rpm; 0-100kph (62mph) 17.3sec; 21.1kg/kW (15.8kg/bhp); fuel consumption 5.1l/100km (55.1mpg).
PRICE L 1986, 1.6L £6002.
PRODUCTION 1,980,100 all Fiesta II.

Ford took time over introducing its own diesel. It waited until it was quite certain that demand was going to be sustained and governments were not going to go back on their taxation policy that generally (except in Britain) encouraged diesel as a key ingredient of good national housekeeping. In 1981 Ford embarked on a joint research programme with Klockner-Humboldt-Deutz AG, German van and lorry manufacturers, waiting for diesel cars to pass five per cent as a trigger for production in the European market. It also waited until it had production plant made available by the conclusion of the Kent engine programme. Its new 1.6-litre diesel was first employed on the Escort and Orion, and would remain a Ford mainstay until the turn of the century. Previewed in May 1983, the new engine had an overhead camshaft, was cast iron throughout, and was on hydraulic mounts to reduce body resonances. Apart from the cylinder spacing there were no hand-me-downs on the new engine. It had conventional indirect injection; a combination gear and toothed belt drive to the overhead camshaft, and slightly offset in-line vertical valves. "Square" bore and stroke dimensions of 80mm would give a capacity of 1608.5cc, yet according to German type-approval papers it could be between 1606.5 and 1611.7 depending on the 1mm machining tolerances.

1983
Orion 1296cc, 1597cc, 1608cc diesel

The Orion was in almost every respect a booted Escort, despite Ford's advocacy of it as a separate model line. It was 10 years before the fiction was ended and the non-hatchback Escort became known simply as an Escort saloon. The Orion's family role was emphasised by the absence of anything racy from its range. It was to be a conventional 3-box car throughout its life, staid, routine, catering for a substantial number of buyers to whom ostentation was anathema. It also had the virtue, through its stiffer bodyshell and enclosed boot instead of a hatchback, of being a good deal quieter and more refined than the Escort. Although quite a lot of the body panels were common to both cars, the roofline was notably different, as was the back, so it was able to accommodate a roomier rear seat. True to its market aims, the Orion's rear backrest sloped at 27deg instead of 24deg, and legroom was increased to 101.6cm (40in) against the Escort's 96.5cm (38in). This was a class-leading dimension, and together with a generous 444.8l (15.7 cu ft) lockable secure boot sustained its market appeal. There were three trim levels, GL, Ghia, and Injection, and four engine options, 1300, 1600, 1600 injection, and 1600 diesel, making the Orion the first Ford with its own Dagenham-made compression ignition engine.

INTRODUCTION July 1983, production to 1986.
BODY saloon; 4-doors, 5-seats; 875kg (1929lb), 1.6 890kg (1962lb), auto 925kg (2039.3lb), diesel 935kg (2061.3lb).
ENGINE 4-cylinders; transverse; 79.96mm x 64.5mm, 1297cc; compr 9.5:1; 50.5kW (67.7bhp) @ 6000rpm; 39.2kW (52.2bhp)/l; 100Nm (74lbft) @ 3500rpm. 1.6: 76.96 x 79.5mm; 1597cc; 58kW (77.8bhp) @ 5800rpm; 36.3kW (48.7bhp)/l; 125Nm (92lbft) @ 3000rpm. Injection model 77kW (103.3bhp), 48.2kW (64.7bhp)/l; 138Nm (102lbft) @ 4800rpm. diesel

1608cc; 39.5kW (53bhp); 24.6kW (32.9bhp)/l.
ENGINE STRUCTURE CVH belt-driven ohc; 2-valves; aluminium cylinder head, iron block; Ford VV carburettor; 5-bearing crankshaft. Injection Bosch K-Jetronic. Diesel Ford KHD; ohc; parallel valves.
TRANSMISSION front wheel drive; sdp clutch; 4-speed synchromesh; 5-speed optional; final drive 3.84:1. 1.6 3.58:1, automatic optional 3.31:1. Injection 3.84:1, diesel 3.58.
CHASSIS steel monocoque; ifs by MacPherson strut; irs by coil springs, pressed lateral arms and trailing tie-

bars; front anti-roll bar; telesc dampers (1.6 front and rear); hydraulic servo brakes, front 24cm (9.4in) dia (1.6 ventilated) discs, rear 18cm (7.1in) drums, dual circuit, rack and pinion; 40l (8.8 gal); 155SR13, or 175/70 HR13 tyres, 5J rims.
DIMENSIONS wheelbase 240cm (94.5in); track 140cm (55.1in) front, 142.4cm (56.1in) rear; length 419.5cm (165.2in); width 164cm (64.6in); height 139.5cm (54.9in); ground clearance 14cm (5.5in); turning circle 10.6m (34.8ft).
EQUIPMENT GL, Ghia and Injection trim levels, all with electric boot release.

PERFORMANCE maximum 157kph (97.8mph), inj 186kph (116mph), diesel 150kph (93.4mph); 29kph (18mph) @ 1000rpm, inj 36.4kph (22.67mph), diesel 38.9kph (24.23mph); 0-100kph (62mph) 13.6sec, inj 9.6sec, diesel 18.8sec; 17.3kg/kW (12.9kg/bhp), 1.6 15.3kg/kW (11.4kg/bhp), diesel 23.7kg/kW (17.7kg/bhp); 7.4l/100km (38.4mpg), inj 8l/100km (35.5mpg), diesel 4.9l/100km (57.3mpg).
PRICE 1.3GL £5905, 1.6 Ghia £7235, 1.6i Ghia £7435, 1.6 GL diesel 1985 £7075.
PRODUCTION 1,857,000 all Escort III models.

RIGHT **Controversial rear suspension was developed for the Escort and Orion. Spring rates, pivot points, and rear wheel location were all in dispute until Ford solved the problem, producing one of the best handling and riding cars of its generation.**

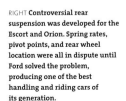

1983
Escort RS1600i

INTRODUCTION 1982, production to 1983.
BODY saloon; 2-doors, 5-seats; weight 920kg (2028.2lb).
ENGINE 4-cylinders; transverse; 79.96mm x 79.52mm, 1596cc; compr 9.9:1; 85.8kW (115bhp) @ 6000rpm; 53.7kW (72.1bhp)/l; 148 (109lbft) @ 5250rpm.
ENGINE STRUCTURE belt-driven overhead camshaft; 2-valves; aluminium cylinder head, finned aluminium rocker cover, iron block; Bosch K-Jetronic fuel injection, breakerless ignition; 5-bearing crankshaft.
TRANSMISSION front wheel drive; 20.3cm (8in) diaphragm spring clutch; 5-speed synchromesh; helical spur final drive 3.84:1.
CHASSIS steel monocoque; ifs by MacPherson struts, coil springs and anti-roll bar; independent variable rate rear suspension by coil springs telescopic dampers and anti roll bar; hydraulic vacuum servo brakes, front 23.9cm (9.4in) dia disc, rear 17.78cm (7in) dia drums, dual circuit; rack and pinion steering; 48l (10.6 gal) fuel tank; SP Sport Super D4 195/50VR15 tyres 6in rims, alloy wheels.
DIMENSIONS wheelbase 240cm (94.5in); track 140cm (55.1in) front, 142.5cm (56.1in) rear; length 397cm (156.3in); width 164cm (64.6in); height 137cm (53.9in); ground clearance 14cm (5.5in); turning circle 10.6m (34.8ft).
EQUIPMENT central locking £136.36, front electric windows £161.41, manual sunroof £258.98, tinted windows £43.08, black paint £80.68, radio cassette £143.25.
PERFORMANCE maximum speed 187kph (116.5mph) *Autocar*; 33.1kph (20.6mph) @ 1000rpm; 0-100kph (62mph) 8.7sec; 10.7kg/kW (8kg/bhp); fuel consumption 10l/100km (28.25mpg).
PRICE £6834.
PRODUCTION 8659.

Shown as a prototype in the autumn of 1981, RS1600i was an XR3 with an 85.8kW (115bhp) fuel injection engine, lowered suspension, and elaborate aerodynamics, intended as a Group A motor sport homologation special. Subject to delays, it tentatively went on sale in the spring of 1982, but deliveries of right hand drive cars did not begin until the end of the year. Since the Advanced Vehicles Operation (AVO) had closed in 1974, responsibility for fast Fords had been taken on by the Motorsport and Rallye Sport (hence RS) divisions in Germany under Mike Kranefuss. Suspension changes included different struts, anti-dive geometry, Koni dampers, thick anti-roll bars, and an aluminium front cross-member. Overall gearing was raised from 4.29:1 on the XR3i to 3.84:1, and in compensation 5th gear was lower, 0.83:1 against the standard car's 0.75. The result was not entirely satisfactory, with top speed in 5th scarcely faster than 4th. External differences were a striped bonnet, a deep front spoiler and a biplane rear wing. The CVH engine was provided with a special cam, solid valve lifters and a high-compression head, the road-going car providing a racy feel but with some coughing and spluttering on start-up. The performance was lively but the RS1600i was only really quick in race tune, when the engine produced half as much power again.

ABOVE **Group A/N regulations demanded the production of 5000 RS1600i Escorts, but strong demand increased it to nearly 9000.**

1983
Sierra XR4i

The most radically-styled Sierra, indeed the most radical-looking Ford since the Probe III concept car, the XR4i featured not only a dramatic biplane rear spoiler but also a unique three window elevation. On sale from June, it had the Cologne V6 engine of the Capri 2.8i and the same 5-speed transmission with close-ratio gears. It faced competition from the Audi Coupe and BMW 320i, the stylish 3-door body and aerodynamic aids distancing it from the run-of-the-mill Sierra, even though a major part of its rationale was to provide the range with some much needed glamour. Sierras never quite raised the market's enthusiasm like other Fords. The lower bodywork was wrapped in polycarbonate cladding, faired round the wheelarches to promote good airflow past the wheels - always a difficult area for aerodynamicists. The wheels stuck further out into the airstream owing to their wide low-profile tyres, and as an additional cosmetic feature the cladding had a contrasting inlaid coloured strip. Suspension modifications included a thicker front anti-roll bar and the addition of a 10mm (.39in) one at the back. Gas filled dampers and bigger brakes completed the performance package. Nothing was skimped on comfort and trim; the interior was equipped with Ghia-style upholstery and accessories, which added to the speed but did not save weight. Despite 3-door bodywork this was the heaviest Sierra yet, weighing more than a 2.8i Capri.

INTRODUCTION April 1983, production to 1985.
BODY saloon; 3-doors, 5-seats; weight 1175kg (2590.4lb).
ENGINE 6-cylinders, 60deg V; in-line; 93mm x 68.5mm, 2792cc; compr 9.2:1; 110.5kW (148.2bhp) @ 5700rpm; 39.5kW (53.1bhp)/l; 216Nm (159lbft) @ 3800rpm.
ENGINE STRUCTURE gear-driven central camshaft; pushrod ohv; 2-valves; iron cylinder head, block;

Bosch K-Jetronic mechanical fuel injection; breakerless ignition; 4-bearing crankshaft.
TRANSMISSION rear wheel drive; diaphragm spring sdp clutch; 5-speed synchromesh; final drive 3.62:1.
CHASSIS steel monocoque; ifs by MacPherson struts; independent rear suspension by semi-trailing arms and coil springs; front and rear anti roll bars; telescopic dampers;

hydraulic servo brakes, front 26cm (10.2in) dia ventilated disc, rear 26cm (10in) dia drums, dual circuit; rack and pinion steering, PAS optional; 60l (13.2gal) fuel tank; 195/60VR14 tyres 5.5J rims.
DIMENSIONS wheelbase 261cm (102.8in); track 145cm (57.1in) front, 147cm (57.9in) rear; length 446cm (175.6in); width 173cm (68.1in); height 139cm (54.7in); ground clearance 12cm (4.7in); turning circle 10.6m (34.8ft).
EQUIPMENT Ford active warning system for fluid levels, brake pad wear; Ford FM/MW/LW radio cassette player.
PERFORMANCE maximum speed 210kph (130.81mph) *Autocar*; 36.2kph (22.6mph) @ 1000rpm; 0-100kph (62mph) 7.7sec; 10.6kg/kW (7.9kg/bhp); fuel consumption 13.3l/100km (21.2mpg).
PRICE 1984 £9946.
PRODUCTION 27,400.

1984
Fiesta II XR2 1597cc

Expanding the Fiesta range, the XR2 had five gears and a 71.6kW (96bhp) version of the CVH engine as used in the original Escort XR3. Low-profile tyres, bigger brakes, up-rated springs and gas-filled dampers, a rear anti-roll bar, wheelarch extensions in smart black plastic and quasi-aerodynamic trappings round the rear window provided more sporting ingredients. Yet it was still a mildly tuned engine; the Escort had already gone on to fuel injection but the Fiesta remained faithful to a Weber twin-choke downdraught carburettor, with a special inlet manifold to ensure everything fitted within the smaller space. The principal feature was an aluminium cylinder head with valves inclined at 45deg and skewed in

relation to one another in plan view by 7deg. This gave the complex valve angles of the Compound Valve angle Hemispherical chamber (CVH) title and, by its nature, a near-hemispherical combustion chamber. The design represented yet another triumph of Ford minimalism, working the valves through a single overhead camshaft, spun by a toothed belt. Inclined valves customarily had to be operated by two cams, or a complicated system of rockers, but the 7deg inclination allowed them to be operated by only one through American-style hydraulic tappets, unusual in a small European engine. XR2 was energetic rather than truly swift and suffered through its thick anti roll bar from a somewhat choppy ride.

INTRODUCTION June 1984, production to 1989.
BODY saloon; 3-doors, 5-seats; weight 840kg (1852lb).
ENGINE 4-cylinders; transverse; 79.96mm x 79.5mm, 1597cc; compr 9.5:1; 70kW (93.9bhp) @ 5750rpm; 43.8kW (58.8bhp)/l; 132Nm (97lbft) @ 4000rpm.
ENGINE STRUCTURE CVH belt-driven overhead camshaft, hydraulic tappets; 2-valves; aluminium cylinder head, iron block; Weber twin-variable-choke downdraught carburettor; breakerless ignition; 5-bearing crankshaft.
TRANSMISSION front wheel drive; sdp 20.3cm (8in) clutch; 5-speed synchromesh; final drive 3.58:1.
CHASSIS steel monocoque structure; ifs by MacPherson struts, coil springs; rear suspension dead axle, trailing links, Panhard rod, anti-roll bar; telescopic dampers; hydraulic, vacuum servo 23.9cm (9.4in) front disc brakes; rear drums 17.8cm (7in); rack and pinion steering; 34l (7.5 gal) fuel tank; radial-ply 185/60HR-13 tyres 6J rims.
DIMENSIONS wheelbase 228.6cm (90in); track 138.5cm (54.5in) front, 134cm (52.8in) rear; length 371cm (146.1in); width 162cm (63.8in); height 136cm (53.5in); ground clearance 14cm (5.5in); turning circle 10.3m (33.79ft).
EQUIPMENT 2-speed intermittent wipers, cloth upholstery, foam headlining, laminated windscreen.
PERFORMANCE maximum speed 165kph (102.8mph) *Autocar*; 27.8kph (17.3mph) @ 1000rpm; 0-100kph (62mph) 10.2sec; 12kg/kW (8.9kg/bhp); fuel consumption 9.4l/100km (30.1mpg).
PRICE £5713.
PRODUCTION 1,980,100 all Fiesta II.

1984–1987
Capri, Tickford Capri

Capri production reached 250,000 in spring 1970, one million in August 1973 and 1.7 million in 1981. Thereafter the pace slackened; Halewood production ceased in October 1971 after 337,491, and the last Cologne Capri was the 1,886,647th. For MY 1985 the 2.8i Injection Special was provided with a limited slip differential, one of the final refinements for a model that had lasted far longer than anyone expected in 1969, production continuing until just before Christmas 1986. The Capri may have lacked sophistication, but its simplicity, compactness, versatility and good value gave it an appeal not unlike that of the pre-war V8 and it enjoyed a similar clientele. Encouraging sales of the 2.8i perhaps gave it delusions of grandeur rather like the Executive Fords, yet it was not only a marketing and commercial success, it was a production triumph, shadowing other models in the Ford range, mainly Cortinas, providing substantial economies of scale in common components. After a lifespan approaching 18 years, the end of the Capri had to be delayed. Enthusiasts held the car in such affection that, like a great diva, its farewell tours

were extended by popular demand. Britain was always its strongest market, so the final 12 months' Cologne production was exclusively right hand drive. The last 280, with metallic green paint and leather interior were known as Capri 280 Brooklands, as a tribute to the birthplace of British motor racing.

Tickford, a division of Aston Martin, developed a premium-priced Capri (left) with Connolly leather upholstery, Wilton carpet, and black ash facia. The engine was turbocharged, intercooled, oil-radiatored and provided with a bigger cooling system. A Getrag gearbox and limited slip differential were installed and gear ratios raised. Air dams, bibs, spoilers, ducts and wheel discs improved the aerodynamics, although not by much. Former Team Lotus driver John Miles, a road tester with Autocar, consulted on the suspension, found better rear axle location vital because the standard single-leaf sprung axle moved 3.8cm (1.5in) sideways during hard cornering, due to deflection in the spring eyes' rubber bushes. Shown at Birmingham in 1982, a few were made in 1983 priced around £15,000 but at £18,581 in 1986 demand was not great.

INTRODUCTION September 1983, production to 1986.
BODY coupe; 2-doors, 4-seats; weight 1230kg (2712lb).
ENGINE Cologne 60deg V6; front; 93.0mm x 68.5mm; 2792cc; compr 9.2:1; 152.9kW (205bhp) @ 5000rpm; 54.8kW (73.4bhp)/l; 192Nm (260lbft) @ 3500rpm.
ENGINE STRUCTURE gear-driven camshaft, pushrod ohv; cast iron cyl head, block; breakerless ign; Bosch K-Jetronic mechanical fuel inj; IHI RHB6 turbocharger with 0.6kg-cm (8.5psi) boost and integral wastegate, equal-length stainless steel manifolds; 4-bearing crankshaft.
TRANSMISSION rwd; diaphragm spring sdp clutch; 4-speed synchromesh; final drive 3.09:1.
CHASSIS steel monocoque; ifs by MacPherson struts; rear susp semi-elliptic springs; 24mm (0.9in) front, 14mm (0.6in) rear anti-roll bars; gas-filled telescopic dampers; hydraulic vacuum servo brakes, 26.2cm (10.3in) ventilated front discs 24.76cm (9.75in) dia, rear 22.9cm (9in) drums, dual circuit; rack and pinion PAS; 59.1l (13gal) fuel tank; 205/60VR13 radial-ply, 7J rims; alloy wheels.
DIMENSIONS wheelbase 256cm (100.8in); track 140cm (55.1in) front, 143cm (56.3in) rear; length 437.5cm (172.2in); width 170cm (66.9in); height 136cm (53.5in); ground clearance 11.5cm (4.5in); turning circle 10.8m (35.43ft).
EQUIPMENT leather and velour upholstery, black ash facia, two pearlescent colours, white and flaxen mist.
PERFORMANCE maximum over 225kph (140.2mph); 41.4kph (25.8mph) @ 1000rpm; 0-100kph (62mph) 6.2sec; 8kg/kW (6kg/bhp); standard non-turbo 2.8i 14.5l/100km (19.5mpg).
PRICE £18,581.

1984
Escort RS Turbo, Escort Cabriolet

The RS Turbo and the Escort Cabriolet were important developments. The RS was a limited production homologation special, designed under the talented Rod Mansfield at Special Vehicle Engineering (SVE) at Dunton, and could be configured to almost any specification. It aimed to meet the regulations for international rallies yet remain flexible enough to suit each event. Replacing the discontinued RS1600i, it used the XR3i as a basis, with a turbocharged version of the 1.6-litre CVH. It also had a viscous coupling limited slip differential, the first application for this ingenious component, which helped banish front wheel drive torque steer. There were the customary extended wheel arches for large fat wheels, Recaro seats and measures to minimise turbo lag. In 1986 the RS Turbo graduated from pure homologation special to proper road car with softer springing, higher gearing, and glass reinforced plastic bodywork panelling. The Cabriolet cost £2000 more than an ordinary Escort and there was a choice of Ghia or XR3i with either 58.9kW (79bhp) or 78.3kW (105bhp) CVH engines. A practical conversion, it was made by the specialists in open-topped bodies, Karmann in Germany, with little loss of interior accommodation except for a smaller boot to give space for the top to fold down.

SPECIFICATION FOR RS
INTRODUCTION 1984, production to 1990.
BODY saloon; 2-doors, 5-seats; weight 940kg (2072lb), Cabriolet 970kg (2138.5lb).
ENGINE 4-cylinders; transverse; 79.96mm x 79.52mm, 1597cc; compr 8.3:1; 97kW (130bhp) @ 6000rpm; 60.7kW (81.5bhp)/l; 180Nm (133lbft) @ 5250rpm. Cabriolet: 77kW (103.3bhp) @ 6000rpm; 48.3kW (64.7bhp)/l; 138Nm (102lbft) @ 4800rpm.
ENGINE STRUCTURE CVH belt-driven overhead camshaft; 2-valves; hydraulic tappets aluminium cylinder head and block; KE-Jetronic fuel injection; Garrett T03 turbocharger; intercooler; breakerless ignition; 5-bearing crankshaft. Cabriolet Bosch K-Jetronic, non-turbo.

TRANSMISSION front wheel drive; 20.3cm (8in) diaphragm spring clutch; 5-speed synchromesh; helical spur final drive 4.27:1; Ferguson limited slip differential. Cabriolet 4.29:1.
CHASSIS steel monocoque; ifs by MacPherson struts, coil springs; irs variable rate by coil springs; telescopic dampers, front and rear anti roll bars; hydraulic vacuum servo brakes, front 23.9cm (9.4in) dia ventilated discs, rear 20.1cm (7.9in) drums; dual circuit; rack and pinion steering; 48l (10.6 gal) fuel tank; SP Sport Super D4 195/50VR15 tyres 6in rims, alloy wheels. Cabriolet 185/60HR14.

DIMENSIONS wheelbase 240cm (94.5in); track 140cm (55.1in) front, 142.5cm (56.1in) rear; length 397cm (156.3in); width 164cm (64.6in); height 137cm (53.9in); ground clearance 14cm (5.5in); turning circle 10.6m (34.78ft).
EQUIPMENT halogen headlights, reversing light, 2-speed and intermittent wipers, laminated windscreen.
PERFORMANCE maximum speed 200kph (124.6mph), Cabriolet 186kph (115.9mph); 32.7kph (20.4mph) @ 1000rpm; 0-100kph (62mph) 8.2sec, Cabriolet 9.7sec; 9.7kg/kW (7.2kg/bhp), Cabriolet 12.6kg/kW (9.4kg/bhp), 10l/100km (28.3mpg), Cabriolet 8.4l/100km (33.8mpg).
PRICE RS £9951, 1.6i Cabriolet £9253.
PRODUCTION RS Turbo 8604, Cabriolet 27,900.

1985
Sierra XR4x4

A rearrangement of the Sierra range took place in 1984 with a 1.6-litre economy model, the E-Max, using a revised Pinto engine of 81.3mm x 77mm instead of 87.67mm x 61mm. Power and torque were about the same as before accompanied by a useful gain in fuel consumption. The newly introduced 3-door body shell was abandoned together with the 2.3-litre V6, while a CVH taxation special was introduced for the business market, on which a 1.8-litre limit had been imposed by income tax "benefit in kind" legislation. An alternative over the 1.8 limit was a new 2.0-litre 85.8kW (115bhp) Sierra with L-Jetronic fuel injection. The major Ford development of 1985, in its determination to match the opposing works teams from Peugeot and Audi, was the employment of 4-wheel drive for rallying with the XR4x4 using two viscous coupling limited-slip differentials. Drawing on Ferguson FF Developments' experience (going back to experimental 4x4 Capris of 1970) 4-wheel drive was used on sporting Sierras and Escort RS Cosworths on and off for a decade. In 1986 Ford confirmed its commitment to the wide non-competition 4-wheel drive market with a 4x4 Ghia Estate that had similar running gear to the XR. The XR4x4 was announced with the 2.0, but by the time it went on sale in May 1985, it was a V6 with K-Jetronic.

INTRODUCTION February 1985, on sale May, production to 1990. Specification for V6 2792cc.
BODY saloon; 5-doors, 5-seats; weight 1175kg (2590lb).
ENGINE 6-cylinders, 60deg V; in-line; 93mm x 68.5mm, 2792cc; compr 9.2:1; 110.5kW (148.2bhp) @ 5700rpm; 39.5kW (53.1bhp)/l; 216Nm (159lbft) @ 3800rpm. 2.0: 4-cylinders; 90.82 x 76.95mm; 1993cc; 9.2:1; 84.5kW (113.3bhp) @ 5200rpm; 42.4kW (56.9bhp)/l; 157Nm (116lbft) @ 4000rpm.
ENGINE STRUCTURE central gear-driven camshaft; pushrods; 2-valves; iron cyl head, block; Bosch K-Jetronic mechanical fuel inj; 4-bearing crank. 2.0 belt-driven ohc; Bosch electronic L-Jetronic and Ford EEC-IV engine management; 5-bearing crankshaft.

TRANSMISSION four wheel drive by Borg Warner Morse Hi-Vo chain and viscous coupling; front drive shaft through engine sump; sdp clutch; 5-speed synchromesh; 37 per cent drive to front, 63 to rear; final drive 3.36:1.
CHASSIS steel monocoque; ifs by MacPherson struts; independent rear suspension by semi-trailing arms and coil springs; front and rear anti roll bars; telescopic dampers; hydraulic servo brakes, front 26cm (10.2in) dia ventilated disc, rear 25.2cm (9.9in) dia drums, dual circuit; rack and pinion PAS; 60l (13.2gal) fuel tank; 195/60VR14 tyres 5.5J rims.
DIMENSIONS track 145cm (57.1in) front, 147cm (57.9in) rear; length 446cm (175.6in); width 173cm (68.1in); height 139cm (54.7in); ground clearance 12cm (4.7in); turning circle 10.6m (34.78ft).

EQUIPMENT split rear seats, door mirror remote control, front electric windows, heated rear window, tinted glass, tailgate wash-wipe, alloy wheels, central locking, radio cassette all standard.
PERFORMANCE maximum speed 201kph (125.2mph) Autocar. 2.0 190kph (118.35mph) estimate; 36.2kph (22.6mph) @ 1000rpm; 0-100kph (62mph) 8.4sec Autocar. 2.0 0-100kph 9.4sec estimate; 10.5kg/kW (7.9kg/bhp); 13.8l/100km (20.5mpg).
PRICE £11,500.
PRODUCTION 23,540.

1985
Sierra RS Cosworth

Launched in March for the Geneva Motor Show, a whole year would elapse before deliveries began of the road car with probably the biggest rear wing ever. The purpose of the RS Cosworth was Group A Touring Car Racing, for which 5000 had to be produced, and although it had the structure of an ordinary Sierra 3-door (stiffer and lighter than the 5-door) and made a splendid road-burner, its speed and performance were aimed principally at motor sport. A newly developed Cosworth-designed engine was built round the Pinto cylinder block, with a turbocharger and a 16-valve twin-cam head.

Following its homologation in 1987, race-prepared engines were giving 223.7kW (300bhp). It even had its cam covers painted vivid red in the best Testarossa tradition, sharing with Ferrari Weber fuel injection and a Marelli electronic ignition system similar to that used in Formula 1. Drive was through a Borg Warner close-ratio gearbox supplied ready-built from the US, and the final drive had a viscous coupled limited slip differential. Ford fitted its own electronic anti-lock braking.

Two journalists on the press launch recalled sweeping down a Spanish motorway, easily keeping station with a Boeing jet, on its final approach to the runway of a nearby airport at around 240kph (150mph). The Boeing's wings were keeping it flying; the Cozzie's were keeping it on the ground, and notably steady.

INTRODUCTION March 1985, production to 1986.
BODY saloon; 3-doors, 5-seats; weight 1240kg (2734lb).
ENGINE 4-cylinders; in-line; 90.82mm x 76.95mm, 1994cc; compr 8.0:1; 150kW (201.2bhp) @ 6000rpm; 75.2kW (101bhp)/l; 276Nm (204lbft) @ 4500rpm.
ENGINE STRUCTURE 2 belt driven overhead camshafts; 4-valves; aluminium cylinder head, iron block; Weber electronic fuel injection, Marelli electronic breakerless ignition; 5-bearing crankshaft; Garrett T3 turbocharger, boost 0.65bar (9psi); intercooler; two electric cooling fans.
TRANSMISSION rear wheel drive; sdp diaphragm spring self-adjusting clutch; Borg Warner manual gearbox 5-speed synchromesh; final drive 3.64:1; limited slip differential.
CHASSIS steel monocoque; ifs by MacPherson struts; anti-roll bars front and back; irs by semi-trailing arms, coil springs, telescopic dampers; hydraulic servo brakes, front 28.3cm (11.1in) dia ventilated disc, rear 27.3cm (10.75in) dia disc, dual circuit, ABS; variable ratio rack and pinion PAS; 65l (14.3 gal) fuel tank; 205/50VR15 tyres, 7Jrims.
DIMENSIONS wheelbase 261cm (102.8in); track 144cm (56.7in) front, 144.5cm (56.9in) rear; length 446cm (175.6in); width 173cm (68.1in); height 137.5cm (54.1in); ground clearance 12cm (4.7in); turning circle 10.6m (34.8ft).
EQUIPMENT electric windows, Recaro seats with height and rake adjustment in Roma cashmere fabric, leather-bound steering wheel all standard.
PERFORMANCE maximum speed 240kph (149.5mph); 36.7kph (22.9mph) @ 1000rpm. 0-100kph (62mph) 6.8sec; 8.3kg/kW (6.2kg/bhp); 14.3l/100km (19.8mpg) *Autocar*.
PRICE £15,950 (1986).
PRODUCTION 6021.

LEFT **Not many years after 75kW (100bhp) per litre was regarded as appropriate for a fragile racing unit, the RS Cosworth was sufficiently tractable and untemperamental to use on the road.**

1985
Granada, Scorpio 1796cc, 1993cc

Demand for big Fords was at best inconsistent at the time decisions were being taken for a new Granada. There was a pressing need, it seemed, to develop as many variants as possible, so a common platform for both cars was a tempting option. "Platform" roughly corresponded to the old chassis, the framework comprising engine and transmission, suspension and running gear, on which a variety of bodies could be mounted. In a monocoque hull, body and platform were wholly integrated, but it was feasible within one overall design to ring the changes with different wheelbases, different tracks, and different body styles. It was a subtler conception than the old Consul and Zephyr of the 1950s, where one was merely a stretched version of the other, with the addition or subtraction of a couple of cylinders and almost everything else identical. The large Granada bore no more than a family resemblance to the mid-size Sierra, except in the centre section and doors and although both were hatchbacks, following the example of Rover and Renault in the luxury market, many customers would scarcely notice the connection. In the UK top of the range models were known as Granada Scorpios, lesser variants were Granadas. It was the first volume production car with electronic ABS as standard from launch, and following the Sierra's near-miss in 1983, it was voted Car of the Year in 1986.

INTRODUCTION 1985, produced until 1998.
BODY saloon; 5-doors, 5-seats; weight 1180kg (2601.4lb), 2.0 1185kg (2612.5lb).
ENGINE 4-cylinders, in-line; 86.2mm x 76.95mm, 1796cc; compr 9.5:1; 66kW (88.5bhp) @ 5400rpm; 36.7kW (49.3bhp)/l; 140Nm (103lbft) @ 3500rpm. 2.0: 90.82 x 76.95mm; 1993cc; 9.2:1; 77kW (103.3bhp) @ 5200rpm; 38.6kW (51.8bhp)/l; 157Nm (116lbft) @ 4000rpm.
ENGINE STRUCTURE belt-driven overhead camshaft; 2-valves; iron cylinder head, block; twin venturi Pierburg downdraught carburettor; Ford ESC II electronic ignition; 5-bearing crankshaft. 2.0 twin venturi Weber.
TRANSMISSION rwd; cable-operated 21.6cm (8.5in) sdp clutch; 5-speed synchromesh; final drive 3.92:1. 2.0: 3.62:1, A4LD automatic option.

CHASSIS steel monocoque; ifs by offset coil sprung MacPherson struts, telescopic twin-tube dampers, anti-roll bar; rear suspension independent with progressive rate coil springs, 18deg semi-trailing arms, telescopic dampers; anti roll bar; automatic self-levelling electric-pumped pneumatic optional; hydraulic servo brakes, front 26cm (10.2in) dia ventilated discs, rear 25.3cm (10in) dia discs, dual circuit, ATE electronic ABS; rack and pinion, hydraulic variable ratio PAS optional; 70l (15.4gal) fuel tank; 175TR14 or 185/70HR14 tyres, 5.5 or 6J rims.

DIMENSIONS wheelbase 276cm (108.7in); track front and rear 147.5cm (58.1in); length 467cm (183.9in); width 176cm (69.3in); height 144cm (56.7in); ground clearance 12cm (4.7in); turning circle 11m (36.1ft).
EQUIPMENT steering wheel adjustable for rake and reach, asymmetrically split rear seat backrests, warning module for fluids and brake pads.
PERFORMANCE maximum 179kph (111.5mph), 2.0 188kph (117.1mph); 36.1kph (22.5mph) @ 1000rpm, 2.0 39.1kph (24.4mph); 0-100kph (62mph) 13.1sec, 2.0 11.5sec; 17.9kg/kW (13.3kg/bhp), 2.0 15.4kg/kW (11.5kg/bhp); 7.9l/100km (35.8mpg).
PRICE 1.8GL £9974, 2.0L £9663.

1985
Granada, Scorpio 2.0 EFI, V6EFI

Despite looking fashionably slippery, the Granada was not especially aerodynamic. Like the Chrysler Airflow of the 1930s it appeared more efficient than it really was, with a Cd of 0.34 instead of the current best practice of under 0.30. It had a smaller frontal area than its Cd 0.44 predecessor, however, and the real drag figure was much the same as the benchmark Audi 100. Detailing was better than the Sierra, with flusher bonded windows, small air intakes, recessed drip rails, and wiper blades that parked out of the draught. Yet in the 1980s luxury-car buyers were tending towards established prestige makes, mostly German, and while Granada sales in Britain were satisfactory, they did not make headway in the rest of Europe. Its 4-cylinder petrol engines were Pinto-based, with the same 76.95mm bore and 86.2 (1.8-litre) or 90.82mm (2.0-litre) stroke. Among the changes that came with the 2.0-litre's Bosch L-Jetronic fuel injection was an intricate cast aluminium inlet manifold, with tuned length tracts of a sort that would gain increasing favour with many designers in years to come. New V6 engines were expected in 1987, so the 1985 one was essentially a stop-gap. It was the end of 1986 before the new engines were announced and the winter of 1986-1987 before the much-altered 60deg V6s of 2.4-litre and 2.9-litre were put into production.

SPECIFICATION FOR 2.0EFI.
INTRODUCTION 1985, production to 1998.
BODY saloon; 5-doors, 5-seats; weight 1185kg (2612.5lb), V6 1310kg (2888lb).
ENGINE 4-cylinders, in-line; 90.82mm x 76.95mm, 1993cc; compr 9.2:1; 84.5kW (113.3bhp) @ 5200rpm; 42.4kW (56.9bhp)/l; 157Nm (116lbft) @ 4000rpm. V6: 93 x 68.5mm; 2792cc; 110.5kW (148.2bhp) @ 5800rpm; 39.6kW (53.1bhp)/l; 219Nm (161lbft) @ 3000rpm.
ENGINE STRUCTURE belt-driven overhead camshaft; 2-valves; iron cylinder head, block; Bosch L-Jetronic fuel injection; Ford EEC IV engine management; 5-bearing crank. V6 gear-driven central camshaft; 4-bearing crankshaft; Bosch LE-Jetronic.
TRANSMISSION rwd; cable-operated 21.6cm (8.5in) sdp clutch; 5-speed

synchromesh; final drive 3.92:1. limited slip 3.64; A4LD automatic option. V6: 3.36 or 3.64:1.
CHASSIS steel monocoque; ifs by offset coil sprung MacPherson struts, telescopic twin-tube dampers, anti-roll bar; irs with progressive rate coil springs, 18deg semi-trailing arms, telescopic dampers; anti roll bar; automatic self-levelling electric-pumped pneumatic optional; hydraulic servo brakes, front 26cm (10.2in) ventilated discs, rear 25.3cm (9.96in) discs, dual circuit, ATE electronic ABS; rack and pinion, hydraulic variable ratio PAS optional, standard on V6; 70l (15.4 gal) tank; 185/70HR14 tyres; 6J rims.
DIMENSIONS wheelbase 276cm (108.7in); track 147.5cm (58.1in); length 467cm (183.9in); width 176cm (69.3in); height 144cm (56.7in); ground clearance 12cm (4.7in); turning circle 11m (36.1ft).

EQUIPMENT steering wheel adjustable for rake and reach, asymmetrically split rear seat backrests, warning module for fluids and brake pads.
PERFORMANCE maximum 193kph (120.2mph), V6 208kph (129.6mph); 35.6kph (22.2mph) @ 1000rpm, V6 41.2kph (25.7mph); 0-100kph (62mph) 10.6sec, V6 9.6sec, auto 11.7sec; 14kg/kW (10.5kg/bhp), V6 11.9kg/kW (8.8kg/bhp); 8.6l/100km (32.9mpg), V6 9.3l/100km (30.4mpg).
PRICE 2.0iGL £10,831, 2.0i Ghia £12,056, 2.8i Ghia £14,306

ABOVE **Later 1990 H registered Scorpio (above) shows few detail changes.**

1985
Granada, Scorpio diesel

It was small wonder that diesel-engined large Fords did not make inroads into the market. Peugeot supplied its 2.1D 2112cc diesel of 1977 that gave 47kW (63bhp), before being replaced by the 2498cc with 51.5kW (69bhp) at 4200rpm. By 1983 the Granada was mature enough to be described by *Autocar* as "much improved," although still not giving much in the way of speed, with a maximum of 139.7kph (87mph), or acceleration, at nearly 28sec to 62mph. An estate car weighed in at 1425kg (3141.6lb) and compared poorly against Rover, Citroen, Vauxhall, Mercedes-Benz and Peugeot rivals. *Autocar* faintly praised the performance as "acceptable", describing the car as a "good all-rounder", as well as saying it was a cheaper alternative to the others. In 1985 the Scorpio was introduced at the Geneva Motor Show in the spring, the 4x4 in the autumn at Frankfurt, and the diesel in January 1986, still with the 51.5kW (69bhp) Peugeot engine. It was 1988 before a newer one, as used in the Peugeot Express van and turbocharged to 68.6kW (92bhp), was fitted, giving a top speed around 173kph (108mph) and cutting the 0-62mph to 13.1sec. The opportunity was taken to fit an M75 gearbox at the same time. The turbo-diesel produced 203Nm (150lbft) of torque at 2250rpm against the non-turbo's 148Nm (109lbft) and most buyers found extra layers of sound-deadening welcome.

INTRODUCTION 1985, production to 1998.

BODY saloon; 5-doors, 5-seats; weight 1350kg (2976lb).

ENGINE 4-cylinders, in-line; 94mm x 90mm, 2498cc; compr 23:1; 51kW (68.4bhp) @ 4500rpm; 20.4kW (27.4bhp)/l; 148Nm (109lbft) @ 2000rpm.

ENGINE STRUCTURE Peugeot XD3 chain-driven camshaft, pushrod ohv; 2-valves; iron cylinder head, block; Bosch EP/VAC fuel injection; 5-bearing crankshaft; block inclined right.

TRANSMISSION rear wheel drive; cable-operated 21.6cm (8.5in) sdp clutch; 5-speed synchromesh; final drive 3.89:1.

CHASSIS steel monocoque; ifs by offset coil sprung MacPherson struts, telescopic twin-tube dampers, anti-roll bar; irs with progressive rate coil springs, 18deg semi-trailing arms, telescopic dampers; anti roll bar; automatic self-levelling electric-pumped pneumatic optional; hydraulic servo brakes, front 26cm (10.2in) ventilated discs, rear 25.3cm (10in) discs, dual circuit, ATE electronic ABS; rack and pinion, hydraulic variable ratio PAS; 70l (15.4 gal) tank; 175TR14 or 185/70HR14tyres, 5.5 or 6J rims.

DIMENSIONS wheelbase 276cm (108.7in); track front and rear 147.5cm (58.1in); length 467cm (183.9in); width 176cm (69.3in); height 144cm (56.7in); ground clearance 12cm (4.7in); turning circle 11m (36.1ft).

EQUIPMENT steering wheel adjustable for rake and reach, asymmetrically split rear seat backrests, warning module for fluids and brake pads.

PERFORMANCE maximum speed 158kph (98.4mph); 39.1kph (24.4mph) @ 1000rpm; 0-100kph (62mph) 19.4sec; 26.5kg/kW (19.7kg/bhp); fuel consumption 7.3l/100km (38.7mpg).

PRICE 2.5LD £10,682.

1985
Granada, Scorpio 4x4

It was debatable how much of the 4x4's crisp handling and responsiveness was down to its 4-wheel drive, and how much to firmer springing and low profile tyres. Either way it was probably the best Scorpio of all. Jensens of 1966, the VW Iltis of 1977, and Audi's pioneering work with the quattro of 1980 had made 4-wheel drive not only respectable but almost commonplace by the time Ford got round to it. And while some manufacturers with front-drive transverse-engined cars went to tortuous lengths to transmit drive round awkward angles, Ford only had to adapt the rear-drive Scorpio/Sierra driveline to achieve the same objective. The epicyclic centre differential sent only 34 per cent of the traction to the front wheels, so the Scorpio's tendency to understeer towards the outside of corners was all but eliminated; it ran true on the motorway and kept an astonishingly firm grip in all weathers. Together with the anti-lock brakes standard since launch on all Granadas, the 4x4 Scorpio was exemplary for all year round mobility. A special feature of the Ford 4x4 was a viscous coupling between central and rear differentials to subdue wheelspin. In December 1986 the Scorpio gained the 2.9-litre V6 with similar power but more mid-range pull, making the performance livelier at some expense to fuel consumption.

INTRODUCTION 1985, production to 1998.
BODY saloon; 5-doors, 5-seats; weight 1385kg (3053.4lb).
ENGINE 6-cylinders, 60deg V; 93mm x 68.5mm, 2792cc; compr 9.2:1; 110.5kW (148.2bhp) @ 5800rpm; 39.6kW (53.1bhp)/l; 219Nm (161lbft) @ 3000rpm.
ENGINE STRUCTURE gear-driven central camshaft; 2-valves; cast iron cylinder head, block; Bosch LE-Jetronic fuel injection; Ford EEC IV engine management; 4-bearing crankshaft.
TRANSMISSION four wheel drive by Borg Warner Morse Hi-Vo chain and viscous coupling; 37 per cent drive to front, 63 per cent to rear; front drive shaft through engine sump; sdp clutch; 5-speed synchromesh; final drive 3.36:1.
CHASSIS steel monocoque; ifs by offset MacPherson struts, telescopic twin-tube dampers, anti-roll bar; irs with progressive rate coil springs, 18deg semi-trailing arms, telescopic dampers; anti roll bar; automatic self-levelling electric-pumped pneumatic optional; hydraulic servo brakes, front 26cm (10.2in) ventilated discs, rear 25.3cm (9.96in) discs, dual circuit, ATE electronic ABS; rack and pinion, hydraulic variable ratio PAS; 70l (15.4gal) tank; 205/60 VR15tyres; 6J rims.
DIMENSIONS wheelbase 276.5cm (108.9in); track front 147.5cm (58.1in), rear 148cm (58.3in); length 467cm (183.9in); width 176cm (69.3in); height 143.5cm (56.5in); ground clearance 12cm (4.7in); turning circle 11m (36.1ft).
EQUIPMENT steering wheel adjustable for rake and reach, asymmetrically split rear seat backrests, warning module for fluids and brake pads.
PERFORMANCE maximum speed 203kph (126.5mph); 41.2kph (25.7mph) @ 1000rpm; 0-100kph (62mph) 9.9sec; 12.5kg/kW (9.3kg/bhp); fuel consumption 12.8l/100km (22.1mpg) *The Sunday Times.*
PRICE £19,680

1985
RS200

Designed as a Group B rally car, the RS200 was turbocharged, mid-engined, light, 4-wheel driven, and fast on any surface, transmitting its substantial power down to the road through fat tyres. It was also the most expensive Ford to date. Group B regulations demanded a production run of 200 cars, so Reliant of Tamworth was commissioned to build them. The prototype was announced in 1984 but did not reach production until 1986, and although it held great promise its rallying career was cut dramatically short. In the Rally of Portugal, notorious for spectators flooding the special stages, an RS200 went off, killing three. Then in the Tour de Corse Henri Toivonen and Sergio Cresto died when their Lancia Delta S4 crashed and caught fire. The Fédération Internationale du Sport Automobile (FISA) immediately banned aerodynamic devices on Group B cars and called a halt to the entire class from 1987. Ford was one of the manufacturers that had invested heavily in the category and, faced with the prospect of scrapping the entire production run, converted them from stark rally cars to Ghia luxury specification, trimmed by Tickford, and put them on sale. Costly, noisy, high-revving, and physically demanding to drive, with a GRP body, cramped interior and lacking an effective heater, the RS200 was spectacularly fast with astonishing roadholding and a surprisingly supple ride.

INTRODUCTION Turin Show 1984, production to 1986.
BODY coupe; 2-doors, 2-seats; weight 1180kg (2601.4lb), rally spec 1050kg (2315lb).
ENGINE 4-cyls, in-line; mid; 86mm x 77.62mm, 1803cc; cr 8.2:1; 184kW (246.7bhp) @ 6500rpm; 102.1kW (136.8bhp)/l; 292Nm (215lbft) @ 4500rpm. Rally versions 283kW (380bhp), track versions 485kW (650bhp).
ENGINE STRUCTURE BDT (Belt Drive camshafts Turbocharged) inclined 23deg right; 2 belt-driven overhead cams; 4-valves; aluminium cylinder head, block; Bosch fuel injection, EEC-IV engine management; 5-bearing crankshaft; Garrett T03/04 turbocharger .8bar (11.6psi), rally version 1.2bar (17.4psi).
TRANSMISSION 4wd with optional rear-drive only; torque split 37%

front 63% rear; lockable centre differential splits 50/50; 5-speed all-indirect gearbox at front separate from engine; diaphragm spring twin plate AP 18.4cm (7.25in) clutch; helical spur primary drive; final drive epicyclic Ferguson with viscous coupling limited slip, 4.375:1.
CHASSIS stressed platform; floor and bulkheads Ciba-Geigy honeycomb sandwich; steel front and rear extensions; bolt-on tubular stiffening subframes link suspension towers to central structure; ifs and irs by double wishbones with twin coil spring damper units and anti-roll bars, adjustable at front; adjustable toe-in control link at rear, alternative ride heights, adjustable spring platform positions; hydraulic servo brakes, 28.5cm (11in) ventilated discs, dual circuit; rack and pinion; 2 tanks 73.6l (16.2 gal) & 41.8l (9.2 gal)

total 115.4l (25.4 gal); Pirelli P700 225/50VR16 tyres, 8in rims, Speedline 3-piece composite alloys.
DIMENSIONS wheelbase 253cm (99.6in); track 150cm (59.1in) front, 149.7cm (58.9in) rear; length 400cm (157.5in); width 176.5cm (69.5in); height varies about 132cm (52in); ground clearance varies about 18cm (7.1in); turning circle 9.6m (31.5ft).
EQUIPMENT road car had insulated cover to sound-damp engine, grey carpet, cloth seats, leather-rimmed steering wheel, no radio.
PERFORMANCE maximum speed 225kph (140.2mph); 32.4kph (20.2mph) @ 1000rpm; 0-100kph (62mph) 6.1sec *Autocar*; 6.4kg/kW (4.8kg/bhp); fuel consumption 17l/100km (16.6mpg).
PRICE £45,000.
PRODUCTION 200.

1986
Fiesta II 1.4 CVH

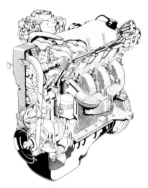

The most contentious aspect of proliferating emission laws was how to achieve the necessary reduction in carbon monoxide (CO) and oxides of nitrogen (Nox). The choice lay between trying to make the combustion process more complete before the exhaust left the engine, or cleaning it up afterwards by means of catalytic converters. Ford advocated the former, more elegant solution, developing CVH or Compound Valve angle Hemispherical chamber technology in its pursuit. Cars with catalytic converters were obliged to run on an air/fuel mixture of 14.7:1, otherwise the cleansing process would not work. The stoichimetric ratio, as it was known, was critical, but unfortunately was responsible for catalytic converter cars using more fuel. In 1986 Ford addressed the difficulty, redesigned the CVH's combustion chambers and piston crowns to promote complete combustion, allowing stoichimetric ratios of 17 or 18:1, so less fuel was used. The resulting Fiesta did 5.4l/100km (52.3mpg) at 90kph (56mph), and 6.8l/100km (41.5mpg) at 120kph (75mph). Power went up by roughly nine per cent, using low-friction piston rings and a sequential carburettor with a manual choke. It was to no avail. Legislators in Europe and America failed to take account of the subtlety, believing the lobbyists for catalytic converters, so carburettors were abandoned and electronic engine management developed. As a direct result of the legislation Fiestas had to be provided with a bigger 40l (8.8 gal) tank.

INTRODUCTION February 1986, production to 1989.
BODY saloon; 3-doors, 5-seats; weight 780kg (1719.5lb).
ENGINE 4-cylinders, in-line; transverse; 77.24mm x 74.3mm, 1392cc; compr 9.5:1; 55kW (73.8bhp) @ 5600rpm; 39.5kW (53bhp)/l; 109Nm (80lbft) @ 4000rpm. With catalyser 44kW (59bhp).
ENGINE STRUCTURE CVH single belt-driven overhead camshaft; 2-valves; hydraulic tappets; aluminium cylinder head, iron block; twin choke Weber DFM carburettor; 5-bearing crankshaft.
TRANSMISSION front rear wheel drive; sdp clutch; 5-speed synchromesh; automatic; final drive 3.842:1.
CHASSIS steel monocoque structure; ifs by MacPherson struts; anti-roll bar; rear suspension dead axle, trailing links, Panhard rod; telescopic dampers; hydraulic, vacuum servo 22.1cm (8.7in) front disc brakes; rear drums 17.78cm (7.0in); rack and pinion steering; 34l (7.5 gal) tank; radial-ply 155/70SR-13 tyres, 4.5 or 5J rims.
DIMENSIONS wheelbase 228.6cm (90in); track 136.5cm (53.7in) front, 132cm (52in) rear; length 365cm (143.7in); width 158.5cm (62.4in); height 136cm (53.5in); ground clearance 14cm (5.5in); turning circle 10.3m (33.79ft).
EQUIPMENT flush wheel covers, cloth seats, body graphics.
PERFORMANCE maximum speed 165kph (102.8mph); 34.7kph (21.6mph) @ 1000rpm; 0-100kph (62mph) 12.1sec; 14.2kg/kW (10.6kg/bhp), with catalyser 17.7kg/kW (13.2kg/bhp); fuel consumption 6.9l/100km (40.9mpg).
PRICE 1.4L £6140, 1.4 Ghia £7554.

1986
Escort 1117cc, 1297cc

The mid-term facelift for all Escorts and Orions included a new facia and a reallocation of engines that would see them through until the end of the decade. As what might be termed a Mark IV Escort range, there was not much new about it, beyond the new Lucas Stop Control System (SCS), a down-market anti-lock braking system optional throughout the range and standard on the RS Turbo. Visual changes were limited to a soft-look front, and a modest change to the tailgate. There were five engine capacities, including the unaltered 1.6 diesel. The petrol engines were 1.1-litre, 1.3-litre, 1.4CVH, and 1.6CVH with carburettor, fuel injection or turbocharger. The 1.3 with 5-speed overdrive gearbox was the most

economical, with new European Legislative Average (ELA) consumption (urban cycle x2 plus steady speed figures divided by four in an effort to de-mysticise the official EEC figures) of 6.4l/100km (44.4mpg). This was some 3.2 per cent better than the 1.1-litre even though it was quite a lot faster. Much of the credit for the superior economy was down to the high 5th gear. It was now acknowledged that the early Escort's indifferent ride had been due to dampers set to give more resilience on bump than rebound. The rear suspension provided more track-change than it should have, so geometry changes were brought in to put things right.

INTRODUCTION Jan 1986, production to 1990.
BODY saloon; 3-doors, 5-seats; weight 825kg (1819lb), 5-door 845kg (1863lb), cabriolet 925kg (2039lb), 3-door estate 850kg (1874lb), 1.3 add 15kg (33.1lb).
ENGINE 4-cylinders, in-line; transverse; 73.96mm x 64.98mm; 1117cc; compr 9.5:1; 37kW (49.6bhp) @ 5000rpm; 33.1kW (44.4bhp)/l; 83Nm (61lbft) @ 2700rpm.
1.3: 73.96 x 75.48mm; 1297cc; 9.3:1; 44kW (59bhp) @ 5000rpm; 33kW (44.25bhp)/l; 100Nm (73lbft) @ 3000rpm.
ENGINE STRUCTURE pushrod ohv, chain-driven camshaft; 2-valves; iron cylinder head, block; Motorcraft VV carburettor; 3-bearing crankshaft. 1.3, 5-bearing.
TRANSMISSION front wheel drive; sdp diaphragm spring clutch; 4-speed synchromesh, 5-speed optional; final drive 3.84 or 4.06:1.
CHASSIS steel monocoque; ifs by MacPherson struts, lower track control arms, anti-roll bar; irs by transverse arms and longitudinal tie-bars, coil springs; telescopic dampers; hydraulic vacuum servo brakes, front 23.9cm (9.4in) discs, rear 18cm (7.1in) drums, dual circuit; rack and pinion steering; 48l (10.6 gal) tank; 145SR13 tyres, 4.5 rims.
DIMENSIONS wheelbase 240cm (94.5in); track front 140.5cm (55.31in), rear 142.5cm (56.1in); length 405cm (159.5in), estate 408cm (160.6in); width 164cm (64.6in); height 137cm (53.9in); ground clearance 14cm (5.5in); turning circle 10.6m (34.8ft).
EQUIPMENT Lucas Girling Stop Control System (SCS) £330.
PERFORMANCE maximum speed 145kph (90.3mph), 1.3 157kph (97.8mph); 28.4kph (17.7mph) @ 1000rpm; 0-100kph (62mph) 18.2sec, 1.3 15.4sec; 22.3kg/kW (16.6kg/bhp), 1.3 19.1kg/kW (14.2kg/bhp); fuel consumption 6.4l/100km (44.4mpg).
PRICE 1.1 Popular 3-door £4921; 1.3L 3-door £5930; 1.3L Estate 3-door £6382.
PRODUCTION 1,885,000 all models.

1986
Escort 1392cc, 1597cc

The Escort's surviving CVH engines, of which Bridgend had already made 2.5 million, had high compression ratios making the combustion chambers not so much hemispherical, like half an orange, as like the peel, squeezed between the humped pistons and valves in the aluminium heads. Only the fuel injection versions had combustion chambers conforming to the old description. Now they became more heart-shaped rather than half-round recesses in the cast aluminium cylinder head. To try and make it easier to burn weaker mixtures, the swirl effect was developed; increasing the turbulence of the incoming charge and making it burn faster. Lean mixtures ignited too slowly. Other improvements to the CVH included a revised water pump, with a cast rotor and a straight inlet pipe. Keen attention was paid to engine breathing in an effort to meet emission requirements, and the new pump met the demands of the RS Turbo, now in main line production. It was no longer a small-numbers specialist build job, each one of which could be modified in any number of ways. Standard on the RS also was SCS anti-lock brakes, available as an option (£330 against the Granada's £800 ABS) throughout the range. The Escort now had Granada-style instrumentation and switchgear, and there was the option of the Granada's electrically heated windscreen to ward off misting and icing.

SPECIFICATION FOR 1.4, 1.6, 1.6i, XR3i.

INTRODUCTION Jan 1986, production to 1990.
BODY saloon; 3-doors, 5-seats; weight 850kg (1874lb), 5-door 870kg (1918lb); cabriolet 950kg (2094.4lb); 5-door estate 895kg (1973lb); 1.6 add 10kg (22lb). XR3i 945kg (2083.4lb); cabriolet 995kg (2193.6lb)
ENGINE 4-cylinders, in-line; transverse; 77.24mm x 74.3mm, 1392cc; compr 9.5:1; 55kW (73.8bhp) @ 5600rpm; 39.5kW (53bhp)/l; 109Nm (80lbft) @ 4000rpm. With catalytic converter: compr 8.5:1; 54.5kW (73.1bhp) @ 5600rpm; 39.1kW (52.5bhp)/l; 103Nm (76lbft) @ 4000rpm. 1.6: 79.96 x 79.52mm; 1598cc; 9.5:1; 66kW (88.5bhp) @ 5800rpm; 41.3kW (55.4bhp)/l; 133Nm (98lbft) @ 4000rpm. 1.6i: 77kW (103.3bhp) @ 6000rpm; 48.3kW (64.5bhp)/l; 138Nm (102lbft) @ 4800rpm. 1.6i with catalytic converter: compr 8.5:1; 66kW (88.51bhp) @5800rpm, 41.3kW (55.4bhp)/l; 123Nm (91lbft) @ 4600rpm.
ENGINE STRUCTURE CVH belt-driven ohc; 2-valves; hydraulic tappets; aluminium cyl head, iron block; Weber 2V carburettor; electronic ignition; 5-bearing crankshaft. 1.6i mechanical Bosch KE-Jetronic fuel injection.
TRANSMISSION front wheel drive; sdp 19cm (7.5in) diaphragm spring clutch; 4-speed synchromesh, 5-speed optional; final drive 3.84 or 4.06:1. 1.6: 21.8cm (8.6in) clutch; opt ATX automatic, 3.58:1 final drive 3.31 automatic. 1.6i: 4.27:1.
CHASSIS steel monocoque; ifs by MacPherson struts, lower track control arms, anti-roll bar; irs by transverse arms and longitudinal tie-bars, coil springs; telescopic dampers; hydraulic vacuum servo brakes, front 23.9cm (9.4in) ventilated discs, rear 18cm (7.1in) drums, dual circuit; rack and pinion steering; 48l (10.6 gal) tank; 155SR13 or 175/70SR13 tyres, 4.5 rims.
DIMENSIONS wheelbase 240cm (94.5in); track front 140.5cm (55.3in), rear 142.5cm (56.1in); length 405cm (159.5in), estate 408cm (160.6in); width 164cm (64.6in); height 137cm (53.9in); ground clearance 14cm (5.5in); turning circle 10.6m (34.78ft).
EQUIPMENT Lucas Girling Stop Control System (SCS) £330, automatic £467.
PERFORMANCE maximum speed 167kph (104mph), 165kph (102.8mph) with cat. 1.6i 185kph (115.2mph); 178kph (110.9mph) with cat. 28.8kph (17.9mph) @ 1000rpm, 1.6i 32.6kph (20.3mph); 0-100kph (62mph) 12.7sec, 13.3sec with cat. 1.6i 10.5sec, 11.5 with cat. 15.5kg/kW (11.5kg/bhp), 1.6 13kg/kW (9.7kg/bhp); fuel consumption 6.8l/100km (41.5mpg), 1.6i with cat 7.9l/100km (35.9mpg).
PRICE 1.4GL 5-door £6919; 1.6L £6712; 1.6 Ghia 5-door £7746.
PRODUCTION 1,885,000 all models.

1986
Escort diesel 1608cc, 1753cc

From its launch in April 1984, the small Ford diesel faced an uphill task in competition with the 1.9-litre Peugeot 309 and Citroen BX, later 205 and Visa. The BX was Britain's best-selling diesel in 1987. One small diesel in three came from PSA against Ford's one in five. Fiat went for bigger capacity diesels to address the power deficit against petrol engines, encouraging Ford to follow suit with the first production engine to use a thermoset plastic manifold, the result of a £50million research programme at the Dunton R&D centre. Plastics under the bonnet faced a hostile environment, but they led to lighter engines and could be made with such accuracy that machining was eliminated, so they were cheap. The new-found power improved the 0-62mph time by 2sec and the engine was also quieter than its predecessor. At the same time as the new diesel, the 1.3-litre petrol was provided with electronic ignition giving an extra 2.2kW (3bhp); road speeds were not much altered but there was a claimed 18 per cent improvement in economy. Escort and Orion also gained variable ratio steering, lighter at slow speeds. Introduced as a 1608cc, the Escort and Orion diesels were enlarged in 1988 to 1753cc, raising power to 44.7kW (60bhp) and torque from 95Nm (70lbft) to 110Nm (81lbft).

INTRODUCTION January 1986, modified MY 1989, production to 1990.

BODY saloon; 3-doors, 5-seats; weight 910kg (2006lb), 5-door 930kg (2050.3lb), 3-door estate 935kg (2061.3lb).

ENGINE 4-cylinders, in-line; transverse; 80mm x 80mm, 1608cc; compr 21.5:1; 39.5kW (52.97bhp) @ 4800rpm; 24.6kW (32.9bhp)/l; 95Nm (70lbft) @ 3000rpm.

ENGINE STRUCTURE Ford KHD, belt-driven overhead camshaft; 2-valves; iron cylinder head, block; mechanical fuel injection; 5-bearing crankshaft.

TRANSMISSION front wheel drive; sdp diaphragm spring 19.1cm (7.5in) clutch; 5-speed synchromesh; final drive 3.84.

CHASSIS steel monocoque; independent front suspension by MacPherson struts, lower track control arms, anti-roll bar; independent rear suspension by transverse arms and longitudinal tie-bars, coil springs; telescopic dampers; hydraulic vacuum servo brakes, front 23.9cm (9.4in) discs, rear 18cm (7.1in) drums, dual circuit; rack and pinion steering; 48l (10.6gal) tank; 155SR13 tyres, 5in rims.

DIMENSIONS wheelbase 240cm (94.5in); track front 140.5cm (55.3in), rear 142.5cm (56.1in); length 405cm (159.5in), estate 408cm (160.6in); width 164cm (64.6in); height 137cm (53.9in); ground clearance 14cm (5.5in); turning circle 10.6m (34.78ft).

EQUIPMENT Lucas Girling Stop Control System (SCS) £330.

PERFORMANCE maximum speed 146kph (90.9mph); 36.2kph (22.65mph) @ 1000rpm; 0-100kph (62mph) 18.9sec; 23kg/kW (17.2kg/bhp); fuel consumption 5.2l/100km (54.3mpg).

PRICE 3-door £6079; L 5-door £7091; GL estate 5-door £7943.

PRODUCTION 1,885,000 all models.

1986
Orion

The 3-box design of the Orion appealed to a clientele that would never buy a hatchback Escort, preferring perhaps to distance itself from the hurly-burly high-speed world of rallying where the Escort had been a consistent and well publicised front-runner. Orion customers were more interested in safety features such as anti-lock brakes; skidding for them remained a worry and if safer brakes could be managed within a smaller budget than the £800 or so asked for them in a Granada, so much the better. The German Anti Block Systeme (ABS), at its sophisticated electronic best, was still a premium-priced option when Lucas-Girling came along with its Stop Control System (SCS). Offered as standard on 1.6 Turbo and XR3i Escorts, or for £330 on 1.4 and 1.6CVH Orions and Escorts, SCS worked well with one wheel on the snowy verge and the other on (relatively) grippy wet tarmac. Its hydro-mechanical system provided commendable security against wheel-locking in emergencies. It was a modest success but never quite as effective as an electronic one, and once real ABS became cheaper SCS was discarded. In 1989 there was an attempt to revive the E for Executive suffix that had been applied so successfully to Escorts, Cortinas, and Corsairs, but the 1600E Orion was little more than a reissue of the 1.6 Ghia and was short-lived.

SPECIFICATION 1.4, 1.6, 1.6i
INTRODUCTION January 1986, produced until 1990.
BODY saloon; 4-doors, 5-seats; weight 875kg (1929lb).
ENGINE 4-cylinders, in-line; transverse; 77.24mm x 74.3mm, 1392cc; compr 9.5:1; 55kW (73.8bhp) @ 5600rpm; 39.5kW (53bhp)/l; 109Nm (80lbft) @ 4000rpm. With catalytic converter compr 8.5:1; 54.5kW (73bhp) @ 5600rpm; 39.1kW (52.5bhp)/l; 103Nm (76lbft) @ 4000rpm. 1.6, 79.96 x 79.52mm; 1598cc; 9.5:1; 66kW (88.5bhp) @ 5800rpm; 41.3kW (55.4bhp)/l; 133Nm (98lbft) @ 4000rpm. 1.6i 77kW (103.3bhp) @ 6000rpm; 48.3kW (64.6bhp)/l; 138Nm (102lbft) @ 4800rpm. 1.6i with catalytic converter compr 8.5:1; 66kW (88.5bhp) @ 5800rpm; 41.3kW (55.4bhp)/l; 123Nm (91lb ft) @ 4600rpm.

ENGINE STRUCTURE CVH belt-driven overhead camshaft; 2-valves; hydraulic tappets; aluminium cylinder head, iron block; Weber DFM carburettor; electronic ignition; 5-bearing crankshaft. 1.6i mechanical Bosch KE-Jetronic fuel injection.
TRANSMISSION front wheel drive; sdp 19cm (7.5in) diaphragm spring clutch; 4-speed synchromesh, 5-speed optional; final drive 3.84 or 4.06:1. 1.6, 21.84cm (8.6in) clutch; optional ATX automatic, 3.58:1 final drive 3.31 automatic. 1.6i 4.27:1.
CHASSIS steel monocoque; ifs by MacPherson struts, lower track control arms, anti-roll bar; irs by transverse arms and longitudinal tie-bars, coil springs; telescopic dampers; hydraulic vacuum servo brakes, front 23.9cm (9.4in) ventilated discs, rear 18cm (7.1in) drums, dual circuit; rack and pinion; 48l (10.6gal) tank; 155SR13 or 175/70SR13 tyres, 4.5 rims. 1.6i 185/60HR14, 5.5 or 6J rims.

DIMENSIONS wheelbase 240cm (94.5in); track front 140.5cm (55.3in), rear 142.5cm (56.1in); length 421.5cm (165.9in); width 164cm (64.6in); height 139.5cm (54.9in); ground clearance 14cm (5.5in); turning circle 10.6m (34.78ft).
EQUIPMENT Lucas Girling Stop Control System (SCS) £330, automatic £467.
PERFORMANCE maximum speed 167kph (104mph), 165kph (102.8mph) with cat, 1.6i 185kph (115.2mph), 178kph (110.9mph) with cat: 32.6kph (20.3mph) @ 1000rpm; 0-100kph (62mph) 12.9sec, 13.35sec with cat, 1.6i 10.5sec, 11.5 with cat; 15.9kg/kW (11.9kg/bhp); fuel consumption 6.8l/100km (41.5mpg), 1.6i with cat 7.9l/100km (35.9mpg).
PRICE 1.4L £6455; 1.6 Ghia £8159; 1.6i Ghia £7586.
PRODUCTION 1,885,000 all models.

1987
Sierra

Constant alterations were necessary to ensure the Sierra's survival. Although it never found a place in the nation's heart like the Cortina did, it sold steadily to the end. By the spring of 1987 there were 18 Sierras and Sapphires with petrol engines from 1.6 to 2.0-litre, and a 2.3-litre diesel. Trim options ranged from basic to Ghia, which had more to do with marketing demarcations than the value of extras. A curiosity of the UK fleet market was that cars, like office carpets or the key to the executive toilet, carried distinctions of status as low-cost as pips and crowns on officers' uniforms. Two-tone paint, plush upholstery, central locking, a box to store cassettes in, tinted windows, a sunroof, and a rev counter hardly amounted to an extra £1000, yet they were crucial in the commercial pecking order. The biggest change to its appearance was more glass area. Among revisions in May 1988 was replacement of the British-built 1.8-litre Pinto engine with one built in America, with different cylinder dimensions but the same power output. Also in 1988, the MT75 5-speed gearbox, bigger and with a synchromesh reverse, was introduced for the more powerful ends of Sierra and Scorpio ranges. In 1989 a new 8-valve 2.0-litre twin cam engine replaced older 2.0-litre Pintos, giving 81.3kW (109bhp) on a carburettor or 93.2kW (125bhp) with fuel injection.

INTRODUCTION February 1987, production to 1992. Specification 2.0EFI and 2.3diesel.
BODY saloon; 5-doors, 5-seats; weight 1060kg (2337lb), estate 1090kg (2403lb), 2.3D 1165kg (2568.4lb).
ENGINE 4-cylinders, in-line; 90.82mm x 76.95mm, 1993cc; compr 9.2:1; 85kW (114bhp) @ 5500rpm; 42.6kW (57.2bhp)/l; 160Nm (118lbft) @ 4000rpm. With catalyser compr 8.5:1; 74kW (99.2bhp) @ 5100rpm; 37.2kW (49.8bhp)/l; 148Nm (109lbft) @ 4000rpm; (lead-free fuel specific). 2.3 94 x 83mm; 2304cc; cr 22.2:1; 49kW (65.7bhp) @ 4200rpm; 21.3kW (28.5bhp)/l; 139Nm (103lbft) @ 2000rpm.
ENGINE STRUCTURE 1 belt-driven overhead camshaft; 2-valves; iron cylinder head, block; Bosch L-Jetronic electronic fuel injection, electronic ignition; 5-bearing crankshaft. 2.3 LXD2 block inclined 20deg to right; chain-driven lateral camshaft;

aluminium cylinder head; Bosch EP/VAC injection.
TRANSMISSION rear wheel drive; sdp diaphragm spring clutch; 5-speed synchromesh; A4LD (automatic 4-speed Lock-up Overdrive) optional; final drive 3.92 or 3.62:1 with catalyser-equipped cars. 2.3, 3.14 or 3.38:1.
CHASSIS steel monocoque structure; MacPherson strut ifs; anti roll bar; independent rear suspension by semi-trailing arms, coil springs; telescopic dampers (GLS and Ghia gas-filled); estate self-levelling; hydraulic servo brakes, front 23.9cm (9.4in) ventilated discs, rear 20.3cm (8in) drums, 24.2cm (9.5in) discs with optional ABS, dual circuit, rack and pinion PAS; 60l (13.2 gal) tank; 195/60HR14 tyres, 5.5in rims, Ghia alloy wheels. 2.3 tyres 165SR/TR 13/14. Estate 175SR/TR 13/14.
DIMENSIONS wheelbase 261cm (102.8in); track front 145cm (57.1in), rear 147cm (57.9in); length 442.5cm

(174.2in); width 169.5cm (66.7in); height 136cm (53.5in); ground clearance 12cm (4.7in); turning circle 10.6m (34.78ft).
EQUIPMENT electrically heated windscreen, 60/40 split rear seat back, high-security locking system, integral radio aerials. Automatic £554.
PERFORMANCE maximum speed 190kph (118.4mph), automatic 184kph (114.6mph), with catalyser 181kph (112.7mph) or 178kph (110.9mph) auto, 2.3 154kph (95.93mph); 33.7kph (21mph) @ 1000rpm, 2.3 42.2kph (26.3mph); 0-100kph (62mph) 11.2sec, 2.3 19.15sec; 12.5kg/kW (9.3kg/bhp), 2.3 23.8kg/kW (17.7kg/bhp); fuel consumption 8.5l/100km (33.2mpg), 2.3 6.6l/100km (42.8mpg).
PRICE 1.6 £7347, 2.0LX £8569, 2.0i Ghia £10,995, 2.3GLD Estate £9889.
PRODUCTION 974,000 all Sierras.

1987
Sierra Sapphire

It took four years to get round to making a Sierra with a boot instead of a hatchback. When the Sierra was facelifted, the Sapphire was enlisted in the battle with the Vauxhall Cavalier, and in defence of Ford's 27 per cent share of the UK market. In one typical January to May the Cavalier was ahead of Sierra with 54,087 sales against 48,290, but in May the Ford edged ahead with 10,028 against 8,984. The traditional fleet market was still strong; company representatives and their contents' insurers often preferring the security of a lockable boot rather than a hatchback with breakable windows, despite its large capacity. One survey showed four buyers out of five demanding more security, so Ford spent £228million adding a boot, among other minor changes. The resulting stiffer shell with its big bonded-in back window was quieter, and although quite shallow with the spare wheel underneath, had useful carrying capacity. Volkswagen had its Jetta, Austin Rover its Montego, Vauxhall had had a 4-door Cavalier from the beginning, and Ford itself had the Orion, all essentially notchback versions of an existing model. There were some engineering changes, including stiffer suspension, but little to the bodywork beyond detail revisions to the front. These were extended throughout the Sierra/Sapphire range, making it a touch less radical but more generally popular.

INTRODUCTION February 1987, production to 1992. Specification 2.0EFI and 1.6 carburettor.

BODY saloon; 4-doors, 5-seats; weight 1095kg (2414lb), 1.6 1025kg (2259.7lb).

ENGINE 4-cylinders, in-line; 90.82mm x 76.95mm, 1993cc; cr 9.2:1; 85kW (114bhp) @ 5500rpm; 42.6kW (57.2bhp)/l; 160Nm (118lbft) @ 4000rpm. With catalyser cr 8.5:1; 74kW (99.2bhp) @ 5100rpm; 37.2kW (49.8bhp)/l; 148Nm (109lbft) @ 4000rpm; (lead-free fuel specific). 1.6 81.3 x 76.95mm; 1598cc; compr 9.5:1; 55kW (73.8bhp) @ 4900rpm; 34.5kW (46.2bhp)/l; 123Nm (91lbft) @ 2900rpm.

ENGINE STRUCTURE 1 belt-driven overhead camshaft; 2-valves; iron cylinder head, block; Bosch L-Jetronic electronic fuel injection, electronic ignition; 5-bearing crankshaft. 1.6 Weber 2V carburettor.

TRANSMISSION rear wheel drive; sdp diaphragm spring clutch; 5-speed synchromesh; A4LD (automatic 4-speed Lock-up Overdrive) optional; final drive 3.92 or 3.62:1 with catalyser cars. 1.6 4-speed, final drive 3.62:1; 5-speed optional.

CHASSIS steel monocoque structure; MacPherson strut ifs; anti roll bar; irs by semi-trailing arms, coil springs; telescopic dampers (GLS and Ghia gas-filled); hydraulic servo brakes, front 23.9cm (9.4in) ventilated disc, rear 20.3cm (8in) drums, 24.2cm (9.5in) discs with optional ABS, dual circuit, rack and pinion PAS optional; 60l (13.2 gal) tank; 195/60HR14 tyres, 5.5in rims, Ghia alloy wheels.

DIMENSIONS wheelbase 261cm (102.8in); track front 145cm (57.1in) rear 147cm (57.9in); length 446.5cm (175.8in); width 170cm (66.9in); height 136cm (53.5in); ground clearance 12cm (4.7in); turning circle 10.6m (34.8ft).

EQUIPMENT electrically heated windscreen £104, trip computer £121, automatic £554, PAS £505, air conditioning £718, Teves ABS £934, headlamp washers £145, trailer coupling £295, high-security locking system, integral radio aerials, electric fan.

PERFORMANCE maximum speed 190kph (118.4mph), automatic 184kph (114.6mph), with catalyser 181kph (112.7mph) or 178kph (110.9mph) auto, 1.6 165kph (102.8mph); 33.7kph (21mph) @ 1000rpm, 1.6 29.9kph (18.6mph); 0-100kph (62mph) 11.2sec, 1.6 14.2sec; 12.9kg/kW (9.6kg/bhp), 1.6 18.6kg/kW (13.9kg/bhp); fuel consumption 8.5l/100km (33.2mpg), 1.6 7.56l/100km (37.4mpg).

PRICE 1.6 £7272, 2.3D £7741, 2.0iGLS £9680, 2.0i Ghia £10,845.

PRODUCTION 974,000 all Sierras.

1987
Sierra Cosworth RS500

Following the success of the 1985–1986 Sierra RS Cosworth, the RS500 evolved as an even more potent Group A racer. Only 500 (thus RS for RennSport 500) had to be manufactured to qualify as "production" according to Touring Car regulations. Although it was nominally no more powerful and not much faster than the road-going car, the RS500's engine could be prepared to produce more than 373kW (500bhp) reliably and consistently. It became almost unbeatable in Group A until the rules were changed to its disadvantage. Sold through specially designated Ford RS dealers this "Evolution" (in touring car race jargon) had a 167kW (224bhp) version of the Cosworth engine, the additional 14.9kW (20bhp)

gained by a Garrett T31/T04 turbocharger and enlarged air-to-air intercooler and induction system. It had twin fuel injectors to each cylinder, pressurised oil cooling to each piston, and larger capacity oil and water pumps. Cooling ducts behind apertures in the front bumper directed air to the intercooler and brakes. Aerodynamic devices included a splitter to enhance downforce, a small lip on the trailing edge of the rear wing and an extra spoiler on the tailgate. Aston Martin Tickford gained the half million pound contract to build 15 cars a day; most of them were painted black with white or blue metallic available to special order only.

INTRODUCTION 1987 production.
BODY saloon; 3-doors, 5-seats; weight 1240kg (2733.7lb).
ENGINE 4-cylinders, in-line; 90.8mm x 77.0mm, 1994cc; compr 8.0:1; 167kW (224bhp) @ 6000rpm; 83.8kW (112.4bhp)/l; 280Nm (207lbft) @ 4500rpm.
ENGINE STRUCTURE two belt-driven ohcs; 4-valves inclined at 45deg; hydraulic tappets; aluminium cyl head, iron block; Weber-Marelli electronic twin-nozzle fuel injection and engine management; 5-bearing crankshaft; Garrett T31/T04 .55bar (7.98psi) turbocharger with air to air intercooler.
TRANSMISSION rwd; sdp diaphragm spring clutch; 5-speed synchromesh; final drive 3.64:1 with viscous-coupling limited slip differential.
CHASSIS steel monocoque; MacPherson strut ifs; irs by semi-trailing arms, coil springs; telescopic dampers anti roll bars front and rear; hydraulic servo brakes, front 28.3cm (11.1in) ventilated discs, rear 27.2cm (10.7in) discs with Teves ABS, dual circuit, rack and pinion PAS; 65l (14.3 gal) tank; 205/50VR15 tyres, 7J rims, alloy wheels.
DIMENSIONS wheelbase 261cm (102.8in); track front 144cm (56.7in), rear 144.5cm (56.9in); length 446cm (175.6in); width 173cm (68.1in); height 137.5cm (54.1in); ground clearance 12cm (4.7in); turning circle 10.3m (33.79ft).
EQUIPMENT front aerodynamic splitter, rear wing.
PERFORMANCE maximum speed 246kph (153.2mph); 36.7kph (22.9mph) @ 1000rpm; 0-100kph (62mph) 6.2sec; 7.4kg/kW (5.5kg/bhp); fuel consumption 11.2l/100km (25.2mpg).
PRICE £19,950.
PRODUCTION 500.

LEFT **Dr Jonathan Palmer flew his Bell 206 JetRanger to Boreham to put his new turbocharged Sierra RS Cosworth through its paces. It was his first season driving with the Formula 1 Tyrrell team when, ironically, he was a consistent winner in the non-turbo field.**

1987
Fiesta II CVT

Continuously Variable Transmission or Constant Velocity Transmission (CVT), or CTX as Ford preferred to call it, was introduced on the engaging but ultimately unsuccessful Daf air-cooled flat-twin of 1959. It was fully automatic, with a centrifugal clutch, limited-slip differential and V-belts running in moveable pulleys. It was simple and efficient, the only point of debate was whether it was worthy because it was cheap, or because it banished gearchanging from small cars. It was only practical because its power losses were negligible, unlike those of conventional automatics with oil-churning torque converters. The solitary control for the driver was a forward and reverse lever, although it took 20 years'

development with V-belts manufactured in steel segments instead of rubber and textiles, redesigned to push and not pull, before CVT was fit for anything as powerful as a Fiesta. The engine still whirred a great deal as it got up to speed ahead, it seemed, of the gearbox. But it was economical, and with electronic controls the constant buzziness of the engine was curbed a little. CVT was optional on the Fiesta and, since it was a joint development between Ford and Fiat, also on the Fiat Uno. In the event, customers did not seem ready for CVT and continued to elect for the clutch and manual gearbox to which they were long accustomed.

INTRODUCTION 1987, produced until 1989.
BODY saloon; 3-doors, 5-seats; weight 785kg (1730.6lb).
ENGINE 4-cylinders, in-line; transverse; 73.96 x 64.98mm; 1117cc; 9.5:1; 37kW (49.6bhp) @ 5000rpm; 33.1kW (44.4bhp)/l; 83Nm (61lbft) @ 2700rpm.
ENGINE STRUCTURE pushrod ohv; chain-driven camshaft; 2-valves; iron cylinder head, block; inverse Ford-Motorcraft VV carburettor; contact-breaker ignition; 3-bearing crankshaft.
TRANSMISSION front wheel drive; automatic continuously variable from 3.67 and 0.63, final drive 3.84:1; single epicyclic gearset for forward and reverse; hydro-mechanical valve block controlled ratio selection and wet multi-plate startup clutches.
CHASSIS steel monocoque; ifs by MacPherson struts, coil springs; rear suspension dead axle, trailing links, Panhard rod; telescopic dampers; hydraulic, vacuum servo 22.1cm (8.7in) front disc brakes; rear drums 17.8cm (7in); rack and pinion steering; 34l (7.5 gal) tank; radial-ply 135SR-13 tyres or 155/70SR13, 4.5 or 5J rims.
DIMENSIONS wheelbase 228.6cm (90in); track front 136.5cm (53.7in), rear 132cm (52in); length 365cm (143.7in); width 158.5cm (62.4in); height 136cm (53.5in); ground clearance 14cm (5.5in); turning circle 10.3m (33.79ft).
EQUIPMENT Ghia trim options.
PERFORMANCE maximum speed 140kph (87.2mph); high ratio 41.3kph (25.7mph) @ 1000rpm; 0-100kph (62mph) 18sec; 21.2kg/kW (15.8kg/bhp); fuel consumption 6.3l/100km (44.8mpg).
PRICE L £4320, 1.1 Ghia £5100.
PRODUCTION 1,980,100 all Fiesta II.

1988
Sierra Cosworth and Sierra Sapphire RS Cosworth

Production of the 3-door Sierra, launched at Frankfurt in 1985, stopped as planned after 5000 had been made for homologation in Group A. Five hundred of the powerful RS500 version were made in 1987, then in 1988 came the less assertive road-going 4-door Sapphire edition. It had a similar engine and transmission and was still often called RS, but it was more of a road car than a detuned racer. With its stiffer bodyshell it reached out to the autobahn-cruising high-speed business market dominated by the classic German makes. Ford's aspirations towards BMW and Mercedes-Benz had been confined to reproducing features, tail-lights, or trim, but now it had a refined road car that reached 60mph

almost as quickly as a Porsche 944 Turbo, and faster than a 928. It outran an Aston Martin V8, a Ferrari Testarossa would be hard-pressed to keep up until 160kph (about 100mph), and it soaked up bumps serenely. Earlier versions had the stiff twitchy feel of a car designed for grip at the expense of comfort. The Design Council praised its value for money. Against a BMW 535iSE at £23,575, an M5 at £34,850, or a Mercedes-Benz 300SE at £27,250 it looked a bargain, even if the pile of the carpets was not so deep, nor the castings finished quite as smoothly as cars from the very top drawer. Genk production began in November 1987.

INTRODUCTION Nov 1987, production to 1990.
BODY saloon; 3-doors, 5-seats; weight 1250kg (2755.8lb).
ENGINE 4-cylinders, in-line; 90.82mm x 76.95mm, 1994cc; compr 8.0:1; 150kW (201.2bhp) @ 6000rpm; 75.2kW (100.9bhp)/l; 276Nm (204lbft) @ 4500rpm.
ENGINE STRUCTURE 2 belt driven overhead camshafts; 4-valves; aluminium cylinder head, iron block; Weber electronic fuel injection, Marelli electronic breakerless ignition; 5-bearing crankshaft; Garrett T03 B turbocharger, boost 0.65bar (9psi); intercooler; two electric cooling fans.
TRANSMISSION rear wheel drive; sdp diaphragm spring self-adjusting clutch; Borg Warner manual gearbox 5-speed synchromesh; final drive 3.64:1; limited slip differential.
CHASSIS steel monocoque; ifs by MacPherson struts; anti-roll bars front and back; irs semi-trailing arms, coil springs, telescopic dampers; hydraulic servo brakes, front 28.3cm (11.1in) ventilated disc, rear 273m (10.8in) disc, dual circuit, Teves ABS; variable ratio rack and pinion PAS; 65l (14.3 gal) tank; 205/50VR15 tyres, 7J rims.
DIMENSIONS wheelbase 261cm (102.8in); track 145cm (57.1in) front, 146cm (57.5in) rear; length 449.5cm (177in); width 170cm (66.9in); height 137cm (53.9in); ground clearance 12cm (4.7in); turning circle 10.6m (34.8ft).
EQUIPMENT electric windows, Recaro seats with height and rake adjustment in Roma cashmere fabric, leather-bound steering wheel all standard.
PERFORMANCE maximum speed 242kph (150.7mph); 36.7kph (22.9mph) @ 1000rpm; 0-100kph (62mph) 6.5sec; 8.3kg/kW (62.kg/bhp); fuel consumption 10.3l/100km (27.4mpg).
PRICE £19,500.
PRODUCTION 11,000.

1989
Fiesta III 1001cc, 1119cc Popular and Popular Plus

The general arrangement of the third generation Fiesta was much as before, albeit on a new platform. The suspension was the same, but the bodyshell was 10.2cm (4in) longer and 5.1cm (2in) wider. Wheelbase was increased by 15.2cm (6in) and, for the first time, it had the option of three or five doors. Torsion beam rear suspension replaced the old dead rear axle and the MacPherson struts at the front were modified, with the lower arms relocated on double bonded vertical bushes. Engine changes were introduced to meet European emission control regulations that would eventually demand catalytic converters. High Compression Swirl (HCS) combustion chambers with new combustion chamber shapes, port profiles and manifolds, contributed to the debate on the merits of lean-burn against exhaust scrubbing as the better means of reducing noxious fumes. The increase in space inside was welcome, as was the 45 per cent bigger boot and the 10 per cent more glass, but the low-geared steering and unresponsive handling made the Fiesta rather a dull car. Still a best seller for 10 of the previous 12 years, production had reached 5million, 1.2million of which were sold in Britain, and it was soon to edge Sierra off the production line at Dagenham. Overall cost of ownership was taken seriously by Ford, with claims that average service costs were 27 per cent lower than before.

INTRODUCTION January 1989. **BODY** saloon; 3/5-doors, 5-seats; 779kg (1717.4lb), 1.1 785kg (1730.6lb). **ENGINE** 4-cylinders, in-line; transverse; 68.7mm x 67.5mm, 1001cc; compr 9.5:1; 33kW (44.3bhp) @ 5000rpm; 33kW (44.2bhp)/l; 74Nm (55lbft) @ 3000rpm. 1.1: 68.7 x 75.5mm; 1119cc; 40kW (53.6bhp) @ 5200rpm; 35.7kW (47.9bhp)/l; 86Nm (63lbft) @ 2700rpm. 1.1 with catalytic converter: compr 8.8:1; 37kW (49.6bhp) @ 5200rpm; 33.2kW (44.3bhp)/l; 83Nm (61lbft) @ 3000rpm. **ENGINE STRUCTURE** HCS pushrod ohv, chain-drive camshaft; 2-valves; iron cylinder head, block; twin choke downdraught Weber carburettor, breakerless electronic ignition; 3-bearing crankshaft.

TRANSMISSION front wheel drive; sdp diaphragm spring clutch; 4-speed synchromesh; final drive 4.06:1. 1.1 5-speed optional; CTX automatic optional with 3.84:1 final drive. **CHASSIS** steel monocoque; ifs by MacPherson struts; irs by trailing arms, torsion beams, coil springs; telescopic dampers; hydraulic brakes, front 24cm (9.5in) discs, rear 180mm (7.5in) drums, dual circuit, SCS optional; rack and pinion steering; 42l (9.2gal) tank; 135SR13 tyres 4.5 or 5J rims. 1.1 145SR13, 155/70SR13, 165/65SR13. **DIMENSIONS** wheelbase 244.5cm (96.3in); track 139cm (54.7in) front, 138.5cm (54.5in) rear; length 374cm (147.2in); width 161cm (63.4in); height 132.5cm (52.2in); ground clearance

14cm (5.5in); turning circle 9.8m (32.2ft). **EQUIPMENT** radio/cassette, four speakers, tinted glass, sunroof, metallic paint all standard. **PERFORMANCE** maximum 139kph (86.6mph), 1.1 145kph (90.3mph), Autocar, 24.7kph (15.4mph) @ 1000rpm, 1.1 33.5kph (20.9mph) 5-speed; 0-100kph (62mph) 20.2sec, 1.1 15.35sec Autocar; 23.6kg/kW (17.6kg/bhp), 19.6kg/kW (14.6kg/bhp) 1.1; 8.5l/100km (33.2mpg) 1.1. **PRICE** Popular 1.0 3-door £5199, 5-door £5476; Popular Plus 3-door £5877; Pop Plus 1.1 3-door £6183, 5-door £6460; 1.1L 3-door £6645, 5-door £6922, LX £7570.

1989
Fiesta III 1392cc, 1596cc

All the engines were modified for Fiesta III. Iron "Valencia" pushrod engines had new cranks and pistons, producing different bore/stroke ratios. The former 957cc engine was over-square at 74x55.7mm, and became 68.7x67.5mm, giving a capacity of 1001cc. Power was unchanged but it was produced at 700rpm less. The High Compression Swirl (HCS) pushrod engines were equipped with fully transistorised ignition using a single flywheel sensor and a pair of dual output coils instead of the old coil and distributor. The 1.1-litre was given a longer-stroke crank to increase the swept volume; it now had a 75.5mm throw, making it 1119cc, improving economy, raising a few bhp extra and giving more torque.

Of the Compound Valve Hemispherical (CVH) overhead cam engines the 1.4-litre gained in power and was the first Ford engine to meet impending European Emission Standards for 1996. The 1.6-litre was a detuned version of the former carburettor XR2 with 67.1kW (90bhp) instead of 70.8kW (95bhp). An additional 1.6-litre was a 16-valve Zetec twin cam as used in the Escort and Mondeo giving 0-60mph acceleration in a fraction over 10sec. Fiestas' variable ratio rack and pinion steering was not unduly heavy, but the optional power assistance reduced the turns lock to lock from the manual's 4.6 to 2.8, enhancing feel and control.

INTRODUCTION January 1989.
BODY saloon; 3/5-doors, 5-seats; weight 815kg (1796.8lb); 1.6 835kg (1840.8lb).
ENGINE 4-cylinders, in-line; transverse; 77.2mm x 74.3mm, 1391cc; compr 9.5:1; 55kW (73.8bhp) @ 5600rpm; 39.5kW (53bhp)/l; 109Nm (80lbft) @ 4000rpm. 1.6, 80 x 79.5mm; 1598cc; 66kW (88.5bhp) @ 5800rpm; 41.3kW (55.4bhp)/l; 133Nm (98lbft) @ 4000rpm.
ENGINE STRUCTURE CVH belt-driven overhead camshaft; 2-valves; hydraulic tappets; aluminium cylinder head, iron block; twin choke downdraught Weber DFM carburettor, breakerless electronic ignition; 5-bearing crankshaft. 1.6 Weber 2V.
TRANSMISSION front wheel drive; sdp diaphragm spring clutch; 5-speed synchromesh; final drive 4.06:1, cat 3.84:1; CTX automatic optional with 3.84:1 final drive 1.6.
CHASSIS steel monocoque; ifs by MacPherson struts; irs by trailing arms, torsion beams, coil springs; telescopic dampers; 1.6 front anti-roll bar; hydraulic vacuum servo brakes, front 24cm (9.5in) discs, ventilated on 1.6; rear 18cm (7.5in) drums, dual circuit, SCS optional; rack and pinion steering; 42l (9.2 gal) tank; 145SR13, 155/70SR13, 165/65SR13 tyres, 5J rims.
DIMENSIONS wheelbase 244.5cm (96.3in); track 139cm (54.7in) front, 138.5cm (54.5in) rear; length 374cm (147.2in); width 161cm (63.4in); height 132.5cm (52.2in); ground clearance 14cm (5.5in); turning circle 9.8m (32.2ft).
EQUIPMENT radio/cassette, four speakers, tinted glass, sunroof, metallic paint all standard.
PERFORMANCE maximum speed 165kph (102.8mph), 1.6 174kph (108.4mph); 33.5kph (20.9mph) @ 1000rpm; 0-100kph (62mph) 12sec, 1.6 10.3sec; 14.8kg/kW (11kg/bhp), 12.7kg/kW (9.4kg/bhp) 1.6; fuel consumption 7.2l/100km (39.2mpg).
PRICE 1.4LX 3-door £7992, 1.6S £7865.

1989
Fiesta III Diesel. Experimental 2-stroke

Even with a larger, more powerful version of Ford's diesel the Fiesta was not lively. Its official fuel consumption figures were not as good as before, either on the urban cycle or at a constant 90kph (56mph), but at 120kph (75mph) it still managed 5.6l/100km (50.4mpg) and its acceleration with the optional 5-speed gearbox was slightly faster than a 1.1-litre petrol car. In 1992 Ford revealed an experiment to equip the Fiesta with an engine that looked as though it had been consigned, through its inability to meet increasingly demanding emission regulations, to the dustbin of technology in the 1960s. The 2-stroke was equipped with a compressed air fuel metering system so precise that its emissions were relatively clean. Unburnt hydrocarbons no longer escaped in such profusion. With the virtues of fewer moving parts the engine was 100mm

(3.9in) lower and 70mm (2.8in) narrower than a 4-cylinder. It had no valves, springs, camshaft or pushrods, weighed 30 per cent less, had 12 per cent better economy and 10 per cent more power, persuading Ford to set up a programme running 50 Fiesta 3-cylinder 1200cc 2-strokes in field trials. They were astonishingly smooth-running with none of the popping and banging associated with old-style 2-strokes. A tank under the bonnet supplied oil to the engine for 12,500 miles without refilling, but it turned out to be problematical in service and the experiment was concluded.

BELOW **Police surveillance. Experiments with orbital engines in patrol cars were carried out over big mileages.**

INTRODUCTION January 1989.
BODY saloon; 3/5-doors, 5-seats; weight 870kg (1918lb).
ENGINE 4-cylinders, in-line; transverse; 82.5mm x 82mm, 1753cc; compr 21.5:1; 44kW (59bhp) @ 4800rpm; 25.1kW (33.7bhp)/l; 110Nm (81lbft) @ 2500rpm. 2-stroke, 1.2-litre; 3-cylinders; 59.7kW (80bhp) @ 5500rpm; 49.75kW (66.7bhp)/l; 122Nm (90lbft) @ 4000rpm.
ENGINE STRUCTURE Ford/KHD belt-driven ohc; 2-valves; iron cylinder head, block; mechanical fuel injection; 5-bearing crankshaft. 2-stroke, reed valve intakes; Sarich forced-air 6bar (87.02psi) fuel injection system by reciprocating pump driven off crankshaft; sealed crankcase; roller-bearing forged one-piece crankshaft; catalytic converter.
TRANSMISSION front wheel drive; sdp diaphragm spring 19.1cm (7.5in) clutch; 5-speed synchromesh; final drive 3.59:1.
CHASSIS steel monocoque; ifs by MacPherson struts; irs by trailing arms, torsion beams, coil springs; telescopic dampers; hydraulic brakes, front 24cm (9.5in) discs, rear 180mm (7.5in) drums, dual circuit, SCS optional; rack and pinion steering; 42l (9.2 gal) tank; 145SR13 tyres.
DIMENSIONS wheelbase 244.5cm (96.3in); track 139cm (54.7in) front, 138.5cm (54.5in) rear; length 374cm (147.2in); width 161cm (63.4in); height 132.5cm (52.2in); ground clearance 14cm (5.5in); turning circle 9.8m (32.2ft).
EQUIPMENT radio/cassette, four speakers, tinted glass, sunroof, metallic paint all standard.
PERFORMANCE maximum 152kph (94.7mph), 2-stroke 168kph (104.7mph); 29.7kph (18.5mph) @ 1000rpm; 0-100kph (62mph) 16sec, 2-stroke 10.7sec; 19.8kg/kW (14.7kg/bhp); fuel consumption 5.1l/100km (55.4mpg), 2-stroke 5.7l/100km (49.6mpg).
PRICE L 1.8D 3-door £7467, LX 1.8D 5-door £8392.
PRODUCTION 50 and some prototypes

1989
Fiesta XR2i

INTRODUCTION January 1989.
BODY saloon; 3/5-doors, 5-seats;
weight 890kg (19623lb).
ENGINE 4-cylinders, in-line;
transverse; 80mm x 79.5mm, 1598cc;
compr 9.75:1; 81kW (108.6bhp) @
6000rpm; 50.7kW (68bhp)/l; 138Nm
(102lbft) @ 2800rpm. With catalytic
converter 76kW (101.9bhp) @
6000rpm; 47.6kW (63.8bhp)/l;
135Nm (100lbft) @ 2800rpm.
ENGINE STRUCTURE CVH belt-
driven ohc; hydraulic tappets;
2-valves; aluminium cylinder head,
iron block; mechanical fuel injection,
breakerless electronic ignition;
5-bearing crankshaft.
TRANSMISSION front wheel drive;
sdp diaphragm spring clutch; 5-
speed synchromesh; final drive
4.06:1.
CHASSIS steel monocoque; ifs by
MacPherson struts; irs by trailing
arms, torsion beams, coil springs;
telescopic dampers; hydraulic
brakes, front 24cm (9.5in) discs, rear
18cm (7.5in) drums, dual circuit, SCS
optional; rack and pinion steering;
42l (9.24gal) tank; 185/60HR13 tyres
5.5J rims.
DIMENSIONS wheelbase 244.5cm
(96.3in); track 141cm (55.5in) front,
138cm (54.3in) rear; length 380cm
(149.6in); width 163cm (64.2in);
height 132.5cm (52.2in); ground
clearance 14cm (5.5in); turning circle
9.8m (32.2ft).
EQUIPMENT radio/cassette, four
speakers, tinted glass, sunroof,
metallic paint all standard.
PERFORMANCE maximum 192kph
(119.6mph), 187kph (116.5mph) with
cat; 32.9kph (20.5mph) @ 1000rpm;
0-100kph (62mph) 9.8sec, 10.15ec
with cat; 11kg/kW (8.2kg/bhp); fuel
consumption 8.2l/100km (34.3mpg)
Autocar.
PRICE £9995

Fast Fiestas began with the XR2 in 1981-1983,
continuing in 1984-1989 with the restyled body. It
gained the 1.6 CVH engine and 5-speed gearbox;
handled well and safely, and with a top speed
comfortably over 168kph (105mph) was a firm
favourite with keen young drivers. The 1989-1992
XR2i had the Mark III body and was still a 2-door.
With fuel injection (necessary for catalytic
converter cars) it had a real turn of speed. The
suspension was tightened down making it a more
sporting car than its predecessors and, although
it never gained the reputation of a VW Golf GTi, it
was nevertheless a worthy contender in the hot
hatch market. Alloy wheels became standard in
the summer of 1990. The fastest Fiesta was the RS
Turbo of 1990, based on the XR2i, with a 99.2kW
(133bhp) CVH engine similar to the Escort RS
Turbo and although not notably economical at
12.3-11.3l/100km (23-25mpg) it reached 60mph in
under eight seconds and had a top speed of
207kph (130mph). Wide wheels and fashionably
fat low profile tyres made the steering heavy at
parking speed; PAS was not considered necessary
and kept the price under £12,000. It had only a
brief production run, being overtaken by the 16
valve RS1800 in 1992. "More fun than a Ferrari at
10 per cent of the price," according to *The Sunday
Times.*

ABOVE **Seven years, 118,000 miles,
reluctant sale of an XR2i on VXR
online.**

1990
Escort, Orion

SPEC 1.4LX NON-CATALYTIC CONVERTER AS SOLD IN BRITAIN.

INTRODUCTION August 1990. BODY saloon; 3-doors, 5-seats; weight 930kg (2050lb), 5-door 950kg (2094.4lb), Orion 985kg (2171.5lb), estate 1005kg (2215.6lb).

ENGINE 4-cylinders, in-line; transverse; 77.24mm x 74.3mm, 1392cc; compr 8.5:1; 52kW (69.7bhp) @ 5600rpm; 37.4kW (50.1bhp)/l; 103Nm (76lbft) @ 4000rpm. Without catalytic converter 54kW (72.4bhp) @ 5500rpm, 108Nm (80lbft) @ 4000rpm.

ENGINE STRUCTURE CVH belt-driven overhead camshaft; hydraulic tappets; 2-valves; aluminium head, iron block; electronic fuel injection (non-cat twin choke carburettor); electronic ignition; 5-bearing crankshaft.

TRANSMISSION front wheel drive; sdp clutch; 5-speed synchromesh; CTX automatic option; limited slip differential; final drive 4.059:1, 3.824:1 non-cat, 3.84:1 with CTX.

CHASSIS steel monocoque; ifs by MacPherson struts, anti-roll bar; semi independent rear by trailing arms, torsion beam axle, telescopic dampers; hydraulic servo brakes, front 23.9cm (9.4in) ventilated discs, rear 18cm (7.1in) drums, dual circuit, Teves ABS optional; variable rate rack and pinion steering; 55l (12.1 gal) tank; 175/70R13 tyres, 5J rims.

DIMENSIONS wheelbase 252.5cm (99.4in); track 144cm (56.7in) front, 146cm (57.5in) rear; length 403.5cm (158.9in). Orion 423cm (166.5in), estate 427cm (168.1in); width 169cm (66.5in); height 139.5cm (54.9in); estate 141.5cm (55.7in); turning circle 10m (32.8ft).

EQUIPMENT ABS £435; automatic £760; metallic paint £175. 4-speaker radio cassette, tinted windows, sunroof standard.

PERFORMANCE maximum speed 164kph (102.2mph); *Autocar*; 34.4kph (21.4mph) @ 1000rpm; 0-100kph (62mph) 12.8sec.; 17.9kg/kW (13.3kg/bhp); fuel consumption 9.7l/100km (29.1mpg).

PRICE £9470.

The Escort and Orion had plenty of life in them yet, but only two years had elapsed since their last makeover. A world wide best seller eight years out of nine, despite differences in the Transatlantic "Escort", Ford had been unnerved in the 1980s by criticism of the Sierra and Escort III, and was determined to do something that would ensure a rapturous reception to the Escort IV. It spent £1billion redeveloping it for 1991. Customers wanted more elbow-room; the body engineers found 7.6cm (3in) extra inside between the B-pillars, while making the outside only 4.6cm (1.8in) wider. The wheelbase was stretched by 12.7cm (5in) and the torsion beam rear suspension was entirely new. Equipment levels were enhanced with power steering, air-conditioning, electronic anti-lock brakes, height and tilt seat adjustments, and an adjustable steering column available as standard on some models or an option on others. Even the basic Escort Popular gained height-adjustable front seat belts. Orions, representing 26 per cent of Escort sales, gained 6 per cent more boot space and among the six engine options were fuel injection and electronic ignition. The RS2000 was available with the 3-door body and prices were only increased by 3 per cent. The Cabriolet lent the range some sparkle with RS2000 firm suspension, and a stiffened body made, as before, by Wilhelm Karmann GmbH of Osnabruck.

1990
Granada Scorpio saloon

Selling what seemed like inflated Sierras to discriminating executives was not getting any easier. Ever since their introduction in 1985, the Granada and Scorpio had been available only as hatchbacks; a notchback met the demand for a secure boot and shelter for rear-seat occupants when the hatch was open. Three-box saloons were quieter and more refined and, with new twin-cam engines, the Granada was becoming sophisticated. The gearbox was improved; just as well in view of growing opposition from Rover working to overcome its quality problems, and improved Vauxhall Carltons and Senators. The Vauxhall Cavalier was once again the best-selling car in Britain, for once dislodging Ford from market leadership. Scorpio saloon's announcement at the Brussels Motor Show in January focused Ford's attention on a Continental Europe that bought Fiestas, Escorts, and Sierras, but not many Granadas. Scorpio was its response to Europeans who regarded large Fords with disdain, relegating Ford to fourth on the Continent behind Volkswagen-Audi, Fiat-Lancia-Alfa Romeo, and Peugeot-Citroen. The British had bought big Fords ever since the V8 of the 1930s, not to mention their love affair with the Zephyr and Zodiac of the 1950s. In the UK one large luxury car in four was a Ford. Things were about to change, even though the clientele of both makes may have regarded the takeover of Jaguar as Ford buying its way into the aristocracy.

SPEC 2.0i AND 2.9V6.
INTRODUCTION January 1990, production to 1992.
BODY saloon; 4/5-doors, 5-seats; weight 1245kg (2744.7lb), 2.9V6 1315kg (2900lb).
ENGINE 4-cylinders, in-line; 86mm x 86mm, 1998cc; compr 10.3:1; 88kW (118bhp) @ 5500rpm; 44.5kW (59.1bhp)/l; 171Nm (126lbft) @ 2500rpm. Without catalytic converter 92kW (123.4bhp) @ 5500rpm; 46kW (61.8bhp)/l; 174Nm (87lbft) @ 2500rpm. V6 6-cylinders 60 deg V; 93 x 72mm; 2935cc; compr 9.5:1; 107kW (143.5bhp) @ 5500rpm; 36.3kW (48.9bhp)/l; 228Nm (168lbft) @ 3000rpm. Non-cat 110kW (147.5bhp) @ 5700rpm; 37.8kW (50.3bhp)/l; 233Nm (172lbft) @ 3000rpm.

ENGINE STRUCTURE 2 chain driven ohcs; 2-valves; aluminium cyl head, iron block; electronic fuel inj, breakerless ignition; 5-bearing crank. V6 hydraulic tappets; chain-driven central camshaft; iron heads and block; 4-bearing crank; Bosch LE/L Jetronic fuel injection.
TRANSMISSION rwd; sdp clutch; 5-speed synchromesh; 4-speed automatic opt; final drive 3.92:1, 3.62:1, 3.64:1 with limited slip differential. V6 final drive 3.64 or 3.36; opt 4x4 34/66 torque split front/rear; 3.62:1 final drive.
CHASSIS steel monocoque; ifs by MacPherson struts; anti roll bar; irs by semi-trailing arms, coil springs; telescopic dampers; hydraulic servo disc brakes, front 26cm (10.24in) ventilated, rear 25.3cm (9.96in), Teves ABS; rack and pinion variable ratio PAS; 70l (15.4gal) tank; 185/70TR/HR 14 or 195/65HR15 tyres, 6Jrims. 4x4 205/60VR15.

DIMENSIONS wheelbase 276cm (108.7in); track 147.5cm (58.1in) front, 150cm (59.1in) rear, 4x4 148cm (58.3in) front; length 467cm (183.9in), saloon 474.5cm (186.8in); width 176cm (69.3in), 4x4 176.5cm (69.5in); height 144cm (56.7in), 4x4 143.5cm (56.5in); ground clearance 12cm (4.7in); turning circle 11m (36.1ft).
EQUIPMENT CD player £215, traction pack £650. Alloy wheels, ABS, automatic, PAS, electric seats, leather trim, 6-speaker radio cassette included in price.
PERFORMANCE maximum speed 180kph (112.1mph); 2.0i automatic *Autocar*; 35.5kph (22.1mph) @ 1000rpm; 0-100kph (62mph) 11.6sec; 14.1kg/kW (10.6kg/bhp), V6 12.3kg/kW (9.2kg/bhp); fuel consumption 11.2l/100km (25.2mpg).
PRICE 2.0i automatic £19,245, 2.9EFi Ghia X £20,895, Scorpio 4x4 £25,350.

1990
Sapphire RS Cosworth 4x4

Cosworth's evolution from racing and high performance engines to production engines was profound. Mercedes-Benz employed the firm to engineer the 190 2.5-16; its casting techniques were world-class, and Ford got it to stiffen V6 engine blocks, reducing resonant noise to produce paragons of smoothness and power. Cosworth engineers reduced turbo lag to an absolute minimum. Four-wheel drive had become more or less obligatory for rallying as well as important for high-speed driving in all weathers. The 4-door Sierra Sapphire body was the stiffest and lightest in the range, so all the elements were brought together, with the MT75 gearbox, in probably the most accomplished Sierra yet. The model may not

have been as universally loved as many Fords and the proportions were never quite right, yet the Sapphire Cozzie 4x4 became such a tempting target for car thieves that Ford claimed it had to be equipped with a special alarm system. Sales were very nearly killed off however, by the steep rise in its insurance premiums. It was well equipped, which went some way towards justifying its premium price, with leather upholstery optional. This was Ford's third try at the performance market and its best and most civilised by far, with neither freakish tyres nor uncomfortably hard springing. Technical difficulties in equipping 4x4s with ABS brakes were overcome and all Ford 4x4s now had them.

INTRODUCTION Feb 1990, production to 1992.
BODY saloon; 4-doors, 5-seats; weight 1290kg (2844lb).
ENGINE 4-cylinders, in-line; 90.8mm x 77mm, 1994cc; compr 8:1; 162kW (217.2bhp) @ 6000rpm; 81.2kW (108.9bhp)/l; 290Nm (214lbft) @ 3500rpm.
ENGINE STRUCTURE 2 belt-drive overhead camshafts; 4-valves; aluminium cylinder head, iron block; Weber-Marelli electronic fuel injection and engine management; 5-bearing crankshaft; Garrett T.03B turbocharger .7bar (10.15psi); air/air intercooler.
TRANSMISSION four wheel drive; sdp clutch; MT75 gearbox 5-speed synchromesh; torque split 34/66 front/rear; limited slip differentials; final drive 3.62:1.
CHASSIS steel monocoque; ifs by MacPherson struts; anti-roll bar; independent rear suspension by semi-trailing arms, coil springs; anti roll bar; telescopic dampers; hydraulic servo disc brakes, front 28.3cm (11.14in) ventilated, rear 27.2cm (10.71in), Teves ABS; rack and pinion PAS; 60l (13.2 gal) tank; 205/50VR15 tyres 7Jrims.
DIMENSIONS wheelbase 261cm (102.8in); track front 145cm (57.1in) rear 147cm (57.9in); length 449.5cm (177in); width 170cm (66.9in); height 135cm (53.2in); turning circle 11m (36.1ft).
EQUIPMENT leather upholstery £500, metallic paint £175. ABS, alloy wheels, PAS, electric windows all standard.
PERFORMANCE maximum speed 232kph (144.5mph) *Autocar*; 35.8kph (22.3mph) @ 1000rpm; 0-100kph (62mph) 6.6sec; 8kg/kW (5.9kg/bhp); fuel consumption 13.1l/100km (21.6mpg).
PRICE £24,995.
PRODUCTION 9250.

LEFT **Cozzie 4x4 with WWII North American B25J Mitchell.**

1991
Escort XR3i, RS2000

Ford celebrated a year's production of the Mark IV Escort by putting the high-performance versions, previewed the year before, on sale. "The Champ is Back" Ford cheerfully asserted at Earls Court Motorfair, the former London Motor Show, in October, at which the RS2000 appeared with a 111.9kW (150bhp) 2.0-litre 16 valve twin cam engine, disc brakes on all four wheels, and profoundly improved handling. Three Escorts were shown with the new engine, built in a new plant at Bridgend in South Wales, and called the Zeta. Lancia soon complained about the name; too close to Beta they said, so it was changed to Zetec. The new factory cost £500million, and could make 500,000 engines a year, more than enough for the entire Escort range. The Zetec, engineered for transverse mounting and front wheel drive, was also to be a key ingredient in the Sierra's successor, the Mondeo, two years hence. Yet even Ford admitted that the engine had had a protracted birth. As late as October 1991 no promises were being made about which Escorts and Orions it would be fitted in, beyond top of the range models already committed to. Consequently most 1.6-litre Escorts were still sold with the 10 year old CVH. Disc brakes were standardised on fast Fords, as was ABS, PAS, and MTX75 close-ratio gears.

INTRODUCTION October 1991.
BODY saloon; 3-doors, 5-seats; weight 1090kg (2403lb), RS 1110kg (2447lb).
ENGINE 4-cylinders, in-line; transverse; 80.6mm x 88mm, 1796cc; compr 10:1; 96kW (128.7bhp) @ 6250rpm; 53.5kW (71.7bhp)/l; 162Nm (119lbft) @ 4500rpm. RS 86 x 86mm; 1998cc; compr 10.3:1; 110kW (147.5bhp) @ 6000rpm; 55.1kW (73.8bhp)/l; 190Nm (140lbft) @ 4500rpm
ENGINE STRUCTURE Zetec 2 belt-driven overhead camshafts; 4-valves; hydraulic tappets; aluminium cylinder head, iron block; electronic multi-point injection, mapped ignition; 5-bearing crankshaft. RS chain-driven camshafts
TRANSMISSION front wheel drive; sdp clutch; 5-speed synchromesh; final drive 3.82:1.
CHASSIS steel monocoque; ifs by MacPherson struts, anti-roll bar; rear suspension, torsion beam, trailing arms, coil springs, anti roll bar, telescopic dampers; hydraulic servo disc brakes, 26cm (10.24in) front (ventilated) and rear, ABS optional; rack and pinion PAS; 55l (12 gal) tank; 185/60VR14tyres 6Jrims; RS 195/50VR15 tyres.
DIMENSIONS wheelbase 252.5cm (99.4in); track front 144cm (56.7in), rear 146cm (57.5in); length 403.5cm (158.9in); width 169cm (66.5in); height 139.5cm (54.9in); turning circle 10m (32.8ft).
EQUIPMENT ABS £505. central locking, electric front windows, electric mirrors, alloy wheels, sunroof, radio cassette, PAS all standard.
PERFORMANCE maximum speed 200.7kph (125mph) Autocar; 33kph (20.6mph) @ 1000rpm; 0-100kph (62mph) 8.6sec, RS 8.4sec; 0-100kph 11.4kg/kW (8.5kg/bhp), RS 10.1kg/kW (7.5kg/bhp); fuel consumption 9.9l/100km (28.6mpg).
PRICE £13,990.

1991
Scorpio V6 24v

"The new Scorpio is either a Jaguar in a plain wrapper or far too good a car to be a Ford. At £27,383 it rubs shoulders with BMWs and Mercedes-Benzes, yet in anything less than a perfect light it could be mistaken for a commonplace Granada at half the price. It is fast enough and very nearly refined enough to be handed to Ford's Coventry subsidiary to be restyled as the medium-sized Jaguar needed for the 1990s. Taking an engine designed by Cosworth Engineering would not cause Jaguar, with its racing engine connections, to lose face. It might hurt to inherit a chassis derived from the humble Sierra but even this has been purified to near-Jaguar standards, though it needs improvements to make the ride smoother. Ford is not planning to use the Scorpio as a basis for a Jaguar but it must be tempting to apply the up-market label and design a body more sophisticated than the rather stodgy six year old Granada... Unfortunately the engine is paired with Ford's A4LD automatic, which changes gear with an audible thump, a matter of calibration to put right says Ford." How prescient of *The Sunday Times* in April 1991, to outline a policy for the Coventry subsidiary acquired in 1989. Ford was careful not to associate the 24-valve Scorpio too closely to Cosworth, it was not a Cosworth Scorpio like a Cosworth Sierra, but it was a sign of things to come.

INTRODUCTION January 1991.
BODY saloon; 4-doors, 5-seats; weight 1385kg (3053.4lb).
ENGINE 6-cylinders, 60deg V; 93mm x 72mm, 2935cc; compr 9.7:1; 143kW (191.8bhp) @ 5750rpm; 48.7kW (65.3bhp)/l; 275Nm (203lbft) @ 4500rpm.
ENGINE STRUCTURE 2 chain-driven overhead camshafts per bank; 4-valves; hydraulic tappets; aluminium cylinder heads, iron block; multi-point Bosch LH-Jetronic fuel injection Ford EEC IV engine management; 4-bearing crankshaft, two 3-way catalytic converters.
TRANSMISSION rear wheel drive; A4LDE Automatic 4-speed Lock-up overdrive; final drive 3.64:1, limited slip differential.
CHASSIS steel monocoque; ifs by struts, coil springs, telescopic dampers, anti-roll bar; irs by semi-trailing arms, coil springs, anti roll bar, telescopic dampers; hydraulic servo ventilated disc brakes, front 27.8cm (10.9in), rear 27.3cm (10.75in), ABS; rack and pinion PAS; 70l (15.4gal) tank; 205/50ZR16 tyres, 6.5Jrims.
DIMENSIONS wheelbase 276cm (108.7in); track 149cm (58.7in) front, 151cm (59.5in) rear; length 474.5cm (186.8in), 5-door 467cm (183.9in); width 176.5cm (69.5in); height 141cm (55.5in); ground clearance 12cm (4.7in); turning circle 11m (36.1ft).
EQUIPMENT alloy wheels, ABS, PAS, air conditioning, electric seats and windows, mirrors and sunroof, cruise control, trip computer, CD player, choice of leather or cloth all standard.
PERFORMANCE maximum speed 225kph (140.2mph); 41kph (25.5mph) @ 1000rpm; 0-100kph (62mph) 8.8sec; 9.7kg/kW (7.2kg/bhp); fuel consumption 12.8l/100km (22mpg) *Autocar.*
PRICE £26,800.

1992
Escort RS Cosworth

Having been the works team's mainstay in rallies since 1990, the RS Cosworth Escort finally went on sale as a road car in the spring of 1992. Essentially a cut-down Sierra Cosworth 4x4 platform with an Escort top half, it had a high-mounted rear aerofoil to provide essential downforce at speed and was only ever available with three doors. The full-sized Sierra Cosworth 4x4 continued in production until the end of 1992, but the smaller car's light weight and responsive handling gave it the edge in competition. In standard road trim the Cosworth YB 16 valve 2.0-litre turbocharged engine gave 169.3kW (227bhp) but works rally cars were developed with anything up to 298kW (400bhp). The handling was astonishingly well controlled and precise, with little of the nervousness associated with quasi-competition cars. Indeed, with performance in the order of a 1960s Ford V8-engined Cobra, the RS in prudent hands had an almost unprecedented margin of safety. A 7-speed gearbox was listed among the homologated optional extras for competition. In due course the authorities deemed such power outputs hazardous and put a limit on turbo-charger pressures. The car was aimed at drivers preoccupied with rallying but unaffordable insurance premiums restricted sales, leading to the abandonment of XR titles in 1994, and the confinement of RS to small runs of specialist rally cars.

INTRODUCTION May 1992.
BODY saloon; 3-doors, 5-seats; weight 1275kg (2811lb).
ENGINE 4-cylinders, in-line; longitudinal; 90.82mm x 76.95mm, 1994cc; compr 8:1; 162kW (217.2bhp) @ 6250rpm; 81.2kW (108.9bhp)/l; 294Nm (217lbft) @ 3500rpm.
ENGINE STRUCTURE Zetec 2 belt-driven overhead camshafts; 4-valves; hydraulic tappets; aluminium head, iron block; Weber-Marelli electronic multi-point injection, mapped ignition; 5-bearing crankshaft, Garrett T3/T04B turbocharger .8bar (11.6psi), with air/air intercooler.
TRANSMISSION four wheel drive; sdp clutch; 5-speed synchromesh; central planetary differential, torque split 34/66 or 40/60 with viscous coupling; final drive 3.62:1.
CHASSIS steel monocoque; ifs by MacPherson struts, anti-roll bar; rear suspension, torsion beam, trailing arms, coil springs, anti roll bar, telescopic dampers; hydraulic servo ventilated disc brakes, 27.8cm (10.9in) front and rear, Teves ABS; rack and pinion PAS; 65l (14.3gal) tank; 225/45ZR16 tyres 8Jrims.
DIMENSIONS wheelbase 255cm (100.4in); track 146.5cm (57.7in) front, 148cm (58.3in) rear; length 414cm (163in); width 174cm (68.5in); height 142.5cm (56.1in); turning circle 10.5m (34.5ft).
EQUIPMENT central locking, electric front windows, electric mirrors, alloy wheels, sunroof, radio cassette, PAS all standard.
PERFORMANCE maximum speed 225kph (140.2mph); 38.1kph (23.7mph) @ 1000rpm; 0-100kph (62mph) 6.1sec; 7.9kg/kW (5.9kg/bhp); fuel consumption 11l/100km (25.7mpg).
PRICE £22,050, Lux £25,590.

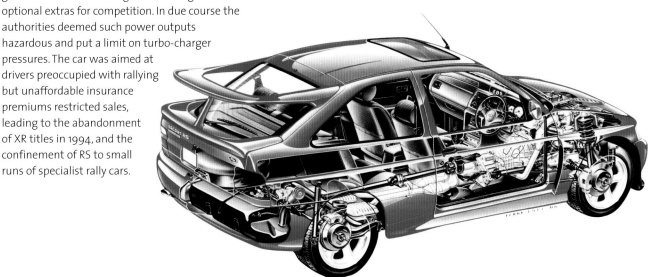

1992
Fiesta RS 1800, RS Turbo

The Peugeot 205 GTi was dominating speedy small cars, and the Fiesta XR2 was not a match for it, even after becoming XR2i in 1989. At around 190kph (118mph) the Ford was fast, but lacked the Peugeot's precision, quick steering, and exquisite balance. The RS Turbo at the Turin Motor Show in April 1990 still fell short. It was coarse and ill-mannered, and although 1.6sec faster than the XR2i to 100kph (62mph), it was slower than the lighter Renault 5GT Turbo. The Fiesta's CVH engine was based on the Escort's, with a Garrett T02 turbocharger and air-to-air intercooler. The steering was higher-geared at 3.75 rather than 4.2 turns from lock to lock, yet still felt unworthy.

The Turbo did not last and in 1992 the RS1800 resurrected the name of an Escort rather than a Fiesta. It was slower than the Turbo, with a 16-valve version of an engine still called Zeta rather than Zetec, but overall a substantial improvement despite its choppy ride, a result of the addition of a rear anti-roll bar. The smooth-running engine was a revelation after the uncouth turbo; it had ample torque, and was agreeably economical. The RS Fiesta had Recaro seats, 5-spoke alloy wheels, and the obligatory cosmetic bounce provided by a colour-keyed spoiler, even though the steering had reverted to over four turns lock to lock.

SPEC RS, 1800 RS TURBO ITEMS LABELLED RST.

BODY saloon; 3/5-doors, 5-seats; weight 995kg (2193.6lb), RST 920kg (2028lb).

ENGINE 4-cylinders, in-line; transverse; 80.6mm x 88mm, 1796cc; compr 10:1; 96kW (128.7bhp) @ 6250rpm; 54.6kW (71.7bhp)/l; 162Nm (120lbft) @ 4500rpm. RST 80 x 79.5mm; 1598cc; compr 8.2:1; 98kW (131.4bhp) @ 5500rpm; 61.3kW (82.2bhp)/l; 184Nm (136lbft) @ 2400rpm.

ENGINE STRUCTURE Zeta, 2 belt-driven overhead camshafts; hydraulic tappets; 4-valves; aluminium cylinder head, iron block; electronic fuel injection, breakerless electronic ignition; 5-bearing crankshaft. RST CVH 1 ohc; 2-valves; Bosch K-Jetronic injection; GarrettT02 turbocharger, intercooler.

TRANSMISSION front wheel drive; sdp diaphragm spring clutch; 5-speed synchromesh; final drive 3.82:1.

CHASSIS steel monocoque; ifs by MacPherson struts; irs by trailing arms, torsion beams, coil springs; telescopic dampers; anti-roll bars front and back; hydraulic brakes, front 24cm (9.5in) ventilated discs, rear 18cm (7.5in) drums; rack and pinion steering; 42l (9.2gal) tank; 185/55VR14 tyres 5.5J rims.

DIMENSIONS wheelbase 244.5cm (96.3in); track front 140.5cm (55.3in), rear 137.5cm (54.1in); length 380cm (149.6in); width 163cm (64.2in); height 132.5cm (52.2in); ground clearance 14cm (5.5in); turning circle 9.8m (32.2ft).

EQUIPMENT radio/cassette, 4-speakers, tinted glass, sunroof, metallic paint all standard.

PERFORMANCE maximum speed 200kph (124.6mph), RST 205kph (127.7mph); 30kph (18.7mph) @ 1000rpm, RST 33.8kph (21.1mph) @ 1000rpm; 0-100kph (62mph) 8.5sec, RST 8.2sec; 10.4kg/kW (7.7kg/bhp), RST 9.4kg/kW (7kg/bhp); fuel consumption 8l/100km (35.3mpg).

PRICE RS Turbo 1991 £11,731, RS1800 1992 £11,615.

1992
16v Zetec Fiesta, Escort, Orion

The new Zetec engine was a long time coming but it was worth the wait. Ford's first mass-market 16-valve 1.8-litre was planned for February 1992, beginning with a 1.6-litre for all three small and medium-sized Fords, Fiesta, Escort, and Orion as well as van derivatives. Later on a more powerful 1.8 was phased in over several months and a 2.0-litre Zetec was planned for the Mondeo - still fully a year ahead. The dohc RS2000 Escort remained and the existing CVH 1.1-litre and 1.4-litre engines were planned to go on for a further three years. The Zetec was to be produced in Cologne and Mexico, as well as Bridgend, a total production capacity of a million a year. Developed by Dunton and Cologne, the design was thoroughly up to date without being radical. There was no variable valve timing, as introduced by Honda, or far-reaching structural innovations like Rover's bolted-sandwich K-series. The Zetec's lightweight valve gear with low-mass anti-syphon hydraulic tappets revved smoothly up to

7000rpm before hitting the rev limiter, its cylinder dimensions were "under-square" and although its block was cast iron in the interests of noise absorption, the 1.8 was still a lightweight. Cam belt replacement was specified at 90,000km (56,000miles), much the same as most of the opposition. After 150,000 hours of dynamometer testing a total of 1260 prototype engines were made, of which 320 were installed in vehicles that covered more than 10million test kilometres (6million miles). In its first form the Zeta was available in two power variants, and it subsequently became available in a variety of sizes. Made from high quality materials, it followed Ford's well-established manufacturing economies in a tradition going back to the 1930s, allowing the bores to be machined on the same equipment as its predecessor. The cylinder centres were exactly the same as those of the CVH it replaced.

INTRODUCTION as Zeta 1798cc, October 1991.

ENGINE weight 122kg (269lb) with oil and principal fixtures; 4-cyls, in-line; transverse; 80.6mm x 88mm, 1798cc; compr 10:1; 77kW (103.3bhp) @ 5500rpm, 42.8kW (57.4bhp)/l; or 96kW (128.7bhp) @ 6250rpm, 53kW (71.6bhp)/l; 153Nm (113lbft) @ 4000rpm or 162Nm (120lbft) @ 4500rpm.

ENGINE STRUCTURE 2 HSN (highly saturated nitrile) toothed belt-driven ohcs; 4-valves, inlet 32mm (1.26in), exhaust 28mm (1.1in); low-mass anti-syphon hydraulic tappets; cylinder head die-cast aluminium, sand-cast grey iron block; chilled cast iron camshafts; high-silicon aluminium pistons; forged steel connecting rods; shell-moulded cast-iron crank with 5 main bearings and 8 counterweights; structural aluminium oil pan; sequential multi-point fuel injection; 16-bit EEC IV engine management computer with 56kB memory; 3-way catalytic converter; fuel requirement 95RON unleaded

1992
Escort, Orion

A good record in the market contradicted the misgivings about the Escort and Orion that surfaced soon after their announcement. Ford, however, played safe and reacted quickly, putting a facelift in hand within months. Renovations surfaced after only two years, improving not only ride and handling, but also the appearance. Ford's style leadership of the 1950s, epitomised by the Zephyr and Zodiac, had seemed to slip from its grasp. There had been eccentricities, like the Mark IV Zephyr, the reverse-rake back windows and the Escort III's "bustle", but by and large Fords had been fashionable, well proportioned, and appealing. The late mind-change on Sierra had shaken confidence, so during the second half of

1992 Escorts and Orions were given a new nose cone, with separate air intake grille and a new rear with bigger tail lights and back window. Road behaviour benefited from extra internal stiffening, including thicker-gauge steel in the forward bulkhead and a facia cross member that braced the steering column to absorb side impacts better. Absorption of frontal crash loads was enhanced by beams extending forward of the suspension turrets and the middle of the car now became an effective safety cage. Power steering became standard throughout the Zetec engined range, CTX automatic was made available, and substantial price cuts to the outgoing models were passed on to the new ones.

SPEC 1.6I 16V.

INTRODUCTION September 1992.
BODY saloon; 3-doors, 5-seats; weight 1085kg (2392lb), 5-doors 1105kg (2436lb), Orion 4-doors 1110kg (2447lb), cabriolet 2-door 1110kg (2447lb), estate car 5-doors 1135kg (2502lb).
ENGINE 4-cylinders, in-line; transverse; 76mm x 88mm, 1597cc; compr 10.3:1; 66kW (88.5bhp) @ 5500rpm; 41.3kW (55.4bhp)/l; 134Nm (99lbft) @ 4000rpm.
ENGINE STRUCTURE 2 belt-driven overhead camshafts; 4-valves; hydraulic tappets; aluminium head, iron block; 5-bearing crankshaft; sequential multi-point fuel injection; EEC IV engine management; 3-way catalytic converter.
TRANSMISSION front wheel drive; sdp clutch; MTX75 5-speed synchromesh; final drive 3.82:1.
CHASSIS steel monocoque; ifs by MacPherson struts, anti-roll bar; rear suspension, torsion beam, trailing arms, coil springs, anti roll bar, telescopic dampers; hydraulic servo brakes, 26cm (10.2in) front ventilated discs, rear 20.3cm (8in) drums, Teves ABS optional; rack and pinion PAS; 55l (12.1gal) tank; 175/70TR13tyres 5Jrims, 155TR13 or 185/60HR14 6Jrims.
DIMENSIONS wheelbase 252.5cm (99.4in) track 144cm (56.7in) front, 146cm (57.5in) rear; length 403.5cm (158.9in), Cabrio 410.5cm (161.6in), Orion 423cm (166.5in), estate 427cm (168.1in); width 169cm (66.5in); height 139.5cm (54.9in), estate 141cm (55.5in); turning circle 10m (32.8ft).
EQUIPMENT CD player £367, ABS £504, manual sunroof, alloy wheels.
PERFORMANCE maximum speed 178.2kph (111mph) *Autocar*; 36.5kph (22.7mph) @ 1000rpm; 0-100kph (62mph) 11.9sec; 16.4kg/kW (12.2kg/bhp); fuel consumption 9.2l/100km (30.7mpg).
PRICE 1.6i LX £11885, 1.6i Ghia 5-door £12,440, Orion 1.8 16v Ghia £12,590, 1.6i LX Estate £12,325.

1993
Maverick 2.4 and 2.7 diesel

Ford was never entirely happy with joint ventures, except those in which it had the upper hand, as with its takeover of Jaguar. The co-operative arrangement with Nissan, under which a new factory was established in Spain to make a strong 4x4, proved short-lived. The Ford Maverick and Nissan Terrano II produced in the former Spanish Motor Iberica SA factory at Barcelona were identical except in badging and cosmetics. The vehicles were designed by Nissan in two wheelbases with 3-doors or 5-doors, had a stout separate chassis with the body mounted at 10 points and a choice of petrol or diesel engines. They were sold through separate dealer organisations, gave a good account of themselves off-road, and although not as refined on-road as rivals such as Land Rover Discovery or Vauxhall Frontera, their build quality was superior to both. In the interests of fuel economy Maverick ran for the most part in rear wheel drive. The 4x4 market showed strong growth, it was a new product line for Ford. In 1996 the diesel had a welcome power increase to 92kW (123.4bhp) with the addition of an intercooler, but the arrangement with Nissan lasted only five years. Double-headed marketing proved fractious, dealers disliked being second-guessed on trade-in prices for a virtually identical model, and in the end Ford decided to make its own 4x4.

INTRODUCTION June 1993.
BODY saloon; 3-doors, 5-seats; weight 1620kg (3571.5lb), 5-door 5-7 seats 1750kg (3858lb), diesels 1730kg (3814lb) and 1850kg (4078.5lb).
ENGINE 4-cylinders, in-line; 89mm x 96mm, 2389cc; compr 8.6:1; 91kW (122bhp) @ 5200rpm; 38.1kW (51.1bhp)/l; 197Nm (145lbft) @ 4000rpm. Diesel 96 x 92mm; 2663cc; compr 21.9:1; 73kW (97.9bhp) @ 4000rpm; 27.4kW (36.7bhp)/l; 221Nm (163lbft) @ 2200rpm.
ENGINE STRUCTURE Z24 chain driven ohc; 3-valves (2 inlet); aluminium head, iron block; electronic fuel injection; breakerless ignition; 5-bearing crank. Diesel TD27T 2-valves; pushrod; gear driven side camshaft; turbocharger.
TRANSMISSION rwd, selectable 4wd; transfer box for high (1.0) or low (2.02) ratio; 24.4cm (9.6in) hydraulic sdp clutch; 5-speed synchromesh; final drive 4.63:1, auto-locking front hubs, limited slip rear axle; diff lock.

CHASSIS box-section ladder frame; ifs by double wishbones and torsion bars, anti-roll bar; rear suspension live axle, five-bar multi-link, coil springs, anti-roll bar; telescopic dampers; hydraulic servo brakes, front ventilated discs, rear drums; recirculating ball PAS; 72l (15.8 gal) tank, 80l (17.6 gal) on lwb; 215SR15tyres, 6Jrims.
DIMENSIONS wheelbase 245cm (96.5in), lwb 265cm (104.3in); track front 145.5cm (57.3in), rear 143cm (56.3in); length 410.5cm (161.6in), lwb 458.5cm (180.5in); width 173.5cm (68.3in); height 180.5cm (71.1in), lwb 181cm (71.3in); ground clearance 21cm (8.3in); turning circle 10.8m (35.4ft), lwb 11.4m (37.4ft); approach angle 35deg, departure angle 36.5deg (lwb 26.5deg) wading depth 45cm (17.7in).
EQUIPMENT alloy wheels on GLX, air conditioning, leather optional. Rear screen wash-wipe, cloth upholstery, RDS radio cassette standard. Accessories included roof rails, nudge bars, running boards, tow bar, lamp guards. 14 equipment packs. 2 solid colours, 8 metallic no extra cost.

PERFORMANCE maximum 159kph (99mph), diesel 147kph (91.6mph); 34.9kph (21.7mph) @ 1000rpm; 0-100kph (62mph) 12.3sec, diesel 19sec; 17.8kg/kW (13.3kg/bhp, diesel 23.7kg/kW (17.7kg/bhp); 14.9l/100km (19mpg), diesel 10.2l/100km (27.6mph).
PRICE swb petrol £15,000; swb diesel £15,500; lwb petrol £17,700, diesel £18,200; lwb GLX petrol £19,200, diesel £19,700.

ILLUSTRATED **The author's Maverick and accessories. A pull-out tray transformed dog-carrying and the Thule luggage carrier increased the holiday loads that could be carried when all three rows of seats were occupied.**

1993
Mondeo 1.6, 1.8, 2.0

The Mondeo was acclaimed critically and commercially from the beginning. Its election as Car of the Year, against keen opposition from the Citroen Xantia and Mercedes-Benz C-class, was testament to qualities worthy of the Cortina in its heyday. Ford promoted it as a car for the world, an ambition on the company wish-list since the Model T, yet no more realistic in the 1990s than it had been in the 1920s. Buyers in different countries had wanted different sorts of Escort, so European and American models had gone their separate ways before production even started. It was much the same with Mondeo although it took longer. Some innovations such as driver airbags, obligatory in America, were incorporated on UK cars although only half as big. Launched as a 4-door saloon, a 5-door hatchback that looked like a saloon and an estate car, a 4x4 was also listed. Five years and £3billion had been spent on five levels of trim and a new range of engines, to provide front wheel drive at last for the mainstream market. No Sierra engine survived, the Mondeo's was mounted transversely, and the only similarity between the cars was size. The Mondeo was 5cm (1.97in) shorter and turned out to be a perfect fit for British garages. Mondeo accumulated many awards, none more significant than the appellation "Mondeo man" signifying the earnest, mobile middle class toiler.

SPEC FOR 1.8I AND 2.0; FOR 1.6 ENGINE SPEC SEE 1992 16V ZETEC.
INTRODUCTION January 1993.
BODY saloon; 4-doors, 5-seats; 1225kg (2700.6lb), 5-door 1245kg (2745lb), estate 1270kg (2800lb); 2.0i plus approx 10kg (22lb).
ENGINE 4-cylinders, in-line; transverse; 80.6mm x 88mm, 1796cc; compr 10:1; 85kW (114bhp) @ 5750rpm; 47.3kW (63.5bhp)/l; 158Nm (117lbft) @ 3750rpm. 2.0 84.8 x 88mm; 1988cc; 100kW (134.1bhp) @ 6000rpm; 50.3kW (67.5bhp)/l; 180Nm (133lbft) @ 4000rpm.
ENGINE STRUCTURE 2 belt-driven ohcs; 4-valves; hydraulic tappets; aluminium head, iron block; 5-bearing crankshaft; sequential multi-point fuel injection; EEC IV engine management; 3-way catalytic converter.

TRANSMISSION front wheel drive; sdp clutch; MTX75 5-sped synchromesh; CD4E automatic option; final drive 4.06:1, automatic 3.92:1.
CHASSIS steel monocoque; ifs by MacPherson struts, coil; springs offset, lower A-arms, anti-roll bar; Quadralink strut-type irs with coil springs; anti roll bar; telescopic dampers, transverse and trailing arms; hydraulic servo brakes, front 26cm (10.2in) ventil discs, rear 22.8cm (9in) drums, ABS opt; rack and pinion PAS; 61.5l (13.5 gal); 185/65HR14, 195/60HR15tyres, 5.5J rims, Si 205/55VR15 6J rims.
DIMENSIONS wheelbase 270.5cm (106.5in); track front 150.5cm (59.25in), rear 148.5cm (58.5in), estate 150.5cm (59.25in) rear; length 448cm (176.4in), estate 463cm (182.3in); width 175cm (68.9in); height 143cm (56.3in), 5-door 142.5cm (56.1in), estate 144cm (56.7in); clearance 12cm (4.7in); turning circle 10.9m (35.8ft).

EQUIPMENT Base, LX, GLX, Ghia, and Si, central locking, driver's airbag, alarm, seatbelt pre-tensioners, and cupholders standard. Traction control, adaptive damping, and cruise control optional on up-market models.
PERFORMANCE maximum 196kph (122mph) Autocar; 35kph (21.8mph) @ 1000rpm; 0-100kph (62mph) 9.6sec; 14.4kg/kW (10.7kg/bhp); fuel consumption 10.1l/100km (28mpg).
PRICE 1.6i 4 door £11,200; 2.0iGhia £17,450; 1.8iGLX Estate £14,155.

1993
Mondeo 1.8 turbodiesel

The Mondeo was made with exterior body panels and almost half the monocoque in galvanised steel. It was heavier than the Sierra not because the body was over-engineered (computer design analyses saw to that) but because of the mechanical sophistication customers were now demanding. The 5-link rear suspension was every bit as heavy as the old Sierra's live rear axle and long transmission shaft. The chassis tuning had been carried out by development and testing chief Richard Parry-Jones and technical counsellor Jackie Stewart. Together they spent two years evaluating and fine-tuning prototypes. The challenge was balance. Stewart: "You can cut down on the compliant bushes that make the car supple and quiet, and make the Mondeo handle like a racing car. Or you can beef them up and make it seem like a limousine, but also make it feel unresponsive." The former world champion gave an assurance that Ford's fabled bean-counters had never stood in their way. "Throughout the programme we were never refused any change we wanted to make on the grounds of cost." The diesel, no longer a poor relation in the engine range, was taken seriously with a turbocharger and intercooler as the market grew more encouraging, yet like the 1.6 and 1.8 petrol, it was not available at first in Ghia trim.

INTRODUCTION January 1993.
BODY Saloon; 4-doors, 5-seats; weight 1285kg (2833lb), 5-door 1305kg (2877lb), estate 1330kg (2932lb).
ENGINE 4-cylinders, in-line; transverse; 82.5mm x 82mm, 1753cc; compr 21.5:1; 65kW (87.2bhp) @ 4500rpm; 37.1kW (49.7bhp)/l; 178Nm (131lbft) @ 2200rpm.
ENGINE STRUCTURE Ford/KHD; gear and belt-driven overhead camshaft; 2-valves; iron cylinder head and block; 5-bearing crankshaft; indirect mechanical fuel injection, Garrett AiResearch T3 turbocharger with intercooler.
TRANSMISSION front wheel drive; sdp clutch; MTX75 5-spd synchromesh; final drive 4.06:1.
CHASSIS steel monocoque; ifs by MacPherson struts, coil springs offset, lower A-arms, anti-roll bar; Quadralink strut-type irs with coil springs; anti roll bar; telescopic dampers, transverse and trailing arms; hydraulic servo brakes, front 26cm (10.2in) ventilated discs, rear 22.8cm (9in) drums, ABS optional; rack and pinion PAS; 61.5l (13.5 gal) tank; 185/65HR14, 195/60HR15tyres, 5.5J rims.
DIMENSIONS wheelbase 270.5cm (106.5in); track front 150.5cm (59.25in), rear 148.5cm (58.5in), estate rear 150.5cm (59.25in); length 448cm (176.4in), estate 463cm (182.3in); width 175cm (68.9in); height 143cm (56.3in), 5-door 142.5cm (56.1in), estate 144cm (56.7in); ground clearance 12cm (4.7in); turning circle 10.9m (35.8ft).
EQUIPMENT Base, LX, GLX, central locking, driver's airbag, alarm, seatbelt pre-tensioners, and cupholders standard.
PERFORMANCE maximum speed 175kph (109mph) *Autocar*; 39.8kph (24.8mph) @ 1000rpm; 0-100kph (62mph) 14.7sec; 19.8kg/kW (14.7kg/bhp); fuel consumption 7.9l/100km (36mpg).
PRICE 1.8TD LX £13,470; estate £14,575.

1993
Escort RS2000 4x4

INTRODUCTION August 1993.
BODY saloon; 3-doors, 5-seats;
weight 1240kg (2733.7lb).
ENGINE 4-cylinders, in-line;
transverse; 86mm x 86mm; 1998cc;
compr 10.3:1; 110kW (147.5bhp)
@ 6000rpm; 55.1kW (73.8bhp)/l;
190Nm (140lbft) @ 4500rpm.
ENGINE STRUCTURE 2 chain-driven
overhead camshafts; 4-valves;
hydraulic tappets; aluminium head,
iron block; electronic multi-point
injection, mapped ignition; 5-
bearing crankshaft.
TRANSMISSION 4 wheel drive; sdp
clutch; 5-speed synchromesh; central
planetary differential, torque split
34/66 or 40/60 with viscous
coupling; final drive 3.56:1.
CHASSIS steel monocoque; ifs by
MacPherson struts, anti-roll bar; rear
suspension, torsion beam, trailing
arms, coil springs, anti roll bar,
telescopic dampers; hydraulic servo
disc brakes, 26cm (10.2in) front
(ventilated) and 27cm (10.6in) rear,
ABS; rack and pinion PAS; 55l (12.1gal)
tank; 195/50VR15tyres, 6J rims.
DIMENSIONS wheelbase 252.5cm
(99.4in); track 144cm (56.7in) front,
146cm (57.5in) rear; length 403.5cm
(158.9in); width 169cm (66.5in);
height 139.5cm (54.9in); turning
circle 10m (32.8ft).
EQUIPMENT central locking, electric
front windows, electric mirrors, alloy
wheels, sunroof, radio cassette, PAS
all standard.
PERFORMANCE maximum speed
208kph (129.6mph); 32.5kph
(20.2mph) @ 1000rpm; 0-100kph
(62mph) 8.7sec; 11.3kg/kW
(8.4kg/bhp); fuel consumption
9.9l/100km (28.6mpg).
PRICE £16,310

Announced at the Geneva Motor Show in March 1993, and expected to be in production by year's end, it was summer 1994 before Escort RS2000 4x4s went on sale. Difficulties at Saarlouis were blamed but in reality engineers were so busy on mainstream cars that none could be spared to develop small-production speciality vehicles. Transverse-engined, unlike the Sierra 4x4, it had the same twin-cam engine as the standard RS2000 with three differentials. In the middle, as it were, was a planetary drive differential, splitting the power and torque 40 per cent to the front and 60 per cent to the rear for sportier handing than the regular front drive car. Escort floorpans had been designed with 4x4 in mind and the rear diff was accommodated without intruding on boot space. Instead of the standard car's semi-independent trailing arm and torsion beam axle, the rear final drive was bolted into its own sub-frame with the back wheels hung on independent semi-trailing arms. The result was astonishing grip and handling in the wet, or on rally special stages, but the additional weight of the complicated drivelines and attendant power losses, added half a second off the 0-100kph (62mph) time and took around 3kph (2mph) off the top speed. It was not much, but together with the higher price buyers seemed to be put off and not many were sold.

LEFT **Scotland. West Coast. Magical Crinan. With seafood at the end of a spectacular road used by Ford for press launches.**

1994
Mondeo V6

World car ambitions saw the Mondeo launched in the United States as the Ford Contour and Mercury Mystique, the smaller with a 2.0-litre 4-cylinder made in Chihuahua Mexico, and the larger a 2.5-litre 24-valve quad-cam 60deg V6 that would become famous as Duratec. With Ford engineering at full stretch, Porsche Engineering at Weissach was recruited as a consultant on the design of the Duratec, an all-aluminium modular engine. This was usually joined to CD4E, Ford's first automatic transaxle designed for full electronic control. Duratec formed the basis of a family of engines between 2.0- and 3.0-litres. It was light, only some 18kg (40lb) heavier than a Zetec 4-cylinder, and it not only had to fit inside the small space available but was also required to deliver good low-speed pulling power. It had to be versatile enough for regular slow-speed passenger cars as well as high-performance sports saloons. In its leisurely applications it was important not to make it feel like a quad-cam multi-valve unit needing high revs to get the best out of it. Bruce Coventry, head of V6 development said: "Low-end torque establishes the character of a vehicle and there won't be a 4-valve V6 that can match our torque curve. From 1500rpm to almost 5200rpm the torque doesn't vary by more than five per cent, so the usable power is good throughout the mid range."

INTRODUCTION January 1994.
BODY saloon; 4-doors, 5-seats; weight 1320kg (2910lb), 5-door 1330kg (2932lb), estate 1380kg (3042.4lb).
ENGINE 6-cylinders, 60deg V; transverse; 82.4mm x 79.5mm, 2544cc; compr 9.7:1; 125kW (167.6bhp) @ 6250rpm; 49.1kW (65.9bhp)/l; 220Nm (162lbft) @ 4250rpm.
ENGINE STRUCTURE 2 chain-driven ohcs per bank; 4-valves; aluminium cylinder heads and block; 4-bearing crankshaft; sequential multi-point fuel injection; electronic engine management.
TRANSMISSION front wheel drive; sdp clutch; 5-speed synchromesh; CD4E automatic option; final drive 4.06:1, automatic 3.77:1.

CHASSIS steel monocoque; ifs by MacPherson struts, coil; springs offset, lower A-arms, anti-roll bar; Quadralink strut-type irs with coil springs; anti roll bar; telescopic dampers, transverse and trailing arms; hydraulic servo ventilated disc brakes, front 27.8cm (10.9in), rear 25.2cm (9.9in), ABS; rack and pinion PAS; 61.5l (13.5gal) tank; 195/60VR15tyres, 5.5J rims. 205/55ZR15, 205/50ZR16 6/6, 5.7J rims.
DIMENSIONS wheelbase 270.5cm (106.5in); track front 150.5cm (59.25in), rear 148.5cm (58.5in), estate 150.5cm (59.25in) rear; length 448cm (176.4in), estate 463cm (182.3in); width 175cm (68.9in); height 143cm (56.3in), 5-door 142.5cm (56.1in), estate 144cm (56.7in); ground clearance 12cm (4.7in); turning circle 10.9m (35.8ft).

EQUIPMENT traction control, air conditioning, ABS, central locking, driver's airbag, alarm, seatbelt pretensioners, and cupholders standard, cruise control, leather trim optional.
PERFORMANCE maximum 225kph (140.2mph); 35.5kph@ 1000rpm; 0-100kph (62mph) 8.6sec, auto 10.4sec; 10.6kg/kW (7.9kg/bhp), estate 11kg/kW (8.2kg/bhp); 9.1l/100km (31mpg).
PRICE £15,970, Ghia £19,950, estate £20,995.

Design brief for the Mondeo V6 aimed at longer service intervals. The aluminium engine needed only fluid and filter changes for its first 160,000km (100,000miles).

1994
Probe 2.0, 2.5 V6

In a bold initiative to re-enter a market that it had dominated with the Capri, Ford brought in the Probe sports coupe early in 1994. It had an intricate pedigree. Engineered by Mazda, in which Ford had a quarter share, it was based on the Mazda 626 and MX-6 platform and assembled using engines and transmissions from Japan in a jointly owned factory at Flat Rock in the United States. It had already been on sale for two years and one version of its V6 engine was successful in the British Touring Car Championship (BTCC) works Mondeo. There was more than nostalgia for the Capri behind the Probe; it faced real competition from the Vauxhall Calibra. In a sense it represented a return to Ford roots as the first whole-car import from the United States since Trafford Park days. The suspension was retuned for Europe, stiffening the front struts and adding Mondeo-like Quadralink rear to provide a firmer ride than its US counterparts. *Motor Trend* was so impressed that it voted the Probe Car of the Year. It cost $13,685 and $16,015 in the US or about £9,120 and £10,700 at the contemporary exchange rate, yet even with the addition of VAT it sold in Britain close to Calibra prices. It did not reach British buyers with the three-year warranty it enjoyed in America, however.

INTRODUCTION 1994.
BODY coupe; 2-doors, 4-seats; weight 1220kg (2689.6lb), automatic 1250kg (2755.8lb), V6 1325kg (2921.1lb).
ENGINE 4-cylinders; transverse; 83mm x 92mm, 1991cc; compr 9:1; 88kW (118bhp) @ 5500rpm; 44.2kW (59.3bhp)/l; 173Nm (128lbft) @ 4500rpm. V6 6-cylinders in 60deg V; 84.5 x 74.2mm; 2497cc; compr 9.2:1; 122kW (163.6bhp) @ 5600rpm; 48.9kW (65.6bhp)/l; 217Nm (161lbft) @ 4000rpm.
ENGINE STRUCTURE 99A 2 belt-driven ohcs; 4-valves; aluminium head, iron block; Mitsubishi electronic fuel injection, electronic engine management; 5-bearing crankshaft. V6 99B 2 gear and belt-driven ohcs, aluminium heads and block; 4-bearing crank; Nippon Denso fuel injection.
TRANSMISSION front wheel drive; sdp clutch; 5-speed synchromesh; automatic optional; final drive 4:1, 3.77:1 automatic.
CHASSIS steel monocoque; ifs by struts, coil springs, anti-roll bar; irs by multi-link, coil springs, anti roll bar; telescopic dampers; hydraulic servo brakes, front 25.8cm (10.16in) ventilated discs, rear drums, or 25.8cm (10.16in) discs when fitted with Sumitomo anti-lock braking; rack and pinion PAS; 59l (12.97gal) tank; 195/65SR14, 205/55SR/HR15 or 225/50VR16 tyres, 5.5,6 or 7J rims.
DIMENSIONS wheelbase 261cm (102.8in); track front 152cm (59.8in); length 454cm (178.8in); width 177.5cm (69.9in); height 131cm (51.57in); ground clearance 16cm (6.3in); turning circle 11.2m (36.8ft).
EQUIPMENT alloy wheels, 2 airbags, electric windows and mirrors standard, leather trim sunroof in Plus Pack.
PERFORMANCE maximum speed 190kph (118.35mph), V6 215kph (133.92mph); 37.7kph (23.48mph) @ 1000rpm, V6 31.7kph (19.75mph); 0-100kph (62mph) 10.4sec, V6 7.9sec; 13.9kg/kW (10.3kg/bhp), V6 10.9kg/kW (8.1kg/bhp); fuel consumption 9.42l/100km (30mpg), V6 11.8l/100km (24mpg).
PRICE 2.0 16v £16,230, 2.5 24v £19,735.

1994
Scorpio

Scorpio received mixed reviews after the Paris Motor Show. The oval grille and ellipsoidal headlights, intended to add distinction, were met with something approaching disbelief. The centre section, the most expensive bit of a car to change, was the same as before, the hatchback abandoned and even though up-market versions were redesigned with wood and leather inside and prices followed those of Vauxhall and Rover, it was the big Ford's last hoorah. The 4-cylinder 16-valve 2.0-litre and Cologne 12-valve 2.9-litre V-6 engines were carried over, and there was a top version with the Cosworth 24-valve. The slow 12-valve V-6 was due to be dropped, but the 2.5-litre turbo-diesel survived. Large Fords seldom sold in big numbers, Britain was usually their best market; on the Continent they tended to be outshone by big Opels and never made the grade against BMW and Mercedes-Benz. The abandonment of the Granada title was imminent, and this Scorpio became the last of a line that went back 45 years to the Zephyr and Zodiac of the 1950s. "Ford is unlikely to stretch a front wheel drive Mondeo the way it did a rear-drive Sierra, when the Scorpio's replacement is due towards the end of the decade. The next big Ford could be called a Jaguar as a means at last of beating Vauxhall, Rover, and Opel." *The Sunday Times*, 31 July 1994.

In 1993 the 2.5-litre diesel supplied by Peugeot was replaced by a turbocharged unit made by the Italian VM company, raising power output from 68.6kW (92bhp) to 85.8kW (115bhp) and improving all-round performance.

INTRODUCTION January 1991.
BODY saloon; 4-doors, 5-seats; weight 1545kg (3406lb).
ENGINE 6-cylinders, 60deg V; 93mm x 72mm, 2935cc; compr 9.7:1; 152kW (203.8bhp) @ 6000rpm; 51.8kW (69.4bhp)/l; 282Nm (208lbft) @ 4200rpm.
ENGINE STRUCTURE 2 chain-driven overhead camshafts per bank; 4-valves; aluminium heads, iron block; multi-point Bosch LH-Jetronic fuel injection Ford EEC IV engine management; 4-bearing crankshaft, two 3-way catalytic converters.
TRANSMISSION rear wheel drive; A4LDE Automatic 4-speed Lock-up overDrive; final drive 3.64:1, limited slip differential.
CHASSIS steel monocoque; ifs by struts, coil springs, telescopic dampers, anti-roll bar; irs by semi-trailing arms, coil springs, anti roll bar, telescopic dampers; hydraulic servo ventilated disc brakes, front 27.8cm (10.9in), rear 27.3cm (10.75in), ABS; rack and pinion PAS; 70l (15.4gal) tank; 205/50ZR16 tyres, 6.5Jrims.
DIMENSIONS wheelbase 276cm (108.7in); track 149cm (58.7in) front, 151cm (59.5in) rear; length 474.5cm (186.8in), 5-door 467cm (183.9in); width 176.5cm (69.5in); height 141cm (55.5in); ground clearance 12cm (4.7in); turning circle 11m (36.1ft).
EQUIPMENT alloy wheels, air conditioning, electric seats and windows, mirrors and sunroof, cruise control, trip computer, CD player, choice of leather or cloth.
PERFORMANCE maximum speed 225kph (140.2mph); 41kph (25.5mph) @ 1000rpm; 0-100kph (62mph) 8.8sec; 10.2kg/kW (7.6kg/bhp); fuel con 12.8l/100km (22mpg) *Autocar*.
PRICE £26,800.

1995
Galaxy 2.0 and V6

Multi purpose vehicles (MPVs), also known quaintly as "people-movers", became one of the fastest-growing automotive sectors, sales doubling between 1990 and 1955. There were forecasts of reaching one new car in 25 within five years. Their essential features were three rows of seats and a one-box body with steeply sloping windscreen. The Renault Espace was pre-eminent. MPVs were adaptable vehicles with practical and flexible accommodation. Opportunists came in with converted forward-control vans, their engines concealed in unlikely places and a turbulent van-like ride, but they were short-lived. Ford and Volkswagen established a joint £1.6billion factory AutoEuropa in Portugal

(Setubal according to Ford, Palmela said VW) to produce one with a flat floor, hinged rather than sliding doors and seats for six that could swivel or be taken out altogether, all within the road space of a Mondeo Estate. Responsibility for the design and engineering lay with VW and production with Ford, so in theory both companies did what they were best at. Unlike Ford's joint venture with Nissan, the Galaxy and VW Sharan (and for a time the Seat Alhambra) coexisted successfully well into the 21st century. Under the codename VX62 the Galaxy used the old 16v 2.0 Scorpio engine and Volkswagen's V6 codenamed VR6. Front suspension was modelled on the Passat, with Ford-inspired MacPherson struts.

INTRODUCTION February 1995.
BODY minivan; 5-doors, 6-seats; weight 1560kg (3439.2lb), V6 1670kg (3681.7lb).
ENGINE 4-cylinders, transverse; 86mm x 86mm, 1998cc; compr 9.8:1; 85kW (114bhp) @ 5500rpm; 42.5kW (57.1bhp)/l; 167 Nm (123lbft) @ 2300rpm. V6: 15deg 81 x 90.3mm; 2792cc; compr 10:1; 128kW (171.7bhp) @ 5800rpm; 45.8kW (61.5bhp)/l; 235Nm (173lbft) @ 4200rpm.
ENGINE STRUCTURE Zetec 2 belt-driven ohc; 4 valve; aluminium head and block; fuel injection, electronic ignition; 5-bearing crank. V6: 2 valves per cyl; sohc per bank; aluminium heads, iron block.
TRANSMISSION front wheel drive; 5-speed synchromesh; 4-speed automatic option; final drive 4.53:1, automatic 4.24; V6 4.06:1 automatic 3.94.
CHASSIS steel monocoque; ifs by MacPherson struts, lower wishbones, anti-roll bar; irs, semi-trailing arms on sub-frames, coil springs, anti roll bar; telescopic dampers; hydraulic servo disc brakes, front 28.8cm (11.3in) ventilated, rear 28cm (11in), ABS; rack and pinion PAS; 75 (16.5gal) tank; 195/65 TR14 tyres, 6J rims, V6 205/60 HR15.
DIMENSIONS wheelbase 283.5cm (111.6in); track 154cm (60.6in) front, 151cm (59.5in) rear; length 461.5cm (181.7in); width 180cm (70.9in); height 172.5cm (67.9in); ground clearance 15cm (5.9in); turning circle 11.7m (38.4ft).
EQUIPMENT V6 electronic traction control standard.
PERFORMANCE maximum speed 176.6kph (110mph), V6 204kph (127.1mph); 31.9kph (19.9mph) @ 1000rpm; 0-100kph (62mph) 12.0sec, V6 10.6sec; 18.4kg/kW (13.7kg/bhp), V6 13kg/kW (9.7kg/bhp); fuel consumption approx 8.8l/100km (32mpg), V6 9.9l/100km (28.6mpg).
PRICE 2.0 Aspen £15,995; GLX V6 £20,550, Ghia V6 £23,300.

1995
Galaxy turbodiesel, 2.3, and 4x4

Galaxy's Volkswagen turbocharged diesel provided good economy and a moderate turn of speed. By the time the Ford 2.3-litre petrol engine was introduced, in March 1997, the model was already taking 30 per cent of the MPV market, its total of 15,000 outselling the VW Sharan in Britain by 8000 in 1996. The new engine, developed by Cosworth, also found a home in the Scorpio and, coming between the 2.0 and V6, soon accounted for up to half of the Galaxys sold. It almost matched the V6's performance while offering something close to the 2.0-litre's economy. The GLX 2.3 had anti-lock brakes, driver's airbag, electric windows and the Ghia added alloy wheels, roof rails and a heated windscreen. There was also a Ghia X with a CD player, fog lights, cruise control, fuel computer and air conditioning. The VW Sharan did not get the 2.3 engine but it did have an exclusive 82kW (110bhp) Audi/VW turbodiesel. The 4-wheel drive Galaxy introduced in January 1997 competed with sports utilities

and came only with the 2.8-litre V6 engine and automatic transmission. The VW Synchro system sent nearly 100 per cent of torque to the front wheels, until slippery conditions were encountered. A viscous coupling then diverted up to 75 per cent to whichever wheels could make best use of it.

INTRODUCTIONS February 1995.
BODY minivan; 5-doors, 6-seats; weight 1670kg (3681.7lb), 2.3 1565kg (3450.2lb), 4x4 1840kg (4056.5lb).
ENGINE 4-cylinders, transverse; 79.5mm x 95.5mm, 1896cc; compr 19.5:1; 66kW (88.5bhp) @ 4000rpm; 34.8kW (46.7bhp)/l; 197Nm (145lbft) @ 1940rpm. 2.3: 108.1kW (145bhp); 203 Nm (150lbft).
ENGINE STRUCTURE Single ohc, cast iron head and block; Bosch VE fuel injection with electronic engine management; turbocharger, air/air intercooler; 5-bearing crankshaft.
TRANSMISSION front wheel drive; 5-speed synchromesh; final drive 4.24:1. 2.3 4.53:1, automatic 4.24. 4x4 3.94:1.
CHASSIS steel monocoque; ifs by MacPherson struts, lower wishbones, anti-roll bar; irs, semi-trailing arms on sub-frames, coil springs, anti roll bar; telescopic dampers; hydraulic servo disc brakes, front 28.8cm (11.3in) ventilated, rear 28cm (11in), ABS; rack and pinion PAS; 75 (16.5 gal) tank; 195/65 TR14 tyres, 6J rims, V6 205/60 HR15.
DIMENSIONS wheelbase 283.5cm (111.6in); track front 154cm (60.6in), rear 151cm (59.5in); length 461.5cm (181.7in); width 180cm (70.9in); height 172.5cm (67.9in); ground clearance 15cm (5.9in); turning circle 11.7m (38.4ft).
PERFORMANCE maximum speed 257kph (160mph) Ford, 2.3 194.2kph (121mph); 40.7kph (25.4mph) @ 1000rpm TD; 0-100kph (62mph) 18sec, 2.3 10.1sec, 4x4 11.6sec; 25.3kg/kW (18.9lg/bhp) TD; fuel consumption approx 6.7l/100km (42.4mpg), 2.3 10l/100km (28mpg).
PRICE Aspen TD £16,995, Ghia TD £20,450. 2.3 GLX £20,205; Ghia £21,585, Ghia X £22,635. 4x4 Ghia £25,750, Ghia X 4x4 £26,810.

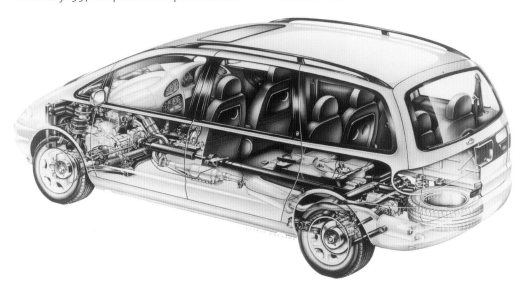

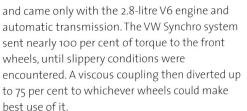

1995
Explorer

A huge success in America where it outsold all its rivals, until suffering in the Firestone tyre debacle, the Explorer was previewed with its native V8 engine in 1995. By the time it appeared at the Birmingham Motor Show in October 1996 it was re-equipped with a new sohc V6 and engineered for right hand drive. Ford was keen to remain in the market for Sports Utility Vehicles (SUVs) following the imminent demise of the Maverick. British drivers generally liked their tough nature and the Explorer exemplified the rugged, businesslike qualities from the spiritual home of the SUV, even though it would not be available with its 156.6kW (210bhp) V8 or as the up-market Mercury Mountaineer. Still, the new engine that

replaced an older 119.31kW (160bhp) V6 gave a good account of itself and was only 3.73kW (5bhp) short. Its automatic was a smooth-shifting five speeder, and the UK market did not import the short wheelbase 3-door version, which had a reputation for over-sensitive handling deemed unsuitable for Europe. Unusually for an American SUV the Explorer was not of unitary construction. It was based on the ladder frame chassis originally designed for the Ranger pick-up. Bulky and not as refined as its European rivals but enormously roomy and well equipped, the Explorer remained the world's most successful SUV with over two million sold.

INTRODUCTION US 1995, Europe December 1996
BODY Saloon; 5-doors, 5-seats; weight approx 1900kg (4188.7lb). ENGINE 6-cylinders, 60deg V; 100.3mm x 84.3mm, 4014cc; compr 9.7:1; 153kW (205.17bhp) @ 5250rpm; 38.1kW (51.2 bhp)/l; 353Nm (260lbft) @ 3000rpm.
ENGINE STRUCTURE chain-driven single ohc per bank; aluminium heads, cast iron block; Ford EEC-V electronic fuel injection; 4-bearing crankshaft.
TRANSMISSION rear wheel drive; electrically engaged four wheel drive; 5-speed automatic; final drive 3.73:1; limited slip differential.
CHASSIS Ladder frame chassis; ifs by short and long arm links, torsion bars, anti-roll bar; rear suspension live axle, leaf springs, anti roll bar; telescopic dampers; hydraulic servo disc brakes, front 28.6cm (11.3in) ventilated, rear 28.5cm (11.2in), ABS; rack and pinion PAS; 72l (15.83gal) tank; 225/705 R16 tyres 7J rims .
DIMENSIONS wheelbase 283cm (111.4in); track 149cm (58.7in); length 453cm (178.3in); width 188cm (74in); height 180cm (70.9in); ground clearance 20cm (7.9in).turning circle 12.5m (41ft).
EQUIPMENT central locking, electric mirrors, seat adjusters, sunroof, and windows, stereo, air conditioning, leather upholstery £1000; 3-year warranty
PERFORMANCE maximum speed 171kph (106.5mph); Ford; 49.1kph (30.6mph) @ 1000rpm; 0-100kph (62mph) 10.9sec; fuel consumption 15.1l/100km (18.7mpg). Autocar.
PRICE 2000 4.0 XLT £26,400 4.0 North Face £27,900.

1995
Escort 1.8i 16v

In a bold return to a 4-year model cycle, the Escort was once again rejuvenated, with a revised front, a small oval grille, a completely redesigned facia and the expenditure of a great deal of effort. The focus was on build quality and the elimination of noise vibration and harshness (NVH). The CE99 programme (subsequently CW170) was co-ordinated with an American initiative, codenamed Helios that began as a response to the

approaching Chrysler Neon, of which much was expected. With the mid-1990s emphasis on the globalisation of Ford there was once again talk of the Escort being a world car on the lines of the Toyota Corolla but, not for the first time, this proved illusory. Mechanically much the same as before, the new Escort was a quieter, more refined car that slightly cast aside the model's traditional emphasis on speed and power. Its launch followed the withdrawal in 1994 of the XR models that had been Ford sporting flagships since 1981. The RS Cosworths had stopped in 1995 and the RS2000 was due to follow in 1996. In some ways the 1995 revisions improved a car that had been rather less than perfect in 1990; the ride was enhanced, the interior was classy, safety improvements such as twin airbags were included, and the entire range from 1.3i to Ghia, 3-door, 5-door, estate, and cabriolet was truly mature.

INTRODUCTION Jan 1995, produced until 1998.

BODY saloon; 3-doors, weight 1065kg (2348lb); 5-doors, weight 1085kg (2392lb), estate 1120kg (2469.2lb), cabriolet 1175kg (2590.4lb), 4/5-seats. ENGINE 4-cylinders; transverse; 80.6mm x 88mm, 1796cc; compr 10:1; 77kW (103.3bhp) @ 5500rpm; 42.9kW (57.5bhp)/l; 156Nm (115lbft) @ 4000rpm.

ENGINE STRUCTURE 2 belt-driven ohc, 4 valves per cylinder; aluminium head, iron block; electronic fuel injection and engine management; 5-bearing crankshaft.

TRANSMISSION front rear wheel drive; 5-speed synchromesh; final drive 3.82:1.

CHASSIS steel monocoque; ifs by struts, coil springs and anti-toll bar; rear suspension torsion beam axle and coil springs; telescopic dampers; hydraulic servo brakes, front 24cm (9.5in) ventilated disc, rear 18cm (7.1in) drums, ABS optional; rack and pinion PAS; 55l (12 gal) tank; 175/65HR14 tyres, 5J rims, various options.

DIMENSIONS wheelbase 252.5cm (99.4in); track 144cm (56.7in) front, 146cm (57.5in) rear; length 413.5cm (162.8in); width 169cm (66.5in); height 139.5cm (54.9in); ground clearance 12cm (4.7in); turning circle 10m (32.8ft).

EQUIPMENT driver's airbag, passenger airbag optional, electric front windows, central locking, electric mirrors £155.

PERFORMANCE maximum speed 187kph (116.5mph) Ford; 36.5kph (22.7mph) @ 1000rpm; 0-100kph (62mph) 10.7sec; 13.8kg/kW (10.3kg/bhp) 3-doors, 14.5kg/kW (10.8kg/bhp) estate; fuel consumption 7.1l/100km (40mpg). **PRICE** £12,255.

Escort range

Engine	Max speed	0–96kph (60mph)	Weight	Trims	Body styles
1.3i 44kW (59bhp)	152.5kph (95mph)	16.4sec	1008kg (2222.2lb)	Encore	3-5-door, estate
1.4i 55.2kW (74bhp)	168.6kph (105mph)	13.5sec	1049kg (2312.6lb)	Encore L, LX	3-4-5-door, estate
1.6i 16v 66.4kW (89bhp)	176.6kph (110mph)	11.5sec	1103kg (2431.7lb)	L, LX, Ghia, Si	3-4-5-door, estate
1.8i 16v 77.6kW (104bhp)	186.2kph (116mph)	10.0sec	1083kg (2387.6lb)	LX, Ghia, Si	3-4-5-door, estate
1.8i 16v 95.5kW (128bhp)	201kph (125.2mph)	9.1sec	1165kg (2568.4lb)	Ghia	Cabriolet
2.0i 16v 110.4kW (148bhp)	208kph (129.6mph)	8.7sec	1165kg (2568.4lb)	RS2000	3-door
1.8D 44kW (59bhp)	152.5kph (95mph)	16.7sec	1100kg (2425.1lb)	Encore, L, LX	3-4-5-door, estate
1.8TD 66.4kW (89bhp)	171.8kph (107mph)	10.8sec	1139kg (2511lb)	Encore, LX, Ghia	3-4-5-door, estate

Equipment	Encore	L	LX	Ghia	Si and RS
Driver's airbag	●	●	●	●	●
Passenger airbag	○	○	○	○	○
Side-impact bars	●	●	●	●	●
Seatbelt pretensioners	●	●	●	●	●
Adjustable lumber support	–	–	●	●	–
Electric front windows	–	●	●	●	●
Electric mirrors	●	●	●	●	●
Power steering	● 1.8TD	● 1.6, 1.8	●	●	●
Central locking	–	–	●	●	●
Engine immobiliser	●	●	●	●	● not diesel
Alarm system	●	●	●	●	●
60/40 split rear seat	●	●	●	●	●
Tinted windows	●	●	●	●	●
RDS radio-cassette	–	–	●	●	●
ABS	–	–	–	–	● RS only

● standard equipment
○ optional
– not available

Prices

3-door
1.3 CFi Encore	£9,495
1.4 EFi Encore	£9,760
1.8d Encore	£9,760
1.4L EFi	£10,095
1.8 LD	£10,095
1.6i 16v	£10,630
1.8 TD Encore	£10,735
1.8 TD L	£11,070
1.4 EFi LX	£11,320
1.8D LX	£11,320
1.6i 16v LX	£11,575
1.6i 16v Si	£11,930
1.8 TD LX	£12,015
1.8 16v Si	£12,255
2.0 EFi 16v RS 2000	£16,315
2.0 EFi 16v RS 2000 4x4	£17,370
2.0 16v RS Cosworth	£23,495
2.0 16v RS Cosworth luxe	£26,925

Estates
1.3 CFi Encore	£10,670
1.6i 16v L	£11,805
1.8 TD LX	£13,190
1.8 Ghia TD	£14,060

5-door
1.3 CFi Encore	£9,915
1.4 EFi Encore	£10180
1.8d Encore	£10,180
1.8 TD Encore	£11,155
1.6i 16v Si	£12,350
1.8i 16v Si	£12,675

4-door/5-door
1.4 EFi L	£10,515
1.8 LD	£10,515
1.6i 16v L	£11,050
1.8L TD	£11,490
1.4 EFi LX	£11,740
1.8D LX	£11,740
1.6i 16v LX	£11,995
1.8i 16v LX	£12,320
1.8 TD LX	£12,435
1.6i 16v Ghia	£12,865
1.8i 16v Ghia	£13,190
1.8 Ghia TD	£13,305

Cabriolet
1.8 16v Si	£16,995

1996
Saetta

Concept Fords like Probe III of 1981 invariably had a purpose. Probe III's had been to accustom public eyes to the lines of the Sierra, due the following year. It was radical, but in the event probably failed in its task. Confidence seemed to give out during the final phases in the Sierra's run-up, but the purpose of the Seatta was to preview the Ka and there was no such faltering. A prototype was shown at the 1994 Geneva Motor Show, ostensibly to gauge reaction, but really the decision to go ahead with the Sub-B class small Ka had already been made. The Geneva car used a shortened Fiesta platform, its overall length 335cm (131.9in), and it was designed by Ford Europe under Claude Lobo. The press speculated about it having the two-stroke engine that had undergone field trials in 50 Fiestas, but there was scant chance. Concept Ka was reputed to be around 755kg (1664.5lb), or 75kg (165.3lb) lighter than a Fiesta (the production car was heavier) and according to Richard Parry-Jones, Ford of Europe's head of product development, the production Ka would have strut front suspension, and he confirmed the likelihood of a Peugeot-style torsion beam rear axle.

By the Turin Motor Show in May 1996, plans for Ka were well advanced and Ghia produced the Saetta, a roadster version of the Ka due to appear at the Paris Motor Show in the autumn. The front was pure Ka, the rear modified and retro-like, in the vogue of the VW concept Beetle and the Renault Fiftie, with a spinal bar following the line of the Ka that probably provided some of the missing roof's structural integrity. Resplendent in blue and silver, Saetta was inspirational, closely following the lines of the approaching production model. The interior was pure Ka, except for patent leather upholstery and silver console mouldings that were a pastiche of 1960s trendiness. Ghia added a tachometer to lend a sporty air, but Saetta was more of a fun roadster than a sports car.

Its real significance lay in the way it introduced so-called New Edge styling that was to play such an important role in shaping Fords of the 1990s and the 21st century. Camillo Pardo, the American who led the Saetta project at Ghia, said: "It is still edge design, but we are exploring surface development and using softer shapes and creases to get away from elliptical shapes."

Saetta created enormous interest at Turin because it represented a profound development in automotive style and above all demonstrated that Ford's hangover from less than chic Sierras and Escorts was finally over. Saetta was proof that modish style was going to be as important in future as technical prowess.

Ford was cautious about Saetta's implications, apart from its obvious relationship to Ka. As soon as the show was over, and *Autocar* had driven it cautiously on a special preview, it was crated up and flown to Detroit to be looked at carefully by senior management.

1996
Ka, Ka2

The production technology that enabled Ka to be made was an important ingredient of its style. Chris Clements, head designer, said that five years earlier Ka would not have been contemplated because body-press techniques could not guarantee its knife-edge fits and close-cut shut-lines. The shape was an ingenious mixture of fluid

curves and near-flat panels, continuous lines between the practical polypropylene mouldings below the waistline, and the sheet steel upper portions providing exquisite balance. The proportions were exemplary, the wide-tracked, wheel-at-each-corner stance a masterpiece, the work of Chris Svensson, a former Royal College of Art student. Production Ka was crisper than the roly-poly prototype shown at Geneva in 1994 and it had the further virtue of cutting 25% off a Fiesta's build time. Ka was as wide as a Fiesta, yet slightly taller, with more head room and shoulder room. There were two equipment levels, Ka and Ka2 and only one engine option, the old pushrod Endura-E that was light and cheap to make. The interior was just as radical as the outside; the facia had sweeping curves and although in reality quite basic, looked stylish and well-resourced. Cars with power steering had 2.9 turns lock to lock instead of 4.2, different castor angles, fatter tyres and shorter gearing satisfying PAS buyers who wanted different driving qualities.

INTRODUCTION 1996. BODY saloon; 3-doors, 4-seats; weight 870kg (1918lb).
ENGINE 4-cylinders; transverse; 75mm x 75.5mm, 1299cc; compr 8.8:1; 44kW (59bhp) @ 5000rpm; 33.9kW (45.4bhp)/l; 103Nm (76lbft) @ 2500rpm.
ENGINE STRUCTURE pushrod ohv; chain-driven camshaft, cast iron cylinder head and block; Ford EEC-V electronic sequential fuel injection and engine management; 5-bearing crankshaft.
TRANSMISSION front wheel drive; 5-speed synchromesh; final drive 4.06:1.
CHASSIS steel monocoque; ifs by MacPherson strut, offset coil springs, lower A-arms, anti-roll bar; rear suspension semi-independent twist beam with coil spring damper units; hydraulic servo brakes, front 24cm (9.5in) disc, rear drums, ABS optional; rack and pinion, optional PAS; 42l (9.2 gal) tank; 165/65R13 tyres, 5J rims.
DIMENSIONS wheelbase 245cm (96.5in); track 139.5cm (54.9in) front, 141cm (55.5in) rear; length 362cm (142.5in); width 164cm (64.6in); height 140cm (55.1in); ground clearance 14cm (5.5in); turning circle 10.3m (33.8ft).
EQUIPMENT Ka rear wash-wipe, driver's airbag, radio/cassette player standard, passenger airbag, air conditioning and alloy wheels option; Ka2 PAS electric windows standard.
PERFORMANCE maximum speed 155kph (96.6mph); 32.4kph (20.2mph) @ 1000rpm; 0-100kph (62mph) 15.4sec; 19.8kg/kW (14.7kg/bhp); 6.7l/100km (42.2mpg).
PRICE £7350; Ka2 £8195.

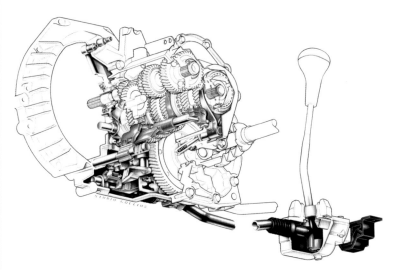

1996
Fiesta Classic

Old habits died hard at Ford, and just as the Populars of the 1950s and 1960s were born-again versions of superseded models, so in the 1990s the Fiesta of the 1980s carried on the tradition. It was not called Popular. A new name had to be coined, implying continuity and good taste, rather than bargain basement, so it was called Classic, and was furnished with 1.1, 1.3, and diesel engines. Different trim versions were distinguished as Quartz and Cabaret 3- and 5-door; prices were the same and power steering was an option (at £430) only on the front-end-heavy diesels. The 1.3 was a 152.5kph (95mph) car and reached 100kph (62mph) in 14.2sec. The more economical diesel,

with much the same power to weight ratio, was only a shade slower at 150.9kph (94mph) and 15.4sec. Launched originally as the front-rank Fiesta in 1976, a lighter car, the design of the all-iron pushrod crossflow 2-valve engine, now designated appropriately Endura-E, went back to the 1967 Cortina Mark II. Despite much modification over the years it was past its best and although it had acquired fuel injection, necessary for stringent emission requirements of the 1990s, it had not much more power. In 1976 the 74mm x 55.7mm 957cc had given 33.6kW (45bhp) @ 6000rpm, and the 74 x 65mm 1117cc 39.5kW (53bhp) @ 6000rpm.

INTRODUCTION 1976 as Fiesta II and 1989 as Fiesta III.
BODY saloon; 3 or 5-doors, 4-seats; weight 825kg (1818.8lb), diesel 875kg (1929lb).
ENGINE 4-cylinders; transverse; 1.1, 68.7 x 75.5; 1119cc; compr 8.8:1; 37kW (49.6bhp) @ 5200rpm; 33.1kW (44.3bhp)/l; 83Nm (61lbft) @ 3000rpm. 1.3: 74mm x 75.5mm, 1299cc; cr 8.8:1; 44kw (59bhp) @ 5000rpm; 33.9kW (45.4bhp)/l; 103Nm (76lbft) @ 2500rpm. Diesel 82.5 x 82mm; 1753cc; compr 21.5:1; 44kW (59bhp) @ 4800rpm; 25.1kW (33.7bhp)/l; 110Nm (81lbft) @ 2500rpm.
ENGINE STRUCTURE pushrod ohv, chain-driven camshaft; cast iron head and block; electronic single point fuel injection; 5-bearing crankshaft.
TRANSMISSION front wheel drive; sdp clutch; 5-speed synchromesh; final drive 4.06:1, diesel 3.59:1.
CHASSIS steel monocoque; ifs by MacPherson struts, coil springs, anti-roll bar; rear suspension torsion beam axle; telescopic dampers; hydraulic, vacuum servo 24cm (9.5in) front disc brakes; rear drums 19.1cm (7.5in); rack and pinion steering; 42l (9.2 gal) tank; 145R-13, 155/70R-13 or 165R-13 tyres, 4.5 or 5J rims.
DIMENSIONS wheelbase 244.5cm (96.3in); track 139cm (54.7in) front, 138.5cm (54.5in) rear; length 374.5cm (147.4in); width 160cm (63in); height 138cm (54.3in); ground clearance 14cm (5.5in); turning circle 10.3m (33.8ft).
PERFORMANCE maximum speed 153kph (95.3mph), 143kph (89.1mph) 1.1, 152kph (94.7mph) diesel); 33.5kph (20.9mph) @ 1000rpm; 0-100kph (62mph) 14.7sec, 18.1sec 1.1, 16sec diesel; 22.3kg/kW (16.6kg/bhp), 19.9kg/kW (14.8kg/bhp) diesel; fuel consumption 8.7-7.4l/100km (33-38mpg), diesel 5.3l/100km (53.3mpg).
PRICE 1997 1.1 £7615-£8015; 1.1 Quartz £8015-8445; 1.3 Cabaret £8415-£8845; 1.8D £8040-£8470; 1.8D Quartz £8440-£8870.

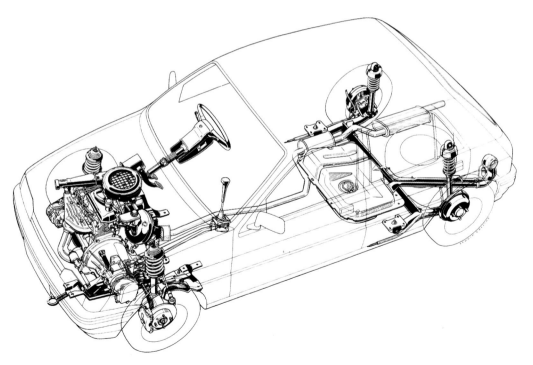

1996
Fiesta 1.25, 1.4, 1.6

BE91 was the codename for a complete reskin of the Fiesta round the 16-valve Zetec-SE engine. The platform was much the same as before, but the body was extensively altered. It failed to gain the Ka's bold New Edge appearance, but with the corporate oval grille looked sufficiently different to make sure customers knew they were buying the latest model. Constant changes in appearance remained a cornerstone of marketing. The Zetec-SE was smoother and quieter than previous Fords and the dohc 16-valve engine represented more than merely a redesign of the combustion process. It was wholly aluminium instead of iron and aluminium, cast-in ribs maintaining the structural stiffness necessary for banishing vibrations. The previous Zetec's hydraulic tappets were discontinued, the new engine reverted to plain mechanical means of operating the valves, yet it marked notable progress towards being almost maintenance free. Oil changes were scheduled for 10,000 miles, new spark plugs at 30,000 miles, and routine valve clearance checks at 100,000 miles. At just 89kg (196.2lb) it weighed less than half its predecessor's 122kg (269lb), not only through the extensive use of aluminium, but also from making components such as the complex inlet valve tracts of plastic, and the cam cover from magnesium alloy. Weight reduction was key to providing a lively performance, improving fuel consumption, and keeping production costs down.

INTRODUCTION January 1996.
BODY saloon; 3/5-doors, 4-seats; weight 940kg (2072.3lb).
ENGINE 4-cylinders; transverse; 71.9mm x 76.5mm, 1242cc; compr 10:1; 55kW (73.8bhp) @ 5200rpm; 44.3kW (59.4bhp)/l; 110Nm (81lbft) @ 4000rpm. 1.4: 76 x 76.5mm, 1388cc; 66kW (88.5bhp) @ 5500rpm; 47.6kW (63.8bhp)/l; 122Nm (90lbft) @ 4000rpm.
ENGINE STRUCTURE 2 belt-driven ohc; 4 valve; aluminium head and block; EEC-V multi-point sequential fuel injection, distributorless electronic ignition; 5-bearing crankshaft.
TRANSMISSION front wheel drive; 5-speed synchromesh; final drive 4.27:1. 1.4, 3.84:1.
CHASSIS steel monocoque; ifs by MacPherson struts, coil springs, anti-roll bar; rear suspension torsion beam axle; telescopic dampers; hydraulic, vacuum servo 24cm (9.45in) front ventilated disc brakes; rear drums 19.1cm (7.5in); rack and pinion PAS; 42l (9.2 gal); 145R-13, 155/70R-13 or 165R-13 tyres, 4.5 or 5J rims.
DIMENSIONS wheelbase 244.5cm (96.3in); track 143cm (56.3in) front, 137.5cm (54.1in) rear; length 383cm (150.8in); width 163cm (64.2in); height 141cm (55.5in); ground clearance 14cm (5.5in); turning circle 10.3m (33.8ft).
EQUIPMENT ABS optional; driver's side airbag, Ford stereo, PAS, electric sunroof standard.
PERFORMANCE maximum speed 170kph (105.9mph), 1.4 171.8kph (107mph); 30.9kph (19.3mph) @ 1000rpm; 0-100kph (62mph) 12.7sec, 1.4 10.7sec; 17.1kg/kW (12.7kg/bhp); fuel con 6l/100km (47.08mpg), 1.4 6.2l/100km (45.6mpg).
PRICE 1.25 Cfi 3-door Encore £9965, 5-door Si £10335, Ghia £10630. 1.4Si £10,750, option packs £395 and £225, air conditioning £470. 1.6i Encore CTX £11,700; 1.6i L CTX £12,135.

1996
Fiesta 1.8 diesel

The new Fiesta handled and held the road better. The platform was reinforced to improve refinement, stretched to include a crushable area at the front and the gearbox casing was webbed and ribbed to reduce noise. Success in the roadworthiness of both Fiesta and Mondeo had been the responsibility of Richard Parry-Jones, the engineer now accountable for all Ford's European small and medium cars. Together with consultant Sir Jackie Stewart he wrought a substantial improvement in the behaviour of the whole Ford range. Ironically it was achieved when Ford's involvement in international motor racing was reduced, even though it kept a low level presence in the world rally championship. Attention was concentrated instead on more practical, seemingly mundane matters, such as the flourishing diesel market. This had been a neglected field because, owing to its dependence on volume production Ford had yet to be wholly convinced the diesel market was going to be sustained. Diesels had never caught on in America and Detroit was suspicious, but fuel prices and fiscal policies in Europe would soon see to it that compression ignition was here to stay. The Fiesta diesel was a development of the overhead cam 1.8-litre from the old CVH range, now known as Endura-D, although it was not yet turbocharged to give it a performance on par with its petrol counterparts.

INTRODUCTION January 1996.
BODY saloon; 3/5-doors, 4-seats; weight 1020kg (2248.7lb).
ENGINE 4-cylinders; transverse; 82.5mm x 82mm, 1753cc; compr 21.5:1; 44kW (59bhp) @ 4800rpm; 25.1kW (33.7bhp)/l; 105Nm (77lbft) @ 2500rpm.
ENGINE STRUCTURE single gear and toothed belt driven ohc; 2 valve; iron head and block; fuel injection.
TRANSMISSION front wheel drive; 5-speed synchromesh; final drive 3.84:1.
CHASSIS steel monocoque; ifs by MacPherson struts, coil springs, anti-roll bar; rear suspension torsion beam axle; telescopic dampers; hydraulic, vacuum servo 24cm (9.5in) front ventilated disc brakes; rear drums 19.1cm (7.5in); rack and pinion PAS; 42l (9.2 gal) tank; 145R-13, 155/70R-13 or 165R-13 tyres, 4.5 or 5J rims.
DIMENSIONS wheelbase 244.5cm (96.3in); track 143cm (56.3in) front, 137.5cm (54.1in) rear; length 383cm (150.8in); width 163cm (64.2in); height 141cm (55.5in); ground clearance 14cm (5.5in); turning circle 10.3m (33.8ft).
EQUIPMENT ABS optional; standard driver's airbag, Ford stereo, electric sunroof.
PERFORMANCE maximum speed 155kph (96.6mph); 34.3kph (21.4mph) @ 1000rpm; 0-100kph (62mph) 17.4sec; 23.2kg/kW (17.3kg/bhp); fuel consumption 5.8l/100km (48.7mpg). PRICE 1.8D Encore £9195; Ghia £11,560.

1996
Mondeo

Three and a half years into Mondeo's term revisions were carefully calculated. A tidier, crisper air intake echoing the shape of the blue oval, wrap-around rear lights, detail changes to the facia and switchgear, new upholstery materials and 4cm (1.6in) more knee-room in the back were among the visible changes. There was a new sporty V6, the ST-24, and an economy 1.6-litre Zetec; the gearshift was now cable-operated and more precise, and a weight-saving programme checked the customary trend for cars to put on unwanted kgs throughout their model cycles. In the interests of performance and economy the Mondeo lost 16-18kg (35.3-39.7lb). A gain in

economy of 16 per cent was expected from taller gearing on the 1.6; 3.84:1 like the 1.8 provided four-gears-plus-overdrive fifth. Safety was given a makeover with modifications aimed at improving crashworthiness; the airbags were brought up to date, side airbags were offered as an option, seat belts given pre-tensioners, and a 3-point belt was introduced in the middle of the back seat. A brake light was positioned high in the tail and on GLX models 4-channel anti-lock brakes were standard. The ST-24 had a 2.5-litre 125.3kW (168bhp) V6, traction control, and specially sporty suspension ensuring the model's continuing sales success and critical acclaim.

SPECIFICATION 2.0 16V.
INTRODUCTION September 1996.
BODY saloon; 4-doors, 5-seats; weight 1240kg (2733.7lb), 5-door estate 1300kg (2866lb).
ENGINE 4-cylinders; transverse 84.8mm x 88mm, 1988cc; compr 10:1; 96kW (128.7bhp) @ 5700rpm; 48.3kW (64.8bhp)/l; 176Nm (130lbft) @ 3700rpm.
ENGINE STRUCTURE 2 belt-driven ohc; 4 valve; aluminium cyl head, iron block; sequential fuel inj; electronic engine management; 5-bearing crankshaft.
TRANSMISSION front wheel drive; 5-speed synchromesh; automatic option; final drive 3.84:1; automatic 3.92:1; traction control option.
CHASSIS steel monocoque; ifs by MacPherson struts, coil springs, anti-roll bar; irs, multi-link coil springs, anti roll bar; telescopic dampers; hydraulic servo disc brakes, front 27.8cm (10.9in) ventilated, rear 25.2cm (10in), ABS; rack and pinion PAS; 61.5l (13.5 gal) tank; 185/65HR14, 195/60HR15, 205/55HR15 tyres, 5.5, 6J rims.
DIMENSIONS wheelbase 270.5cm (106.5in); track front 150.5cm (59.25in), rear 148.5cm (58.5in); length 456cm (179.5in); width 175cm (68.9in); height 148cm (58.3in); ground clearance 12cm (4.7in); turning circle 10.9m (35.8ft).
EQUIPMENT automatic £495, metallic paint £230, passenger airbag £325, air conditioning £470.
PERFORMANCE maximum speed 200.7kph (125mph) *Autocar*; 32kph (19.9mph) @ 1000rpm; 0-100kph (62mph) 9.8sec; 12.9kg/kW (9.6kg/bhp), estate 13.5kg/kW (10.1kg/bhp); fuel consumption 10.5l/100km (26.8mpg).
PRICE 1.6 Aspen £12,395; 2.0LX £13,500; 2.0 Ghia £15,995; 2.5 24v V6 Ghia X £20,850; 2.0Si estate £15,950.

1996
Scorpio 2.3 16v

Revisions to the Scorpio took place over two years. In 1994 the Ultima was introduced with the 24-valve Cosworth V6 and the old Cologne V6 phased out. This left a gap in the engine range between the economy 2.0 16-valve and the powerful Cosworth, with £10,000 between them. Accordingly in 1996 the 2.0 was dropped and a new 2.3 introduced with more power than the old V6, 111kW (149bhp) against 108kW (145bhp), but short of two cylinders. Accounting for something like half of Scorpio sales, its executive-class drivers had to be persuaded that it was as smooth running as a six, so the redoubtable Dr Frederick Lanchester (1868-1946) was called upon for a solution. His contra-rotating balancer shafts, with equal and opposite unbalanced weights to cancel out-of-balance engine tremors, were invoked to secure a noise reduction of 6dB and minimise vibration. Despite the complications, the engine was actually 3.4kg (7.5lb) lighter than the old 2.0-litre and although it demanded over 3,000rpm to get the best out of it, served the Scorpio well in its declining years. Gearing was raised over the 2.0, making the 2.3 a relaxed motorway car, which the optional 4-speed automatic transmission with electronic control of shifting complemented in both its Sport and Economy modes. Ride and handling were improved with Mondeo-style revisions to the front suspension.

INTRODUCTION August 1996.
BODY saloon; 4-doors, 5-seats; weight 1440kg (3174.6lb), estate 1495kg (3295.9lb).
ENGINE 4-cylinders; 89.6mm x 91mm, 2295cc; compr 10:1; 108kW (144.8bhp) @ 5600rpm; 47.1kW (63.1bhp)/l; 202Nm (149lbft) @ 4500rpm.
ENGINE STRUCTURE 2 belt-driven ohc, 4-valve; aluminium head, iron block; EEC-V electronic fuel injection and engine management; 5-bearing crankshaft; two balancer shafts running x 2 engine speed.
TRANSMISSION rear wheel drive; 5-speed synchromesh; 4-speed automatic option; final drive 3.91:1.
CHASSIS steel monocoque; ifs struts and lower wishbones, coil springs, anti-roll bar; irs semi-trailing arms, coil springs, anti roll bar; telescopic dampers; hydraulic servo disc brakes, front 25cm (9.8in) ventilated, rear 25.3cm (10in), ABS; rack and pinion PAS; 70l (15.4 gal) tank; 195/65HR15, 205/60VR15, 215/60VR15 tyres 6J, 6.5J rims.
DIMENSIONS wheelbase 277cm (109in); track 148cm (58.3in) front, 149.5cm (58.9in) rear; length 482.5cm (190in); width 176cm (69.3in); height 140cm (55.1in); ground clearance 12cm (4.7in); turning circle 10.4m (34.1ft).
EQUIPMENT Ghia; alloy wheels, stereo, all electric windows, central locking, electric mirrors, alarm.
PERFORMANCE maximum speed 195.9kph (122mph) *Autocar*; 36kph (22.4mph) @ 1000rpm; 0-100kph (62mph) 10.3sec; 13.3kW (9.9kg/bhp), estate 13.8kg/kW (10.3kg/bhp); fuel consumption 10.5l/100km (26.9mpg).
PRICE £18,370.

1997
Puma 1.7

INTRODUCTION Feb 1997, production to November 2001.
BODY coupe; 2-doors, 2+2-seats; weight 1039kg (2290.6lb). ENGINE 4-cylinders; transverse; 80mm x 83.5mm, 1679cc; compr 10.3:1; 92kW (123.4bhp) @ 6300rpm; 54.8kW (73.5bhp)/l; 157Nm (116lbft) @ 4500rpm.
ENGINE STRUCTURE Zetec-SE twin belt-driven ohc, 4-valve; variable camshaft timing; aluminium head, and block; Ford EEC-V multipoint fuel injection, electronic ignition; 5-bearing crankshaft.
TRANSMISSION front wheel drive; 5-speed synchromesh; final drive 3.82:1.
CHASSIS steel monocoque; ifs by MacPherson strut, offset coil springs, lower A-arms, anti-roll bar; rear suspension semi-independent twist beam with coil spring damper units; hydraulic servo brakes, front 24cm (9.5in) disc, rear drums, ABS; rack and pinion variable PAS; 42l (9.2gal) tank; 195/50R15 tyres, 6J rims.
DIMENSIONS wheelbase 245cm (96.5in); track 145cm (57.1in) front, 141cm (55.5in) rear; length 398.5cm (156.9in); width 167.5cm (65.9in); height 134cm (52.8in); ground clearance 14cm (5.5in); turning circle 10.4m (34.1ft).
EQUIPMENT alloy wheels, metallic paint £240, passenger airbag £300, air conditioning £350.
PERFORMANCE maximum 197.5kph (123mph) Autocar; 31.4kph (19.6mph) @ 1000rpm; 0-100kph (62mph) 8.6sec; 11.3kg/kW (8.4kg/bhp); fuel consumption 7.4l/100km (38.2mpg).
PRICE £14,550.
PRODUCTION 45,000 UK sales.

With the RS and XR models gone, new ways were found of making Fords glamorous. It remained important to get the most out of each platform and SE161 was a coupe based, like the Ka, on the much-improved Fiesta and introduced at the 1997 Geneva Motor Show. The Lynx concept at 1996 Geneva, like the Saetta, had curved roof hoops of carbon fibre but extended, rather than foreshortened, the Fiesta framework by 25cm (9.8in) to 408cm (160.6in), 4cm (1.6in) longer than an Escort. The production Puma retained the Fiesta wheelbase and introduced Ka-type New Edge styling, rounded off to Ian Callum's design in tune with the sporty theme. Instead of the Ka's modest pushrods, it had the Yamaha-inspired 16-valve Zetec-SE with Variable Camshaft Timing (VCT), shifting the inlet valves' phasing though not their lift or dwell, according to engine speed and load. A unique feature of VCT was continuous electronic operation rather than prompting by anything mechanical. A stiffer body shell than Fiesta, 1mm extra on the front anti-roll bar, five per cent up on spring rates, and 30 per cent on the rear suspension's twist beam made Puma a real driver's car. The 2000-strong limited edition Racing Puma had 114.1kW (153bhp) and extended aluminium wheel arches, for £22,750, and last of all the £13,995 Puma Thunder came in Magnum Grey, or Moondust with black leather trim.

1998
Puma 1.4i, 1999 Puma Racing ST160

In the summer of 1998 a 1.4-litre Puma was presented as an alternative to the 1.7. It cost some £1500 less, was 28kg (61.7lb) lighter, and took 2sec longer to reach 100mph (62mph). It was 19.3kph (12mph) slower but had a fuel consumption advantage of some 15 per cent. The Zetec-SE engine, from the 1.4 Fiesta, was smoother running than the 1.7, the difference in performance quite small and the car ran on the same 15in alloy wheels and 195/50 tyres as the 1.7, so the handling was every bit as good. There was less likelihood of wheelspin in the wet, or on loose surfaces, but as a stylish two-plus-two coupe it suffered from the same cramped rear seats and unevenly shaped

boot. In 1999, encouraged by a 223.7kW (300bhp) concept Puma with stretched wheelbase and four wheel drive (it was an Escort Cosworth with longitudinal engine and steroid Puma bodywork) another concept car, the ST160, was exhibited at the Geneva Motor Show. This was developed by the Ford Racing Division at Boreham, based more on the production car, with 119.3kW (160bhp), front wheel drive, and limited slip differential. Brakes were bigger, with Alcon racing calipers, it did 225kph (140mph) and in the autumn the go-ahead was given for up to 1000 to be built for racing by Tickford at Daventry, Northamptonshire. It was priced at £23,000.

INTRODUCTION June 1998, production to November 2001.
BODY coupe; 2-doors; 2+2-seats; weight 1035kg (2281.8lb).
ENGINE 4-cylinders; transverse; 76mm x 76.5mm, 1388cc; compr 10.3:1; 66kW (88.5bhp) @ 5500rpm; 47.6kW (63.8bhp)/l; 123Nm (91lbft) @ 4000rpm.
ENGINE STRUCTURE Zetec-SE twin belt-driven ohc, 4-valve; aluminium head, and block; Ford EEC-V multipoint fuel injection, electronic ignition; 5-bearing crankshaft.
TRANSMISSION front wheel drive; 5-speed synchromesh; final drive 4.19, 4.25:1.
CHASSIS steel monocoque; ifs by MacPherson strut, offset coil springs, lower A-arms, anti-roll bar; rear suspension semi-independent twist beam with coil spring damper units; hydraulic servo brakes, front 24cm (9.5in) disc, rear drums, ABS optional; rack and pinion variable PAS; 42l (9.2gal) tank; 195/50R15 tyres, 6J rims.
DIMENSIONS wheelbase 245cm (96.5in); track 145cm (57.1in) front, 141cm (55.5in) rear; length 398.5cm (156.9in); width 167.5cm (65.9in); height 134cm (52.8in); ground clearance 14cm (5.5in); turning circle 10.4m (34.1ft).
EQUIPMENT alloy wheels, metallic paint £240, passenger airbag £300, air conditioning £350, ABS £390.
PERFORMANCE maximum 178.2kph (111mph) Autocar; 31.6kph (19.7mph) @ 1000rpm; 0-100kph (62mph) 10.6sec; 15.7kg/kW (11.7kg/bhp); fuel consumption 7.1l/100km (39.9mpg).
PRICE £13,200.
PRODUCTION 45,000 UK sales.

1998
Cougar V6, ST200

Announced at the Detroit Motor Show at the turn of the year, the Cougar was based on a Mondeo platform clad in a sleek coupe body with plenty of space for the two occupants in the front, but not much headroom for the plus two in the back. A replacement for the Probe, or a successor to the Capri, as Ford preferred, it was an American-inspired project developed in Europe. The Probe was a critical success but perhaps remained too transatlantic. The suspension was ST24 with firmer springs, dampers and anti-roll bars, yet even with a body shell 20 per cent stiffer than a Mondeo the handling was touring rather than sporting. Luggage space was enormous and could

be doubled by folding the split rear backrests flat. The modified 2.0-litre Zetec engine came from Bridgend, the V6 Duratec was American. A 234.9kW (315bhp) V6 with a Jaguar 4x4 powertrain was floated as an idea at the 1999 Los Angeles Motor Show but, renamed ST200 at the Frankfurt Motor Show in September, it remained front wheel drive only with the MTX-5 manual gearbox. Using the same ST200 engine as Mondeo, a Duratec V6 with dual-inlet air cleaner, revised camshafts, and free-flowing exhaust, it also had thicker anti-roll bars. Had it reached production it would have been one of the fastest-ever Fords sold in the UK.

INTRODUCTION January 1998, production to 2001.
BODY coupe; 3-doors, 2+2-seats; weight 1315kg (2900lb), V6 1390kg (3064.4lb).
ENGINE 4-cylinders, in-line; 84.8mm x 88mm, 1988cc; compr 10:1; 96kW (128.7bhp) @ 5600rpm; 48.3kW (64.7bhp)/l; 178Nm (131lbft) @ 4000rpm. V6: 82.4x79.5mm; 2544cc; 9.7:1; 125kW (167.6bhp); 49.1kW (65.9bhp)/l; 220Nm (162lbft).
ENGINE STRUCTURE Zetec-E; 2 belt-driven ohc; 4-valves; aluminium head and block; fuel injection and EEC-V electronic engine management; 5-bearing crankshaft. Duratec V6, 2 chain-driven ohc per block, 4-valves; 4-bearing.
TRANSMISSION front wheel drive; 5-speed synchromesh; automatic option; final drive 3.82:1, automatic 3.92. V6 3.82/3.77.
CHASSIS steel monocoque; ifs MacPherson struts, anti-roll bar; Quadralink irs; coil springs, anti roll bar; telescopic dampers; hydraulic servo disc brakes, front 26cm (10.3in) ventilated rear 25.2cm (9.9in) (V6 all ventilated), ABS; rack and pinion PAS; 60l (13.2 gal) tank; 205/60R15, 215/50R16 tyres, 6, 6.5Jrims.
DIMENSIONS wheelbase 270.5cm (106.5in); track front 150.5cm (59.25in); rear 149cm (58.7in); length 470cm (185in); width 177cm (69.7in); height 132cm (52in); turning circle 11m (36.1ft).
EQUIPMENT airbags, alloy wheels, ABS, A/C, electric mirrors and windows, leather, CD player extra.
PERFORMANCE maximum speed 209kph (130.2mph), V6 225kph (140.2mph); 35.3kph (22mph) @ 1000rpm; 0-100kph (62mph) 9.6sec, V6 8.1sec; 13.7kg/kW (10.2kg/bhp); fuel consumption 8.3l/100km (34mpg).
PRICE £19,845, V6 £20,845, X-pack automatic £22,820.

1998
Focus 1.4, 1.6, 1.8

Replacing the Escort after 30 years and 20m cars, the Focus was first shown at the Geneva Motor Show in March, and went on sale in the autumn of 1998. More sophisticated than its predecessor, and although only 1.1cm (.43in) longer and 1cm (.39in) wider, it was 8cm (3.15in) taller, so the occupants sat more upright within a wheelbase 7cm (2.76in) longer. The result was a substantial improvement in legroom and headroom and almost as much space inside as a Mondeo. The emphasis was less on speed than comfort, safety, and style. Refinement was improved by making the body 35 per cent stiffer, and reinforcing suspension attachment points to reduce their potential for generating resonance. The redesign of the front suspension offset the coil springs of the MacPherson struts in order to reduce "stiction," so long a bugbear of the system. The rear suspension was entirely new, a double wishbone arrangement with coil springs that was just as effective as, and a good deal cheaper than, a complex multi-link system. The Focus was 30kg-50kg (66lb-110.2lb) lighter than the Escort, which together with better aerodynamics made it, according to Ford, 25 per cent more fuel-efficient. Power trains for the petrol-engined cars were the familiar 1.4 Zetec-SE from the Fiesta, a new 1.6 version of the same engine, and a 1.8 and 2.0 as used in the Mondeo.

INTRODUCTION autumn 1998.
BODY saloon; 3, 4 or 5-doors, estate car 5-doors; 5-seats; weight 1070kg (2358.9lb), 1.8 1125kg (2480.2lb).
ENGINE 4-cylinders; transverse; 76mm x 76.5mm, 1388cc; compr 11:1; 55kW (73.8bhp) @ 5000rpm; 39.6kW (53.1bhp)/l; 123Nm (91lbft) @ 3750rpm. 1.6: 76 x 81.4mm; 1596cc; 11:1; 74kW (99.2bhp); 46.4kW (62.2bhp)/l; 145Nm (107lbft). 1.8: 80.6 x 88mm; 1796cc; 10:1; 85kW (114bhp); 47.3kW (63.5bhp)/l; 158Nm (117lbft).
ENGINE STRUCTURE Zetec-SE or Zetec-E; 2 belt-driven ohc; 4-valves; aluminium head and block; fuel injection and electronic engine management; 5-bearing crankshaft.
TRANSMISSION front wheel drive; 5-speed synchromesh; final drive 4.06:1. 1.6 3.82; 1.8 4.06.
CHASSIS steel monocoque with sub-frames; ifs by MacPherson struts, angled coil spring damper units, and lower wishbones, anti-roll bar; irs by control blade multi-links, anti roll bar; telescopic dampers; hydraulic servo brakes, front 25.8cm (10.2in) ventilated discs; rear drums (1.6, 1.8 discs), dual circuit, ABS optional; rack and pinion PAS; 55l (12.1gal) tank; 175/70R14, 185/65R14, 195/55R15 tyres 5.5, 6J rims.
DIMENSIONS wheelbase 261.5cm (103in); track front 149.5cm (58.9in), rear 148.5cm (58.5in); length 415cm (163.4in); width 170cm (66.9in); height 143cm (56.3in); turning circle 10.9m (35.8ft).
EQUIPMENT various option packs Climate, reflex, Styling, Luxury; CX, Zetec, LX and Ghia, CD upgrade, metallic paint.
PERFORMANCE maximum speed 171kph (106.5mph), 1.6 185kph (115.2mph), 1.8 198kph (123.3mph); 36.8kph (22.92mph) @ 1000rpm; 0-100kph (62mph) 14.1sec, 1.6 10.9sec, 1.8 10.2sec;19.5kg/kW (14.5kg/bhp), 1.8 13.2kg/kW (9.9kg/bhp); fuel consumption 6.4l/100km (44.1mpg).
PRICE 1.4CL 5-door £12,850; 1.6 Zetec £13,350; 1.8 Ghia £14,350.

1998
Focus 2.0

INTRODUCTION autumn 1998.
BODY saloon; 3, 4 or 5-doors, estate car 5-doors, 5-seats; weight 1145kg (2524.3lb).
ENGINE 4-cylinders; transverse; 84.8mm x 88mm, 1988cc; compr 10:1; 96kW (128.7bhp) @ 5750rpm; 48.3kW (64.8bhp)/l; 174Nm (128lbft) @ 3750rpm.
ENGINE STRUCTURE Zetec-E; 2 belt-driven ohc; 4-valves; aluminium head and block; fuel injection and EEC-V electronic engine management; 5-bearing crankshaft.
TRANSMISSION front wheel drive; 5-speed synchromesh; final drive 4.06:1.
CHASSIS steel monocoque with sub-frames; ifs by MacPherson struts, angled coil spring damper units, and lower wishbones, anti-roll bar; irs by control blade multi-links, anti roll bar; telescopic dampers; hydraulic servo disc brakes, front 25.8cm (10.16in) ventilated; rear 25.3cm (9.96in), dual circuit, ABS optional; rack and pinion PAS; 55l (12.1gal) tank; 175/70R14, 185/65R14, 195/55R15 tyres 5.5, 6J rims.
DIMENSIONS 4-door wheelbase 261.5cm (103in); track front 149.5cm (58.9in), rear 148.5cm (58.5in); length 436.2cm (171.7in); width 170cm (66.9in); height 143cm (56.3in); turning circle 10.9m (35.78ft).
EQUIPMENT various option packs Climate, reflex, Styling, Luxury; CX, Zetec, LX and Ghia, CD upgrade, metallic paint.
PERFORMANCE maximum speed 201kph (125.2mph); 36.1kph (22.5mph) @ 1000rpm; 0-100kph (62mph) 9.2sec; 11.9kg/kW (8.9kg/bhp); fuel consumption 8.9l/100km (31.7mpg).
PRICE 2.0 Ghia 5-door £15,350, estate £15,850.

The Focus name had been used in 1992 for a concept roadster based on the Escort Cosworth, a voluptuous design shown at the Turin Motor Show as an experiment in exotic materials such as Kevlar and carbon fibre. A 3-piece fold away roof was tried but its market niche would have been small and nothing more was heard of it until it was sold at Christie's 2002 auction in Detroit for $1million. Production of Focus was in Saarlouis and Valencia, capable of 450,000 a year, the rate at which Escort had been made and a notchback saloon and estate car joined the model line-up. The 2.0-litre engine from the Mondeo was stiffened to reduce vibration so that it revved cheerfully to 6900rpm before invoking the rev-limiter. Mondeos had been criticised for harshness at such speeds but although power output was quite modest, its willingness to rev and low gearing gave it a lively turn of speed. Anti-roll bars were increased from 20mm (.79in) to 21mm (.83in) and the wheel arches were flared to accommodate wider tyres, a modification that seemed to suit the Focus well. Interiors followed the Ka's curvaceous style and the 2.0 was given a mock titanium finish to match the modernist character. Accolades came thick and fast. An international panel of artists, designers, and architects elected it the world's most beautiful car, and automotive journalists voted it Car of the Year 1999.

1998
Focus turbodiesel

Diesel technology advanced a step with development of the ohc 2-valve 44kW (59bhp) engine from the 1996 Fiesta. Direct injection into the combustion chambers rather than the inlet tract, together with precise electronic metering, turbocharger and intercooler, added 23kW (30.8bhp) for the Focus. Emissions were reduced and direct injection also raised the torque over earlier versions by 11 per cent, so it pulled strongly between 1500 and 3600rpm, until the fuel cutoff point at 4800rpm. Once the turbocharger was integrated into the exhaust manifold it was also more economical and refined. Oil-filled engine mountings and fixings for the exhaust well

outside the floor area of the cabin were further enhancements. In 2001 the diesel was brought completely up to date with the Duratorq TDCi common-rail version that averaged 4.4l/100km (65mpg) and was expected to save its owner £300 in fuel costs before the time of its first service. Routine maintenance was claimed to cost 28 per cent less than the previous Fiesta after service intervals were increased to 20,000km (12,500miles). Bumpers were strengthened and bolt-on wings made repairs cheaper. A CO_2 rating of only 119g/km was significant in view of a new tax structure, introduced to the UK in April 2002, which took account of vehicle emissions.

INTRODUCTION autumn 1998.
BODY saloon; 3, 4 or 5-doors, estate car 5-doors, 5-seats; weight 1185kg (2612.5lb).
ENGINE 4-cylinders; transverse; 82.5mm x 82mm, 1753cc; compr 19.4:1; 67kW (89.9bhp) @ 5000rpm; 38.2kW (51.3bhp)/l; 200Nm (148lbft) @ 2000rpm.
ENGINE STRUCTURE Endura Di; one chain and belt-driven ohc; 2-valves; aluminium head and block; fuel injection; 5-bearing crankshaft, turbocharger, intercooler.
TRANSMISSION front wheel drive; 5-speed synchromesh; final drive 3.56:1.
CHASSIS steel monocoque; ifs by MacPherson struts, angled coil spring damper units, and lower wishbones, anti-roll bar; irs by control blade multi-links, anti roll bar; telescopic dampers; hydraulic servo brakes, front 25.8cm (10.16in) ventilated discs; rear drums, dual circuit, ABS optional; rack and pinion PAS; 55l (12.1gal) tank; 185/65R14, 195/55R15 tyres 5.5, 6J rims.
DIMENSIONS estate wheelbase 261.5cm (103in); track 149.5cm (58.9in) front, 148.5cm (58.5in) rear; length 443.8cm (174.7in); width 170cm (66.9in); height 144.7cm (57in); turning circle 10.9m (35.8ft).
EQUIPMENT various option packs Climate, reflex, Styling, Luxury; CX, Zetec, LX and Ghia, CD upgrade, metallic paint.
PERFORMANCE maximum speed 184kph (114.6mph); 45.8kph (28.5mph) @ 1000rpm; 0-100kph (62mph) 12.4sec; 17.7kg/kW (13.2kg/bhp); fuel consumption 4.9l/100km (57.6mpg).
PRICE 5-door 1.8l Ddi Ghia £14,850; estate 1.8TDdi LX £14,850.

1999
Fiesta range, Zetec-S

The 1996 changes transformed Fiesta from merely workmanlike into a best-selling class leader. For MY 2000 it was fine-tuned, with Endura petrol and diesel editions chugging on in the bargain basement and 1.25 and 1.4 remaining mechanically unchanged, all gaining a facelift with a lower bonnet line and trapezoidal headlights. Trying to disguise old presswork was not an unqualified success, showing that as long as basic ingredients of cost, economy, roadworthiness, and proportions were right, the rest could look after itself. Efforts at a flagship Fiesta had been sometimes undistinguished and it took three years to produce a new one after 1996. Key ingredients were the 1.6 Zetec-S engine

and the transformation in handling. The sporty Fiesta took the Zetec-S title, and wheels, tyres, gearbox, and interior changed. Suspension was lowered 13mm (.5in) in front and 10mm (.4in) at the back, the front anti-roll bar thickened by 2mm to 17mm (.7in) and the rear twist beam stiffened 42 per cent, aimed at flatter roll-free cornering. Importantly the steering gained a heavier rack to improve its feel and it reverted to 2.8 turns lock to lock. A fashion fad was a mesh grille over the oval air intake, imitating the wire screens that 1930s sports racing cars wore to protect headlamps and radiator cores from the flying stones with which racetracks, particularly Le Mans, once abounded.

SPECIFICATION ZETEC-S

INTRODUCTION Oct 1999, production to 2002.
BODY saloon; 3-doors, 4-seats; weight 975kg (2149.5lb).
ENGINE 4-cylinders; transverse; 79mm x 81.4mm, 1596cc; compr 11:1; 76kW (101.9bhp) @ 6000rpm; 47.6kW (63.8bhp)/l; 145Nm (107lbft) @ 4000rpm.
ENGINE STRUCTURE twin belt-driven ohc, 4-valve; aluminium head, and block; Siemens electronic fuel injection, electronic engine management; 5-bearing crankshaft.
TRANSMISSION front wheel drive 5-speed synchromesh; final drive 4.25:1; traction control.
CHASSIS steel monocoque; ifs by MacPherson struts, coil springs, anti-roll bar; rear suspension torsion beam axle; telescopic dampers; anti-roll bar; hydraulic, vacuum servo 25.8cm (10.2in) front ventilated disc brakes; rear19cm (7.5in) drums; ABS; rack and pinion PAS; 42l (9.3 gal) tank; 195/55R15 tyres, 6J rims.
DIMENSIONS wheelbase 244.5cm (96.3in); track 143cm (56.3in) front, 137.5cm (54.1in) rear; length 383cm (150.8in); width 163cm (64.2in); height 141cm (55.5in); ground clearance 14cm (5.5in); turning circle 10.3m (33.8ft).
EQUIPMENT 15-spoke alloy wheels, CD player; electric front windows; 1.25-litre available with CVT optional £1000; Zetec-S 3-door only.
PERFORMANCE maximum speed 182kph (113.4mph); 33.7kph (21mph) @ 1000rpm; 0-100kph (62mph) 10.2sec; 12.8kg/kW (9.6kg/bhp); fuel consumption 6.9-6l/100km (40.9-47.1mpg).
PRICE 3-door 1.3 Encore £7750; 1.25LX £9750; 1.4 Zetec £9750; 4-door 1.4 Ghia £11,850.

1999
Focus WRC

The Focus was a winner almost from the start in the World Rally Championship (WRC). Colin McRae finished third in the Monte Carlo Rally, only to be excluded on a technicality, an oversized water pump resulting in a 2-week development programme reputedly costing £500,000 to make certain a standard one would work just as well. The turbocharged and intercooled engine was a close relative of the production Focus. It used a standard iron block, conformed strictly with the design criteria as rebuilt by Mountune with design tolerances and electronics eliminating turbo lag. The drive was taken by a bevel gear from the tilted transverse engine to a longitudinal six-speed gearbox to all four wheels by way of a central differential that split the torque 50:50 through two more diffs at the front and back. The front and central diffs had hydraulic locks, controlled by microprocessor programs, to deal with the broadside cornering required for loose-surface high speed driving. A regulation safety roll cage gave immense strength to a body shell that looked every inch a Focus, keeping many of the standard car's features at least in spirit if not exactly. MacPherson struts front and rear replaced Focus's own control blade system, increasing suspension travel to 20cm (7.9in) to suit gravel stages.

BODY saloon; 3-doors, 2-seats; weight 1230kg (2711.7lb).
ENGINE 4-cylinders; transverse, 1989cc; 223.7kW (300bhp) @ 6000rpm; 112.5kW (150.8bhp)/l; 551Nm (406lbft) @ 4000rpm.
ENGINE STRUCTURE 2 belt-driven ohc; 4-valves; aluminium cylinder head, iron block; Garrett turbocharger, electronic engine management; 5-bearing crankshaft.
TRANSMISSION four-wheel drive; M-Sport X-Trac 240; 6-speed sequential; final drive to choice; electronic control of locking differentials.
CHASSIS steel monocoque supported by roll cage; reinforced chassis rails; ifs by MacPherson struts and adjustable links; adjustable telescopic dampers; hydraulic servo 30cm (11.8in) ventilated disc brakes; ABS; rack and pinion PAS; 120l (26.4 gal) tank; 7Jx15in wheels, choice of tyres.
DIMENSIONS wheelbase 263.5cm (103.7in); length 415.2cm (163.5in); width 177cm (69.7in); height 142cm (55.9in).
EQUIPMENT Sparco seats, safety harness, intercom, calculating and navigation equipment.
PERFORMANCE maximum speed approx 225kph (140mph); 0-100kph (62mph) 4.3sec, 0-160kph (100mph) 10.0sec; 5.5kg/kW (4.1kg/bhp).

Third on its second WRC event in Sweden, it won on its third appearance, in Kenya. It won again in Portugal on its fourth and was in contention for the world title in only its second season.

1999
Fiesta diesel

Secure in the improvements to ride, handling, comfort, equipment and refurbishment of its appearance, entry-level 1999 Fiestas carried on with much the same mechanicals as before, including the normally aspirated and rather noisy Endura D diesel. While it offered comparable power against rivals, it took half a second longer than the Volkswagen Polo to 100kph (62mph) and was around 6kph (4mph) down on top speed. Both used indirect injection, while many of their contemporaries were moving on to direct injection, and some even to common rail diesels. Even though it had power steering, sunroof, driver's airbag, and a radio that could be upgraded to Radio Data System (RDS) for £60, it had not

kept pace with the improvements to the chassis. Fiesta diesel seemed well down the pecking order when it came to updating, until March 2000, when it inherited the turbocharged Focus TDdi, which also went into the small Fiesta and Courier panel vans. Performance was on a par with the 1.25 petrol Fiesta, it used less fuel (5.3l/100km (53.3mpg) against 6.1l/100km (46.3mpg)), but more importantly it was a match in smooth running and enjoyed a reduction in vibration. The price of the new generation diesel Fiesta was the same as the outgoing model and it came in 5-door form. Option packs to upgrade the specification continued.

INTRODUCTION Oct 1999, production to 2002.
BODY saloon; 3-doors, 5-doors; weight 1015kg (2237.7lb); TD 1010kg (2226.7lb).
ENGINE 4-cylinders; transverse; 82.5mm x 82mm, 1753cc; compr 21.5:1; 44kW (59bhp) @ 4800rpm; 25kW (33.7bhp)/l; 105Nm (77lbft) @ 2500rpm. TD compr 19.4; 55kW (73.8bhp) @ 4000rpm; 31.3kW (41.1bhp)/l; 140Nm (103lbft) @ 1900rpm.
ENGINE STRUCTURE Endura DE, 1 gear and belt driven ohc, 2-valve; iron head, and block; fuel injection; 5-bearing crankshaft. Endura DI-TD direct injection, turbocharger.
TRANSMISSION front wheel drive 5-speed synchromesh; final drive 3.84:1, TD3.61.
CHASSIS steel monocoque; ifs by MacPherson struts, coil springs, anti-roll bar; rear suspension torsion beam axle; telescopic dampers anti-roll bar; hydraulic, vacuum servo 24cm (9.45in) front disc brakes; rear 19cm (7.5in) drums; ABS; rack and pinion PAS; 42l (9.2 gal) tank; 165/70R13, 185/55R14 tyres, 5.5, 6J rims.
DIMENSIONS wheelbase 244.5cm (96.3in); track 143cm (56.3in) front, 137.5cm (54.1in) rear; length 383cm (150.8in); width 163cm (64.2in); height 141cm (55.5in); ground clearance 14cm (5.5in); turning circle 10.3m (33.8ft).
PERFORMANCE maximum speed 155kph (96.6mph), TD168kph (104.7mph); 34.3kph (21.37mph) @ 1000rpm; 0-100kph (62mph) 17.2sec, TD14.3sec; 23.1kg/kW (17.2kg/bhp), TD 18.4kg/kW (13.7kg/bhp); fuel consumption 7.9-5l/100km (35.8-56.5mpg), TD 6.5-4.2l/100km (43.5-67.3mpg).
PRICE 1.8TDdi LX £10,850.

1999
Focus saloon and estate

SPECIFICATION 2.0.

INTRODUCTION January 1999.
BODY saloon; 4-doors, 5-seats; weight 1160kg (2557.3lb), estate 1197kg (2639lb).
ENGINE 4-cylinders; transverse; 84.8mm x 88mm, 1988cc; compr 10:1; 96kW (128.7bhp) @ 5500rpm; 48.3kW (64.8bhp)/l; 178Nm (131lbft) @ 5500rpm.
ENGINE STRUCTURE Zetec-E; 2 belt-driven ohc, 4-valves; aluminium head and block; sequential fuel injection, EEC-V electronic engine management; 5-bearing crankshaft.
TRANSMISSION front wheel drive; 5-speed synchromesh; final drive 4.06:1.
CHASSIS steel monocoque; ifs by MacPherson struts, coil springs, anti-roll bar; multi-link irs; anti roll bar; telescopic dampers; hydraulic servo disc brakes, front 25.8cm (10.2in) ventilated, rear 25.4cm (10in) ; ABS; rack and pinion PAS; 55l (12.1 gal) tank; 195/60R15 tyres 5J rims, alloy wheels.
DIMENSIONS wheelbase 261.5cm (103in); track 148.5cm (58.5in) front, 147.5cm (58.1in) rear; length 436.2cm (171.7in)/443.8cm (174.7in); width 169.9cm (66.9in); height 148cm (58.3in)/149.7cm (58.9in); turning circle 10.9m (35.8ft).
PERFORMANCE maximum speed 201kph (125.2mph); 36.1kph (22.5mph) @ 1000rpm; 0-100kph (62mph) 9.2sec/9.6sec;12.1kg/kW (9kg/bhp); fuel consumption 9l/100km (31.4mpg).
PRICE 4-door £15,500, estate £16,000.

Having started with good proportions, by the beginning of 1999 the Focus range was expanded to improved its appearance and enhance its market prospects. Like the Orion (and the Escort saloon) before it, the Focus 4-door was aimed at a different sort of buyer from the hatchback. It was 21cm (8.3in) longer and 4cm (1.6in) taller, and the spring rates were softened to give a more compliant ride. The absence of a large hatchback opening in the rear stiffened the bodyshell, enhancing roadworthiness, improving refinement, and making the car quieter. Rounding off the up-market presentation, the 4-door came only as a 1.6 or 2.0 Ghia, with air conditioning and CD prominent in a long list of standard equipment, topped off with timber-look trim round the facia, Ghia badges and additional chrome. The Focus lent itself well to an estate car configuration. The already low-line suspension was flattened further to reduce intrusions into the loading space and triple-rate springs made allowance for heavy weights in the back. The roofline was made an extra 1.7cm (0.7in) taller, the modifications and the extra glassware increasing its weight by 41kg (90.4lb). Loadspace capacity was further improved by making the estate car's tailgate upright. Saloon Focus prices were the same as those for the 5-door hatchback, and the estate was only £500 more.

2000
Galaxy

Successful models, such as the well-established multi-purpose vehicle, required only a light touch rather than a full makeover. Tear-drop headlights and a narrow grille gave it a Ford family identity, while it gained new mechanical packages with 24-valve heads for the V6 and a new turbodiesel, in addition to the existing 2.3 petrol. The V6 came with Electronic Stability Programme (ESP) as standard. ESP detected the onset of skidding by sensors measuring yaw, sideways acceleration, steering wheel angle, and road speed. The on-board computer worked out a combination of throttle responses and judicious braking of individual wheels, to bring the vehicle back on course. Traction control was also optional with the 2.3. Further novelties included a 6-speed manual and the option of 5-speed automatics with a capacity for push-pull manual sequential operation. The completely revised interior included so-called technical grain surface treatment for the facia, stemming from the texture of modern lightweight carbon fibre or bonded metallic materials. Optional satellite navigation, standard parking distance sensors, and a multi-media system providing screens on the backs of the front seats for videos or games, were among the high-tech features of this modern Ford. All Galaxy models had seven seats as standard, with the option of six "captain's chairs" with integral armrests on the Ghia.

INTRODUCTION March 2000.
BODY minivan; 5-doors, 7-seats; weight 1650kg (3637.6lb); V6 1700kg (3748lb); turbodiesel 1666kg (3673lb).
ENGINE 4-cylinders; transverse; 89.6mm x 91mm, 2259cc; compr 10:1; 107kW (143.5bhp) @ 5500rpm; 47.36kW (63.5bhp)/l; 203Nm (150lbft) @ 2500rpm. V6: 81x 90.3mm; 2792cc; 150kW (201.2bhp); 53.7kW (72bhp)/l; 264Nm (195lbft). 1.9TDi: 1896cc; 66kW (88.5bhp) or 85kW (114bhp).
ENGINE STRUCTURE chain-driven 2 ohc; 4-valve; aluminium head, iron block; EEC-V engine management, and SEFI multi-point fuel injection; 5-bearing crankshaft. V6 2 chain ohc per bank; Bosch engine management; 4-bearing. Diesel, belt-driven sohc EDC16 management, turbocharged, intercooled.

TRANSMISSION front wheel drive; hydraulic clutch; gearbox 5-speed synchromesh; automatic optional; final drive 4.231:1, V6 and diesel 3.591, automatics 4.572, 3.684, 2.87.
CHASSIS steel monocoque; ifs by MacPherson struts, lower wishbones, offset coil springs; irs by semi-trailing arms, coil springs; anti roll bars; gas-filled telescopic dampers; hydraulic servo disc brakes, 28cm (11in) front ventilated (V6 both ventilated, 31.3cm (12.2in) and 29.4cm (11.6in); ABS; dual circuit; rack and pinion PAS; 70l (15.4 gal) tank; 195/65TR15; 205/60HR15, 215/55WR16.

DIMENSIONS wheelbase 283.5cm (111.6in); track front 152.6cm (60.1in), rear 151.2cm (59.5in); length 464.1cm (182.7in); width 181cm (71.3in) without mirrors; ht 173.2cm (68.2in) without roofrail; turning circle 11.1m (36.4ft).
EQUIPMENT optional xenon lights, air conditioning standard.
PERFORMANCE maximum 197kph (122.7mph), V6 217kph (135.2mph); 34kph (21.2mph), V6 41.5kph (25.9mph) @ 1000rpm; 0-100kph (62mph) 12.3sec, V6 9.9sec; 15.4kg/kW (11.5kg/bhp), V6 11.3kg/kW (8.4kg/bhp), TD 25.2 or 19.6kg/kW (18.8kg or 14.6kg/bhp); 10.1l/100km (28mpg), TDi 6.5l/100km (43.5mpg).
PRICE 2.3LX £18,245, 2.8 Ghia £24,245, 1.9TD Ghia automatic £23,740.

2000
Transit

It took the best part of 40 years for the Transit to embrace front wheel drive but eventually, for lighter loads at any rate, the advantages of a low floor and better driving qualities won through. A transverse-engined front end was added to the long-standing range of ladder-frame rear-drive chassis; both sorts sharing 95 per cent of their components. Front wheel drive suited vans, while chassis-cabs had a ladder-type frame with rear wheel drive and the option of twin wheels for extra traction. Front wheel drive enabled all the mechanical units to be packaged together, making it easy to ring changes in wheelbases, load lengths, roof heights and body styles, crucially with no propeller shaft, a low floor, low door openings and more headroom in the back. It had more cube space, and the medium wheelbase model could take four Europallets, 1.2m (3.9ft) x 0.8m (2.6ft). The technical challenge was to provide for both longitudinal (rear drive) and transverse (front-drive) engines. Cabs could have 3-abreast seats, separate chassis-cabs or extended accommodation with dual passenger and load-carrying roles. Manufactured in the former Spitfire factory at Southampton, following a £600m investment, the Transit had a bewildering range of petrol and diesel engines. 4 valves per cylinder, once the prerogative of grand prix cars, and turbochargers made the Transit feel more like a car than ever.

ABOVE **Workhorse of the World. Five generations of Transit van. For the new millennium Transit service intervals were extended to 25,000km (15,000miles) and warranty to three years or 160,000kms (100,000miles). The 3-piece easily repairable front bumper was no reflection on van drivers' skill.**

INTRODUCTION January 2000.
BODY cab, chassis-cab, various; SWB 260 2.0Di low roof van 2455kg (5412lb); LWB 350 med roof van 2.4Di 3500kg (7716lb).
ENGINES 4-cyls; transverse or in-line; diesel 2.0 DuraTorq Di: 55kw (73.8bhp) @ 3300rpm; 180Nm (133lbft); @ 2250rpm. 74kw (99.2bhp) @ 4000rpm; 230Nm (170lbft) @ 2000rpm. 2.4: 55kw (73.8bhp) @ 3500rpm; 185Nm (137lbft) @ 2000rpm. Fuel injection direct Bosch VP30, 66kw (88.5bhp) @ 4000rpm; 200Nm (148lbft) @ 1800rpm. 88kw (118bhp) @ 4000rpm; 240Nm (177lbft) @ 2300rpm. Petrol 2.3dohc: 107kw (143.5bhp) @ 5700rpm; 200Nm (148lbft) @ 2500rpm. 2.0 diesel: 86mm x 86mm; 1998cc; compr 19:1; chain-driven dohc; aluminium 2-piece head, 4-valves; cast iron block with aluminium ladder frame; cast iron exhaust manifold with integral turbocharger; Ford EEC-V engine management. 2.4 diesel: 89.9mm x 94.6mm; 2402cc; cr 19.0:1. 2.3L 16v petrol; 89.6mm x 91.0mm; 2295cc; compr 10:1; aluminium head, iron block; chain-driven dohc; Ford EEC-V engine management; electronic fuel injection.
TRANSMISSION 2.0L DuraTorq Di, front wheel drive; Ford VXT75 transmission; hydraulic clutch; 5-speed synchro; final drive 4.23:1 or 4.54 for towing. 2.4L DurtaTorq Di and 2.3L petrol rear wheel drive Ford MT75 transmission, final drive 4.63:1 or 5.13 for towing.
CHASSIS steel monocoque cab or van; ifs by MacPherson struts; rear suspension dead beam; RWD live axle, leaf springs; gas-pressurised telescopic dampers; hydraulic servo brakes, front 27.6cm (10.9in) ventilated disc, rear 25.4cm (10in) drums, RWD 29.4cm (11.6in) and 28cm (11in); optional ABS, dual circuit; rack and pinion PAS; 80l (17.6 gal) tank; 195/70R x 15C tyres, RWD 215/75R x 16C.

DIMENSIONS wheelbase van 330cm (129.9in), 375cm (147.6in), chassis-cab 313.7cm (123.5in), 350.4cm (138in), 395.4cm (155.7in); length medium van 520.1cm (204.8in), long van 565.1cm (222.5in), medium chassis 545.2cm (214.7in); width 197.4cm (777.2in) excluding mirrors; height medium roof 235.3cm (92.6in), high roof 258.2cm (101.7in); turning circle 11.4m (37.4ft) SWB to 13.9m (45.6ft) LWB.
EQUIPMENT driver airbag, radio standard, passenger's airbag, perimeter alarm, metallic paint, electric mirrors, electric windows, heated windscreen, tow bar, CD player, parking sensor, tachograph, vinyl seat trim, air conditioning optional.
PRICE from £12,686.

2000
Mondeo

In common with most of the British motor industry, Ford prices edged downwards at the turn of the century, and Mondeo prices were reduced by 8.8 per cent. New equipment with a (Ford) estimated value of £825 was added so, together with the price reduction, the customer gained 14 per cent more moneysworth. Three body styles, four engine options and five levels of trim, LX, Zetec, Zetec-S, Ghia, and GhiaX added up to 51 different Mondeos, all with ABS, airbags, electric windows, CD player, air conditioning and heated windscreen. All Fords now had a three-year 60,000mile warranty. The first European Ford to be created digitally, Mondeo showed close attention to detail. An increase in wheelbase of 5cm (2in) gave a disproportionate increase in rear seat room. Raising the seats by 1.5cm (0.6in) in front and 1.7cm (0.7in) in the back and enlarging the doors made access easier. An extra 15cm (5.9in) in length provided a full 500l (17.65cuft) of luggage capacity. A computer tool was used to analyse various luggage space designs, using a wide range of simulated real world cargos from suitcases to push chairs. The rear seat cushion folded forward allowing the seatbacks to be folded downward, providing a larger flat floor. First-aid kit and warning triangles were cleverly stowed to take up as little room as possible.

SPEC 2-LITRE

INTRODUCTION October 2000.
BODY saloon; 4/5-doors, 5-seats; weight 1245kg (2744.7lb), estate 1300kg (2866lb).
ENGINE 4 cylinders; transverse; 84.8mm x 88mm, 1988cc; comp 10:1; 96kW (128.7bhp) @ 5600rpm; 48.3kW (64.8bhp)/l; 178Nm (131lbft) @ 4000rpm.
ENGINE STRUCTURE Zetec-E; 2 belt-driven ohc; 4-valves; aluminium head, iron block; electronic fuel injection, EEC-V engine management; 5-bearing crankshaft.
TRANSMISSION front wheel drive; 5-speed synchromesh; automatic option; final drive 3.82:1; automatic3.92:1; traction control option.
CHASSIS steel monocoque ; ifs by MacPherson struts, coil springs, anti-roll bar; irs, multi-link coil springs, anti roll bar; telescopic dampers; hydraulic servo ventilated disc brakes, front 26cm (10.2in) , rear 25.2cm (9.9in), Teves ABS; rack and pinion PAS; 61.5l (13.5 gal) tank; 185/65HR14, 195/60HR15, 205/55HR15 tyres, 5.5J rims.
DIMENSIONS wheelbase 270.5cm (106.5in); track front 150.5cm (59.25in), rear 148.5cm (58.5in); length 456cm (179.5in), estate 467cm (183.9in); width 175cm (68.9in); height 142cm (55.9in), estate 151cm (59.5in); ground clearance 12cm (4.7in); turning circle 10.9m (35.7ft).
EQUIPMENT automatic £1000, traction control £495.
PERFORMANCE maximum speed 206kph (128.3mph), estate 199kph (124mph); 32kph (19.9mph) @ 1000rpm; 0-100kph (62mph) 10sec, estate 10.2sec; 13kg/kW (9.7kg/bhp) fuel consumption 11.7-5.9l/100km (24.2-47.88mpg).
PRICE 2.0i £16,095, 2.0i Ghia X £19,395.

2001
Maverick

The Maverick developed with Nissan in the 1980s was built like the traditional 4x4, with a stout separate chassis and firm springing. The new Maverick was smaller, of unitary construction, and although its cross-country credentials were good, it rode and handled more like a car. In a reversal of its older namesake, it was front wheel drive until told otherwise; if the front wheels lost grip Control Trac chipped in, diverting pull to the rear as well. A manual 4x4 override helped establish its towing capacity of 1700kg (3747.8lb), about the weight of a small boat. A versatile Sport Utility, it had plenty of space for five to sit in comfort with 92.5cm (36.4in) legroom in the rear. The rear seat back split 60:40 or could be folded away to provide 1830l of load space. Displaying environmental credentials for a growing clamour of greens lobbyists, Ford studied a hybrid-electric Maverick. The Maverick HEV was to have regenerative braking, could be stopped and started almost instantaneously, yet was still capable of 6.01l/100km (47mpg). It could thus be driven 800km (around 500m) on a single tank with acceleration similar to a Maverick V6. Sophisticated motor generators saved fuel by shutting down the engine when coasting or stopped, restarting when the driver stepped on the accelerator.

INTRODUCTION April 2001.
BODY saloon SUV; 5-doors, 5-seats; weight 1470kg (3240.8lb).
ENGINE 4-cylinders; transverse; 84.8mm x 88mm, 1988cc; cr 9.6:1; 95kW (127.4bhp) @ 5400rpm; 48.8kW (65.4bhp)/l; 183Nm (135lbft) @ 4500rpm. V6: 89 x 79.5mm; 2967cc; compr 10:1; 149kW (199.8bhp) @ 6000rpm; 50.2kW (67.3bhp)/l; 272Nm (201lbft) @ 4750rpm.
ENGINE STRUCTURE 2 belt-driven ohcs; 4-valves; aluminium head, iron block; sequential electronic fuel injection, EEC-V engine

BELOW **First launched in the United States as the Ford Escape in August 2000, Maverick collected media awards and sold 75,000 in its first three months.**

management, distributorless ign; 5-bearing crank. V6 60 deg; aluminium heads and block; 2 chain-driven ohc per bank; 4-bearing crank, Ford coil-on-plug ignition.
TRANSMISSION front wheel drive; G5M 5-speed manual transaxle; final drive 4.588:1 Power Take Off (PTO) 2.928:1. Control Trac II 4wd full-time dual mode central viscous coupling, PTO for power transfer to rear axle, Rotary Blade Coupling (RBC) for front/rear proportioning. V6 CD4E 4-speed automatic transaxle final drive 3.770:1, PTO 2.927:1.
CHASSIS steel monocoque; ifs by MacPherson struts; independent multi-link rear; anti roll bars front & rear; tele dampers; hydraulic servo brakes, front 27.8cm (10.9in) ventilated discs, rear 23cm (9in) drums, ABS with electronic brake-force distribution; rack and pinion PAS; 58l (12.8 gal) tank; 225/70R15, V6, 235/70R16tyres, alloy wheels.

DIMENSIONS wheelbase 262cm (103.2in); track 155.5cm (61.2in) front, 155cm (61in) rear; length 439.5cm (173in); width 178cm (70.1in); height 170cm (66.9in); ground clearance 20cm (7.9in); turning circle 10.8m (35.4ft).
EQUIPMENT cruise control, CD player, leather trim standard on V6, ABS, EBD, air-con standard throughout.
PERFORMANCE maximum 166kph (103.4mph), V6 190kph (118.4mph); 45kph (28mph) @ 1000rpm, V6 48.5kph (30.2mph); 0-100kph (62mph) 13.55sec, V6 10.55sec; 15.5kg/kW 911.5kg/bhp); 10.3l/100km (27.5mpg), V6 13.6l/100km (20.8mpg).
PRICE 2.0 £17,995, 3.0 £20,995.

2001
Fiesta 1.3 8v and 1.6 16v

Announced at the Frankfurt Motor Show on 11 September 2001, a completely new Fiesta entered an uncertain world. Production was not scheduled to start until the following spring, bringing a 25 year old name firmly into the 21st century with a stylish new body shell and more space inside, promising fuel economy that only a few years previously would have been dismissed as freakish. Replacing Endura E, the petrol 1.3-litre Duratec's combined figure of 6.2l/100km (45.6mpg) was attainable in everyday driving, as was the 1.4 diesel Duratorq's 4.3l/100km (65.7mpg). The Fiesta's driving quality was well received and it was equipped with the IPS intelligent safety system with up to six airbags. The small Duratec 8-valve engine achieved economy by reducing internal friction. The camshaft drive was a roller chain instead of the usual toothed belt, the valve stems were reduced to 6mm (.24in) diameter, and the sophisticated electronic system kept the stoichiometric (petrol and air) mixture so consistent that emissions were controlled more than before so nearly 90 per cent of maximum torque was available between 1500rpm and 4500rpm. A compact engine 5.3cm (2.1in) less than before top to bottom, and 3mm (.12in) shorter end to end, it also featured a new Powertrain Control Module (PCM), electronic throttle control, for the first time in a small Ford.

INTRODUCTION January 2002.
BODY saloon; 5-doors, 5-seats; weight 1045kg (2303.8lb), 1.6 1040kg (2292.8lb).
ENGINE 4-cylinders; transverse; 74mm x 75.5mm, 1299cc; compr 10.2:1; 50kW (67.1bhp) @ 5500rpm; 38.5kW (51.6bhp)/l; 106Nm (78lbft) @ 2800rpm. 1.6: 79 x 81.4mm; 1596cc; compr 11:1; 76kW (101.9bhp) @ 6000rpm; 47.6kW (63.8bhp)/l; 145Nm (107lbft) @ 4000rpm.
ENGINE STRUCTURE Duratec 8V; chain-driven ohc; 2-valves; aluminium head, iron block; sequential multipoint electronic fuel injection, Siemens integrated engine management, distributorless ignition; 5-bearing 4-counterweight crank. 1.6 Duratec 16V; 2 belt-driven camshafts; 4-valves; 8-counterweight crank.

TRANSMISSION front wheel drive; hydraulic single plate diaphragm spring clutch; gearbox 5-speed synchromesh; final drive 4.06:1, 1.6, 4.25:1.
CHASSIS steel monocoque; ifs by MacPherson struts with offset spring-damper units, lower arms on separate cross-member; semi-independent rear suspension twist-beam, coil springs; telescopic dampers; hydraulic servo brakes dual circuit diagonally split, front 25.8cm (10.2in) discs, rear 20.3cm (8in) drums, optional 4-channel ABS; rack and pinion PAS; 45l (9.9 gal) tank; 175/65R14 tyres, 5.5J rims.
DIMENSIONS wheelbase 248.6cm (97.9in); track front 147.5cm (58.1in), rear 144.5cm (56.9in); length 391.7cm (154.2in); width 168.3cm (66.3in); height 146.3cm (57.6in); ground clearance 14cm (5.5in); turning circle 10.3m (33.8ft).

EQUIPMENT optional Blaupunkt satellite navigation.
PERFORMANCE maximum speed 158kph (98.4mph), 1.6, 185kph (115.2mph); 34.8kph (21.7mph) @ 1000rpm, 1.6 32.9kph (20.5mph); 0-100kph (62mph) 15.8sec, 1.6 10.6sec; 20.9kg/kW (20.3kg/bhp), 1.6 13.7kg/kW (10.2kg/bhp); fuel consumption 6.2l/100km (45.6mpg), 1.6, 6.6l/100km (42.8mpg).
PRICE 1.3 Finesse £8,495, 1.3LX £8995; 1.6 Ghia £11,195.

2001
RS Focus

It had been five years since RS (variously Rallye Sport or Renn Sport) featured as a premium sporting brand name. To motorsport purists it still meant a no-compromise road-going rally car, inspired by Ford's World Rally Championship (WRC) programme. Short of a works drive it was the closest most people would get to a WRC Focus, the ultimate road-going car with front wheel drive and a turbocharged 2.0-litre Duratec. On the outside it had the rally car's aerodynamics, inside it was functional with a racing appearance that included carbon-fibre-type panels, supportive bucket seats, and even a WRC-style engine start button. The Focus RS was a small-volume production car like its predecessors, with 70 per cent of the standard components re-engineered or replaced. These included the Quaife automatic torque-biassing differential that detected the output to each wheel and redistributed it to reduce wheelspin. Colin McRae helped to provide the rally-driver's eye ingredients essential to a true driver's car, even at the expense of ride and refinement. Along with the other works drivers Carlos Sainz and Pierro Latti, McRae drove prototypes on special stages to match chassis calibration to that of the works cars. Saarlouis-built RS Focus cars were sold through regular dealers, although they could be collected from Ford's WRC headquarters in Cumbria.

INTRODUCTION October 2000, on sale spring 2001.

BODY saloon; 3-doors.

ENGINE 4-cylinders; transverse; 84.8mm x 88mm, 1988cc; compr 10.1; 158kW (211.9bhp) @ 5500rpm; 79.48kW (106.6bhp)/l; 310Nm (229lbft) @ 3500rpm.

ENGINE STRUCTURE Duratec RS; 2 belt-driven ohc; sodium-filled exhaust valves; 4-valves; aluminium head, iron block; sequential electronic fuel injection (SEFI); Ford EEC-V electronic engine management; electronic distributorless ignition; 5-bearing crankshaft; Garrett stainless steel water-cooled turbocharger, 1bar (14.5psi) max boost; water-cooled intercooler.

TRANSMISSION front wheel drive; heavy-duty AP racing clutch; 5-speed synchromesh; Quaife automatic torque biasing differential.

CHASSIS steel monocoque; ifs by MacPherson struts with uprated offset coil springs, Sachs racing dampers, 18mm (.71in) anti-roll bar; irs by control blade multi-link, Sachs racing dampers with internal rebound spring; anti roll bar; hydraulic servo disc brakes, front Brembo 4-pot twin opposed piston callipers, 33.5cm (13.2in) ventilated front, rear 28cm (11in) discs and 2-pot calipers, Bosch MK25 ABS; rack and pinion PAS; 55l (12.1 gal) tank; Michelin Pilot Sport 225/40R18 tyres, 8in rims, OZ wheels.

DIMENSIONS wheelbase 261.5cm (103in); track 148.5cm (58.5in) front, 147.5cm (58.1in) rear; length 429cm (168.9in); width 170cm (66.9in); height 148cm (58.3in); turning circle 10.9m (35.8ft).

EQUIPMENT Sparco race-style leather and Alcantara seats. Carbon-fibre console.

PERFORMANCE maximum speed 230kph (143.3mph); 36.9kph (23.1mph) @ 1000rpm; 0-100kph (62mph) 6.4sec; fuel consumption 10.1l/100km (27.9mpg).

PRICE £15,995.

Mondeo ST220

Sport Technology (ST) was a new branding term for "Accessible and dependable performance derivatives, reflecting the character and extending the core strengths of foundation models," according to Jost Capito, director of Special Vehicle Engineering Ford of Europe. Essentially they were what were once called Stage 1 performance conversions, less aggressive than Rallye Sport (RS), and in the case of the Mondeo ST220, introduced as what Ford liked to call a grand tourer version of the saloon. RS was for "performance purists", while ST was aimed at a broader group of enthusiasts who wanted a turn of speed without sacrificing practicality, dependability and creature comforts. Critics acclaimed the ST220 a resounding success. *Auto Express* rated it best against keen rivals MG ZT+190, Vauxhall Vectra GSi, and Honda Accord Type R. The Ford's composure on twisty roads earned it praise, as did its luxurious interior and 500l (17.65cuft) boot. Subtly altered bumpers and grille, and 16-spoke alloy wheels gave it a purposeful appearance, along with being 15mm (.59in) lower than standard. The stiffer springing affected the ride and compromised refinement but it avoided some of the noise and harshness associated with more extreme competition cars. More significantly the price of this executive express overlapped the bottom end of the associated Jaguar range.

INTRODUCTION March 2002.
BODY saloon; 4/5-doors, 5-seats; weight 1385kg, estate 1445kg (3185.7lb).
ENGINE Duratec ST 6-cylinders, 60 deg V; transverse; 89mm x 79.5mm; 2967cc; compr 10:1; 166kw (222.6bhp) @ 6150rpm; 55.9kw (75.1bhp)/l; 280Nm (207lbft) @ 4900rpm.
ENGINE STRUCTURE 2 chain-driven ohc per bank; 4-valves; aluminium heads and block; sequential electronic fuel injection; Ford Black Oak engine management; electronic distributorless ignition; 4-bearing crankshaft.
TRANSMISSION front wheel drive; MTX75; hydraulic single plate 24cm (9.45in) diaphragm spring clutch with dual-mass flywheel; gearbox 5-speed synchromesh; final drive 3.56:1.
CHASSIS steel monocoque; ifs by MacPherson struts with angled coil-spring units, lower control arms on subframe; anti roll bar; irs by quadralink and struts; telescopic dampers; hydraulic servo disc brakes, front 24cm (9.5in) ventilated, rear 30.5cm (12in), dual circuit, ABS and Electronic Stability Programme (ESP), emergency brake assist; rack and pinion PAS; 61l (13.4 gal) tank; 25/40R18tyres, 7J rims.
DIMENSIONS wheelbase 275.5cm (108.5in); track front 152cm (59.8in), rear 153.5cm (60.4in); length 473cm (186.2in), estate 480.5cm (189.2in); width 181cm (71.3in); height 144.5cm (56.9in), estate 145.5cm (57.3in); ground clearance 12cm (4.7in); turning circle 11.1m (36.4ft).
EQUIPMENT Recaro heated leather front seats, optional satellite navigation, telematics.
PERFORMANCE maximum speed 243kph (151mph); 0-100kph (62mph) 6.8sec; 8.3kg/kW (6.2kg/bhp); fuel consumption 10.2l/100km (27.7mpg).
PRICE £21,745.

2002
ST170 Focus

When ST (Sport Technology) was applied to the Focus the result, according to Andy Barratt, medium car brand manager, was refined performance, accessible value, and everyday practicality. A keen driver's car, it was a step below a World Rally Championship contender, with a 2.0-litre Duratec engine and a notable Getrag close-ratio twin-layshaft 6-speed gearbox weighing only 46kg (101.4lb). Each layshaft had its own final-drive ratio; one of 2.88:1 contained first, second, third, and fifth gears, the second with 4.25:1 fourth, sixth and reverse. One small family Ford in four sold through UK dealers was a performance or sporting derivative, so the ST170 with Duratec and variable valve timing (VVT) was important and profitable. The intake camshaft had an electro-mechanical and hydraulic control, varying the valve opening through 60deg according to engine speed, load and temperature. VVT calibrated combustion so precisely on cold start-ups that the exhaust catalyst worked straight away. The fuel injection was so exact that no return loop had to be plumbed into a system that met Euro Stage IV emissions requirements. The car was also swift as a result of VVT together with 33.5mm (1.3in) inlet valves and stiffer valve springs allowing it to rev to a red line at 7200rpm and electronic limiter at 7350rpm.

INTRODUCTION March 2002.
BODY saloon; 3-doors, 5-seats; weight 1208kg (2663lb), 5-door 1239kg (2731.5lb).
ENGINE 4-cyls; transverse; 84.8mm x 88mm, 1988cc; compr 10.2:1; 127kW (170.3bhp) @ 7000rpm; 63.9kW (85.7bhp)/l; 197Nm (145lbft) @ 5500rpm.
ENGINE STRUCTURE 2 belt-driven ohcs with variable valve timing; 4-valves; aluminium head, iron block; sequential multipoint fuel injection; Ford Black Oak electronic engine management; electronic distributorless ignition; 5-bearing crank.

TRANSMISSION front wheel drive; hydraulic 22.8cm (8.98in) clutch, dual-mass flywheel; Getrag twin layshaft gearbox 6-speed synchromesh; automatic; final drive see text.
CHASSIS steel monocoque; ifs by MacPherson struts with angled coil springs and A-arms on separate sub-frame; control blade multi-link rear suspension; 21mm (.83in) anti roll bars; telescopic dampers; hydraulic servo disc brakes, front 30cm (11.8in) ventilated, rear 280mm (11.1in), dual circuit diagonally split, ABS, optional Electronic Stability Programme (ESP); rack and pinion PAS; 50l (11 gal) tank; 215/45R17tyres, 7Jrims, 15-spoke alloy wheels.

DIMENSIONS wheelbase 261.5cm (103in); track front 148.5cm (58.5in), rear 147.5cm (58.1in); length 429cm (168.9in); width 170cm (66.9in); height 148cm (58.3in); turning circle 10.9m (35.8ft).
EQUIPMENT xenon self-levelling headlamps, arc-shaped tailgate spoiler, leather upholstery, Recaros optional; a/c, CD player, leather sports seats std.
PERFORMANCE maximum 210kph (131mph); 37kph (23.1mph) @ 1000rpm; 0-100kph (62mph) 7.95sec; 9.5kg/kW (7.1kg/bhp); 9.1l/100km (31mpg).
PRICE £15,995.

3-door Fiesta 1.4 and diesel

First publicised at the Paris Motor Show, along with the Street Ka, the 3-door Fiesta made its UK debut a few weeks later at Birmingham. In Finesse, LX and Zetec trim its sportier sloping roofline and angled tailgate were, Ford claimed, to be aimed at younger drivers. In fact it was identical to the more upright 5-door below the body crease line. To achieve a separate identity the 3-door's roof was lowered from the top of the A-pillar towards the back, and the C-pillar brought forward by 75mm (2.95in), creating a vaguely coupe appearance. This meant losing 8mm (.31in) in rear-seat headroom but by way of compensation there was more stowage in bigger front door bins along with pockets beside the back seat. VDA boot volume was slightly smaller at 268l (9.5cuft) against 284l (10cuft) for the 5-door. There were two engine options; the diesel Duratorq TDCi 1.4-litre, an early product of an agreement between Ford and PSA Peugeot Citroën, or the petrol Duratec 16v 1.4-litre, with electronic, drive-by-wire throttle control. The arrival of the 3-door coincided with Durashift EST (Electronic Shift Technology) an automatic-shift transmission providing the flexibility of manual shifting with the ease of an automatic. The driver could choose between fully automatic, or a sequential shift actuated by three electric motors, two shifting gears, one operating the clutch.

INTRODUCTION October 2002. **BODY** saloon; 3-doors, 5-seats; weight 1035kg (2281.8lb), diesel 1065kg (2347.9lb).
ENGINE 4-cyl; transverse; 76mm x 76.5mm, 1388cc; compr 11:1; 58kW (77.8bhp) @ 5700rpm; 41.8kW (56.1bhp)/l; 124Nm (92lbft) @ 3500 rpm. TDCi: 73.7 x 82mm; 1399cc; compr 18:1; 50kW (67.1bhp) @ 4000rpm; 35.8kW (47.9bhp)/l; 160Nm (118lbft) @ 2000rpm.
ENGINE STRUCTURE Duratec; 2 belt-driven ohcs; 4-valves; aluminium head and block; Siemens electronic fuel injection, electronic EEC-V engine management, breakerless ignition; 5-bearing crankshaft. Duratorq TDCi 1 overhead camshaft; common rail direct injection with turbocharger.

TRANSMISSION front wheel drive; hydraulic 18cm (7.1in) clutch; 5-speed synchromesh; automatic; final drive 4.06:1. Diesel 21cm (8.27in) clutch, final drive 3.37:1.
CHASSIS steel monocoque; ifs by MacPherson struts with offset coil spring, lower arms on subframe; rear suspension torsion beam axle; telescopic dampers anti-roll bar; hydraulic, vacuum servo, diagonally split dual circuit brakes 25.8cm (10.2in) front ventilated discs; rear 20.3cm (8in) drums; ABS and 4-channel electronic brake distribution; rack and pinion PAS; 45l (9.9 gal) tank; 175/65R14tyres, 5.5, 6J rims.

DIMENSIONS wheelbase 248.7cm (97.9in); track front 147.5cm (58.1in), rear 144.4cm (56.9in); length 391.7cm (154.2in); width 168cm (66.1in); height 141.7cm (55.8in); ground clearance 12cm (4.7in); turning circle 10.3m (33.8ft).
EQUIPMENT passive anti-theft system D-PATS.
PERFORMANCE maximum speed 168kph (104.7mph), TDCi 164kph (102.2mph); 34.3kph (21.4mph) @ 1000rpm, TDCi 42.8kph (26.7mph); 0-100kph (62mph) 13.2sec, TDCi 14.9sec; 17.9kg/kW (13.3kg/bhp), TDCi 21.3kg/kW (15.9kg/bhp); fuel consumption 6.4l/100km (44.1mpg), TDCi 4.3l/100km (65.7mpg).
PRICE 1.6 Ghia 11,195, TDCi £10,965.

2002
Fusion

The Fusion concept at the 2001 Frankfurt Motor Show wore the customary aspect of an off-road adventure vehicle embarking on a safari. At Geneva six months later, in production form, it emerged as a practical highly adaptable mini-MPV, with five seats that could be folded flat to provide the load space of an estate car several sizes bigger. With ample compartments for maps, picnic items, and family paraphernalia, the Fusion was a versatile small car on the Fiesta platform, with all the Fiesta's roadworthiness and refinement. The obligation for a volume car manufacturer to produce as many variations on a platform as possible brought Ford into a diverse, flourishing market, but the Frankfurt Fusion's turbocharged direction-injection petrol engine with Variable Cam Timing (VCT), automated Durashift Electronic Select Transmission, navigation system with telematics and integrated multi-media entertainment system was not carried through to production. Instead, the Geneva car was an Urban Activity Vehicle (UAV) with a sensible choice of TDCi common rail turbodiesel, or two 16-valve petrol engines. With its tall body easy to get in and out of and clever detailing like a front passenger seat that folded into a table, Fusion provided taxi-like maneuverability, along with roominess for the urban dweller, within the footprint of a compact car.

INTRODUCTION spring 2002.
BODY saloon; 5-doors, 5-seats; 1070kg (2359lb), 1.6 1080kg (2381lb), TDCi 1102kg (2429.5lb).
ENGINE 4-cyls; trans; 76mm x 76.5mm, 1388cc; cr 11:1; 58kW (77.8bhp) @ 5700rpm; 41.8kW (56bhp)/l; 124Nm (92lbft) @ 3500 rpm. TDCi: 73.7 x 82mm; 1399cc; cr 18:1; 50kW (67.1bhp) @ 4000rpm; 35.8kW (47.9bhp)/l; 160Nm (118lbft) @ 2000rpm. 1.6: 79 x 81.4mm; 1596cc; cr 11:1; 76kW (102bhp) @ 6000rpm; 47.6kW (64bhp)/l; 145Nm (107lbft) @ 4000rpm.
ENGINE STRUCTURE Duratec; 2 belt-driven ohcs; 4-valves; aluminium head and block; Siemens electronic fuel inj, electronic EEC-V engine management, breakerless ign; 5-bearing crank. Duratorq TDCi 1 ohc; common rail direct injection with turbocharger.

TRANSMISSION front wheel drive; hydraulic 18cm (7.1in) clutch; 5-speed synchro; auto; 4.25:1. 1.6 and diesel 21cm (8.27in) clutch, diesel 3.37:1.
CHASSIS steel monocoque; ifs by MacPherson struts, offset coil spring, lower arms on subframe; rear susp torsion beam axle; telesc dampers; anti-roll bar; hydraulic, vacuum servo, diagonal split dual circuit brakes 25.8cm (10.2in) front ventilated discs; rear drums 20.3cm (8in); ABS and 4-channel electronic brake force distribution; rack and pinion PAS; 45l (9.9 gal) tank; tyres 195/60R15 or 195/60R15 with alloy wheels, 5.5, 6J rims.
DIMENSIONS wheelbase 248.5cm (97.8in); track 147.4cm (58in) front, 143.5cm (56.5in) rear; length 402cm (158.3in); width 172.1cm (67.8in); height 152.8cm (60.2in); clearance 12cm (4.7in); turning circle 9.9m (32.5ft).

EQUIPMENT 60/40 split rear seat, dual-stage front airbags, Ambiente, Trend, and Elegance trims.
PERFORMANCE max 1.4 163kph (102mph), 1.6 180kph (113mph), TDCi 159kph (99.4mph); 0-100kph (62mph) 1.4 13.7sec, 1.6 10.9sec, TDCi 15.5sec;18.4kg/kW (13.8kg/bhp), 1.6 14.2kg/kW (10.6kg/bhp), TDCi 22kg/kW (16.4kg/bhp); 6.5l/100km (43.5mpg), 1.6 6.6l/100km (42.8mpg), TDCi 4.4l/100km (64.2mpg).
PRICE 1.4 £9995; 1.4TD £10,665; 1.6 £11,495.

Transit Connect, Tourneo Connect

Light and sub one tonne vans at the Amsterdam RAI Commercial Vehicle Show in February 2002 incorporated the Transit name, which after 35 years meant almost as much as "Ford" did. Connect extended the Transit pedigree to the light commercial load-box market. Not a car-derived van, it had been designed, engineered, tested and constructed as a commercial vehicle. The bodyshell was toughened with high-strength steel, double-skinned body sides, two side cross members and a boron steel front cross member. It was reinforced underneath and the suspension strengthened for off-road. Anti-roll bars gave car-like stability and handling. There was a high-roof long wheelbase derivative, and a short wheelbase light commercial, a choice of petrol, diesel and turbo diesel engines and either a bulkhead or sliding side-load doors. The swb Transit Connect was the only vehicle in its class that could take two Europallets, 1.2m (3.9ft) x 0.8m (2.6ft), through the rear doors. Sloping body sides made best use of the load-box area and the folding passenger seat provided a long flat floor up to the footwell. An ingenious flexible load restraint system allowed customers to install their own racking. Tourneo offered van ability during the week, car qualities at the weekend, and warranty terms were two years with a 10 year anti-perforation body guarantee.

INTRODUCTION spring 2002.
BODY saloon; 5-doors, 5-seats; weight swb Transit 1345kg (2965.2lb), lwb 1380kg (3042.4lb); Tourneo swb 1420kg (3130.5lb), lwb 1475kg (3251.8lb).
ENGINE 4-cylinders; transverse; 80.6mm x 88mm, 1796cc; cr 10:1; 86kW (115.3bhp) @ 5750rpm; 47.9kW (64.2bhp)/l; 160Nm (118lbft) @ 4400rpm. TDdi: 82.5 x 82mm, 1753cc; cr 19.4:1; 55kW (73.8bhp) @ 4000rpm; 31.4kW (42.1bhp)/l; 175Nm (129lbft) @ 1800rpm. TDCi: 66kW (88.5bhp), 37.7kW (50.5bhp)/l; 220Nm (162lbft) @ 1700rpm.
ENGINE STRUCTURE Duratec; belt-driven two ohc; 4-valves; aluminium head, iron block with aluminium ladder frame; Visteon Bosch sequential fuel inj; Visteon PCM

engine management; breakerless ignition; 5-bearing crank. TDdi and TDCi all iron engine, 2-valves, single belt-driven ohc, turbocharger, intercooler, TDdi Visteon PCM management Bosch inj, TDCi Ford SMECU Delphi direct inj.
TRANSMISSION front wheel drive; MTX75; hydraulic 22cm (8.7in) single plate clutch; 5-spd synchro; final drive 4.06:1. TDdi 23.8cm (9.4in) clutch, TDCi 22.8cm (9in).
CHASSIS steel monocoque; ifs by MacPherson struts, gas pressurised dampers and anti-roll bar; rear susp dual rate multi-leaf springs, gas pressurised dampers; anti-roll bar; hydraulic servo brakes, front 27.8cm (10.9in) ventilated discs, rear 22.8cm (9in) drums, 27.8cm (10.9in) discs optional; ABS and Traction Assist opt with rear discs; rack and pinion PAS; 60l (13.2 gal) tank; 195/65R15 reinforced radial-ply tyres.

DIMENSIONS wbase swb 266.4cm (105in), lwb 291.2cm (115in); track front 150.5cm (59.25in), rear 155.2cm (61.1in); length swb 427.8cm (168.4in), lwb 452.5cm (178in); width swb 179.5cm (70.7in), lwb 190.6cm (75in); height swb 173.9cm (68.5in), lwb 190.6cm (75in); ground clearance 16.7cm (6.6in); turning circle swb 11m (36.1ft), lwb 11.9m (39ft).
PERFORMANCE maximum speed 165kph (mph); 0-100kph (62mph) 12.7sec; fuel consumption 9.7l/100km (29.1mpg).
PRICE LX £16,560.

2002
Ford GT

INTRODUCTION Detroit 2002.
BODY coupe; 2-doors, 2-seats; weight 1496.9kg (3300lb).
ENGINE 8-cylinders, 90deg V; mid; 90.2mm x 105.8mm, 5408cc; compr 8.5:1; 372.9kW (500bhp) @ 5250rpm; 68.9kW (92.5bhp)/l; 678Nm (500lbft) @ 3250rpm.
ENGINE STRUCTURE 2 chain-driven overhead camshafts per bank; 4-valves; aluminium cylinder heads and block; Bosch port fuel injection, 2 injectors/cylinder; electronic returnless fuel delivery; 5-bearing crankshaft; Eaton-Lysholm supercharger and intercooler; Ford EEC-V engine management
TRANSMISSION rear wheel drive; RBT transaxle; hydraulic twin plate 24cm (9.45in) clutch; gearbox 6-speed synchromesh; limited slip differential.
CHASSIS aluminium space frame, aluminium body shell, selected composite panels; front and rear independent suspension by unequal length control arm with coil-over spring-damper units; anti roll bars front and rear; 35.6cm (14in) hydraulic servo disc brakes, cross-drilled Brembo ventilated discs and 4-piston calipers; rack and pinion hydraulic PAS; 71.9l (15.8 gal) tank; 235/45R18 and 315/40R19tyres, 18 x 8in x 10in wheels.
DIMENSIONS wheelbase 271cm (106.7in); track 159cm (62.6in) front, rear 160.8cm (63.3in); length 463.3cm (182.4in); width 194.4cm (76.5in); height 112cm (44.1in); ground clearance 14cm (5.5in); turning circle 12.2m (40ft).
PERFORMANCE maximum speed in excess of 305kph (190mph); 0-100kph (62mph) 4.0sec; 4kg/kW (3kg/bhp); fuel consumption 25.7-17.7l/100km (11-16mpg).

In sporting terms the most famous car to carry the Ford blue oval without any qualification, like Lotus or Cosworth, was the GT40. The series of sports-racing coupes culminated in the mighty J-car and Mark IV, but it was always known by its earliest title, signifying Grand Touring and the 40 inches (101.6cm) it stood from the ground to the top of the roof. Yet although the reproduction shared the mystique and the name and even a robust American V8 amidships, it shared not a single dimension. The new car was more than 45.7cm (18in) longer and at 111.8cm (44in) tall could well have been called the GT44. Ford said its lines drew from, and refined, "the best features of GT40 history expressing the car's identity through modern proportion and surface development." The 5.4-litre engine looked the part, with a complex array of polished stainless-steel header pipes and braided stainless steel fuel lines with anodized aluminum fittings, although it now had a supercharger and an intercooler. Instead of the semi-monocoque hull of 23swg (.024in) sheet steel with square tube stiffening, it had an aluminium spaceframe. The interior, beneath doors cut away into the roof, was a more faithful reproduction with ventilated seats, the same instrument layout with analogue gauges and big tachometer, and modern versions of traditional toggle switches.

2002
StreetKa

The StreetKa roadster was a concept at the Turin Motor Show in 2000. Public and press reaction to it was good, and by Geneva the following spring Ford confirmed that it would go into production, with the Duratec 1.6 8-valve engine. Designed by David Wilkie of the Turin Ghia Studio, it was turned into a production reality, ironically by Ghia's old rival Industrie Pininfarina SpA. Under Wilkie's supervision Pininfarina engineered it for volume production and launch in 2003. "We drew crowds whenever we showed it," said Martin Leach, Ford of Europe's vice president of product development. Ford wanted to find a new way of reaching customers unconnected from motor sport, yet exemplifying the nature of the Ford range. StreetKa teamed up with Kylie Minogue (below) as a sponsor of her 39-date 2002 European Fever Tour, from Cardiff to Barcelona. The production StreetKa featured in photographs with Kylie, providing a preview before it went on sale in 2003. "The partnership with Kylie was the perfect way to show off StreetKa ahead of its launch," said Peter Fleet, marketing director. "StreetKa and Kylie had a lot in common; they were both small, beautiful and stylish." The car was formally unveiled to the public at the Paris Motor Show in September 2002.

INTRODUCTION 2003.
BODY roadster; 2-doors, 4-seats; weight 1061kg (2339.1lb).
ENGINE 4-cylinder; transverse; 82.07 x 75.48mm; 1597cc; compr 9.5:1; 70kW (93.9bhp) @ 5500rpm; 43.8kW (58.8bhp)/l; 135Nm (100lbft) @ 4250rpm.
ENGINE STRUCTURE Duratec 8V; chain-driven overhead camshaft; 2-valves; aluminium cylinder head, iron block; sequential multipoint electronic fuel injection, Siemens integrated engine management, distributorless electronic ignition; 5-bearing 4-counterweight crankshaft.
TRANSMISSION front wheel drive; hydraulic single plate diaphragm spring clutch; gearbox 5-speed synchromesh; final drive 4.25:1
CHASSIS steel monocoque; independent front suspension by MacPherson struts with offset spring-damper units, lower arms on separate cross-member; anti-roll bar; semi-independent rear suspension twist-beam, coil springs; telescopic dampers; hydraulic servo brakes dual circuit diagonally split, front 25.8cm (10.16in) ventilated discs, rear 20.3cm (8in) drums, 4-channel ABS optional on left hand drive; rack and pinion PAS; 42l (9.2gal) tank; 195/45R16tyres, 5J rims six-spoke alloy wheels.
DIMENSIONS wheelbase 244.8cm (96.4in); track front 141.7cm (55.8in), rear 145.2cm (57.2in); length 365cm (143.7in); width 169.5cm (66.7in); height 133.5cm (52.6in); ground clearance 14cm (5.5in); turning circle 11.1m (36.4ft).
EQUIPMENT Ford 6000 RDS/EON two-channel radio/CD player; air conditioning, leather upholstery optional.
PERFORMANCE maximum speed 173kph (108mph); 0-100kph (62mph) 12.1sec; 15.2kg/kW (11.3kg/bhp); fuel consumption 7.9l/100km (35.8mpg).
PRICE: Convertible £12,512; Winter Edition Convertible £14,812.

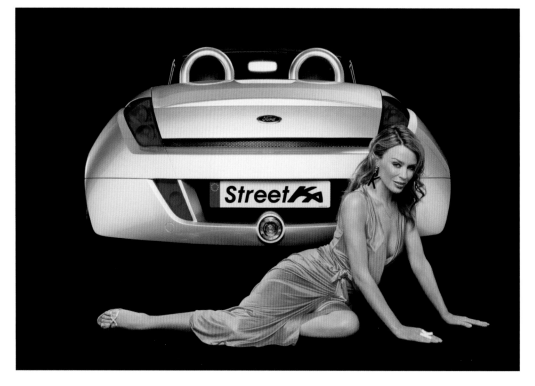

2003
SportKa 1.6

When Ka sales exceeded a million, the StreetKa roadster and SportKa versions brought the range to three. Brentwood could not resist "zesty" and "sparkling" when the SportKa was first exposed at the Paris Motor Show in the autumn of 2002, for launch in Ford America's centenary year. The "coolest Ka" had lower, stiffer springing with different toe-in and camber, and a South Africa-made engine with a close-ratio gearbox. Identified by flared wheel arches, and 16in instead of 13in alloy wheels with low-profile tyres, together with a sporty spoiler blending into the wrap-round rear bumper, the Sport had the Street's curious central round reversing light and the option of unique Imperial Blue paintwork. Sportka adopted a similar grille and body-coloured front bumper, and among features borrowed from the soon to be discontinued Puma was its aluminium ball gearshift. More resistance to body roll was achieved by a 64 per cent increase in anti-roll bar firmness and the front spring rates were 30 per cent higher. Rear roll stiffness on the Fiesta's twist-beam rear suspension was 45 per cent more and rear spring rates went up seven per cent. The 8-valve Duratec delivered 90 per cent of its torque between 1500-4500rpm and also met Euro Stage IV emission regulations. A 1.3 70PS version was available in some markets.

INTRODUCTION 2003.
BODY coupé; 2-doors, 4-seats; weight 1300kg (2865.9lb).
ENGINE 4-cylinders; transverse; 82mm x 75.5mm, 1597cc; compr 9.5:1; 70kW (93.9bhp) @ 5500rpm; 43.8kW (58.8bhp)/l; 135Nm (100lbft) @ 3000rpm.
ENGINE STRUCTURE Duratec 8v; chain-driven overhead camshaft, aluminium cylinder head and block; Ford EEC-V electronic sequential fuel injection and engine management; 5-bearing crankshaft.
TRANSMISSION fwd; 5-speed synchromesh; final drive 4.06:1.
CHASSIS steel monocoque; ifs by MacPherson strut, offset coil springs, lower A-arms, anti-roll bar; rear semi-independent twist beam with coil spring damper units; hydraulic servo brakes, front 24cm (9.45in) ventilated disc, rear drums, ABS; rack and pinion PAS; 42l (9.2 gal) tank; 195/45R16 tyres, 6J rims.
DIMENSIONS wheelbase 244.8cm (96.4in); track front 141.7cm (55.8in), rear 139.3cm (54.8in); length 365cm (143.7in); width 164cm (64.6in); height 143.6cm (56.5in); turning circle 10.4m (34.1ft).
EQUIPMENT leather steering wheel; optional black perforated leather upholstery; passive anti-theft PATS immobiliser.
PERFORMANCE maximum speed 174kph (108mph); 32.4kph (20.2mph) @ 1000rpm; 0-100kph (62mph) 9.7sec; 18.6kg/kW (13.8kg/bhp); fuel consumption 7.6l/100km (37.2mpg).
PRICE £10,295; SE £11,295.

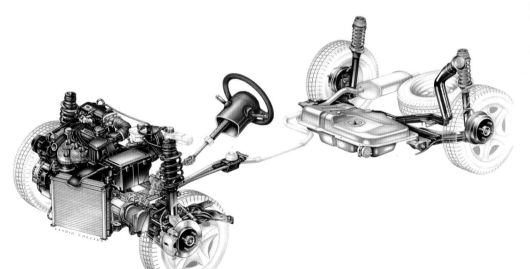

2003

Focus C-MAX 1.6 and 1.8 petrol; 1.6 and 2.0 TDCi

C-Max underpinnings anticipated the following year's Focus, in a package Ford tried to avoid calling an MPV. Yet multi-purpose it was, with five adaptable seats in a one-box body. Brand manager Joerg Pfisterer explained C indicated comfort, confidence and control; max just meant maximum. Load capacity was 1692l (59.7cuft) and Trends and Ghias came with an electronic parking brake, which dispensed with a lever. New Duratorq high-pressure common rail turbocharged diesels had been developed with PSA Peugeot-Citroën, and the 2-litre had a 6-speed manual Getrag-Ford Durashift gearbox. Using variable-nozzle Garrett turbochargers the new engines were certified to Euro Stage III and particulate filters were available, which reduced soot by 95 per cent. With an extra 2.5cm (1in) wheelbase and 4cm (1.5in) wider track than Focus, the first Ford with electro-hydraulic power assisted steering required 20 per cent less effort at parking speeds. Dispensing with an engine-driven servo pump saved three per cent of fuel. Dual automatic temperature control was standard on Ghia, optional elsewhere, self-adjusted according to cabin warmth, power train configuration, engine temperature and speed. Rear passengers could have a roof-mounted screen for DVDs or video games. After a year Durashift CVT automatic became available on the 2-litre petrol and the 1.6 TDCi. There were four trim levels.

INTRODUCTION preview Paris 2002; Geneva and Frankfurt 2003.
PRODUCTION June 2003.
BODY saloon; 5-doors, 5-seats; weight 1260kg (2778lb); 1.8 1345kg (2965lb); 1.6TDCi 1390kg (3064lb); 2.0 TDCi 1505kg (3318lb).
ENGINE 4-cylinders; transverse; 79mm x 81.4mm, 1596cc; compr 11:1; 74kW (100bhp) @ 6000 rpm; 46.3kW (62bhp)/l; 146Nm (107.7lbft) @ 4000rpm. 1.8 83mm x 83mm; 1798cc; cr 10.8:1; 88kW (118bhp) @ 6000rpm; 48.9kW (65.6bhp)/l; 166Nm (122.4lbft) @ 4000rpm. 1.6TDCi 75mm x 88.3mm; 1560cc; cr 18.3:1; 80kW (107.3bhp) @ 4000rpm; 51.3kW (68.8bhp)/l; 240Nm (177lbft) @ 1750rpm. 2.0TDCi 85mm x 88mm; 1997cc; cr 18:1; 100kW (134.1bhp) @ 4000rpm; 50.1kW (67.2bhp)/l; 320Nm (236lbft) @ 4500rpm.
ENGINE STRUCTURE Duratec 1.6; 16 valves; 2 belt-driven ohc with Ti-VCT; 1.8, 2 chain-driven ohc; aluminium head, block; Siemens integrated PCS engine management, Visteon sequential electronic multipoint fuel injection; electronic distributorless ignition; 5-bearing nodular cast iron crankshaft, 8 counterweights. Duratorq diesels; 2 belt-driven ohc; 1.8 Bosch fuel injection, 2.0 Siemens; Garrett turbochargers w electronic management; intercoolers.
TRANSMISSION fwd; hydraulic sdp clutch; 5-speed synchromesh with facia manual control; final drive 4.06:1, 1.6 TDCi 3.41, 2.0 TDCi 6-speed MMT6; 2.85:1.
CHASSIS steel monocoque, front and rear sub-frames; ifs twin-tube MacPherson struts; trailing arm control blade irs; coil springs; anti roll bar; gas-filled telescopic dampers; hydraulic servo brakes, front discs 27.8cm (10.9in), rear 30cm (11.8in). ABS, optional ESP; electric-hydraulic PAS; 55l (12.1gal) tank; 195/65R15, 205/55R16, 205/50 R17 tyres, 6/6.5J rims.

DIMENSIONS wheelbase 264cm (103.9in); track front 153.5cm (60.4in), rear 153cm (60.2in); length 433.5cm (170.7in); width 182.5cm (71.9in); height 156cm (61.4in); turning circle 10.7m (35.1ft), 11.2m (36.7ft).
EQUIPMENT Sony audio, optional satnav and rear-seat entertainment, DEATC climate control (standard on Ghia). Folding and demountable rear seat.
PERFORMANCE maximum speed 175kph (109mph), 1.8 195kph (121mph), 1.6 TDCi 185kph (115mph), 2.0 200kph (124.6mph); 32.5kph (20.2mph) @ 1000rpm, 1.8 33.5kph (20.9mph), 1.6TDCi 48kph (29.9mph), 2.0 57kph (35.5mph); 0-100kph (62mph) 12.9sec, 1.8 10.8sec, 1.6 TDCi 11.3sec, 2.0 9.6sec; fuel consumption EU av 7.2l/100km (39.5mpg), 1.8 7.6l/100km (37.2mpg), 2.0 7.6l/100km (37mpg).
PRICE 1.6 Studio £13,490, 1.8LX £14,565, 2.0 Ultima £18,250.

2003
Mondeo 1.8 SCi and 6-speed

The tenth anniversary Mondeo was not much changed, but gained more names beginning with Dura. Chrome highlights on the grille and a reprofiled bumper freshened the appearance. Trapezoidal fog lamps, bigger mirrors that folded away on Ghia, Ghia X and ST220, and puddle lamps that shone on the ground were practical enhancements. Tail lamps gained silvered indicator lenses, while what Ford called chrome accents on the upper doorline, door handle inserts, and tailgate handle completed the premium look. Estate car customers could specify metallic roof rails. The important innovation was the Duratec SCi (Smart Charge injection), which was Ford's first direct-injection petrol engine. This improved fuel economy over the preceding model, *What Car?*'s 2001 Car of the Year, by six to eight per cent. Durashift was a 6-speed manual transmission for higher-powered Mondeos, manufactured in Cologne under code-name MMT6, it was the main product of a joint venture between Ford and Getrag. Durashift 5-tronic automatic had an F1-style steering-wheel mounted paddle shift option. Among refinements to the Duratorq TDCi common-rail turbodiesel engine were a revised cylinder head and injectors that made it quieter starting up from cold. The satellite navigation system option brought in DVD-based route guidance and a colour touch screen.

INTRODUCTION June 2003.
BODY saloon; 4/5-doors, 5-seats; weight 1290kg (2843.9lb); estate 1355kg (2987.2lb).
ENGINE 4-cylinders; transverse; 83mm x 83.1mm, 1798cc; port fuel injection cr 10.8:1; 92kW (123.4bhp) @ 6000rpm; 51.2kW (68.6bhp)/l; 170Nm (125.4lbft) @ 4500rpm). direct injection cr 11.3:1; 96kW (128.7bhp) @ 6000rpm; 53.4kW (71.6bhp)/l; 175Nm (129lbft) @ 4250rpm.
ENGINE STRUCTURE Duratec HE 16-valves; 2 inverted-tooth chain-driven ohc; low pressure cast aluminium head, aluminium block; 120bar direct common rail fuel inj; piston recesses; direct-fire ignition with coil-on-plug; 4-electrode surface-spark plugs; 5-bearing cast iron counterweighted crank.

TRANSMISSION fwd; MMT6 hydraulic single plate diaphragm spring clutch with dual-mass flywheel; Durashift 6-speed synchromesh; final drive 4.36:1; 5-speed 3.05:1; Durashift 5-tronic sequential with ACTU.
CHASSIS steel monocoque; ifs by MacPherson struts with angled coil spring units, lower control arms on subframe; anti roll bar; irs by quadralink and struts; telescopic dampers; hydraulic servo ventilated disc brakes, front 30cm (11.8in), rear 28cm (11in), diagonally split dual circuit, ABS and Electronic Stability Programme (ESP) and emergency brake assist; rack and pinion PAS; 58.5l (12.9gal) fuel tank; 205/55 R16, 205/50 R17, 225/40 R18 tyres 6/7J rims.
DIMENSIONS wb 275.5cm (108.5in); track front 152cm (59.8in), rear 153.5cm (60.4in); length 437cm

(172in); estate 480.5cm (189.2in); width 181cm (71.25in); height 146cm (57.5in); estate 147cm (57.9in), 151cm (59.4in) with racks; ground clearance 12cm (4.7in); turning circle 11.1m (36.4ft).
EQUIPMENT climate front seats; heated rear seats; power folding mirrors; auto headlamps.
PERFORMANCE maximum speed 207kph (128.9mph); 42.6kph (26.5mph) @ 1000rpm; 0-100kph (62mph) 10.5sec; fuel consumption 9.9l/100km (28.5mpg), 5.7l/100km (49.5mpg), 7.2l/100km (39.2mpg).
PRICE July 2004 1.88 LX 4-door £14,900; estate £15,900; Zetec 5-door 2.0 automatic £17,800; Zetec-S 2.0tdci 130PS £19,150; Ghia 1.8Sci 4-door 6-speed manual £17,500; Ghia X 1.8Sci 6-speed £19,700; ST220 4-door 3.0 £23,100.

2004
Fiesta, Fusion 1.6 TDCi

The Fiesta reached maturity with a glowing reputation for space and practicality, yet some disappointment perhaps over the cabin materials, low-speed ride, and refinement. However most drivers were happy to trade a bit of firm springing for good road grip and safe, enjoyable handling. The engine range was wide: 1.3 8-valve; 1.25 16-valve; 1.4, 1.4TDCi and 1.6 16-valve. Furthermore the Fiesta had a good name for safety and security equipment, with standard passenger airbags and antilock brakes. Fusion, with which Fiesta shared a platform, gained some cosmetic enhancements at the Geneva Motor Show 2003 and was called Fusion Plus. For only the second time on a UK Ford it had DVD rear seat entertainment; it gained an extra 10.7l (0.38cuft) stowage space and the optional Electronic Stability Programme (ESP). The DVD's infra-red headsets eliminated tangled cables, and the system functioned for half an hour after the car was switched off, before shutting down to preserve battery life. Fusion had three engine choices, the 1.4-litre 68PS TDCi, 1.4-litre 80PS and 1.6-litre 100PS 16v. Small-engined Fiestas were manual 5-speeders. The 1.4L and 1.4TDCi could have manual or EST advanced manual and for 2004 both Fusion and Fiesta gained a new fully automatic transmission for the 1.6 16v, a conventional 4-speed with hydraulic clutches, brakes and planetary gears.

ABOVE **The third generation high-pressure common rail diesel 90PS Duratorq 1.6L TDCi joined the existing 68PS 1.4 8-valve to take Fiesta and Fusion into the growing "premium diesel" sub segment. This accounted for nearly a quarter of B class sales in the UK, Germany, France and Spain.**

INTRODUCTION Fiesta Autumn 2004; Fusion 1.6 spring 2005.
BODY Fiesta: saloon; 3-5 dr, 4 seats; weight 1.3, 1.4, 1030kg (2270.7lb); 1.6 1040kg (2293lb), TDCi 1060kg (2337lb). Fusion 1070kg (2359lb).
ENGINE 4-cylinders; transverse; 76mm x 76.5mm, 1388cc; cr 11:1; 58kW (77.8bhp) @ 5700rpm; 41.8kW (56.1bhp)/l; 124Nm (91.5lbft) @ 3500rpm. 1.6: 79mm x 81.4mm; 1596cc; 74kW (99.2bhp) @ 6000rpm; 46.4kW (62.2bhp)/l; 146Nm (108lbft) @ 4000rpm. 1.4 TDCi: 73.7mm x 82mm; 1399cc; compr 17.9:1; 50kW (67.1bhp) @ 4000rpm; 35.7kW (47.8bhp)/l; 160Nm (118lbft) @ 2000rpm. 1.6TDCi 75mm x 88.3mm; 1560cc; compr 18:1; 66kW (88.5bhp) @ 4000rpm; 42.3kW (56.7bhp)/l; 204Nm (150.5lbft) @ 1750rpm.
ENGINE STRUCTURE 1.3 chain driven single ohc 8-valves; 1.4, 1.6 petrol, 2 belt-driven ohc; 16-valves; aluminium head, block; fuel injection, Siemens engine management; 5-bearing crank. TDCi 1.4, 1 belt-driven ohc; 8-valves, 1.6 2 belt-driven ohc 16-valves; common rail diesels turbocharged.
TRANSMISSION fwd; hydraulic diaphragm spring sdp clutch; 5-speed synchro manual or Durashift EST; 1.6 opt automatic; final drive 4.06:1, EST 4.25:1, automatic 4.28:1, diesels 3.37:1. Fusion 4.25:1, auto 4.28:1.
CHASSIS steel monocoque; ifs by MacPherson struts, offset coil spring, lower arms on subframe, rear torsion beam axle; tele dampers; anti roll bar; hydraulic vacuum servo split dual circuit disc (Fusion ventilated) and drum brakes, ABS, front discs 25.8cm (10.2in); PAS; 45l (9.9gal) fuel tank; 175/64R14 tyres 5J rims.
DIMENSIONS wb 248.5cm (97.8in); track front 147.5cm (58.1)(Fusion 148cm (58.3in), rear 144.5cm (56.9in); length 391.5cm (154.1in); width 168cm (66.1in); height 146cm (57.5in); ground clearance 14cm (5.51in), Fusion 16cm (6.29in); turning circle 10.3m (33.8ft).

EQUIPMENT Fiesta 4 trim levels: Finesse, Zetec, LX, Ghia airbags, deadlocks, CD player all standard. LX electric windows and mirrors, air conditioning. Zetec alloys.
PERFORMANCE max 1.4/16 167kph (104mph); 1.6 183kph (113.9mph); TDCi 1.6 180kph (112.1mph). Fusion 163kph (101.5mph); 178kph (110.9mph), 176kph (282.5kph). 34.5kph (21.49mph), 32.9kph (20.49mph), 42.8kph (26.7mph) @ 1000rpm; 0-100kph (62mph) 13.2sec, 10.6sec, 11.9sec. Fusion 13.7; 10.9, 12.9sec; fuel con 6.6l/100km (42.8mpg), 6.9l/100km (40.6mpg), 4.7l/100km (60.6mpg).
PRICE Fiesta 1.25 £8495, 1.6 £10,645, 1.4TDCi £9695. Fusion 1.4 £9925, 1.6 £11,525, TDCi £10,695.

2004
Fiesta ST, Zetec S

The Sports Technologies (ST) Fiesta recreated the excitement and sportiness of the 1981 XR2, the 1989 XR2i (qv) and later versions, of which British enthusiasts bought 34,000. The ST was the first road car from the Team RS organisation within Ford, and besides the customary colour-keyed body details, fancy bumpers, rubbing strips, outside mirror finishers and 17in 11-spoke alloy wheels, it had a vigorous 2-litre engine and chassis tuning to provide handling that matched its speed. Racing style seats were trimmed in black leather with bold red centre sections bearing an ST logo. A leather steering wheel and metal pedals completed the sporty picture. By the time the car reached its first buyers in 2005, the rear spoiler was altered to achieve less drag and more downforce, the steering ratio was raised and the seats were more supportive. Fiesta ST achieved the competitive insurance rating of 13E. Late in 2004, with more enthusiasts appreciating the ambitious torque of modern turbo-diesels, it was time for the Fiesta Zetec S. This shared some of the dynamics and cosmetics of the ST, including discreet side skirts and the rear spoiler on the roof trailing edge, with the 1.6 TDCi engine. Zetec S was also available with the 1.6 16-valve petrol engine, and a choice of four colours including an exclusive Magnum Grey metallic.

INTRODUCTION Geneva Motor Show 2004, on sale January 2005.
BODY saloon; 3-doors, 4-seats; weight 1060kg (2337lb).
ENGINE 4-cylinders; transverse; 87.5mm x 83.1mm, 1999cc; compr 10.8:1; 110kW (147.5bhp) @ 6000rpm; 55kW (73.8bhp)/l; 190Nm (140lbft) @ 4500rpm. 1.6TDCi 75mm x 88.3mm; 1560cc; compr 18:1; 66kW (88.5bhp) @ 4000rpm; 42.3kW (56.7bhp)/l; 204Nm (150.5lbft) @ 1750rpm. 1.6, 79mm x 81.4mm; 1596cc; 74kW (99.2bhp) @ 6000rpm; 46.4kW (62.2bhp)/l; 146Nm (107.7lbft) @ 4000rpm.
ENGINE STRUCTURE Duratec 2.0; 2 belt-driven ohc; 16-valves; aluminium head, block; fuel inj, Siemens engine management; 5-bg crankshaft. TDCi 1.6; 2 belt-driven ohc 16-valves; common rail diesel, turbo. 1.6 petrol, 2 belt-driven ohc; 16-valves; fuel inj, Siemens engine management.
TRANSMISSION fwd; hydraulic diaphragm spring sdp clutch; 5-speed synchro; ST final drive 3.82:1
CHASSIS steel monocoque; ifs by MacPherson struts, offset coil spring, lower arms on subframe, rear torsion beam axle; tele dampers; anti roll bar; hydraulic vacuum servo split dual circuit disc brakes, 25.8cm (10.2in); ABS; PAS; 45l (9.9gal) tank; 195/45 R16; 205/40 R17 tyres, 6.5, 7J rims.
DIMENSIONS wb 248.5cm (97.8in); track front 147.5cm (58.1in), rear 144.5cm (56.9in); length 391.5cm (154.1in); width 168cm (66.1in); height 146cm (57.5in); clearance 14cm (5.5in); turning circle 10.3m (33.8ft).
EQUIPMENT optional twin body stripes £150, side stripes £75.
PERFORMANCE maximum 208kph (129.5mph), TDCi 179.8kph (112mph), 1.6 183kph (114mph); ST 31.8kph (19.8mph) @ 1000rpm; ST 0-100kph (62mph) 8.4sec, TDCi 11.2sec, 1.6 petrol 9.9sec, ST 5.7l/100km (49.6mpg).
PRICE ST £13,595; TDCi £12,495; Zetec S petrol £11,595.

2004
Focus 3/5 door

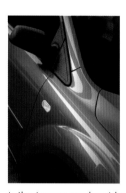

Changes to the Focus in 2004 included a completely new front. The A-post was more steeply raked, the bonnet rose more sharply, the trapezoidal grille was given a chrome surround, the high tail lamps were slimmed down, and the tailgate was made wider and deeper, making it easier to load bulky items. But the biggest change was on the body sides. Since 1998 the Focus had distinctive wheelarches, which curved into the doors and side rubbing strip, and now they were subdued and less of a feature. The effect was less crisp, more conformist, yet the model's success remained undiminished as a 3-door and 5-door with a choice of six engines 1.4, 1.6, (100 and 115ch) 2.0, and 1.6 and 2.0 TDCi. The new body was said to be 10 per cent stiffer with a robust new front subframe. The facia lost its voluptuous Ka-style curves to emphasise clarity and practicality. As a result of the steeper-raked windscreen, solar reflective glass could be used to block nearly five times the radiation of standard tinted glass, improving air conditioning efficiency. Among the additional options were headlights that guided the beams to follow the steering, Bluetooth hands-free phones, voice control of audio, telephone, climate control, and in-car navigation. The 12l (0.4cuft) facia compartment could keep refreshments chilled in cars with air-conditioning.

INTRODUCTION autumn 2004. **BODY** saloon; 3-doors, 5-doors, 5-seats; weight 1150kg (2535.3lb), 2.0 1230kg (2711.6lb), TDCi 1260kg (2777.8lb) and 1300kg (2866lb). **ENGINE** 4-cylinders; transverse; 76mm x 76.5mm, 1388cc; compr 11:1; 59kW (79.1bhp) @ 5700rpm; 42.5kW (56.1bhp)/l; 124Nm (91.4lbft) @ 3500rpm. 1.6, 79mm x 81.4mm; 1596cc; 74kW (99.2bhp) @ 6000rpm; 46.4kW (62.2bhp)/l; 146Nm (107.7lbft) @ 4000rpm, or 84kW (112.6bhp) @ 6000rpm; 52.6kW (70.5bhp)/l; 55Nm (114lbft) @ 4150rpm. 2.0 87.5 x 83.1mm, 1999cc; cr 10.8:1; 107kW (143.5bhp) @ 6000rpm; 63.5kW (85.2bhp)/l; 185Nm (136.5lbft) @ 4500rpm. 1.6 TDCi 75mm x 88.3mm; 1560cc; cr 18:1; 80kW (107.3bhp) @ 4000rpm; 51.3kW (68.8bhp)/l; 204Nm (150.5lbft) @ 1750rpm. 2.0TDCi 85mm x 88mm; 1997cc; compr 18:1; 100kW (134.1bhp) @ 4000rpm; 50.1kW (67.2bhp)/l; 320Nm (236lbft) @ 4500rpm. Overboost 1.6 260Nm (191.7lbft), 2.0 340Nm (250.7lbft).

ENGINE STRUCTURE 1.4, 1.6 petrol, 2 belt-driven ohc; 16-valves; aluminium head, block; fuel injection, Siemens electronic engine management; 5-bearing crank. 2.0 Duratec, 2 belt driven ohc; 16-valves; aluminium head, block; fuel inj, Siemens engine management; 5-brg crank. TDCi; 2 belt-and-chain driven ohc 16-valves; 1.6 aluminium block, steel liners, aluminium head; 2.0 iron block aluminium head; 1600bar common rail diesel with Garrett turbocharger and intercooler. **TRANSMISSION** fwd; hydraulic diaphragm spring sdp clutch; 5-speed synchro; final drive 4.06:1; TDCi 1.6 3.41:1; TDCi 2.0 6-speeds, final drive 2.85:1. 1.6TDCi opt CVT. **CHASSIS** steel monocoque; ifs by MacPherson struts, offset coil spring, lower arms on subframe, gas-filled dampers; irs short-long arm control blade, anti-roll bar; gas-filled dampers; anti roll bar; hydraulic vacuum servo split dual circuit disc brakes, 27.8cm (10.9in), 30cm (11.8in) ventilated front; 26.5cm (10.4in), 28cm (11.02in) rear; ABS; rack and

pinion PAS (electro-hydraulic on 2.0, and TDCi); 55l (12.1gal) tank; 195/65 R15; 205/55 R16 tyres, 6/6.5/7J rims. **DIMENSIONS** wb 264cm (103.9in) track front 153.5cm (60.4in), rear 153cm (60.2in); length 434cm (170.9in); width 184cm (72.4in); height 149cm (58.7in); ground clearance 14cm (5.5in); turning circle 10.7m (35.1ft). **EQUIPMENT** dual single-stage front airbags, optional thorax side airbags, full-length inflatable side-curtains, pyrotechnic pretensioner retractor front seat belts, collapsible pedals. **PERFORMANCE** maximum 1.4 164kph (101mph), 1.6 180kph (111mph), 2.0 206kph (127mph), 2.0TDCi 203kph (125mph); 1.4 32.5kph (20.24mph), 2.0 36kph (22.4mph), 2.0 TDCi 57.2kph (35.6mph) @ 1000rpm; 0-100kph 14.1sec, 9.2sec, 9.3sec; 6.6l/100km (42.7mpg); 7.1l/100km (39.8mpg); 5.6l/100km (51.4mpg). **PRICE** 1.4 Studio 3-door £10,895, 5-door £11,495; 2.0 Zetec 3-door £14,195, 5-door £14,795; 2.0 TDCi Titanium 5-door £17,675.

2004
Maverick, Escape 2.3 16v, 3.0V6

Maverick put on weight. Between its launch in 2001 and Geneva 2004, when it was restyled and enhanced with a Duratec 2.3litre 4-cylinder engine in place of the 2.0litre, it gained 55kg (121.2lb). Longer and wider, it had an improved version of the front wheel drive transmission which, sensing when it was losing grip, turned automatically to four wheel drive. A member of Ford's global 4-cylinder family, the engine was certified to Euro Stage IV emissions, with a balancer shaft improving smoothness and refinement. Safety was enhanced with side-impact protection and pretensioners that tightened the front safety belts in the first moments of a crash. Energy management retractors then gradually slackened them to reduce pressure on the occupant's chest. Emergency Brake Assist was power assistance that recognised hard braking and helped the driver apply maximum effort. The air bags recognised less severe frontal crashes, inflating with reduced force, or not at all. Mavericks now had disc brakes on all four wheels. The V6 came with a 4-speed automatic and was configured for smoother idle through new mountings and optimal throttle feel by a Black Oak powertrain management computer. The refreshed appearance included a new interior and central console and the rear liftgate had flip-up glass to improve luggage access. Maverick was also made in the United States, where it was known as the Escape.

INTRODUCTION 2004, Geneva.
BODY SUV; 5-doors, 5-seats; weight 1525kg (3362lb); 3.0 1589kg (3503.1lb).
ENGINE 4-cylinders, in-line; 87.5mm x 94mm, 2261cc; compr 9.7:1; 110kW (147.5bhp) @ 5700rpm; 48.7kW (65.3bhp)/l; 200Nm (147.5lbft) @ 4000rpm. 3.0 60 deg V6; 89mm x 79.5mm; 2967cc; comp 10:1; 149kW (199.8bhp) @ 6000rpm; 50.2kW (67.3bhp)/l; 262Nm (193.2lbft) @ 4850rpm.
ENGINE STRUCTURE 4-valves 40deg; 2 chain-driven ohc; aluminium head, block; electronic fuel injection; 5-bearing crankshaft. 3.0 Duratec V6; 4-valves; 2x2 chain-driven ohc; aluminium; Ford EEC-V electronic injection; 4-bearing crank.
TRANSMISSION front wheel drive; automatic engagement 4wd; variable distribution through central viscous coupling; 5-speed synchromesh; final drive 4.43:1. 3.0 4-speed automatic, 3.77:1
CHASSIS steel monocoque; ifs by MacPherson struts; multi-link irs; anti roll bars; telescopic dampers; hydraulic servo 30.3cm (12in) disc brakes, ventilated at front; ABS; PAS; 62l (gal) tank; 215/70 R16 tyres, 7Jrims.
DIMENSIONS wheelbase 262cm (103.2in); track front 155.5cm (61.2in), rear 155cm (61in); ground clearance 21cm (8.3in); length 444cm (174.8in); width 182.5cm (71.8in); height 176cm (69.3in).
EQUIPMENT Spare tyre under boot floor; centre console with stowage bin, 12-volt power point, air-con, adjustable cupholders; optional micro-perforated leather upholstery.
PERFORMANCE maximum speed 171kph (106.2mph); 36.1kph (22.4mph) @ 1000rpm; 0-100kph (62mph) 10.7sec; fuel consumption 10.6l/100km (26.65mpg). 3.0 188kph (116.8mph); 49kph (30.4mph); 10.5sec; 12.2l/100km (23.2mpg).
PRICE 2.0 XLT £17,815; 3.0 £20,815.

2005
Focus 4-door saloon, Wagon

Four doors and a boot put the Focus saloon slightly up-market, albeit a slightly older market perhaps than the 3- or 5-door, one that would appreciate the better proportions and tranquility that came with the stiffer construction round the partition between the passengers and luggage. The weight difference between 5- and 4-door was negligible, however the estate car version introduced in 2004, with its extra 13.5cm (5.3in) overall length, did carry a penalty of 50kg-70kg (110-154lb). The 4-door's engine choice started at 1.6-litre, it was built with Ghia or Titanium trim at Valencia in Spain, and shared the same front end with the 3-door, 5-door, estate and Focus C-Max. Its boot space was 526l (18.6cuft), and with a 102cm (40.2in) lid and 104.8cm (41.25in) between the wheel arches it was roomier and more accessible than the previous Focus. Liftover height was 65.6cm (25.8in) and the 60/40 split rear seat back allowed for long loads. The Focus Wagon, no longer with a 1.4-litre option, had 475l (16.8cuft) of carrying capacity, extendable to 1525l (53.8cuft) with the back seats folded flat. Known within Ford as the C-car, something like three million Focuses of all types had been built at Saarlouis and Valencia and build quality was constantly improved. Laser sighting and laser welding robot construction, with x-ray checking of welds, reduced panel gaps to 3.5mm with tolerances of just 1mm.

INTRODUCTION 4-door on sale 21 May 2005.
BODY saloon; 4-doors, 5-seats; weight 1150kg (2535lb), 2.0 1230kg (2712lb), Wagon 1285kg (2833lb), TDCi 1260kg (2778lb), Wagon 1310kg (2888lb) and 1300kg (2866lb), Wagon 1370kg (3020lb).
ENGINE 4-cylinders; transverse; 79mm x 81.4mm; 1596cc; 74kW (99.2bhp) @ 6000rpm; 46.4kW (62.2bhp)/l; 146Nm (107.7lbft) @ 4000rpm, or 84kW (112.6bhp) @ 6000rpm; 52.6kW (70.5bhp)/l; 155Nm (114lbft) @ 4150rpm. 2.0 87.5 x 83.1mm, 1999cc; cr 10.8:1; 107kW (143.5bhp) @ 6000rpm; 63.5kW (85.2bhp)/l; 185Nm (136.5lbft) @ 4500rpm. 1.6 TDCi 75mm x 88.3mm; 1560cc; cr 18:1; 80kW (107.3bhp) @ 4000rpm; 51.3kW (68.8bhp)/l; 204Nm (150.5lbft) @ 1750rpm. 2.0TDCi 85mm x 88mm; 1997cc; compr 18:1; 100kW (134.1bhp) @ 4000rpm; 50.1kW (67.2bhp)/l; 320Nm (236lbft) @ 4500rpm. Overboost 1.6 260Nm (191.7lbft), 2.0 340Nm (250.7lbft).

ENGINE STRUCTURE 1.6 and 2.0 Duratec, 2 belt-driven ohc; 16-valves; aluminium head, block; fuel inj; Siemens electronic engine management; 5-brg crank. TDCi; 2 belt-and-chain driven ohc 16-valves; 1.6 aluminium block, steel liners, aluminium head; 2.0 iron block aluminium head; 1600bar common rail diesel with Garrett turbocharger and intercooler.
TRANSMISSION fwd; hydraulic diaphragm spring sdp clutch; 5-spd synchro manual gearbox; final drive 4.06:1; TDCi 1.6 3.41:1; TDCi 2.0 6-spd, final drive 2.85:1. 1.6TDCi optional CVT.
CHASSIS steel monocoque; ifs by MacPherson struts, offset coil spring, lower arms on subframe, gas-filled dampers; irs short-long arm control blade, anti-roll bar; gas-filled dampers; anti-roll bar; hydraulic vacuum servo split dual circuit disc brakes, 27.8cm (10.9in), 30cm (11.8in) ventilated front; 26.5cm (10.4in), 28cm (11in) rear; ABS; rack and pinion PAS (electro-hydraulic on 2.0, and TDCi); 55l (12.1gal) tank; 195/65 R15; 205/55 R16 tyres, 6/6.5/7J rims.

DIMENSIONS wheelbase 264cm (103.9in); track front 153.5cm (60.4in), rear 153cm (60.2in); length 434cm (170.9in), Wagon 447.5cm (176.2in); width 184cm (72.4in); height 149cm (58.7in); ground clearance14cm (5.5in); turning circle 10.7m (35.1ft).
EQUIPMENT dual single-stage front airbags, optional thorax side airbags, full-length inflatable side-curtains, pyrotechnic pretensioner retractor front belts, collapsible pedals.
PERFORMANCE maximum speed 1.6 180kph (111mph); 2.0 206kph (127mph); 2.0TDCi 203kph (125mph) 2.0 36kph (22.4mph); 2.0 TDCi 57.2kph (35.6mph) @ 1000rpm; 0-100kph (62mph) 1.6 15.1sec, Wagon 15.5sec, 2.0 9.2sec, Wagon 9.4sec; 9.3sec Wagon 9.5sec; fuel consumption 6.6l/100km (42.7mpg); 7.1l/100km (39.8mpg); 5.6l/100km (51.4mpg).
PRICE 1.6 Wagon LX £12,798; 1.6 TDCi Titanium £17,425; 2.0 TDCi £18,525. 4-door. 4-door 1.6 Ghia £15,020; 2.0 Titanium £16,520; 2.0TDCi Titanium £17,875.

2005
Fiesta

Following the new edition at Frankfurt in 2001, and new engines in autumn 2004, the Fiesta 3-door and 5-door was given what Ford called a designer makeover for the 2006 model year. This amounted to new bumpers and grille, new headlamps and rear lamps, thicker body side mouldings, body-coloured handles and mirrors on "selected models". The interior was a little more daring, but not much. A new facia and better materials with a "soft-feel" upper section made up some of the ground that was being lost to competitors. The Fiesta remained good to drive. Many testers reckoned it was the best-handling supermini and it was rated highly for practicality. Interior space was generous, with the increase in size achieved over the previous model especially in the back, and although the boot was small it was a good shape for luggage. The diesels earned almost universal praise, although the 1.25 and 1.4 petrol cars gained more credit for their economy than their speed. To try and keep Fiesta British sales at the commendable level of 100,000 (along with Fusion) in the year, a number of features were added, including rain sensing wipers, automatic "home safe" headlight mode, air conditioning, one touch down driver's electric window, and MP3-compatible stereo.

ABOVE **Fiesta came joint top with the Nissan Micra in** *What Car?***'s security tests. Burglars were unable to break through the fixed allocation of deadlocks inside two minutes.**

INTRODUCTION November 2005. **BODY** saloon; 3 or 5-doors, 5-seats; weight 1.4, 1030kg (2270.7lb), 1.25 1100kg (2425lb), 1.6 1040kg (2292.8lb), TDCi1060kg (2336.9lb). **ENGINE** 4-cylinders; transverse; 71.9mm x 76.5mm; 1242cc: cr 10.1:1; 55kW (73.8bhp) @ 6000rpm; 44.3kW (59.4bhp)/l; 110Nm (81.1lbft) @ 4000rpm. 74 x 75.5mm; 1299cc; cr 10.2:1; 51kW (68.4bhp) @ 5600rpm; 39.2kW (52.6bhp)/l; 106Nm (18.2lbft) @ 2600rpm. 76mm x 76.5mm, 1388cc; cr 11:1; 59kW (79.1bhp) @ 5700rpm; 42.5kW (56.9bhp)/l; 124Nm (91.4lbft) @ 3500rpm. 79mm x 81.4mm; 1596cc; 74kW (99.2bhp) @ 6000rpm; 46.4kW (62.2bhp)/l; 146Nm (107.7lbft) @ 4000rpm, or 84kW (112.6bhp) @ 6000rpm; 52.6kW (70.5bhp)/l; 155Nm (114lbft) @ 4150rpm. 87.5 x 83.1mm, 1.4TDCi 73.7mm x 82mm; 1399cc; compr 17.9:1; 50kW (67.1bhp) @ 4000rpm; 35.7kW (47.9bhp)/l; 160Nm (118lbft) @ 2000rpm. 1.6 TDCi 75mm x 88.3mm; 1560cc; cr 18:1; 80kW (107.3bhp) @ 4000rpm; 51.3kW (68.8bhp)/l; 204Nm (150.5lbft) @ 1750rpm. **ENGINE STRUCTURE** 1.25 and 1.6 petrol 16-valves; 2 belt-driven ohc; aluminium head, block; fuel inj; Siemens electronic engine management; 5-brg crank. 1.3 8-valve 2 belt-driven ohc; TDCi 1.4 8-valves 1 chain driven ohc, 1.6 16-valves, 2 chain-driven ohc; aluminium. **TRANSMISSION** fwd; hydraulic sdp clutch; 5-speed synchromesh manual gearbox; final drive 3.37:1 1.4, 1.25, 4.25:1 1.6, 4.25 and 4.28; TDCi 1.4 3.37:1. **CHASSIS** steel monocoque; ifs by MacPherson struts, offset coil spring, lower arms on subframe, rear torsion beam axle; telescopic dampers; anti-roll bar; hydraulic vacuum servo split dual circuit, 25.8cm (10.2in) ventilated front disc and drum brakes, ABS; PAS; 43l (9.5gal) tank;195/60R15, 195/55R16 tyres 6J rims.

DIMENSIONS wheelbase 248.5cm (97.8in); track front 147.5cm (58.1), rear 144.5cm (56.9in); length 391.5cm (154.1in); width 168cm (66.1in); height 146cm (57.5in); ground clearance 14cm (5.5in); turning circle 10.3m (33.8ft). **EQUIPMENT** rain-sensing wipers; optional satellite navigation; MP3 connection. **PERFORMANCE** maximum speed 1.3 160kph (99.6mph), 1.25 163kph (101.5mph), 1.4 166kph (103.4mph), 1.6 TDCi 180kph (112.1mph); 34.8kph (21.7mph) @ 1000rpm, 1.4 34.5kph (21.5mph), 1.6 TDCi 42.8kph (26.7mph); 0-100kph (62mph) 17.3sec, 1.4 13.2sec, 1.6 TDCi 11.9sec; fuel consumption (mean official figs) 6.24l/100km (45.2mpg), 1.4 6.4l/100km (44.1mpg); 1.4TDCi 4.33l/100km (65.1mpg). **PRICE** 1.25 16v Studio 3-door £8,395; 1.6 Ghia 5-door £12,545; 1.6 TDCi £12,495.

2005
Fusion

Bluetooth hands-free technology, relaying the caller's voice over the car speakers when the hands-free phone was in use, was one of the Fusion's features for MY 2006. Sales were pushed at dealerships to sustain what was, in effect, a taller multi-purpose Fiesta that had more space, a higher driving position and good visibility. Fiesta and Fusion were Britain's third best-selling model and second-best supermini to the Vauxhall Corsa. Like all Fiesta based Fords from the Puma to the Ka, it enjoyed a favourable reputation for being satisfactory to drive, although it weighed more. New colours came in for the new season, with a trip computer giving miles to empty, average and actual fuel consumption, average speed, trip distance and outside temperature. Optional air conditioning had automatic temperature control. Powered and heated mirrors folded away when central locking was activated or they could be moved away manually for parking in tight spaces. Fusion had a choice of two petrol and two diesel engines, 5-speed gearbox, or two sorts of automatic transmission. The comprehensive list of options could be rationalised into packs; Reflex (side thorax airbags, side air-curtain airbags and centre rear head restraint, together with Electronic Stability Programme ESP); Smokers (ashtray and cigar lighter), and interior styling (colour co-ordinated mats and interior appliqué).

INTRODUCTION November 2005. **BODY** estate; 5-doors, 5-seats; weight 1070kg (2359lb); TDCi 1.4 1100kg (2425lb); TDCi 1.6 1085kg (2392lb). **ENGINE** 4-cylinders; transverse; 76mm x 76.5mm, 1388cc; cr 11:1; 59kW (79.1bhp) @ 5700rpm; 42.5kW (56.9bhp)/l; 124Nm (91.4lbft) @ 3500rpm. 79mm x 81.4mm; 1596cc; 74kW (99.2bhp) @ 6000rpm; 46.4kW (62.2bhp)/l; 146Nm (107.7lbft) @ 4000rpm. 1.4TDCi 73.7mm x 82mm; 1399cc; cr 17.9:1; 50kW (67.1bhp) @ 4000rpm; 35.7kW (47.9bhp)/l; 160Nm (118lbft) @ 2000rpm. 1.6 TDCi 75mm x 88.3mm; 1560cc; cr 18:1; 66kW (88.5bhp) @ 4000rpm; 42.3kW (56.7bhp)/l; 204Nm (150.5lbft) @ 1750rpm.

ENGINE STRUCTURE 16-valves; 2 belt-driven ohc; aluminium head, block; fuel inj, Siemens electronic engine management; 5-brg crank. TDCi 1.4 8-valves; 1 belt-driven ohc; iron block; aluminium head. 1.6 aluminium block, steel liners, aluminium head; 1600bar common rail diesel with Garrett turbocharger and intercooler. **TRANSMISSION** fwd; hydraulic sdp clutch; 5-speed synchromesh; final drive 1.4, 1.6, 4.25:1, TDCi 3.37:1. **CHASSIS** steel monocoque; ifs by MacPherson struts, offset coil spring, lower arms on subframe; rear torsion beam axle; telescopic dampers; anti roll bar; hydraulic vacuum servo split dual circuit, 25.8cm (10.2in) ventilated front disc and drum brakes, ABS; PAS; 43l (9.5gal) tank; 195/60R15, 195/55R16 tyres 6J rims. **DIMENSIONS** wheelbase 248.5cm (97.8in); track front 148cm (58.3in), rear 144.5cm (56.9in); length 402cm (158.3in); width 172cm (67.7in); height

153cm (60.2in); ground clearance 16cm (6.3in); turning 10.3m (33.8ft). **EQUIPMENT** 9 or 7 spoke alloy wheels £250-£350; privacy glass £100; sat nav £1,000; leather trim £750; ST Sport heated leather seats £750; Bluetooth hands-free phone and voice control system £250-£300. **PERFORMANCE** maximum speed 163kph (101.5mph); TDCi 1.6 176kph (109.6mph) 35kph (21.8mph) @ 1000rpm; TDCi 1.6 42.8kph (26.7mph) 0-100kph (62mph) 14sec; TDCi 1.6 12.9sec; fuel consumption (av) 6.4l/100km (44.1mpg), TDCi 1.6 4.8l/100km (58.9mpg). **PRICE** Studio 3-door 1.25 £8,227; Style 5-door 1.4 TDCi £10,347; Zetec Climate 1.6 TDCi £11,547; Ghia 1.6 100 automatic £13,232.

2005
Focus ST

Sports Technologies (ST) Fiestas were already well established when the formula was applied to the Focus, with the addition of a 225 PS 2.5-litre 5-cylinder turbocharged engine. Ford was able to draw on technology developed elsewhere within the Premier Automotive Group, and the Volvo-sourced engine not only propelled the ST to 60mph inside 6.5sec, but also into *What Car?*'s honours for 2006 as best hot hatch against the VW Golf Gti, arguably the archetype of the category, and the Skoda Octavia RS. Here was a car to form the basis of a World Rally Championship contender using Ti-VCT (twin independent variable cam timing), which produced formidable torque, flat-lining the full 320Nm (236lbft) from a meagre 1600rpm right up to 4000rpm, before tapering gently away to 6500rpm at the peak of the power range. With 30 per cent stiffer springing, five per cent firmer anti-roll bar recalibrated dampers and lowered by 1.5cm (.59in), the ST's agility and smooth ride matched its speed. The styling was sharpened to a WRC contender profile and the inverted trapezoidal grille added to the dramatic effect. Inside the customary red and black, with the option of Performance Blue or Electric Orange, created a strongly competition ambience. Best of all the ST was priced £1,500 less than its closest rival.

INTRODUCTION Geneva 2005, on sale Autumn 2005.
BODY saloon; 3/5-doors, 4-seats; weight 1315kg (2899lb)/1360kg (2998.3lb).
ENGINE 5-cylinders; transverse; 83mm x 93.2mm, 2522cc; cr 9.0:1; 166kW (222.6bhp) @ 6100rpm; 65.8kW (88.2bhp)/l; 320Nm (236lbft) @ 1600-4000rpm.
ENGINE STRUCTURE 20-valves; 2 belt-driven ohc; variable valve timing; direct-acting shimless tappets; aluminium head, block; sequential electronic fuel injection; Bosch engine management; KKK-Warner integrated turbocharger; intercooler; 6-bearing crankshaft.
TRANSMISSION fwd; sdp clutch; 6-speed synchromesh; final drive 4.0:1.
CHASSIS steel monocoque; ifs MacPherson struts with offset coil springs; anti roll bar; irs short-long arm control blade multi-link; coil springs; telescopic dampers; hydraulic servo brakes, diagonally split; front 32cm (12.6in) ventilated disc, rear 28cm (11in); ABS; rack and pinion PAS; 55l (12.1gal) tank; 225/40R18 tyres; 8J rims; cast aluminium alloy wheels.
DIMENSIONS wheelbase 264cm (103.9in); track front 153.5cm (60.4in), rear 153.1cm (60.3in); length 436.2cm (171.7in); width 184cm (72.4in); height 144.7cm (56.9in); ground clearance 12.5cm (4.9in); turning circle 11.7m (38.4ft).
EQUIPMENT Recaro seats; front and side airbags; pyrotechnic seat belt pretensioners; neck injury protection system on front seats.
PERFORMANCE maximum speed 241kph (150mph); 41.5kph (25.9mph) @ 1000rpm; 0-100kph (62mph) 6.8sec; fuel consumption combined 9.3l/ 100km (30.4mpg).
PRICE from £17,520.

2005
Mondeo

Launched in 1993, equipped with the 2.5-litre V6 in 1994, restyled in August 1996, relaunched as a new edition in 2000, enhanced by the addition of the sporting ST220 in the autumn of 2002, restyled again and given the 1.8Sci direct injection engine in June 2003, freshening up of the Mondeo fell due in 2005. "Mondeo has been in the top 10 best selling cars in Britain since its launch. It is currently the second best selling diesel and a firm favourite with both retail and fleet customers," according to Jon Gunn-Smith, large car brand manager Ford of Britain. Changes to the exterior across the range gave a new appearance to the front bumper and a chrome grille. New Titanium and Titanium X versions, introduced as special editions in 2004, gave more choice to premium buyers alongside the existing Ghia and Ghia X. A 6-speed transmission became available and the addition of the 155PS TDCi made the Mondeo one of the most powerful diesels in the segment. Known first as the ST TDCi as part of the Sports Technologies Mondeo range, this engine later became available on Zetec models as well. Meeting the Euro Stage IV emission regulations, which became mandatory on 1 January 2006, the engine had an electrically actuated variable turbocharger, bringing the usable power band down to 1250rpm.

INTRODUCTION May 2005, Stage IV 90PS TDCi August 2005. Specifications for 1.8 125PS, 2.0 145PS, 2.0 130PS TDCi:
BODY Saloon/Wagon; 4/5-doors, 5-seats; weight 1285kg (2832.9lb)/1360kg (2998.3lb). TDCi 1390kg (3064.4lb)/1460kg (3218.7lb).
ENGINE 4-cylinders; transverse; 83mm x 83mm, 1798cc; cr 10.8:1; 92kW (123.4bhp) @ 6000rpm; 51.2kW (68.7bhp)/l; 170Nm (125.4lbft) @ 4500rpm. 2.0 87.5mm x 83mm; 1999cc; cr 10.8:1; 107kW (143.5bhp) @ 6000rpm; 53.5kW (71.7bhp)/l; 190Nm (140lbft) @ 4500rpm. TDCi 86mm x 94mm; 2198cc; cr 17.5:1; 114kW (152.9bhp) @ 3500rpm; 51.9kW (69.6bhp)/l; 360Nm (265.5lbft) @ 1800rpm.
ENGINE STRUCTURE Duratec HE 1.8 and 2.0; 16-valve; 2 chain-driven ohc; aluminium head and block;

electronic fuel injection, engine management, and fuel system; 5-bearing crankshaft. TDCi 2 belt-and-chain driven ohc 16-valves.
TRANSMISSION front wheel drive; hydraulic sdp clutch; 5-speed synchromesh; final drive 3.82:1; 2.0 4.07:1; CD4E automatic 4.23:1; TDCi 6-speed, final drive 4.07 and 2.85:1.
CHASSIS steel monocoque with front and rear sub-frames; ifs by twin-tube MacPherson struts; trailing arm Control Blade irs; coil springs; anti roll bar; gas filled telescopic dampers; hydraulic servo ventilated disc brakes, front 30cm (11.81in) , rear 28cm (11in). ABS, optional ESP; PAS; 58l (12.75gal) tank; 205/55 R16, 205/50 R17, 225/40 R18 tyres 6.5J rims.
DIMENSIONS wb 275.5cm (108.5in); track front 152cm (59.8in) rear 153.5cm (60.4in); length 473cm

(186.2in); width 181cm (71.25in); height 146cm (57.5in); ground clearance 11.6m (38.1ft) turning circle 10.7m (35.1ft), 11.2m (36.7ft).
EQUIPMENT Titanium X 18in alloys, Alcantara/leather trim; ESP; climate seats.
PERFORMANCE maximum speed 205kph (127.7mph); 215kph (133.9mph) (automatic 190kph) (118.4mph); 220kph (137mph) 35.2kph (21.9mph), TDCi 57.2kph (35.6mph) @ 1000rpm; 0-100kph (62mph) 10.9sec, 9.6sec auto 11.4sec, 8.9sec; fuel consumption 8.4l/100km (33.8mpg), 8.6l/100km (33mpg), 6.4l/100km (44.1mpg).
PRICE LX1.8 4-door, £15,800; estate £16,800; Zetec 2.0 automatic 5-door £18,300; 2.2 TDCi 6-speed estate £19,800.

2006
S-MAX

A new monospace 7-seater with transverse engine and front wheel drive, the S-Max was a new model for Ford, filling the space between the Mondeo Wagon and the Galaxy MPV. Under Ford's shared technologies strategy, which allowed input between brands and models, within the Premier Automotive Group, the S-Max shared ingredients with other Ford and PAG models. As a means of reducing costs and spreading development load the arrangement worked well, with most customers unaware of it, the rest seemingly unaffected. Aimed squarely at buyers with an active lifestyle, the major S-Max feature was a second and third row of seats that could provide 32 variations of space and seating arrangement. Each seat folded flat, second row seats slid and tilted, and the third row tilted, so S-Max could be configured for combinations of people or large loads of baggage. There were 26 stowage compartments under the floor, in the seats and in the facia, together with an array of optional items that included dog guards, roof boxes, a coolbox, bicycle carrier, towbar and an "activity kit" using aluminium bars and attachments to lock other sporting or recreational items in place. Customers had a choice of two petrol and two diesel engines. Trim options were LX, Zetec, and Titanium.

INTRODUCTION Geneva Motor Show, on sale June 2006.
BODY one-box people carrier; 5-doors, 7-seats; weight 2.0 1605kg (3538.4lb); 2.5 1681kg (3705.9lb); 1.8 and 2.0 TDCi 1736kg (3827.2lb).
ENGINE 2.0 4-cylinders; transverse; 87.5 x 83.1mm, 1999cc; cr 10.8:1; 107kW (143.5bhp) @ 6000rpm; 63.5kW (85.2bhp)/l; 190Nm (140.5lbft) @ 4500rpm. 2.5, 5 cylinders; 83mm x 93.2mm, 2522cc; cr 9.0:1; 162kW (217.2bhp) @ 6100rpm; 64.3kW (86.2bhp)/l; 324Nm (238.9lbft) @ 1600-4000rpm. 1.8 TDCi 82.5mm x 82mm; 1753cc; cr 18.1:1; 92kW (123.4bhp) @ 3700rpm; 52.5kW (70.4bhp)/l; 320Nm (236lbft) @ 1500-4800rpm. 2.0 TDCi 85mm x 88mm; 1997cc; cr 18.1:1; 105kW (140.8bhp) @ 4000rpm; 52.6kW (70.5bhp)/l; 340Nm (250.8lbft) @ 4500rpm.
ENGINE STRUCTURE 2.0 16-valves; 2 chain-driven ohc; aluminium head and block; electronic fuel injection, engine management, and fuel system; 5-bearing crankshaft. 2.5, 20-valves; 2 belt-driven ohc; variable valve timing; direct-acting shimless tappets; aluminium cylinder head, block; sequential electronic multipoint fuel injection; Bosch engine management; KKK-Warner integrated turbocharger; intercooler; 6-bearing crankshaft, dual mass flywheel. 1.8 TDCi 1 belt driven ohc; cast iron head and block; common rail multi-point fuel injection; electrically actuated variable geometry Garrett GT18 turbocharger, intercooler and transient torque overboost. 2.0 TDCi 16-valves; dohc; iron block, aluminium head.

TRANSMISSION front wheel drive; hydraulic sdp clutch; MTX75 5 or 6-speed double synchromesh; final drive 1.8, 3.56:1, 2.0, 4.067:1, 2.5 4:1. 6-speed 4.0 and 2.9.
CHASSIS steel monocoque with front and rear sub-frames; independent front suspension by twin-tube MacPherson struts; trailing arm Control Blade irs; coil springs; anti roll bar; gas-filled telescopic dampers with CCD; hydraulic servo disc brakes, ventilated front 30cm (11.81in), rear 30.2cm (11.88in);

electronic parking brake; ABS, EBD; rack and pinion HPAS (2.0TDCi EHPAS); 70l (15.4 gal) tank; 215/60 R16, 225/50 R17, 235/45 R18 tyres 6.5J rims.
DIMENSIONS wheelbase 285cm (112.2in); track front 158.9cm (62.6in) rear 160.5cm (63.2in); length 482cm (189.7in); width 185.4cm (72.9in); height 165.8cm (65.3in); turning circle 11.9m (39ft).
EQUIPMENT LX 16in steel wheels; fog lights; power-operated and heated mirrors; steering wheel toggle controls; a/c; electric front windows; ABS; heated windscreen; stereo radio CD RDS EON.
PERFORMANCE maximum speed 2.0, 197kph (122.7mph); 2.5 230kph (143.3mph); 1.8 TDCi 187kph (116.5mph); 0-100kph (62mph) 10.5sec; 7.5sec; 11.3sec; 11.3sec fuel consumption 8.1l/100km (34.9mpg); 7.1l/100km (39.8mpg); 6.4l/100km (44.1mpg).
PRICE 2.0 LX £16,995; 1.8TDCi Zetec £19,295; 2.0TDCi Titanium £21,495.

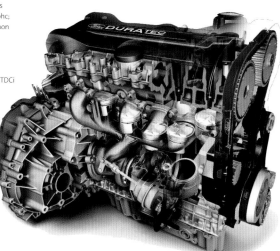

2006
Galaxy

By way of distinguishing it from the S-Max, the Galaxy, which had a broadly similar shape and specification, was priced a notch or two higher, as befitted a flagship. The Galaxy's important merit was that unlike the previous model, developed and manufactured in conjunction with the Volkswagen group, it was an in-house Ford product. It was aimed moreover at comfort and quality. Telling it apart from the S-Max was not easy however, apart from the front wheelarch air exit grilles, but closer observation would show different window profiles, and the more sporty S-Max was 6.7cm (2.6in) lower and 5cm (1.9in) shorter. The Galaxy had a squared-off rump by way of emphasising the essentially people-carrying and perhaps less frantically "lifestyle" role expected of it. S-Max drivers had a "cockpit" instead of a Galaxy's "command bridge", its seating was described as 5+2 instead of the Galaxy's simple seven, and the more luxurious model had two extra stowage compartments, making 31 with a combined capacity of 110l (3.9cuft). The air-conditioning cooled the facia glove box, where the family could keep its drinks cool. Galaxy trim levels were LX, Zetec, Ghia, and Ghia X. There was one-third more luggage room compared with the previous model, 435l (15.4cuft) against 335l (11.8cuft) even with all seven seats in place.

INTRODUCTION Geneva Motor Show, on sale June 2006.
BODY one-box people carrier; 5-doors, 7-seats; weight 2.0 1605kg (3538.4lb); 2.5 1681kg (3705.9lb); 1.8 and 2.0 TDCi 1736kg (3827.2lb).
ENGINE 2.0 4-cylinders; transverse; 87.5 x 83.1mm; 1999cc; cr 10.8:1; 107kW (143.5bhp) @ 6000rpm; 63.5kW (85.2bhp)/l; 190Nm (140Slbft) @ 4500rpm. 2.5 5-cylinders; 83mm x 93.2mm, 2522cc; cr 9.0:1; 162kW (217.2bhp) @ 6100rpm; 64.3Kw (86.2bhp)/l; 324Nm (238.9lbft) @ 1600-4000rpm. 1.8 TDCi 82.5mm x 82mm; 1753cc; cr 18:1; 92kW (123.4bhp) @ 3700rpm; 52.48kW (70.4bhp)/l; 320Nm (236lbft) @ 1500-4800rpm. 2.0 TDCi 85mm x 88mm; 1997cc; cr 18:1; 105kW (140.8bhp) @ 4000rpm; 52.6kW (70.5bhp)/l; 340Nm (250.8lbft) @ 4500rpm.
ENGINE STRUCTURE 2.0 16-valves; 2 chain-driven ohc; aluminium head and block; electronic fuel inj, and engine management; 5-brg crank. 2.5, 20-valves; 2 belt-driven ohc;

variable valve timing; direct-acting shimless tappets; aluminium head, block; sequential electronic multipoint fuel inj; Bosch engine management; KKK-Warner integrated turbocharger; intercooler; 6-bearing crank, dual mass flywheel. 1.8 TDCi 1 belt driven ohc; cast iron head and block; common rail multipoint fuel injection; electrically actuated variable geometry Garrett GT18 turbo, intercooler and transient torque overboost. 2.0 TDCi 16-valves; dohc; iron block, aluminium head.
TRANSMISSION fwd; hydraulic sdp clutch; MTX75 5 or 6-spd double synchro; final drive 1.8, 3.56:1, 2.0 4.067:1, 2.5 4.1. 6-spd 4.0 and 2.9.
CHASSIS steel monocoque with front and rear sub-frames; ifs by twin-tube MacPherson struts; trailing arm Control Blade irs; coil springs; anti roll bars; gas-filled telescopic dampers with CCD; hydraulic servo disc brakes, ventilated front 30cm (11.8in), rear 28cm (11in); electronic parking brake; ABS, EBD; rack and pinion HPAS (2.0TDCi EHPAS); 70l (15.4 gal) tank; 215/60 R16, 215/60 R16, 225/50 R17, 235/45 R18 tyres 6.5J rims.

DIMENSIONS wb 285cm (112.2in); track front 158.9cm (62.6in), rear 160.5cm (63.2in); l 482cm (189.7in); w 185.4cm (72.9in); h 172.5cm (67.9in); turning circle 11.9m (39ft).
EQUIPMENT Zetec. Air conditioning, overhead console. Ghia; chrome elements on outside; distinctive seat trim, standard cruise control, auto lighting, rain sensing wipers, full-length overhead console; Ghia X leather trim, panorama roof.
PERFORMANCE maximum speed 2.0, 194kph (120.8mph); 2.5 230kph (143.3mph); 1.8 TDCi, 187kph (116.5mph); 0-100kph (62mph) 10.5sec, 7.5sec, 11.3sec; fuel con 8.1l/100km (34.9mpg); 7.1l/100km (39.8mpg); 6.4l/100km (44.1mpg).
PRICE 2.0 LX £19,495; 1.8TDCi Zetec £22,295; 2.0TDCi Ghia £23,995

Both S-Max and Galaxy had Continuously Controlled Damping (CCD), an adaptive damper system controlling pitch and roll by monitoring and adjusting damper rates every two tenths of a second. Drivers could choose their own setting, Sport, Normal, or Comfort.

2006
Focus Coupe Cabriolet

The first production powered convertible was a French décapotable électrique of 1934. In 1957 Ford of America's Fairlane 500 Skyliner had a metal hardtop that retracted into the long boot, nearly 21,000 of which were sold at $2942. It continued with a restyled version of 1959 in the Galaxie sub-series until after 12,915 sales, too few for Ford, the $3349 "retrac" was discontinued. Almost 50 years later the theme was revived in Europe and Ford of Britain's first was a Coupe-Cabriolet (CC), joining the Focus range, at £200 cheaper than its GM rival and £2,575 less than the nearest competitor from VW. The CC's fully retractable two-piece hardtop opened and closed in 29 seconds. With the roof in place it had 534l (18.8cuft) of luggage boot space, while retracted there was still a useful 248l (8.8cuft), claimed as best in class. "The initial design of the Vignale Concept remained almost untouched during its transition to the production CC," according to Chris Bird, director of design Ford of Europe. Developed in partnership with Pininfarina in Italy, where it was to be produced, the CC was equipped with a Rollover Protection Device (RPD). On detecting an imminent overturning, two safety roll-bars extended by up to 20cm (7.9in), providing a supportive strut, protecting the occupants in conjunction with the strong windscreen pillars.

INTRODUCTION Vignale concept Paris 2004, shown Geneva and London 2006. On sale October 2006. **BODY** roadster; 2-doors, 4-seats; 1413kg-1631kg (3115.2-3595.7lb). **ENGINE** 4-cyl; transverse; 79mm x 81.4mm; 1596cc; 74kW (99.2bhp) @ 6000rpm; 46.4kW (62.2bhp)/l; 146Nm (107.7lbft) @ 4000rpm. 87.5 x 83.1mm, 1999cc; cr 10.8:1; 107kW (143.5bhp) @ 6000rpm; 63.5kW (85.2bhp)/l; 185Nm (136.5lbft) @ 4500rpm. 2.0TDCi 85mm x 88mm; 1997cc; cr 18:1; 100kW (134.1bhp) @ 4000rpm; 50.1kW (67.2bhp)/l; 320Nm (236lbft) @ 4500rpm. Overboost 1.6 260Nm (191.7lbft), 2.0 340Nm (250.7lbft).

ENGINE STRUCTURE 1.6 petrol 16-valves; 2 belt-driven ohc; aluminium head, block; fuel inj, Siemens electronic engine management; 5-bearing crank. 2.0 Duratec, 2 belt-driven ohc; 16-valves; aluminium head, block; fuel inj, Siemens electronic engine management; 5-bearing crank. 2.0 TDCi iron block aluminium head; 1600bar common rail diesel with Garrett turbo and intercooler. **TRANSMISSION** fwd; hydraulic sdp clutch; 5-speed synchro; final drive 4.06:1, TDCi 1.6 3.41:1, TDCi 2.0 6-speeds, final drive 2.85:1. 1.6TDCi optional CVT.

CHASSIS steel monocoque; ifs by MacPherson struts, offset coil spring, lower arms on subframe, gas-filled dampers; irs short-long arm control blade, anti-roll bar; gas-filled dampers; anti roll bar; hydraulic vacuum servo split dual circuit disc brakes, 27.8cm (10.9in), 30cm (11.8in) ventilated front, 26.5cm (10.4in), 28cm (11in) rear; ABS; rack and pinion PAS (electro-hydraulic on 2.0, and TDCi; 55l (12.1gal) tank; 195/65 R15; 205/55 R16 tyres, 6/6.5/7J rims. **DIMENSIONS** wb 264cm (103.9in); track front 153.5cm (60.4in), rear 153cm (60.2in); length 434cm (170.9in); width 184cm (72.4in); height 149cm (58.7in); ground clearance 14cm (5.51in); turning circle 10.7m (35.1ft). **EQUIPMENT** CC-1 alloys; CD, a/c. CC-2 10-spoke Vignale wheels; leather steering wheel; Sony MP3; quickclear windscreen. CC-3 leather trim, cruise control; Sony 6CD, auto lights/wipers/ mirror; chrome detail grille surround. **PERFORMANCE** maximum speed 2.0 206kph (127mph); 0-100kph (62mph) 9.2sec; fuel consumption 7.1l/100km (38mpg). **PRICE** Focus CC-1 £16,795; CC-2 £17,795; CC-2 diesel £19,270; CC-3 £18,795, and £20,210.

2006
Transit

After 40 years of unbroken success, the Transit was restyled, re-designed and re-engineered in Ford of Britain's research centre at Dunton, Essex. The interior was reconfigured with a facia-mounted gearshift making it more car-like, safety was improved, and the range widened to encompass 60 basic structures and body styles. Front wheel drive Transits were available with three east-west mounted Duratorq TDCi 2.2-litre diesels (85PS/250Nm, 110PS/285Nm, and 130PS/310Nm) developed at the Dagenham diesel centre, the first dedicated commercial vehicle powertrain under the partnership between Ford and PSA Peugeot-Citroën. Rear wheel drive Transits had a choice of

three Duratorq TDCi 2.4-litre diesels facing north-south (100PS/285Nm, 115PS/320Nm and 140PS/375Nm). The 2.4-litre was exclusively Ford. The seventh new engine was a petrol-LPG-compatible new Duratec 2.3-litre (145PS/200Nm) petrol unit, essentially the Mazda MZR assembled in Mexico. With Lanchester balancer shafts for smoother running, this had Electronic Throttle Control (ETC) for smoother response, a mechanical returnless fuel system and a smart fuel pump to regulate pressure. The engine met Stage IV emission legislation and had 20,000km or one-year oil service intervals. Hardened valve seats allowed conversion to LPG or CNG.

INTRODUCTION 2006.
BODY low, medium, and high roof panel van, high roof Jumbo, chassis cab, double cab, M2 and M1 people mover; up to 5-doors, up to 17-seats; 2200kg (4850lb) to 3300kg (7275lb).
ENGINE 4-cylinders; transverse or in-line; 2.2 TDCi 86mm x 94.6mm, 2198cc; cr 18:1; 96kW (128.7bhp) @ 3500rpm; 43.6kW (58.5bhp)/l; 319Nm (228.6lbft) @ 1600rpm. 2.4TDCi 89.9mm x 94.6mm; 2402cc; 103kW (138.1bhp) @ 3500rpm; 42.9kW (57.5bhp)/l; 375Nm (276.6lbft) @ 2000rpm. 2.3 petrol 87.5mm x 94mm; 2261cc; 107kW (143.5bhp) @ 5250rpm; 47kW (63bhp)/l; 200Nm (147.5ftlb) @ 3850rpm.
ENGINE STRUCTURE TDCi, 2 belt-and-chain driven ohc; aluminium head, block; common rail multi-point fuel inj; turbocharger and intercooler; transient torque overboost function; electronic throttle; dual mass flywheel; 5-bearing crankshaft.
TRANSMISSION fwd or rwd see text; hydraulic sdp clutch; 5 or 6-speed synchro; final drive, choice of 7.
CHASSIS steel; ifs by MacPherson struts; variable rate coil springs; stabilizer bar; rear suspension leaf springs; gas-filled dampers front and back; hydraulic dual circuit servo disc brakes; EBD; PAS; 80l (17.6gal) tank; choice of tyres, rims, wheels.
DIMENSIONS wb 293.3cm (115.5in); 330cm (129.9in); length 486.3cm (191.4in); width 523cm (205.9in) with mirrors 236cm (92.9in); height 198.9-260.2cm (78.3-102.4in) depending on configuration; turning circle 10.8m (35.4ft); 11.9m (39ft); 13.3m (43.6ft).
EQUIPMENT optional heavy duty front axle for "blue light" emergency services; two sizes of side door loading; 500 body variants; 8 year antiperforation warranty; optional satellite navigation system; air conditioning; cruise control, CD player.
PRICE 280 SWB 85PS panel van £13,650. Panel vans to £23,550.

2007
Mondeo 1.6, 2.0, 2.3

After it was introduced in January 1993, Mondeo gained a 2.5 V6 in June 1994. The ST220 came out in Autumn 2002 and the range was spruced up with a 1.8SCi engine in June 2003. Previewed at the Paris Motor Show close to production in September 2006, the new edition was introduced at Geneva the following March with what Ford called the kinetic design first seen on the Iosis Frankfurt Concept in 2005. Martin Smith, Ford Europe's Design Director, who had brought kinetic into production on the S-Max and Galaxy, said, "The Mondeo takes the next major step towards a more expressive and emotional Ford range." Chamfered corners, a deep offset between the top of the bonnet and front wings, and a three-plane plan formed the visual link to Iosis, creating a new 'family' face with a large upper and inverted trapezoidal lower grille. Big headlamps and lower foglamps disguised the bulk required to meet pedestrian safety legislation. Mondeo represented a €715million investment to develop Genk in Belgium into a flexible manufacturing plant. The common architecture and technology of the Mondeo, in all its three body styles, together with S-Max and Galaxy, allowed them to be produced on the same assembly lines. The 1.6 Duratec petrol engine was derived from the one fitted to the S-Max.

INTRODUCTION 2007.
BODY saloon/hatchback; 4 or 5-doors, 5-seats; weight 1360kg (2998.2lb), estate 1380kg (3042.3lb). 2.0 1400kg (3086.4lb). 2.3 1465kg (3229.7lb).
ENGINE 4-cylinders, transverse; 79mm x 81.4mm, 1596cc; compr 11:1; 81kW (108.62bhp) @ 6300rpm; 50.7kW (68bhp)/l; 160Nm (118lbft) @ 4100rpm, or 92kW (123.4bhp) @ 6300rpm; 160Nm (118lbft) @ 4100rpm. 2.0 87.5 x 83.1; 1999cc; cr 10.8:1; 107kW (143.5bhp) @ 6000rpm; 185Nm (136.4lbft) @ 4500rpm. Duratec HE 2.3 87.5 x 94; 2261cc; 10.6:1; 118kW (158.2bhp) @ 6500rpm; 208Nm (153.2lbft) @ 4200rpm.
ENGINE STRUCTURE Duratec Ti-VCT; 4-valves; 2 belt-driven ohc; aluminium head, block; Siemens fuel injection, 2.0, 2.3 sequential; Visteon engine management; 5-bearing crankshaft. 2.0, 2.3 chain-driven 2ohc.
TRANSMISSION front wheel drive Durashift iB5; hydraulic sdp clutch; 5-speed synchromesh; final drive 4.06:1. 2.0 4.07. 2.3 6-speed AWF21 automatic with Sport mode; 3.75:1.
CHASSIS steel monocoque, Boron A and B pillars; MacPherson strut ifs; SLA irs; subframes front and back; telescopic dampers; hydraulic servo disc brakes, front ventilated 30cm (11.8in), rear 30.2cm (11.9in), ABS; ESP; rack and pinion PAS; 70l (15.4gal) tank; 205/55R16, 215/55R16, 235/45R17, 235/40R18 tyre; 6.5J, 7.5J, 8J, rims.
DIMENSIONS wheelbase 285cm (112.2in); track front 159cm (62.6in); rear 160.5cm (63.2in); length 478cm (188.2in); width 188.5cm (74.2in); height 150cm (59in).
EQUIPMENT Boron bumper beams; 7 airbags; DEATC air conditioning; Edge, Zetec, Ghia and Titanium X options.
PERFORMANCE maximum speed 190kph (118.6mph); 0-100kph (62mph) 12.7sec; fuel consumption 7.2l/100km (39.2mpg). 2.0 210kph (130mph); 9.9sec; 7.9l/100km (35.8mpg). 2.3 207kph (128.6mph); 10.5sec; 9.9l/100km (28.5mpg).
PRICE 1.6 Edge £14,780; 2.0 Ghia X £20,492; 2.3 Zetec estate £19,690.

Mondeo 2.5 Turbo

Relinquishing Jaguar and the Premier Automotive Group provided an opportunity to regain ground in the premium market, neglected since the Granadas and Scorpios of the 1990s. A good deal had changed. Buyers were choosy about refinement and up-market rivals had introduced models well into traditional Ford territory. The new Mondeo was 4.7cm (1.8in) longer, 12cm (4.7in) wider, 7cm (2.7in) taller and the wheelbase was 9.6cm (3.8in) longer than its predecessor. A measure of success was Jeremy Clarkson's enthusiasm for it, although he remained typically blunt about cash-strapped Ford: "It has sold Aston Martin, it is shutting 14 plants, shedding 30,000 jobs and that's why the new Mondeo contains, as far as I can tell, no new technology at all. The Focus, designed in a bath of cash, had expensive independent rear suspension. The Mondeo has no similar technological leaps. What you do get is tried and tested. Largely parts come from the S-Max and the forthcoming Volvo V70. All Ford has done is screw them together properly." The rest of the press agreed that the driving appeal of the turbocharged flagship Mondeo matched that of BMWs and Audis, although, as Clarkson also pointed out: "That's before we get to the price. Whatever model you choose is going to be thousands and thousands cheaper than anything from Audi or BMW. And about a million less than anything from Stuttgart."

INTRODUCTION March 2007. BODY saloon/hatchback; 4 or 5-doors, 5-seats; weight 1490kg (3284.8lb) Estate +20kg (44.1lb).
ENGINE 5-cylinders; transverse 83mm x 93.2mm, 2521cc; compr 9:1; 162kW (217.2bhp) @ 5000rpm; 64.3kW (86bhp)/l; 320Nm (236lbft) @ 1500-4800rpm.
ENGINE STRUCTURE Duratec-HE, 4-valves; 2 belt-driven ohc; aluminium head, block; sequential fuel injection; Bosch engine management; coil on plug ignition; 6-bearing crankshaft; KKK turbocharger, intercooler.

TRANSMISSION front wheel drive; dual mass flywheel; hydraulic sdp clutch; 6-speed synchromesh M66; final drive 4.0:1.
CHASSIS steel monocoque, Boron A and B pillars; MacPherson strut ifs; SLA irs; subframes front and back; telescopic dampers; hydraulic servo disc brakes, front ventilated 30cm (11.8in), rear 30.2cm (11.9in), ABS; ESP; rack and pinion PAS; 70l (15.4gal) tank; 235/45R17, 235/40R18 tyre; 7.5J, 8J, rims.
DIMENSIONS wheelbase 285cm (112.2in); track front 159cm (62.6in); rear 160.5cm (63.2in); length 478cm (188.2in); width 188.5cm (74.2in); height 150cm (59in).

EQUIPMENT Boron bumper beams; 7 airbags; DEATC air conditioning; Edge, Zetec, Ghia and Titanium X options. 6cd autochanger, MP3 compatible 3.5mm auxiliary connection socket in glove box. Bluetooth hands free telephone option. DVD sat nav. HLA hill launch assist, IVDC, Adaptive Cruise Control.
PERFORMANCE maximum speed 245kph (152.2mph); 0-100kph (62mph) 7.5sec; fuel consumption 9.3l/100km (30.4mpg).
PRICE Ghia X £22,992.

2007
Mondeo 1.8, 2.0, 2.2 TDCi, estate

The Paris debut had previewed an estate car, and the complete 4- and 5-door saloon range became available in the second quarter of 2007. "The wagon bodystyle was important in the CD segment so it was appropriate to show it in Paris first," said Martin Smith. "It emphasised the sporty, dynamic and premium appearance of the new range. Above all, we managed to achieve this 'Kinetic' look without compromising luggage capacity. New Mondeo challenged perceptions of a big Ford." Detailing was good, with tie-down points and hooks in the luggage area, which at 1745l (62.6cuft) in 2-seat mode was 45l (1.6cuft) more than before. There were new "infotainment" systems, with Ford's Human Machine Interface (HMI) steering-wheel toggle switches as seen on Galaxy and S-Max, and a central LCD screen. John Fleming, President and CEO of Ford Europe called the new car "critical to the Ford of Europe business. (It) has always been a major player in the European CD segment, and with over four million owners looking for us to deliver something special, we have every intention of meeting their expectations." Among the premium-class innovations was green or blue tinted glass. Blue glass was traditionally used on premium cars and was standard for the techno contemporary look of the Titanium X. Green tinted glass was fitted to Edge, Zetec and Ghia, and all Mondeos were available with a solar reflect front windscreen.

INTRODUCTION March 2007 **BODY** saloon/hatchback; 4 or 5-doors, 5-seats; weight 1430kg (3152.6lb), 5-door estate +20kg (44lb). 2.0 1480kg (3262.8lb) **ENGINE** 4-cylinders, transverse; 82.6mm x 82mm, 1753cc; compr 18.5:1; 74kW (99.2bhp) @ 3850rpm; 56.6kW (75.9bhp)/l; 280Nm (206.5lbft) @ 1800rpm. Or 92kW (123.4bhp); 320Nm (236lbft). 2.0 85 x 88; 1997cc; 17.9:1; 85kW (114bhp) or 96kW (128.7bhp) or 103kW (138.1bhp) @ 4000rpm; 300Nm (221.3lbft) or 320Nm (236lbft) @1750-2250rpm.

ENGINE STRUCTURE 1.8L Duratorq 2-valves; sohc chain and belt drive; cast iron head, block; variable nozzle Garrett GT18 turbo with intercooler; Delphi common-rail fuel injection. 2.0L aluminium head, iron block; variable geometry turbo; common rail Ford multiple fuel injection; 5-bearing crankshaft. **TRANSMISSION** front wheel drive; hydraulic sdp clutch; 5-speed synchromesh; 2.0 6-speed; final drive 3.65:1. 2.0 2.77:1 or 2.95:1. Automatic 3.33:1

CHASSIS steel monocoque, Boron A and B pillars; MacPherson strut ifs; SLA irs; subframes front and back; telescopic dampers; hydraulic servo disc brakes, front ventilated 30cm (11.8in), rear 30.2cm (11.9in), ABS; ESP; rack and pinion PAS; 70l (15.4gal) tank; 235/45R17, 235/40R18 tyre; 7.5J, 8J, rims. **DIMENSIONS** wheelbase 285cm (112.2in); track front 159cm (62.6in); rear 160.5cm (63.2in); length 478cm (188.2in); width 188.5cm (74.2in); height 150cm (59in). **EQUIPMENT** Boron bumper beams; 7 airbags; DEATC air conditioning; Edge, Zetec, Ghia and Titanium X options. 6cd autochanger, MP3 compatible 3.5mm auxiliary connection socket in glove box. Bluetooth hands free telephone option. DVD sat nav. HLA hill launch assist, IVDC. **PERFORMANCE** maximum speed 185kph (115mph); 0-100kph (62mph) 12.3sec; fuel consumption 5.8l/100km (48.7mpg). 2.0 210kph (130mph); 9.5sec; 5.9l/100km (47.9mpg) **PRICE** 2.0 LX £18,022; 2.5 Titanium X £23,992.

2007
C-MAX

Focus was dropped from the C-MAX title during a freshening-up coinciding with the election of S-MAX as 2007 Car of the Year. The creation of one-box people-movers increased the volumes of existing platforms. New top presswork was relatively cheap, drivelines and running gear expensive, and more than 470,000 had already been built at Saarlouis to improve Focus economies of scale. The new variant kept its flexible three rear seats, the middle one folding away to allow the outer ones to converge diagonally, moving rearwards to provide extra leg and shoulder room for two. For utmost luggage carrying, all could be individually tipped, tumbled or removed. The front was 'kinetic', combining hard lines and flowing forms said to represent energy even when stationary. First seen in the Galaxy and S-MAX, this revised the face of 5-seat C-MAX, alongside the 5+2 S-MAX and 7-seat Galaxy. Buyers could ring the changes with petrol engines; 1.6-litre, 1.8-litre, and 2.0-litre between 100 PS (74 kW) and 145 PS (107 kW). The 1.8-litre HE Flexifuel could run on any mixture from 100 per cent petrol to an 85 per cent bio-ethanol fuel (E85). Bio-ethanol, derived from renewable biomass, reduced CO_2 emissions by up to 80 per cent. Flexifuel was part of a portfolio of environmentally friendly technologies. The 2.0-litre Duratec HE could be ordered in some places fully converted for Liquefied Petroleum Gas (LPG) or Compressed Natural Gas (CNG).

INTRODUCTION 2007, spec for 2.0 Duratec petrol and 2.0TDCi Duratorq.
BODY MPV; 5-doors, 5-seats; weight 1320kg (2910lb); TDCi 1415kg (3119.5lb).
ENGINE 4-cylinders; transverse; 87.5mm x 83.1mm, 1999cc; compr 10.8:1; 107kW (143.5bhp) @ 6000rpm; 53.5kW (71.7bhp)/l; 185Nm (136.4lbft) @ 4000rpm.TDCi, 85 x 88mm; 1997cc; cr 18:1; 100kW (134.1bhp) @ 4000rpm; 50.1kW (67.2bhp)/l; 320Nm (236lbft) @ 2000rpm

ENGINE STRUCTURE 4-valves; chain-driven dohc; aluminium head, block; Visteon engine management, electronic fuel injection; 5-bearing iron crankshaft. TDCi 4-valve belt and chain dohc; Siemens engine management; common rail injection; low inertia turbocharger; forged steel crankshaft.
TRANSMISSION front wheel drive; dual mass flywheel; hydraulic 24cm (9.4in) sdp clutch; Getrag 5-speed synchromesh; automatic option; final drive 4.06:1, auto 4.2. TDCi 6-speed; 3.81:1/2.77:1

CHASSIS steel monocoque; Macpherson strut ifs; anti roll bar; multi-link control blade irs; anti roll bar; hydraulic servo dual circuit diagonal split disc brakes, front 30cm (11.8in) ventilated, rear 28cm (11in), ABS, optional ESP; electronic-hydraulic r&p PAS; 55l (12.1gal) tank; TDCi 53l (11.6gal); 205/55R16/17 tyres, 6.5J/7.5J 16/17rims, alloy wheels.
DIMENSIONS wheelbase 264cm (103.9in); track front 153.5cm (60.4in), rear 153cm (60.2in); length 433.5cm (170.7in); width 182.5cm (71.8in); height 156cm (61.4in).
EQUIPMENT optional panorama laminated layer glass roof with integral blinds. Style, Zetec, Ghia, Titanium; X-pack available for Ghia and Titanium; Sport pack for Zetec and Titanium.
PERFORMANCE maximum speed 203kph (126.1mph); 36kph (22.4mph) @ 1000rpm; 0-100kph (62mph) 9.8sec; fuel consumption 7.3l/100km (38.6mpg). Auto 8.1/34.8. TDCi 200kph (124.3mph); 57kph (35.4mph) @ 1000rpm; 9.6sec; 5.8l/100km (48.6mpg)
PRICE 1.6 Studio £12,805; 1.8FFV Titanium £16,300; 2.0TDCi Titanium £18,555.

2008
Galaxy 2.2 TDCi

Business Car's Multi Purpose Vehicle of the year, the Galaxy gained the prolific (Peugeot; Citroën; Jaguar; Land Rover; Volvo; Mazda) Duratorq 175PS 2.2 TDCi, the largest and most powerful diesel in a European Ford passenger car. There was also an extra 10PS for 2.0 diesel S-Max and Galaxy models with automatic transmission and a 2.0 Flexifuel. Following its new freedom in the premium market after the dissolution of Premier Automotive, Ford sold the new Galaxy only with Ghia trim, well equipped with accessories such as wireless Bluetooth mobile phone connectivity. *Autocar* thought the refined and smooth-running 2.2 well suited to automatic transmission and was disappointed it was not available, as on the

2.0. The testers thought it maintained a decent cruise and picked up speed quite quickly, although suffering from diesel rattle on startup. The extra torque proved a boon when the Galaxy's seven seats were occupied; it was no lightweight at some 375kg (626.7lb) more than a Mondeo and at 176m (69.3in) tall against the saloon's 150cm (59in), carried a lot of built-in headwind. In the autumn Galaxy buyers were offered a free panorama roof, worth £700, and following the (temporary) 2.5per cent reduction in VAT, an effective price reduction of around £500. Galaxy was also one of the first to be available with Digital Audio Broadcasting (DAB) radios as standard on Titanium, X and X Sport derivatives.

INTRODUCTION May 2008.
BODY MPV; 5-doors, 5/7-seats; weight 1775kg (3913.2lb).
ENGINE 4-cylinders; transverse; 85mm x 96mm, 2179cc; compr 16.6:1; 129kW (173bhp) @ 3500rpm; 59.2kW (79.4bhp)/l; 400Nm (295lbft) @ 1750-2750rpm.
ENGINE STRUCTURE 2-valves; sohc chain and belt drive; cast iron head; variable nozzle VNG turbocharger with intercooler; common-rail fuel injection; 5-bearing crankshaft.
TRANSMISSION front wheel drive; hydraulic 22.8cm (9in) sdp clutch; 6-speed synchromesh; ESP; final drive 4.27:1.
CHASSIS steel monocoque, Boron A and B pillars; MacPherson strut ifs; SLA irs; subframes front and back; telescopic dampers; hydraulic servo disc brakes, front ventilated 30cm (11.8in), rear 30.2cm (11.9in), ABS; ESP; rack and pinion PAS; 70l (15.4gal) tank; 215/60R16, 225/50R17 tyre; 6.5J, 7J, rims.
DIMENSIONS wheelbase 285cm (112.2in); track front 158cm (62.2in), rear 160cm (63in); length 482cm (189.8in); width 188.5cm (74.2in); height 176cm (69.3in).
EQUIPMENT 10-spoke alloy wheels; solar reflect windscreen; rear compartment a/c. Ghia X Plus-pack 18in alloys; bi-xenon lights; leather trim.
PERFORMANCE maximum speed 208kph (129.2mph); 0-100kph (62mph) 9.6sec; fuel consumption 7l/100km (40mpg).
PRICE Ghia £25,775.

2008
Kuga 2.0 TDCi, 2.5T

Crossover was coined to describe a vehicle built on a car platform with the tall interior, high seating position, generous ground clearance and four wheel drive capability of a Sports Utility Vehicle. Good crossovers felt like saloon cars to drive, with secure handling and a smooth ride. The Kuga effectively replaced the Maverick and was sold in Britain mostly with the Duratorq 2.0 turbodiesel, although a few came with the alternative 2.5 petrol engine. Growing demands from green lobbyists gave the diesel a best in class CO2 figure of 169g/km and a particulate filter was standard equipment. The C-car architecture of the Focus and C-Max provided a satisfactory balance of comfort and control

although critics thought the steering lifeless and the luggage space of 360l (12.7cuft), smaller than a Focus, ungenerous. With the back seats flat it was 1355l (47.8cuft). Underseat storage beneath the rear seats and boot floor were practical Sports Utility features. The back seats had a 60/40 split and the tailgate a flat glass upper section that opened separately. The engine was outstandingly refined and wind and road noise subdued to levels more like a saloon than an SUV. Titanium Kugas had rain sensing wipers, partial leather trim, cruise control, blue tinted glass and among the options was a rear-facing camera for safe reversing. Both diesels produced the same torque, the 5-cylinder through a wider rev range.

INTRODUCTION March 2008 on sale June.
BODY SUV; 5-doors, 5-seats; weight 1500kg (3307lb), 2.5 1530kg (3373lb).
ENGINE 4-cylinders, transverse; 85mm x 88mm, 1997cc; compr 17.9:1; 100kW (134bhp) @ 4000rpm; 50.1kW (67.1bhp)/l; 320Nm (236lbft) @ 2000rpm. 2.5, 5-cylinders 83 x 93.2; compr 9:1; 147kW (197.1bhp) @ 6000rpm; 320Nm (236lbft) @1600-4000rpm.
ENGINE STRUCTURE DW10, 4-valves; 20hc belt and chain; aluminium head, block; common rail direct injection; VNG turbo and intercooler; 5-bearing crankshaft. 5-cylinder 6.
TRANSMISSION fwd, automatic engagement 4wd; MMT6 sdp clutch; 6-speed Getrag synchromesh; electronic Haldex torque distribution; final drive 3.24:1, AWD 4.53:1. 5-cyl 5-speed, 6-speed automatic option, final drive 2.65:1.
CHASSIS steel monocoque; ifs struts; irs multi-link; anti roll bars; telescopic dampers; hydraulic servo disc brakes, front 30cm (11.8in) ventilated, rear 30.2cm (11.9in), ABS, EBD; rack and pinion PAS; 66l (14.5gal) tank; 235/55R17 tyres, 7J, 7.6J rims, wheels.
DIMENSIONS wheelbase 269cm (105.9in); track front 158cm (62.2in), rear 159cm (62.6in); length 444.3cm (174.9in); width 184cm (72.4in); height 171cm (67.3in).
EQUIPMENT Keyless start, a/c, ESP, MP3 connector, 230v/150w socket, cruise control standard. Optional panoramic roof, DAB radio.
PERFORMANCE maximum speed 182kph (mph); 0-100kph (62mph) 10.6sec; fuel consumption 6.4l/100km (44.1mpg). 5-cyl 205kph (mph); 8.8sec; 8.1l/100km (28.5mpg)
PRICE £21,502 Zetec, £27,252 Titanium.

2008
Ka 1.2, 1.3 TDCi

Radical when it first appeared in 1996, the Ka's origami style was successful, providing a useful increase in the volume and lowering the cost of its Fiesta underpinnings. Its numbers would barely have justified it as a stand-alone model however, so when a replacement fell due Ford and Fiat found common cause in co-producing two models on the same basis. Fiat's plant at Tychy, Poland had been making Pandas since 2003; production reached 360,000 in 2007, with the introduction of the Fiat 500. Adding the Ka took this to over half a million, making the factory viable and competitive. Ford's version was by all accounts better, changes to the suspension and steering improving its ride and handling. *Autocar*

columnist Steve Cropley had no doubts: "Ford needs to embody modern design values, not pick up a lot of retro cues like the Fiat. Ford has amassed a great reputation for providing some of the best-handling mainstream cars, but it has never been required to use someone else's suspension. Ford insiders confirmed that they examined the Fiat hardware (while it was in the very last design stages) and satisfied themselves that it could work under a Ford." *What Car?* confirmed Cropley's confidence: "It's nimble through corners and accurate to steer. The ride is surprisingly good for such a small car – more settled than the Fiat."

INTRODUCTION Paris, 2008 on sale January 2009.
BODY saloon; 3-doors, 4-seats; weight 865kg (1907lb), 1.3TDCi 980kg (2160.5lb).
ENGINE 4-cylinders, transverse; 70.8mm x 78.9mm, 1242cc; compr 11.1:1; 51kW (68.4bhp) @ 5500rpm; 41kW (55bhp)/l; 102Nm (75.2lbft) @ 3000rpm. 1.3 69.6 x 82; 1248cc; compr 17.6:1; 55 kW (73.8bhp) @4000rpm; 145Nm (106.9lbft) @ 3500rpm
ENGINE STRUCTURE 2-valves; belt driven ohc; aluminium head, block; fuel injection; 5-bearing crankshaft. 1.3, 2 chain-driven ohc; direct injection, turbocharger, intercooler
TRANSMISSION front wheel drive; hydraulic sdp clutch; 5-speed synchromesh; final drive 3.44:1.
CHASSIS steel monocoque; MacPherson strut ifs; anti-roll bar; rear folded sheet steel torsion beam axle; telescopic dampers; anti roll bar; hydraulic servo brakes, front 24cm (9.4in) disc, rear 18cm (7in) drums, ABS, EBD; r&p electric PAS; 35l (7.7gal) tank; 175/65 R14, 195/50 R15 tyres, 5.5, 6J rims. 1.3 ventilated discs
DIMENSIONS wheelbase 230cm (90.5in); track front 141cm (55.5in), rear 140cm (55.1in); length 362cm (142.5in); width 166cm (65.4in); height 150.5cm (59.2in). 1.3, 151cm (59.4in).
EQUIPMENT a/c on Edge, Zetec, Titanium; optional ESP.
PERFORMANCE maximum speed 159kph (98.8mph); 0-100kph (62mph) 13.1sec; fuel consumption 5l/100km (55.4mpg). 1.3 4.2l/100km (67.3mpg).
PRICE Studio £7995, 1.3 Zetec £10,195.

2008
Fiesta 1.2, 1.4, 1.6 TiVCT; 1.4 and 1.6TDCi

'Global' cars were an automotive Holy Grail for a hundred years. The Model T came close and so was its only rival in production longevity, universal recognition and the total number made, the Volkswagen Beetle. Nothing else came close. World-wide single designs languished on manufacturers' wish lists throughout the 20th century. Ford managed cars with the same name in different places, but the practicalities of actually making them the same proved insurmountable. Basing a world class Fiesta on the Mazda 2 brought the goal closer. If the fundamentals suited Europe and Asia, and they demonstrably did, North America, China, Australia and South Africa would surely follow. Fiesta was described as the first Ford under what was called the Global

Product Development System (GPDS) and more were promised. Adjustments were made to meet different countries' requirements, better ride and handling to suit European driving styles, for example, and important innovations were made in engines. Better fuel economy and emissions were crucial in ecologically-charged times. Emissions of CO_2 were reduced against previous Fiestas. There was an ultra-low CO_2 ECOnetic model with emissions of 98g/km and a top range 1.6-litre Duratec Ti-VCT petrol. Developments in responsiveness, economy and emissions came through improvements to 1.4 and 1.6litre Duratorq TDCi diesels. Electric PAS made a small contribution to greenery, as well as avoiding the expense and complication of hydraulics.

INTRODUCTION Geneva March, on sale October 2008.
BODY saloon/hatchback; 3/5-doors, 5-seats; 1.2 weight 965kg (2127.4lb). 1.6TiVCT 970kg (2138.4lb). TDCi 1025kg (2259.7lb)
ENGINE 1.6TiVCT 4-cylinders; transverse; 79mm x 81.4mm, 1596cc; compr 11:1; 88kW (118bhp) @ 6000rpm; 73.9kW (99bhp)/l; 152Nm (112.1lbft) @ 4050rpm. 1.6TDCi ECOnetic 75 x 88.3; 1560cc; compr 18.3:1; 66kW (88.5bhp) @ 4000rpm; 204Nm (150.5lbft) @ 1750rpm.
ENGINE STRUCTURE 4-valves; 2 belt-driven ohc; aluminium head, block; Siemens fuel injection; 5-bearing crankshaft. TDCi 2 belt and chain ohc; common rail Bosch direct injection; turbocharger; intercooler; Perlitic cast iron crankshaft.
TRANSMISSION front wheel drive; 5-speed synchromesh; ESP; final drive 3.82:1. TDCi 3.37:1; Econetic 3.05:1
CHASSIS steel monocoque; Macpherson strut ifs; anti roll bar; twist-beam rear suspension, coil springs; anti roll bars; telescopic dampers; hydraulic servo brakes, front 25.8cm (10.2in) ventilated disc, rear 20cm (7.9in) drums, ABS; electric PAS; 45l (9.9gal) tank; 175/65R14, 195/45R16, 205/40R 17 tyres.
DIMENSIONS wheelbase 249cm (98in); track front 147.5cm (58in), rear 146cm (57.5in); length 395cm (155.5in); width 172cm (67.7in); height 148cm (58.3in).
EQUIPMENT ECOnetic, lowered suspension, low rolling resistance tyres, special aerodynamic profile, specially calibrated Duratorq 1.6 TDCi, low 98g/km CO_2 exempt from road tax .
PERFORMANCE maximum speed 193kph (120mph); 0-100kph (62mph) 9.9 sec; fuel consumption 5.8l/100km (47.9mpg). TDCi 175kph (mph); 42.8kph @ 1000rpm; ECOnetic 3.7l/100km (76.3mpg).
PRICE Studio £8695, Style £9295, Style+ £10,395, Zetec £10,995, Zetec S 12,595, Titanium £12,095, ECOnetic £11,845.

2009
Focus RS Mk 2

Previewed in 2007 on the restyled Focus at Frankfurt, the Mark 2 RS was worth waiting for. *What Car?* called the handling sublime. "The RS practically explodes off the mark, hitting 62mph in just 5.9 seconds, and doesn't give up until it reaches 163mph. Driven gently it is surprisingly civilised." The Focus of 2004 gained the so-called Kinetic style of the 2006 Galaxy, S-Max and Mondeo. The overall shape was maintained, yet most body panels except the roof were reworked. Trapezoidal grilles, swept back headlamps and sculpted wheelarches made the RS look like a works rally car. Four wheel drive was rejected as heavy and complicated so the RS had innovative front suspension known as a RevoKnuckle, designed to reduce torque steer, troublesome on powerful front wheel drive cars and usually worse with wide tyres and limited-slip differentials. RevoKnuckle worked in conjunction with a Quaife automatic torque biasing limited-slip differential. RS engineers worked with the Advanced Research Centre in Aachen to develop the suspension around the simplicity of a McPherson strut, with geometry settings minimising disturbances principally a reduction in steering offset. Space-saving rear suspension, introduced by Richard Parry-Jones in 1998, gave good body control and an absorbent ride. The multi-link used trailing arms, giving the geometry of double wishbones. Control Blade had wide and simple uniformly thick pressed steel trailing arms with hub carriers in place of two longitudinal locating rods.

INTRODUCTION July 2008.
BODY saloon; 2-doors, 4-seats; weight 1468kg (3236lb).
ENGINE 5-cylinders, transverse; 83mm x 93.2mm, 2522cc; compr 8.5:1; 221kW (296.4bhp) @ 6500rpm; 87.6kW (117.5bhp)/l; 440Nm (324.5lbft) @ 2250-4500rpm.
ENGINE STRUCTURE 4-valves; chain-driven dohc; aluminium head, block; Bosch ME 9.0 Motor-Management sequential injection and ignition; 6-bearing forged steel crankshaft; Borg-Warner K16 integral turbocharger, intercooler.
TRANSMISSION front wheel drive; dual mass flywheel; sdp clutch; 6-speed synchromesh; ESP; Quaife automatic torque biasing limited-slip differential; final drive 4:1.
CHASSIS steel monocoque; Macpherson strut ifs; independent rear suspension control blade multi-link; 24mm (.095in) anti roll bars; telescopic dampers; hydraulic servo disc brakes, front 33.6cm (13.2in) ventilated, rear 30.2cm (11.9in), EBD, ABS; rack and pinion PAS; 55l (12gal) tank; 235/35R19 tyres.
DIMENSIONS wheelbase 264cm (103.9in); track front 158.6cm (62.4in), rear 158.7cm (62.5in); length 434cm (170.9in); width 184.2cm (72.5in); height 148.4cm (58.4in).
EQUIPMENT .
PERFORMANCE maximum speed 263kph (163mph); 0-100kph (62mph) 6sec; fuel consumption 9.9l/100km (28.5mpg).
PRICE £24,995.

2009
S-Max, 2008 2.2 TDCi

Following the May 2008 changes announced for MY 2009, the 175PS 2.2 Duratorq TDCi engine was extended to MPVs. The alterations provided an increase from 130PS to 140PS for the 2.0 diesel in S-MAX and Galaxy, with a choice of 6-speed manual or automatic gearboxes. An optional flexifuel engine could run on any mix of bio-ethanol and petrol and for 2010 the 2.0 SCTi, a 203PS turbocharged petrol engine, made use of EcoBoost, a global Ford initiative for high-volume engine technology. This ranged from small cars to large trucks, aimed to use 20 per cent less fuel, and cut CO2 from four and six cylinder engines by 15 per cent. Ford claimed that compared to expensive hybrids and diesel engines, EcoBoost improved the existing petrol engine without compromising performance. Entry-level versions of the S-Max were renamed Edge instead of LX. Wireless Bluetooth mobile phone connectivity became standard and by the time it was revised in 2010 the price had gone up to £20,645. S-Max gained two *Fleet News* awards for its Easy Fuel System (preventing inadvertent filling with the wrong one) as Best Technical Innovation. It was also Best MPV, beating five others thanks to "good design, practicality, high quality, flexibility and driver appeal. This car will appeal to both finance and HR-led fleets – allowing employees to choose a people carrier without feeling they are driving a big car."

INTRODUCTION May 2008.
BODY one-box people carrier; 5-doors, 7-seats; weight 1725kg (3802.9lb).
ENGINE 2.2 TDCi 85mm x 96mm; 2179cc; compr 16:1; 129kW (172.9bhp) @ 3500rpm; 59.2kW (79.4bhp)/l; 400Nm (295lbft) @ 1750--2750rpm.
ENGINE STRUCTURE 2-valves; sohc chain and belt drive; cast iron head, block; variable nozzle VNG turbocharger with intercooler; common-rail fuel injection; 5-bearing crankshaft.
TRANSMISSION front wheel drive; hydraulic sdp clutch; 6-speed synchromesh; ESP; final drive 4.27:1.
CHASSIS steel monocoque with front and rear sub-frames; independent front suspension by MacPherson struts; trailing arm Control Blade irs; coil springs; anti roll bar; gas-filled telescopic dampers with CCD; hydraulic servo disc brakes, ventilated front 30cm (11.81in), rear 30.2cm (11.88in); electronic parking brake; ABS, EBD; rack and pinion HPAS; 70l (15.4 gal) tank; 235/45 R18 tyres 7, 8J rims.
DIMENSIONS wheelbase 285cm (112.2in); track front 158.9cm (62.6in) rear 160.5cm (63.2in); length 477cm (187.8in); width 188.4cm (74.2in); height 177.5cm (69.8in); turning circle 11.9m (39ft).
EQUIPMENT optional seat pack; space pack; Titanium X pack with keyless entry, panorama roof, Bi-xenon headlights, Alcantara/leather trim.
PERFORMANCE maximum speed 212.4kph (132mph); 0-100kph (62mph) 9.1sec; fuel consumption 6.6l/100km (42.8mpg).
PRICE £17,800.

2010
Galaxy

After ten years with the Portuguese-made Galaxy, Ford started making its own in 2005 at Genk along with the S-Max on the Mondeo platform. The S-Max grew sportier and the Galaxy more luxurious with seats that folded away yet could carry seven with space to spare. As veteran tester Honest John wrote, "You could put a couple of kids in the rearmost seats, slide them forward a bit and have plenty of room for a family's holiday luggage without having to fit a big box on the roof. Or you could become a part-time antique dealer, carrying sideboards from auction one day and little old ladies to bridge schools the next." With a higher centre of gravity the Galaxy was scarcely a seven-seat sports car like the S-Max.

The ride was softer, so there was more body roll and understeer. In 2008 fresh engines included EcoBoost and for 2010 a 2.0 Duratorq TDCi diesel, with either 140PS or a new 163PS, which rendered the 175PS 2.2 TDCi redundant, all-aluminium engines reducing weight by 155kg (341.7lb) so performance was unaffected. PowerShift double wet-clutch transmission was standard with EcoBoost and optional with Duratorq. Blind Spot Information, a radar-based system warning drivers of vehicles close by was introduced at the Brussels Motor Show. An Adjustable Speed Limiter Device (ASLD) avoided disobedience of traffic regulations. *BusinessCar* made it Best MPV for the fourth year in a row.

INTRODUCTION January 2010. Spec 2.0 EcoBoost SCTi Powershift; 2.0 Duratorq TDCi 163PS manual
BODY MPV; 5-doors, 5/7-seats; weight 1727kg (3807.3lb); 1733kg (3820.lb).
ENGINE 4-cylinders; transverse; 87.5mm x 83.1mm, 1999cc; compr 10:1; 149kW (199.8bhp) @ 6000rpm; 74.5kW (99.9bhp)/l; 300Nm (221.3lbft) @ 1750-4500rpm. Dq 2.0 85 x 88mm; 1997cc; cr 17.9:1; 120kW (160.1bhp) @ 3750rpm; 340Nm (250.8lbft) @ 2000-3250rpm.
ENGINE STRUCTURE 4-valves; 2 chain driven ohc; aluminium head, block; turbocharger with intercooler; 5-bearing crankshaft. Dq 2.0; 2-valves; sohc chain and belt drive; aluminium block; variable nozzle VNG turbocharger with intercooler; common-rail fuel injection.
TRANSMISSION front wheel drive; Powershift 6-speed dual clutch automatic; final drive 3.93 or 2.68:1. Dq 2.0 manual 6-speed synchromesh; 4.06 or 2.96:1. 6-speed Powershift auto 4.06 or 2.91:1
CHASSIS steel monocoque, Boron A and B pillars; MacPherson strut ifs; SLA irs; subframes front and back; telescopic dampers; hydraulic servo disc brakes, front ventilated 31.6cm

(12.4in), Dq 2.0 ventilated; rear 30.2cm (11.9in); ABS; ESP; rack and pinion PAS; 70l (15.4gal) tank; 215/60R16, 225/50R17 tyre; 6.5J, 7J, rims.
DIMENSIONS wheelbase 285cm (112.2in); track front 158cm (62.2in), rear 160cm (63in); length 482cm (189.8in); width 188.5cm (74.2in); height 176cm (69.3in).
EQUIPMENT Titanium, Titanium X Sport, silver bars in grille, silver roof rails. LED tail lights; air conditioner temperature and humidity sensor; easyfuel capless filler; solar reflect windscreen.
PERFORMANCE maximum speed 217kph (134.8mph); 46.7kph (29mph) @ 1000rpm; 0-100kph (62mph) 8.8sec; fuel consumption 8.1l/100km (34.9mpg). Dq 2.0, 203kph (126mph); 52.1kph (32.4mph) @1000rpm; 9.8sec; 6.0l/100km (47.1mpg)
PRICE Titanium X £28,965, Dq Zetec £25,785, Dq Titanium X £30,835

2010
Transit

Celebrating 45 years meant Transit had lasted twice as long as the Model T. Celebration Hallmark models had marked its 30th and 40th year, and on 30 April 2010 a special edition Transit Sapphire came off the line at Southampton. The six millionth Transit, made in three distinct series at 22 factories, was celebrated with simultaneous ceremonies across the globe when European manufacturing vice president, Ken Macfarlane handed its keys to Paul Hendy, managing director of Britain's first Ford dealer, which was reaching a centenary of its own.

Over 2 million Transits had been sold in Britain since 1965 when the British Transit replaced the 400E Thames Trader, a small narrow-track forward control van. First to carry the Transit title was the FK1000 (Ford Köln 1000kg) of 1953, renamed Taunus Transit in 1961 and discontinued in 1965 when the new short wheelbase, petrol-engined 610kg (12cwt) Transit cost £542 and the most expensive was a 15-seat Custom bus at £997. The Mark 1 Transit was built at the former Hawker Hurricane factory at Langley, and continued until 1978. In 1971 production moved to the ex-Supermarine Spitfire factory next to Southampton airport. Engines for the original 78 derivatives included the Essex V4 1.7 and 2.0, a 32kW Perkins diesel, requiring a longer bonnet, replaced in 1974 by Ford Yorks. Police and ambulance Transits had a 3litre V6. Suspension was by live axles front and back.

Transit was restyled in 1978, the Essex V4 replaced by the Cortina Pinto engine and two years later by the 1.6 Kent cross-flow. The York diesel lasted until 1984 when it gained direct injection during a further facelift. A true second generation platform was introduced in 1986 with an essentially one-box design and independent front suspension for short wheelbase models. This was extended throughout the range in 1992. Further changes in 1994 included a high roof option and 16-valve engines as used in Scorpio, Escort, Galaxy and Jaguar X-type followed the principle established in 1965 of using common components from across the passenger car range for the Transit line.

After 45 years buyers were able to choose from 600 varieties including a 3.5 tonne 14-seat Minibus costing £25,400, with a choice of three 2.4-litre TDCi powertrains. All rear-wheel-drive models now had six-speed transmissions and Transit became the first medium CV to have DAB radio as standard. After 2011 the four wheel drive (AWD) range was extended to over one tonne. *Practical Motorhome* judged the Tribute T620 motorhome, built by Auto-Trail and based on the Transit motorhome chassis, best budget-buy motorhome and motorhome of the year 2010.

BELOW **Sir Henry Cooper OBE, KSG, aged 76, celebrated 45 years of the Transit. (see Transit entry of 1965)**

2010
Mondeo

Mondeo changed less radically in 17 years than Cortinas I to V had in the 20, between 1962 and 1982. It came out in 1993, a second generation followed in 2000, restyled five years later and a proper third edition in 2007. In 2010 revisions were mainly mechanical with the iron 2.2-litre TDCi replaced by an aluminium 2.0 along with an EcoBoost petrol injection turbo. Since ECOnetic technologies were delivering fuel consumption of 5.3l/100km (53.2mpg) and the diesels CO2 emissions of 139g/km, there was no longer a dedicated ECOnetic model. Like the Galaxy, with which it shared the Genk production line, the Mondeo gained PowerShift, which proved a good match for both the petrol direct-injection engine, where it was standard, and TDCi common-rail diesels where it was optional. PowerShift was two transmissions in parallel, each with its own wet-clutch unit, one intermediate shaft carrying gears one, three and five, and the other two, four and six, so it effectively had two final drive ratios. Shifts could be made by pre-selecting the next gear at full power. Unlike conventional automatics, it needed no power-sapping torque converters, planetary gear sets or multiple bands. PowerShift provided the ease and convenience of automatics with the sporty smooth performance of a manual. There were useful cosmetic changes and new driver assistance features including lane departure warning and reversing TV monitor.

INTRODUCTION Moscow motor show August 2010. Spec 2.0 EcoBoost SCTi 203PS; 2.0 Duratorq TDCi 140PS Powershift

BODY saloon; 4/5-doors, 5-seats; weight 1480kg (3262.8lb); estate +20kg (44lb).

ENGINE 4-cylinders; transverse; 87.5mm x 83.1mm, 1999cc; compr 10:1; 149kW (199.8bhp) @ 6000rpm; 74.5kW (99.9bhp)/l; 300Nm (221.3lbft) @ 1750-4500rpm. Dq 2.0 85 x 88mm; 1997cc; cr 17.9:1; 103kW (138.1bhp) @ 4000rpm; 320Nm (236lbft) @ 1750-2250rpm.

ENGINE STRUCTURE 4-valves; 2 chain driven ohc; aluminium head, block; turbocharger with intercooler; 5-bearing crankshaft. Dq 2.0; 2-valves; sohc chain and belt drive; aluminium block; variable nozzle VNG turbocharger with intercooler; common-rail fuel injection.

TRANSMISSION front wheel drive; Powershift 6-speed dual clutch automatic; final drive 3.81 or 2.77:1. Dq 2.0 manual 6-speed synchromesh; 3.33:1. optional 6-speed Powershift.

CHASSIS steel monocoque; MacPherson strut ifs; SLA irs; subframes front and back; telescopic dampers; hydraulic servo disc brakes, front ventilated 30cm (11.8in); rear 30.2cm (11.9in); ABS; ESP; rack and pinion PAS; 70l (15.4gal) tank; 205/55R16, 215/55R16, 235/45R17, 235/40R18 tyre; 6.5J, 7.5J, 8Jrims.

DIMENSIONS wheelbase 285cm (112.2in); track front 159cm (62.6in), rear 160.5cm (63.2in); length 484cm (190.6in); width 188.5cm (74.2in); height 150cm (59in).

EQUIPMENT

PERFORMANCE maximum speed 232kph (144.2mph); 53.7kph (33.4mph) @ 1000rpm; 0-100kph (62mph) 7.9sec; fuel consumption 7.7l/100km (36.6mpg). Dq 2.0, 209.2kph (130mph); 53.7kph (33.4mph) @1000rpm; 9.5sec; 5.3l/100km (53.2mpg)

PRICE £22,095, estate £23,195; Dq £19,245, £20,745 with Powershift, estate £20,345

2010
Sporty C-Max and Grand C-Max

Industry market segments were always imprecise. The European C-segment comprised 16 per cent of saloons and hatchbacks between about 1300cc and two litres, costing around €15,000. In Britain C-segment was nearer 20 per cent, so it was important. Designers aimed at the widest market, especially as America tended towards something the same as Europe. Ford showed its C-car intentions in 2010 with the C-Max on the platform of the 2011 Focus. A compact multi activity vehicle (MAV) with five seats, it was accompanied by Grand C-Max with seven seats and, for the first time on a Ford car, sliding doors. The Grand had a 14cm (5.5in) longer wheelbase and was 4cm (1.6in) taller. Powertrains included a 1.6litre EcoBoost petrol with independently variable timing on both intake and exhaust camshafts, and a ten per cent reduction in CO2 to 154 g/km. The 1.6 and 2.0litre Duratorq TDCi diesels were uprated. The first Ford of Europe model with Active Park Assist, C-Max had a system that automatically steered it into parking spaces identified on either side of the road. It could steer quickly and accurately, with the driver operating brake and accelerator, forwards or reverse, into spaces a metre longer than the car. Two ultrasonic sensors scanned for gaps and audible warnings helped in tight spaces. Blind Spot Information System alerted drivers to passing vehicles hidden in blind spots. Rear bumper radar modules illuminated LEDs on each mirror.

INTRODUCTION Geneva 2010, spec for 1.6 Ecoboost, Grand 2.0TDCi.
BODY MPV; 5-doors, 5-seats; weight 1385kg (3053.4lb); 1575kg (3472.2lb).
ENGINE 4-cylinders; transverse; 79mm x 81.4mm, 1596cc; compr 10:1; 132kW (177bhp) @ 5700rpm; 82kW (111bhp)/l; 240Nm (177lbft) @ 1600-5000rpm. 2.0TDCi, 85mm x 88mm; 1997cc; cr 16:1; 120kW (161bhp) @ 3750rpm; 60kW (80.5bhp)/l; 340Nm (250.8lbft) @ 2000-3250rpm.
ENGINE STRUCTURE 4-valves; belt-driven dohc w variable cam timing; aluminium head, block; Bosch MED17 engine management, direct fuel injection; Borg Warner KP39 low inertia turbo; 5-bearing counterweight iron crankshaft. TDCi 4-valve belt and chain dohc; iron block, aluminium head; Ford 2nd generation common rail management; 8-hole solenoid direct injectors; Garrett variable geometry turbo; forged steel 5-bearing 8-counterweight crankshaft.
TRANSMISSION front wheel drive; Durashift B6 6-speed synchromesh; TDCi MMT6 or Powershift 6 speed dual clutch electronic automatic; final drive 000, auto 000. TDCi 6-speed; 3.81:1/2.77:1 Powershift +60kg (132.3lb).

CHASSIS steel monocoque; Macpherson strut ifs; anti roll bar; multi-link control blade irs; anti roll bar; hydraulic servo dual circuit diagonal split 27.8cm (10.9in) disc brakes, front ventilated. 30cm (11.8in) Grand, 1.6 EcoBoost, and 2.0TDCi; ABS, ESP, EBD, REBA, EBP, HRB, Torque vectoring; r&p EPAS; 60l (13.2gal) tank; 215/50R17, 235/40 R18 tyres, alloy wheels.
DIMENSIONS wheelbase 264.8cm (104.2in), Grnd 278.8cm (109.8in); track 155.1cm (61in); length 438cm (172.4in), G 452cm (177.9in); width mirrors flded 185.8cm (65.27in); height 162.6cm (64in), G 168.4cm (66.3in), 169.8cm (88.85in) w roof rails.
EQUIPMENT Zetec or Titanium trim; alloy wheels, air conditioning, leather steering wheel, Thatcham cat 1 alarm, DAB radio/CD and Bluetooth with USB connectivity.
PERFORMANCE maximum speed 217kph (134.8mph); 0-100kph (62mph) 8.5sec; fuel consumption 6.6l/100km (42.8mpg). TDCi 210kph (130mph); 8.6sec; 5.1l/100km (55.4mpg). Grnd 215kph (133.6kph); 8.9sec; 6.8l/100km (41.5mpg). 205kph (127.4mph); 9.2sec; 5.3l/100km (53.3mpg).
PRICE Zetec £16,745; Grand Zetec £18,745, Grand Zetec 1.6TDCi £19,745.

2011
Focus 1.6, 1.6 EcoBoost

On sale by Ford of Britain's centenary, Focus was the second of ten models based on C-car underpinnings. Following Ford's commitment to five electrified vehicles in North America and Europe by 2013, a battery-electric Transit Connect and a battery-electric Focus were planned for 2012. Two C-Max derivatives of the C-car were to be made in Valencia, a full hybrid electric and a plug-in hybrid electric. Meanwhile the 5-door Focus launched, ready for production, in Paris was followed by an estate car in summer 2011. The Focus was to sell a million a year in 120 markets, 80 per cent of its components common to all of them. Production of three body styles began in

Saarlouis and Michigan, where there was an additional 4-door 2litre saloon shown at Detroit in January 2010. The coupé-like style of the Focus was not extended to 3-door or Coupé-Cabriolets. There were two 1.6litre engines, a non-turbo Ti-VCT with either 105PS or 125PS, and a new EcoBoost with 150PS or 180PS. Appearing for the first time, the *Low Speed Safety System* was designed to avoid frontal collisions in congested traffic. At under 30 km/h (20 mph) its optical sensor detected anything in its way and calculated how hard it needed to apply the brakes to avoid impact, taking over from the driver if necessary.

INTRODUCTION Paris 2010, on sale March 2011. spec EcoBoost
BODY saloon; 3/5-doors, 4-seats; weight 1505kg (3318lb).
ENGINE 4-cylinders; transverse; 79mm x 81.4mm, 1596cc; compr 10:1; 132kW (177bhp) @ 5700rpm; 82kW (111bhp)/l; 240Nm (177lbft) @ 1600-5000rpm.
ENGINE STRUCTURE 4-valves; belt-driven dohc w variable cam timing; aluminium head, block; Bosch MED17 engine management, direct fuel injection; Borg Warner KP39 low inertia turbo; 5-bearing counterweight iron crankshaft.
TRANSMISSION front wheel drive; Durashift B6 6-speed synchromesh; or Powershift 6 speed dual clutch electronic automatic, Powershift +60kg (132.3lb).
CHASSIS steel monocoque; Macpherson strut ifs; anti roll bar; multi-link control blade irs; anti roll bar; hydraulic servo dual circuit diagonal split 27.8cm (10.9in) disc brakes, front ventilated. 30cm (11.8in) 1.6 EcoBoost; ABS, ESP, EBD, REBA, EBP, HRB, Torque vectoring; rack and pinion EPAS; 60l (13.2gal) tank; 215/50R17, 235/40 R18 tyres, alloy wheels.
DIMENSIONS wheelbase 264.8cm (104.2in); track 155cm (61in); length 435.8cm (171.6in); width 182.3cm (71.8in); height 146.9cm (57.8in).
EQUIPMENT Active park assist, lane keeping aid, traffic sign recognition, adaptive cruise control, blind spot information, power child locks, optional rear view camera.
PERFORMANCE maximum speed 215kph (133.6mph); 0-100kph (62mph) 8sec; fuel consumption 6.5l/100km (43mpg).
PRICE £16,500-£21,000 est.

2011
Focus 1.6, 2.0 TDCi

INTRODUCTION March 2011.
BODY saloon; 3/5-doors, 4-seats;
weight 1565kg (3450.2lb).
ENGINE 1.6TDCi ECOnetic 75 x 88.3;
1560cc; compr 18.3:1; 66kW (88.5bhp)
@ 4000rpm; 204Nm (150.5lbft) @
1750rpm. 2.0 4-cylinders; transverse;
85mm x 88mm; 1997cc; cr 16:1;
120kW (161bhp) @ 3750rpm; 60kW
(80.5bhp)/l; 340Nm (250.8lbft) @
2000-3250rpm.
ENGINE STRUCTURE 4-valve belt
and chain dohc; iron block,
aluminium head; Ford 2nd
generation common rail
management; 8-hole solenoid direct
injectors; Garrett variable geometry
turbo; forged steel 5-bearing
8-counterweight crankshaft.
TRANSMISSION front wheel drive;
MMT 6-speed synchromesh or
Powershift 6 speed dual clutch
electronic automatic. TDCi 6-speed;
3.81:1/2.77:1 Powershift +60kg
(132.3lb).
CHASSIS steel monocoque;
Macpherson strut ifs; anti roll bar;
multi-link control blade irs; anti roll
bar; hydraulic servo dual circuit
diagonal split 30cm (11.8in) disc
brakes, front ventilated; ABS, ESP,
EBD, REBA, EBP, HRB, Torque
vectoring; r&p EPAS; 60l (13.2gal)
tank; 215/50R17, 235/40 R18 tyres,
alloy wheels.
DIMENSIONS wheelbase 264.8cm
(104.2in); track 155cm (61in); length
435.8cm (171.6in); width 182.3cm
(71.8in); height 146.9cm (57.8in).
EQUIPMENT Active park assist, lane
keeping aid, traffic sign recognition,
adaptive cruise control, blind spot
information, power child locks,
optional rear view camera.
PERFORMANCE maximum speed
200kph (125.5mph); 0-100kph
(62mph) 9.1sec; fuel consumption
4.2l/100km (67mpg) CO2 109g/km.
PRICE £16,500-£21,000 est

Once the basis of the C-car was decided, the
engines were modified and choice of power
output was widened. The fuel injection and
turbocharger of the 1.6 Duratorq TDCi underwent
change so it became available with 95PS or 115PS;
the more powerful with transient overboost
increasing torque from 270 Nm to 285 Nm during
acceleration. The changes were achieved without
affecting economy or CO2 emissions. The 2.0 took
over where the 1.6 left off at 115PS, or it could be
further amplified to 140 or 163PS with a 6-speed
manual transmission. PowerShift 6-speed dual-
clutch automatic was available with all but the
lowest powered. The first Ford to standardise
Auto-Start-Stop, which turned off the engine at
traffic halts. As a result the 1.6litre EcoBoost petrol
and the 1.6litre TDCi diesel Focus, representing
half those sold in Europe, could reduce urban fuel
consumption and CO2 emissions by 10 per cent.
Later in the year the Focus range was available
with a dedicated, ultra-low CO2 ECOnetic
derivative. The car's slippery profile and steeply
raked windscreen provided satisfactory
aerodynamics and it followed the Mondeo with
an active grille shutter, stemming airflow through
the cooling system. This kept drag down to a
coefficient (CD) of 0.27, compared to 0.30 for
the outgoing model, Ford's most significant
nameplate with over 10 million sold since 1998.

2012
Focus ST

Enthusiasts were dismayed when the ST's charismatic 2005 Volvo-inspired 5-cylinder 2.5litre engine was replaced by a 4-cylinder 2.0litre. Moreover, since the car was announced at Paris in 2010 only as a 5-door, it looked as though the model was more mainstream than its neo-competition predecessor, which had been the basis of a World Rally Championship contender. By way of recompense the new one was introduced resplendent in Tangerine Scream, a new colour reflecting its energetic credentials, yet it was perhaps just as well that Ford introduced its new challenger for the 2011 FIA World Rally Championship at Paris. The Fiesta RS (right) announced at the same time, in the familiar striking blue and grey livery, restated the company's well established commitment to motor sport. It was just as well, also, that the 4-cylinder had a generous 25PS advantage over the earlier car and 40Nm (29.5lbft) more torque. It also had Torque Vectoring Control, which acted like a differential constantly balancing the distribution of pulling power between the front wheels. The effect was to reduce understeer, improve traction and "turn-in", or steering response. This was especially effective accelerating out of corners, by imperceptibly braking the inside front wheel, sending more engine torque to the wheel with better grip.

INTRODUCTION 2011
BODY saloon; 5-doors, 4-seats; weight 1400kg (3086lb).
ENGINE 4-cylinders, transverse; 87.5mm x 83.1mm, 1999cc; compr 10:1; 197kW (246bhp) @ 6500rpm; 98.3kW (132bhp)/l; 360Nm (265lbft) @ 1800-4750rpm.
ENGINE STRUCTURE 4valves; 2 chain driven ohc; aluminium head, block; turbocharger with intercooler; 5-bearing crankshaft.
TRANSMISSION front wheel drive; dual mass flywheel; sdp clutch; 6 speed synchromesh; limited slip differential.
CHASSIS steel monocoque; Macpherson strut ifs; anti roll bar; multi-link irs; anti roll bar; hydraulic servo brakes, dual circuit diagonal split 30cm (11.8in) ventilated disc, ABS; ESP, EBD, REBA, EBP, HRB, torque vectoring r&p EPAS; 60l (13.2gal) tank; 235/40 R18 tyres, alloy wheels.
DIMENSIONS wheelbase 264.8cm (104.2in); track 155 cm (61in); length 435.8cm (171.6in); width 182.3cm (71.8in); height 146.9cm (57.8in).
EQUIPMENT Recaro seats
PERFORMANCE maximum speed 250kph (155mph); 0-100kph (62mph) 6sec; fuel consumption 7.8l/100km (36mpg); CO2 180g/km.
PRICE £24,000 est.

Chronology

1896
JUN Henry Ford drives Quadricycle in Detroit.

1903
JUN 16 Henry Ford and eleven investors sign US incorporation papers.
■ Motor Car Act raises British speed limit to 20mph (32.1kph).

1904
Percival Perry, accessory and component salesman, uncrates Fords imported by Aubrey Blakiston's American Motor Car Agency (AMCA), 117 Long Acre, London.
MAR Model A exhibited by AMCA in Cordingly Show at Agricultural Hall, Islington.
NOV 18 Central Motor Car Company, capital £10,000, takes over Blakiston's Agency.

1905
Central Motor director Perry tries Model B in London taxi market. Sells three.

1906
Blakiston resigns, Perry managing director. Gordon McGregor Ford Canada, waives Ford rights in Britain. Perry gains concession for UK and Europe.
NOV Olympia. Model N, £120, cheapest 4-cylinder in UK.

1907
Central Motor Car Company liquidated. Perry, Thornton & Schreiber sells 50 Model Ns.

1908
Perry, Thornton & Schreiber moves to Westminster Bridge Road.
NOV 13–21 First Model Ts at Olympia, London.

1909
Perry, Thornton & Schreiber wound up.
APR Petrol duty introduced; 3d (1.5p) a gallon.
OCT Henry Ford sets up London saleroom with Perry. 55–59 Shaftesbury Avenue sells 400 Detroit-made cars.

1910
Lloyd George budget (passed 1909) imposes Horse Power tax: £3.00 from 6½HP to 12HP up to £42 for 60HP.

1911
MAR 8 Certificate of Incorporation, Ford Motor Company (England) Limited. Pays £2000 to lease 5½ acres at Trafford Park Manchester.
MAY Henry Alexander takes Model T to top of Ben Nevis.
OCT 23 Model T at Trafford Park is first Ford assembly outside US.

1912
Annual production 3000. Ford Britain's biggest car manufacturer. Model Ts race at Brooklands. Henry Ford watches dealer AE George win.
■ Model T Landaulette, Town Car popular taxi. Running costs £233 for 744 gal petrol (£72 19/-) driver's wages (£67.15/4d), operating profit £206 12/3d.

1913
JAN 5 US Ford employees' pay rises to $5 per day.
APR 1 Detroit introduces moving assembly line.
AUG Trafford Park introduces moving assembly.
■ Annual production outsells combined Wolseley, Morris, Austin, Singer and Rover.

1914
Ford builds 8300 cars to sell through 1000 UK dealers.

1915
War production. 100 Model Ts a day.
■ McKenna Duties apply 33 per cent tax to imported cars and parts.

1915
Millionth Ford car. British Government buys 30,000 Model Ts for troop carrying, ambulance duty and moving munitions.

1916
Model T Fords on war service with Lawrence of Arabia.
■ Perry establishes Automobiles Ford in Paris.

1917
JUL Henry Ford & Son Inc registered. Ford family shareholders.
■ Fordson tractor production, Dearborn.
■ Percival Perry arranges Fordson tractor test with UK Board of Agriculture & Fisheries.
■ Government orders 6000. *The Motor* complains on behalf of UK industry.

■ Perry appointed CBE.
■ First Fordson tractor from Detroit to Manchester. Perry made deputy controller, mechanical warfare, Ministry of Munitions.

1918
Percival Perry knighted KBE.

1919
JAN 1 Edsel Ford succeeds Henry Ford as president.
■ Perry buys factory site with frontage on Southampton Water.
MAY Perry resigns over policy.
■ September 1919 to December 1920, Trafford Park builds 46,000 vehicles.
■ Tractor production starts at Cork.
■ Henry Ford buys Ford stock of outside shareholders.

1920
Trafford Park makes left hand drive for export.
■ Ford makes half the world's cars.
JUL Sir Herbert Austin suggests an alliance; rebuffed by Henry Ford.
■ Percival Perry and Noel Mobbs set up Slough Trading, refurbishing war-surplus vehicles.

1921
Car tax set at £1 per HP. Calculated on cylinder bore makes Model T annual £23. Motor Car Acts abolish petrol tax, introduce log books and tax discs. Petrol costs 3/5d (17p) a gallon.

Model Ts await dispatch from the former tramcar factory at Trafford Park.

1922

FEB 4 Ford buys Lincoln for $8 million; Ford first to make million cars a year.
■ Trafford Park research laboratory gets test microphotography.
■ Cork tractor production discontinued.
■ Dagenham (Essex) chosen for new factory.
■ Production starts Rue Dubois, Antwerp, Belgium.
■ Perry retires to Channel Islands.

1923

MAY Montier-Ford finishes 14th at Le Mans.

1924

MAY Dagenham, 295acres (119.4hectares) bought from Samuel Williams' Docks Company for £150,000.
■ McKenna Duties repealed; UK imports 47,677 cars.
■ Ford production in Copenhagen for Scandinavia.

1925

APR 250,000th Trafford Park Model T.
■ McKenna Duties reintroduced.
APR 13 Inaugural flight of first company airline, Ford Airport Dearborn, to Chicago.
■ German Ford factory, Berlin-Plotzensee
NOV 24 General Motors pays £510,000 to control Vauxhall.

1926

Edsel Ford reports to Henry Ford, "We know we have been defeated and licked in England."
■ Southampton Water site sold to city Corporation for £3,600. Becomes Ocean Terminal.

1927

APR British Ford buys Cork tractor plant from Henry Ford for $2million.
MAY US Model T production ends at 16.5million.
AUG 19 11.58am Trafford Park.

Model T production ends at 301,980.
DEC 2 Model A production starts; Model T production ends in Cork.

1928

MAR Henry Ford visits UK.
APR Wall Street unsteady. Henry Alexander takes Model A up Ben Nevis.
JUN Ford Tri-motor at Olympia Aviation Show.
DEC 7 Ford (England) Ltd floated as Ford Motor Company Ltd. Stanford Cooper secretary.
■ Ford Motor Company Ltd issues capital of £7million; 40% UK 60% US. Buys US Ford's nine European companies for £2.8million.

1929

MAY 16 Edsel Ford inaugurates Dagenham construction.
OCT Wall Street crashes. Perry visits European factories with Maurice Buckmaster.
■ Cork recommences tractor production with Model N serial 757369.

1930

Britain abolishes 20mph limit. Introduces compulsory car insurance.
OCT Henry Ford visits partly complete Dagenham.
■ Ford Belgium moves to purpose-built factory.
■ Perry takes offices opposite new London showroom, 88 Regent Street.

Land's End Hotel. The 250,000th Ford, a Model T, made in Britain sets off to celebrate its manufacture on Apl 17, 1925, before going on to the British Empire Exhibition at Wembley.

1931

First Cologne Ford; Morris introduces £100 Minor 2-seater.
FRIDAY SEP 27 Trafford Park closes.
TUESDAY OCT 1 Dagenham opens. First vehicle Model AA truck.
■ British Highway Code introduced.
■ Patrick Hennessy production manager, Dagenham.
■ Perry asks Dearborn for small car. It designs Model Y.
DEC Rowland Smith goes to America to monitor Model Y. Trafford Park sold.

1932

Dearborn evaluates the competition.
FEB 19 Model Y launch at White City.
FEB Irish tariffs compel tractor production transfer; Cork to Dagenham.
■ Cork makes last Model N, serial 779135.
MAR 9 US launch Ford V8. Briggs Motor Bodies and Kelsey Hayes Wheel open in Dagenham.
■ Model B production begins. Ford Aviation closes
AUG Model Y production starts. Dagenham occupies 600acres (242.8hectares)
■ AA 1-ton truck with 3.3litre 4-cylinder side-valve engine.
OCT V8-18 on sale. Ford Motor Show, Royal Albert Hall.
■ Ford Britain declares loss of £682,000.

1933

FEB 19 Model N tractor production, Dagenham with no 779154.

■ Model Y takes 19% of market against Austin 29% and Morris 27%.
OCT V8-40 introduced in Britain; Ford Motor Show, Royal Albert Hall.
■ Fordson named 2-ton truck. 3.6litre V8 on 20-seat coach.
■ Dagenham makes 2778 tractors in first year.

1934
MAR–MAY Model A driven India to London, 8075miles (12,995km).
MAR Road Traffic Act introduces driving tests, urban speed limits, pedestrian crossings.
JUL 13 HRH Prince of Wales drives round Dagenham in V8-40 Phaeton with Sir Percival Perry and manager AR Smith.
■ Dagenham blast furnace inaugurated.
■ V8 with half-elliptic springing in 2-ton truck, sliding roof in forward control cab.
■ Fordson truck payloads 5cwt to 2tons include 6x2 Surrey, 6x4 Sussex 2-tonner.
OCT 1 Model C 10HP production starts. Ford Motor Show, Royal Albert Hall.

1935
JAN Ford V8s four of the first ten in Monte Carlo Rally. JH Walley of Bishop's Stortford fifth.
MAR 12 V8-48 on sale in Britain. V8 engine available on trucks.
JUL 17 First Dagenham V8 engine: Jul 25, first V8 car.
SEP 1 V8-60 22HP introduced.
OCT 15 Model CX production; Harris V8, Jensen and Dagenham Motors specials at Ford Motor Show, Royal Albert Hall.

From 1932 to 1937 Ford showed disdain for the SMMT London Motor Show at Olympia and held its own at the Royal Albert Hall. The £100 Model Y was the centrepiece in 1934.

OCT 17 Perry announces £100 Model Y; Fordson Tug 3-wheeled truck.
NOV 12 V8-68 on sale in Britain.

1936
JAN PG Christea and I Zamfirescou (Ford V8) win Monte Carlo Rally.
JUN 24 V8-62 22HP introduced; discontinued Feb 3, 1940.
OCT Ford Motor Show, Royal Albert Hall. Fitzmaurice streamlined V8.
■ Dagenham makes 12,675 tractors. V8 engine standard in trucks from 15cwt upwards.

1937
JAN Mme Hellé-Nice and Mlle Marinovich (Matford V8) win Monte Carlo Rally Ladies Award.
JAN 25 V8-78 on sale in Britain. 25cwt truck with 2.2litre V8 and forward cab.
MAR 22 Model 7W 10HP in production.
SEP 1 Model 7Y 8HP in production; V8-62 gets outside opening boot.
OCT Ford Motor Show, Royal Albert Hall.
■ Fordson tractors dark blue changes to orange.
■ Safety glass and speedometers mandatory.

1938
JAN G Bakker Schut and K Ton (Ford V8) win Monte Carlo Rally.
■ Sir Percival Perry becomes Lord Perry of Stock Harvard.
MAR V8-78F on sale in Britain.
APR 22 V8-81A on sale in Britain.

MAY Sir Malcolm Campbell director Ford Motor Company Limited.
■ Car tax 15/- (75p) per horse power, petrol tax 9d (3.75p) per gallon.
SEP 8HP Model 7Y in production at Dagenham.
OCT 3 Prefect 10HP E93A in production, 10cwt van 30HP E83W.
DEC 13 V8-91A introduced; discontinued Jan 16, 1940.
■ Henry Ford and Harry Ferguson agree joint tractor.

1939
FEB E93A Prefect coupe.
SEP 16: petrol rationing.
OCT V8 30HP Model 91A. Air Ministry invites Ford Britain to make Rolls-Royce Merlins.
OCT 31 Anglia 8HP E04A production starts.
■ Commercial Vehicle Division abandons move to Manchester. Fordson tractors modified for Tractor Vaporising Oil (TVO).

■ Perry and Hennessy make wartime provision for 3000 tractors painted green.
■ Patrick Hennessy general manager, Dagenham.
■ Thames replaces Fordson on medium and heavy trucks.

1940
33% Purchase Tax on cars introduced. Night time 20mph speed limit. Road deaths peak at 8609 in a year.
■ Factory at Urmston Manchester set up for Rolls-Royce Merlins.
DEC Urmston factory bombed.

1941
Rowland Smith made MD.
MAR–MAY Urmston bombed again.
■ Patrick Hennessy leaves for Ministry of Aircraft Production.
JUNE Merlin engines in production.
JULY Hennessy knighted. Maurice Buckmaster joins Special Operations Executive (SOE).

Wartime production lined up. The armed services, particularly the Royal Air Force, had priority for the supply of tractors.

Ford foundry raises £7,500 for Hornchurch Spitfire. Ford has 400-strong Home Guard.
DEC Wartime government demands agreement with Amalgamated Engineering Union (AEU) at Urmston; first Ford trade union recognition.

1942
North African front gets 3637 boxed vehicles. Ford Industrial Engines formed to deal with surplus engines. Swiss machine tools supplied to Ford through German-occupied France, and Spain.

1943
MAY 26 Death of Edsel Ford, aged 49.
■ First Ford industrial action – union activists occupy offices.
■ Wings for Victory week, Ford workers buy five Spitfires

1944
Rowland Smith knighted.
JUN 6 Ford develops Trinadite vehicle waterproofing for D-Day.
■ V1 and V2 missiles narrowly miss Dagenham plant.

1939–1945
Production of 262,007 V8 engines. 5cwt van EO4C. 4-cylinder reinstated for trucks. 12,707 vehicles assembled from US and Canadian components; 184,579 2 and 4-wheel drive vehicles, 137,483 tractors, 2-ton fire engines made with Jensen bodywork for National Fire Service; 15 and 30cwt 4x2s; 30cwt and 3-ton 4x4s; 3-ton 6x4s for military. Henry and Edsel Ford's trust fund for 410 Emergency Ford food vans, maintained free of charge by dealers, served 18,649,741 Blitz meals. Two hundred bombs fall on Dagenham plant. War casualties: Trafford Park, three dead eight injured. Dagenham, five dead 24

injured. Ford Cologne plant little damaged by bombing, wrecked by retreating German artillery.

1945
MAR Sir Patrick Hennessy joins Ford Britain board.
MAR 19 Fordson Major E27N tractor production at Dagenham.
■ Tractors change from green to blue. Vans 5cwt and 10cwt in production; forward control V8 trucks 2-5 tons.
JUN Anglia 8HP in production at Dagenham.
Petrol 2/- (10p) a gallon.
SEP Henry Ford retires, grandson Henry Ford II (28) takes over.

1946
Dagenham builds millionth vehicle, 10HP Prefect.
■ Tractor 9N introduced. Ferguson alleges patent infringement. Sues for $340million.
■ Ford of Britain average annual profit £633,000.

1947
APR 7 Death of Henry Ford (83). Car Purchase Tax doubles to 66.6%.
■ Stanley James Gillen joins Ford Britain from GM Michigan.
JUN Dagenham 25,000th tractor.
JUL 16 V8 Pilot E71A; 1937 middle; Don Ward chief body engineer adds new bonnet and boot.
AUG 14 Pilot press view, Rembrandt Hotel South Kensington.
■ Petrol ration cut.

1948
JAN 1 Flat £10 annual car tax introduced.
FEB Henry Ford II drives 250,000th postwar Ford off Dagenham line. Cancels proposed Pilot made from Humber body dies.
OCT 27 Anglia 8HP E94A in production.
■ Sir Patrick Hennessy appointed managing director; Lord Perry (70) retires.
OCT 27 First post-war Earls Court Motor Show.
DEC 21 Prefect 10HP E493A in production.
■ Dagenham record 50,561 tractors. First Perkins P6 diesel for E27N.
■ First British Ford cars to USA.
■ Bulk spares storage; Langley, Bucks, former aircraft factory.
■ Ford leads British market – first time since Model T.

1949
Ken Wharton and Joy Cooke win Tulip Rally in Anglia.
■ Van 5cwt E494C, E83W estate car launched.
SEP Pound devalued by 30% from US $4.03 to $2.80.
■ Briggs Motor Bodies acquires former Spitfire factory at Southampton.
■ Thames normal control 4x2s, 6x4s artic and PSV chassis, 2-8tons.
■ Car and Truck Engineering Department, Rainham, Essex.
■ Perkins P6 diesel option on trucks. Hydraulic servo brakes standard.
Ford America sets up International Division

1950
Ken Wharton (V8 Pilot) wins Tulip and Lisbon Rallies.
■ Car Engineering and Truck Engineering divide. Staff Engineer for each.
APR Petrol tax doubles to 1s 6d (7.5p). Gallon costs 3s 0d (15p).
■ Car Purchase Tax restored to 33.3%.
MAY Petrol rationing ends.
OCT Consul and Zephyr at Earls Court Motor Show London.
■ Sir Rowland Smith appointed chairman.

1951
JAN 1 Consul EOTA production starts.
FEB 12 Zephyr Six EOTTA production starts. Consul, Zephyr Convertibles.
■ Government buys 5000 army 4x4s, 2E and 3E – Canadian V8 engine Commer cab.
■ Petrol Tax increased, new car double Purchase Tax reintroduced.
■ Fordson Major tractor.

1952
JAN SH Allard wins Monte Carlo Rally in Allard P1 with Ford V8 engine.
APR Harry Ferguson settles for $9.25 million, pays $4million legal costs.
■ Petrol tax increases.
■ British Motor Corporation formed; sells more cars than Ford.
■ Fordson New Major multi-fuel tractor, Smithfield Show.

1953
JAN M Gatsonides and P Worledge (Zephyr Six) win Monte Carlo Rally. Two millionth British made Ford, a Zephyr Six.

FEB Ford buys five UK Briggs Motor Bodies plants (inc Doncaster, Croydon, Romford) for £3.2million. Share exchange takes cost to £5.6million.
APR Car Purchase Tax 50%.
AUG 8 Popular production moves to Briggs, Doncaster. Model Y line closes.
OCT 7 Popular 10HP 103E production.
■ Pool petrol ends, branded fuels return.
■ Southampton plant makes 50,000 commercial vehicles.
■ Thames truck V8 replaced by 3.6litre 52.2kW (70bhp) ohv 4-cylinder.
■ Ken Wharton (Consul) wins Tulip Rally.
OCT 28 Anglia, Prefect 100E and Popular 103E.
NOV 2 Zephyr Zodiac EOTTA. Dec 17: Prefect 100E.

1954
Thames Trader 2-5 tons forward control, tipper, artic, first Ford diesel.
■ Ford France sold.
■ Terry Beckett Briggs styling manager.

1955
AUG Dagenham 250,000 sqft £10million Paint, Trim and Assembly (PTA).
SEP 13 100E Escort estate.
SEP 23 100E Squire estate.
■ Car Purchase Tax 60%. HP min deposit 15% repayment 24 months.

Ford Köln's 1950s Taunus, like the Consul and Zephyr, followed Detroit's lead, with 3-box shape and a hint of jet intake in front.

1956
Sir Patrick Hennessy chairman, Sir Rowland Smith retires.
FEB Mark II Consul, Zephyr, Zodiac.
APR Government fixes minimum 50% car HP deposits.
■ Prefect wins Canadian Winter Rally.
OCT Consul Mk II Estate in production.
■ Suez Crisis. Petrol rationing until May 1957.
■ Dagenham's 2millionth vehicle.

1957
Electric clutch two pedal option on Anglia and Prefect. About 50 made.
■ Ford Taunus 12M, 15M and 17M imported to UK.
APR Official opening of Aveley, Essex parts centre.
JUN 17 Death of Lord Perry
■ Unit construction 10/15cwt Thames van with ifs, side loading, replaces E83W 10cwt.

■ Thames Trader forward control 4.9litre petrol and 5.4litre diesel 6cyl 1.5-7tons.

1958
Keith Duckworth and Mike Costin form Cosworth Engineering.
■ Ford first British motor company with computer. It occupies entire air conditioned room. Computer used for 15-acre spare parts facility at Belhus.
■ HP restrictions lifted.
DEC First British motorway, 8.5 mile Preston bypass.

1959
APR Car Purchase Tax reverts to 50%; Zephyr down from £916 to £865.
■ Ford computer investigates suspension geometry and vibration.
■ Dagenham builds millionth commercial.

- James Allen Barke director product division
- **MAY 5** Prefect 107E.
- **AUG 25** Popular 100E.
- **SEP** 3 997cc Anglia 105E and Popular 100E.
- Ford team prize in Safari.
- **NOV 2** M1 opens, minister of transport Ernest Marples "appalled".
- G Burgess, S Croft-Pearson (Zephyr) win RAC Rally.
- First race for Cosworth-modified 105E Anglia engine, Brands Hatch.

1960

- **JAN** Ford buys 346 acres near Liverpool.
- Ford USA buys privately-held shares in Ford Britain for £128.5million.
- **MAR 19** Jim Clark wins Formula Junior Goodwood with Ford Cosworth engine.

MAY Jaguar buys Daimler. Project Archbishop (Cortina) approved to compete with German equivalent (Cardinal).
- Thirty years' truck-making ends at Dagenham. £70million moves heavy commercial vehicles to Langley, former Hawker Hurricane factory.
- Thames PSV double-deck special carries cyclists through Dartford-Purfleet tunnel.
- Front disc brakes optional on Consul, Zephyr, Zodiac.
- Ford team prize in Safari.
- **AUG** Design and engineering staff move to Aveley, Essex. Edsel designer Roy Brown appointed to style studio.
- **NOV** Clay model Archbishop approved.
- Ford plans tractor factory on 100 acres at Basildon, Essex, general manager William Batty.

1961

- **JAN** Joint Ford Britain MD J Allen Barke reports to Ford US Convention.
- **JAN 23** Frank Keighley, National Provincial Bank, draws cheque on Lazard Bros, Ford America merchant bankers for £119,595,645, to credit Ford Britain.
- **APR** Classic 109E, Anglia 5 and 7cwt van production.
- **JUN 1** "Archbishop" programme; £13million approved by Board in Regent Street. Deadline for production June 1962.
- **JUL** Capri 109E production. Ford team prize in Safari. Last Ford Prefect.

1962

Walter Hayes, former editor of *The Sunday Dispatch*, joins Ford Public Affairs.
- Stan Gillen made chairman of subsidiary Autolite
- Truck Engineering Division moves to Gants Hill, Ilford; Administration to £13million Warley office. Ford International sets up in Brussels under Leo Beebe. Ford Britain and Ford Germany compete with Cortina and Taunus 12M prototypes.
- Normal control Traders have curved screens; options five gears and 2-speed axles.
- Special Vehicle Operations tailors 7000 trucks, vans to customers' requirements.

Peter Hughes' notable victory in the East African Safari was a landmark for the recently launched Cortina. Ford competitions stalwarts include Peter Ashcroft on extreme left, Bill Barnett (third left standing) and multi-talented driver Vic Elford (back left).

- 1.6 Perkins diesel alternative to Consul 1.7litre in Thames van.
- **SEP** 2-seater Cortina Saxon abandoned.
- **NOV** Car Purchase Tax reduced from 55% to 45%.
- Fordson tractors change from blue and orange, to blue and grey. New Dexta model.

1963

- **JAN** Cortina 1500 production starts, Lotus Cortina made by Lotus.
- Ford Ferrari bid fails; Ford Advanced Vehicles, Slough set up.
- **MAR 8** First Anglia from new Halewood plant on Merseyside.
- Production at former Briggs factory in Doncaster transferred to Dagenham.
- **OCT** Halewood 328acre site officially open after £30million investment
- Jack Sears (Cortina GT) wins British saloon car championship.

1964

- **APR 1** GT40 prototype; Halewood transmission plant opens.
- Peter Hughes (Cortina) wins Safari Rally.
- William Batty director of car and truck group.
- 100-acre tractor plant opens at Basildon, new 2000, 3000, 4000, and 5000 models.
- **JUN** Le Mans, Fords fail.
- Jim Clark (Lotus Cortina) wins British saloon car championship. Aeroflow ventilation introduced.

1965

Carroll Shelby takes over Ford racing team; 7.0litre GT40 Mark II.

- Thames name dropped from commercials, range discontinued except for K-series.
- Ford makes 85,000 commercial vehicles, launches D-series for heavy duty sector.

MAY Jim Clark wins Indianapolis 500 in Lotus-Ford 38.

- Borg Warner Model 35 automatics optional Cortina, Corsair.
- V4 and V6 engines introduced by Ford Germany.
- Roger Clark (Cortina) wins Gulf London and Scottish Rallies.

JUN Le Mans, Ferrari 1-2-3, six Fords fail.

- Lotus Cortina A frame discontinued, leaf-spring suspension introduced.

AUG 1 Autolite chairman Stan Gillen succeeds J Allen Barke as MD and CEO.

AUG 9 First Transits from Langley and Germany replace 10/15cwt Thames.

OCT Transit goes on sale.

- Sir John Whitmore (Lotus Cortina) wins European saloon car championship.

DEC 70mph (112.4kph) "temporary" speed limit imposed in Britain.

1966

APR launch of Mk IV Zephyr/Zodiac. Harley Copp, Director of Engineering

- Ford wins team prize in Safari.
- Car Purchase Tax increased from 25% to 27.5%, petrol tax raised. American J-cars unready for Le Mans.

JUN Mk II GT40s stage formation finish 1-2-3 at Le Mans.

SEP Cortina Mark II production; millionth Cortina.

- Bengt Söderström, Gunnar Palm (Lotus Cortina) win Acropolis and RAC Rallies.
- John Fitzpatrick (Anglia) wins British Saloon Car Championship.
- US enacts car safety and emission legislation.
- Ford Britain's number one commercial vehicle producer at 113,623.
- Cortina best-selling car in Britain; UK imports 6% of its cars.

1967

JAN 1 Slough factory taken over by JW Automotive Engineering.

- Approval given for Escort Twin-Cam, codename J25.

MAR Lotus-Cortina Mark II to be made at Dagenham.

- Ford team prize in Safari.

JUN 4 Jim Clark wins Dutch Grand Prix, Zandvoort with Lotus-Ford 49.

JUN Mark IV J-cars win Le Mans. Comuta electric car.

- Ford of Europe created. Chairman John Andrews. Stan Gillen President, Vice President Ford USA, Leonard Crossland succeeds Gillen.
- Transit automatic transmission optional.
- Bengt Söderström (Lotus Cortina) wins Swedish Rally.

SEP 1300 and 1600 crossflow Kent engine.

OCT 12 Prime Minister Harold Wilson opens Research and Development centre, Dunton

NOV 17 Escort, replacement for Anglia, begins at Halewood.

- Pound devalued from US $2.80 to $2.40.

1968

JAN 17 Escort launched, Halewood makes 500 a day.

MAR 1 Group 3 homologation agreed for Escort with Type 49 strong bodyshell.

- Car Purchase Tax raised to 33.3%.
- Road tax up from £17.10s (£17.50) to £25. Petrol 6s od (30p) a gallon.
- Group 6 F3L sports prototype.

APR Escort van.

MAY 1 Escort Group 2 homologated.

MAY 3 Sir Patrick Hennessy retires, Len Crossland chairman, William Batty MD.

SEP John Wyer Mirage Gulf GT40s win Le Mans.

NOV 36.66% petrol tax. New car HP deposit 40%; 1,144,770 cars sold in Britain 102,276 imported.

- Harry Ferguson Research builds 20 Zephyr 4WD police cars.
- Graham Hill world champion with Ford-Cosworth engine.

1969

JAN Capri; 26 variants. Cosworth develops 16-valve twin cam Kent engine.

MAY MOT Test for cars over three years old.

JUN John Wyer Mirage Gulf GT40s win Le Mans. P1075 first car to win twice.

- GT40 Mark III announced. Jackie Stewart world champion with Ford-Cosworth engine.

1970

JAN Halewood makes first RS1600 Escort; production to Aveley

OCT Ford Advanced Vehicle Operations (AVO) established at Aveley

- Hannu Mikkola, Gunnar Palm (Escort) win World Cup Rally to Mexico.
- BP explores Forties Field for oil.

The late Bob Guccione's *Penthouse* magazine sponsored a team of Escorts in the increasingly popular series of saloon car races in 1975. Penthouse Pets duly turned out, with their Transit, in a supporting role.

■ Advanced Vehicles Operation (AVO) builds RS1600 and Escort Mexico.
■ Jochen Rindt posthumous world champion, with Ford-Cosworth engine.

1971
JAN GT70 rally car proposed.
EASTER MON Thruxton, Transit Supervan with Eagle V8 of 320.7kW (430bhp).
JUL Car Purchase Tax reduced from 36.6% to 30%.
■ Perkins diesels discontinued in Transit, diesels now Ford-made.
■ Transit production transfers to Southampton.
OCT Escort Sport launched; millionth Escort made for William Young, Wigan.
■ Ford production hit by nine-week strike. Market share falls to 16% in first half.
■ Jackie Stewart world champion with Ford-Cosworth engine.

1972
Metropolitan Police votes Transit Britain's Most Wanted. A perfect getaway van.
■ Hannu Mikkola, Gunnar Palm (Escort) first non-Africans to win Safari Rally.
■ Car Purchase Tax reduced to 25%; UK produces record 1,971,311 cars.
■ Transit diesel – three world records Monza. 10,000km (6214mls) 120.4kph (75mph).
■ 2.5litre V6 option for Transit, also light artic and high capacity parcels van.
■ Emerson Fittipaldi world champion with Ford-Cosworth engine.
NOV Roger Clark, Tony Mason (Escort RS1600) win RAC Rally.

1973
JAN Radial-ply tyres standard for all but cheapest fleet Escorts.
JAN 8 Ford takes minority holding in Ghia of Turin.

MAR Escort 1300E made at Aveley
■ William Batty appointed Chairman, knighted.
■ A-series light/medium commercials fill gap between Transit and D-series.
■ Arab oil embargo; 50mph (80.3kph) UK speed limit; fuel ration cards printed.
APR Purchase Tax ends, VAT + 10% Special Car Tax (almost) keeps status quo.
JUL RS2000 announced from AVO.
SEP Halewood's millionth Escort. Production of 1300E transferred.
■ Spanish factory planned to make front wheel drive Ford.
NOV RS3100 Capri production starts at Halewood.
■ Timo Makinen, Henry Liddon (Escort RS1600) win RAC Rally.
■ Capri RS3100 enters touring car racing.
DEC Capri Mark II production; national three-day week response to strikes.
■ Jackie Stewart world champion with Ford-Cosworth engine. DFVs win every race.

1974
JAN 16 Granada Ghia, first European Ghia-badged production model.
MAR VAT on petrol; price rises from 42p a gallon to 74p a gallon by year end.
APR Capri II Ghia 2000, 3000; French-built C3 automatic replaces BorgWarner.

APR Escort 1300E 4-door made for export.
MAY Economy 50mph (80.26kph) limit rescinded.
■ Safety belt fitments compulsory. Design Council Award for Cortina Mark III.
SEP Cortina Mk III 2000E Estate launched; Consul name dropped.
NOV Timo Makinen, Henry Liddon (Escort RS1600) win RAC Rally.
■ Emerson Fittipaldi world champion with Ford-Cosworth engine.

1975
JAN 24 Ford Advanced Vehicles Aveley closes – oil crisis.
MAR Capri Mark II S shown at Geneva; John Player Special livery option.
■ Launch of Mark II Escort van.
APR launch of Transcontinental truck.
■ CRS, French riot police CRS buys Transit buses with steel mesh screens.
■ H-series Transcontinental trucks and chassis cabs 16-19tons; Cummins diesels.
■ 1.6litre Crossflow 4-cylinder replaces V4 in Transit; production passes 1million.
■ Sir William Batty relinquishes chairmanship, becomes president of Society of Motor Manufacturers and Traders and member of the Engineering Industries Council.
OCT 21 Millionth Cortina Mark III made at Dagenham
NOV Timo Makinen, Henry Liddon (Escort RS1600) win RAC Rally.

1976
UK inflation 24%; British Leyland goes into state ownership.

FEB 2.0litre economy Granada.

■ Walter Hayes Vice President Ford Europe

JUL Granada production to Germany.

OCT Capri production to Germany.

NOV Roger Clark, Stuart Pegg (Escort RS1600) win RAC Rally.

■ Escort Britain's top-selling car with 133,959.

■ James Hunt world champion with Ford-Cosworth engine.

1977

Cortina becomes Britain's best-selling car – remains so until 1981

■ Ford best-selling tractor and truck maker.

■ UK car imports 52%.

JAN Ford Bordeaux C3 automatic replaces Borg Warner in Transit.

■ UK inflation 16%; car prices go up every 90 days or so.

FEB Fiesta launched in Britain (produced in Spain 1976).

■ Jody Scheckter (Wolf-Ford) scores Ford DFV's 100th grand prix win; Monaco.

■ OPEC raises oil prices 10% in January, 5% in Jul; UK petrol 86p a gallon.

SEP 2.3litre V6 for Cortina GL, Ghia, and S; 1298cc engine added to Fiesta.

NOV Björn Waldegård, Hans Thorzelius (Escort RS) win RAC Rally.

■ Fiesta third in Car of the Year (COTY) behind Rover 3500 and Audi 100.

1978

MAR Capri Mark III in production at Cologne.

MAR 9 Major changes to Transit, redesigned suspension, new ohc engines.

■ Fiesta van launched.

■ Bridgend, South Wales, £180million engine plant opens, capacity 500,000 per year.

JUN 75 year anniversary of Ford Motor Company; special Fiesta launched.

JUL Death of Stan Gillen (67)

■ Nine-week strike by 57,000 at Halewood and Dagenham costs £200million lost sales.

OCT First Motor Show at NEC, Birmingham; Ford stand empty due to strike.

NOV Hannu Mikkola, Arne Hertz (Escort RS) win RAC Rally.

■ Mario Andretti world champion with Ford-Cosworth engine.

■ Granada 3rd in COTY behind Porsche 928 and BMW 7-series.

1979

JAN Dagenham produces millionth Dorset Diesel engine.

MAR millionth Fiesta; special edition of 3100.

■ OPEC raises oil price 9%, petrol £1 then £1.22 a gallon. Second Oil Crisis.

AUG Cortina modifications "Mark IV½" Cortina 80.

NOV Hannu Mikkola, Arne Hertz (Escort RS) win RAC Rally.

■ Björn Waldegård wins world rally drivers' championship with Ford.

■ Ford wins 1979 world manufacturers' rally championship with Hannu Mikkola.

■ Oil price effectively doubles in year, $12 to $26 a barrel.

Jackie Stewart (Tyrrell-Ford) 1973 world champion.

1980

FEB Inauguration of Special Vehicle Engineering under Rod Mansfield.

MAR Philip Caldwell succeeds Henry Ford II. Walter Hayes Vice President Ford USA

JUL Rear wheel drive Escort stops, including RS2000.

AUG Escort Mark III production begins at Halewood, Saarlouis and Valencia.

SEP XR designation for XR3 Escort.

OCT Sir Terence Beckett director-general of the CBI. Sam Toy Ford chairman.

■ Alan Jones world champion with Ford-Cosworth engine.

1981

MAR Death of Sir Patrick Hennessy.

■ Launch of Cargo truck.

■ LPG available for Transit.

■ Special Vehicle Engineering set up at R&D, Dunton.

■ Nelson Piquet world champion with Ford-Cosworth engine.

APR Vatanen wins world rally drivers' championship with Ford.

■ Escort RS1600i shown; Granada gets mid-life facelift; Probe III shown.

■ Escort COTY ahead of Fiat Panda and Austin Metro.

1982

FEB Henry Ford II appointed Honorary Knight of the British Empire. Walter Hayes made CBE

SEP Sam Toy drives the last Cortina off Dagenham production line.

■ Toy appointed SMMT vice-president.

■ Ford Britain lends Ford US £961million.

OCT Sierra, Cortina's replacement goes on sale.

OCT 13 2 millionth Escort built at Halewood.

■ Keke Rosberg world champion with Ford-Cosworth engine.

1983

JAN 31 Seat belt wearing compulsory

MAY New diesel previewed. Thames foundry closes

■ Ford workforce reduced by 21,000 between 1980 and 1983

JUN Sierra XR4i with biplane spoiler.

SEP Escort sells 174,190, third highest ever.

■ Sierra 2nd in COTY behind Audi 100.

■ Ford and Cosworth Engineering form partnership for grand prix engine.

1984

MAR E-Max 1.6 Sierra announced.

APR Transit launch. Industry's first direct-injection diesel engine.

■ Petrol increases to £1 a gallon.

■ New paint shop £30million.

■ Cork factory closed.

■ Lead-free fuel proposed for 1989.

■ Group B RS200 mid-engined 4WD rally car

■ Diamond white XR3i is four millionth Halewood car.

■ Dagenham-made diesel engine for Fiesta/Escort/Orion.

SEP Six-year anti corrosion guarantee.

OCT Repairs lifetime guarantee.

1985

FEB Donald Petersen Chairman.

MAR Sierra RS Cosworth basis for Group A racing car.

APR Vehicle Excise Duty rises to £100, petrol over £2 a gallon.

JUL 25 Two millionth Transit.

■ Eltec ELectronic TEChnology concept car with microprocessors and multiplexing

■ Supervan II with Cosworth V8 does 279.3kph (174mph).

OCT 23 Ford celebrates 75th anniversary of UK manufacture. Sam Toy retires, becomes president of SMMT.

1986

JAN New Transit range.

July 1985, Eltec ELectronic TEChnology concept car with microprocessors and multiplexing.

■ M25 completed; Ford fails to buy Austin-Rover or Alfa Romeo.

JUL Fiat and Ford Europe's truck divisions merge to form Iveco.

■ Scorpio COTY ahead of Lancia Y10 and Mercedes-Benz 200.

■ Group B rally cars banned following fatal accidents.

NOV Dagenham engine plant wins British quality award.

DEC Last Capri of 1.9million sold since 1969.

1987

Ron Mellor, VP Car Engineering Ford Europe, retires to Anglia Ruskin University

■ Ford has 29% of UK market with 178,000 Escort, 153,000 Fiesta, 140,000 Sierra.

■ CVT transmission option on Fiesta.

■ Sierra Cosworth RS500 wins World Touring Car Championship.

OCT Ford acquires 75% of Aston Martin.

■ Sierra Cosworth RS500 wins British Touring Car Championship.

1988

FEB British Design Award for Sierra Cosworth.

■ Dagenham makes 2 millionth Sierra.

■ MT75 5-speed gearbox in Sierra, Granada, Scorpio.

■ Death of Sir Rowland Smith, aged 100.

■ Sierra Cosworth RS500 wins European Touring Car Championship.

■ Sierra Cosworth RS500 wins British Touring Car Championship.

AUG Death of Enzo Ferrari aged 90.

■ Small Ford diesel enlarged from 1608cc to 1753cc.

1989

Ford Cosworth DFX scores 151 Indycar wins since 1976.

■ Record Escort sales, 181,218. Walter Hayes retires from Ford of Europe.

■ Sierra Cosworth RS500 wins British Touring Car Championship.

NOV Ford buys Jaguar for £1.6billion.

■ Car market 2,373,391; 1,370,589 imports includes Fords and Vauxhalls.

1990

Car market drops by 300,000. £78million modernisation at Dagenham

■ Ford's Bill Hayden MD of Jaguar replacing John Egan.

■ Sierra final facelift, 1.8 Ford turbodiesel replaces Peugeot-made engine.

■ Sierra Cosworth RS500 wins British Touring Car Championship.

■ New Escort and Orion – £1billion investment.

■ Fiesta third in COTY behind Citroen XM and Mercedes-Benz SL.

1991

Dagenham one-car plant building Fiesta. Diesel facilities cost £91million.

MAR Geneva. Ghia concept CW170, later Focus

OCT Zeta engine previewed; changed to Zetec after Lancia objects.

■ Walter Hayes succeeds Victor Gauntlett as chairman of Aston Martin.
■ Ian Gerald McAllister Ford managing director

1992
MAR Special Car Tax (extra rate of VAT on cars) reduced from 10% to 5%.
■ Escort RS Cosworth on sale; fuel injection standard throughout Ford.
NOV Special Car Tax abolished; mid-range Escort £400 cheaper.
■ Ian McAllister chairman and managing director. Nick Scheele chairman and CEO Jaguar.

1993
JAN catalytic converters compulsory; airbags standard or optional.
MAR Annual Vehicle Excise Duty (VED) goes up to £125.
■ Mondeo replaces Sierra.
■ Maverick Spanish joint venture with Nissan.
■ Paul Radisch (Mondeo) wins FIA Touring Car World Cup.
■ Nigel Mansell wins Indycar championship in Lola-Ford T3.
■ Ayrton Senna wins five grands prix for McLaren-Ford.
■ François Delecour (Escort) wins World Rally Championship in Portugal.
■ Driver airbags standard on all Fords.
NOV Alexander James Trotman becomes first Ford chairman born outside USA.

1994
XR designations discontinued.

■ Sam Toy appointed OBE.
■ Ford acquires remaining 25% of Aston Martin. Walter Hayes retires. François Delecour (Escort) wins Monte Carlo Rally.
■ Michael Schumacher world champion with Ford-Cosworth engine.
■ Ford-Cosworth 40th anniversary, 175 Grand Prix wins, 10 world constructors' championships, 13 world drivers' championships; used by 56 teams, 186 Indycar race wins, 11 CART championships, 11 Indianapolis 500 wins
■ Mondeo wins World Touring Car Championship.
■ Mondeo wins COTY.

1995
Escort's last year as best-selling car in UK; over 4 million made at Halewood.
■ Supervan III has Cosworth F1 of 484.7kW (650bhp).
■ Dagenham builds 28 millionth engine
■ Alex Trotman launches Ford 2000 aimed at consolidating Ford round the world
■ Saetta concept car at Geneva.

1996
JUN Ford of Britain Heritage centre opened
OCT 8 250 millionth world Ford, a Fiesta, is Dagenham's 20 millionth since 1931.
■ Ian McAllister CBE president SMMT.
■ Alex Trotman knighted.

1997
JAN Ford makes five-year agreement for Stewart Grand Prix.

■ Tremor concept SUV
APR Ford wins Queen's Award for Export
MAY 15 Henry Ford statue, Dagenham
MAY 30 Jim Clark statue, Kilmany, Fife
SEP J Mays succeeds Jack Telnack as head of global design
■ Ka 2nd in COTY behind Renault Megane.

1998
European Escort production moves to Halewood.
FEB £36million plan for Southampton
MAR Prince of Wales opens technology centre, Bridgend
■ Escort replacement named Focus
■ Cougar maintains New Edge styling introduced 1966 Ka.
■ Annual road deaths 3421, lowest since recording began in 1924
SEP Ford acquires Cosworth Racing; CR-2 for Jaguar F1, XF for CART.
SEP 17 Dagenham engine plant produces 30 millionth engine
NOV Ford Focus (COTY) and Scottish Car of the Year (SCOTY)
DEC RSA honours Alex Trotman.

1999
JAN Alex Trotman, chairman and CEO retires, William Clay Ford Jr is chairman, Jacques Nasser president and CEO. Roger Clark Memorial, Mallory Park
■ Ford buys Volvo for $6.45billion.
MAR Alex Trotman life peer, Baron Trotman of Osmotherley, North Yorkshire
■ Colin McRae 1995 World Rally Champion joins Ford for £6million.

May 30, 1997, Jim Clark statue unveiled, Kilmany, Fife.

Drives Focus in WRC. Wins Safari and Portugal rallies twice
■ Premier Automotive Group - Jaguar, Volvo, Aston Martin, Lincoln-Mercury.
APR Dagenham builds 4 millionth 1.6/1.8litre diesel.
■ Elevated A13 built across Ford site.
■ Ford Motor Company buys Kwik-Fit for $1.6billion.
■ Johnny Herbert wins European Grand Prix with Stewart Ford V10 CR-1.
■ Focus voted COTY.
AUG 5 Death of Sir Leonard Crossland (85).

DEC International motor journalists elect Model T Car of the Century.

2000

JAN Focus North American Car of the Year.

FEB Dagenham cuts daily output from 1200 to 560.

MAR Ford buys Land Rover from BMW for £1.7billion.

MAY Announcement of closure of paint, trim, and assembly at Dagenham, new £500million diesel engine complex. Fiesta production transfer to Germany.

JUL 21 Ford Europe chairman Nick Scheele drives last Escort off line.

■ Halewood made 5,202,412 Escorts, 1 million Anglias, Capris, and Corsairs.

■ Halewood turned over to Jaguar.

SEP Duke of Edinburgh visits Dunton

■ Ford Team Mondeo wins manufacturers' British Touring Car Championship.

■ Alain Menu (Mondeo) wins driver's BTCC from team-mates Reid and Rydell.

■ Ford's 500th BTCC win, Menu at Oulton Park.

■ Colin McRae 4th in WRC.

OCT Transit Van of the Year

DEC 26 Death of Walter Hayes (76).

2001

JAN Ford Europe Chairman Nick Scheele CEO. Mondeo *What Car?* Car of the Year. £360million investment, Bridgend

FEB Ford appoints Pininfarina to produce StreetKa; first Ford built in Italy.

■ Ford 25 years Britain's best-selling make, 36 and 23 years best in commercials.

MAR Ford first road hydrogen car in UK

JUN Nick Scheele knighted in Queen's Birthday Honours

■ Colin McRae 2nd in WRC after winning in Argentina, Cyprus and Greece

March 2002, StreetKa. Ford sponsored Kylie Minogue's European Fever Tour.

OCT Sir Nick Scheele president and COO Ford Global Operations Mondeo gains 21 awards.

2002

MAR StreetKa Ford sponsors Kylie Minogue's European 'Fever' Tour.

MAR GT40 reintroduced. Ian McAllister CBE retires as chairman and managing director Ford of Britain.

■ Roger Putnam succeeds as chairman.

McRae wins Safari Rally to post record in WRC events.

2003

Ford retains title of Britain's best selling nameplate for 26th consecutive year.

MAY Car production ceases at Dagenham, Ford's global centre of diesel engine manufacture.

JUN 16 Detroit Ford centenary celebrations led by chairman and CEO Bill Ford.

JUL Biggest celebration of Ford centenary outside US, at Goodwood Festival of Speed.

OCT 31 Death of Sir William Batty (90).

NOV PM Tony Blair opens £325million Dagenham Diesel Centre.

■ 300 millionth Ford built at Dearborn. "A million of anything is a great many": Henry Ford.

2004

Martin Smith made executive director of design.

FEB Transit diesel-electric hybrid research begun.

MAR Three millionth European Focus

MAY C-Max new engines and transmissions. Focus C-Max Ultima

JUN Auto China debut for 4-door Focus concept, Mondeo Duratec V6

■ Ford GT sets 330kph (205mph) top speed

Auto Express Used Car Honours appoints Focus TDCi Best Diesel.

■ Bridgend makes engine for Land Rover Discovery 3.

JUN Focus C-Max wins British Insurance Car Security Award. World championship rallying Ford's primary motor sport activity for 4 years.

2005

Diesel-electric Transit Hytrans goes on test.

FEB Sir Nick Scheele (60) retires as president Ford Motor Company

APR Ford voted most responsible and trusted car brand in Britain.

APR 25 Death of Lord Trotman (72).

■ Roger Putnam retires as chairman, replaced by Stephen Odell. Joe Greenwell vice-president governmental affairs.

■ John Fleming appointed CEO Ford of Europe

■ 5 millionth Transit made at Southampton.

■ *Auto Express* votes Focus Car of the Year.

SEP Bridgend makes premium Jaguar coupe engine.

OCT Ford-Peugeot-Citroën more diesel co-operation

■ Focus Flexi-Fuel goes on test.

■ Focus voted Scottish family car of the year.

2006

Ford named Fleet Manufacturer of the Year for second time.
JAN 6 EcoBoost programme promises 20 per cent better economy on half a million Ford, Lincoln and Mercury vehicles annually.
FEB 1 Roelant de Waard chairman and managing director Ford of Britain
■ Sir Digby Jones appointed Ford's corporate and governmental affairs advisor.
■ Bridgend £100m investment for new 6-cylinder engine.
■ Bridgend builds 13,000,000th engine.
JUN Ford leads UK market by 18,000 units.
■ Millionth Focus at London Motor Show.
NOV Ford 2006 World Rally Manufacturers' Champion.

2007

MAR 12 Aston Martin sold to David Richards' consortium for £480million.
JUN 11 Ford announces Jaguar Cars is for sale.
JUN Roger Putnam appointed CBE.
JUL Mondeo Auto Express COTY.
SEP 15 Colin McRae MBE dies in helicopter accident.
NOV Mondeo SCOTY.
■ Ford 2007 World Rally Manufacturers' Champion.
DEC S-Max COTY.

2008

JAN 1 Tata Motors preferred bidder for Jaguar Cars.
■ Mondeo and Verve Concept win categories in *What Car?* Awards.
■ *BusinessCar* awards to Mondeo, S-Max, Galaxy.
MAR 24 Death of Sam Toy (84).
MAR 26 Ford sells Jaguar Land Rover to Tata Motors for $2.3billion Ian McAllister knighted.
■ John Fleming Chairman and CEO Ford of Europe
AUG Ford fits DAB radios.
■ Olga Kurylenko to drive Ka in Bond movie Quantum of Solace.
SEP Stephen Odell appointed president and CEO Volvo.
■ Mondeo wins second *Towcar of the Year.*
OCT £70million Bridgend investment for low CO2 engines.
NOV Fiesta SCOTY.
DEC Roeland de Waard VP sales, Ford Europe.

2009

JAN 1 Joe Greenwell chairman Ford of Britain, Nigel Sharp MD. Greenwell president SMMT.
JAN 15 Business secretary visits engine plant.
JAN 23 Fiesta *What Car?* Car of the Year.
FEB Ranger Pickup in Europe
MAR Iosis Max Concept at Geneva.
■ Ford's third Fleet Manufacturer of the Year.
■ Weak pound forces UK price increases.
APR Fiesta *What Diesel?* best small car and car of the year.

■ Transit and Fiesta van Econetic models.
JUN Electric prototypes for UK low carbon vehicle flee
JULY Alistair Darling visits Bridgend plant.
AUG Fiesta *Auto Express* Car of the Year.
SEP Bridgend's 15,000,000th engine.

2010

JAN Focus RS is Heritage Collection's 100th.
■ Ford offsets VAT 2.5% increase. Scrappage scheme brings 35,500 extra sales
■ C-platform Focus prototype shown in Detroit
MAR Global electric vehicle plan in Europe; five promised by 2013.
APR 23 *Auto Week* nominates Ford Start Best Concept at Beijing Motor Show.
APR 30 Southampton. Special edition of 1150 £14,995 Transit Sapphires.
MAY *Fleet World* names Focus Best

Fleet Car; Transit Connect World's Best Small Van; ECOnetic CVs Best Innovation.
JUN *BusinessCar* gives Galaxy overall MPV award fourth year running. S-MAX gains Mini-MPV award; S-Max Best MPV
JUN 28 Prince of Wales at Bridgend; EcoBoost engine and plant's 30th anniversary.
JUL 7 Global electric vehicle plan deploys 5-passenger Transit Connect demonstrators
JUL 12 Contracts signed for £1.5billion investment at four UK facilities
JUL 15 Volvo CEO Stephen Odell (55) appointed CEO Ford of Europe as Zhejiang Geely Holding Group buys Volvo from Ford. John Fleming (58) appointed head of Ford global manufacturing and labour affairs.
AUG 2 Sale of Volvo to Zejiang Geely for $1.8billion completed.

2011

MAR 8 Centenary, Ford of Britain.

2009 Focus Battery Electric Vehicle (BEV).

Afterword

We knew from the beginning that Ford in Britain was, for the most part, well documented and cheerfully imagined that this might make compilation effortless. In some ways it helped, even though the volume of information available was overwhelming. It became a question not of what to put in, so much as what to leave out. Compression of the data into key facts, within a manageable format, was challenging.

Innovations in **The Ford File** in response to requests, often from journalists who are the books' keenest users, include production figures and prices wherever possible. Metric and Imperial conversions are used throughout, Imperial given first up to 1950 when this would have been the norm, Metric thereafter. Engine power is quoted in kilowatts and brake horse power, net wherever possible and mostly in modern times from internationally posted certifications, which means they do not invariably conform with manufacturers' publicity figures. Prices are converted from £sd to decimal. Performance data has been mostly researched from published road tests, the sources shown when known; those not attributed may be taken as the manufacturers' own. The same goes for homologated weight. All CO_2 emissions figures in g/km and most fuel consumption figures are from official tests following EC Directive 93/116/EC.

Each entry has a text of around 220 words and the specification contains over 70 separate pieces of information, sometimes more. With around 250 entries in the model-by-model section and the other tables, this comes to something like 120,000 words and 50,000 facts. As with all our books we have tried to make **The Ford in Britain Centenary File** as accurate as we can. Yet even with an accuracy of 99.9%, it follows that some 170 inexactitudes may have occurred. Specialists in one make or model may spot them. If they think they have marked an error, anomaly or even an omission, let us know and we shall try to put it right in subsequent editions. Write with details, and whatever references you can obtain, to the publishers, not to Ford Motor Company. Although Ford was given opportunities to correct errors of fact, since this is an independent publication, the opinions it contains are those of the author.

The Ford in Britain Centenary File has been compiled with the help of a large number of individuals, and if we have missed any of them out in the acknowledgements, we apologise. We hope it is a useful aid to study, enjoyable to browse through, and successful as a source of reference. Compiling it has been absorbing.

Eric Dymock, **Ruth Dymock**, 2011.

Acknowledgements

The publishers thank successive Executive Directors Communications and Public Affairs at Ford of Britain Michael Callaghan and Tim Holmes and their staff, in particular Brian Bennett. Our thanks are also due to former Ford Chairman Roger Putnam, a friend since his days at Lotus Cars, together with many generations of public relations officials at Ford, including Syd Wheelhouse, Harry Calton, John Southgate and the late Walter Hayes for making available for test almost every Ford model since the 1950s. Thanks are also due to Alastair Smith AMA FSA Scot, of the Museum of Transport, Glasgow, Trevor Cockburn and Gordon Brennan for information on flathead V8s and Andy Anderson of Anderson Project Management Ltd for information on the GT70 restoration. Ford dealers down the years have had a talent for public relations. Thanks go to the late Jimmy Nicholson of Hamilton who entrusted the author with his new Mark I Zodiac, the late Morris Smellie of Braedale Garage, Motherwell whose 105E Anglias he drove in the 1950s, Skelly's of Motherwell for Fords driven in the 1960s, and Jim Duncan of Rothesay who gave practical help with research into tractors. Thanks also to the library service in Rothesay for finding obscure books including Hilary St George Saunders's invaluable Ford at War. As with other books in the File series thanks go to David Fletcher of the Tank Museum at Bovingdon for his prompt, courteous, and unfailingly accurate information on obscure military matters, also Caroline Johnson, library administrator at the National Motor Museum, Beaulieu, Hants. Fran Chamberlain of Ford Photographic and Heritage Administrator John Nevill were invaluable in our quest for photographs. Among the photographic sources we used was the National Motor Museum at Beaulieu. As with all Dove Publishing books, thanks are due to publishing director Mike Roberts, production consultant David Bann, and Andrew Barron of Thextension for the jacket design and redesign for the enlarged and revised Centenary edition. Book creation, typesetting and production for earlier editions were by Ruth Dymock, sub-editing by Joanna Dymock.

The publishers owe grateful thanks to Ford of Britain chairman Joe Greenwell for his generous Foreword as well as his enthusiasm for our series of File books.

Bibliography

The Motoring Encyclopediae, Amalgamated Press
Fleetway, 1936 and 1938.
Ford at War, Hilary St George Saunders,
Ford Motor Co Ltd, 1947
The Lotus 49, David Hodges, Lionel Leventhal, 1970
The Ford GT40, David Hodges, Lionel Leventhal, 1970
The Encyclopaedia of Motor Sport, Rainbird, 1971
Military Wheeled Vehicles, Olyslager, Ward Lock 1972
British Cars series, Olyslager , Warne 1973
Transport Treasures of Trafford Park, Dennis Gill MAIE,
Transport Publishing 1973
Let's Call it Fiesta, Edouard Seidler, Edita SA & Patrick
Stephens 1976
V8, Michael Frostick, Dalton Watson 1979
Illustrated Encyclopedia of Military Vehicles, Ian Hogg,
John Weeks, Hamlyn 1980
Capri, Jeremy Walton, Foulis 1981
A-Z of Cars 1920s–1980s, Sedgwick, Gillies, Robson,
Baldwin, Lewis, Bay View Books
Ford Popular, Dave Turner, Osprey 1984
Ford & Fordson Tractors, Michael Williams,
Blandford Press 1985
Ford, Robert Lacey, William Heinemann 1986
British Family Cars of the Fifties, Michael Allen,
Haynes, 1987
Ford File, Graham Robson, Temple Press 1987
Ford Vans, Trucks, and PSVs, Michael Allen, Les Geary,
Foulis, 1988
British Family Cars of the Sixties, Michael Allen,
Haynes, 1989
Henry, Walter Hayes, Weidenfeld & Nicholson 1990
Consul Zephyr Zodiac Executive Fords, Michael Allen,
MRP 1990
Complete Catalogue of Ford Cars, David Burgess-Wise,
Bay View Books 1991
Mondeo, World Publishing & Publicity SA 1992
World War Two Military Vehicles, G N Georgano,
Osprey 1994
The Cosworth Fords, Jeremy Walton, PSL Haynes 1994
Ford Transit to 1986, Ed. Trevor Alder,
Transport Source Books 1995
Ford's Kent Crossflow Engine, Peter & Valerie Wallage,
Haynes 1995
Cars in the UK, Vol 1 and Vol 2, Graham Robson, Motor
Racing Publications 1997
Ford Chronicle, Flamming, Lewis, Consumer Guide 1997

A-Z of British Coachbuilders, Nick Walker,
Bay View Books 1997
Cortina, The Story of Ford's Best-Seller, Graham Robson,
Veloce 1998
Fordson Tractors, Robert N Pripps, Motorbooks
International
Lotus 49, Michael Oliver Veloce 1999
Catalogue of British Cars, Culshaw & Horrobin,
Veloce 1999
The Model T Ford, Jonathan Wood, Shire, 1999
The Beaulieu Encyclopædia of the Automobile,
The Stationery Office 2000
Ford Model Y, Sam Roberts, Veloce 2001
Ford at Dagenham, Detroit in Europe, David Burgess-Wise,
Breedon Books 2001
Ford in Touring Car Racing, Graham Robson,
Haynes, 2001

Among the sources used in research were the author's
archive collections of the annuals *Automobil Revue/Revue
Automobile* published by BTM AG Bern, *Automobile Year*
published by Editions J-R Piccard and Phillipsen,
Autocourse published by Hazleton and CMG, *The Motor*
Year Books, Temple Press 1949–1957, Ford Motor Company
press books, statements and reprints, other material from
*The Motor, The Autocar, Autosport, Automotive News
Europe, Motor Sport, Classic Car, Classic Car Profiles, Classic
& Sportscar, The Automobile, On Four Wheels, Automobile
Quarterly, Veteran & Vintage*, and *Glass's Information
Services* publications, to all of whose contributors and
proprietors motoring historians owe continuing thanks.

Index